Disability, Society, and the Individual

Disability, Society, and the Individual

Second Edition

Julie Smart, PhD, CRC, LPC,
NCC, ABDA, CCFC, BCPC

pro·ed
An International Publisher

8700 Shoal Creek Boulevard
Austin, Texas 78757-6897
800/897-3202 Fax 800/397-7633
www.proedinc.com

© 2009, 2001 by PRO-ED, Inc.
8700 Shoal Creek Boulevard
Austin, Texas 78757-6897
800/897-3202   Fax 800/397-7633
www.proedinc.com

Permission granted by Ann Landers and Creators Syndicate
to reprint Exhibits 3–1, 3–2, 3–5, 4–1, 5–1, 6–1, and 6–2

Library of Congress Cataloging-in-Publication Data

Smart, Julie.
   Disability, society, and the individual / Julie Smart. — 2nd ed.
      p. cm.
   Includes bibliographical references and index.
   ISBN-13: 978-1-4164-0372-2
   1. People with disabilities—Social conditions.   2. Discrimination
against people with disabilities.   3. Sociology of disability.   I. Title.
HV1568.S63 2008
305.9'0816—dc21
                                                        2007031967

Art Director: Jason Crosier
Designer: Vicki DePountis
This book is designed in Janson Text, Gill Sans, and Triplex.

Printed in the United States of America

1   2   3   4   5   6   7   8   9   10   17   16   15   14   13   12   11   10   09   08

This book is dedicated to my dear parents,
Helen and Ben Fishler.

Contents

Acknowledgments

Obviously, writing a second edition is a different experience than writing the initial version of the book. I feel that I was given the opportunity to "get it right," or perhaps better stated, "to say more" about the various topics. For this second edition, I was also able to consider the comments of readers—both students and professors. These viewpoints were helpful and I have tried to incorporate many of these suggestions. Interestingly, as I contemplated the organization of this new edition, I decided that the arrangement of the sections still made sense to me; therefore, I decided to retain the three-section format.

I have used many excerpts from various writers, people with disabilities, and disability scholars, and there probably would be no book (or second edition) without their contributions. I have long respected the ideas and scholarship of these individuals, and their work certainly strengthens and broadens the scope of this book. Also, I don't think the work of these individuals has received the recognition and consideration it deserves. Many of my sources are books from university presses, typically small and esoteric publishers who publish books that very few students read and study. Therefore, I have tried to bring many of these authors "together" in a single book and give a broader context to this often hidden scholarship.

Utah State University and the Department of Special Education and Rehabilitation gave me a sabbatical, and I am very grateful for the time to focus on a second edition. My colleagues have been both encouraging and supportive, and this professional respect has certainly facilitated my writing.

Finally, I wish to thank my students. Over the years, I have taught a course entitled "Psychosocial Aspects of Disability" in a master's degree program in rehabilitation counseling, during which the students and I have discussed the ideas in this book. Also at Utah State University, this book is used for a General Education Social Sciences undergraduate course entitled "Society and Disability." In this course, students of any major are provided some introductory understanding of disability. If I have managed to present many sides of a single issue, much of this is a result of these classroom discussions. In addition, students and graduates send me articles, e-mails, and other materials, knowing that I am deeply interested in issues related to disability. Many of these materials have been used in this book. As I re-read what I have written, I am struck by—and feel grateful for— the many contributions of my students.

Julie Smart
Utah State University
June 2007

Abbreviations and Terms

ADA   Americans with Disabilities Act

ADL   Activities of daily living, such as eating, bathing, grooming, doing household maintenance tasks, conducting necessary business, and shopping

ASL   American Sign Language

CRAB   Currently regarded as able-bodied

IL   Independent Living

PWD   Person or people with disabilities

PWOD   Person or people without disabilities

TAB   Temporarily able-bodied

Note: "Deaf" with a capital "D" indicates the Deaf Culture (sometimes referred to as the Deaf community), while "deaf" with a small "d" refers to the disability of deafness. Individuals who are Deaf do not consider themselves to have a disability; instead, they view themselves as part of another culture that speaks another language. Indeed, the symbol of their oppression—sign language—has evolved into a symbol of unity and community.*

---

*Jankowski, K.A. (1997). *Deaf empowerment: Emergence, struggle, and rhetoric.* Washington, DC: Gallaudet University.

Introduction

On the first day of class I ask my students: "When you walk into any major chain bookstore do you find any books about people with disabilities?" All of my students are smart, but it takes them a bit of time to think about this. Eventually, they answer: Helen Keller, Christopher Reeve, and the blind guy who climbed Mt. Everest. But all of these individuals are considered to be super crips, individuals with many more resources than the typical person with a disability. Recently, students have begun answering, "the Pulitzer Prize-winning book about finding the cure for polio." This isn't a book about people who *experienced* polio but about the professional researchers/ scientists, Jonas Salk and Albert Sabin, who developed the polio vaccines. Given the fact that nearly one fifth (18%) of the American population has a disability (NOD/Harris Survey, 2004), it is surprising that there isn't a section in the bookstore devoted to "Disability History." I ask this question because I want my students to think about the invisibility of people with disabilities in our society and culture. People with disabilities, and their experiences, knowledge, and accumulated wisdom, are invisible in our society and culture; furthermore, this invisibility is not noticed or discussed. No one questions why there are no books written by people with disabilities, or better stated, why books written by people with disabilities are not widely available.

John Hockenberry, a journalist with a spinal cord injury, describes the invisibility of people with disabilities in textbooks and the curriculum:

> Why is it that a person would not be considered educated or privileged if he went through school and never learned there was a France or a French language? But if a person went through school and knew

nothing about disability, never met a disabled person [*sic*], never heard of American Sign Language, he might be considered not only educated, but also lucky? (cf. Fleischer & Zames, 2001, p. 205).

In spite of this invisibility, disability is being redefined as a social construct; people with disabilities are beginning to develop a collective identity, and the number of those with disabilities continues to climb. Furthermore, "We want more disabled people [*sic*], not fewer" (Cook, as cited in Stalcup, 1997, p. 175). Perhaps most important, all of us have the possibility of acquiring a disability, or marrying someone with a disability, or having a child with a disability.

The threefold purpose of this book is to look at the disability experience from the perspective of the individual who has a disability, to discuss how disabilities are viewed by society, and to consider the relationship between these two viewpoints. As this book emphasizes, a perfect world is not a world without disabilities; it is a world in which accommodations for people with disabilities (PWDs) are provided and artificial barriers are removed. It is also a world that does not stigmatize or discriminate against those with disabilities, a world that accords basic human rights to PWDs. Note: the acronyms PWD and PWOD (and their plurals) will be used throughout the book for the purposes of clarity and brevity. PWD denotes a person or people *with* disabilities and PWOD denotes a person or people *without* disabilities.

I wanted to write a book that, in a single place, would consider the overall, broad, comprehensive experience of disability. It was important for me that readers gain an introductory understanding of the way in which three broad areas relate to each other. These areas are as follows: definitions of disability, societal response to PWDs, and the experience of disability. To my knowledge such a book has not been available. Of course, there are excellent books on each of three broad areas, and I have used these works in my research and writing and have referenced each, if the reader wishes more depth and detail. Therefore, I have deliberately sacrificed detail and depth to provide a broad overview of the disability experience. Some sort of organization and conceptualization, even if artificial, is necessary. Hence, these three sections of the book (and the *sequence* of the sections) are provided to facilitate learning. Whenever possible, these interrelationships are noted.

Clearly, the most important section of this book deals with the experience of the PWD. It may appear counterintuitive that the most important section of the book is also the final section. After much consideration, I decided that it is impossible to understand the experiences of PWDs without first learning about the differing definitions and models of disability and how these affect the daily lives of PWDs. The services PWDs receive, whether they live in the community or in an institution, or whether they live (at all) are all determined by definitions and models of disability. Hence, the first section defines disability. The second section deals with societal responses to disability. The PWD is greatly affected by the way in which society views him or her and the disability. Indeed, many PWDs declare that coping with prejudice and discrimination is a greater concern than the disability itself. Further, because everyone's self-identity is partially determined by one's culture and society, it makes sense to consider the way in which society views (and has viewed) PWDs before discussing the experience of PWDs.

Do these well-defined sections represent the reality of any one person? Of course not. No book can truly communicate someone's experience. Moreover, there are no neat divisions between defining disability, society's response, and the individual's experience of living with a disability. Certainly, all three of these concepts interact with each other and no one truly conceives of his or her life in these three neat, clean paradigms.

In contrast to most textbooks on disability, this book is not organized by the various diagnostic categories of disability, with each chapter discussing a specific disability, such as blindness, mental illness, paraplegia, or mental retardation. Rather, broad similarities and differences across a wide range of disabilities are considered. There are many psychosocial issues, responses, and tasks required of PWDs; therefore, this book discusses these broad issues. Society's view of disability and PWDs are also discussed in terms of a wide spectrum of disabilities, rather than discussing society's view of and response to each disability type.

The first section defines disability and normality and the various models of disability. Normality and disability are defined in relation to each other, and the definition of neither is straightforward or clear-cut. (I recently saw a bumper sticker on a car that read, "Normal at our house is just a setting on the clothes dryer.") Some of this section is devoted to what a disability is *not*. Models of disability, at first glance, appear to be theoretical abstractions; however, these models determine the daily lives of PWDs. Six reasons why there are more disabilities than ever before are discussed in addition to the Americans with Disabilities Act (ADA). The ADA was passed in 1990, leading many in the Disability Rights Movement to term PWDs as the "last and least minority." Certainly, most other minority groups in the United States were accorded their civil rights before 1990. These first two chapters also present the rationale underlying the correct terminology for describing disability and PWDs. Much of the research for this section is focused on demographic data and legal scholarship.

The second section of the book discusses society's responses to disability and PWDs—most of which have included prejudice and discrimination. Chapters 4, 5, 6, and 7 discuss 10 sources of prejudice and discrimination. Each PWD, regardless of his or her achievements, economic resources, or privilege, understands that he or she belongs to a devalued group. PWDs are often faced with the need to negotiate a relationship with a society that, in many cases, rejects them. The focus of these four chapters is on the effect of prejudice on PWDs; however, the way in which people without disabilities (PWODs) pay for their prejudice is also reviewed. Prejudice is expensive. Prejudice against any groups literally costs the larger group, and eliminating prejudice against the minority group improves the economy. By systematically refusing to allow members of one group the right to fulfill their potential, the larger group forfeits economic benefits. Further, PWODs pay for their prejudice by losing the creativity and diversity of ideas that PWDs could provide, if allowed. For example, most universities offer women's studies courses and African American courses, but the incorporation into the undergraduate curriculum of disability history or disability studies lags far behind. Finally, PWODs pay for their prejudice against PWDs by losing an opportunity to grow because of the fear of acquiring a disability. If PWDs and their experiences were socially validated, PWODs could understand the disability experience and not fear it as much.

Some concepts in this second section are difficult to understand. First, as a society, we have never viewed disability as an ordinary human experience. Indeed, many PWDs report that they would not wish to be "cured" of their disability; instead they would rather simply be treated as individuals whose disability does not make them un-ordinary or less than fully human. When the public views disability as heroic or tragic, not only is this an inaccurate perception of the lives of PWDs, but it also does not allow PWDs to be regarded as and judged like everyone else. Second, the idea that disability is a collective concern may appear illogical; nonetheless, these chapters attempt to show that disability concerns everyone. Finally, and most difficult, many readers have questioned my arguments against telethons, simulation exercises, and other "well-intentioned handicapism." I think it is important to think about the *results* of some of these practices. Without question, the *motives* of those who support telethons and simulations are well-intentioned; however, the costs to PWDs and the *results* have set the Disability Rights Movement back. Indeed, many PWDs point out that there are no telethon or simulation exercises for other minority groups. Many PWDs consider charity of any type, including telethons, to have relieved general society of any need to provide civil rights for PWDs. Titles of many books stress the contradiction between civil rights and charity, including Shapiro's (1993) *No Pity: People with Disabilities Forging a New Civil Rights Movement*; Fleischer and Zames' (2001) *The Disability Rights Movement: From Charity to Confrontation*; and Scotch's (1984) *From Good Will to Civil Rights: Transforming Federal Disability Policy*. Much of the literature for this section was taken from works on the sociological view of disability and books on disability rights.

The focus changes in Chapters 8, 9, and 10. In these chapters, the individual's response to disability is considered, especially considering the factors of the disability itself and factors in the environment. Types of onset, varied courses, levels of severity, degree of visibility, the presence of chronic pain, and the degree of stigma and prejudice directed toward that particular disability are all known to have an effect on the individual's response. Disability scholars recognize that factors in the environment have an important impact on the individual's response to the disability. Of course, most PWDs think of the disability as a personal attribute, not as a tragic problem. For many PWDs, the disability is not the single most important self-identifier. Further, the only shared identity is the prejudice and discrimination they experience. Other than this devalued position in society, it is safe to state that there is no single disability experience.

At the end of each chapter I suggest viewing several videos that I like. I hope that reading and discussing the various chapters will provide context and background for the videos. In other words, after reading each chapter, viewers will more completely understand the videos. These videos show PWDs relating their experiences and viewpoints and allow the viewers to see PWDs in many different settings: in their homes, in hospitals, at work, with their friends, or in school. Some of these videos follow a PWD for a long time, providing viewers with a long-term perspective of a disability. In other videos, family members, friends, professional caregivers, in addition to the PWD, discuss their responses to the PWD and the disability. This provides a multifaceted picture of the disability experience. Some videos show historical scenes of hospitals and institutions that have been closed for decades, and two videos show the institutions in Nazi Germany where PWDs were murdered. In other videos, major players in the Disability Rights Movement recount their experiences and the difficulties in obtaining basic civil rights for Americans with disabilities. It is my hope that this book will provide the foundation and background for viewing these videos; moreover, it is clear that these videos will add richness, detail, and immediacy in understanding disabilities and the people who experience them.

As a society, we are increasingly understanding the pervasiveness, significance, and value of the disability experience. It is hoped that this book will lend support to a transformation of the way in which we view ourselves.

References

Fleischer, D. Z., & Zames, F. (2001). *The disability rights movement: From charity to confrontation.* Philadelphia: Temple University.

National Organization on Disability/Harris Survey of Americans with Disabilities. (2004). New York: Harris Interactive.

Scotch, R. K. (1984). *From good will to civil rights: Transforming federal disability policy.* Philadelphia: Temple University.

Shapiro, J. P. (1993). *No pity: People with disabilities forging a new civil rights movement.* New York: Times Books.

Stalcup, B. (Ed.). (1991). *The Disabled, Current Controversies Series.* San Diego, CA: Greenhaven.

Definitions
of Disability

Defining Disability

- Is disability truly universal?
- Does anyone know what "normal" is?
- Darwin's theory of evolution and "survival of the fittest" posited that humankind would eventually be free of disability. Has this happened?
- Why is it necessary to define or categorize disabilities?
- Why are labels and diagnoses depersonalizing for the individual?
- Does everybody have a disability of some sort?
- Can environmental factors—such as the labor market or societal prejudice and discrimination—change the definition of disability?
- If medicine and medical technology have made such great advances, why are there more disabilities than ever before?
- Why is the increase in disabilities considered to be progress?

The Universality of Disability, or Disability Is a Natural Part of Everyone's Life

> **In this section, look for—**
>
> - Why disability is an "equal opportunity situation"
> - How many PWODs choose to deny or minimize the possibility of acquiring a disability
> - How disability concerns all of us

Disability has been present throughout human history in every culture and society, yet there never has been a universal definition of disability (Hirandini, 2005). Disability is a permanent part of human history, and the number of people with disabilities continues to increase. Of course, not everyone has a disability or will have a disability; but everyone has the potential to acquire a disability and every child born has the potential for a congenital disability—a disability present at birth. Clay Haughton, director of Civilian Equal Opportunity for the Department of Defense, explained:

> No one is immune to developing a disability, and almost no one, regardless of race, gender, religion or economic status, will go through life without suffering from some form of physical impairment. It's truly the equal opportunity situation, and those of us who are disabled are a constant visual reminder of the frailty of each member of the human race. And so, accepting this possibility and adjusting to disability, those are matters that concern us all. (Fleischer & Zames, 2001, p. 109)

While Haughton terms the acquisition of a disability an "equal opportunity situation," Berube, a university professor, refers to the potential for anyone to acquire a disability as follows:

> [a] category whose constituency is contingency itself. Any of us who identify as "nondisabled" must know that our self-designation is inevitably temporary, and that a car crash, a virus, a degenerative genetic disease, or a precedent-setting legal decision would change our status in ways over which we have no control whatsoever. (1998, p. viii)

So, rather than thinking of disability as something abnormal, exotic, or marginal to our interests, we see that disability concerns all of us (Smart, 2004).

Does Anyone Know What "Normal" Is?

> **In this section, look for—**
>
> - The reasons why diagnoses of exclusion are frequently ambiguous
> - The idea that normalcy is a changing, elastic concept
> - Three factors that affect society's determination of normalcy

The question that heads this section is an important one because the answer has a great impact on the self-concepts of individuals, on how people treat each other, and on the allocation of public resources for services and benefits. Other questions follow. Is it always positive to be labeled "normal"? Where can we see pictures of "normal" people? Is "abnormal" always a negative label, indicating someone as inferior, deviant, or deficient? Is there one fixed, correct pattern of human development? Or, is the concept of normalcy a dynamic, changing concept (in contrast to a fixed, unchanging idea)? Does the concept of normalcy always imply progress for humankind? A disability scholar stated that normalcy was ". . . a dynamic concept for a changing and progressing world, the premise of which was that one could discern from observation of human behavior the direction of human evolution" (Baynton, 1997, p. 83). Indeed, disabilities or people with disabilities were either absent or invisible in the futuristic books of the 1950s that envisioned the great scientific and technological advances of the 21st century.

Often, normal is defined solely as the absence of deviance, illness, or disability so that the definition becomes a definition of exclusion. In other words, if deviance, illness, or disability is not present, the person is judged to be normal. No definition of exclusion is very helpful. After all, only eliminations are made, usually of those factors considered to be undesirable; no further guidelines or clarifications are given. Diagnoses of exclusion, including the determination of normalcy, are frequently given as a result of the ambiguity and lack of specificity of these types of diagnoses. Consequently, there are more clear-cut, standardized, measurable, and objective guidelines for the definition of abnormal than there are for the definition of normal.

Conceptualizing normalcy as the ideal, as the standard against which everything is measured, is another invalid assumption. For many, normal means perfect. Assumptions, accurate or not, can remain intact throughout centuries of human history. Davis (1997) summarized the long history of the concept of normalcy: "A common assumption would be that some concept of the norm must have always existed. After all, people seem to have an inherent desire to compare themselves to others" (p. 9). Those who subscribe to this assumption believe that anything, or anyone, that does not meet all the prescribed criteria, guidelines, and standards is abnormal. Indeed, Wolfensberger (1972) stated, "Normalcy is often confused with humanity." In the third section of this book, we will see that PWDs often redefine normalcy, and the way in which PWODs define normalcy is often not valued by PWDs.

Following these types of logic—that normalcy means only the absence of abnormalcy or that normal is considered to be the standard of evaluation—the determination of normalcy would depend on the combination of three elements: (1) the characteristic(s) to be judged, (2) the environment in which the characteristic(s) appear, and (3) the individual(s) who are making the judgment. Defining power is the authority to determine who or what is normal. Normalcy is, in many ways, in the eyes of the beholder; indeed, the determination of normalcy and abnormalcy may tell us more about the people making the determinations than about the people being judged. The most clear-cut example of defining power is the example of Nazi Germany and the Holocaust. The Nazis defined the criteria of being "normal" and then killed all those who did not meet these criteria, including German children and adults with disabilities (Friedlander, 1996). Nazi pseudoscientists "confirmed" these criteria with "data."

In the original sense of the word, "normal" carries no value judgment; normal is neither good nor bad. Normal simply means typical, prevalent, customary, routine, commonplace, in the middle, and to be expected (Davis, 1997). Normal means average, ordinary, and common. Nonetheless, most people aspire to be normal but not average! Remember the radio program "A Prairie Home Companion" that told of a fictional town, called Lake Wobegon, in which all of the children were "above average"? Both "normal" and "abnormal," therefore, can also be good or bad. Here is an example of abnormalcy: "I am abnormal because I am extremely beautiful, I am an Olympic athlete, and I have a genius-level IQ." Consider this example: "It is normal for 500 murders to be committed each year in the City of Oz." Accordingly, the determination of normalcy or abnormalcy is not an evaluation because these concepts have no inherent value; rather, it is a simple determination based on how typical an event, a characteristic, or a behavior is. Normalcy, then, is more of a statistical concept, which includes the ideas of "most commonly occurring and most likely to happen."

One disability scholar states: "There is no flesh-and-bones human body that is normal; the only 'normal body' is the one constructed from the 'bare bones' of statistics . . . . This is the fiction presented to disabled people [sic]" (Michalko, 2002). Of course, PWODs, people who consider themselves to be "normal," often do not realize that these categories exist. Murphy, a university anthropology professor who became paralyzed because of a spinal tumor, explained that the identity of "normal" is an elite category, just as "White" is thought to often be the valued category in racial/ethnic classifications and therefore neither the "normals" nor the "Whites" are required to think of themselves as being in these categories. Murphy recalled a discussion with a Black anthropology colleague in which the colleague stated, "I always think of myself as being Black just as you always think of yourself as being White." With Murphy's disability came a realization that "I would no more have thought of myself as White than I would have thought of myself as walking on two legs" (Murphy, 1990, pp. 102–103). In other words, when one is within the so-called "normal" group, the individual is often unaware that there is a classification. Indeed, while most PWDs think of themselves as someone with a disability, most PWODs would not describe themselves as able-bodied persons.

The Link Between the Academic Discipline of Statistics and Eugenics

In this section, look for—

- The definition of eugenics
- The link between statistics and eugenics
- The lack of a disability identity for D/deaf people on Martha's Vineyard
- How the definition of normalcy is becoming more constricted as a result of managed care
- Cost-containment policies

Quantification, measurement, statistical methodologies, and counting of human characteristics all carry the potential to be distorted into value judgments. Eugenics, the study of hereditary improvements of the human race by controlled selective breeding and, in its extreme form, by the elimination of those with disabilities, was a direct result of statistical analyses of biological traits measured on large samples of people. These analyses then led to theories that created the concept of the "normal distribution" curve and the concept of the "norm." Sir Francis Galton (1869), Karl Pearson (originator of the Pearson Product Moment Correlation statistic), and Sir Ronald Fisher, considered to be the "fathers" of the academic discipline of statistics, were eugenicists or, as they are sometimes called, population geneticists (Leakey, as cited in Darwin, 1979). Galton was cousin, friend, and colleague of Charles Darwin's. It was Galton who coined the term "eugenics" and wrote numerous books, including *Hereditary Genius* (1887) and *Inquiries into Human Faculty and Its Development* (1883). Fisher used statistical analyses in the book he wrote, *The Genetical Theory of Natural Selection*. Pearson, another British statistician, argued that "genetically inferior people were outbreeding [having more children than] superior ones and that the human species was degenerating by dysgenics" (*L.A. Times*, October 23, 1994; as cited in Jacoby & Glauberman, 1995, p. 386).

Davis (1997) pointed to this link:

> The rather amazing fact is that almost all early statisticians had one thing in common: they were eugenicists. . . . While this coincidence seems almost too striking to be true, we must remember that there is a real connection between figuring the statistical measures of humans so that deviations from the norm diminish. . . . Statistics is bound up with eugenics because the central insight of statistics is the idea that a population can be normed. (p. 14)

Eugenicists then implemented mathematical, scientific, and statistical methodology to define that which was normal and that which was deviant. The debate continues, at least for intellectual and cognitive disabilities. Books such as *The Bell Curve* (Herrnstein & Murray, 1994), *Measured Lies: The Bell Curve Examined* (Kincheloe, Steinberg, & Gresson, 1997), and *The Mismeasure of Man* (Gould, 1981) have all focused on the relationship between scientific, statistical concepts and the definition of "normal" intellectual and cognitive functioning. Eugenics often included physical attractiveness or the lack of it. "Eugenics promised to make humanity not just strong and smart, but beautiful as well. Being hereditarily fit included being visually attractive. Ugliness, according to these scientists, was a hereditary disease" (Burch, 2007, p. 242).

Darwin's theory of evolution and natural selection, sometimes referred to as the "survival of the fittest," and the improvement of "mammiferous animal species" (including humans) postulated that eventually there would be no individuals with defects or disabilities. Indeed, Darwin posited that variations considered to be harmful would be eliminated. Herbert Spencer (1884) applied Darwin's theories specifically to humans and was a leader in the Social Darwinism movement. Spencer believed that "under the natural order of things society is constantly excreting its unhealthy, imbecile, slow, vacillating, faithless members" (p. 355). Note the use of the word "excreting." Ironically, the opposite has occurred. Today, a greater proportion of humankind has disabilities than ever before. (These increases in disability rates and their sources will be discussed later in this chapter.) These scholars/ writers contributed to the false idea that normalcy is natural and the converse, that abnormalcy is unnatural. Nevertheless, Darwin wrote with clarity and force and in a style easily understood by the general public, and his theories had, and continue to have, a tremendous influence on the public consciousness (Hofstadter, 1955). Certainly, "the theory of evolution is considered to be one of the fundamental principles that govern the universe" (White & Gribbin, 1995, p. 3).

Notwithstanding the important and widespread acceptance of Darwin's Theory of Natural Selection, this theory does not apply to humans. (Darwin's theory has been scientifically proved for plants and animals but not for humans.) Indeed, the major thesis of this book stands in direct opposition to Darwin's Theory of Natural Selection. At the time that Darwin and his disciples were developing this theory, advances in medicine that would preserve and prolong life were impossible to predict. Darwin's theory is based on natural processes operating without the effect of human intervention (Diamond, 1999). But humankind has always struggled, and in many ways has succeeded, in overcoming the effects of nature. As we shall see later in this chapter, medical advances have indirectly increased the number of individuals with disabilities. More and more people have disabilities, and, furthermore, because of longer life spans and sophisticated medical management, individuals who have disabilities are living longer. These higher disability rates may, at first glance, appear to be at odds with the trajectory of progress that science and civilization provide. However, considering that the alternative would be death, higher rates of disability are certainly advances. Indeed, Wendell (1997) suggests that society's inability to foresee those scientific and technological advances would result in greater numbers of disabilities and labels it "[b]ad social planning that is based on the illusion that everyone is young, strong, and healthy" (p. 260).

Olkin (1999) pointed out that society's efforts to eliminate disability can lead to the idea that *people* who have disabilities should also be eliminated. Olkin listed 13 "Human Rights of Children with Disabilities" and included the following:

> Right 6: To not be made to feel that "people like them" should be prevented. Much of the financial resources, most of the charities, and now prenatal screening, put the emphasis on preventing disabilities. It is psychologically hard for children to know that if their mother could have screened for and found out about the condition the child has, the pregnancy may well have been terminated. . . . We might well say to these children that it is not them [sic], but the disability that we are trying to prevent, but this is a sham message when we're also trying to encourage incorporation of this disability into a self-concept. (p. 101)

In the United States in the early 1900s a new discipline, "anthropometry," was developed at three institutions: Harvard University, Columbia University, and the Smithsonian. The discipline of anthropometry concerned itself with developing "standardized measures of the 'average' body" (Urla & Swedlund, 2005, p. 291). These norms were then applied to everyone, in spite of the fact that they were only a table of statistical averages, or an abstraction. By 1945 Norman and Norma had appeared. These were life-sized statues based on the composite measurements of thousands of White 18–25-year-old subjects (Urla & Swedlund, 2005, p. 291). These statues were exhibited as the prototypes for "normal" Americans. With the patriotism that accompanied the end of World War II, the media emphasized that if the United States were to retain its status as a world power, Americans had "a national responsibility" to be healthy and follow the lead of Norman and Norma. Brettell and Sargent (2005) explained: "Norma and Norman were thus always more than statistical composites; they were prescriptive ideals" (p. 292).

Thus, we can see that prestigious American institutions supported and developed eugenic standards. American scientists then used these "standards," mistakenly thought to be objectively, scientifically quantified and proven, to judge the value of lives. Later in this book we shall learn of the Nazi murder of 200,000 German citizens with disabilities. No other government has this type of record and, furthermore, "the Nuremberg court did not require that reparations be paid to the families of those with disabilities who were killed, nor that their murderers be punished" (Fleischer & Zames, 2001, p. 139). We should also remember that the Nazis received their initial training in eugenics in the United States and Great Britain.

Confusing Normalcy With the Ideal

According to Davis, eugenics had the effect of making the physical body the individual's most important source of identity. The individual became his or her body, an organic entity, a mechanical machine that either functioned correctly and efficiently or did not function. With the appearance of statistics, the normal curve, and eugenics, the concept of normalcy was enshrined as the desired status. Disability scholars (Davis, 1997; Wendell, 1997) assert that society has confused normalcy with the ideal. With the concept of normalcy, society confers a desirable status on some people (the "normal" ones). In contrast, with the concept of the ideal, everyone falls short. No one has the ideal characteristics (or is supposed to). Indeed, the concept of the ideal often embodied spiritual/philosophical/mythical/religious meanings in which divine beings are ideal. In some belief systems, humans can become ideal but only in some sort of afterlife. Further, in many spiritual orientations, the individual is not his or her body—the main identity of the individual is his or her eternal spirit. Therefore, in these belief systems the spirit could not be measured (as the body can be in statistics). The idea that humans (rather than deity) have the capability to measure the worth of an individual (such as eugenics) would seem without reason in many religious/ spiritual belief systems.

The Social Construction of Normalcy and Disability

The increasing proportion of the population with disabilities adds a new dimension to the concept of normalcy. If normalcy is based on numbers, with those in the numerical majority considered to be "normal" and those in the numerical minority considered to be "abnormal," then as more individuals acquire the identification of having a disability, will the definitions of normalcy and disability change? An unusual example of a substantial number of individuals having a disability (albeit not a majority) and not being perceived as having a disability because of their large proportion in the population is described in Groce's book *Everyone Here Spoke Sign Language: Hereditary D/deafness on Martha's Vineyard* (1985). In 1694, the first D/deaf resident of Martha's Vineyard, Jonathan Lambert, arrived. Lambert was a sailor who brought an inherited trait that causes D/deafness. Geographic isolation and intermarriage resulted in D/deafness for many individuals; many families had members who were D/deaf. By 1850, one in 25 residents of the town of Chilmark was D/deaf, and in one neighborhood, the ratio was one in four. What is truly unusual about the story is the lack of a disability identity on the island. On Martha's Vineyard D/deafness was a natural part of human existence. D/deafness was unremarkable; marriages took place between D/deaf individuals and hearing individuals and the birth of a D/deaf baby was not regarded as a tragedy. Moreover, as the title of Groce's book suggests, the use of sign language was not regarded as an accommodation and, indeed, the widespread use of a communication system that everyone could understand probably contributed to the lack of a disability identity. Also, because telecommunications had not yet been introduced, most long-distance communication used the written word. Thus, people who were D/deaf were not disadvantaged, socially or economically. People who were D/deaf were viewed as different but not as deviant or pathological. Researchers asked residents on Martha's Vineyard if there were any people with disabilities on the island. All of the respondents answered "yes," giving examples of people who were blind or had orthopedic impairments. No one described a D/deaf person as a person with a disability. Many disability advocates have theorized that it is not biological conditions that "make" disabilities; rather, it is the lack of accommodations (Higgins, 1992; Liachowitz, 1988; Scott, 1969). The story of Martha's Vineyard lends support to this theory.

Often termed "the universality of disability," the theoretical model of everyone in a community having the same disability helps us to understand the social construction of disability. For example, if no one could walk, the community would be completely accessible for wheelchairs. Even more important, there would be no stigma, prejudice, or stereotypes about people who could not walk. The community would adjust to the inability to walk, with both universal accessibility and the corresponding absence of prejudice and discrimination.

If a spaceship from another planet landed and the aliens could walk, they would find all the drinking fountains in this community to be too low because the fountains would be at wheelchair height. Also, the aliens would probably experience a great deal of prejudice, discrimination, and stereotyping because of their deviance (their ability to walk). If, instead of the ability to walk, the universal disability was D/deafness, there would be the same conditions: (1) universal accommodations and (2) lack of prejudice and discrimination against people who are D/deaf, which, of course, would be everybody. A third result occurs: the identity of people who are D/deaf then becomes a cultural and social/linguistic identity and not a disability identity.

In spite of the complexities of defining normalcy/abnormalcy, some widely accepted standards of normalcy must be established, depending on both the characteristic(s) and the environment. How can society operate without some broad guidelines to provide services that are most appropriate? Naturally, determination of normalcy/abnormalcy must (occasionally) be made, but it is important to consider the following when making these types of assessments:

- Value judgments that may mistakenly interfere
- The environment in which the person functions
- Who is making the determination and what their motives are (Remember, it is "normals" who have defining power. "Normals" define "nonnormals," not the other way around, so it is not a matter of equal differences. "Normal" people, whoever they might be, have power and "nonnormal" people, whoever they might be, do not have power.)
- The purpose of the assessment
- The diagnostic tools, instruments, and classification system used

All five of these considerations are subject to adaptation and revision. We may like to think that our value systems are fixed and unchanging, but societal values do shift, environments evolve, clinicians change their diagnostic criteria and methods, and policymakers pass in and out of power. What is considered to be normal today might not be normal tomorrow (Brown, 1991; Smart, 2005; Smart & Smart, 1997).

Especially with intellectual disabilities and mental/emotional disabilities, it is important to understand that the diagnostic instruments and tools and the classification systems are very much linked to the environment/culture in which they are developed and implemented. Smart and Smart (1997), for example, studied the *Diagnostic and Statistical Manual of Mental Disorders–Fourth Edition* (*DSM-IV*) published by the American Psychiatric Association (1994). The *DSM-IV* is the classification system used to diagnose psychoses, personality disorders, mental retardation, and other types of mental illness. Many clinicians must render a diagnosis of some sort from the *DSM-IV* to be paid for services. As described by Smart and Smart, the *DSM-IV* does not take into account the individual's culture or religious/

spiritual background. Indeed, Kirk and Kutchins (1992) detailed a highly critical account of the DSM as a *political* rather than a *scientific* classification system. They labeled the *DSM-IV* as "lily white" (p. 103), questioning the validity of using DSM diagnoses for people of color. Seem and Hernandez (1997, as cited in Ivey & Ivey, 1998) conducted an analysis of the *DSM-IV* and determined that more attention should be paid to feminist issues. This is not to advocate that the use of the *DSM-IV* should be discontinued. These cautions, however, clearly point out the necessity of a critical awareness that every diagnosis based on *DSM-IV* criteria always occurs in the broad sociocultural context of the North American culture. As Allen Frances, the chief architect of the American Psychiatric Association's *Diagnostic and Statistical Manual, DSM–IV,* said, "The special features (of the new edition) are . . . elimination of the term 'organic mental disorder' because it incorrectly implied that other psychiatric disabilities did not have a biological contribution" ("Mental Disorders," 2000). In other words, it took 42 years for the American Psychiatric Association to acknowledge that biological and physical factors contribute to the causality of mental illnesses and other psychiatric disabilities.

Having discussed the most widely used classification system for mental retardation and mental illness (the *DSM-IV*), it is important to make a brief statement about the diagnostic tools and instruments used to make these types of diagnoses. Many psychological tests have a "fundamental negative bias" (as cited in McCarthy, 1993) in that only pathology is noted and described. Many widely used instruments, such as the *Minnesota Multiphasic Personality Inventory–Second Edition* (MMPI-2; Butcher, Dahlstrom, Graham, Tellegen, & Kaemmer, 1989), tap only negative traits and do not give a picture of the individual's adaptive functioning. Surely, if the tools clinicians use are based on deficit and pathology, disability diagnoses will be given. Further, groups considered to be inferior, such as women, gay men and lesbians, and racial/ethnic minorities, will be given diagnoses of pathology more often than individuals who are not considered inferior.

Finally, the reason why the assessment of normalcy is made is important. We like to think that "society" is committed to providing the best services for those with disabilities; however, occasionally the considerations of convenience, cost, and the comfort of those without disabilities receive first priority (Hahn, 1988, 1991). Managed care reforms, cost-containment efforts, and financial risk shifting may work together to more narrowly define both disability and normalcy (Vernellia, 1994). It should also be remembered that there are many situations in which such assessments of normal/abnormal are unnecessary and irrelevant.

It is important to discuss the concept of normalcy/abnormalcy early on because everything that follows—the categorization of disability, the individual's adjustment to disability, and society's reaction to those with disabilities—will directly relate to these ideas.

Categorizing Disabilities

> ### In this section, look for—
>
> - Reasons why it is necessary to categorize disabilities
> - How diagnoses often affect self-image
> - The short leap from categorization to stereotyping
> - Why categorization of disabilities is based on symptom manifestation and not etiology
> - The four broad categories of disabilities
>   1. Physical disabilities
>   2. Intellectual disabilities
>   3. Cognitive disabilities
>   4. Psychiatric disabilities

Categorization of disabilities is necessary to provide benefits and services to those who need them (Albrecht, 1976). Government agencies must design some sort of counting and data collection system to estimate the resources necessary to serve the needs of their mandated populations and also to establish policy (Thompson-Hoffman & Storck, 1991). The determination of eligibility for services and benefits, the agencies from which applicants are allowed to receive services, and the settings in which individuals live (institutions or in the community) are closely related to the categorization of the disability (Matson & Barrett, 1993). In the move toward managed care and cost containment (which often includes benefit limitations), the categorization, diagnosis, and definition of disability are important, but complex and detailed, considerations. Simply stated, without a diagnosis, third-party payers will not reimburse, nor will government agencies provide services and benefits (Ivey & Ivey, 1998). Advocacy groups, usually individuals with disabilities, need information in understandable categories to represent their legislative and judicial interests. Categorization of disabilities also exerts a powerful effect on the type of prejudice and discrimination directed toward individuals with disabilities (Szymanski & Trueba, 1994). The relationship between disability categorization and societal responses will be discussed in Chapter 4. Finally, and most important, the categorization of the disability affects the self-identity of the individual with the disability, as will be seen in Chapter 6. Professional vocabulary, including diagnoses, often affects self-images of those who are given these diagnoses. Physicians, psychologists, and other clinicians know that the diagnosis describes a condition a person has and not the person himself or herself. However, diagnosis often sculpts the self-image of those who receive the diagnosis. A textbook for nursing students illustrates the effect of a diagnosis or disability on the individual:

> When a veterinarian diagnoses a cow's condition as an illness, he does not merely, by diagnosis, change the cow's behavior . . . but when a physician diagnoses a human's condition as an illness, he changes the man's behavior by diagnosis: a social state is added to a biophysiological state by assigning the meaning . . . . (Lubkin & Larsen, 2006, p. 23)

Further, one disability scholar (Langer, 1983) found that labels affected the performance of those who received them and, moreover, the clinicians formed their expectations of patients based on the label given. Those individuals who received labels of low competence performed poorly (as expected by their physicians), and those individuals who received labels of high competence performed well. This process is known as a self-fulfilling prophecy (Hannah & Midlarsky, 1987).

Categorization of these diagnoses, while necessary, is also fraught with difficulties, and no classification system truly represents the reality and experience of the individual with the disability. Categorization may lead to false stereotypes, such as the stereotype that all or most individuals with the same disability share important characteristics, experiences, or perceptions (for example, "Most people who are D/deaf are shy"). It is a short leap from categorization to stereotyping (McCarthy, 1993; Wright, 1991). Also, in theory, these are classifications and categories of disabilities that people experience and not classifications of people themselves. In practice, however, many individuals with disabilities are consigned to categorization. Indeed, to be perceived as a person with a disability is to be immediately, and often incorrectly, categorized (for example, a rehabilitation counselor who states, "I have four quads on my caseload"). Any categorization scheme tends to emphasize differences *between* categories and emphasizes the similarities *within* categories (Schmelkin, 1988). Further, simply because the focus of most categorization systems is on the disability, the strengths, abilities, assets, and resources of the individual are not considered. Finally, and most important, these categorization schemes of disability do not take into account the self-identities of the individuals with disabilities. Two people who experience the same type and severity of disability have differing circumstances, resources, values, interests, and abilities. Everyone has multiple identities, and for people with disabilities, the disability is only one aspect of their identity. Finally, the diagnosis may not fit the individual's self-concept, and these individuals may be surprised or resentful that they are considered to have a particular diagnosis. Having explained (1) the necessity for categorization and (2) the effects of categorization, it is important to emphasize that categories are only abstractions and never can fully describe or capture anyone's reality.

Although there is no one universally accepted categorization of disabilities (Olkin, 1999), the most widely accepted categorization is organized by the symptoms and manifestations of disabilities and not by the cause (etiology) or the source (pathogenesis) of the disability (Bowe, 1981, 1984, 1985, 1993; Bradsher, 1997; Brown, 1991). For example, schizophrenia is considered to be a psychiatric disability, but if disabilities were categorized according to etiology, schizophrenia, and many other mental illnesses, would be considered a physical disability because it has been proved that many mental illnesses are caused by physical factors. Defining or categorizing disability by the etiology or pathogenesis would be difficult because (1) for many disabilities, the cause is not known; (2) for some disabilities, there are multiple causes, such as mental illness (Kiesler, 1999); (3) clinicians may change their hypotheses concerning the cause of a specific disability; and (4) for some disabilities, the same treatments might apply, regardless of cause. It should also be noted that while professionals know that diagnoses do not carry any implications about cause, many nonprofessionals—including individuals who are given these diagnoses—are unaware that most diagnoses are based only on symptoms and other clinical features, saying nothing about possible causes. Certainly, the categorization of disabilities by their symptoms, whether they are physical, intellectual, cognitive, or psychiatric, has the longest history in both medicine and the social sciences. Another advantage of this categorization system is the treatment and management plans that result from looking at the course, type, and severity of symptoms. Notwithstanding the present wide acceptance of categorization of disabilities by their symptoms, efforts to refine these classification systems continue. This book will use this categorization system, unless otherwise noted.

Some disabilities are chronic illnesses, such as diabetes, lupus, arthritis, and multiple sclerosis. Nonetheless, health conditions and chronic illnesses are considered to be disabilities. Injuries often result in disabilities. So, while injuries are not discussed in the following sections, it should be remembered that following medical stabilization, many injuries do result in disabilities.

Thus, there are four broad categories of disability—physical, intellectual, cognitive, and psychiatric—all of which are based on symptoms. Individuals with physical disabilities experience physical symptoms, those with intellectual disabilities experience intellectual manifestations, those with cognitive disabilities have cognitive manifestations, and psychiatric symptoms are present in those individuals who have been diagnosed as having a psychiatric disability. Many individuals have more than one disability, and, in these cases, one disability is typically labeled the "primary" disability and the other disabilities are labeled "secondary," and so on.

Physical Disabilities

> ### *In this section, look for—*
> - Visual impairments
> - Hearing impairments
> - Dual sensory loss, such as D/deaf—blindness
> - Mobility impairments
> - Health disorders

Physical disabilities include mobility impairments; neurologic impairments such as cerebral palsy and seizure disorders; traumatic brain injuries; musculoskeletal conditions, such as muscular dystrophy and arthritis; sensory loss; and health disorders. Most people would be surprised to learn that many experts consider arthritis to be the most frequently occurring disability in the United States (LaPlante, 1991, 1993, 1996, 1997). In Chapter 4, the societal prejudice, discrimination, and stigma directed toward individuals with disabilities will be discussed, and we will see that of the four broad categories of disabilities (physical, intellectual, cognitive, and psychiatric), individuals with physical disabilities experience the least amount of prejudice and discrimination. Because government policymakers are subject to the same flawed human perceptions as the general public, we will learn that individuals with intellectual, cognitive, and psychiatric disabilities received government funding for benefits and services long after those with physical disabilities. Moreover, intellectual, cognitive, and psychiatric disabilities were not considered to be disabilities until the 20th century. The longer history of service provision and allotment of resources to individuals with physical disabilities has resulted in more professional experience and knowledge in dealing with physical disabilities (DeJong & Lifchez, 1983). This longer history of self-identification has resulted in stronger advocacy groups, such as the National Federation for the Blind (NFB), established in 1940 (Berkowitz, 1987).

Physical disabilities lend themselves to objective, quantifiable diagnoses, often with standardized laboratory procedures. In contrast, the diagnosis of intellectual, cognitive, or psychiatric disabilities requires more subjective, impressionistic, clinical judgment. Indeed, some disability advocates regard many psychiatric diagnoses as thinly veiled moral judgments (Szasz, 1961). The most clear-cut illustration of a diagnosis of pathology (not a disability) reflecting society's moral judgment is outlined in Clendinen and Nagourney's (1999) book *Out for Good: The Struggle To Build a Gay*

Rights Movement in America. The authors devote a chapter to describing the struggle to remove homosexuality as a diagnosis of pathology from the American Psychiatric Association's *Diagnostic and Statistical Manual of Mental Disorders.*

Visual Impairments

Visual impairments include total blindness from birth; the gradual loss of vision; muscular disorders, such as strabismus, or "crossed eyes"; and loss of acuity across the visual field, such as tunnel vision (Falvo, 1991; Rosenthal & Cole, 1993). People who wear eyeglasses or contact lenses are not considered to have a visual impairment simply because the use of a common and easily obtainable device, such as eyeglasses, restores the individual to full functioning. Indeed, to be considered a visual impairment, the condition must be severe enough to limit daily functioning. Degenerative conditions, affecting the retina or optic nerve, include retinitis pigmentosa, retinal detachment, and glaucoma (Carroll, 1961). Visual impairments may also be caused by genetic factors such as malformations or may be acquired from infections, inflammations, accidents, or tumors (Panek, 1992). However, a large percentage of visual impairments have unknown causes. LaPlante (1991) estimated that approximately 1.5 million individuals of all ages have visual impairments.

The age distribution of visual impairments is different from that of other disabilities inasmuch as these impairments occur, for the most part, at the beginning of life (before the age of 1 year) or at the end of life (after the age of 70 years). Indeed, it is estimated that 60% of all visual impairments occur before the age of 1. Two factors that, in the past, led to thousands of cases of blindness in newborn infants have now been virtually eliminated. These two factors are maternal rubella and excess oxygen administered to premature infants, which resulted in retrolental fibroplasia. The rubella vaccine and incubators introduced in the 1960s, that control the amount of oxygen, have almost eliminated blindness from these causes. However, many adults born before the 1960s have experienced lifelong blindness as a result of these two causes.

There is a larger percentage of visual impairments than ever before in the United States because of the larger percentage of elderly people (Silverstone, Lang, Rosenthal, & Faye, 1999). Visual impairments are positively correlated with age, and as the population ages, the number of people with visual impairments increases. Advances in medicine and medical technology have greatly decreased the number of infants born with blindness and yet have also indirectly increased the number of elderly individuals who are blind. Because medical advances have lengthened the life span of elderly individuals, they now survive with disabilities, many of which are visual impairments.

Individuals with visual impairments, especially those w blind since birth, often have been educated in specialized resid (Warren, 1984, 1989). Although these residential schools are b with specialized programs in regular schools, there are many .... today who were educated in these segregated schools (Tuttle, 1984). Most people with other types of disabilities, except for hearing impairments and mental retardation, were not educated in schools that required them to live apart from their families. Before the advent of special education programs in the public schools, parents had little choice other than to send their children to boarding schools that were equipped with the educational resources, including teachers, to help their children reach their academic potential. Nonetheless, the emotional cost, for the child sent to school, the parents, and the siblings, was high. In Chapter 8 we will discuss the effects of segregation on the individual and the costs to society of segregating groups.

Historically, people who are blind have been viewed as receiving preferential treatment (Berkowitz, 1987) inasmuch as more services and benefits have been accorded to them. Individuals with visual impairments, as a group, have been the beneficiaries of legislation that offered services only to those who are blind. The original Social Security Act allowed only those who were blind to qualify for public assistance (welfare), and today, individuals who are blind automatically qualify for Social Security benefits. The Randolph-Sheppard Act allowed only people who were blind to operate vending stands in federal buildings, and the Wagner O'Day Act of 1938 required the federal government to purchase products produced in workshops by people who are blind. No other disability group has had legislation and policy written exclusively for it. There is a box on federal income tax forms where taxpayers can indicate if they are blind. Most states (approximately 32) have separate agencies for individuals who are blind. (People with all other types of disabilities are served by a single agency: Vocational Rehabilitation.)

Hearing Impairments

Most people have viewed closed-captioned television programs and watched sign language interpreters at meetings and in the classroom, and a few have had to make accommodations for elderly relatives and friends with hearing loss. Indeed, according to Livneh and Antonak (1997), hearing impairments are among the most prevalent types of physical disability in the United States. In some ways, then, individuals with hearing impairments have achieved some measure of visibility and integration within the broader American culture (Moore, 1987).

Hearing loss is measured in decibels, but in defining the exact level of loss, two other factors are considered: age of onset and site of the loss. Prelingual D/deafness occurs before the individual develops speech, usually before the age of 2 years, and postlingual D/deafness occurs after the age of 2. Obviously, the functional limitations of prelingual D/deafness are greater than those of postlingual D/deafness because with the latter, the individual usually has the capacity to speak. The site of the loss often determines treatment, such as surgery or the use of hearing aids. Estimates of the prevalence of hearing loss in the United States are as high as 28 million people, or 11% of the population.

The cause of more than 25% of all hearing loss is unknown. Nonetheless, hearing impairments are often the result of many known conditions, which are divided into two broad categories: congenital and acquired. Congenital, meaning existing at birth, includes hereditary factors, such as those that cause otosclerosis, and prenatal disease, such as rubella. Acquired hearing loss includes postnatal infections, such as scarlet fever, measles, mumps, influenza, typhoid fever, meningitis, and otitis media. As would be expected, the development of antibiotics has greatly decreased the number of individuals with postlingual D/deafness (Higgins, 1980). Environmental factors, such as physical abuse and exposure to prolonged loud noise, can also cause hearing loss.

The presence of a hearing loss in a child often requires parents to make important decisions early in the child's life (Moore, 1987). The type of education, the means of communication, and the use of technology such as cochlear implants and hearing aids are decisions that will have lifelong effects, yet these decisions must be made early on, when the child is too young to be accorded a great deal of input.

Nonetheless, many individuals with hearing impairments and D/deafness consider themselves to be part of a different culture—D/deaf Culture—claiming individual identity as members of a linguistic culture, rather than as individuals with a disability (Bauman & Drake, 1997; Stokoe, Croneberg, & Casterline, 1965; Van Cleve & Crouch, 1989). Individuals in no other disability category consider themselves to be a different culture. Those who advocate for the identification of a D/deaf Culture cite the use of a different language, American Sign Language (ASL), and the fact that individuals who are D/deaf tend to marry other individuals who are D/deaf. The fact that many of these individuals were educated at residential schools may also contribute to their self-identity as a separate culture. Certainly, their unwillingness to accept "the disabled role" of impairment, deviance, and inferiority plays a large part in the D/deaf Culture movement. The impetus for D/deaf Culture came from within the group of people who are D/deaf and was motivated, for the most part, by the need for solidarity and mutual support. In addition, many D/deaf Culture scholars assert that it is impossible to understand the motivations behind the D/deaf Culture without understanding the tragic history of oralism, in which D/deaf children were not allowed to use sign language and were forced to use oral communication (speaking). Alexander Graham Bell, the inventor of the telephone, was a teacher of D/deaf children, an oralist, and a eugenicist. Although he believed that D/deaf people should be allowed to live, Bell did not believe that D/deaf people should be allowed to marry and have children. In Bell's time, it was not widely known that most D/deaf parents have hearing children.

D/deaf Culture does not view D/deafness as pathology or disability. Jankowski, in her book *D/deaf Empowerment: Emergence, Struggle and Rhetoric* (1997), emphasizes that those in the D/deaf Culture have been opposed to cochlear implants, devices that have the capability to restore some hearing. Jankowski told of a hearing mother in Canada who claimed the right to have her D/deaf child implanted with this device, giving her reason as "it would make him more like her, a hearing person." A former Ontario legislator, Gary Malkowski, replied, "Then you presumably have no objection to D/deaf parents requesting surgery to make their hearing child D/deaf" (p. 145). The D/deaf Culture, at its most extreme, refuses services, accommodations, and cochlear implants and did not support the Americans with Disabilities Act (ADA).

Acceptance into the D/deaf Culture can be narrowly defined. Heather Whitestone, Miss America of 1995, is D/deaf. Whitestone's parents insisted that she learn to speak and therefore she was not fluent in American Sign Language. Ironically, in 1992, Ms. Whitestone competed in the Miss D/deaf Alabama competition "where she was trounced because . . . [she was] unable to fully understand the ASL of the interviewer (or the judges)—and their inability to understand her ironically 'handicapped' Whitestone . . . ." As Whitestone wrote in her autobiography, "Just because I spoke . . . they (Miss D/deaf Alabama pageant officials) decided that I could not fit into the D/deaf culture, that I was not an 'ideal D/deaf person'" (Burch, 2007, p. 255). So, while Whitestone was not considered "D/deaf enough" in the D/deaf Culture, the Miss America Pageant considered her to be D/deaf.

Dual Sensory Loss: D/deaf—Blindness

As would be expected, individuals who are both D/deaf and blind experience severe communication deficits. Another obstacle to the education and rehabilitation of individuals who are D/deaf–blind is the fact that this type of disability is a low-incidence category. Simply because there are so few people whose disabilities fall within this category, it is difficult to provide services and benefits. A biographer of Helen Keller explained the disability of D/deaf–blindness: "Today, relatively few D/deaf–blind people suffer [*sic*] from Helen Keller's condition—that is, being completely D/deaf and blind from an early age. The life-threatening childhood infections such as meningitis and scarlet fever have been for the most part eradicated, and the simultaneous onset of blindness and D/deafness seldom occurs . . . . In general, D/deafness precedes blindness. Today 50 percent of the D/deaf-blind population suffer [*sic*] from Usher syndrome, a genetic condition characterized by hearing loss and by retinitis pigmentosa, an irreversible condition causing . . . eventual total blindness in middle age" (Hermann, 1998, p. 340).

As with simple D/deafness or blindness, time of onset has an important impact on the functional limitations of the individual. Learning to speak is a difficult task for these individuals. Individuals with low-incidence disabilities of any type are often educated in residential schools, far from their homes. Communication is an overriding issue. Helen Keller, probably the most well-known person with dual sensory loss, reported a lifetime of difficulty in distinguishing between her own ideas and the ideas of others because most of what she learned she received literally "secondhand." Information was finger-spelled into her hand (Hermann, 1998).

Mobility Impairments

Mobility impairments interfere with the individual's movement and coordination. Examples of such impairments are spina bifida; cerebral palsy; spinal cord injuries; paraplegia; quadriplegia; muscular dystrophy; and amputations, including congenital limb deficiencies.

Many of these conditions are the result of hereditary conditions; others occur before or during birth, and others occur because of injury or infection. For example, the single largest cause of amputation in the United States is therapeutic surgical procedures necessitated by complications and secondary infections resulting from diabetes. Spinal cord injuries, which often result in paraplegia (paralysis of the lower limbs) or quadriplegia (paralysis of all four limbs and the trunk), are caused by automobile accidents, falls, gunshot wounds, and stabbing, among others. More than 80% of individuals with spinal cord injuries are male. Thus, spinal cord injuries are the only physical disability that is more prevalent among one sex.

Mobility impairments are visible to others, and many individuals with these conditions also experience other disabilities, such as hearing loss, intellectual deficits, and general perceptual difficulties. Some mobility impairments, such as muscular dystrophy, will eventually result in death, but most are stabilized after the acute phase.

Health Disorders and Chronic Illness

Health disorders such as diabetes, seizure disorders, multiple sclerosis, hemophilia, sickle cell anemia, AIDS, and cystic fibrosis are considered to be disabilities because they limit functioning; require treatment, care, and management; and often force individuals with these conditions to be the target of discrimination and prejudice. However, health disorders are different from sensory loss or orthopaedic disabilities in some important aspects. For example, some health disorders are invisible and thus the individual must balance the costs of disclosure against the need for accommodation

(Livneh & Antonak, 1997). Some health disorders, such as diabetes, are asymptomatic and the individual may not be aware that he or she has the disorder. Indeed, some health disorders may be somewhat "invisible" to the individual who has the condition because when symptoms subside, the individual may no longer continue treatment/management, feeling that he or she no longer has the condition. Lifelong management needs and quality-of-life issues are important to individuals with health disorders. The terminal course of some health disorders (the individuals will eventually die from the disorder or complications from the disorder) renders these disabilities different from other disabilities that are stable. Another difference in course or progression of the disability is the episodic nature of many health disorders. Relapses, seizures, or "flare-ups" are often unpredictable and frequently are exacerbated by stress. So, exactly when the individual wants to be symptom-free, such as for job interviews or in social situations, stress may help to bring on an episode of the health disorder.

Intellectual Disabilities

In this section, look for—

- How mental retardation is more than 7 times as prevalent as blindness or D/deafness and 10 times as prevalent as physical disabilities
- Mild mental retardation
- Moderate mental retardation
- Severe mental retardation
- Profound mental retardation

Intellectual disabilities include mental retardation, Down syndrome, and autism. As stated previously, these disabilities are grouped together because of their similar symptoms or manifestations, yet the range of these symptoms is broad. Government funding for education and services for individuals with intellectual disabilities was initiated only recently. Special education in neighborhood schools began in the 1970s (Hardman, Drew, Egan, & Wolf, 1993), and adult services were authorized in 1943. Therefore, today there are many adults with these types of disabilities who either remained at home in the care of the family or were institutionalized. Now, there are both community services and specialized education in regular schools for individuals with these disabilities, allowing the majority to live at home with their families while they receive an education.

Mental Retardation

Mental retardation is defined by the American Association on Intellectual and Developmental Disabilities (AAIDD; formerly known as the American Association on Mental Retardation, or AAMR) as "significantly subaverage general intellectual functioning resulting in or associated with concurrent impairments in adaptive behavior, and manifesting during the developmental period" (Grossman, 1983, p. 11). Individuals with IQs in the range of 55–70 would be considered to have mild mental retardation; those with IQs in the range of 40–54 would be considered to have moderate retardation; those with IQs in the range of 25–39 would have severe retardation; and IQs in the range of 24 or lower indicate profound mental retardation (AAIDD, 1992; American Psychiatric Association, 1994). Adaptive behavior is defined as those behaviors that are necessary to function, such as social, self-help, communication, and occupational behaviors. As with IQ scores, there is a wide range of adaptive behavior, and these levels of functioning are also labeled "mild," "moderate," and "severe." To distinguish mental retardation from disabilities that occur later in life (for example, senile dementia), this diagnosis is determined in the developmental period between birth and age 22 (Drew, Logan, & Hardman, 1992).

It is estimated that approximately 6 million people in the United States (3% of the population) can be classified as having mental retardation, with 90% of these classified as having mild mental retardation (Joseph P. Kennedy, Jr. Foundation, 1991). Mental retardation is more than 7 times as prevalent as blindness or D/deafness and 10 times as prevalent as physical disabilities. Causes of mental retardation include maternal infection during pregnancy, most often congenital rubella or fetal alcohol syndrome; birth trauma (most often lack of oxygen); postnatal infections such as encephalitis or metabolic problems that result in the body's inability to process certain substances; and chromosomal abnormalities.

Cognitive Disabilities

> **In this section, look for—**
> - Traumatic brain injury
> - Learning disabilities

Cognitive disabilities impair perception, memory, information processing, reasoning, sensory discrimination (auditory and visual), and attention. Learning disabilities and traumatic brain injury are cognitive disabilities

(Cruickshank, 1990; Gaddes, 1985; Hallahan, Kauffman, & Lloyd, 1985). The first indication that a child may have a learning disability usually occurs when parents and/or teachers notice a discrepancy between the child's achievement in school and his or her measured intelligence or potential. The child with a learning disability scores lower on achievement tests than his or her classmates but also scores lower than would be expected given his or her assessed level of intelligence/potential (i.e., IQ scores). These discrepancies are a result of the fact that school achievement tests, such as spelling, arithmetic, and handwriting, require skill and facility in the cognitive areas of perception, visual discrimination, auditory discrimination, and information processing (Houck, 1984). Often, individuals with learning disabilities are clumsy, are unable to distinguish their right from their left, have no sense of direction, transpose numbers, are unable to distinguish between sounds of different words, and have poor handwriting skills.

Once considered to be a disability that an individual "outgrew" or, at a minimum, to be a disability only in academic settings, learning disabilities are now known to be lifelong impairments (Johnston, 1987). It is difficult for adults to totally avoid tasks that require reading, writing, or math skills, and, furthermore, the individual knows that he or she is intelligent but is unable to explain his or her difficulties in academic areas (even to himself or herself). Often, spouses of adults with learning disabilities undertake the financial responsibilities for the family and all other family tasks that require writing and math. Also, adults with learning disabilities are frequently underemployed, meaning they work in jobs that do not utilize their full potential.

Hypotheses of the causation generally fall into two categories: neurological causes or genetic causes. Damage to the central nervous system, usually occurring at birth, such as anoxia or abnormal fetal position, or infections are thought to be associated with learning disabilities. Genetic abnormalities are also thought to be linked to learning disabilities. Traumatic brain injuries can be caused by accidents, strokes, or infections. Traumatic brain injuries are the leading cause of death and disability among children and adolescents; these injuries occur most frequently to individuals aged 15 to 24 years. Of those who sustain traumatic brain injuries, 80% are male.

Psychiatric Disabilities

> ### In this section, look for—
> - Mental illness
> - Autism
>
> (continues)

- Chemical and substance abuse
- The relationship between the advent of psychotropic medications and the deinstitutionalization movement
- How the success of psychotropic medication "humanized" mental illness

Psychiatric disabilities, the disability category that was the last to receive government funding for services and benefits, includes mental illness, autism, and chemical and substance abuse. The disabilities in this category are often viewed by the general public as self-imposed and being caused, or at least exaggerated, by the individual's lack of character or willpower.

Indeed, more than any other disability group, the families of individuals with psychiatric disabilities are often blamed for the disability. The combination of societal stigma and a short history of government funding for services renders the category of psychiatric disabilities vulnerable to reduction in social services and discontinuity of care.

Mental illness includes schizophrenia, delusional disorders, bipolar affective disorders, major depression, and anxiety/panic disorders (American Psychiatric Association, 1994). The treatment of mental illness underwent a dramatic shift with the introduction of psychotropic medications. Before the introduction of these medications, individuals with severe psychoses were institutionalized for decades; many individuals lived in institutions for their entire lives. Medications, although certainly not without problems, triggered the deinstitutionalization movement and allowed these former patients to integrate into the community. Perhaps even more important than community integration, the success of psychotropic medication has "humanized" the disability, helping the general public to understand the role of organic/biological factors in the causation of these mental illnesses (Deegan, 1997).

Does Everyone Have a Disability of Some Sort?

In this section, look for—

- How disadvantage is not disability
- Examples of "perceived disabilities"
- The Americans with Disabilities Act definition of disability
- The difference between eligibility programs and entitlement programs

The answer to the question "Does everyone have a disability of some sort?" will affect an individual's self-concept, determine funding and benefits for government services, and assist individuals without disabilities to better understand those who do have disabilities. It is often stated that everyone has limitations, challenges, and problems. This is true. However, disadvantage is not disability. The ADA (1990) clearly defines disability by providing three general guidelines, all of which are necessary: (1) the presence of a physical, cognitive, intellectual, or psychiatric condition, or a combination of conditions; (2) pervasive impairment in social and occupational functioning; and (3) individuals with these impairments are the target of prejudice, discrimination, stigma, and reduced opportunities. So, it can be seen that disability is a combination of the condition, limitations in functioning, and societal prejudice and discrimination.

Are prejudice and discrimination always inherent in the definition of disability? Societal negative response to individuals with disabilities will be discussed in detail in Chapter 3. However, the example of facial disfigurement will illustrate this relationship. There are no functional limitations in many individuals with facial disfigurements, but, not surprisingly, these disabilities are among the most limiting simply because of the reaction of others to the individual with the disfigurement. So, in spite of the fact that the individual has no functional limitations, he or she is often not employed and lives a life of isolation and reduced opportunity. "Perceived" disabilities, such as obesity and stuttering, usually do not involve functional limitations, but individuals who experience these conditions are subject to reduced opportunity, prejudice, and discrimination. The ADA provides protection to people who are *"regarded* as having a disability." Other well-documented examples of visible physical conditions leading to reduced opportunities are lack of height for boys and men and obesity for girls and women. Looking at the newspaper article that described a longitudinal study in Great Britain (1994) (see Exhibit 1–1), it can be seen that, over the lifetime, short men and fat women earned less money. Therefore, individuals with both of these physical traits, the majority of whom experience no functional limitations, fight long-standing prejudice and discrimination. Many of these individuals, as high school students, probably did not get dates for the prom and then continued to be devalued through their lifetimes. This study quantifies the devaluation in terms of lifetime salaries. For the individuals whose daily lives were summarized, categorized, and interpreted in this study, the low salaries and the lack of occupational success and opportunities are probably less hurtful than the social discrimination and alienation they have been forced to endure. There is an interesting aspect to the prejudice and discrimination directed toward height and weight in that the prejudice seems to be gender-specific. Lack of height among women is not generally considered as negative (short women are described by the positive term "petite"), and obesity in men is more accepted by the general public than obesity in women. Men who are overweight are described by such positive terms as "stocky" or "husky."

Exhibit 1-1

Girls' Weight, Boys' Height Affect Earning Power

CHICAGO (AP)—Obese teenage girls and short teenage boys make less money when they become young adults than others their age, a study of thousands of British youths found.

The study doesn't indicate whether the culprit is discrimination or some internal factor such as low self-esteem, but it suggests appearance can have a big effect on teens' transition from school to work, the research said in the July issue of the *Archives of Pediatrics and Adolescent Medicine.*

Dr. James D. Sargent, lead author of the study, said obesity needs to be prevented by teaching children to eat properly. But he said he is also concerned that women are starving themselves or purging to achieve the ideal of thinness prized in British and U.S. society.

Previous studies, including a recent survey of more than 10,000 Americans ages 16 to 24, found that overweight people, especially women, are far less likely to get married or make a comfortable living when they get older.

Dr. William H. Dietz, who led that study, said that the new work "provides once again pretty compelling evidence that obesity is a major social handicap as well as physical handicap."

He said it matters little whether discrimination or factors such as low self-esteem were behind the findings, because both result from societal attitudes.

The new study looked at 12,537 people in England, Scotland, and Wales, where all children born between March 3 and 9, 1958, were enrolled in a national child development study and have been tracked ever since.

The study found that girls in the heaviest 10 percent of their age group at age 16 earned 7.4 percent less than their non-obese peers by the time they reached 23; and those in the heaviest 1 percent earned 11.4 percent less at age 23.

For boys, obesity did not appear to affect earnings, but height did. For every four inches less height at age 16, boys earned 2 percent less at age 23, the researchers found.

Another clear-cut example of a disability with few, if any, functional limitations is provided by Shapiro (1993) in his book *No Pity.* Shapiro told the story of Paul Steven Miller, a top graduate of Harvard Law School and a dwarf. Miller was told by a law firm in Philadelphia that, although the firm was impressed with his credentials, they would not hire Mr. Miller because clients, on meeting Mr. Miller, would, in the words of the interviewer, "think we're running some sort of circus freak show" (p. 28).

Someone who uses eyeglasses does have a vision loss, thus meeting the criterion of the first guideline, but is not considered to have a disability because the use of a simple, easily obtainable technology (eyeglasses or contact lenses) allows the individual to function without impairment. Based on the same argument, that an easily available intervention can restore an individual to full functioning (in this case, medication), the U.S. Supreme Court ruled that a mechanic with high blood pressure did not have a disability and, therefore, was not protected under the ADA (*Murphy v. United Parcel Service*, 141 F.3d 1185, 97-1992). Furthermore, most people who wear eyeglasses have not experienced a great deal of prejudice and discrimination. Also, a severe case of flu is not comparable to the experience of a disability. Although the flu can limit an individual's activities and is an unpleasant and painful episode, it is not a long-term condition. Furthermore, people who have or have had the flu are not the target of prejudice and discrimination, and finally, a bout with the flu has little effect on a person's self-identity. Extreme fear of speaking in public is certainly a limitation, but it is not considered to be a disability because, in addition to the difficulty in documenting a physical condition, people with stage fright experience little functional impairment because they can simply avoid the need to speak in public. Disadvantage is not a disability. In an empirical study published in *Rehabilitation Psychology* in 1996 (Zea, Belgrave, Townsend, Jarama, & Banks, 1996), the authors stated: "Some of the (Latino) participants referred to their disability as 'lack of English'" (p. 235). It appears that 13 subjects, or 26% of the Latino sample, listed lack of English as their disability. Not being able to speak English in the United States is a disadvantage, but it is not a disability. These individuals, who did not have a disability, were compared to others with "physical (disabilities), emotional (disabilities), substance abuse, and cognitive (disabilities)" (p. 230). In spite of the fact that multivariate analyses were used, one fourth of one sample did not have a disability.

Most public agencies that are mandated to serve people with disabilities provide benefits, funds, and services only after eligibility has been determined. Therefore, the individual must apply for services; provide evidence of the disability, which sometimes includes submitting to extended evaluation procedures; and then be determined "eligible for services" or "not eligible." The three guidelines established by the ADA comprise the eligibility criteria for most of these agencies. Rather than an entitlement program, in which individuals who are part of a mandated population are automatically accepted for services, services for people with disabilities are usually eligibility programs and applicants must prove their eligibility. Public education is an entitlement program, but most disability agencies (including vocational rehabilitation) are eligibility programs.

Another difference between entitlement and eligibility programs concerns funding. In entitlement programs, such as income support programs (Social Security Disability Income [SSDI] and Supplemental Security Income [SSI]) and Medicaid and Medicare, individuals are provided services regardless of the availability of funds. In contrast, individuals in eligibility programs may not receive services if funds are not available (McDonnell,

Hardman, McDonnell, & Kiefer-O'Donnell, 1995). Most entitlement programs are federal programs, and eligibility programs are administered by the state.

There Are More Disabilities Than Ever Before

In this section, look for—

- The differing definitions of disability used by government agencies
- The six reasons why there are more disabilities than ever before
- The increase in disability is progress—both for individuals with disabilities and society
    1. Advances in neonatal medicine
    2. Advances in emergency medicine and trauma care
    3. Aging of the population
    4. Longer life spans of PWDs
    5. Liberalization and expansion of the definition of disability
    6. More accurate counting
- The alternative (to having a disability) for the first four reasons would be the death of the individual

Disability is a natural and ordinary part of life, and there is a larger proportion of the population with disabilities today than before. It seems likely that this number will continue to grow. An important point to remember is that these increasing rates of disability are advances (both for the individual and society) because, in most cases, the alternative to the acquisition of a disability would be the individual's death. Modern medicine has increased the number of individuals with disabilities, increased their life spans, and improved their quality of life. People who would have died now survive with a disability. It is estimated that the number of people with disabilities exceeds 45 million (Americans with Disabilities Act, 1990; Equal Employment Opportunity Commission, 1991; Ficke, 1992; Hahn, 1991, 1993; LaPlante, 1991, 1997). One factor that makes it difficult to determine accurate disability counts is the difference in the definition of disability (LaPlante, 1997; Pfeiffer, 1993; Zola, 1993).

There is no uniform definition of disability because government agencies define disability differently (Zola, 1993). Further clouding the picture is the fact that some health demographers (people who count and categorize the number of health conditions and disabilities) do not define disability as completely as do rehabilitation demographers. For example, while rehabilitation demographers define alcohol abuse and learning disorders as disabilities, health demographers do not. Finally, rehabilitation demographers are also concerned about health conditions such as obesity, diabetes, and hypertension, which, if not defined as disabilities, are disposing factors that lead to disability.

Some federal programs such as SSDI and SSI define disability in terms of activity limitations either in "major life activities" or "work limitations." This functional limitation definition of a disability, especially with regard to work limitations, is economically motivated. Children younger than age 16 and individuals older than age 65 are not typically included in these surveys because they are thought to be "excused" from work. Medical organizations and the diagnostic manuals they produce, such as the *International Classifications of Impairments, Disabilities, and Handicaps* (Thompson-Hoffman & Storck, 1991; World Health Organization, 1980), define disabilities in terms of pathology, losses, disorders, impairments, defects, and abnormalities in physical, psychological, or anatomical structure or function.

A disability scholar, Walkup (2000) views the "definitional diversity" of disability as necessary and as an ascendant trajectory because when both professionals and the public understand the various factors in the definition of disability, deeper understandings will result. Rather than simply viewing disability as a physical impairment, disability is now defined much more broadly, taking interactional factors, such as the environment and the individual's resources, into account. Walkup pointed out that more consistent, standardized communication among professionals, policymakers, and the public is "no mere housekeeping" task:

> Although not posing any problem in principle, standardization of concepts and measures is no mere "housekeeping" task. Definitional diversity is partly maintained because, even under the best of circumstances, extensive amounts of hard thought and labor are required to operationalize a concept. Moreover, even when all parties can agree that new concepts or measures are needed, disability definitions carry consequences for agencies, professionals, advocates, and politicians. (Walkup, 2000, p. 411)

In 2001, the World Health Organization published a comprehensive classification system, the *International Classification of Functioning, Disability and Health* (ICF; WHO, 2001). Indeed, the ICF appears to have surmounted many of the conceptual inadequacies of the International Classification of Impairments, Disabilities, and Handicaps (or ICIDH, as it was previously known). In Chapter 2, when we discuss the Functional Model of Disability, features of the ICF will be presented.

Challenges in Counting Disability

There is no way to know the exact number of disabilities. Surveys are a major undertaking, both expensive and time-consuming. It is necessary to design and develop a questionnaire, implement accurate sampling procedures, and create interviewing and coding procedures. Field-testing of procedures is lengthy and expensive. Data analysis is complex. However, there are surveys that seek to learn the number and types of disabilities. There are three major sources of federal data and, although none of these sources allows for a determination of causality, all three surveys have different purposes (Thompson-Hoffman & Storck, 1991). The goals of some of these survey programs are simply to gather economic and social data on the *entire* population and include some questions about disability. The goal of the second type of national survey is to collect data on the health status of all Americans, and we have seen that health demographers define disability differently than disability programs do. The goal of the third type of national survey is to assess the number of individuals who are receiving benefits and services from federal disability agencies and programs; therefore, only recipients are surveyed. Obviously, there are many PWDs who are not recipients of services; therefore, these types of surveys would grossly underestimate the number of disabilities. Advocacy groups (nonprofit, consumer-driven groups that typically represent one type of disability) use government survey data because such groups would not have the resources to undertake large-scale national surveys.

In addition to the logistical challenges of collecting data, the prevalence of disability is underreported because some disabilities are still considered to be stigmatizing and individuals are reluctant to report family members who have these disabilities. In addition, there are many individuals who have disabilities, such as learning disabilities, but are not aware that they do, in fact, have a disability.

It is probably safe to assume that the narrow definitions and the lack of consistency among agencies and different demographic methods result in underestimations and underreporting of the prevalence of disability. Nonetheless, it is widely understood that the higher rates of disability result from the six factors explained in the following section (Jones, Sanford, & Bell, 1997; Kaye, LaPlante, Carlson, & Wenger, 1997; Pope & Tarlov, 1991).

Considering only disability costs, "in the United States, annual disability costs have doubled in the past 10 years to approximately $23 billion a year. During this time, the number of beneficiaries of public disability income support has increased by 57% from 4 million to 5.3 million citizens" (Kouzis & Eaton, 2000, p. 908).

Six Reasons for Increasing Disability Rates

Advances in Neonatal Medicine

There are more congenital disabilities (disabilities present at birth) than ever before as a result of the capabilities of neonatal medicine to sustain life. Neonatal medicine is a specialty that concerns itself with newborn infants. Infants who in the past would have died now undergo treatment in the uterus and receive better monitoring and care during the birth process and advanced treatment during the first few months of life. As a result, more babies are born, and more babies live, with cerebral palsy, spina bifida, and mental retardation. For example, babies who are premature and have low birthweight experience high rates of neurological conditions. In the past, premature infants who weighed less than 3.3 pounds rarely survived. Today, it is commonplace for infants as small as 1.5 pounds to survive. The increasing number of births to teenage mothers also contributes to greater incidence of congenital disabilities because teenage mothers have higher rates of babies who are premature or have low birthweight, or both (Himmelstein, Woolhandler, & Wolfe, 1992). Medical advances and technology, such as fertility enhancement, have brought about multiple births. This increased prevalence of multiple births has also augmented the number of congenital disabilities. For example, there is a fourfold increase in the probability of an infant's having cerebral palsy if the infant is part of a multiple birth. The strides of neonatology have resulted in higher rates of cerebral palsy, mental retardation, and spina bifida.

Advances in Emergency Medicine and Trauma Care

The Vietnam War was a great impetus to the development of emergency medicine and trauma care, and the larger medical community incorporated these military methods of evacuating people with injuries and providing trauma care while en route to the hospital. As a result of these advances, victims of accidents or trauma experience high survival rates because they are evacuated from the scene quickly, treated, and stabilized while being transported to the hospital. Fewer individuals die before they reach the hospital. In 1980, for example, less than 10% of individuals with traumatic brain injury or spinal cord injuries survived. Today, the survival rate for individuals with these disabilities is higher than 90%.

Individuals with spinal cord injuries experience permanent paralysis and other health problems such as decubitus ulcers or pressure sores (bed sores) and respiratory and bladder complications. Antibiotics that treat, and cure, these secondary infections allow individuals with spinal cord injuries (and amputations) to experience long life spans (Crewe, 1993). After World

War I, there were 400 American men with battle injuries that paralyzed them from the waist down. Of these men, 90% died before they reached home, most as a consequence of secondary infections. After World War II and the discovery of antibiotics, there were 2,000 veterans with paraplegia and 85% were alive 20 years later (Shapiro, 1993). Indeed, most individuals today with paraplegia or quadriplegia consider themselves to be healthy (some consider themselves athletes), controlling infections and other complications with the use of antibiotics. It should be noted that individuals with paraplegia or quadriplegia do not live as long as individuals without these conditions; nonetheless, these individuals usually live for a long period after the onset of their disability.

Aging of the Population

It is clear that as an individual ages, he or she has a greater probability of acquiring a disability, most often a chronic illness. It is also clear that as a large proportion of a population ages, such as is occurring in the United States presently, the population becomes more disabled. Two social workers summarized the aging of the American population in this way: "The aging are coming and they are us" (Galambos & Rosen, 2000, p. 13). In the 20th century, "the percentage of Americans ages 65 and older . . . more than tripled and the number . . . increased 11 times" (Galambos & Rosen, 2000). In the year 2030, more than one in five people will be older than age 65, and by the year 2050, if current trends continue, the percentage of older adults in the population will exceed the percentage of children (Conway-Giustra, Crowley, & Gorin, 2002).

Medicine and medical technology have lengthened the life span of Americans. For example, since the 1970s stroke *mortality rates* have decreased significantly, but the *incidence* of stroke has not decreased. Obviously, more individuals survive strokes, many with disabilities.

Arthritis is very common among older individuals, but arthritis, although disabling, is rarely fatal. Of all therapeutic amputations performed in the United States today, 75% are performed on people older than age 65. Most of these amputations are the result of complications of diabetes. Diabetes, a condition often associated with old age, is the leading cause of blindness in the United States. Mobility impairments and sensory loss are prevalent among elderly people. As Americans live longer, they will continue to experience higher disability rates (Higgins, 1992; Zola, 1989). Indeed, by the year 2040, when the younger baby boomers are 85 years old, the number of Americans with disabilities will be triple what it is today. Also, those individuals with congenital disabilities or disabilities acquired early in life are experiencing longer life spans (Wilkins & Cott, 1993).

Nonetheless, it is now thought that the rate of disability among older Americans has been overestimated (Jacoby, 2002). Health demographers are not quite sure what is contributing to these lower disability rates among older people, but they consider the lower rates of smoking and drinking, healthier lifestyles, and medications for heart disease and high blood pressures to be contributing factors.

People With Disabilities Live Longer

Not only are there more people with disabilities, but people with disabilities live longer with the disabilities than before (Becker & Kaufman, 1988; Benedict & Ganikos, 1981; Brody & Ruff, 1986; Mitchell & Kemp, 1996). Trieschmann (1987) noted:

> Aging is synonymous with living. . . . The issue of aging with a disability is a new problem for western societies, one that has caught our health care system by surprise. Currently, individuals who have lived with spinal injury, polio, and other disabilities for 30, 40, and 50 years are arriving in physicians' offices with a variety of complaints that the physicians have not been taught to handle. (p. 1)

The overall increase in the life span contributes to the longer lives of people with disabilities; but even more important are the scientific, technological, and medical advances in the management and treatment of chronic disabilities. To cite a single example, 50 years ago, many parents of infants with disabilities were told by physicians that their babies would not survive to adulthood. Fifty years ago, this was an accurate prognosis. Now, the situation is very different, and most infants with congenital or early-onset disabilities survive to adulthood. Indeed, more than 90% of children with disabilities survive into adulthood (White, 2002). Living longer with a disability has implications for the individual, the family, and the larger society.

For example, individuals with Down syndrome (a genetic condition that causes mental retardation) are living twice as long as they did 20 years ago. The average life span of someone with Down syndrome in 2007 was 56 years, while in 1983, the average life span was 25 years. Better medical care and advances in surgery have led to these longer life spans. Before the 1980s there were no programs for adults with Down syndrome simply because there were very few adults with this condition.

Harriet McBryde Johnson, a 39-year-old lawyer, was born with muscular dystrophy. Her parents were told that she would die in her teenage years. In an article entitled "Too Late to Die Young," s] childhood, "The death sentence hangs over my childhood (Johnson, 2005, p. 44). McBryde Johnson describes her life: continues to deteriorate, my life looks more and more n I leave the cozy comfort of home to go to law school. I figure]

I finish; if I go now I can probably practice for a couple of years. By this time, the thought is almost subconscious: when I die I might as well die a lawyer" (p. 46). She concludes, "My plan to die young hasn't worked out . . . . It's too late to die young."

The combination of the longer lives of PWDs and the survival rates of individuals with certain types of disability results in challenges for newly trained medical professionals. In a study entitled *Health and Wellness: People with Disabilities Discuss Barriers and Facilitators to Well Meaning* (Putnam, Greenen, Powers, Saxton, Finney, & Dautel, 2003), researchers stated:

> A common complaint was the lack of knowledge medical professionals have in general about disabilities, such as spinal cord injuries, polio, multiple sclerosis, cerebral palsy, and amputation. One participant said, "We have doctors now that are so young they've never even seen a case of polio. And several of my doctors, I've had to educate them and send them materials and talk to them about it because they have no experience." Another stated, "In my condition as a paraplegic, I find that the medical profession is . . . ignorant in most things, dealing with a person who's a paraplegic because they have no concept of what I can or cannot do, and they're afraid to ask." (p. 42)

Stubbins (1988) asserted that medical science has not only increased the number of people with disabilities but also changed the experience and personal significance of disability: "Medical advances have transformed the central meaning of disability from physical survival to the search for meaning when one is socially isolated, unemployed, or underemployed, and lacking essential environmental accommodations" (p. 24). Furthermore, the health care financing system and federal agencies and programs have not kept pace with the increased life spans of PWDs. Additionally, there are young adults with disabilities who want to become independent and obtain education, jobs, and marriage, and there are few policies or agencies in place to assist them.

Liberalization and Expansion of the Definition of Disability

The expansion or liberalization of the definition of disability has resulted in higher numbers of disabilities. This is termed a "statistical" cause because the number of people with these types of disabilities did not increase; rather, the way in which their disability was defined or diagnosed changed. Nonetheless, changes in definition result in greater numbers of people to be served and more people who consider themselves to have a disability.

Disability used to be thought of as only physical disability by both the general public and government policymakers. Even today there are many who think of disability solely in terms of physical disabilities. Nonetheless, such impairments as mental illness, learning disabilities, and alcohol dependence and substance abuse are defined as disabilities, and individuals who experience these conditions are eligible for services and accommodations. It should be noted that there are a few experts who do not consider conditions such as alcoholism to be diseases or disabilities (Fingarette, 1988; Peele, 1989). Last to be legally recognized as disabilities, psychiatric and cognitive disabilities are the first to be eliminated in government agency guidelines. For example, in 1997 the Social Security Administration ruled that individuals with alcohol or chemical dependency were no longer eligible for benefits (Watkins & Podus, 2000).

In addition to the liberalization of the definition of disability, it is safe to state that there has also been an expansion in the definition of disability. Examples such as AIDS, post-polio syndrome, and chronic fatigue syndrome illustrate that the number and types of disabilities are expanding. The *Diagnostic and Statistical Manual of Mental Disorders–Fourth Edition* (*DSM-IV;* American Psychiatric Association, 1994) contains 120 more diagnoses than its predecessor, the *Diagnostic and Statistical Manual of Mental Disorders–Third Edition, Revised* (*DSM-III-R;* American Psychiatric Association, 1987). Although most of these 120 new diagnoses are simply refinements or subcategories of long-established diagnoses, several diagnoses are new. Indeed, the editors stress the evolving nature of the *DSM*. It is interesting that some clinicians (Turner & Hersen, 1997) have noted that many of these new diagnoses fail to make a clear distinction between the disorder and normal functioning. (It should be noted that not all psychiatric disorders are considered to be disabilities.) Other diagnostic guidebooks, such as the *International Classification of Diseases* (ICD, World Health Organization, 1980), also continue to add diagnoses (Wallis, 2007).

Learning disabilities provide an illustration of the liberalization of the definition and the way in which such definitions reduce stigmatization and allow for accommodations. John R. Horner flunked out of the University of Montana six times, but later "his brilliant synthesis of evidence . . . forced paleontologists to revise their ideas about dinosaur behavior, physiology, and evolution" (West, 1994, p. 334; cf. Gerber & Brown, 1994). Horner related the stigma of learning disabilities: "Back in the days when I was growing up, nobody knew what dyslexia was . . . . So everybody thought you were lazy or stupid or both. And I didn't think I was, but I wasn't sure" (Gerber & Brown, 1994).

Not everyone accepts some of the more recently defined disabilities as legitimate disabilities that are protected under the Americans with Disabilities Act and therefore require accommodations. "Barbara Bateman (1992), one of the most respected leaders in the field of learning disabilities, noted that even after a quarter of a century of evolution in this field, we still find individuals who believe that learning disabilities do not exist. Unfortunately, there are still individuals directing universities, graduate schools, medical schools, and corporate training programs who think that a learning disability is just another fancy excuse for getting special attention" (Brinkerhoff, 1997, p. 145).

More Accurate Counting

As both the general public and government policymakers become more clear on the definitions of disability, the numbers of all individuals *reported* to have disabilities continue to climb. Essentially, more accurate counting is another "statistical" cause for the higher disability rates because the number of people with disabilities did not increase, only the number of people who are counted or reported as having a disability. Further, disability and health demographers consider the reported number of disabilities to be an underestimation, simply because there are many individuals who do not wish to identify themselves as having a disability. Another illustration of more individuals reporting disabilities concerns the inverse relationship between the economy and disability rates (Yelin, 1992). During economic slumps and depressions, more individuals claim disabilities; most of these individuals are unemployed and need to claim their disability to receive financial benefits. In times of prosperity, the number of disability claims decreases. Therefore, the number of people with disabilities did not increase, but rather the number of people *reporting* disabilities.

Table 1–1 is a graphic representation of defining (and counting) disability in terms of work limitations. Looking across the first row, it can be seen that a much higher percentage of working-age Americans have "any work disability" than have a "severe work disability." (Of responders, 2.8% report "not severe work disability" and 7.5% report "severe work disability.") There appears to be little difference between males and females in either disability category. There are five age categories and, in both categories of disabilities, the percentage goes up as age goes up. (Statisticians state, "There is a positive relationship between prevalence of disability and age.")

The biggest single percentage increase is found in the severe disability category from the ages of 45 to 54 and 55 to 64 years. The 45- to 54-year-old group reports 9.5%, and the 55- to 64-year-old group reports almost twice the percentage (15.7%).

Figure 1–1 shows the increase, from 1981 to 2004, in the percentage of the U.S. population with a disability. Disability is defined as "work limitation." Each increment on the chart represents 1 percentage point. It can be seen that in 1984, approximately 14.5% reported a "work limitation," while in 1994, this percentage had increased to 15%–16%. This increase may not appear, at first glance, to be significant, but the increase in percentage represents tens of thousands of individuals.

Other information on disability from the U.S. Census Bureau includes the following:

Population Distribution

- 51.2 million Americans have some level of disability. They represent 18% of the population.
- 32.5 million Americans have a severe disability. They represent 12% of the population.
- 4 million children, ages 6 to 14, have a disability. They represent 11% of the population of children.
- 72% of people older than age 80 have a disability. This is the highest percentage of any age group.
- 20% of females have a disability, which is higher than the 17% of males. However, among children younger than age 15, boys are more likely than girls to have a disability (11% versus 6%).

Specific Disabilities

- 1.8 million people who are aged 15 and older report a visual impairment.
- 1 million people who are age 15 and older report a hearing impairment.

Table 1-1

Prevalence of Work Disability Among Persons Aged 16–64 by Gender and All Education Levels, 2005

| | | With a Work Disability | | | |
| | | Not Severe | | Severe | |
	Total (thousands)	Number (thousands)	Percentage of total	Number (thousands)	Percentage of total
All persons aged 16–64	190,023	5,413	2.8	14,242	7.5
Males	93,551	2,715	2.9	6,952	7.4
Females	97,472	2,698	2.8	7,290	7.6
Ages 16–24	36,589	510	1.4	1,199	3.3
Ages 25–34	38,990	739	1.9	1,736	4.5
Ages 35–44	43,057	1,067	2.5	2,697	6.3
Ages 44–54	41,869	1,394	3.3	3,987	9.5
Ages 55–64	29,518	1,703	5.8	4,623	15.7

U.S. Census Bureau, Disability Selected Characteristics of Persons 16–74: 2005. Retrieved June 19, 2007, from http://www.census.gov/hhes/www/disability/cps/cps105.html.

Figure 1–1 Percentage of men and women aged 18–64 who reported a work limitation in the U.S. from 1981 to 2004. Houtenville, A. J., Erickson, W. A., Lee, C. G. (2007, March 16). Disability Statistics from the American Community Survey (ACS). Ithaca, NY: Cornell University Rehabilitation Research and Training Center on Disability Demographics and Statistics (StatsRRTC). Retrieved June 18, 2007 from www.disabilitystatistics.org.

- 2.6 million people who are aged 15 and older have some difficulty in having their speech understood by others. Of this number, 610,000 were unable to have their speech understood at all.

- 14.3 million people report a limitation in cognitive functioning or a mental or emotional illness that interferes with their daily activities. This includes those with Alzheimer's disease, depression, and mental retardation. This group comprises 6% of the population.

Military Veterans

- 2.6 million veterans received compensation for service-related disabilities as of 2004. Of these veterans, 506,000 served in World War II; 237,000 in Korea; 1 million in Vietnam; and 540,00 in the Persian Gulf.

Medical Advances and Societal Advances

Certainly there have been societal advances that have eliminated some disabilities and reduced the number of other types of disabilities. Workplace safety, public sanitation, and more widely available health insurance are all examples of societal advances that have reduced the number of disabilities. Large-scale epidemics, such as polio epidemics, have been eradicated in the Western, developed world; however, there are probably more disabilities caused by recreational/sports injuries than in the past. Wars continue to produce disabilities and, indeed, the combat survival rates continue to climb along with the disability rate.

There is a widespread belief that if medical and scientific communities had the capability to prevent all congenital disabilities, there would be no babies born with disabilities. For example, a producer's description of a videotape about children with disabilities concludes with this sentence: "The program also addresses the growing likelihood that prenatal testing and advances in gene technology may make the current generation of those with physical challenges [*sic*] the last (generation)." Of course, medical researchers and other scientists should work to prevent disability, but this does not imply that all parents would choose to terminate a pregnancy rather than to give birth to a baby with a disability. Perhaps even more important is society's conceptualization of the "problem."

Such a quick and facile acceptance of the desirability of ending all congenital disabilities demonstrates the widely perceived source of the "problem." The problem is erroneously thought to be the person with the disability. It is more accurate to think of the environment as the problem. For example, the decision-making process of prospective parents who learn that their baby will be born with a disability would be very different if the following conditions were present: (1) all PWDs were accorded full equality and participation in society, including social and intimate relationships; (2) all PWDs had access to the adaptive technology they need and want; (3) all PWDs were provided with the medical resources to manage and control their disabilities; and (4) all PWDs were provided ethical and capable personal care attendants, if needed. Reviewing this list, it is possible to see that none of these conditions relates to the *presence* of disability itself. None of these four conditions proposes to *prevent* or *cure* disability. These conditions propose change—not in the individual with the disability or his or her parents, but in the broader environment.

In-Class Video

■ View the 17-minute video "Understanding Hearing Loss" by Films for the Humanities and Sciences (P.O. Box 2053, Princeton, NJ 08543-2053, 800-257-5126, www.films.com). The producers describe this video: "This program explains sound, hearing, hearing loss, and the relationship between listening to speech and the different kinds of hearing loss. It includes realistic simulations of what speech sounds like with different kinds of hearing loss and useful hints on improving communication."

- View the video "Asperger's: Living Outside the Bell Curve." One of the parents of a child with Asperger's syndrome makes this statement, "It's sad that we can no longer just be quirky or odd, but that we must have a diagnosis." Another parent states, "Society does force people who are different from the norm to explain why they are different." Discuss these statements, relating them to concepts of normalcy in this chapter and the value of a diagnosis. Read the book review entitled "What Autism Epidemic?" in *Time Magazine* (January 22, 2007, p. 69). Compare the arguments for defining autism as a disability and the arguments against such a definition.

- View the 29-minute video "Dyslexia: A Different Kind of Mind," by Films for the Humanities. This program from *The Doctor Is In* explores how students with dyslexia learn and how new teaching techniques are helping them succeed in school. Thomas West, author of *In the Mind's Eye*, discusses our society's need for the visual talents, possessed by many people with dyslexia.

Learning Activities

1. Read the book *A Nearly Normal Life* by Charlie L. Mee (1999, New York: Little, Brown). Focus on Mee's definition of normal and the "desirability of normal" and his own "deviance from normalcy." What does the author mean by "The need to expand our concept of normalcy"? Why does he think this is necessary?

2. Read the book *Three Quarters, Two Dimes, and a Nickel* by Steve Fiffer (1999, New York: Free Press). Write a short paper explaining why the title of the book is not *One Dollar*.

3. Read Zola's paper on the various definitions of disability and how each of these definitions reflects the needs and values of the definers ("The Politics of Disability" in *Disability Studies Quarterly, 12,* 1992). Read Hahn's (1993) paper "The Political Implications of Disability Definitions and Data." Write a summary paper.

4. Listen to *On a Roll: Talk Radio on Life and Disability* with host Greg Smith. *On a Roll* airs on 36 radio stations across the country, as well as the Internet live every Sunday at 9:05 p.m. Eastern time. The program also has Internet-only streaming audio segments at www.thestrengthcoach.com. *On a Roll* is sponsored by Microsoft (www.microsoft.com/enable), the Action Storm Series Power Chairs (www.invacare.com), EasyStand (www.easystand .com), and NeverLand Adventures (619-696-6068).

5. Read the special issue *Disability Policy Studies* (1993, 1994) that discusses the differing definitions of disability. Write a paper describing these differing definitions; the source and rationale of each definition; and the legal, clinical, and personal implications of each definition.

6. Give the definition of disability found in the following legislation: SSDI-SSI and ADA. Write a short paper outlining the similarities and differences among the definitions and the implications these conflicting definitions have for individuals with disabilities.

7. Taking the example of the space aliens given earlier in this chapter, write a short paper describing the prejudice, discrimination, and stereotyping the aliens would encounter.

8. Go to the library and access the second edition of Radius CD-ROMs. These 19 CD-ROM data sets are the largest single source on disability. Students can analyze disability in terms of demographic, health, employment, and other social variables.
Find this CD-ROM: "1998 National Organization of Disability Survey of Americans with Disabilities" and write a paper on some aspect of disability and its relation to demographic variables such as sex, age, geographic area, income, level of education, or ethnicity/race. Note: These data include 438 variables and 1,000 case studies. Radius 1999 Edition is available at most university libraries. Their Web site is www.socio.com and their e-mail address is socio@socio.com.

9. Go to the Web site for the National Dissemination Center for Children with Disabilities Clearinghouse for National Information Center for Child and Youth with Disabilities (www.nichcy.org).

Writing Experience

Using any of the nine "bullet" questions listed at the beginning of this chapter, write a paper that responds to one of these questions.

References

Albrecht, G. L. (Ed.). (1976). *The sociology of physical disability and rehabilitation*. Pittsburgh, PA: University of Pittsburgh Press.

American Association on Intellectual and Developmental Disabilities. (1992). *Mental retardation: Definition, classification, and systems of supports* (Special 9th ed.). Washington, DC: Author.

American Psychiatric Association. (1994). *Diagnostic and statistical manual of mental disorders* (4th ed.). Washington, DC: Author.

Americans with Disabilities Act of 1990, 42 U.S.C. § 12101 *et seq.* Available: www.usdoj .gov/crt/ada/adahomal.htm.

Bauman, H. D. L., & Drake, J. (1997). Silence is not without voice: Including D/deaf culture within the multicultural curricula. In L. J. Davis (Ed.), *Disability studies reader* (pp. 307–314). New York: Routledge.

Baynton, D. C. (1997, Spring). Disability: A useful category of historical analysis. *Disability Studies Quarterly, 17* (2).

Becker, G., & Kaufman, S. (1988). Old age, rehabilitation, and research: A review of the issues. *The Gerontologist, 28,* 459–468.

Benedict, R., & Ganikos, M. (1981). Coming to terms with ageism in rehabilitation. *Journal of Rehabilitation, 47*(4), 10–18.

Berkowitz, E. D. (1987). *Disabled policy: America's programs for the handicapped.* London, England: Cambridge University.

Berube, M. (1998). Foreword. In S. Linton (Ed.), *Claiming disability: Knowledge and identity* (pp. vii–xv). New York: New York University.

Bowe, F. (1981). *Demography and disability: A chartbook for rehabilitation.* Hot Springs, AR: University of Arkansas, Arkansas Rehabilitation Services, Arkansas Rehabilitation Research and Training Center.

Bowe, F. (1984). *U.S. Census and disabled adults.* Hot Springs, AR: University of Arkansas, Arkansas Rehabilitation Services, Arkansas Rehabilitation Research and Training Center.

Bowe, F. (1985). *Black adults with disabilities.* Washington, DC: U.S. Census Bureau.

Bowe, F. (1993). Statistics, politics, and employment of people with disabilities. *Journal of Disability Policy Studies, 4,* 83–91.

Bradsher, J. E. (1997). Disability among racial and ethnic groups, #10 [On-line]. *Disability Statistics Abstract.* San Francisco: University of California at San Francisco. Available: www.dsc.ucsf.edu.

Brettell, C. B., & Sargent, C. F. (Eds.). (2005). *Gender in cross-cultural perspective* (4th ed.). Upper Saddle River, NJ: Prentice Hall.

Brinkerhoff, L. C. (1997). Students with learning disabilities in graduate or professional programs: Emerging issues on campus and challenges to employment. In P. J. Gerbert & D.S. Brown (Eds.), *Learning disabilities and employment* (pp. 143–164). Austin, TX: PRO-ED.

Brody, S., & Ruff, G. (Eds.). (1986). *Aging and rehabilitation: Advances in the state of the art.* New York: Springer.

Brown, S. C. (1991). Conceptualizing and defining disability. In S. Thompson-Hoffman & I. F. Storck (Eds.), *Disability in the United States: A portrait from national data* (pp. 1–14). New York: Springer.

Burch, S. (2007). "Beautiful, though D/deaf": The D/deaf American Beauty Pageant. In B. J. Brueggemann & S. Burch (Eds.), *Women and D/deafness: Double visions* (pp. 242–261). Washington, DC: Gallaudet University.

Butcher, J. N., Dahlstrom, W. G., Graham, J. R., Tellegen, A., & Kaemmer, B. (2001). *Minnesota multiphasic personality inventory* (2nd ed.). Bloomington, MN: NCS Pearson.

Carroll, T. J. (1961). *Blindness: What it is, what it does, and how to live with it.* Boston: Little, Brown.

Clendinen, D., & Nagourney, A. (1999). *Out for good: The struggle to build a gay rights movement in America.* New York: Simon & Schuster.

Conway-Giustra, F., Crowley, A., & Gorin, S. H. (2002). Crisis in caregiving: A call to action. *Health and Social Work, 27,* 307–311.

Crewe, N. M. (1993). Aging and severe physical disability: Patterns of change and implications for change. In M. Nagler (Ed.), *Perspectives on disability* (2nd ed., pp. 355–361). Palo Alto, CA: Health Markets Research.

Cruickshank, W. M. (1990). Definition: A major issue in the field of learning disabilities. In M. Nagler (Ed.), *Perspectives on disability* (pp. 389–406). Palo Alto, CA: Health Markets Research.

Darwin, D. (1979). *The illustrated origin of species (abridged and introduced by Richard E. Leakey)*. New York: Hill and Wang.

Davis, L. J. (1997). Constructing normalcy: The bell curve, the novel, and the invention of the disabled body in the nineteenth century. In L. J. Davis (Ed.), *Disability studies reader* (pp. 307–314). New York: Routledge.

Deegan, P. E. (1997). Recovery: The lived experience of rehabilitation. In L. Spaniol, C. Gagne, & M. Koehler (Eds.), *Psychological and social aspects of psychiatric disability* (pp. 92–98). Boston: Boston University, Center for Psychiatric Rehabilitation.

DeJong, G., & Lifchez, R. (1983). Physical disability and public policy. *Scientific American, 248*(6), 40–49.

Diamond, J. (1999). *Guns, germs, and steel: The fate of human societies*. New York: W. W. Norton.

Drew, C. J., Logan, D. R., & Hardman, M. L. (1992). *Mental retardation: Life cycle approach* (5th ed.). Columbus, OH: Merrill.

Equal Employment Opportunity Commission Office of Program Publications. (1991). *National database: Americans with Disabilities Act receipts 100194-093095*. Washington, DC: Author.

Falvo, D. R. (1991). *Medical and psychosocial aspects of chronic illness and disability*. Gaithersburg, MD: Aspen.

Ficke, R. C. (1992). *Digest of data of persons with disabilities: 1992*. Washington, DC: National Institute on Disability and Rehabilitation Research.

Fingarette, H. (1988). *Heavy drinking*. Berkeley, CA: University of California.

Fisher, R. A. (1958). *The genetical theory of natural selection* (2nd ed.). New York: Dover.

Fleischer, D. Z., & Zames, F. (2001). *The disability rights movement: From charity to confrontation*. Philadelphia, PA: Temple University.

Friedlander, H. (1996). *The origins of Nazi genocide: From euthanasia to the final solution*. Chapel Hill, NC: University of North Carolina.

Gaddes, W. H. (1985). *Learning disabilities and brain function: A neuropsychological approach* (2nd ed.). New York: Springer-Verlag.

Galambos, C. M., & Rosen, A. (2000). The aging are coming and they are us. In S. M. Keigher, A. E. Fortune, & S. L. Witkin (Eds.), *Aging and social work: The changing landscapes* (pp. 13–19). Washington, DC: NASW Press.

Galton, F. (1869). *Hereditary genius*. London: Macmillan.

Galton, F. (1883). *Inquiries into human faculty and its development*. New York: Dutton.

Galton, F. (1887). *Hereditary genius: An inquiry into its lows and consequences*. New York: Appleton.

Gerber, P. J., & Brown, D. S. (Eds.). (1997). *Learning disabilities and employment*. Austin, TX: PRO-ED.

Girls' weight, boys' height affects earning power. (1994, July 13). *Standard-Examiner*, p. A4.

Gould, S. J. (1981). *The mismeasure of man*. New York: W.W. Norton.

Groce, N. (1985). *Everybody here spoke sign language: Hereditary D/deafness on Martha's Vineyard*. Cambridge, MA: Harvard University.

Grossman, H. J. (Ed.). (1983). *Manual on terminology and classification in mental retardation*. Washington, DC: American Association on Mental Deficiency.

Hahn, H. (1988). The politics of physical differences: Disability and discrimination. *Journal of Social Issues, 44,* 39–47.

Hahn, H. (1991). Foreword. In R. P. Marinelli & A. E. Dell Orto (Eds.), *The psychological and social impact of physical disability* (3rd ed., pp. ix–x). New York: Springer.

Hahn, H. (1993). The political implications of disability definitions and data. *Journal of Disability Policy Studies, 4,* 41–52.

Hallahan, D. P., Kauffman, J. M., & Lloyd, J. W. (1985). *Introduction to learning disabilities* (2nd ed.). Englewood Cliffs, NJ: Prentice Hall.

Hannah, M. E., & Midlarsky, E. (1987). Differential impact of labels and behavioral descriptions on attitudes toward people with disabilities. *Rehabilitation Psychology, 32,* 227–238.

Hardman, M. L., Drew, C. J., Egan, M. W., & Wolf, B. (1993). *Human exceptionality: Society, school, and family* (4th ed.). Boston: Allyn & Bacon.

Hermann, D. (1998). *Helen Keller: A life*. New York: Alfred A. Knopf.

Herrnstein, R., & Murray, C. (1994). *The bell curve: Intelligence and class structure in American life*. New York: Free Press.

Higgins, P. C. (1980). *Making disability: Exploring the social transformation of human variation*. Springfield, IL: Charles C. Thomas.

Higgins, P. C. (1992). *Outsiders in a hearing world: A sociology of D/deafness*. Newbury Park, CA: Sage.

Himmelstein, D. U., Woolhandler, S., & Wolfe, S. M. (1992). The vanishing health care safety net: New data on uninsured Americans. *International Journal of Health Services, 22,* 381–396.

Hirandini, V. (2005). Rethinking disability in social work: Interdisciplinary perspectives. In G. E. May & M. B. Raske (Eds.). *Ending discrimination in social work: Strategies for social workers* (pp. 71–81). Boston: Allyn & Bacon.

Hofstadter, R. (1955). *Social Darwinism in American thought* (rev. ed.). Boston: Beacon.

Houck, C. K. (1984). *Learning disabilities: Understanding concepts, characteristics, and issues*. Englewood Cliffs, NJ: Prentice Hall.

Ivey, A. E., & Ivey, M. B. (1998). Reframing the *DSM-IV*: Positive strategies from developmental counseling and therapy. *Journal of Counseling and Development, 76,* 334–350.

Jacoby, R., & Glauberman, N. (Eds.). (1995). *The bell curve debate: History, documents, options*. New York: Random House.

Jacoby, S. (2002). Living better, longer. *American Association of Retired Persons Bulletin, 11,* 14.

Jankowski, K. A. (1997). *D/deaf empowerment: Emergence, struggle and rhetoric*. Washington, DC: Gallaudet University.

Johnson, H. B. (March/April 2005). Too late to die young. *American Association of Retired Persons Bulletin, 44,* 46, & 99.

Johnston, R. B. (1987). *Learning disabilities, medicine, and myth: A guide to understanding the child and the physician*. Boston: Little, Brown.

Jones, M., Sanford, J., & Bell, R. B. (1997). Disability demographics. How are they changing? *Team Rehab Report, 38,* 36–44.

Joseph P. Kennedy, Jr. Foundation. (1991). *Facts about mental retardation*. Washington, DC: Author.

Kaye, H. S., LaPlante, M. P., Carlson, D., & Wenger, B. L. (1997). Trends in disability rates in the United States, 1970–1994, #17 {On-line}. *Disability Statistics Abstract.* San Francisco: University of California at San Francisco. Available: www.dsc.ucsf.edu. Retrieved August 1, 2007.

Kiesler, D. J. (1999). *Beyond the disease model of mental disorders.* Westport, CT: Praeger.

Kincheloe, J. L., Steinberg, S. R., & Gresson, A. D., III (Eds.). (1997). *Measured lies: The bell curve examined.* New York: St. Martin's.

Kirk, S. A., & Kutchins, H. (1992). *The selling of the DSM: The rhetoric of science in psychiatry.* New York: Aldine Degruyter.

Kouzis, A. C., & Eaton, W. W. (2000). Psychopathology and the initiation of disability payments. *Psychiatric Services, 15,* 908–913.

Langer, E. J. (1983). *The psychology of control.* Beverly Hills, CA: Sage.

LaPlante, M. P. (1991). The demographics of disability. In J. West (Ed.), *The Americans with Disabilities Act: From policy to practice* (pp. 55–80). New York: Milbank Memorial Fund.

LaPlante, M. P. (1993). State estimates of disability in America. *Disability Statistics Abstracts No. 3.* Washington, DC: National Institute on Disability and Rehabilitation Research.

LaPlante, M. P. (1996). Health conditions and impairments causing disability. *Disability Statistics Abstracts No. 16.* Washington, DC: National Institute on Disability and Rehabilitation Research.

LaPlante, M. P. (1997). How many Americans have a disability: #5 {On-line}. *Disability Statistics Abstract.* San Francisco: University of California at San Francisco. Available: www.dsc.ucsf.edu. Retrieved August 1, 2007.

Liachowitz, C. H. (1988). *Disability as a social construct: Legislative roots.* Philadelphia: University of Pennsylvania.

Livneh, H., & Antonak, R. F. (1997). *Psychosocial adaptation to chronic illness and disability.* Gaithersburg, MD: Aspen.

Lubkin, I. M., & Larsen, P. D. (Eds.). (2006). *Chronic Illness: Impact and interventions* (6th ed.). Sudbury, MA: Jones and Bartlett.

Matson, J. L., & Barrett, R. P. (Eds.). (1993). *Psychopathology in the mentally retarded* (2nd ed.). Boston: Allyn & Bacon.

McCarthy, H. (1993). Learning with Beatrice A. Wright: A breath of fresh air that uncovers the unique virtues and human flaws in us all. *Rehabilitation Education, 10,* 149–166.

McDonnell, J. L., Hardman, M. L., McDonnell, A. P., & Kiefer-O'Donnell, R. (1995). *An introduction to persons with severe disabilities: Educational and social issues.* Boston: Allyn & Bacon.

Mental disorders are not diseases. (2000, January). *USA Today,* pp. 30–31.

Michalko, R. (2002). *The difference disability makes.* Philadelphia: Temple University.

Mitchell, J. M., & Kemp, B. J. (1996). The Older Adult Disability Scale: Development and validation. *Rehabilitation Psychology, 41,* 187–203.

Moore, D. F. (1987). *Educating the D/deaf: Psychology, principles, and practices* (3rd ed.). Boston: Houghton Mifflin.

Murphy, R. (1990). *The body silent in America.* New York: W. W. Norton.

Olkin, R. (1999). *What psychotherapists should know about disability.* New York: Guilford.

Panek, W. C. (1992). Visual disabilities. In M. G. Brodwin, F. Tellez, & S. K. Brodwin (Eds.), *Medical, psychosocial, and vocational aspects of disability* (pp. 217–230). Athens, GA: Elliott & Fitzpatrick.

Peele, S. (1989). *The diseasing of America.* Boston: Houghton Mifflin.

Pfeiffer, D. (1993). The problem of disability definition. *Journal of Disability Policy Studies, 4,* 77–82.

Pope, A. M., & Tarlov, A. R. (Eds.). (1991). *Disability in America: Toward a national agenda for prevention.* Washington, DC: National Academy Press.

Putnam, M., Greenen, S., Powers, L., Saxton, M., Finney, S., & Dautel, P. (2003). Health and wellness: People with disabilities discuss barriers and facilitators to well being. *Journal of Rehabilitation, 69,* 37–45.

Rosenthal, B. P., & Cole, R. G. (1993). Visual impairments. In M. G. Eisenberg, R. L. Gluekauf, & H. H. Zaretsky (Eds.), *Medical aspects of disability* (pp. 38–67). Springfield, IL: Charles C. Thomas.

Schmelkin, L. P. (1988). Multidimensional perspectives in the perception of disabilities. In H. E. Yuker (Ed.), *Attitudes toward persons with disabilities* (pp. 127–137). New York: Springer.

Scott, R. A. (1969). *The making of blind men: A study of adult socialization.* New York: Sage.

Shapiro, J. P. (1993). *No pity. People with disabilities forging a new civil rights movement.* New York: Random House.

Silverstone, B., Lang, M. A., Rosenthal, B. P., & Faye, E.E. (Eds.). (1999). *The Lighthouse handbook on vision impairment and vision rehabilitation.* New York: Oxford University Press.

Smart, D. W., & Smart, J. F. (1997). *DSM-IV* and culturally sensitive diagnosis: Some observations for counselors. *Journal of Counseling and Development, 75,* 392–398.

Smart, J. F. (2004). Models of disability: The juxtaposition of biology and social construction. In T. F. Riggar & D. R. Maki (Eds.), *Handbook of rehabilitation counseling* (pp. 25–49). New York: Springer.

Smart, J. F. (2005). The promise of the International Classification of Functioning, Disability, and Health (ICF). *Rehabilitation Education, 19,* 191–199.

Spencer, H. (1884). *Social statics: Or the conditions essential to human happiness.* New York: Appleton.

Stokoe, W. C., Croneberg, C., & Casterline, D. (1965). *Dictionary of American Sign Language* (2nd ed.). Washington, DC: Gallaudet College.

Stubbins, J. (1988). The politics of disability. In H. E. Yuker (Ed.), *Attitudes toward persons with disabilities* (pp. 22–23). New York: Springer.

Szasz, T. S. (1961). *The myth of mental illness.* New York: Harper.

Szymanski, E. M., & Trueba, H. T. (1994). Castification of people with disabilities: Potential disempowering aspects of classification in disability services. *Journal of Rehabilitation, 60*(3), 12–20.

Thompson-Hoffman, S., & Storck, I. F. (Eds.). (1991). *Disability in the United States: A portrait from national data.* New York: Springer.

Trieschmann, R. B. (1987). *Aging with a disability.* New York: Demos.

Turner, S. M., & Hersen, M. (Eds.). (1997). *Adult psychopathology and diagnosis* (3rd ed.). New York: Wiley.

Tuttle, D. (1984). *Self-esteem and adjusting to blindness.* Springfield, IL: Charles C. Thomas.

Urla, J., & Swedlund, A. C. (2005). Measuring up to Barbie: Ideals of the feminine body in popular culture (pp. 285–298). In C. B. Brettell & C. F. Sargent (Eds.), *Gender in cross-cultural perspective* (4th ed.). Upper Saddle River, NJ: Prentice Hall.

Van Cleve, J. V., & Crouch, B. A. (1989). *A place of their own: Creating the Deaf community in America.* Washington, DC: Gallaudet.

Vernellia, R. R. (1994). Impact of managed care organizations on ethnic Americans and underserved populations. *Journal of Health Care for the Poor and the Underserved, 5,* 224–237.

Walkup, J. (2000). Disability, health care, and public policy. *Rehabilitation Psychology, 45,* 409–422.

Wallis, C. (2007, Jan. 22). What autism epidemic? *Time,* 69.

Warren, D. H. (1984). *Blindness and early childhood development.* New York: American Foundation for the Blind.

Warren, D. H. (1989). Implications of visual impairments for child development. In M. C. Wang, M. C. Reynolds, & H. J. Walberg (Eds.), *Handbook of special education: Research and practice. Vol. 3. Low-incidence conditions* (pp. 155–172). Oxford, England: Pergamon.

Watkins, K. E., & Podus, D. (2000). Alcohol and drug abuse: The impact of terminating disability benefits for substance abusers on substance abuse and treatment participation. *Psychiatric Services, 51,* 1371–1381.

Wendell, S. (1997). Toward a feminist theory of disability. In L. Davis (Ed.), *Disability studies reader* (pp. 260–278). New York: Routledge.

West, T. G. (1997). Slow words, quick words—Dyslexia as an advantage in tomorrow's work place. In P. J. Gerber & D. S. Brown (Eds.), *Learning disabilities and employment* (pp. 349–370). Austin, TX: PRO-ED.

White, M., & Gribbin, J. (1995). *Darwin: A life in science.* New York: Simon and Schuster.

White, P. H. (2002). Access to healthcare: Health insurance considerations for young adults with special health care needs/disabilities. *Pediatrics, 110,* 1328–1336.

Wilkins, S., & Cott, C. (1993). Aging, chronic illness, and disability. In M. Nagler (Ed.), *Perspectives on disability* (2nd ed., pp. 363–377). Palo Alto, CA: Health Markets Research.

Wolfensberger, W. (1972). *The principle of normalization in human services.* Toronto: National Institute on Mental Retardation.

World Health Organization. (1980). *International classification of impairments, disabilities and handicaps: A manual of classification relating to the consequences of disease.* Geneva, Switzerland: Author.

Wright, B. A. (1991). Labeling: The need for person–environment individuation. In C. R. Snyder & D. R. Forsyth (Eds.), *Handbook of social and clinical psychology: The health perspective* (pp. 469–487). New York: Pergamon.

Yelin, E. H. (1992). *Disability and the displaced worker.* New Brunswick, NJ: Rutgers University.

Zea, M. C., Belgrave, F. Z., Townsend, T. G., Jarama, S. L., & Banks, S. R. (1996). The influence of social support and active coping on depression among African Americans and Latinos with disabilities. *Rehabilitation Psychology, 41,* 225–242.

Zola, I. K. (1989). Toward a necessary universalizing of a disability policy. *Milbank Quarterly, 67,* 401–428.

Zola, I. K. (1993). Disability statistics: What we count and what it tells us. *Journal of Disability Policy Studies, 4,* 9–39.

Models of Disability:
The Biomedical Model,
the Environmental Model,
the Functional Model, and
the Sociopolitical Model

- How does the Biomedical Model of disability differ from the Environmental and Functional Models?

- How does the Sociopolitical Model of disability differ from the other three models?

- Can disabilities be socially and culturally constructed, or are disabilities only biological phenomena?

- What are the advantages and disadvantages of diagnoses?

- What is the difference between an invisible and a visible disability?

- What is the difference between a congenital disability and a disability acquired late in life?

- Why shouldn't we use the words "cripple," "victim," or "handicapped"? Regardless of which words are used, isn't the meaning the same?

In the preceding chapter, we learned about the difficulty of determining normalcy and the reasons why there are more disabilities than ever in history. In this chapter, we shall discuss the ways in which normalcy is enforced—both clinically and legally. To gain some understanding of both society's response to disability and the PWD's response to disability, it is necessary to discuss the various models of disability.

What Are Models of Disability?

> ### In this section, look for—
> - Why models of disability are important
> - How models define our world and influence our attitudes and actions
> - The functions of models

One way in which to conceptualize disability concerns the different models for disability that can be implemented. A model is a set of guiding assumptions, concepts, and propositions about the nature of phenomena or human experience. Models have often been defined as human-made tools for understanding and human-made guidelines for action. As would be expected, treatment and intervention strategies are guided by the type of disability model used. There are four basic models of conceptualizing disability: (1) the Biomedical Model, (2) the Environmental Model, (3) the Functional Model, and (4) the Sociopolitical Model. Different models of disability have different uses, and each model has its advantages and disadvantages. However, all models are, to some extent, incomplete and subject to error, simply because models are *human-made representations* of experiences and phenomena.

Nonetheless, these models are important both to individuals with disabilities and to those without disabilities. It is essential to be clear and explicit—especially to ourselves—about the models we use. Occasionally, we should question and examine models to which we subscribe and we should question our ways of explaining the world. Indeed, models define our world and influence our attitudes and actions. Each of the following models formed the basis for the development of different types of government-sponsored services (Bickenbach, 1993; Moore & Feist-Price, 1999; Stone, 1984).

Models of disability provide definitions of disability. In spite of the fact that each model defines disability in a narrow fashion, each model answers the question, "What is a disability?" A second function of models of disability is to help identify the location of the "problem" and, subsequently, identify who is to be held responsible for the solution. Determination of the location of the problem is referred to as the *causal attribution*, and determination of who is to solve the problem is referred to as the *responsibility attribution*. A third function of models of disability is to determine needs. For example, if all needs of a PWD are considered to be medical, then all resources will be allocated to meet medical needs. Fourth, models guide the formulation and implementation of policy. Laws such as the Social Security laws, the Vocational Rehabilitation Acts, the Individuals with Disabilities Education Act, and the Americans with Disabilities Act (ADA) all derive from different models. Fifth, models determine which academic disciplines study and learn about the experience of disability. If disability is thought to be a social construction, then the social sciences and political sciences would teach about disability, whereas if disability is thought to be solely a medical phenomenon, only those in the medical/health sciences will learn about disability. Sixth, models shape the self-identity of those with disability. Because models provide definitions, diagnoses, and theories of causation and responsibility, based on seemingly authoritative and prestigious sources, PWDs often accept these concepts as self-identifiers. Finally, models can cause prejudice and discrimination. Two of the models, the Biomedical and the Functional Models, have a normative basis, meaning that the absence of a disability is considered to be better than the presence of a disability and because of this normative basis, prejudice results.

Models of disability are abstractions or theories and do not exist in reality. However, they are *not* harmless abstractions. Models guide legislation and determine the service settings for PWDs and where PWDs live (or if they live at all). Models guide the training of professionals who serve PWDs, and models have a significant impact on the popular media. Most of all, models determine the daily, lived experience of having a disability.

The Biomedical Model of Disability

> **In this section look for—**
>
> - The strengths of the Biomedical Model
>   —The model with the strongest causal attribution
>   —The model with standardized objective diagnoses
> - The weakness of the Biomedical Model
>   —Did not take the individual's environment into account
>   —Relieved society of any responsibility for PWDs
>   —Objectified PWDs

The Biomedical Model is the most familiar and best understood conception of disease and disability, probably because this model has the longest history. (The only other model with a longer history is called the Moral or Religious Model, in which disability was thought to be the result of sin or evil.) The Biomedical Model uses objective, clear-cut, standardized measures and, as the name suggests, uses experts, such as physicians, to provide defining characteristics, causes, prognoses, and methods of treatment (Fowler & Wadsworth, 1991). There are two dimensions of this model, normal and pathological, with the diagnosis of normal often defined as simply the absence of any pathology. As would be expected, the Biomedical Model focuses on the anatomy and physiology of the individual and uses standardized procedures to make diagnoses. These standardized procedures allow different medical experts to arrive at the same diagnosis. Because of the high levels of skill and knowledge necessary to render both diagnoses and treatment, the Biomedical Model of disability relies on the use of experts, usually physicians. While the contributions of the profession of medicine cannot be overstated, there are deficiencies in the Biomedical Model; however, conscious wrongdoing on the part of medical professionals is not implied. After all, it is society who has endowed the medical professions with these responsibilities.

In the Biomedical Model, pathology, abnormality, and deviance are present in the individual. Bickenbach (1993) described this definition of disability as deviance:

> The most commonly held belief about [this model of] disablement is that it involves a defect, deficiency, dysfunction, abnormality, failing or medical "problem" that is located in an individual. We think it is so obvious as to be beyond serious dispute that disablement is a characteristic of a *defective person*, someone who is functionally limited or anatomically abnormal, diseased, or pathoanatomical, someone who is neither whole nor healthy, fit nor flourishing, someone who is biologically inferior or subnormal. The essence of disablement, in this view, is that there are things *wrong* with people with disabilities. (p. 61)

As a result of this deficit orientation of this model, an individual with a disability understands that he or she is a member of a devalued group—the disabled—regardless of any personal qualities, resources, or advantages of the individual (Smart, 2006). This also means that society often considers that the life of a PWD is worth less investment than the life of a PWOD (McCarthy, 1993). Indeed, taken to an extreme, society could endow the medical profession with the mandate to eliminate disabilities and the people who experience them (Singer, 1981, 1995, 2000).

Therefore, disability is viewed as an individual tragedy (Shell, 2005). Society is effectively absolved of all responsibility for disability because society relinquished authority to the medical profession. Conrad (2004) described the way in which society has endowed the medical professions with the power to remove the experience of disability from attention and concern of the general public:

Because of the way the medical profession is organized and the mandate it receives from society, decisions related to medical diagnoses and treatment are virtually controlled by the medical professions . . . . By defining a problem as medical, it is removed from the public realm where there can be discussion by ordinary people and put on a plane where only medical people can discuss it. (p. 22)

It is only within the last 100 years that physicians have faced the challenge of helping patients to manage and treat conditions over the life span. For centuries, medical treatment had two outcomes: a total cure or the death of the person. Hahn (2005) stated that in this two-outcome paradigm, diagnosis was straightforward—the patient was either dead or cured. Of course, there were exceptions to this, such as mental illness or sensory loss. The flu epidemics illustrate the two outcomes: individuals either died of the flu (500,000 died in the United States) or they recovered completely. However, the polio epidemics produced three outcomes: the individual died, the individual recovered completely, or he or she lived with an orthopedic disability. Thus, the polio epidemics produced tens of thousands of individuals with disabilities. For many conditions, such as diabetes, there wasn't any management or treatment available and individuals with diabetes died. People with amputations did not survive long after the procedure because, before the advent of antibiotics, infections, which are secondary to amputations, killed them. People today live with many conditions, both physical and emotional, that are neither acute nor curable but that could result in death or further disablement if the conditions are not managed and controlled.

The lingering effects of this two-outcome paradigm of the Biomedical Model are experienced by people with disabilities today. For example, many individuals with disabilities are very healthy and do not require referral to medical specialists when they have commonplace illnesses that are not related to their disabilities or even when they need routine physical or dental examinations. Yet, many physicians refer individuals with disabilities to seek treatment from specialists. Indeed, many individuals with disabilities must undergo hospitalization needlessly to have simple dental work performed. Another example of the vestiges of the two-outcome paradigm is found in insurance policies that do not provide payment for services after medical stabilization has been reached. Therefore, such services as marriage counseling to deal with the acquisition of a disability, treatment for secondary conditions and complications, and medical services to deal with the interaction of the aging process and the disability are typically not funded (Smart, 2005a). After medical stabilization, most insurance policies do not fund services.

The focus of the Biomedical Model on pathology and on the biology and physiology of the patient has, for the most part, ignored the individual's role functioning and his or her environmental demands (Smart, in press). Disability concerns are divorced from social factors in the Biomedical

Model. Indeed, the Biomedical Model conceived the "problem" as existing entirely within the individual and focused all efforts on "fixing" the individual, rarely acknowledging the social construction of and societal reaction to disability (Phillips, 1990; Sinacore-Guinn, 1995; Szasz, 1961, 1976). The individual with a disability, however severe the disability, is a complete person with family, work, and community responsibilities, all of which affect the diagnosis of the disability. To cite a single example, to determine level of benefits, physicians will often render a numerical rating of a disability, such as 25% or 35%, not taking into account such factors as the degree of stigma toward the disability, the individual's family support, or the individual's coping resources. Two clear-cut examples of disabilities that are very limiting, but not from any functional or organic limitations, are the disabilities of Paul Steven Miller, found in Chapter 1, and the disabilities of individuals with facial disfigurements. The Biomedical Model, with its emphasis solely on the individual, is not broad enough to describe these individuals' experiences or generate plans to change their situations. Two people with the same diagnosis, at the same numerical rating, may have different prognoses. The solution, of course, is multidisciplinary case management in which disability professionals, with their complementary knowledge, skills, and perspectives, provide a complete range of services, including medical, educational, and vocational.

The perspective of the Biomedical Model often objectified people with disabilities because these individuals were viewed as a body part, a specific organ, or a type of disability. The PWD becomes a "quad," or a "schizophrenic," or a "diabetic." Clearly, some of this objectification and impersonal treatment of the PWD assists physicians in maintaining an objectivity and emotional distance/detachment. It appears that, rather than easing the discomfort of the patient, physicians have chosen to respond to their own discomfort. The Biomedical Model, in its most extreme form, holds that if physicians view patients as whole people and as collaborators in the diagnosis and treatment of their conditions, the effectiveness of physicians will be compromised. As technology and laboratory diagnostic procedures proliferate, less emphasis will be placed on history taking and learning about the patient from the patient. Thus, in the name of medical pragmatism, the individual and his or her environment are ignored (Cameron, 1982). Leonard Kriegel, who contracted polio, effectively captures the power of the Biomedical Model and the objectification. Notice that Kriegel compared himself to a monster, the creation of Dr. Frankenstein:

> Filled with pride in their technological prowess, the three of them (bracemakers) stood in front of me, admiring their skills. Had I been created in the laboratory of Mary Shelley's Dr. Frankenstein, I could not have felt myself any more the creature of scientific pride. (Kriegel, 1997, p. 41)

The Biomedical Model is often perceived to be that of experts delivering services to passive recipients who are expected to be compliant and to whom little information and few treatment options are provided. This "expert-in-control" is referred to as the "omniscience of the experts" (DeLoach & Greer, 1981). Paternalism probably began in the Biomedical Model (Smart, 2004). A practicing attorney with a severe congenital disability stated, "Doctors never bothered asking me what my life could become" (Mikata, 1995). Disability advocates report stories of experts and physicians who did not listen to individuals with disabilities and their family members; other experts who viewed the individuals' disabilities as tragic flaws; and experts who did not have the experience of living with disabilities 24 hours a day, 7 days a week. In the National Public Radio (NPR) Disability History Project, a parent of a child with spina bifida stated, "Parents endow the doctors with more understanding than they often have."

Although these patterns are changing, many individuals with disabilities have felt themselves to have been devalued and treated as inferior by medical professionals and were allowed very little control over their treatment (Smart, 2005a,b). Today, some adults with disabilities feel resentment toward their parents, believing that the parents unquestioningly submitted them to all the treatments, procedures, hospitalizations, and institutionalizations "prescribed" by doctors. However, at that time, parents had few options.

A pediatrician, Perri Klass, has described a possible result of the Biomedical Model:

> If we are at war, then who is the enemy? Rightly the enemy is the disease, and even if that is not your favorite metaphor, it is a rather common way to think of medicine: we are combating these deadly processes for the bodies of our patients. They become battlefields, lying there passively in bed while the evil armies of pathology and the resplendent forces of modern medicine fight it out. Still, there are some very good doctors who seem to think that way, who take disease as a personal enemy and battle it with fury and dedication. The real problem arises because all too often the patient comes to personify the disease and somehow the patient becomes the enemy. (Klass, as cited in Couser, 1997, pp. 26–27)

One of the greatest leaders in the Disability Rights Movement was Ed Roberts. However, physicians had seen little value in his life when he was a teenager and contracted polio. Furthermore, Roberts internalized those views. He was respirator-dependent. With others, Roberts later founded the Independent Living Movement and the World Institute on Disability. He fought to graduate from high school and to be admitted to the University of California at Berkeley, and he organized the "Rolling Quads" to fight for the right to live outside the campus hospital. Roberts was appointed by

Governor Jerry Brown to be director of the California State Department of Rehabilitation. He died in 1995.

Shapiro (1993) described the effect of the Biomedical Model of disability on Roberts:

> Roberts saw himself as a "helpless cripple" overwhelmed by depression, powerlessness, and self-hatred. He asked his parents if he would ever go to college, marry, or hold a job. The answer, based on what doctors, nurses, and counselors had said, was always no. It would have been more humane, a doctor had told his mother, if the high fever of polio had killed him quickly. (p. 42)

Because of its long history, most of which was involved with the treatment of physical conditions, the Biomedical Model does not lend itself well to intellectual, cognitive, or psychiatric disabilities (Helms, 1992). Only recently have intellectual, cognitive, and psychiatric disabilities been recognized as disabilities. Furthermore, these disabilities are conditions that are, for the most part, managed and treated over the life span of the individual. The Biomedical Model, with its emphasis on finding, treating, and curing a problem that exists solely within the individual (without taking the environment into consideration), does not describe cognitive, intellectual, or psychiatric disabilities very well. Polio illustrates the Biomedical Model's complete lack of interest in the psychological and sociological aspects of disability. Wilson, a polio survivor, collected and studied hundreds of first-person accounts of polio in the United States and Canada. Wilson summarized:

> While physicians, surgeons, physical therapists, and nurses focused on rehabilitating the body, the polio survivors of whatever age were largely left alone to deal with the significant emotional and psychological responses to physical crippling and extended rehabilitation hospitalization. The cost was tremendous. (Wilson, 1990, p. 67)

Polio survivors, many of them young children, had endured months of separation from their families and had experienced many treatments and therapies. They had also seen their roommates die and had wondered if they would survive to leave the hospital. When they returned home, many had orthopedic disabilities. Most difficult, these polio survivors returned to a society in which there were no accommodations, little assistive technology, and no peer support groups. One polio survivor (Mee, 1999) told of his father's only reference to his polio: "The world is not going to change for you." Yet, in spite of all this, professionals never saw the need for emotional or psychological counseling and support for polio survivors or their families.

Also, concerning the dominance of the Biomedical Model in shaping the polio experience, authors have noted that Franklin Delano Roosevelt, the president of the United States who was a polio survivor and a consummate politician, regarded polio as a personal tragedy for which society should provide charity. Rather than seeking to bring about national legislation that would provide civil rights, services, and public accommodations for polio survivors, Roosevelt began the first nationwide charity drives, and the first poster children were the creation of the March of Dimes. Indeed, many disability scholars refer to Roosevelt as a "handicapitalist" and the father of the charity telethons, such as Jerry Lewis's Muscular Dystrophy telethon. Of course, it should be remembered that FDR provided millions of dollars for the treatment and care of individuals with polio, and, perhaps most important, he served as a role model for Americans with all types of disabilities.

It is interesting that most writings by and directed to physicians refer to the Biomedical Model as the disease model. Medical methodology and mindsets were applied to social institutions. Physicians were often the directors of state residences and schools for PWDs, although training and education was the central mission of these homes and schools. Policymakers felt that any services related to disability were to be rendered by physicians. Conrad (2004) called this the medicalization of disability.

The Environmental Model of Disability

> **In this section look for—**
>
> - Prejudice and discrimination are not an inherent aspect of a disability
> - The environment can cause, define, or exaggerate disability

The Environmental Model posits that the individual's environment—both social and physical—can cause, define, or exaggerate disability. It is easy to see the relationship between disability and the physical environment. "Disability is viewed as . . . a product of a disabling, unresponsive, or insensitive environment" (Hursh, 1995, p. 322). Essentially, environments can limit physical access and opportunities for work, education, and social participation (Tannebaum, 1986). If a person with paraplegia does not have a wheelchair, then the impact of the paraplegia is greater. Barriers in the physical environment can hinder the individual with a disability, and the ADA is helping to make the environment accessible for all citizens. We shall see in Chapter 5 that the physical world has been designed on the (false) assumption that everyone can walk, everyone can hear, and everyone can see.

It is a little more difficult to understand the relationship between disability and the social and cultural environment. For example, in Manchurian China, infant girls from upper-class homes had their feet bound tightly until the bones were broken and twisted; as a result, these girls and women were unable to walk. Furthermore, to most people today who look at photographs of these Manchurian girls and women, the feet of the girls and women appear to be deformed. But, the Manchurian people considered the feet of these women to be beautiful and, moreover, judged the inability to walk or stand to be a sign of prestige and status because these girls and women came from rich homes and, therefore, were not required to work. This is an unusual example, but it does illustrate that disability is not only a biological construction; it is also the result of social and cultural definitions.

Another example of a disability that is often environmentally defined is a learning disability. Learning disabilities, the result of neurological malfunction, probably were not noticeable in preliterate societies. In modern times, individuals with learning disabilities are often called "6-hour retardates" by others and by themselves because their learning disabilities seem environmentally specific during the 6 hours they are in school. Another example of environmental factors defining disability, rather than anything related to the disability itself, is described by Sobsey (1994). Sobsey recounted that many men with disabilities left institutions during World War I and World War II to fight in the United States military. One institution in Connecticut, Southbury Training School, released 13 men who then enlisted to fight in World War II. Four of these 13 men were wounded in combat and seven were promoted to higher ranks. When the war ended, most of these soldiers were returned to institutions.

While there is an environmental factor to all types of disability, the Environmental Model may more completely provide a solution to psychiatric disabilities. A legal scholar, Stefan (2001) explained that psychiatric disabilities are as follows:

> . . . episodic, highly responsive to context and environment, and exist along a spectrum, which theoretically can be cause for hope—people with mental disabilities are frequently strong, talented, competent, and capable, and their environments can be structured in a way to support and increase their strengths, talents, competence, and capabilities. (p. 10)

Today, there are many environmental changes that have transformed the definition of disability. For example, the introduction of psychotropic medications, which allow many individuals with mental illnesses to control their symptoms, has dramatically changed the ways in which both society and the individual view mental illness. Of course, these medications do not work for everyone, and there are many side effects, but nonetheless, these medications have brought about many changes. We can see that this is an environmental change and not a change in mental illness. Other environmental changes that have affected the definition of disability include supported employment and supported living. Used primarily for individuals with mental retardation and individuals with mental illness, these types of community jobs and apartment living are supervised and assisted by professional service providers. Individuals who in the past would not have been thought to be capable of working or living outside an institution now do both. Once again, these types of professional services are environmental changes and are not changes in the disabilities. Finally, the accordance of civil rights to PWDs by the ADA is another straightforward example of environmental shifts that have transformed the meaning of disability.

Prejudice, discrimination, and stigma are not an inherent part of a disability; instead, they are part of the environment (Balcazar, Bradford, & Fawcett, 1988). These attitudes needlessly hinder PWDs. More relevant today as examples are individuals with mental illness who manage their illnesses with medications and, yet, because of societal prejudice, discrimination, and stigma, are hindered unnecessarily.

Society has created many barriers, both physical and attitudinal, for people with disabilities. For example, in the United States today the attributes of health, strength, youth, fitness, and beauty are highly valued (Buss, 1998), and the emphasis on these attributes increases the impact of disability. In the chapter on society's response to disability, the societal/cultural construction of disability will be discussed more thoroughly.

The Functional Model of Disability

> ## In this section look for—
>
> - The relationship between disability and society's roles and functions
> - The relationship between disability and the individual's roles and functions
> - The way in which assistive technology can change the definition of disability

The Functional Model of disability theorizes that the functions of the individual influence the definition of disability. Individuals who enjoy physical activities would probably be more affected by a mobility impairment than those who do not care for such activities. Also, individuals whose work does not require physical strength, movement, or stamina would be less affected by mobility disability. The example most often used to illustrate the Functional Model of disability is that of the professional pianist who has one finger amputated. The loss of one finger would probably not be considered a disability for most people, and yet, because of the impairment in occupational functioning for the concert pianist, the amputation would be a life-changing disability. Individuals who are visual learners and lose their vision probably experience a greater sense of loss than auditory learners who lose their sight. The relationship between functioning and disability can be very specific to the individual. For example, Stephen Hawking, professor of physics at Cambridge University and world-famous theoretical physicist, considers his disability, amyotrophic lateral sclerosis (ALS), which greatly limits mobility and impairs speech, to be an advantage because it allows him more time to think. Two people can have the same type and degree of disability, but because of their functions and environments, they have a very different disability experience.

Judy Gilliam, a Government Service 15 (top-level) manager at the Defense Department, was described by her supervisor as follows:

> She's a quadriplegic, Phi Beta Kappa, and she says it this way, "I can't dress myself. I can't walk. I can't drive. I can't pick up a glass of water. But I can work." And her work, I am here to tell you, is consistently characterized by superior quality and productivity. (Fleischer & Zames, 2001, p. 131)

Another example of the way in which the vocational environment may change the definition of disability concerns learning disabilities. In the same way that machines replaced the need for human muscle power at the time of the Industrial Revolution, computers may replace the need for many human clerical skills.

> Over the lifetime of today's students, many of the basic verbal and clerical skills that have long dominated education at all levels will cease to be important in an economy and marketplace where these tasks will be increasingly taken over by semi-intelligent machines. With these changes, the visual-spatial talents, global thinking mental models, pattern recognition, creative problem solving and other nonverbal abilities often associated with dyslexia are expected to become increasingly important in tomorrow's workplace, as greater use is made of data visualization, computer graphics, and interactive multi-sensory technologies to understand and communicate information about complex systems and discontinuous trends. As everyone struggles to accommodate themselves to deep changes in thinking and working, some dyslexics [sic] will doubtless play, once again, their oft-repeated role—working creatively at the edge of a new frontier, reading little but learning much, experimenting, innovating, establishing a path forward—learning from direct experience, anticipating where things are going, taking risks. (West, 1997, p. 350)

Which functions should be included in the Functional Model (Boorse, 1986)? The examples of Stephen Hawking and the concert pianist consider work and wage-earning functions. Work is an important function for many reasons, including financial security. In addition, in the United States a great deal of our social status is determined by the work we do (or whether we do work at all). Should nonessential functions such as leisure and sports be included in the Functional Model of disability? Most Functional Models, at present, include only work activities and activities of daily living (ADLs), which assist PWDs in getting to jobs. As a result of this exclusive focus on work and ADLs, many individuals in the Disability Rights Movement regard the Functional Model of disability as an economic model. According to these advocates, the Functional Model is primarily concerned with the earning capacity of the PWD.

The Functional Model of disability, of course, is closely related to the availability of adaptive technology and the capability of such technology to assist in role functioning (Spechler, 1996). A professor in a wheelchair can perform his or her occupational functions; an individual who is blind who uses a computer with a speech synthesizer, a brailler, and other assistive technology can perform successfully in many vocational roles. Weisgerber (1991) told of a man named Manny Guitierrez, with Down syndrome, who works with archaeologists from the University of Arizona. Mr. Guitierrez tags all the artifacts unearthed on the digs. Weisgerber summarized: "His work does not entail intellectual tasks but rather the ability to label archaeological artifacts, a task at which he excels" (p. 179). Another example of the importance of assistive technology is the emergence of wheelchair athletes. There were no wheelchair athletes until a particular wheelchair was developed.

Three scholars/researchers who study the sources of attitudes toward people with disabilities (Langer, Bashner, & Chanowitz, 1985) found that children can understand disability from a Functional Model. After speaking to a group of children about disabilities and discussing the various jobs at which PWDs are successful, the researchers showed the children two pictures of male newscasters; one newscaster was in a wheelchair and the other newscaster did not have a visible disability. The children rated both newscasters as equally qualified to perform the job. The children could see that the mobility impairment would not impede the newscaster on the job.

In addition to role functions of individuals, there are role functions of society in general, which also affect the definition of disability (Smart, 2005a). The shift of the economy of the United States from an economy that depended on physical labor such as farming, mining, and manufacturing to an economy based on service and information processing has influenced the definition of disability. In an economy based on physical labor, many individuals with cognitive disabilities, such as learning disabilities or mild mental retardation, were successful workers. In contrast, in that economy, an individual (especially a man) with a physical disability would have been severely limited. In today's economy, a cognitive disability is much more limiting than a physical disability because service jobs and technological/

information-processing jobs require high levels of cognitive functioning. Today, an individual with a physical disability who has the use of assistive technology has many employment options (Smart & Smart, 2006).

Before the advent of industrialized, urban society, disability was defined and treated differently. In small, rural communities in which members of families worked side by side, day after day, and everyone in the small community knew everyone else, PWDs had their basic needs met and were accorded a place in their community. As described by a noted disability scholar: "In small scale societies, nondisabled citizens knew disabled citizens. People many of us take to be 'bizarre' or 'disturbed' in today's urban areas would often have become familiar, accepted (if not well understood) neighbors of rural communities" (Higgins, 1992, p. 191).

For everyone in these small communities, with or without disabilities, home and family were the basis of everyday life. Everyone was perceived as a unique individual, with both a history and place in the community before the standardization and anonymity of large cities. It was the environment that influenced the status and perception of PWDs and not anything inherent in the disabilities. Another disability scholar described the place of the PWD in these small communities:

> [In preindustrial communities] rigid separation had not yet been made between home and work and where travel was difficult for anyone, citizens with disabilities may not have been exposed to some of the egregious inequities that have subsequently become apparent in highly impersonal autonomous cultures. . . . Deviant or atypical personal characteristics that may have become familiar in a small community seemed bizarre or disturbing in an urban milieu. (Hahn, 1997, pp. 177–178)

The impact on a PWD of moving from a small community to a larger, more anonymous community also occurs today. Casey Roberts Dunham, former Miss South Central Georgia, who has Tourette's syndrome, a neuropsychiatric disability that causes involuntary behaviors, explained:

> I was brought up in a small town and went to school with the same kids for years. They took it as something I always did—grunted and made facial expressions. But by the time I was 13 or 14 years old and went to Wayne County, where there was a bigger and more diverse crowd of kids, it was harder. They made smart remarks and I had no ammo for fighting back . . . . My confidence was beat to the dirt. (*Living with Tourette Syndrome: A Family Portrait*)

Scheer and Groce (1988) summarized the negative effect: "Americans have lost familiarity with disabled [*sic*] people so common in small-scale societies" (p. 33). It is interesting that Scheer and Groce view this loss to be greater for PWODs than for PWDs.

Ryan and Thomas (1980) explained the way in which industrialization altered the definition of mental retardation: "The speed of factory work, the enforced discipline, the timekeeping and production norms—all of these were a highly unfavourable change from the slower, more self-determined and flexible methods of work into which many handicapped [*sic*] people had been integrated" (p. 101).

Thirty years ago, Farber and his colleagues (Farber, 1968; Farber & Lewis, 1976; Heiney, 1976) incorporated the Functional Model of disability into their label for people with disabilities: "surplus populations." People with disabilities, according to these disability scholars, are thought of as surplus populations by the general public because they are not considered to be necessary for institutional efficiency and progress.

Changes in social role functioning also alter the definition of disability (Quinn, 1995). For example, elderly people today live far more active lives than their counterparts did 100 years ago, with many today working until age 75 and many more engaging in active community work and physical activity in their retirement years. Today, an older person who experiences a disability, such as blindness or a mobility impairment, probably considers the disability to be limiting rather than simply an expected outcome of aging. As can be seen from these examples, large-scale changes in functioning alter the definition of disability.

Assistive technology also changes the functional definition of disability because these devices allow PWDs to perform many functions and activities (Smart, in press). Mobility devices include power wheelchairs, sonic guides, vision enhancement devices, and functional electronic stimulation (FES). In FES, successive bursts of low-level, controlled electricity stimulate paralyzed muscles to contract according to patterns programmed into a computer. This allows the return of coordinated movement to paralyzed muscles, such as those needed for walking. It is used with persons whose muscles have not been damaged and with persons, such as those with spinal cord injuries, whose movements have been blocked by the inability of messages from the brain to get through the spinal cord and to the muscles (Scherer, 1993, p. 18).

There are also augmentative and alternative communication devices that help the individual to "speak"; environmental control devices that allow the individual to lock doors, operate the thermostat, and operate other household appliances; and sensory devices that read for people who are blind.

Scherer (1993) explained the rapid increase in the use of assistive technology. "Each passing year has seen the numbers of assistive technologies in use increase exponentially. . . . As recently as the early 1960s, most equipment available to individuals wth disabilities was only of a mechanical nature. Wheelchairs were literally chairs on wheels. Artificial limbs were plastic or, earlier, metal and wooden replacements for lost arms or legs" (p. 19).

The Sociopolitical Model of Disability

> ### In this section, look for—
>
> - The Sociopolitical Model considers disability to be a collective concern
> - The Sociopolitical Model is a reaction against the Biomedical Model
> - The Sociopolitical Model includes prejudice and discrimination as causal factors in disability
> - The Sociopolitical Model advocates for an accommodating society rather than requiring the PWD to "take the world as it is"
> - The Sociopolitical Model advocates for civil rights rather than charity or pity
> - Proponents of this model want to form a group identity and identity politics
> - PWDs want their civil rights as American citizens while at the same time maintaining their identity as PWDs

The Sociopolitical Model is also referred to as the Minority Group Model or the Independent Living Model. This model is a radical shift and, at first glance, may be difficult to understand. Proponents of this model posit that disability is a societal concern (May, 2005). Society causes disability and it is society, rather than the individual, who should bear the responsibility for dealing with disability. A disability scholar explained:

> The idea that disability is a collective issue, however, is not easy to grasp. It seems to run counter to the traditional Western social and political philosophies, influenced by the Enlightenment, that places tremendous importance on the individual. Combine this emphasis with belief in the superiority of reason and mind over the passions and vicissitudes of the body, also a legacy of the Enlightenment, and we can begin to understand why the disability has long been conceived of as only an individual issue. (Michalko, 2002, p. 6)

If we review the six reasons why there are more disabilities than ever before, not *in spite of* medical advances but *because* of medical advances, the idea that society plays a part in causing disabilities becomes clearer.

Thinking in terms of large populations (demographics), it has long been acknowledged that societal influences such as lack of health insurance, lack of education, and poverty are associated with higher rates of disability.

Those without insurance, those with less than an eighth-grade education, those who work in dangerous and physically demanding jobs, and those who live below the poverty line are at greater risk for acquiring a disability (Smart & Smart, 1997). It is clear that all of these societal problems can be eliminated, or, at minimum, improved.

The Sociopolitical Model, because of its emphasis on demographics and large groups, has the capability to consider other social identities of the individual with a disability, such as gender, religion, sexual orientation, or racial/ethnic/cultural identity. Such recognition of these other statuses can more completely describe the individual's experience of disability. On a demographic level (looking at large populations of people), the Sociopolitical Model recognizes that those of racial/ethnic minority status have a greater probability of experiencing a disability (with the exceptions of Asian and Pacific Islanders). An excellent summary is provided by disability demographers Thompson-Hoffman and Storck (1991):

> There is a higher concentration of disability among blacks and, in most cases there is a lower concentration among Hispanics. Where breakdowns are available on Native Americans, they consistently form the subgroup with the largest percentage of disabled persons. Disability prevalence rates for Asians and Pacific Islanders are markedly below national estimates. (p. 25)

Disability demographers have posited some possible causes for these higher rates of disability, including less insurance coverage, higher employment rates in physically demanding and dangerous jobs, lower educational levels, and high rates of poverty. It can be seen that *all* of these hypothesized causes are the result of societal conditions. If these societal conditions could be changed, reduced, or improved, it stands to reason that the higher rates of disabilities for minorities would be reduced.

Proponents of the Sociopolitical Model assert that many of the difficulties PWDs experience are caused by society. Disability is not a private concern because disability is defined as a social and political construction. We can recall the example of Martha's Vineyard, in which people who were Deaf were not considered to be socially different and did not experience lives of reduced opportunity, and most important, PWODs accommodated the Deaf by learning sign language. Isolation of PWDs, reduced opportunities for PWDs, and legalized discrimination against PWDs are all socially constructed and not related to any biological or emotional condition of the individual.

The Sociopolitical Model recognizes that there is a biological component to disability but also holds that there is nothing in the disability or the PWD that warrants prejudice or discrimination (Smart, 2004). Any inferiority experienced by PWDs is the inferiority conferred on them by society. Therefore, if disability is socially constructed, it can also be socially deconstructed.

While the Biomedical Model may seek to address disability by eliminating, preventing, or curing disability, the Sociopolitical Model views the solution of the "problems" of disability to be the lack of civil rights and accommodations. In contrast to the Sociopolitical Model, the shortcomings of the Biomedical Model are seen in the following statement:

> . . . society sees its responsibility to disability in the provision of preventive, curative, and rehabilitative measures. Disability must be prevented; failing this, it must be cured; if it can be neither prevented nor cured, society must see that the person is rehabilitated, the "final solution." These responses are in keeping with the biomedical version of what it means to be human. This version, which emphasizes adjustment and adaptation, plays a dominant role in the contemporary understanding of disability. Unfortunate as it is, disability is something that *happens* to some of us and it is up to us to take advantage of what society gives us in the form of medical and rehabilitation programs—and adjust. (Michalko, 2002, pp. 6–7)

The ADA is based on the Sociopolitical Model. Much of the impetus (and methodology) of the Sociopolitical Model is derived from the Civil Rights Movement of the 1960s. While the advocates of this model recognize that not every PWD, or even most PWDs, will become political activists, they also understand that collective gains will result in individual successes. In the NPR Disability History Project, a mother of a child with a disability related: "When my daughter was young, people would ask, 'Is she going to school?' I feel that I owe a debt to the older generation for creating the cultural and educational opportunities that my daughter has. They insured the basic human rights for people [PWDs] whose very existence was not acknowledged" (National Public Radio, Disability History Project, Overdue Revolution).

Comparison of the Four Models

Each of these models contributes to the understanding of the disability experience and provides guidelines for action. In the Biomedical Model, treatment methods are concerned with changing the individual; in the Functional Model, intervention methods are aimed at adapting the functions of the individual; in the Environmental Model, professionals seek to change both the physical and social environments of the individual; and in the Sociopolitical Model the provision of civil rights and equal social status is the goal. In only one of the four models, the Biomedical Model, is the "problem" viewed as entirely within the individual. Nonetheless, biology and organic functioning are important. No one would advocate that individuals who are blind should be bus drivers. The clear point, however, is that biology is not as important as it was previously thought to be.

No one today subscribes to a single disabilit^
safe to state that for centuries there was only one
Model. There is a purpose for each model, and co
tion of models can result in greater accuracy and
the disability experience. It is important to under
of disability relate to each other. For instance, the
of differing models of disability concerns deafness. For some, deafness is
viewed from the Biomedical Model as a biological loss/dysfunction that requires some sort of treatment to the individual. In contrast, the Deaf Culture views deafness from the Environmental Model and regards individuals
who are deaf as members of a different culture who use a different language.
In fact, many in the Deaf Culture feel more identification with Hispanics
because many Hispanics speak a different language.

Models of Disability, American Legislation, and Agencies That Serve Persons With Disabilities

> **In this section, look for—**
>
> ■ Social Security programs based on the Biomedical Model of disability,
>
> ■ How the ADA follows the Functional and Sociopolitical Models of disability

The sequence of American disability legislation closely parallels the history of models of disability. Social Security programs, in place since 1935,
are based on the Biomedical Model because the presence of a disability
must be established and the benefits provided are intended to pay living
and disability-related expenses, not to assist individuals in finding employment. The Social Security Administration (SSA) funds two programs for
Americans with disabilities. The first is the Supplemental Insurance Income
(SII) and the second is Social Security Disability Income (SSDI). In contrast, the state/federal system of vocational rehabilitation (VR) is based on
the Functional Model of disability because, to be declared eligible for services, it must be established that the disability impairs the ability of the
individual to obtain employment. The workers' compensation system is
also based on the Functional Model because the eligibility is granted when
the individual proves that he or she can no longer perform the job. The
ADA appears to have been derived from two models: the Functional Model
and the Sociopolitical Model. The courts are defining disability, under the
ADA, according to the Functional Model. For example, an individual who

could control his high blood pressure with medication was judged not to have a disability because his functioning was intact (*Murphy v. United Parcel Service*, 1992). The ADA derives much of its basis from the Environmental Model of disability because the statute clearly delineates the prejudice and discrimination that has needlessly hindered Americans with disabilities.

Thus, the history of American disability legislation closely parallels the sequence of the models of disability. The first model of disability was the Biomedical Model; therefore, the first disability legislation was based on the Biomedical Model. The second model of disability was the Functional Model, and the next "generation" of disability legislation was based on this model. The newest model of disability is the Environmental Model, and the Sociopolitical Model is gaining momentum; the ADA is based on these two models. Indeed, in the next chapter, we shall read Section 2 (Findings and Purposes) of the ADA that outlines the "handicaps" found in the American environment. When more than one model provides the basis for laws, politics, and service agencies, the onus for change rests with both the individual with the disability and the environment.

This parallel between models of disability and American disability legislation makes sense because American legislation, of any kind, is simply institutionalized public opinion. The Biomedical Model of disability (and the resulting legislation and service agencies) theorized that the individual is responsible for solving his or her disability "problem" and, if it could not be "solved," then government should provide financial benefits ("income maintenance"). The Functional Model, and the resulting legislation and service agencies, advocated looking at the functional requirements of work and considering ways in which the functions could be changed. The Environmental Model, and the ADA, mandate that environments, both physical and social, must change.

Dichotomy or Continuum?

> **In this section, look for—**
>
> - How dichotomies are impermeable and exclusionary— disability or no disability.
> - The cut-off point on the continuum (disability or no disability), which often changes positions

Another conceptualization of disability, which takes into account all three models, views the disability experience as either a dichotomy or a continuum. The dichotomy is simple: disability is either present or absent. All individuals must identify with one of the two categories and no one can identify with both categories. A true dichotomy does not allow the categories of "both" or "neither"; the boundaries of the two categories are impermeable and exclusionary.

In contrast, a continuum view of disability has two polar opposites: the presence of a disability or the absence of a disability, but accommodates positions between these extremes (see Figure 2–1). The closer the individual identifies with either of these polar opposites, the more clear-cut the disability status. Near the end of the continuum designated as "presence of a disability" would be individuals with severe and multiple disabilities, while near the end of the continuum designated as "absence of a disability" would be individuals who have no disability. Somewhere along the continuum there must be a cut-off point that separates individuals with disabilities from individuals who do not have disabilities. Mild disabilities, which would fall in the middle of the continuum, are more difficult to quantify.

Such a cut-off point requires accurate and sophisticated measuring instruments. Examples of disabilities whose diagnoses rely on accurate diagnostic tools are blindness and deafness. Indeed, diagnostic accuracy and diagnostic reliability are two hallmarks of blindness and deafness. Examples of disabilities for which diagnoses are not the result of precise, reliable diagnostic tools might include mental illness or learning disabilities. Because the diagnosis of these disabilities relies more on clinical judgment, impressionistic data, and psychological measures, there is less diagnostic precision. Certainly, the cut-off points for both blindness and learning disabilities must be considered a range of points rather than a single point, but the range or variability in the cut-off point required for blindness would be smaller than the range of scores required for learning disabilities. Simply stated, the precision in the cut-off point of this disability dichotomy would be directly related to the precision in the diagnostic tools and procedures. Furthermore, some disability experts consider cut-off points for all types of disabilities to be arbitrary. For example, in Chapter 1, we learned that mental retardation is diagnosed as mild, moderate, severe, or profound. It is easy to see that the cut-off point between the low end of mild mental retardation and the high end of moderate retardation (to use a single example) might be difficult to establish.

The continuum view of disability allows the cut-off point to change positions—both for society as a whole and for individuals. Therefore, cut-off points are temporary and subject to change. For example, the American Diabetes Association has lowered the diagnostic threshold for diabetes in

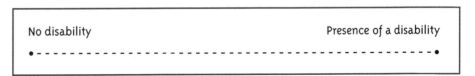

Figure 2–1 The continuum view of disability (in contrast to discrete categories).

an effort to diagnose more cases in the early stages and thus avoid many of the secondary complications. The new threshold is 126 milligrams of sugar per deciliter of blood after an 8-hour fast. The previous diagnostic threshold was 140. Legislation, public opinion, the labor market, changes in medicine, and the development of assistive technology adjust the position of the cut-off points. Changes that affect large numbers of people include changes in policy and legislation that redefine what is considered to be a disability. For example, in 1998 the Social Security Administration ruled that alcohol and substance abuse were no longer defined as disabilities and individuals with these conditions were no longer eligible for benefits. Changes that affect an individual might include the development and acquisition of some assistive technology that allows the individual to work.

Cross-Categorical Definitions of Disability: Clinical, Legal, Cultural, and Personal

There are four general categorical definitions of disability: clinical, legal, cultural, and personal. Most of the time, these four definitions of disability are in agreement, although occasionally these cross-categorical definitions may differ. Clinical definitions of disability are usually those found in medical and psychiatric diagnostic manuals, and clinical diagnoses do not always qualify as legal definitions. For example, the *Diagnostic and Statistical Manual of Mental Disorders–Fourth Edition* (*DSM-IV;* American Psychiatric Association, 1994), published by the American Psychiatric Association, includes many psychiatric disorders that are not legally defined as disabilities. For example, individuals who are clinically diagnosed as having a substance abuse disorder are not protected under the ADA if they are actively using illegal drugs. Nor would gambling addiction be considered a disability when applying for benefits and services, although the American Psychiatric Association considers gambling addiction to be a disorder. Further complicating the picture is the fact that the clinical professions define disability differently, and various government agencies, laws, and policies also often define disability based on different criteria.

Earlier, we read of a single example of a cultural definition of a disability—actually a nondefinition of disability. The example of the bound feet of Manchurian baby girls is an example of cultural definitions of disability that contradict the biological/impaired functioning constructions of disability. More on cultural definitions of disability will be presented in Chapter 7 on the individual and disability.

As expected, the single most important definition of disability is the individual's definition of his or her disability. This personal definition may differ from the clinical, legal, and cultural definitions. For example, a person with diabetes may not view himself or herself as a person with a disability although the individual monitors his or her blood sugar and takes daily injections of insulin. Failure to monitor and control the diabetes would result in death. Yet, because there are few functional limitations and diabetes is an invisible disability, many individuals with diabetes do not consider themselves to have a disability. However, legally and clinically, diabetes is defined as a disability. The Deaf Culture provides the most clear-cut example of the way in which personal definitions of disability can conflict with clinical and legal definitions. Individuals in the Deaf Culture do not consider themselves to have a disability. The personal definition of disability merits a thorough discussion, and this will be presented in Chapter 7 on the individual and disability. Many in the Deaf Culture refuse accommodation, do not support the use of cochlear implants (which have the potential to improve hearing), and did not advocate for the passage of the ADA.

To summarize, the most widely accepted definition of disability includes three elements: (1) a physical, intellectual, cognitive, or psychiatric condition is involved; (2) this condition impairs functioning; and (3) the individual is subject to prejudice, discrimination, and reduced opportunity because of the condition.

Additional Categories of Disabilities

> **In this section, look for—**
>
> ■Categorization of disabilities according to severity
>
> ■Reasons why individuals with severe disabilities often require case management services
>
> ■Information on congenital and acquired disabilities
>
> ■Information on invisible and visible disabilities

Disabilities also are categorized according to their degree. Basically, there are three levels: mild, moderate, and severe. Severe disabilities, sometimes referred to as profound disabilities, are those that impair the individual in several areas of functioning (Matson & Barrett, 1993). For some individuals, a severe disability is a single disability, such as profound mental retardation, because mental retardation impairs functioning in almost every environmental setting. For others, a severe disability is actually multiple disabilities, such as dual sensory loss. Profound cerebral palsy is considered to be a severe disability because this condition can affect the individual's speech, motor abilities, and intellectual functioning. For each type of disability, there are criteria and standards for determining the degree of disability and for assigning the designations of mild, moderate, or severe. For example, mild hearing losses are defined as loss of hearing in the better ear of 25–40 decibels, moderate hearing losses (or being hard of hearing) are defined as loss of hearing in the 40–60-decibel range, and severe hearing losses are losses of 60–80 decibels. Severe mental retardation is defined as 3 standard deviations below normal. Thus, each type of disability has specific diagnostic criteria for determining the degree of impairment.

Individuals with severe disabilities require services from caregivers from many different professions (for example, medical, special education, physical therapy, speech pathology, and vocational rehabilitation). Therefore, case management is important for individuals with disabilities. Case management is the coordination of services of many different professionals to provide comprehensive and continuous care for a single individual. In contrast, many individuals with mild disabilities usually do not need case management. For example, a person with a mild case of diabetes would only need services from a physician.

Severe disabilities, as explained when we discussed the concept of disabilities existing along a continuum, are more evident than mild or moderate disabilities. Thus, severe disabilities are more easily and quickly diagnosed (and therefore treated) than are mild disabilities. However, almost all severe disabilities are also visible disabilities, and the individual is therefore subjected to more prejudice and discrimination. Furthermore, in a time of "rationing" of benefits and services provided to people with disabilities, those whose disabilities meet the criteria for "severe" may or may not receive services. Essentially, when there are not enough resources to serve everyone with a disability, there are two basic choices: (1) serve *many* people with mild disabilities, or (2) for the same amount of money, serve *a few* people with severe disabilities. Certainly, these two options are a simplification; nonetheless, government agencies often are forced to use waiting lists or to give priority for services to people with certain types or degrees of disabilities. On first glance, serving many people with mild disabilities appears economically sound; however, serving only a few people who have severe disabilities may be, in the long run, more economically practical because these people are those who would not be able to integrate into the broader society without these benefits and services.

Finally, in the past, those with severe disabilities were more likely to have been institutionalized. Case management was not considered to be necessary because the people with severe disabilities were literally under a single roof. In the chapter on the individual and disability, a more complete discussion of the effects of institutionalization—on the individual and on society—will be discussed.

Congenital or Acquired

Congenital disabilities are those that are present at birth or shortly thereafter. Acquired disabilities are those that occur some time later. For some disabilities, such as blindness or deafness, there are critical differences in the age of onset. Further, it is safe to say that for all disabilities, the age of onset is important in the adjustment process and in the way in which society views and treats the individual with the disability. The same type and degree of disability—for example, blindness present at birth—would be a different experience than blindness acquired in old age. For some disabilities, time of onset cannot be determined because the onset is insidious. Therefore, for these types of disabilities, it is the time of diagnosis, rather than time of onset, that is considered.

Invisible or Visible

Some disabilities are visible to others, whereas other disabilities are invisible. People with mobility impairments have visible disabilities, whereas people with learning disabilities have invisible disabilities. This visibility of the disability takes many forms: aspects of the disability itself, such as congenital limb deficiencies; the use of assistive devices, such as white canes, hearing aids, and wheelchairs; unusual behaviors that result from the disability, such as responding verbally to hallucinations; or aspects of the treatment/management of the disability, such as side effects from medications or the need to attend therapy meetings. As would be expected, the experience of an invisible disability is different than the experience of a visible disability because society responds to individuals with invisible disabilities differently than it does to individuals with visible disabilities. People with invisible disabilities have the option of disclosure—being able to choose when, or if ever, to disclose. However, they are not automatically offered accommodations. It should be remembered that invisible disabilities can be severely limiting and present severe impairments for the individual. In Chapter 6 we shall learn of the hypervisibility, overobservation, and loss of privacy that individuals with visible disabilities experience.

The Americans With Disabilities Act: Equal Opportunity Under the Law

> ### In this section, look for—
> ■ The five titles of the ADA:
> 1. Title I: Employment
> 2. Title II: Transportation
> 3. Title III: Public Accommodations and Services
> 4. Title IV: Telecommunications
> 5. Title V: Miscellaneous

The ADA, which was signed into law by President George Bush in 1990, is considered to be the civil rights law for people with disabilities. There are three components of the ADA: (1) the statute itself; (2) regulations, policy guidance, and technical assistance manuals; and (3) court decisions, or what is called "case law." Indeed, the provisions of the ADA are considered to be an application of civil rights principles. "Reasonable accommodations" in policies, practices, and procedures must be put in place to end discrimination against people with disabilities. Guidelines must be decided on a case-by-case basis. The ADA has five main sections, or titles, each addressing a particular issue and each with different enforcing bodies. In addition to the enforcement by federal bodies, individuals can file lawsuits. A brief summary of each of the five titles of the ADA follows.

Title I: Employment

All employment aspects, including hiring, pay, benefits, job training, promotion, tenure, and termination, are covered in Title I. It is important to understand that current users of illegal drugs are not protected by the ADA. No employer with 15 or more employees can discriminate against an individual with a disability who is qualified and capable of performing the essential functions of the job. Further, employers must provide "reasonable accommodations" such as adaptations in employment testing procedures, assistive technology, job restructuring, provision of written materials in alternative formats such as Braille, provision of sign language interpreters, time off for visits to therapists, and architectural access for their employees with disabilities. Employment-testing accommodations include extra time for taking the test, someone to read the test, sign language interpreters, oral tests, large print, allowing the use of a magnifying glass, assisting in marking the answer sheet, and Braille presentations. The rationale behind the provision of these accommodations is to allow the test-taker to demonstrate his or her skill and knowledge level while still maintaining the validity of the test. (Of course, for some jobs, such as air traffic controller, speed of response is an integral part of the job and therefore some accommodations on preemployment tests, such as extended time, cannot be given.) These reasonable accommodations must be provided unless employers can prove the accommodation(s) present an "undue hardship." Applicants or employees who pose a direct threat to the health and safety of other individuals may be refused a job or may be fired. Employers cannot make blanket inquiries about the presence of disabilities, such as health "checklists" on application forms, nor are they allowed to ask, verbally or in writing, if the applicant has a disability. Also, employers are allowed to require preemployment medical examinations only after a conditional offer of employment has been made. Of course, individuals whose disabilities are readily visible, such as those who use a sign language interpreter or individuals who use wheelchairs, would not have the option of disclosing the presence of a disability.

Employers must pay employees with disabilities at the same rate as comparable employees without disabilities. This equal pay provision extends to benefits, including health insurance. (Health insurance is very important to people with disabilities.) The ADA also prohibits employers from assigning employees who have disabilities to the "back room." In other words, employers are not allowed to segregate an employee because of his or her disability. The Equal Employment Opportunity Commission enforces this title. Private clubs, organizations and churches, and Native American tribes are exempt from this title.

Title II: Transportation

Public entities, such as airplanes, buses, and trains, must provide vehicles that are accessible to people with disabilities. These accessible vehicles must be of a comparable level and comparable response time as vehicles used for people without disabilities. Therefore, accessible public transportation must provide the same schedules and routes that are available to everyone. The Architectural and Transportation Barriers Compliance Board, with members appointed by the President, devises standards for compliance, and the Department of Transportation enforces this title.

Title III: Public Accommodations and Services

Individuals with disabilities cannot be denied full and equal enjoyment of public accommodations solely on the basis of their disability. Public accommodations are hotels, motels, restaurants, theaters, art galleries, libraries, shopping malls, banks, professional offices, recreational facilities, parks, and zoos. For example, movies such as *Titanic*, *Mask of Zorro*, and *Star Wars: The Phantom Menace* have been audio-described for people who are blind and closed-captioned for people who are deaf, allowing many PWDs to "go to the movies" if the theater is physically accessible. These public facilities may be exempted from compliance if they can demonstrate that the adaptations are not "readily achievable." Private organizations and religious organizations are exempt. The Attorney General enforces this title.

Title IV: Telecommunications

Individuals with speech and hearing disabilities have the right to rapid, efficient, nationwide telephone and telecommunications systems (Equal Access to Software and Information, 1999). Therefore, all telephone companies must provide public telephones that are accessible to people with speech and/or hearing impairments 24 hours a day, 7 days a week, to and from the United States, at no extra cost to the user. These devices include TDDs (telecommunication devices for the deaf). Federally funded public service announcements must include closed captions.

Frank Bowe (1993) described accessibility to television: "The Television Decoder Circuitry Act of 1990 (P.L. 100-431) requires that all 13-inch or larger television sets sold or manufactured in the United States after July 1993 include built-in chips enabling the set to receive and display captions or subtitles. The chips themselves cost under $10 to manufacture and are included as part of the purchase price of the set. Broadcasters, advertisers, and others pay the cost of producing the captions themselves" (p. xii).

This title is enforced by the Federal Telecommunications Commission. Electronic databases, Web sites, and e-mail must be available in alternative formats for individuals who are blind or who have learning disabilities.

Title V: Miscellaneous

Guidelines for making historical sites and wilderness accessible to individuals with disabilities are included. Accessible wilderness areas, including hunting and fishing locations, were mandated under Section 502 of the Rehabilitation Act of 1973 (Sullivan, 1998). The government must ensure that Americans with disabilities are able to engage in outdoor activities in the national parks and all other federal lands. The ADA strengthened and reinforced this mandate.

What the ADA Does Not Cover

Clearly noted is the fact that individuals who use illegal drugs and those who have received diagnoses of sexual behavior disorders, kleptomania, pyromania, substance abuse disorders, or compulsive gambling are not covered by the ADA. Individuals must present documented evidence of a disability, and employers can ask for a second opinion. Further, the individual must be qualified to do the job to receive job accommodations under Title I. Employers are not required to lower performance or production standards. Meltsner (1998) stated:

> [Employers] do not have to tolerate theft, chronic lateness, insubordination, lewdness, violence, or other clearly inappropriate behavior. The disabled person [*sic*] can be disciplined. It is not discrimination to criticize or to fire for cause. Companies are not required to accommodate low education levels, lack of credentials, or other limitations unrelated to the person's disability. . . . Nor do [employers] have to make a particular accommodation just because it's requested. Some requests . . . are truly unreasonable. (pp. 46–47)

Private houses are exempt from the provisions of the ADA, and transit authorities have 30 years to make existing stock accessible to PWDs.

The Intent/Rationale of the Americans With Disabilities Act

The ADA clearly states the rationale of this statute: "Individuals with disabilities are a discrete and insular minority who have been faced with restrictions and limitations, subjected to a history of purposeful unequal treatment and relegated to a position of political powerlessness in our society." A bill much like the Civil Rights Act of 1964 was needed to extend legal protection against discrimination to citizens with disabilities. People with disabilities often jokingly refer to the intent of the ADA as "boldly going where everybody else goes." Before the passage of the ADA, it was legal to discriminate against a qualified job applicant solely on the basis of disability. Employers could, and did, candidly inform applicants with disabilities that they did not obtain a job simply because of the presence of a disability, and individuals who acquired a disability while they were employed, which did not render them unqualified or incapable of performing the functions of a job, often were terminated. These individuals had no legal recourse.

Furthermore, it makes economic sense to facilitate the employment of capable, qualified people who want to work. Job accommodations that allow people with disabilities to work have been found to be affordable, especially when the reduced costs of public assistance (welfare payments) and the payment of taxes are taken into consideration (Spechler, 1996). Indeed, many consider the passage of the ADA to be based on the economic benefits argument rather than on the argument of according rights to a group of Americans.

President George Bush understood this dollars-and-cents approach when he stated, "When you add together state, local, and private funds it costs almost $1200 billion annually to support Americans with disabilities, in effect to keep them dependent" (cited in Imrie, 1996, p. 64).

Senator Edward Kennedy also emphasized the economic benefits of the ADA, commenting, "Some will argue that it costs too much to implement this bill. But I reply, it costs too much to go on without it. Four percent of the American gross domestic product is spent on keeping disabled people [*sic*] dependent" (cited in Imrie, 1996, p. 64).

Two disability analysts, Batavia and Schriner (2001), described the *intent* of the ADA; however, they also point out the need for further laws to mandate specific needs of PWDs. Notice within this quote the words "in the mainstream of our society." These analysts are pointing out that "separate is not equal" and that the intent of the law is to minimize segregation and institutionalization.

Although the ADA was intended to achieve social reform primarily on a case-by-case basis, it does provide some insight into how broader issues should be addressed. It indicates, through the general intent of Congress, that a major goal of disability policy in this country is to ensure the inclusion of people with disabilities in the mainstream of our society, and that people with disabilities are to be treated as first-class citizens. Using the ADA as a philosophical statement reflecting our national disability policy provides guidance and is valuable to keep us focused on ultimate policy goals. However, legally, it is no substitute for the laws needed to achieve such goals as access to health insurance, personal assistance services, employment, smoke-free environments, and the electoral process. (p. 363)

The ADA Definition of Disability

In this section, look for—

- The ADA definition of disability
- The ADA definition of "undue hardship"
- The ADA definition of "qualified" individual

The ADA defines mental impairment as "any emotional or psychological disorder, such as mental retardation, organic brain syndrome, emotional or mental illness, or specific learning disabilities" (29 CFR Part 1630.1 [h2]). To be considered an "individual with a disability," the person must document a physical or mental impairment and "substantial limitation" in one or more major life activities. It can be seen that the ADA defines disability from the Biomedical Model and the Functional Model. Reasonable accommodations mandated by the ADA include job restructuring (working part-time, flex time, modified work schedules, telecommunicating, etc.), provision of assistive technology such as computers, and removal of architectural barriers. Indeed, many of the court cases testing the ADA focus on defining disability.

The ADA, as with most laws, must demonstrate general applicability and, at the same time, it should be specific enough to apply to individual circumstances. The regulations and technical assistance manuals provide flexibility and further explanations of how to interpret the statute. Nonetheless, one of the most difficult issues in the implementation of Title I of the ADA is whether the employer is required to make accommodations. As you will recall, Title I states that if the provision of these accommodations causes "undue hardship," the employer is not required to offer these adaptations. The definition of accommodation, with certain disabilities such as learning disabilities and mental illness, is often hard to establish. Physical disabilities, especially those that are clearly visible, present little difficulty in documentation or in determining the necessary accommodations (O'Keeffe, 1994). Wider doorways for wheelchair users or voice-activated computers for workers who are blind are accommodations that are easily understood. In contrast, the determination and provision of accommodations for workers with cognitive and psychiatric disabilities are often more complex and much less understood.

The ADA Does Not Require Preferential Treatment for People With Disabilities

The ADA is a federal law, although it is not totally universal in its application because private organizations, religious organizations, and Native American tribes are not required to comply. Much of the general public mistakenly believes that the ADA designates Americans with disabilities as eligible for preferential treatment such as lowering or waiving requirements. The ADA clearly states that the individual must be qualified, or, stated another way, the individual must be able to perform the essential functions of the job (with or without accommodations) and is not exempted from any legitimate requirement or qualification. In Chapter 4, on societal response to disability, a discussion of the differences between ensuring equal opportunity and extending preferential treatment will be presented. The ADA ensures equal opportunity for qualified individuals, based on their American citizenship, and does not require or encourage preferential treatment for people with disabilities.

Before the ADA, Some Employers Could Legally Discriminate Against Qualified Applicants/Employees Solely on the Basis of Disability

The ADA states, "Individuals with disabilities are a discrete and insular minority who have been faced with restrictions and limitations, subjected to a history of *purposeful unequal treatment* [italics added] and relegated to a position of political powerlessness in our society." Before the passage of the ADA, there were a few laws that protected the civil rights of individuals with disabilities, and these few laws were enforced on a very limited basis. The story of Paul Steven Miller in Chapter 1, the Harvard Law School graduate who was told by the Philadelphia law firm that he would not be hired because of his disability, illustrates the legality of such actions. Naturally, the law firm was aware that it was totally legal to candidly tell Mr. Miller the reason why he would not be hired. The law firm's actions may have been unethical or immoral, but they were legal at that time.

Before the passage of the ADA, if parents wanted to take their children for a family fun night to the new Disney movie at the neighborhood theater, they would have to leave one child at home—the child who uses a wheelchair. Before the passage of the ADA, some individuals with disabilities could use accessible public buses. However, most often there were so few of these types of buses that they ran on very limited schedules. An accessible bus that travels each route only once a week would now be illegal because of the ADA. So, it can be seen that it is not only the provision of the accessible bus but also the fact that these buses have comparable schedules and routes to the nonaccessible buses that fulfill the requirement of equal public transportation for people with disabilities.

Weinberg (1988) reported on her study that asked people with physical disabilities, "If there were a surgery available that was guaranteed to completely cure disability with no risk, would you be willing to undergo the surgery?" (p. 144). Twenty-two individuals participated in intensive interviews that varied in duration from 2 to 16 hours. Weinberg's study took place before the passage of the ADA (in 1988), and the interviewees clearly outlined the difficulties that lack of accommodations and accessibility played in their lives. It is not the disability that the fantasy surgery would "cure" but the lack of accommodations that make life difficult for many of these individuals. For example, Weinberg reported, "Another respondent, Lois, whose job involves the supervision of teachers, said that her inability to observe classrooms on the second floor of her school building is an obstacle in her effectively carrying out her present position as well as a hindrance to her chances for promotion" (p. 144). Lois does not need surgery; she needs an elevator. It is not her disability that is obstructing a job promotion; it is the lack of an elevator. Furthermore, the surgery is not possible—it is only a hypothetical example, but the installation of the elevator is a very workable and practical solution. Finally, when Lois is not promoted, PWODs will probably attribute this failure to Lois's lack of motivation and lack of desire for achievement, never stopping to consider that the absence of essential environmental accommodations prevented her job promotion (and her higher salary).

In another example, Sharon L., a medical social worker in Ogden, Utah, received her bachelor's and master's degrees before passage of the ADA. The difficulties she experienced in obtaining her education would not be legal today. Sharon uses a wheelchair, and the university in her hometown is very hilly and also very snowy during the winter, making the campus difficult to navigate. Indeed, she simply stayed at home during winter quarter every year. (This is an illustration of reduced opportunities for people with disabilities.) Naturally, her inability to go to school during winter quarter delayed her graduation. In addition, because there were no elevators, when Sharon had a class on the second or third floor of a building, she would roll up to the staircase and wait for any fellow students who appeared to be "strong and kind-looking men" and ask one to carry her up the stairs and the other to carry her chair. (This is an illustration of why individuals with disabilities want their rights and not charity.) Sharon had to rely on the kindness of others and submit to the humiliation of being carried in the arms of a stranger of the opposite sex. Nonetheless, she graduated twice—once with an undergraduate degree and again with a graduate degree. Now, because of the passage of the ADA, students with disabilities do not face these obstacles.

Before the ADA, There Was Only Limited Legal Protection and Limited Enforcement

Until the passage of the ADA, restrictions on discrimination against people with disabilities in the workplace applied to only a few workplaces; some states had laws, and Section 504 of the Federal Rehabilitation Act of 1973 prohibited employers who received federal contracts from discriminating on the basis of disability (Perlman & Kirk, 1991). Sections 503 and 504 of the Rehabilitation Act of 1973 offered some protection against discrimination in employment, and Section 502 mandated architectural access. However, the Rehabilitation Act of 1973 applied only to federal employers or employers who received federal contracts. The Civil Rights Law of 1964 applied only to individuals of racial/ethnic minorities and to women; people with disabilities were not included in this civil rights legislation.

The Supreme Court had only one opportunity to rule on the provision of accommodations (under the Rehabilitation Act of 1973). In *Southeastern Community College v. Davis* (1979), the Court held that the college was not required to admit an applicant with a hearing loss to the nursing program or to provide accommodations for her training. The fact that only one case concerning the enforcement of the Rehabilitation Act of 1973 was brought to the Supreme Court demonstrates that this act had little relevance for most Americans with disabilities.

Before the ADA, there was no federal mandate that required telecommunications, public places of entertainment, or transportation facilities to be available to people with disabilities. This type of widespread and blatant discrimination was legal until 1990. It would be unthinkable, and justifiably so, if any racial, ethnic, political, cultural, gender, sexual preference, or religious group in the United States experienced such discrimination. Americans with disabilities received their civil rights in 1990.

Resistance to the Americans With Disabilities Act

Why would there be resistance to the ADA? First, there is the mistaken belief that the ADA is reverse discrimination in that people with disabilities are now being given privileges and opportunities and also being afforded exemptions from valid employment and educational qualifications. Accommodations for disabilities are sometimes erroneously confused with special privileges. Indeed, the cost of most job accommodations has been found to be in the $100 to $500 range.

Definitions of such concepts as "disability" and "undue hardship" have been debated in court cases. You will remember that accommodations are not required if it can be proved that the provision of these accommodations causes undue hardship. There have been cases of people who do not have disabilities (as defined by the ADA) and, in spite of this, have sought protection and accommodations under the ADA. These types of cases are abuses of the ADA and may make it more difficult for those with legitimate disabilities to assert their rights. For example, many high school students are now claiming learning disabilities and asking the Scholastic Aptitude Test (SAT) administrators to allow them extra time in which to take this college entrance examination. Never before have such large numbers of high school seniors claimed a learning disability and asked for accommodation in testing. The majority of these claimants do not have learning disabilities nor are they eligible for the accommodations. The Supreme Court ruled that an individual who wore eyeglasses did not have a disability and therefore was not protected under the ADA. If the court had ruled in this individual's favor, then more than two thirds of all American adults, those who wear eyeglasses, would be considered to have a disability, "including the seven out of nine justices who heard this case while wearing glasses" (Becker, 1999, p. 9). Nonetheless, such abuses make it more difficult for those who truly do have learning disabilities to receive the appropriate accommodations. Read the newspaper article in Exhibit 2–1 about athletes who claimed false disabilities to receive permits to park in "handicapped parking."

Becker, a Nobel Prize winner and a professor at the University of Chicago, wrote an editorial in *Business Week* entitled "Are We Hurting or Helping the Disabled [*sic*]?" Considering the ADA only as employment legislation, Becker (1999) questioned the passage of the ADA, stating, "The ADA passed without evidence of systematic discrimination against the disabled [*sic*] workers in any way comparable to the discrimination against blacks that gave rise to the civil-rights legislation of the 1960s" (p. 9).

Becker pointed out a weakness in the ADA: "Congress allowed the definition of disability in the act to be vague. I predicted in this magazine that the vagueness of the ADA and the litigious nature of the judicial system would encourage lawyers and workers to widen the concept of disability to absurd extremes" (p. 9).

According to Becker, "the truly disabled [*sic*] may be the principal victims. . . . To prevent costly lawsuits, many companies apparently avoid hiring job applicants whom they believe would prove litigious under the ADA" (p. 9). Many disability advocates would agree with many of Becker's arguments. The ADA has spawned a great deal of litigation, and the overall employment rate of people with disabilities has probably decreased, for the

Exhibit 2-1

Athletes Face Charges Over Handicapped Parking Scam

LOS ANGELES (AP)—The fourteen men listed a smorgasbord of complaints—knee and back injuries, asthma, Bell's palsy—to justify requests for handicapped parking permits, authorities said.

In truth, they were arguably among the most able-bodied men on the UCLA campus: members of the football team.

The men, current and former Bruin players, won the permits by claiming fake injuries, investigators said Friday. They were charged Thursday with misdemeanors of illegally possessing the blue handicapped parking placards.

Each count carries a maximum six months in jail and $1,000 fine. One person who allegedly obtained two placards was charged with four counts.

The players' applications to the state Department of Motor Vehicles claimed knee injuries, back injuries, back surgery, torn ligaments, Bell's palsy, and asthma.

All of the claims were bogus, said Mike Qualls, spokesman for the city attorney's office.

---

reason that Becker advanced. However, most disability advocates consider the ADA, despite these flaws, to be a landmark piece of legislation that has transformed the lives of many Americans.

Another source of resistance toward the ADA may simply stem from a dislike for governmental interference in such a broad array of public institutions. Some have complained that by allowing access to Americans who have disabilities, liability insurance premiums will increase or employers will not be able to fire incompetent workers who have disabilities; others complain of the inconvenience, and still others insist that the presence of people with disabilities in public life will make others feel ill at ease, uncomfortable, distressed, and embarrassed. Some employers have been fearful that if they hire someone with a disability, coworkers, supervisors, and customers will all be "freaked."

Some of the criticisms of the ADA are humorous (and ill-informed). Brian Doherty (1997), an assistant editor for *Reason*, a monthly libertarian periodical, wrote an article entitled "ADA Compliance Is Too Expensive." Doherty states, "Sometimes it makes more sense to help a person in a wheelchair up a step or two than to spend thousands of dollars on ramps" (p. 53). We have learned that the provision of civil rights is never based on cost and, therefore, such statements are without basis. Moreover, there are many people in wheelchairs who would need help with those one or two steps. Bovard (1997) wrote an article entitled "The ADA Defines Disability Too Broadly." Bovard made the following statements, "The ADA is also exploding like a series of cluster bombs across the budgets of local governments across the country" (p. 54). "The ADA is sometimes said to stand for

'Attorneys' Dreams Answered' " (p. 59) and "At colleges, the ADA has been a godsend to shirking students" (p. 60).

Robert Burgdorf (2002) is a professor of law who wrote the original draft of the ADA. In 2004 Burgdorf wrote, "Fourteen years ago, as I drafted the original version of the Americans with Disabilities Act, I never dreamed that this landmark civil rights law would become so widely misunderstood and my words so badly misinterpreted particularly by the body meant to protect the very rights guaranteed by the law."

Results of the ADA

> **In this section, look for—**
>
> - Why the ADA has spurred advances in assistive technology
> - Why the ADA has contributed to a collective identity for PWDs
> - How the ADA has increased the employment rate of PWDs

As would be expected, the ADA has, in the last 17 years, facilitated the access of people with disabilities into many aspects of public life. In addition, the ADA has spurred many advances in telecommunications, assistive technology, and job restructuring. Many of these advances have also benefited people without disabilities. For example, closed-captioned television, originally developed for viewers who are deaf, has also been helpful for elderly individuals or people who are learning English, and much of the assistive technology developed for people who are blind is used as memory aids for forgetful people who are not blind. Ramps into buildings that facilitate access for people who use wheelchairs also facilitate access for anyone or anything on wheels, such as strollers, carts, and wheeled suitcases. The first use of the transistor tube, which led to the computer revolution, was in a hearing aid.

The ADA has also contributed to a collective identity of people with disabilities. Although this group identity did not begin with the ADA, the ADA has fostered the growth, pride, and awareness of their rights and responsibilities under the law. For example, in the state of Utah, a man named Robert Irons undertook a project to contact people with disabilities and assist them in becoming registered to vote. Mr. Irons helped 900 people to register and then organized telephone committees to ensure that each of these 900 people had transportation to the polls on voting days. Mr. Irons simply informed individuals with disabilities about their large numbers and their ability to vote on legislation that would be favorable to them. It is safe to state that the ADA has increased group solidarity of Americans with disabilities.

Has the ADA increased the rate of employment for people with disabilities? The Harris Survey commissioned by the National Organization on Disability in 1994 showed that people with disabilities were not experiencing higher employment rates. In contrast, in 1996 the U.S. Census Bureau Survey of Income Programs and Participation found a 27% decrease in employment of people with severe disabilities. Once again, the conflicting results of these studies can be explained by the differing definitions of "disability" and "work." Some scholars believe that employment of PWDs has increased in small- and medium-sized companies (that employ fewer than 15 workers) because these companies are not afraid of litigation: small- and medium-sized companies are exempt from compliance with the ADA. Nonetheless, it is safe to state that the passage of the ADA has not facilitated the employment of as many individuals as anticipated.

Talking About Disability

> ### In this section, look for—
>
> - How language can be demeaning, distancing, and polarizing
> - How language can determine job opportunities, educational opportunities, and social participation for PWDs
> - How language can communicate deficit

Using language that conveys respect for people with disabilities is, at times, cumbersome and awkward, and for most of us, there is new terminology to be learned. Language is more than political correctness or semantics. Listening to the NPR Disability History Project, especially the segment "Tomorrow's Children," we can learn the way in which the words used to describe people directly resulted in their deaths. "Newspapers and medical journals of 1915 referred to people with disabilities as 'defective,' 'idiot,' and 'imbecile.' These were incredible value judgments. They didn't see the hostility, the contempt, the subjectivity. They thought they were making technically valid, objective decisions. Chloroform unfit children. Show them the mercy we show beasts that are no longer fit to live" (NPR, 2004). Assumptions about the value of lives often derive from their perceived value to society and to themselves. Often, the language used to refer to PWDs implies that their lives are not worth living (Marks, 1999, p. 38).

Language is powerful, and the use of words clearly communicates attitudes toward people. For example, there are many unacceptable words for individuals of various racial, cultural, and ethnic groups. If a parent were to hear his or her child use one of these words, the parent would automatically correct the child, explaining why the word the child used is offensive and what the correct word is.

Language is a mirror that reflects society's views toward certain groups, and the words that are used very accurately reveal social and cultural history. There are many words that are offensive, demeaning, and out of date and lead to inaccurate stereotypes. Indeed, much of the objection to many words used to describe PWDs is derived from the history of their use, rather than from their actual meaning. Much of the language used to describe the disability experience comes from the Bible, illustrating the long history of underlying attitudes toward people with disabilities. Indeed, in reviewing the history of any group of people that has been the target of prejudice, discrimination, and reduced opportunity, we find that the language used by the broader society to speak about these people has these characteristics: (1) The words used to describe these people are both offensive and demeaning; (2) the identifying words that are used to set these people apart from the broader society make very clear that these people do not "belong" with everybody else (this is called "distancing" or "polarization"); (3) usually the language is not a self-identification—people don't use these terms to describe themselves; (4) the language usually "lumps" all the people perceived to be in the group together regardless of individual differences; (5) the labels used to describe people with disabilities describe, often inaccurately, only one aspect of an individual's identity (this is called "reductionism"); and (6) society is very reluctant to change individual language use, using the defense of ease of use or freedom of speech. Legislation cannot control language, but educating the public about the correct way to discuss disability and the underlying rationale behind this language is a first step in integrating people with disabilities into society.

In the case of people with disabilities, the language used can determine job opportunities, educational opportunities, and social participation (Hahn, 1993). Before behavior and attitudes can be changed, language must be changed. In the chapters on society and disability, it will become clear that people with disabilities have experienced pervasive, systematic, institutionalized prejudice and discrimination and, naturally, the language used by society very clearly reflected these attitudes (Rossides, 1990). Language forces people into pejorative categories.

Language That Communicates Deficit, Inferiority, and Pathology

The language used to describe disabilities and the people who experience disabilities communicates deficit and inferiority. The prefixes *dis-* and *dys-* mean difficult, impaired, or absent. Words such as *disorder, disability, disease, dyslexia*, *dystrophy*, and *dysfunction* reflect these meanings. The prefixes *im-* and *in-* mean absence or lack; therefore, the word *invalid* means without value or validity, *impairment* means without strength or quality (or spoiled), and *infirm* means without strength. The prefix *para-* (in *Paralympics*) means subsidiary. (Note: Paralympics are competitions for athletes with physical disabilities, and the Special Olympics are competitions for people with intellectual disabilities.) It is not surprising that most PWODs think of disabilities as deficits and inferiority because language shapes our attitudes. In Chapters 5, 7, and 8 we will see that many PWDs do not think of their disabilities as losses or as the absence of something. Moreover, many PWDs consider their disabilities to be assets and an integral part of their self-identities. For example, Dr. Irving King Jordan, former president of Gallaudet University, who is deaf, made this statement: "If there are 1,000 aspects of being deaf, 998 are good and 2 are bad." By quantifying the experience of deafness, Dr. Jordan is making the point that his disability has been an asset and not a deficit.

Person-First Language

There are some basic guidelines. The first, and most well known, is the "people-first" approach. It is the Americans with Disabilities Act and not the Disabled Americans Act because this federal legislation is based on people's American citizenship and not their disability. They are Americans first. Also, it is correct to say "individual with a disability," not "a disabled individual." It is correct to say "a person who is blind," not "a blind person." It is "an athlete with a disability" or, even better, simply "an athlete." In spite of this, the term "disabled athletes" often is used. Person-first language may appear to be more cumbersome, but it serves the purpose of emphasizing that the individual is a person first and the disability is secondary. In the past, it was legal in many places to institutionalize, sterilize, and even kill people with disabilities because they were not considered to be fully human. Therefore, the importance of "people-first" language can be seen. However, individuals who are deaf, especially those in the Deaf Culture, prefer to be referred to as "a Deaf person" (Stalcup, 1991). You will see that the word "Deaf" is capitalized. This insistence on putting the word "Deaf" before the word "person" is based on the Deaf's identity as a culture, as a group not unified by a disability, but rather unified by shared experiences and a common language. Incidentally, the use of the expression "the Deaf" is acceptable. However, it is not correct to use these types of expressions with other disability groups.

A few people do not like the person-first language because they feel that the disability is an important part of their identity. Sobsey (1994) reported, "One physically disabled person [*sic*] told [me] that she is not *a woman with a disability*, she is a *disabled woman*. She feels strongly that her life-long disability is as essential a part of her as her gender or heritage, and she feels that the person-first rule fails to recognize this critical aspect of her identity. People should have the right to reject any labels that they do not like and forcing an unwanted label on anyone is abusive" (p. 320).

Olkin (1999) succinctly remarked, "When we talk about using 'person-first' language . . . this is what we mean. It's not semantics. It's a way of looking at us and seeing us, not the disability" (p. 89).

"Person-first" language is not new; in fact, Beatrice Wright, in her classic book *Physical Disability: A Psychological Approach*, published in 1960, advised against using "shortcuts" in speaking about people with disabilities. Wright explained: "Then, a physically disabled person is also a physically *abled* person. There are things that he [*sic*] *can* do as well as things that he [*sic*] *cannot* do. We may conclude that the designation 'a physically disabled person' is a shortcut to the more involved but psychologically sounder expression, 'a person with a physical disability.' Such a reformulation is far reaching. . . . The shortcut distorts and undermines" (pp. 7–9). Although Wright was speaking only of physical disabilities, for the last 40 years she has advocated the use of language that separates the disability from the total person.

The Person Is Not the Condition

The second basic guideline is often referred to as "the person is not the condition." So, there are no "diabetics," "schizophrenics," or "quadriplegics," but rather "individuals with disabilities, schizophrenia, or quadriplegia." Once again, this type of language communicates that the individual is not the condition or the disability. No one would speak of a group of people diagnosed with cancer as "the cancerous," but we often hear and read the phrase "the mentally ill" or "the deaf," or "the blind." Sometimes, people with disabilities are identified by their use of assistive technology. A server in a restaurant said, "I have three wheelchairs and two white canes." (Wheelchairs don't eat, they don't pay restaurant bills, and they don't leave tips.) Also, because most people with disabilities are not sick, it is inappropriate to refer to them as "patients." For example, Bickenbach (1993) made the observation that "many people with disabilities make no more use of medical services than anyone else" (p. 83). In 1999 a publisher of a book for psychologists and psychiatrists advertised a book on adjustment to chronic disease with a photograph of a man in a wheelchair reaching out to a nurse. Most people in wheelchairs do not have a chronic disease, but the media, including a publisher for professionals, presents the idea in a very subtle way that disability (in this case, the wheelchair) and sickness (the title and subject of the book) are synonymous.

The disability should not be mentioned if it is not relevant, and it is surprising how often the disability simply is not pertinent. The following is an example of an inappropriate statement: "Dr. Smith, who uses a wheelchair, gave a brilliant lecture." Certainly, it is important to mention the use of a wheelchair when planning accommodations such as a lowered podium from which to deliver the lecture or ramps up to the podium. Nonetheless, in the sentence used here, the use of the wheelchair should not be mentioned. When the media include the disability when it is not relevant, they are giving the incorrect impression that the disability is the focus of the individual's life or that everyone should view the person as his or her disability. Indeed, most of the time, it is probably more accurate to use "people" rather than "people with disabilities." No one likes to be referred to, or thought of, as only one aspect of his or her nature. No single label can capture the meaning of an entire person's personality and character.

Avoiding Sensational and Emotional Terms

Sensational and emotional words should be avoided because these types of words are demeaning. The word "survivor" is preferred over "victim," and it is more correct to say that an individual "experiences" a certain disability rather than that he or she "suffers from" the disability (Lynch & Thomas, 1994). A humorous bumper sticker on a car reads, "I don't suffer from insanity. I enjoy every minute of it." Clearly, the message of the bumper sticker is twofold: (1) avoid the use of emotional terms such as "suffer," and (2) no one, except for the individual with a disability, can describe the experience. It is better to use the expression "congenital disability" rather than "birth defect." A person uses a wheelchair and is not "confined to" a wheelchair. Words such as "cripple," "lame," "dumb" (meaning someone who does not speak), "afflicted," "stricken," "maimed," "invalid," "infirm," "misshapen," or "withered" communicate a condescending attitude. Also, instead of the word "fit," "seizure" is considered to be more accurate.

According to Michalko, a disability scholar, when a PWD is said to "suffer" a disability, it "discursively points to and constructs the value of able-bodiedness while devaluing disability. It implies that disability is a life bereft of value, and not only is this idea offensive to those of us who are disabled, but it is also not true" (Michalko, 2002, p. 51). Disability is difficult, time-consuming, and expensive, and it can be painful. Nonetheless, PWDs do not exist in a continuous state of suffering and misery, uninterrupted by pleasure and satisfactions, and it is clear that this type of language conveys the false idea that a disability automatically results in a low quality of life. Linton (1998) states that sensational language "attributes life, power, and intention to the condition (the disability) that disempowers the person with the disability, rendering him or her helpless and passive" (p. 25)

The History of Certain Words

For the most part, certain words, such as "cripple" or "maimed," were not consciously used to be demeaning and insulting. Sinason (1992) stated, "Each worker introducing a new term hopes that the new word brings new hope and a period of historical change. Each time the new word is coined, it is coined honorably. . . . It is therefore doing a grave disservice to past pioneers to point contemptuously to their chosen term" (p. 40). Nonetheless, their use has become demeaning, insulting, and often inaccurate. The word "handicap" should be avoided simply because of its history. Many believe that the word derived from the act of begging because beggars had their "cap in their hand." It should be noted that this story has no basis in fact. However, in the past, many individuals with disabilities, in the absence of any other opportunity, begged for a living. Certainly today, when it is stated that anyone has "his or her cap in hand," the unstated message is that the person is perceived as humble or inferior. Indeed, the first disability laws in the United States were enacted in the 1860s, when Civil War veterans with disabilities were seen begging on the streets of American cities. Therefore, it is best to use the word "disability." Incidentally, the first hospital for children with orthopedic impairments was established in New York City during the Civil War. The name of the hospital was the New York Hospital for the Ruptured and Maimed (Byrom, 2004).

Some disability advocates do use the word "handicap" to describe obstacles and impediments in the environment but never in reference to a condition an individual experiences (Nagi, 1991). The following sentence is an illustration: "The lack of health insurance benefits was a handicap to Ms. Lupino's accepting the position."

"Special" and "exceptional" are words that many people with disabilities dislike because these words invoke a history of segregation. There are many stories of parents being told that their child was going to be placed in a "special" classroom or a "special program." The words "special" and "exceptional" also have a euphemistic quality. "Special" and "exceptional" are labels that people with disabilities instantly recognize as meaning segregated and inferior. They are not innocuous terms because they imply difference and thus are polarizing. Individuals in "exceptional" or "special" programs "are then stigmatized as those who cannot 'get by' under programs designed to meet basic needs" (Bickenbach, 1993, p. 201). One disability scholar explained the use of the word "special" in this way:

> Labeling education and its recipients special may have been a deliberate attempt to confer legitimacy on the educational practice and to prop up a discarded group. It is also important to consider the unconscious feelings such a strategy may mask. It is my feeling that the nation in general responds to disabled [sic] people with great ambivalence. Whatever apathy and disdain is felt is in competition with feelings of empathy, guilt, and identification. (Marks, 1999, p. 158)

An article once appeared in the *Disability Rag*, a publication written by and for PWDs, titled "Getting Rid of Special" (Woodward, 1991). The author was clearly opposed to the use of the word "special" to describe PWDs or the services PWDs receive. However, the author understood that, even among PWDs themselves, there is disagreement about the word's use. The author quoted a National Spinal Cord Injury Association advertisement that showed a sign for "disabled parking." The advertisement read, "We're asking for a special place in your hearts, not just in your parking lots" (p. 41).

Euphemisms

Euphemisms are insulting because their use implies that the reality of the disability is negative and unfortunate. Much of the language used to speak about the disability experience has been condescending, trivializing, or euphemistic. Expressions such as "physically challenged" or "mentally different" are both condescending and euphemistic, suggesting that disabilities cannot be discussed in an open and candid manner. The use of these expressions also trivializes the disability experience, suggesting that disabilities are only minor inconveniences. Richard Harris, director of the Office of Disabled Student Development at Ball State University in Indiana, reported that a "point of view article in the May 1991 *Paraplegia News* entitled 'Cripplespeak' poked some fun at the newest 'acceptable term,' which is 'people of differing abilities.'" The coiner of this term won $50,000. Additionally, the article expressed mild amusement at Michigan's politically correct term for an individual with a disability: handicapper (Harris, 1992, p. 210).

Erik Weihenmayer, who climbed Mt. Everest and who is blind, wrote about the use of euphemisms:

> Isn't it interesting . . . that the problem isn't always blindness, but all the false assumptions surrounding blindness, and that includes your own. Once a lady wanted to ask me how long I had been blind, but she was too afraid to use the word *blind*. Maybe she thought that blindness was a kind of demon and just the mere mention of the word might give it the power to rise up and crush my spirit. So instead, she asked, "How long have you been a person of sightlessness?" (2001, p. 84)

People, in their attempts to be positive and complimentary, often inadvertently use insulting qualifying statements such as "Even though she uses a wheelchair, she is beautiful—or intelligent, or funny, or generous, or hardworking, or honest" or "I don't think of you as having a disability." While these types of statements are not intended to be hurtful and condescending, they are both because they clearly communicate the speaker's bias against people with disabilities. (It's like the compliment "You don't sweat much for a fat girl.") The speaker is acknowledging an exception but, at the same time, holding on to the biases and prejudices held against the larger group: people with disabilities.

Defiant Self-Naming, or Gimp Pride

Many PWDs use words to describe themselves and their experience that are not appropriate for PWODs to use. The use of slang, imitation of PWODs, and exaggeration are ways to fight against prejudice and discrimination of the larger culture. This type of terminology is called "in-group" language and often is a challenge to PWODs and a reclamation of the in-group's right to name and describe their identity. Defiant self-naming celebrates and takes pride in disability. Linton (1998) explained: "Cripple, gimp, and freak are used by the disability community. They are personally and politically useful as a means to comment on oppression because they assert our right to name experience" (p. 17). In later chapters, we will learn that PWDs have rarely been allowed to establish a group identity. Many in the Gimp Culture consider the use of this in-group language to be therapeutic. Nancy Mairs (as cited in Thompson, 1997) illustrated the power of the self-labeling:

> People . . . wince at the word, "cripple." Perhaps I want them to wince. I want them to see one tough customer, one to whom the fates/gods/viruses have not been kind, but who can face the brutal truth of her existence squarely. As a cripple, I swagger. (p. 284)

"But, there is a paradox to labels. They can also be a language of empowerment," stated Sue Souter, former U.S. Commissioner of Rehabilitation and former President of the World Institute on Disabilities Services (1993). Souter relates that the Deaf Culture does not endorse the term "hearing impaired," preferring the word "deaf." They are determined to retain the power to define and label themselves. Nonetheless, most legislation, including the ADA, uses the term "hearing impaired" because it is considered to be a sensitive term. To the Deaf Culture, the term "hearing impaired" is a euphemism imposed by outsiders.

Finally, it should be noted that these guidelines are used in American English and not necessarily used in British English or other languages. For example, one disability scholar (Charlton, 1998) noted:

> The struggle to change language describing disability is particularly interesting in Spanish. The most common expression in Latin America is *minasvalidas*, which translates as "less valid." The term *discapitados* (less capable) is also very common. Pejorative terminology about disabilities abounds in Spanish and, in fact, there is not one politically correct term describing disability in the dictionary. We in the disability rights movement created our own terms, *personas con deshabilidades*, or persons with disabilities. The word *deshabilidades* is not in the dictionary. When people point this out, believing that this means we cannot use the word, we proudly tell them we will not accept the language of

the oppressors just because some book perpetuates the stereotypes and myths that we are fighting to break down. (p. 67)

Another example of the use of language to describe PWDs has been provided by Ong (1993): "The Chinese term for disabled is 'canfei,' meaning crippled and useless. It depicts the Chinese view of disability" (p. 9).

Labels That Attempt To Describe All Those Different From the Majority

In this section, look for—

- What are "catch-all" categories
- Why "crips can call themselves anything they want"

In an effort to organize and simplify, administrators implement labels to describe people that often become "catch-all" categories. Catch-all categories have often included "exceptional," "multicultural," and "special." People included in these categories often are people with disabilities, people who are intellectually gifted, people of differing cultural/racial/linguistic/ethnic groups, and people of differing sexual orientations (Artiles & Trent, 1994; Pugach & Seidl, 1996). Looking at these various types of people, it becomes clear that they have little in common, with the exception of two factors. First, they all have been targets of prejudice and discrimination, and second, administrators and policymakers often view these different types of people as a single group simply because the "regular" places and services are not viewed as appropriate for any of these people. It is as if everything, and everybody, that defies easy labeling and categorization is put together into a single undifferentiated category. In essence, these catch-all categories are diagnoses of exclusion. These are diagnoses of exclusion in which most of the exclusions are positive and those characteristics or needs that remain are placed in catch-all categories. While it may only be thoughtlessness or an attempt to limit the number of categories, the use of catch-all terms communicates that "these people" are different from the majority, stating, "We don't know who you are, we only know who you are *not*—mainstream." Ironically, "these people" may also be different from others in the same catch-all category—perhaps more different from them than from the majority.

Experts in racial/ethnic/linguistic issues deplore linking racial/ethnic groups with disability groups. Pugach and Seidl (1996) stated this objection: "Unless special educators are willing to view current interpretations of the disability–diversity relationship as problematic in the first place, the richness of cultural diversity will always be transformed into a deficit" (p. 5). These highly educated university professors are stating that disability is a deficit, but cultural diversity is richness. Furthermore, it appears that these special education professors' only concern with including disability groups with racial and cultural groups is the prejudice by association that racial and cultural groups will experience by being somehow related to disability groups, rather than considering that these two groups (both of which are "rich" and neither of which is a "deficit") do not belong together simply because their needs are very different. For example, in public education, what is the commonality, in terms of learning, of a child who does not speak English and a child who speaks English and uses a wheelchair?

In contrast to all of the above, people who have disabilities can speak about their disabilities, often referring to themselves as "crips" or using other seemingly derogatory terms. Such in-group language reflects their (1) anger at their treatment by people without disabilities, (2) need to choose their own identifiers, and (3) identity of belonging to a group as a sign of solidarity with other people with disabilities. As with all in-group language, it is not appropriate for individuals without disabilities to use these terms.

Many agencies, legislation, and acronyms of organizations use incorrect language because they were created and named before the use of correct language. Therefore, there is the Equal Education for All Handicapped Children Act of 1975 and the ARC, which stands for Association of Retarded Citizens. The correct usage today would be Individuals with Disabilities Education Act of 1990 and the Association for Individuals with Mental Retardation. (ARC still uses the acronym but has changed the name of the organization.)

In the chapters on society and disability, we will see more clearly the direct relationship between demeaning language and prejudice and discrimination. After reviewing the history of treatment of people with disabilities, the correct language will not seem awkward, cumbersome, or difficult to use.

In-Class Videos

All of the following videos (except for "Ways to Move") show different types of disabilities. After viewing each of these videos, discuss the following in class. If your class is large, divide into groups.

1. In which of the four categories (physical, intellectual, cognitive, or psychiatric) would this disability be placed?
2. Use the Functional Model to describe this disability.
3. Use the Environmental Model to describe this disability.
4. Is this disability an invisible disability or a visible disability?
5. What types of accommodations (mandated by the ADA) would be necessary for an individual with this type of disability?

- View the 60-minute video "Ways to Move" by Films for the Humanities and Sciences (P.O. Box 2053, Princeton, NJ 08543-2053, 800-257-5126, www.films.com). The producers describe the video in this way: "This program contains three stories that explore the debate between what has been called the Biomedical Model of disability, in which disability is a challenge to be cured, and the independence model, in which the challenge is to make society more accessible. Viewers meet individuals who shatter stereotypes about disability."

- View the 26-minute video "Muscular Dystrophy" by Films for the Humanities and Sciences. The producer states, "This program from 'The Doctor Is In' looks at how individuals with muscular dystrophy deal with the disease: a young boy gets physical therapy at an Easter Seals Center, bracing helps a six-year-old girl with spinal muscular atrophy, and a young mother with myasthenia gravis gets help from surgery and medication. The program also covers the search for a cure and the available treatments."

- View the 21-minute video "Diagnosing and Treating Cystic Fibrosis" by Films for the Humanities and Sciences. According to the producers, this video is "divided into four segments and examines the presentation, diagnostic testing, treatment, and biochemistry of CF. Computer graphics and endoscopic imagery enhance this informative program."

- View the 19-minute video "Advancements in Traumatic Brain Injury" by Films for the Humanities and Sciences. The producers describe this video: "Dr. George Zitnay, president of the Brain Injury Association, and other experts discuss the various types of brain injuries within the context of new diagnostic methods and treatments. Innovative rehabilitation techniques are illustrated on actual brain injury sufferers [sic]. Several people with brain injuries reveal how the injuries have impacted their lives and the lives of their families."

- View the 19-minute video "The Injured Brain: Closed Head Traumas" by Films for the Humanities and Sciences. The producers state that the video "explains the types and symptoms of closed head injuries—anything from temporary loss of consciousness to coma—though some patients show almost no symptoms." It shows the tests used to determine the nature and extent of the injury, treatment, the problems of recovery, and the role of rehabilitation.

- View the 30-minute video "Mentally Handicapped and Epileptic: They Don't Make a Fuss" by Films for the Humanities and Sciences. The producers state: "This program deals with the combination of mental handicap and epilepsy, showing extensive footage of actual seizures, discussing the special psychosocial implications of this combination of problems, and dealing with first aid, risk-taking, and prognosis." The conclusion is that, despite intractable seizures and limited horizons, even severe mental handicaps and severe epilepsy need not preclude a happy and fulfilling life.

- View the 56-minute video "Breaking the Silence Barrier: Inside the World of Cognitive Disabilities." The producers describe this video as reporting "on the creative technologies and multimedia software programs that are being used to help people with autism, traumatic brain injuries, and learning and speech disabilities. Temple Grandin, an autistic woman [sic] with a Ph.D. in animal science, explains how deep pressure therapy helped her. Renowned neurologist Oliver Sacks shares his views on autism. Also profiled is Bob Williams, who is the first person with a significant speech disability to hold a major federal office."

- View the 35-minute video "Mental Disabilities: Organic Disorders" by Films for the Humanities and Sciences. The producers state, "This program demonstrates clinical organic disorders, their characteristics, and differential diagnoses. The disorders discussed include those relating to psychoactive substance use, schizophrenia and delusional disorders; and mood, neurotic stress-related, and somatoform disorders. Each disorder is explained and identified by its characteristics. Included are Alzheimer's, Pick's disease, Huntington's disease, Parkinson's disease, Creutzfeldt-Jakob disease, and HIV dementia. Also included are organic personality disorders, frontal lobe syndrome, primary cerebral disease, systemic disease, endocrine disorders, exogenous toxic substance, and temporal lobe epilepsy."

- View the 46-minute video "Schizophrenia and Delusional Disorders" by Films for the Humanities and Sciences. The producers describe the video in this way: "Schizophrenia, acute and transient psychoses, persistent delusional disorders, and schizoaffective disorders are examined. Their principal abnormalities are divided into the following psychiatric phenomena: disordered thinking, delusions, hallucinations, and abnormal behavior. Specific symptoms of each disorder are discussed."

- View the 24-minute video "Fetal Alcohol Syndrome: Life Sentence" by Films for the Humanities and Sciences. The producers describe the video in this way: "Fetal alcohol syndrome is the result of permanent organic injury to the brain of the fetus, caused by maternal drinking during pregnancy. That injury leads to learning disabilities, poor judgment, antisocial behavior, and worse, if a recent study is correct. This program discusses FAS within the context of that study, which suggests that 20 to 25 percent of all prison inmates may suffer from the condition. The program examines how early identification and treatment of children with FAS can help prevent extreme antisocial behavior in adulthood."

- View the 49-minute video "Empowering People with Disabilities through Technology" by Films for the Humanities and Sciences.

The producers describe this video: "In this program, three people determined to be doers, not viewers, demonstrate the adaptive technology that is improving the quality of their lives. For Larry, an adult quadriplegic, mouth-activated remote controls allow him to do high-end computer drafting and even sail a boat. For Carol, born with an underdeveloped visual cortex, an enhanced computer enables her to attend college. And for Matthew, a child born with cerebral palsy, an orthotic walking device has him up and around while helping him condition his bones and muscles. Other innovations include Braille PCs (personal computers), talking book scanners, and a remarkable hands-free office."

- View the 60-minute video "Redesigning the Human Machine" by Films for the Humanities and Sciences. The producers state, "This program explores the use of technological advances. Virtual reality is being used as a learning tool for children with disabilities, as an assistive technology for Parkinson's disease patients, and as a form of empowerment for the disabled [*sic*]. The program also examines the potential use of robotics to assist people with limited mobility. Cochlear implants are also explained."

- View the 60-minute video "Ready to Live" by Films for the Humanities and Sciences. The producers describe this video as looking "at ways adaptive technologies help people with disabilities find independence. Included are profiles of a world-class runner who uses an advanced prosthetic leg, a former Bosnian soldier whose life was transformed by a pair of artificial hands, one of the founders of the 'Independent Living Movement,' and a woman who inspired a revolution in wheelchair design and construction."

- View the 30-minute video "Open to the Public: Complying with the Americans with Disabilities Act" from Aquarius Productions. The producers describe this video as providing "an overview of the Americans with Disabilities Act as it applies to state and local governments. The ADA doesn't provide recommendations for solving common problems, but this film could provide enough information for governments to solve some common problems without turning to high-priced consultants."

- View the 30-minute video "Right at Home: The Fair Housing Act Explained" from Aquarius Productions. The producers describe this video as showing "simple solutions for complying with the Fair Housing Act amendments. Emphasizes low-cost, practical solutions and working with people with disabilities to find the best applicable solution. Ideal for people with disabilities, university courses, and disability awareness organizations."

- View these three 15-minute videos: "Lily: A Longitudinal View of Life with Down Syndrome" produced by Insight Media. The producers describe these videos as follows: "Lily's enormous spirit and openness in discussing her situation provide views with insights to the possibilities and challenges of living with Down Syndrome. "Lily: A Story About a Girl Like Me" (1978) examines her life at age 10, when she was mainstreamed because her district lacked facilities for her. "Lily: A Sequel" (1988) was shot when she was 20, and shows her graduation from high school and life in a group home. She also shares her wishes for more independence and a fuller social life. "Lily at Thirty" (1997) interviews her when she has her own apartment and works in a supermarket." #TAH3295

■ View the 53-minute video "Refrigerator Mothers" produced by Fanlight Productions. The producers describe this video: "From the 1950's through the 1970's, mental health and medical professionals claimed that autism was caused by mothers who were cold, rejecting, unable to 'bond properly.' They were labeled 'refrigerator mothers.' This film profiles seven courageous women who refused to be crushed by the burden of blame. Today, they have strong, supportive relationships with their now adult sons and daughters and, in a variety of ways, have helped them to find their place in the world." Order no. JF-346.

■ View the 51-minute video "Spinal Impact" produced by Films for the Humanities and Sciences. The producers describe this video: "When a spinal cord injury occurs, both the life and the quality of life hang in the balance. This program explores the most promising scientific breakthroughs in the treatment of spinal cord injuries, including nerve regeneration and electrical stimulation devices. Compelling case studies of survivors of spinal cord injuries address the various degrees of paralysis and explain why swift and aggressive care at the time of the injury is crucial to all levels of recovery. A Discovery Channel Production." #GXY11046.

■ View the 55-minute video "Working Like Crazy" produced by Fanlight Productions. The producers describe this video: "An estimated 85% of people labeled 'mentally ill' are unemployed, and often viewed as incapable of working, hopeless, helpless, maybe dangerous besides. 'Working Like Crazy' challenges these stereotypes. This is a fresh, engaging look at the struggles and victories of six former mental health patients. Though once labeled 'unemployable,' they now work in businesses run and staffed by other psychiatric survivors—places where they can make a living, rebuild their lives, connect with others, and contribute to society." Order no. HN-333.

Learning Activities

1. Give a class presentation on one type of disability, such as blindness, schizophrenia, or mental retardation. Describe this disability

from each of these models: the Biomedical Model, the Environ-mental Model, the Functional Model, and the Sociopolitical Model.

2. View the video "My Body Is Not Who I Am" by Lisa Shaffer of the Albany Medical School and Aquarius Productions. Write a short paper listing how the individuals in this video view the Bio-medical Model of disability. For example, why does one of the in-terviewees make this statement: "I was angry with my parents for jumping to the beck and call of the doctors. When you're a child and have 'corrective surgeries,' you go through life thinking you're defective"?

3. View the two videos "Open to the Public: Complying with the Americans with Disabilities Act" and "Right at Home," both by Aquarius Productions. Then, document places in your community that are not architecturally accessible.

4. After obtaining an ADA technical manual, which will give precise measurements and specifications for accessibility, visit various places in your community, such as entertainment facilities, sports facilities, workplaces, schools, and churches and other places of worship and write a short paper describing their accessibility.

5. Write a paper or report to class on ADA litigation using these Web sites. After briefly describing each case, either defend the court's ruling or explain why you consider the ruling to be contrary to the intent of the ADA.
   - Americans with Disabilities Act: www.usdoj.gov/crt/ada/adahom1.htm.
   - President's Committee on Employment of People with Intel-lectual Disabilities: www.acf.hhs.gov/programs/pcpid/.
   - Disability Statistics Center: www.dsc.ucsf.edu/main.php.
   - The Disability Link Barn: www.accessunlimited.com/html/link_barn.html.

6. Look up different types of assistive technology available by using ABLEDATA (ABLEDATA, Silver Spring Centre, 8455 Colesville Road, Suite 935, Silver Spring, MD 20910-3319, 800-277-0216). ABLEDATA is a CD-ROM database and is usually available for public use at most independent living centers. Manufacturers and vendors of assistive technology (both commercial and noncom-mercial) put information about their products on this CD-ROM database. Users may access information by typing a category of disability or by typing in the function of the assistive technology. Information about the functions, costs, maintenance requirements, and other related equipment is provided.

7. Access the following sources:
   - Equal Opportunity Commission, Office of Program Opera-tions. (1993a). National database: Americans with Disabilities Act receipts 072692-072593. Washington, DC: Author.

- Equal Opportunity Commission, Office of Program Operations. (1993b). National database: Americans with Disabilities Act receipts 100192-093093. Washington, DC: Author.
- Equal Opportunity Commission, Office of Program Operations. (1994). National database: Americans with Disabilities Act receipts 100193-093094. Washington, DC: Author.
- Equal Opportunity Commission, Office of Program Operations. (1995). National database: Americans with Disabilities Act receipts 100194-093095. Washington, DC: Author.

8. Determine the total number of ADA complaints filed with the Equal Employment Opportunity Commission (EEOC). Are there trends? Of the 35 types of disabilities, which two categories have the highest frequency and percentage of complaints? List the 12 categories of discriminatory behavior.

Writing Experience

Write a paper that responds to one of the seven "bullet" questions listed at the beginning of this chapter.

References

American Psychiatric Association. (1994). *Diagnostic and statistical manual of mental disorders* (4th ed.). Washington, DC: Author.

Athletes face charges over handicapped parking scam. (1999, July 11). *Herald Journal*, p. 2. Associated Press.

Artiles, A. J., & Trent, S. C. (1994). Overrepresentation of minority students in special education: A continuing debate. *The Journal of Special Education, 27*, 410–437.

Balcazar, Y., Bradford, B., & Fawcett, S. (1988). Common concerns of disabled Americans: Issues and options. In M. Nagler (Ed.), *Perspectives on disability* (pp. 3–12). Palo Alto, CA: Health Markets Research.

Batavia, A.I., & Schriner, K. (2001). The Americans with Disabilities Act as an engine of social change: Models of disability and the potential of a civil rights approach. *Disability Policy Studies Journal, 29*, 690–702.

Becker, G. S. (1999, August 2). Are we hurting or helping the disabled? *Business Week* 3635, p. 9.

Bickenbach, J. E. (1993). *Physical disability and social policy.* Toronto: University of Toronto.

Boorse, C. (1986). Concepts of health. In D. Van De Veer & T. Regan (Eds.), *Health care ethics: An introduction* (pp. 359–393). Philadelphia: Temple University.

Bovard, J. (1997). The ADA defines disability too narrowly. In B. Stalcup (Ed.), *The Disabled, Current Controversies Series* (pp. 47–53). San Diego, CA: Greenhaven.

Bowe, F. (1993). Preface. In M. J. Scherer (Ed.), *Living in the state of stuck: How technology impacts the lives of people with disabilities* (pp. xi–xvi). Cambridge, MA: Brookline.

Burgdorf, R. (2002). *Supreme Court decisions thwart intent of ADA.* San Diego, CA: Center for an Accessible Society.

Buss, D. M. (1998). *Evolutionary psychology.* Boston: Allyn & Bacon.

Byrom, B. (2004). A pupil and a patient: Hospital-schools in progressive America. In S. Danforth & S. D. Taff (Eds.), *Crucial readings in special education* (pp. 25–37). Upper Saddle River, NJ: Pearson.

Cameron, J. (1982). *For all that has been: Time to live and time to die.* New York: Macmillan.

Charlton, J. I. (1998). *Nothing about us without us: Disability oppression and empowerment.* Berkeley, CA: University of California.

Conrad, P. (2004). The discovery of hyperkinesis: Notes on the medicalization of deviant behavior. In S. Danforth & S. D. Taff (Eds.), *Crucial readings in special education* (pp. 18–24). Upper Saddle River, NJ: Pearson.

Couser, G. T. (1997). *Recovering bodies: Illness, disability, and life writing.* Madison, WI: University of Wisconsin.

DeLoach, C., & Greer, B. G. (1981). *Adjustment to severe physical disability: A metamorphosis.* New York: McGraw-Hill.

Doherty, B. (1997). ADA compliance is too expensive. In B. Stalcup (Ed.), *The Disabled, Current Controversies Series* (pp. 54–61). San Diego, CA: Greenhaven.

Equal Access to Software and Information. (1999). Available: www.rit.edu/-easi. Accessed July 24, 2000.

Farber, B. (1968). *Mental retardation: Its social context and social consequences.* Boston: Houghton Mifflin.

Farber, B., & Lewis, M. (1976). Compensatory education and social justice. *Peabody Journal of Education, 49,* 85–96.

Fleischer, D. Z., & Zames, F. (2001). *The Disability Rights Movement: From Charity to Confrontation.* Philadelphia: Temple University.

Fowler, C. A., & Wadsworth, J. S. (1991). Individualism and equity: Critical values in North American culture and the impact on disability. *Journal of Applied Rehabilitation Counseling, 22,* 19–23.

Gerber, P. J., & Brown, D. S. (Eds.). (1997). *Learning disabilities and employment.* Austin, TX: PRO-ED.

Hahn, H. (1993). The political implications of disability definitions and data. *Journal of Disability Policy Studies, 4,* 41–52.

Hahn, H. (1997). Advertising the acceptably employable image: Disability and capitalism. In L. J. Davis (Ed.), *The disability studies reader* (pp. 172–186). New York: Routledge.

Hahn, H. (2005). Academic debates and political advocacy: The U.S. disability movement. In G. E. May & M. B. Raske (Eds.), *Ending disability discrimination: strategies for social workers* (pp. 1–24). Boston: Pearson.

Harris, R. W. (1992). Musings from 20 years of hard-earned experience. *Rehabilitation Education, 6,* 207–211.

Heiney, R. W. (1976). Renaissance or retreat for special educators: Issues to explore before 1984. *The Journal of Special Education, 10,* 415–425.

Helms, J. E. (1992). Why is there no study of cultural equivalence in standardized cognitive ability testing? *American Psychologist, 47,* 1083–1101.

Higgins, P. C. (1992). *Making disability: Exploring the social transformation of human variation.* Springfield, IL: Charles C. Thomas.

Hursh, N. C. (1995). Essential competencies in industrial rehabilitation and disability management practice: A skills-based training model. In D. E. Shrey & M. Lacerte (Eds.), *Principles and practices of disability management in industry* (pp. 303–354). Winter Park, FL: GR Press.

Imrie, R. (1996). *Disability and the city: International perspectives.* New York: St. Martin's Press.

Individuals with Disabilities Education Act of 1990, 20 U.S.C. § 1400 *et seq.*

Kriegel, L. (1997). Falling into life. In K. Fries (Ed.), *Staring back: The disability experience from the inside out.* (pp. 37–50). New York: Plume.

Langer, E. J., Bashner, R. S., & Chanowitz, B. (1985). Decreasing prejudice by increasing discrimination. *Journal of Personality and Social Psychology, 49,* 113–120.

Linton, S. (1998). *Claiming disability: Knowledge and identity.* New York: New York University.

Living with Tourette Syndrome: A Family Portrait. Available: www.tsa-usa.org/People/ LivingWithTS/LivingTS.htm.Accessed August 7, 2007.

Lynch, R. T., & Thomas, K. R. (1994). People with disabilities as victims: Changing an ill-advised paradigm. *Journal of Rehabilitation, 69*(1), 8–11.

Marks, D. (1999). *Disability: Controversial debates and psychosocial perspectives.* London: Routledge.

Matson, J. L., & Barrett, R. P. (Eds.). (1993). *Psychopathology in the mentally retarded* (2nd ed.). Boston: Allyn & Bacon.

May, G. E. (2005). Changing the future of disability: The disability discrimination model. In G. E. May & M. B. Raske (Eds.), *Ending discrimination in social work: Strategies for social workers* (pp. 82–98). Boston: Allyn & Bacon.

McCarthy, H. (1993). Learning with Beatrice A. Wright: A breath of fresh air that uncovers the unique virtues and human flaws in us all. *Rehabilitation Education, 7,* 149–166.

Mee, C. L. (1999). *A nearly normal life: A memoir.* Boston: Little Brown.

Meltsner, S. (1998). Psychiatric disabilities: What's real, what's protected. *Business Health, 16*(6), 46–47.

Michalko, R. (2002). *The difference disability makes.* Philadelphia: Temple University.

Mikata, S. (1995, November). Presentation given at the annual meeting of the Utah Rehabilitation Association, Salt Lake City.

Moore, C. L., & Feist-Price, S. (1999). Societal attitudes and the civil rights of persons with disabilities. *Journal of Applied Rehabilitation Counseling, 30,* 19–24.

Murphy v. United Parcel Service, 97-1992. 526 U.S. 1036.

Nagi, S. Z. (1991). Disability concepts revisited: Implications for prevention. In Institute of Medicine (Ed.), *Disability in America: Toward a national agenda for prevention* (pp. 309–327). Washington, DC: National Academy Press.

National Public Radio. (May 1998). *Disability History Project: A little history worth knowing.*

O'Keeffe, J. (1994). Disability, discrimination, and the Americans with Disabilities Act. In S. M. Bruyere & J. O'Keeffe (Eds.), *Implications of the Americans with Disabilities Act for psychology* (pp. 1–14). Washington, DC: American Psychological Association [co-published with Springer Publishing, New York].

Olkin, R. (1999). *What psychotherapists should know about disability.* New York: Guilford.

Ong, W. A. (1993). *Asian American cultural dimensions in rehabilitation counseling.* San Diego, CA: San Diego State University, Rehabilitation Cultural Diversity Initiative (RCDI).

Perlman, L. B., & Kirk, F. S. (1991). Key disability and rehabilitation legislation. *Journal of Applied Rehabilitation Counseling, 22*(3), 21–27.

Phillips, M. J. (1990). Damaged goods: Oral narratives of the experience of disability in American culture. *Social Science Medicine, 30,* 849–857.

Pugach, M. C., & Seidl, B. L. (1996). Deconstructing the diversity connection. *Contemporary Education, 68,* 5–8.

Quinn, P. (1995). Social work and disability management policy: Yesterday, today, and to-morrow. *Social Work in Health Care, 20*(3), 67–82.

Rehabilitation Act of 1973, 87 Stat. 355, 29 U.S.C. § *701 et seq.*

Rossides, D. W. (1990). *Social stratification: The American class system in comparative perspective* (2nd ed.). Englewood Cliffs, NJ: Prentice-Hall.

Ryan, J., & Thomas, F. (1980). *The politics of mental handicap.* Harmondsworth, UK: Penguin.

Scheer, J., & Groce, N. (1988). Impairment as human constraint: Cross cultural and historical perspectives on variation. *Journal of Social Issues, 44*, 23–37.

Scherer, M. J. (1993). *Living in the state of stuck: How technology impacts the lives of people with disabilities.* Cambridge, MA: Brookline.

Shapiro, J. P. (1993). *No pity: People with disabilities forging a civil rights movement.* New York: Times Books.

Sinacore-Guinn, A. L. (1995). The diagnostic window: Culture and gender-sensitive diagnosis and training. *Counselor Education and Supervision, 35*, 18–31.

Shell, M. (2005). Polio and its aftermath. Cambridge, MA: Harvard.

Sinason, J. (1992). *Mental handicap and the human condition.* London: Free Association Books.

Singer, P. (1981). *The expanding circle: Ethics and sociobiology.* New York: Farrar, Straus, & Giroux.

Singer, P. (1995). *Rethinking life and death: The collapse of our traditional values.* New York: St. Martin's Press.

Singer, P. (2000). *Writings on an ethical life.* New York: Ecco/Harper Collins.

Smart, J. F., & Smart, D. W. (2006). Models of disability: Implications for the counseling profession. *Journal of Counseling and Development, 84*, 29–40.

Smart, J. F. (2004). Models of disability: The juxtaposition of biology and social construction. In T. F. Riggar & D. R. Maki (Eds.), *Handbook of rehabilitation counseling* (pp. 25–49). New York: Springer.

Smart, J. F. (2005a). Challenges to the Biomedical Model of disability: Changes to the practice of rehabilitation counseling. *Directions in Rehabilitation Counseling, 16*(4), 33–43.

Smart, J. F. (2005b). The promise of the International Classification of Functioning, Disability, and Health (ICF). *Rehabilitation Education, 19*, 191–199.

Smart, J. F. (2006). Challenging the biomedical model of disability. *Advances in Medical Psychotherapy and Psychodiagnosis, American Board of Medical Psychotherapists, 12*, 41–44.

Smart, J. F. (in press). The power of models of disability. *Journal of Rehabilitation.*

Smart, J. F., & Smart, D. W. (1997). The racial/ethnic demography of disability. *Journal of Rehabilitation, 63*, 9–15.

Sobsey, D. (1994). *Violence and abuse in the lives of people: The end of silent acceptance.* Baltimore: Brookes.

Southeastern Community College v. Davis 99 S. Ct. 2361 (1979).

Souter, S. (1993, August 16). *Women with disabilities: How to become a boat rocker in life.* Paper presented at the Ethics in Rehabilitation Conference, New Zealand Rehabilitation Association, Dunedin, N.Z.

Spechler, J. W. (1996). *Reasonable accommodation: Profitable compliance with the Americans with Disabilities Act.* Delray Beach, FL: St. Lucie Press.

Stalcup, B. (Ed.) (1991). *The Disabled, Current Controversies Series.* San Diego, CA: Greenhaven.

Stefan, S. (2001). *Unequal rights: Discrimination against people with mental disabilities and the Americans with Disabilities Act.* Washington, DC: American Psychological Association.

Stone, D. A. (1984). *The disabled state.* Philadelphia: Temple University.

Sullivan, D. M. (1998). Hunting and fishing: Ways of life in rural America. In T. S. Smith (Ed.), *Rural rehabilitation: A modern perspective* (pp. 292–312). Amaudville, LA: Bow River.

Szasz, T. S. (1961). *The myth of mental illness.* New York: Harper.

Szasz, T. S. (1976). *Heresies.* New York: Anchor.

Tannebaum, S. J. (1986). *Engineering disability: Public policy and compensatory technology.* Philadelphia: Temple University.

Thompson, R. G. (1997). Feminist theory, the body, and the disabled. In L. Davis (Ed.), *The disability studies reader* (pp. 279–292).

Thompson-Hoffman, S. & Storck, I. F. (Eds.) (1991). *Disability in the United States: A portrait from national data.* New York: Springer.

Weihenmayer, E. (2001*). Touch of top of the world: A blind man's journey to climb farther than the eye can see.* New York: Dutton.

Weinberg, N. (1988). Another perspective: Attitudes of people with disabilities. In H. E. Yuker (Ed.), *Attitudes toward persons with disabilities (pp.* 141–153). New York: Springer.

Weisgerber, R. A. (1991). *Quality of life for persons with disabilities: Skill development and transitions across life stages.* Gaithersburg, MD: Aspen.

West, T. G. (1997). Slow words, quick words—Dyslexia as an advantage in tomorrow's work place. In P. J. Gerber & D. S. Brown (Eds.), *Learning Disabilities and Employment* (pp. 349–370). Austin, TX: PRO-ED.

Wilson, D. J. (1990). *Living with polio: The epidemic and its survivors.* Chicago, IL: University of Chicago.

Wright, B. (1960). *Physical disability: A psychological approach.* New York: Harper & Row.

Woodward, J. (1991, November/December). Getting rid of special. *The Disability Rag,* pp. 35–41.

Society and Disability

PART

Sources of Prejudice and Discrimination, Part 1

- Does physical, intellectual, mental, or emotional disability always lead to social inferiority?
- Is disability entirely a social construction, or does biology matter?
- Can legislation (such as the Americans with Disabilities Act [ADA]) completely eradicate prejudice, discrimination, and segregation?
- Since the ADA, has the overall position in society of people with disabilities advanced, stayed the same, or fallen behind?
- Why has a society been created that excludes PWDs?
- Why is handicapism the only "ism" to which everyone is susceptible?
- What do PWDs want from society?
- Why were German citizens with disabilities the first targets of the Nazi Holocaust?
- Why are eugenics movements economically motivated?
- Why is assisted suicide for PWDs often supported?
- How can assisted suicide lead to infanticide of babies with severe disabilities?

Societal Prejudices Often Become Self-Identifiers

In this section, look for—

■ Why there is no clear demarcation between society's perception of disability and the individual's perception of his or her disability

In reality there is no clear demarcation between society's perception of disability and the individual's adjustment to his or her disability because the individual internalizes a great deal of society's judgments and reactions to the disability (Albrecht, 1976; Gove, 1976; Ince, 1980; Phillips, 1992; Schur, 1971, 1979). For anyone, with or without a disability, society contributes to the individual's sense of self (Allport, 1954, 1958). Perceptions of disability labels, expectations of people with disabilities, and ascribed meanings of the experience of disability are all shaped by the broader culture (Albrecht, 1992). Feedback from seemingly competent sources and continual reinforcement from the media work together to shape much of an individual's self-concept (Hormuth, 1990). Of course, the degree to which society shapes the identity of the person with the disability depends on several factors (which are discussed in the next chapter). Not all individuals are equally affected by society's judgments. Do you remember in the preceding chapter from the video "My Body Is Not Who I Am" the man who states that when he was a child the label used to describe his surgeries, "corrective surgeries," made him think that there was something wrong with him? This is an example of a disability label profoundly affecting an individual's self-concept. In another video, "Tell Them I'm a Mermaid," a woman states, "[Before I acquired a disability] I used to think I had to feel sorry for disabled people [*sic*]. That they were weirdos and creeps." Irving Zola (1982) contracted polio at age 15 and was in an auto accident when he was 19. Zola described the way in which PWODs internalize the prejudices against PWDs:

> Born for the most part into normal families, we are socialized into that world. The world of sickness is one we enter only later, poorly prepared and with all the prejudices of the normal. The very vocabulary we use to describe ourselves is borrowed from that society. We are de-formed, dis-eased, dis-ordered, abnormal and, most telling of all, called an invalid. (p. 206)

False stereotypes can become self-identifiers, and PWDs, like anyone else, internalize the hidden, unquestioned assumptions and values of the larger society. J. Morris (1991) reminds us that most PWDs live their lives in the company of PWODs and "our ideas about disability and about ourselves are generally formed by those who are not disabled" (p. 37). Rod Michalko (2002), who is blind, observed: "I was conditioned by my society to view my disability as a misfortune. The most salient sense of the world I had during adolescence came to me in terms of a dichotomy; there were those who could see naturally and well and those who could not; there were those who were fortunate and those who were not; there were those who were normal and those who wanted to be . . . there was everyone else and there was me" (pp. 22–23). "Unfortunately, the stereotype of the disabled [*sic*] person as dependent, helpless, weak, and passive is still prevalent, particularly among the disabled [*sic*] public, but also among people with disabilities" (Phillips, 1992, p. 220).

Another example of the interrelationship between society's judgments and the individual's self-concept is found in the book *The Making of Blind Men: A Study of Adult Socialization* (1969) by Robert Scott. Early in the book, Scott summarized his relationship: "The disability of blindness is a learned social role. The various attitudes and patterns of behavior that characterize people who are blind are not inherent in their condition but rather are acquired through ordinary processes of social learning . . . . Blind men are made, and by the same processes of socialization that have made us all" (p. 14). In spite of this interrelationship between society and the individual in ascribing meaning to the disability experience, this chapter will focus on society, and Chapters 7, 8, and 9 will discuss the individual and his or her reaction to a disability.

By Any Standard, People With Disabilities Have Experienced More Prejudice and Discrimination Than Any Other Group in History

Disability has been present in all societies in the world throughout history. In spite of the long history and the universality of disability, almost without exception, people with disabilities have been discriminated against, with that discrimination ranging from minor embarrassment and inconvenience to relegation to a life of limited experience and reduced social opportunity and civil rights (Biklen, 1986; Biklen & Bailey, 1981; Bogdan, 1988; Bogdan & Biklen, 1977; Bogdan & Knoll, 1995; Bowe, 1978, 1990). Although there have been a few exceptions of humane treatment, or even veneration, most societies have stigmatized their members with disabilities (Eisenberg, 1982). No other racial, cultural, ethnic, linguistic, religious, political, national, sexual orientation, or gender group has experienced this degree of pervasive and generalized prejudice and discrimination, which included killing babies with disabilities, forced sterilization of PWDs, institutionalization, and mass murder. For example, individuals of racial and ethnic groups are typically not targets of discrimination in their homeland, nor are members of certain religious groups discriminated against in every setting. Certainly history reveals many more attempts to systematically eliminate PWDs than efforts to eliminate racial/ethnic/cultural/religious groups. In contrast, PWDs have been segregated, sterilized, or killed in almost every culture throughout history.

Davis (1997) summarized the prejudice and discrimination against PWDs: "People with disabilities have been isolated, incarcerated, observed, written about, operated on, instructed, implanted, regulated, treated, institutionalized, and controlled to a degree probably unequal to that experienced by any other minority group" (p. 1).

Prejudice Against People With Disabilities (PWDs) Today in the United States

In this section, look for—

- The definition of prejudice
- The definition of handicapism or ableism
- The ADA's summary of the prejudice against PWDs in the United States

Prejudice, according to Allport (1986), is "an avertive or hostile attitude toward a person who belongs to a group simply because he belongs to that group, and is therefore presumed to have the objectionable qualities ascribed to in that group" (p. 7). Allport defined discrimination as follows:

> . . . detrimental distinctions of an active source . . . exclud[ing] all members of the group in question from certain types of employment, from residential housing, political rights, educational or recreational opportunities, churches, hospitals, or from some other social privileges. Segregation is an institutionalized form of discrimination, enforced legally or by common custom. (pp. 14–15)

We can simplify by stating that *prejudice* is attitudes and beliefs and *discrimination* is behavior. Therefore, it is easier to disguise prejudice, but discrimination is overt (visible) and can be witnessed by others. Prejudice is hard to challenge and confront, but it is possible to counter blatant discrimination. Handicapism is defined as a set of assumptions and practices that promote the differential and unequal treatment of people because of apparent or assumed physical, mental, or behavioral differences (Fleischer & Zames, 2001).

It should be noted that certain legislation and public policy addressed the needs of PWDs before the passage of the ADA. However, these focused on the *service* needs of PWDs, such as education and rehabilitation, rather than focusing on their *civil rights*. The ADA's main thrust is to guarantee the civil rights of PWDs (Moore & Feist-Price, 1999).

The following is the Findings section of the ADA (1990). It is presented in its entirety here for the following reasons: (1) Reading the Findings section is one of the best ways to understand the rationale and intent of the law, and (2) this section of the ADA is perhaps the most concise and precise summary of the history of prejudice and discrimination toward PWDs in the United States.

The Congress finds that

1. some 43,000,000 Americans have one or more physical or mental disabilities, and this number is increasing as the population as a whole is growing older;
2. historically, society has tended to isolate and segregate individuals with disabilities, and, despite some improvements, such forms of discrimination against individuals with disabilities continue to be a serious and pervasive social problem;
3. discrimination against individuals with disabilities persists in such critical areas as employment, housing, public accommodations, education, transportation, communication, recreation, institutionalization, health services, voting, and access to public services;
4. unlike individuals who have experienced discrimination on the basis of race, color, sex, national origin, religion, or age, individuals who have experienced discrimination on the basis of disability have often had no legal recourse to redress such discrimination;
5. individuals with disabilities continually encounter various forms of discrimination, including outright intentional exclusion; the discriminatory effects of architectural, transportation, and communication barriers; overprotective rules and policies; failure to make modifications to existing facilities and practices; exclusionary qualification standards and criteria; segregation; and relegation to lesser services, programs, activities, benefits, jobs, or other opportunities;
6. census data, national polls, and other studies have documented that people with disabilities, as a group, occupy an inferior status in our society and are severely disadvantaged socially, vocationally, economically, and educationally;

7. individuals with disabilities are a discrete and insular minority who have been faced with restrictions and limitations, subjected to a history of purposeful unequal treatment, and relegated to a position of political powerlessness in our society, based on characteristics that are beyond the control of such individuals and resulting from stereotypical assumptions not truly indicative of the individual ability of such individuals to participate in and contribute to society;

8. the nation's proper goals regarding individuals with disabilities are to ensure equality of opportunity, full participation, independent living, and economic self-sufficiency for such individuals; and

9. the continuing existence of unfair and unnecessary discrimination and prejudice denies people with disabilities the opportunity to compete on an equal basis and to pursue those opportunities for which our free society is justifiably famous, and costs the United States billions of dollars in unnecessary expenses resulting from dependency and nonproductivity.

The Outcomes of the ADA

> **In this section, look for—**
>
> ■ The reasons why many experts believe that the economic position of PWDs continues to fall behind that of PWODs
>
> ■ The difference between *de facto* and *de jure* segregation

The reforms of recent years do not appear to have produced much change in the overall position in society for Americans with disabilities. Americans with disabilities have, of course, made advances, but Americans without disabilities have achieved many *more* gains. Thus the gap between Americans without disabilities and Americans with disabilities has continued to grow (Hahn, 1987). For example, a sociologist (Rossides 1990) reported, "Federal aid may have provided better education for all, but without changing relative differences" (p. 352). Rossides was speaking only about one social benefit, that of mass public education, but his statement illustrates this growing gap in spite of government efforts. Liachowitz (1988), a legal scholar, described the denial of federal aid to PWDs and the failure of the United States to provide education to all children with disabilities before 1975 as institutionalized prejudice. In Liachowitz's view, PWDs, as a group, are denied rights and a share of the nation's resources.

At first glance, it may seem incongruous that federal laws (such as the Americans with Disabilities Act of 1990 and the Equal Education Act) and government programs are resulting in advances for people with disabilities, and yet their relative position in society continues to decline (Silvers, 1996). Simply stated, PWDs are obtaining more jobs, but PWODs are obtaining even more and better jobs. PWDs and other disenfranchised groups are adversely affected by changes in the labor market, technological advances, inflation, the global economy, and economic depressions (National Disability Statistics and Policy Forum, 1995). Of course PWODs are also affected by these negative conditions, but they are not affected as greatly. Gains for PWDs must be judged relative to gains for PWODs (Hahn, 1987). Of course, there is presently low unemployment and a corresponding need for workers. This type of labor market will naturally assist PWDs. However, this type of labor market also assists PWODs *more*.

Government legislation has effectively eliminated *de jure* segregation of people with disabilities, but *de facto* segregation continues. No government can legislate public attitudes and beliefs (Bryan, 1996). It should also be remembered that in addition to the passage of legislation, the issues of funding and of enforcement often decide the impact of the legislation. In other words, if there are no funds allocated to enforce the law, there will be few actual benefits. Further, if the government does not actively enforce the law, the status quo continues. Nonetheless, legislation such as the ADA and government and private efforts of self-empowerment are increasing equal opportunity and social justice for PWDs. Later in this chapter we will discuss disability rights groups and their successes in securing civil rights.

Without such legislation, government can implicitly legitimize the failure and disadvantaged status of people with disabilities (Charlton, 1998). The ADA clearly states that PWDs in the United States have experienced pervasive discrimination and therefore much (but not all) of their low employment and other disadvantaged and unequal status can be attributed to society. Before the ADA, most Americans considered the disadvantaged status of PWDs to be the result of their own failings and shortcomings (Wright, 1988), which naturally led to the conclusion that the solution for the situation is the responsibility of PWDs. The ADA explicitly and clearly states that the disadvantaged status of PWDs is not solely the result of their organic impairments and functional limitations (Moore & Feist-Price, 1999; Perlman & Kirk, 1991; Shapiro, 1993; Tucker & Goldstein, 1991).

In a book on social stratification and the class system, Rossides (1990) effectively describes both the circular relationship between PWDs' low position and the prejudice and handicapism of society:

> Although there is a great deal of heterogeneity among persons with disabilities, in the aggregate persons with disabilities have not made any significant relative gains vis-à-vis people without disabilities. They also suffer from a low prestige evaluation (largely associated with their historic subordination). People with disabilities are barred from full or even adequate participation in American society. The vicious process

in which low class (income, wealth, occupation, education) leads to low prestige (through handicapism, residential segregation, interactional segregation) which in turn reinforces low class is an institutionalized pattern that will not be easy to break. (p. 419)

"Pervasive Disadvantages" Found by the National Organization on Disability

The National Organization on Disability (NOD) commissioned Harris Interactive to direct surveys to determine the progress of PWDs in key areas of American life. Surveys were undertaken in 1986, 1994, 1998, 2000, and 2004. At a Congressional hearing in Washington, DC, the NOD, in comparing the results of the 1986 survey with the 2004 survey, found "slow and modest progress" in the lives of Americans with disabilities. Some of the 2004 findings included the following:

- Only 35% of PWDs reported being employed full- or part-time, compared with 78% of those who do not have disabilities.
- Three times as many PWDs (as PWODs) live in poverty with annual household incomes of less than $15,000 (26% versus 9%).
- PWDs remain twice as likely to drop out of high school (21% versus 10%).
- PWDs are twice as likely to have inadequate transportation (31% versus 13%), and a much higher percentage go without needed health care (18% versus 7%).
- PWDs are less likely to socialize, eat out, or attend religious services than their counterparts who are not disabled.
- Although 22% of employed PWDs report encountering job discrimination, this is a dramatic decrease from 36% 4 years ago.
- The severity of the disability makes a significant difference in all of the gap areas, and people with severe disabilities have much greater disadvantages.
- PWDs are much more worried (than are PWODs) about their future health and well-being. Half are worried about not being able to care for themselves or being a burden to their families, compared with one fourth of other Americans.
- Americans with disabilities rely on assistive technology, and one third say they would lose their independence without this technology.
- PWDs are more likely to have a common sense of identity with other PWDs; 56% now say they do, compared to 47% in 2000.

Considering a single issue in this list, we can quickly see that Americans with disabilities did not have the opportunities for entertainment, such as attending movies and eating in restaurants. With the passage of the ADA, it is now illegal for theaters and restaurants to fail to provide accommodations, and it is likely that more PWDs than ever before are availing themselves of entertainment options. Nonetheless, it was not free market forces that opened restaurants and theaters to PWDs; it required the force of law. It is safe to state that most of the rights to which PWDs are now legally entitled would not have been provided if the federal government did not make it illegal to withhold them.

Examining Prejudice and Discrimination Against PWDs

In this section, look for—

- Undetected prejudice and discrimination against PWDs
- Society as ambivalent toward disability
- Society has never allowed PWDs to be ordinary citizens
- Whose "problem" is handicapism?

Fleischer and Zames in their book *The Disability Rights Movement: From Charity to Confrontation* (2001) observed:

> Unkind words against homosexuals, African Americans, Hispanics, and other minorities at least prompt rebuke from people who, though not members of these stigmatized groups, still recognize the prejudice. But prejudice against individuals with disabilities commonly goes undetected by a general public too unaware of its own feelings to recognize what has been said or written as prejudicial. (p. xv)

These authors point to the unacknowledged and unresolved feelings of PWODs about disability as a source for much of the prejudice and discrimination. Furthermore, Fleischer and Zames assert that society does not recognize these attitudes (and their results) as discrimination. Although no one probably ever wishes to have a disability, most PWDs state that their disabilities are not as tragic and difficult as most PWODs consider them to be. PWDs know that disabilities are time-consuming and expensive and functions are lost; however, many would choose not to relinquish the disability if they were given the choice. Most PWODs view disability as a totally negative experience, whereas most PWDs do not.

Ironically, disability is the only "open" minority group, but many PWODs deny this reality. One mother of a child with a disability asked the following:

> What is our fear of disability about? Of course, there is more work and more costs for everyone. But, time and money are insufficient explanations for the terror of disability. Few things are as difficult to face as disabilities they themselves do not have. Few differences, such as race, gender, religion, are as threatening to a person's sense of worth. . . . the able-bodied can be turned into the disabled at the next turn of the road. You would think that prejudice would be contained, because at any time, I could turn into them. (May, 1998, National Public Radio, "Beyond Affliction: The Disability History Project, Tomorrow's Children")

Some PWODs might argue that PWDs are, in truth, biologically inferior and therefore deserve their social inferiority. Those who hold this view would remind us that, although lamentable, it is a reasonable conclusion. A legal scholar (Liachowitz, 1988) showed that these false conclusions have influenced legislation. "The growth of these ideas is demonstrated here by analyzing laws and public documents that were developed prior to the early twentieth century. These early records suggest that the cultural practice of translating physical abnormality into social inferiority is too deeply rooted as to have had an almost certain impact on both the formulation and implementation on public policy" (p. 1).

However, most PWDs consider their difficult problems to be the lack of accommodations and the prejudice and discrimination they encounter (Hahn, 2005). Madeleine Will (as cited in Weisgerber, 1991), former assistant secretary for education and head of the Office of Special Education and Rehabilitative Services (OSERS), emphasized:

> Most disabled people [*sic*] . . . will tell you that despite what everyone thinks, the disability itself is not what makes everything different. What causes the disabilities is [*sic*] the attitudes society has about being disabled, attitudes that make a disabled person embarrassed, insecure, uncomfortable, dependent. Of course, disabled people [*sic*] rarely talk about the quality of life. But it has precious little to do with deformity and a great deal to do with society's own defects. (p. 6)

Often, PWODs mistakenly believe that the stigma and prejudice ascribed are natural results of PWDs' biological inferiority when the stigma is actually a reflection of value judgments of PWODs. In much the same way, the lack of physical accommodations, or Braille, or sign language interpreters is not part of the "natural" world; rather, the absence of these accommodations is part of the world that PWODs chose to construct. Moreover, PWDs are increasingly confronting and naming this prejudice and discrimination (Morris, 1991).

Society Is Ambivalent Toward PWDs

Liachowitz (1988) stated, "We have never allowed people with disabilities to be ordinary citizens" (p. 108). Society considers PWDs to be recipients of charity or some other types of preferential treatment but not as ordinary American citizens with civil rights, including guaranteed access to resources and protection under the law. A political scientist asked:

> The United States also falls short of its ideals but Americans don't know this. Why is there not deeper questioning? Why is there no concerted attack on the systems of society that perpetuate these inequalities? People with disabilities are excluded from valued rights and forms of social participation . . . . Disability is not a disqualification for citizenship or an occupation . . . All evidence points to systematic and stable injustice for large portions of the American population. (Rossides, 1990, p. 419)

The ambivalence toward PWDs may be seen in the way in which the U.S. Congress has passed legislation that has prohibited discrimination of PWDs and then subsequently failed to provide the necessary funding, enforce these laws, or both. Indeed, the beginnings of the Disability Rights Movement may be dated from the 1977 sit-in protest by PWDs of a federal building in San Francisco, forcing then secretary of Health, Education, and Welfare (HEW) Joseph Califano to issue regulations for Section 504 of the Rehabilitation Act of 1973. Section 504 guaranteed civil rights for PWDs in programs receiving federal financial assistance. No Congress wished to be seen as not according civil rights to Americans with disabilities and yet, at the same time, "many institutions—including hospitals, colleges, and universities, as well as local governments—whose federal funding would soon be affected by signing of HEW's Section 504 regulations" feared costly and burdensome requirements (Fleischer & Zames, 2001, p. 52). Therefore, the federal government's ambivalence about the civil rights of PWDs was demonstrated in their willingness to sign federal law but not to issue the regulations so that the law could be carried out and enforced.

On a personal level, Murphy (1987) describes this ambivalence: "There is a deep and uneasy ambivalence in relations between the able-bodied and the disabled, for how is one supposed to act toward a quasi-human, a person who literally arouses fear and loathing? While at the same time, these are sentiments that must remain hidden at all costs, for they fly in the teeth of values that dictate concern and kindness to the handicapped [*sic*]" (p. 145).

Whose Problem Is Handicapism?

The problem of handicapism or ableism belongs to PWODs, in the same way that racism is the problem of "whiteness." Amundson (2000) explained: "In order to study racism, or any scholarship on racism, we must first study whiteness" (p. 78). Davis (1997) commented, "So much of writing about disability has focused on the disabled [*sic*] person as the object of study, just as the study of race has focused on the person of color . . . the 'problem' is not the person with the disabilities; the problem is the way that normalcy is constructed to create the 'problem' of the disabled [*sic*] person" (p. 9). Longmore (2003) summarized the long history of handicapism: "What we fear, we often stigmatize and shun" (p. 132). There is a tendency to regard anything that threatens our sense of self as alien.

What Do PWDs Want?

People with disabilities want full citizenship, including accommodations for their disabilities. At the same time, they do not wish to relinquish their identity as a person with a disability and they do not want their disability experiences to be hidden, minimized, or ignored (Pfeiffer, 2005). In the past, many PWDs have felt that they needed to hide, "pass," or minimize their disability to gain "honorary able-bodied status." In addition, PWDs want the disability experience to become part of the broader American culture, in much the same way that American ethnic groups have enriched the entire culture. We shall discuss these ideas at greater length in the Epilogue.

Sources of Prejudice and Discrimination Against People With Disabilities

Here is a brief list of all 10 sources of prejudice discussed in Chapters 3 and 4:

1. The economic threat
2. The safety threat
3. The ambiguity that PWODs ascribe to PWDs
4. The salience or perceived defining nature of the disabilities
5. The spread or overgeneralization of the effects of the disability
6. The idea of moral accountability for the cause of the disability
7. The idea of moral accountability for the management of the disability
8. The inferred emotional consequences of the disability
9. The emphasis on beauty, fitness, and youth
10. The fear of acquiring a disability among PWODs

Many of the sources of prejudice against PWDs are the same sources of prejudice directed toward individuals of certain racial/ethnic/cultural/linguistic groups or any other minority group. PWDs, however, experience prejudice and discrimination from additional sources. This appears to be a reasonable assertion because, as previously noted, it is known that throughout history, PWDs have experienced more prejudice and discrimination than any other single group.

Sources of prejudice against people with disabilities include (1) the economic threat; (2) the safety threat; (3) the ambiguity that PWODs ascribe to PWDs; (4) the salience of the disability or the perceived defining nature of the disability; (5) the concept of spread or overgeneralization; (6) the idea of moral accountability for the cause of the disability; (7) the idea of moral accountability for the management of the disability; (8) the inferred emotional consequences of disability; (9) the emphasis on beauty, fitness, and youth; and (10) the fear of acquiring a disability among PWODs, sometimes referred to as "existential angst." It is interesting that there is not "equal prejudice" toward all PWDs because some types of disabilities, such as mental illness, are the target of a greater degree of prejudice (Abroms & Hodera, 1979; Antonak, 1980; Obermann, 1965). The first five sources of prejudice listed are also sources of prejudice directed at other minority groups. Using racial groups as an example, it is well known that individuals of racial minority are often perceived by the majority as an economic threat and a safety threat, and ambiguous and racial-identifying characteristics are often thought to be the sole determinant of the individual's attitudes, character, and behavior. However, racial/ethnic minority individuals do not experience prejudice from the five sources listed last. Individuals in a racial/ethnic minority group are not thought to be "responsible" for their ethnic membership; there is not the inferred emotional consequences to being a member of certain racial/ethnic groups, and people of the majority (those in power) do not express fear or anxiety that someday they might become part of a racial/ethnic/cultural group. Furthermore, there is nothing inherently negative about being a member of a racial/ethnic group minority, while there are negative aspects of a disability.

With the possible exception of fear of acquiring a disability (or existential questioning), all of the sources of prejudice against PWDs are irrational. We shall now discuss each of these 10 sources of prejudice in greater detail. There is a great deal of overlap among all 10.

The Economic Threat

In this section, look for—

- The three factors that are considered when determining the economic costs of disabilities
- The economic motivation of the eugenics movement

(continues)

- The dollar costs of job accommodations that allow PWDs to work
- The effect of financial disincentives on the employment of PWDs
- The way in which PWDs have been an industrial reserve army

Throughout history, PWDs have been perceived as "burdens" or "drains" on the resources of the community (Berkowitz, 1987). Disability reformers at the beginning of the 20th century "believed cripples became immoral characters who siphoned off the lifeblood of the economy" (Byrom, 2004, p. 25). Thinking in terms of three factors—(1) the loss of tax dollars from PWDs who do not work; (2) tax dollars spent on government programs for PWDs, such as special education, vocational rehabilitation, Social Security Disability Insurance (SSDI), and public assistance (welfare); and (3) the increased insurance premiums for all policy holders as a result of the high costs of disability—it can be seen that disability is expensive and everyone, willingly or unwillingly, bears the cost (Albrecht, 1976: Anderson & Glesnes-Anderson, 1987; Anthony & Young, 1984; Bayles, 1987; Brown, 1987; Ferrans, 1987).

Disability is expensive—both for the individual and for society. It is expensive to live with a disability and, at the same time, maintain a reasonable quality of life. One PWD summarized:

> I think we would all agree that the cost for health and maintaining health for Americans with disabilities is a lot more. It costs a lot more . . . in terms of motorized wheelchairs . . . "accessible technology" or devices to help with activities of daily living. Unless we can get hired at jobs that pay enough for us to be able to afford these particular items, we . . . can't get those items. (Putnam et al., 2003, p. 89)

In a climate of "scarcity of resources," waiting lists, rationing of services, and cost containment, the statement "A tax dollar spent on you is a tax dollar NOT spent on me" appears to be rational. Read two letters written to Ann Landers (Exhibits 3–1 and 3–2).

A writer, "Roanoke," previously had written complaining that PWDs "lie around sucking up taxpayers' money," and the two letters reprinted here are responses to Roanoke. In the first letter, S.H.J. from Oakland begins the letter by describing the resentful attitudes he or she held toward "freeloaders" and "lazy" people and then goes on to describe his or her own history of independence and hard work, including 90-hour work weeks. S.H.J. briefly describes some of the effects of his or her disability, such as

Exhibit 3-1

Dear Ann: I want to respond to "Roanoke," who said people on disability would rather sit back and suck up the taxpayers' money than work. A few years ago, I was singing that same ignorant tune. I had worked hard since I was 14 years old and had no respect for anyone on welfare. I put myself through college and graduate school and always had jobs that paid well. I thought, "If I can do it, why can't they?" I remember using words such as "lazy" and "freeloaders."

I am now disabled by what they used to call a "nervous breakdown." Those 90-hour work weeks eventually caught up with me. I have learned, to my sorrow, that in spite of all the therapy and medication, I will have to struggle with my emotional fragility the rest of my days. I would give anything to lead a normal life again, but I know this is impossible.

I am unable to fill out a form or stand in line in a pharmacy or a bank without fearing that I will suddenly go to pieces. Yesterday I had a crying spell in the supermarket because I couldn't find the bouillon cubes. Any little frustration can set me off.

There are many honorable, hard-working people who used to earn their own way but can no longer do so because they are now mentally ill. Most of us manage to make it back into the workplace, but many do not, and we must rely on the generosity of the American taxpayer. Please ask your readers not to condemn the entire system because of a few perceived abuses. We really do hate being dependent, but we have no choice.
—S.H.J., Oakland, Calif.

Dear Oakland: I'm sure you have the heartfelt gratitude of all the people for whom you spoke today. Your eloquent plea for compassion touched millions of readers. Thank you for a letter that will make a difference.

---

crying in the supermarket and not being able to stand in a line at the pharmacy. By telling us that he or she cannot do these simple, routine tasks, S.H.J. is proving to us that he or she is truly incapable of holding a job. S.H.J. ends the letter by saying, "There are many honorable, hard-working people who used to earn their own way but can no longer do so because they are mentally ill."

The second writer, from Greensboro, North Carolina, describes his or her disability and then makes the main point, "I don't feel that I am a burden to the taxpayers. I earn my disability check because I worked for 36 years and paid into Social Security for my retirement." Note that Greensboro explains (or defends) receiving SSDI funds by telling (1) the severity of the disability (he or she almost died) and that he or she continues to experience pain and other symptoms, (2) he or she paid into the SSDI fund for 36 years, and (3) he or she "contributes to society" by doing volunteer work (with people "more needy," i.e., children and immigrants who do not speak English).

Exhibit 3–2

Dear Ann: I agree with the reader from Oakland who defended people on welfare after "Roanoke" criticized them so harshly. I am not lying around "sucking up taxpayers' money" as Roanoke would have you believe.

I am on disability because of a head injury. I taught school for 36 years and was told not to go back to full-time teaching because the stress would be too much. I also became an epileptic because of my head injury.

When my family went to the hospital at the time of the accident, they were told I would either die or become a vegetable. I was in a coma for weeks. It took me nine months to learn to walk and write again. I saw double for months.

As long as I stay on my medication and avoid stress, life is beautiful. I don't feel that I am a burden to the taxpayers. I earn my disability check because I worked for 36 years and paid into Social Security for my retirement.

I do volunteer work at the public schools and am helping children learn to read. I also work with adults who come from other countries and want to learn English.

I still have some pain and my neurologist says the Fourth of July is still going on in my head, but I am not complaining. I consider myself one of the lucky ones. I hope Roanoke sees this.
—Greensboro, N.C.

Paul Longmore (2003), a disability scholar and activist, told of Richard Lamm, governor of Colorado and U.S. Senate candidate, who was "a long-time opponent of lift-equipped buses and special education for severely disabled [*sic*] children, both of which are not 'cost-effective.' Lamm talks about 'hard choices.' Hard on whom? And whose choice? Once again, a politician is telling us [PWDs] that our basic needs . . . are too expensive and unimportant. In times of economic hardship and tight resources" (p. 207), the needs of PWDs are not considered important enough.

Economic calculations of "cost–benefit ratio" and "cost–value" often consider disability as a negative factor, for both society and the individual with the disability. If the lives of PWDs are considered to be of less value than the lives of PWODs and if the lives of healthy people are considered to be more valuable than the lives of people who are not healthy, the concept of utilitarianism becomes relevant. In utilitarianism, economic resources will not be allocated to PWDs. Hahn (2005) explained: ". . . choice often implies a trade-off between people or goods of greater or less value. Thus, health care practices that yield the most benefit for the largest number of people ordinarily can be expected to provide rewards primarily for the non-disabled segment of the population" (p. 15).

The father of James, a child with Down syndrome, wrote:

Among the many things I fear coming to pass in my children's lifetime, I fear this above all: that children like James will eventually be seen as "luxuries" employers or insurance companies cannot afford, or as "luxuries" the nation or the planet cannot afford. I do not want to see a world in which human life is judged by the kind of cost-benefit analysis that weeds out those least likely to attain self-sufficiency and to provide adequate "returns" on social investments. (Berube, 1996, p. 52)

A woman (Vash, 1981) who contracted polio at age 16 spoke of how she feels she is a burden ("drag") on society and the way in which she, unlike PWODs, feels that she must constantly "earn" her right to live:

I felt I had been slated to die but somehow tricked the great scythe wielder and lived . . . to be a damn drag on a number of people. A lot of my achievement trip was feeling I had to earn and re-earn my right to a place on the planet. What looked like ambition was actually paying penance for not having been gracious enough to just die. (p. 10)

A legal scholar (Liachowitz, 1988) reminds us that PWDs, especially those with severe and multiple disabilities, are permitted to live only by the generosity of society.

Quantifying the Value of a Human Being

What is the value of an individual? Courts of law often calculate the earning power of the individual to arrive at a figure of economic value (Anthony & Young, 1984). The legal system realizes, of course, that economic value is only a single aspect of the individual, but in the absence of any other quantifiable measure, the courts utilize the measure of lifetime earnings. The value of humans is immeasurable; nonetheless, we often assume that economic value is a valid and complete measurement.

Putting a dollar value on a person with a disability presents more ethical difficulties. A disability scholar stated, "Utility, even more so than charity, cheapens people with disabilities. Charity exceeds utility in its concern for those with disabilities, no matter how pitying that concern may be. Utility merely 'uses' disabled [sic] people. If they (and the policy addressed toward them) cannot produce a 'profit' (i.e., if benefits do not exceed costs), then they have little or no value" (Higgins, 1992, p. 199).

Therefore, societies care for their babies and children because babies and children grow up to become economically valuable, and societies care for their elderly because, in the past, these elderly individuals have been economically valuable. Neither group, children nor the elderly, can care for themselves and, because of this, they are vulnerable. How does society justify caring for people with severe disabilities who are also vulnerable but who never have and never will economically contribute (Beck, 1999; DeJong & Lifchez, 1983; Eisenberg, Griggins, & Duval, 1982)? If, indeed, the only value a person has is his or her economic value (or potential), then questions about the value of people with severe and multiple disabilities arise.

Furthermore, people with severe and multiple disabilities not only do not work and produce resources, but also consume resources. Collectivistic societies throughout history, who believed that the group is more important than individual members, often viewed PWDs as burdens. It was a short leap to segregate PWDs; provide them with a low quality of life and care to save money; forcibly sterilize them; and, in extreme cases, abandon them to die or kill them outright. Most eugenic movements have had economic motivations (Gallagher, 1990). One scholar (Pelka, 1997) stated, "Eugenicists opposed social programs for people who were poor and disabled [*sic*], believing such programs aided the unworthy in the struggle for survival" (p. 115). Friedlander (1995), in his book *The Origins of Nazi Genocide: From Euthanasia to the Final Solution*, quoted a German legal scholar in the Nazi era, Karl Binder, who spoke of institutionalized Germans with disabilities and the care they received as "the greatest care of beings who are not only worthless but even manifest negative value" (p. 15).

Reading the publisher's summary from Friedlander's book, as seen on the next page, several points underscore our discussion of the relationship between economics and eugenics. First, note that the first step to murder (not euthanasia) was to reduce the amount of money spent on the care of PWDs. The administrators of institutions complained of overcrowding or of having too many residents. One of their first steps was to reduce the amount of food given to the residents. Second, note how the use of language facilitates mass murder. By referring to Germans with disabilities as "life unworthy of life" it became easier to "eliminate these people." Note how unconcerned the Nazi officials were about the method of death. "Just beat them to death" was good enough. Ironically, euthanasia is generally thought of as a merciful, painless, dignified, and peaceful death (Battin, 1986). Although the Nazis called the murder of Germans with disabilities "euthanasia," it was indeed murder and the motivation was economic savings for the Nazi regime, not concern for the individual (Exhibit 3–3). Finally, notice how the killing of adults (after the killing of children had been in progress) was carefully timed to coincide with Germany's invasion of Poland (September 1939) to take advantage of the fact that the German public would be distracted. Physicians, who subscribed to the Hippocratic Oath, which states, "First, do no harm," starved, beat, and gassed their patients.

Hugh Gallagher, in his book *By Trust Betrayed: Patients, Physicians, and the License to Kill in the Third Reich* (1990), quoted a deposition given by a psychologist, Ludwig Lehner, at the Nuremberg trials. A physician, Dr. Pfannmuller, killed children with disabilities by starving them. Part of Lehner's deposition stated: "I remember the gist of the following remarks of Pfannmuller":

"These creatures [he meant the children] naturally present for me as a National Socialist only the burden for the healthy body of our *Volk*. We

Exhibit 3-3

An Excerpt from The Origins of Nazi Genocide

The move to rid Germany of institutionalized handicapped adults might have been expected. As we have seen, the funds spent for the upkeep of institutionalized patients had already been reduced drastically, and it had become customary to refer to them as "life unworthy of life." Hitler, who had told Gerhard Wagner in 1935 that he would institute compulsory euthanasia once war came, had not been alone in this desire. At a 1938 meeting of government officials responsible for the administration of mental institutions, for example, one speaker concluded that "a solution for the field of mental health would simply require that one eliminates those people." Fritz Bernotat, the Nazi radical who administered state hospitals in Hessen-Nassau, was later more explicit when he told a meeting of institutional directors who were complaining about overcrowding: "If you have too many patients in your institution, just beat them to death, and then you will have space."

In the summer of 1939 Hitler initiated the policy of killing handicapped adults. This killing operation would involve far larger numbers of victims than the relatively limited operation against children [who were disabled]. Hitler turned first to the government agency normally responsible for public health. The Fuhrer sent for Leonardo Conti, who would soon succeed the deceased Wagner as Reich physician leader. Unlike Wagner, who had held only a Nazi party office, Conti also occupied the newly created position of state secretary for health in the RMdI [Reich Ministry of Interior].

do not kill [he could have used a euphemistic expression for this word kill] with poison, injections, etc.: then the foreign press and certain gentlemen in Switzerland [the International Red Cross] would only have new inflammatory material. No, our method is much simpler and more natural, as you see." With these words, he pulled, with the help of a . . . nurse, a child from its little bed. While exhibiting the child like a dead rabbit, he asserted with a knowing expression and cynical grin, "For this one it will take two or three more days." (p. 127)

One book, *Hitler's Pope: The Secret History of Pius XII* (Cornwell, 1999), sought to access and understand the Catholic Pope's reaction to the Nazi Holocaust. The author concluded that the Pontiff was aware of the mass killings but refused to speak out publicly, citing a desire to protect the neutrality of the Vatican and the Catholic church. Long before the mass extermination of Jewish people, the Romany (gypsies), and political prisoners, the Nazis exterminated Germans with disabilities, many of whom were Catholics and living in Catholic institutions under the care of nuns. When the murder of these Germans with disabilities began, German Catholic clergy implored Pope Pius XII to intervene. The Pope refused and remained silent. Many German clergy did speak out vehemently against the killing of Germans who had disabilities; the most well known of these was Count von Galen, the Bishop of Munster. Many Holocaust scholars posit that Hitler and the Nazis began mass extermination of certain groups of people and waited for world and church leaders to react, and when these leaders did not protest, the Nazis moved on to exterminate another group of people. (Of course, the Nazis carried out their killings in secret, but there is documented evidence that world leaders knew about the killings.) Disability scholars recognize the significance of the Nazis' first choice of victims: Germans with disabilities. Of all the groups of people exterminated by the Nazis, people with disabilities were the most stigmatized. Both disability scholars and Holocaust scholars have questioned whether the Holocaust would have taken place if world leaders had protested the killing of Germans with disabilities.

Dr. Hans Sewering, who has been documented as taking part in the killing of Germans with disabilities, was elected president of the World Medical Association in 1992. However, he was forced to resign when protesters objected to his history of mass murder (Sobsey, 1994).

The mass murder of PWDs occurred only in Germany, but the eugenics movement had widespread support in both the United States and Great Britain. "A Gallup poll in 1937 showed that 45% of Americans favored euthanasia for 'defective infants' and in 1942 the official journal of the American Psychiatric Association called for the killing of all 'retarded' children aged over five" (Proctor, 1988, p. 180).

Read the following Associated Press newspaper article of June 30, 1999. The article presents evidence from recently declassified East German documents that many Germans who were aware of the government-sponsored murder of PWDs attempted to solicit international support to stop the killings.

> The death notices appeared in German newspapers in suspicious numbers in the fall of 1940, twenty-two in two weeks, and the families placing them used strikingly similar phrases about the fates of their loved ones, patients in mental asylums.
>
> "After days of uncertainty we received the unbelievable news of the sudden death of my beloved wife, the mother of our little Christa," said one.
>
> "After anxious uncertainty, I received from Grafeneck in Wurttemberg the unbelievable news that my beloved husband, our dear son-in-law and brother-in-law, the glass handicraftsman . . . closed his dear eyes forever," said another.
>
> On they went, "unbelievable" deaths after periods of "uncertainty."
>
> In their bewildered sorrow, these families were uncovering a Nazi horror. They were signaling to fellow citizens that terrible acts were going on in the sanitariums of southern Germany. The U.S. vice

consul in Leipzig, Paul Dutko, understood what was happening and cabled superiors.

Bur recently declassified documents do not show anything was done about that warning and others in the months before Germany's "euthanasia" programs became undeniably known and the full weight of the Holocaust descended.

"Details so far gathered concerning these notices give them a 'Frankenstein' setting; their attendant circumstances, described in this dispatch, are fantastic and gruesome," Dutko wrote in his October 1940 cable.

"Opinion has been expressed that incurable mental patients [*sic*] of Germany are being eliminated in this manner to reduce mouths to feed and that this is but a beginning."

Documents found in the National Archives by the Simon Wiesenthal Center, a Los Angeles research organization named after the famed Nazi hunter, point to a series of early communications by U.S. officials about Nazi Germany's systematic killing of its own mentally ill or deformed citizens [*sic*].

In one German letter, an anonymous correspondent wrote to NBC in New York saying thousands of mental patients [*sic*] were being killed monthly in southern Germany.

Hurry, the correspondent wrote, "and with your expressions of horror prevent further murders!"

"Humanity will thank you." ("Holocaust Foreshadowed," 1999)

Nazi Germany and mass murder of people with disabilities may seem far removed from present-day circumstances and attitudes. Nonetheless, Olkin (1999) demonstrated the power of what she terms "the burden literature" (p. 47) by listing many articles about PWDs from scholarly, academic, and research-oriented journals that use the word "burden" in their titles. Olkin explained that all of these articles have publication dates of 1990 or later. "Then it is not just the disability that is a burden but the person with a disability" (p. 47). Research and scholarly writing mirror the culture in which they originate, and scholars/researchers/writers perpetuate (albeit in a very sophisticated manner) the prejudices and misconceptions of the general society. By beginning with the (false) premise that PWDs are burdens to PWODs, these writers then arrive at (false) conclusions.

Disability Losses

It is impossible to quantify the worth of a person. In contrast, it is a relatively simple and straightforward process to calculate the economic impact of disability in the United States. Weisgerber (1991) reported that adding the total "aggregate economic losses" and the total "value of resources that are allocated to interventions for persons with disabilities" will result in a number, called national "disability losses." Weisgerber stated:

> Chirikos (1989) estimated that at a national level the annual economic losses (due to disability) for persons with moderate disabilities are $54.1 billion and for persons with severe disabilities, $122.6 billion. In contrasting employability versus dependency, it is estimated that the losses for persons with disability of working age (15 to 64) are about $111.5 billion, for those outside those ages (0 to 14 and 65 and over), the estimated loss is $65.2 billion. (p. 189)

Weisgerber concluded: "These losses amounted to 6.9% of the gross national product in 1980," or "alternatively, as Chirikos pointed out, the losses can be characterized as a 'tax of about $800 levied on each and every American'" (p. 190). Bickenbach (1993) has termed these tax dollars "coerced charity." When the dollar figure of the cost of ADA litigation is added, disability losses will increase.

In spite of these high unemployment rates, most people with disabilities report that they want to work, according to Louis Harris polls (1986, 1994) commissioned by the International Center for the Disabled (ICD). Allowing PWDs to work in the open economy would offset these "disability losses." (The emotional and social benefits of working for PWDs would perhaps be far greater than the economic benefits.) One of the rationales of the passage of the ADA was to allow people with disabilities the opportunity to work. The cost of job accommodations for people with disabilities has been found to be very low. The U.S. General Accounting Office (USGAO, 1990) reported that the average cost of making 34 business facilities accessible was less than 1 cent per square foot (USGAO, 1990). In 1982 the GAO reported that 51% of the accommodations cost nothing; 30% cost less than $200, and another 20% cost less than $500. Those accommodations that were most expensive were audiovisual aids. When comparing the cost of workplace accommodations that allow PWDs to work to the cost of aggregate disability economic losses, which annually costs billions of dollars, it becomes apparent that workplace accommodations make sound economic sense. Bowe (1980) found that architectural accessibility was less expensive than carpet cleaning, stating, "A National League of Cities study found that it costs less than one half of one percent of the total cost of constructing a new building to make it completely accessible and usable by disabled [sic] people."

We will discuss in greater detail the reasons why the unemployment and underemployment rates of PWDs are so high. Nonetheless, for the sake of brevity, it can be summarized that these high unemployment rates are the result of prejudice and discrimination on the one hand and the financial disincentives that are built into many government programs on the other hand. Financial disincentives occur when individuals are faced with the loss of benefits, including their health insurance, if they accept a job. For a

PWD, accepting most jobs would be economic stupidity because of the low salaries paid, especially if the individual has to pay a personal care attendant or has to manage the disability with expensive medication (Berkowitz, 1987; Berry, 1995; Chubon, 1994; DeJong & Batavia, 1990; McCarthy, 1982). Of course, the government is working to dismantle this system of these financial disincentives.

Another way in which the "costs" of disability are perceived to be borne by those who do not have disabilities can be seen in the attitude of many parents whose children do not have disabilities. Turner and Louis (1996) observed, "Children with disabilities in the classroom were seen as taking away from the educational experience of others" (p. 136). Turner and Louis quote from *Beyond Normal*, written by a mother and educator who chose to remain anonymous. She wrote: "I believe that children with disabilities do not take away from the other children. They do not diminish the community" (p. 136). Certainly, this mother is aware of the public perception that children with disabilities compromise the quality of education for the children without disabilities. Nonetheless, it has been found that whenever PWDs are integrated, the quality of both services and products increases.

PWDs have often been viewed as an "industrial reserve army" (Hahn, 1997, p. 173), in both a figurative and a literal sense, for the American economy. Many men left institutions during World War I and World War II to fight in the U.S. military. Sobsey (1994) told of 13 men from an institution in Connecticut who, in spite of being labeled as having mental retardation, enlisted to fight in World War II. Four of these men were promoted to higher ranks and seven were wounded in action. In spite of their war records, most of these men returned to the institution after the war.

Sobsey (1994) concluded, "Wars and labor shortages have repeatedly redefined who has mental retardation" (p. 132), thus lending support to viewing disability as a continuum, rather than as two discrete categories of disability or no disability. Conditions in the broader environment, such as labor shortages and wars (rather than anything to do with the disability), can change the cutoff point on the continuum. Hahn (1997) reported, "In World War II, physical exams and other conditions of employment were waived by many corporations to open up jobs for disabled [*sic*] persons, and other members of the industrial reserve, who compiled favorable records of productivity and work performance. During the war, the unemployment rate among disabled [*sic*] adults temporarily declined, only to rise again when these job requirements were reinstated to permit the hiring of returning veterans" (p. 173).

Hahn illustrated that when the American economy needs more workers, PWDs are hired and perform well. Obviously, neither the disabilities nor the PWDs have changed; their sudden employability is a result of fluctuations in the labor markets. Therefore, much, if not most, of the unemployment and underemployment of PWDs results from lack of opportunity and discrimination, rather than any functional limitations imposed by the disability. The important issue of functional limitations, or better stated, *imputed* functional limitations, is subject to questions when, during periods of great labor needs, PWDs are able to perform all sorts of jobs.

The Safety Threat

> **In this section, look for—**
>
> ■ The two causes for perceiving PWDs as dangerous:
>
> 1. Safety
>
> 2. Contagion

People with disabilities are perceived to be a threat to the physical safety of PWODs in two ways: (1) violence, destructiveness, aggression, and antisocial behavior (Hyler, 1988; Hyler, Gabbard, & Schneider, 1991), and (2) contagion and contamination. Society's perception of a threat posed by PWDs has, throughout the centuries, led to institutionalization for PWDs. Nonetheless, documented facts have shown that it is PWDs who have much more violence, hostility, and aggression directed toward them from PWODs. Yet, deeply ingrained misconceptions persist, including that PWODs have cause to be afraid of PWDs. For millennia, people with disabilities have been institutionalized and subsequently subjected to neglect, abuse, and death (Craine, Henson, Colliver, & McLeland, 1988; Ulicny, White, Bradford, & Matthews, 1990; Waxman, 1991). Ironically, the stated rationale for institutionalization was for the safety of the person with the disability (i.e., "He or she might hurt someone or he or she might hurt himself/herself"). Tragically, once institutionalized, it was the PWD who was hurt by the "caregivers." Much of the rationale for sterilization of female residents of institutions was based on the (resigned) expectation that they would be raped, and sterilization was the only way to avoid unwanted pregnancies (Sobsey, 1994). Violence, including assault, robbery, murder, and rape, toward PWDs in the community (rather than in an institution) is also much more common than violence toward PWODs (Cole, 1984, 1991; Sobsey & Mansell, 1993). Reasons for these higher rates of violence are that PWDs are more physically vulnerable; they are often unable to get help; and they interact on a daily basis with a wide range of caregivers, many of whom have not been screened for previous arrest records.

Nonetheless, we should briefly discuss the reasons why PWDs would be perceived as a safety threat. Individuals with intellectual or mental disabilities, or both, are often thought to be dangerous, as can be seen in the following example. A young man working in a sandwich shop had a diagnosis of schizophrenia. His coworkers, aware of the diagnosis, were frightened every time this young man picked up a knife to chop lettuce. This expectation of violent behavior is a misconception because symptoms of many mental disabilities include social withdrawal and, furthermore, many individuals with mental disabilities take daily medication that sedates and calms them. Indeed, it has been proved that people with these types of disabilities are actually less violent than the general population (Schmitt, 1999). In one remarkable case, patients and staff at the Utah State Hospital exploited the public's fear of people with mental illness. For many years, they sponsored a Halloween "spook alley" and "haunted house" during the month of October. This was a very successful fundraiser for the hospital.

Why, then, is there this persistent misconception? A great deal has to do with the media and the portrayal of the "psychotic" killer in movies, television, and books (Bower, 1980; Byrd & Elliott, 1988; Hyler, 1988; Hyler, Gabbard, & Schneider, 1991; Kriegel, 1987; Longmore, 1985a, 1985b; Safran, 1998; Zola, 1985, 1992). Of course, there have been psychotic killers, but such incidences are relatively rare. Irving Zola, a person with a disability (he contracted polio when he was young) and a disability advocate and scholar, loved to read murder mysteries. Zola made a comprehensive study of more than 1,000 murder mysteries, sampling 150, and titled his study "Any Distinguishing Features? The Portrayal of Disability in the Crime-Mystery Genre" (1992). Zola concluded that "villainy has long been associated with abnormality—whether physical, psychological, or mental—and is documented in nonfiction as well as fiction. Thus, from the earliest crime-fiction writing as well as in illustrations and silent films, one could easily recognize the villain by his or her features. She or he was inevitably unkempt, ugly, slobbering, sneering, and often scarred" (p. 236).

Zola observed that it was highly significant that, until recently, the single most watched program in the history of American television was an episode of *The Fugitive*. Zola commented: "Here the wrongly accused hero finally caught the heretofore unseen killer of his wife, the . . . man with one arm" (p. 236). All the years of chasing a murderer, of whom only one characteristic was known—he had one arm—finally ended. Simply because disability issues were part of his consciousness, Zola was able to point out how pervasively the media links disability with violent and criminal behavior.

Today, when we think of fear of contagion, we probably think of acquired immunodeficiency syndrome (AIDS). However, overwhelming evidence has shown that fears of contagion from AIDS were unfounded. In the 1940s, during the polio epidemics, mothers were afraid to kiss their children who had contracted the polio virus and nurses and doctors wore masks (PBS, *1999—Paralyzing Fear: The Story of Polio in America*). One author, a polio survivor, explained the fear that polio engendered before the availability of vaccines. "Polio's suddenness and unpredictability—the unknowability of where it came from, when and where it might strike, and how severely—gave it the mystique and fearsomeness almost of the bubonic plague as it swept through the country" (Mee, 1999, p. 50). The treatment for polio included the unnecessary isolation of the patient from his or her family. Regardless of whether the patients with polio were infants, children, or adults, they were not allowed contact with their family because of the fear of contagion. However, this fear was groundless because once the individual's polio became apparent, all of the family members had been exposed. At the time of the polio epidemics, very little was known about the spread of the disease.

Shell (2005) summarized this fear: "Fear of contagion and contagion itself changed forever familial relations, both intergenerational and intragenerational" (p. 79). Many pregnant women who survived polio underwent abortion because physicians feared "intrauterine polio." Many more pregnant women who lived in homes where polio had been found (or simply suspected) had abortions. Several national publications urged these women to have abortions. Of course, there is no such disease as "intrauterine polio," and all of the abortions were unnecessary.

The polio epidemics were the result of cleanliness and better public sanitation. It was unknown at the time of the epidemics that the very circumstances that prevented most other diseases—cleanliness and public sanitation—brought about the epidemics because children never developed an immunity to polio. Therefore, when the polio virus (which is spread through fecal contamination) was brought into a community, thousands contracted polio. It is probably no accident that the two largest polio epidemics in history occurred on islands—Tasmania and Iceland. Because of their geographic isolation, these populations did not have immunity to polio. The polio epidemics (in the United States) can be dated to the first in 1893 (at the time of great public health sanitation measures) to the last in the 1950s, when the polio vaccines were widely disseminated. The history of the polio epidemics and the race to develop vaccines may help us to understand the AIDS epidemics better.

Currently, while a few disabilities are contagious, most are not, and, as stated previously, most people with disabilities are in very good health. Nonetheless, PWODs often feel that they must "maintain a safe distance."

Another way in which to view the perceived threat of contagion, or the idea that one individual can "give" a disability to someone else, is clearly demonstrated by Mackelprang and Salsgiver (1999):

> People with disabilities were to be prevented from marrying or having children for fear of propagating their imperfections. As the 19th century progressed, the number of institutions to deal with the threat and nuisance of persons with disabilities increased dramatically; people with disabilities were increasingly isolated, sometimes under subhuman conditions. (p. 39)

Those who believe in such practices as preventing PWDs from marrying or having children, and believe in the rationale for these practices, which is that PWDs will propagate their imperfections, are not worried that the general public will acquire the disability or imperfection but that, nonetheless, the disability will be passed on to others (Harrison, 1987; Higgins, 1992; Van De Veer & Regan, 1987). Fine and Asch (1988a) reported that until recently, many states had laws that banned individuals with epilepsy or individuals with psychiatric disabilities from marrying.

The Ambiguity of Disability

In this section, look for—

- The tendency to ascribe negative aspects or greater limitations to the disability
- The definition and effects of interaction strain

Stereotyping, making generalizations and categorizations, and sorting people by medical diagnoses all help to simplify and give meaning to a vast array of information. Generating expectations, making sensible judgments or decisions, and feeling in control are all difficult when the environment is novel or ill-defined or lacks meaning. Furthermore, the more ambiguous the situation, the more the individual is required to "guess" about the meaning of the situation and what his or her responses should be. This type of guessing to make sense of a situation is called personal inference. Personal inference is based on personal factors (including value systems, past experiences, and education) and therefore reveals more about the observer than the observed. For example, the Rorschach inkblot test is not designed to gather information about the inkblots; rather it is to learn about the observer. In much the same way, the perceptions that PWODs have of PWDs often reveal more about PWODs.

Learned responses and attitudes, which in the past were adaptive, may not be appropriate in ambiguous circumstances. Indeed, using learned responses, which were adaptive in other situations, in a novel and ambiguous environment may actually be harmful. Frequently people make inappropriate responses and occasionally they are not aware that their responses have been inappropriate. Finally, an ambiguous environment is automatically assumed to be negative or hostile, even when it is not. This is often called "fear of the unknown." In short, we don't feel in control when our environment, and the people in it, are ambiguous.

This tendency to attribute negative aspects or greater limitations to PWDs simply because they appear ambiguous is found, occasionally, at the professional level. For example, individuals with communication limitations, such as individuals who are deaf or people with cerebral palsy, have been given diagnoses that underestimate their intellectual capabilities merely because these individuals are not able to communicate articulately and fluently, and this ambiguity makes an accurate diagnosis difficult. Nonetheless, the direction of error in these diagnoses is most often downward, ascribing *more* limitation to the individual's functioning.

The opposites of ambiguity are clarity, meaning, and an abundance of previous experience with this type of environment. People feel comfortable, competent, and in control in these types of situations. In fact, people actively seek out these types of environments and experiences. They are able to make fine discriminations and distinctions; the world is not just black or white or comprised of only a few types of people. Well-defined environments are automatically assumed to be pleasant and safe. Individuals in clear-cut situations are able to make sensible decisions and evaluations; they know that their responses are adaptive, and they are able to interpret feedback about themselves. In well-defined environments, there may be decision points or danger points, but people are aware of these and have both the experience and the expertise to successfully negotiate these. And simply because people have a tendency to seek out well-defined situations, PWODs often seek out other PWODs and avoid PWDs.

The word *ambiguous* comes from the Latin word *ambos*, which means *both*, and the dictionary definition of the word is "having contrary values or qualities, of doubtful classification." A related word, *ambivalent*, has the Latin *ambos*, and the second part of the word means *equivalent*. So ambivalent literally means *both equivalent*. Disability, for many, appears to be ambiguous, and the response is often one of ambivalence. The ambiguity leads to tension, discomfort, and ambivalence, all of which are unpleasant, and the PWOD often seeks to reduce or eliminate the ambiguity. There are two equal, but contrary, reactions to the PWD. On the one hand, the observer feels intense aversion and hostility, but on the other hand, he or she also feels strong sympathy and compassion (Antonak, 1985; Bettancourt & Dorr, 1998; Bogdan & Taylor, 1976, 1982; Ferguson, Ferguson, & Taylor, 1991; Gellman, 1959; Goffman, 1963). Often, the tension of this ambivalence leads to what is called *response amplification*, or overreacting. Such response amplification can be exaggerated kindness and solicitude or a quick escape (aversion) from the PWD, the source of the ambivalence and tension. Although the need or desire to reduce tension is somewhat understandable, PWDs are aware that people often overreact to their disability (Hastorf, Wildfogel, & Cassman, 1979; Kleck, 1968).

The discomfort, tension, and ambiguity often lead to what has been termed *interaction strain* (Fichten, 1986; Fichten, Robillard, Tagalakis, & Amsel, 1991; Gouvier, Coon, Todd, & Fuller, 1994; Siller, 1976). Interaction strain has been measured in research studies and is most often found to include such factors as (1) shorter duration of contact/conversation—the PWOD wants to leave as quickly as possible; (2) less eye contact and physical contact; and (3) avoidance of personal topics during conversation and a greater focus on impersonal, trivial, polite "small talk" (Antonak, 1988; Belgrave, 1984; Belgrave & Mills, 1981; Gouvier, Steiner, Jackson, Schlater, & Rain, 1991; Grand, Bernier, & Strohmer, 1982; Hannah & Midlarsky,

1987; Livneh, 1982, 1983, 1991; Strohmer, Grand, & Purcell, 1984). Some sophisticated research studies have monitored the autonomic responses of PWODs interacting with PWDs, such as pupil dilation, heart rate, blood pressure, galvanic skin (perspiration), and voice pattern (Vander Kolk, 1976a, 1976b). These studies showed that certain types of disabilities elicit more discomfort than other types of disabilities.

Obviously, many PWODs do not feel comfortable, competent, and in control when interacting with PWDs (Safilios-Rothschild, 1970). PWODs may make all sorts of "mistakes" in their interactions with PWDs and may not even be aware of some of their mistakes. The environment is so ambiguous and stressful that PWODs have no way to evaluate their own behavior and the effect their behavior has on others. Also, PWODs often interpret the sometimes hard-to-understand behavior of PWDs as negative. If the individual in the wheelchair falls asleep during a meeting, PWODs may interpret the behavior as rudeness and boredom when the behavior is actually a side effect of medication. Indeed, many adaptive coping responses of PWDs are misperceived by PWODs. It is not an enjoyable experience to feel uncomfortable and incompetent, and for many PWODs, the solution is to avoid the experience altogether. Also, the PWD recognizes that he or she (or his or her disability) makes others uncomfortable and that others avoid him or her. Thus, the interaction strain can become circular.

The preferential treatment given by public agencies to those individuals who are blind (discussed in Chapter 1) is thought to result from the lack of ambiguity ascribed to blindness. In other words, PWODs think they understand blindness. Deshen (1992) stated, "Blindness has an essential distinctiveness and lack of ambiguity relative to other conditions . . . . There is an immediate visible link between the condition and its behavioral manifestations, such as an impaired mobility and lack of ability to read print" (p. 4). Mirzoeff (1997) explained the relative lack of ambiguity of blindness when compared to deafness: "Medico-psychology thus considered the loss of sight to be far less grievous a blow than deafness. This sense that the blind are more 'human' than the deaf has persisted to the present and accounts for the greater sympathy and funding that is available for the blind" (p. 390).

Note that Mirzoeff sees a relationship between perceived degree of loss and perceived degree of humanity. In other words, the smaller the perceived loss (disability), the more humanity ascribed to the individual. Ironically, the fact is that "sign language can remedy the 'communication disorder' of deafness in a way that nothing seems to repair the perceptual deficit of blindness" (Couser, 1997, p. 240).

Of course, part of the interaction strain is probably a result of the PWOD's awareness that disability is a natural part of life and that he or she could acquire a disability. Nevertheless, most PWDs are acutely aware of this interaction strain and have developed strategies to reduce this. Some PWDs, however, feel that the discomfort of PWODs is the "problem" of the PWODs and feel no need to take steps to make others feel comfortable in their presence. PWDs whose disability can be concealed often choose to avoid this interaction strain by hiding the disability. For example, people with hearing impairments often choose to not wear their hearing aid in public, making a conscious decision to sacrifice the ability to hear for the appearance of being a hearing person (Blood, 1997). Many individuals who are missing a hand choose not to wear the hook in public and wear a prosthetic hand instead. The hook, which is much more functional, is used at home in private, but these individuals know that they can avoid a great deal of interaction strain if the cosmetic hand, which is practically useless in terms of functioning, is worn in public. In reality, probably no one ever thinks that the prosthetic hand is a real hand, but a prosthetic hand does not elicit the intense reaction that a hook does. The following letter illustrates this interaction strain from the perspective of the PWD:

> Soon after I learnt that my failing sight would ultimately lead to blindness, I passed on the information by letter to two old and true friends. In each case I had by letter a warm and sympathetic response, but in each case, when next I came in personal contact with these friends, I sensed at once a nervous reaction, a doubt as to what changes they would find in me and what was the right way to behave . . . . It was a useful experience, teaching me right at the beginning that besides learning to take blindness in my stride, I had to persuade my friends to take it in theirs. (Mitchell, as cited in Tuttle, 1984, p. 76)

The fact that the strain was felt by "two old and true friends" rather than strangers underscores the discomfort that disability elicits. Mr. Mitchell was aware that his blindness would cause his friends discomfort, and he sought to reduce this discomfort by writing a letter before meeting his friends for the first time as a person who was blind. Like most PWDs, Mr. Mitchell was aware that others would view him as inferior and somehow changed in character and personality. Mr. Mitchell assumed from their "warm and sympathetic" letters that his friends were not uncomfortable with his blindness. Note that Mr. Mitchell suddenly learns that he has a double task—to deal with the blindness and to deal with his friends' reactions to the blindness. Rather than looking to friends for support and assistance in this time of change, Mr. Mitchell must carefully consider and negotiate his friends' reactions. This is a valuable experience because it clearly illustrates how the salience of disability overrides years of "old and true" friendship.

The Heightened Ambiguity of Episodic and Invisible Disabilities

Research has consistently shown that there is a great deal more prejudice and stigma associated with disabilities that have episodic courses. Disabilities such as psychiatric disabilities or chronic illness often have periods of remission offset by flare-ups or symptom exacerbation. In contrast to disabilities with a stable course, such as blindness or deafness, episodic-course disabilities result in ambiguity, and this ambiguity leads to stigma and prejudice. "Do you have a disability or not?" and "Do I have a disability or not?" are questions that are often asked. Once again, in the presence of ambiguity, bad motives are often inferred by others. Nonetheless, the defining characteristics of these disabilities are periods of high functioning interspersed with times of low functioning or no functioning.

Disabilities that are not visible to others also appear ambiguous, thus increasing the stigma. In later chapters, we will learn that there is no correlation between degree of impairment and degree of visibility. In other words, invisible disabilities can lead to great functional limitations. To further complicate the picture, there are many disabilities that are both episodic and invisible.

Stefan (2001) undertook a national survey. Her findings included the following:

> One of the most striking aspects of the survey responses was the percentage of people who described themselves as disabled but said that other people did not regard them as so, saying things such as, "even the people who know of my psychiatric history do not know what a struggle it is for me to maintain my balance." Another wrote "Friends and family—they don't understand my illness/disability—they think I am getting away with something—that there is nothing wrong with me. (p. 57)

The stigma and prejudice directed toward individuals with psychiatric disabilities result from a combination of several factors. All of these factors come together to produce powerful, longstanding, and institutionalized prejudice and discrimination.

The Perceived Ambiguity of Psychiatric Disabilities

- Psychiatric disabilities are invisible disabilities
- Psychiatric disabilities are typically episodic disabilities

(Note: Visible disabilities with stable courses typically are less stigmatizing.)

The Moral Accountability for the Cause and the Management

- Individuals with psychiatric disabilities are often thought to have caused their disability or, at minimum, to have not done all that is possible to avoid the disability. Families are often blamed.
- Society does not consider psychiatric disabilities to be congenital disabilities despite the fact that the genetic predisposition to acquire a psychiatric disability is present at birth.

- Individuals with psychiatric disabilities may appear to not manage their disability very well. They may appear to survive from one crisis to the next.
- Individuals with psychiatric disabilities may be perceived as violent or dangerous.

To reduce prejudice and discrimination, a starting place may be the examination of these factors, including the reasons why these false beliefs continue to be accepted.

The Salience of the Perceived Defining Nature of the Disability

> **In this section, look for—**
> - The definition of salience and its effects on PWDs
> - Why the PWD is often viewed as only the disability

Salience of the disability simply means that the disability is the most important, or the only, aspect of the individual. Nothing else about the individual is acknowledged or noticed, including race, gender, or sexual orientation (Antonak, 1985; Chubon, 1994; Coleman, 1997; Covey, 1998; Davis, 1997; Eisenberg, 1982; Fine & Asch, 1988b; Henderson & Bryan, 1997; Roessler & Bolton, 1978). One woman remarked: "People meet you the disability before they meet you" (National Public Radio, 1998, Inventing the Poster Child). Another PWD stated: "You want to be yourself and the world asks you to be your disability" (National Public Radio, 1998, Inventing the Poster Child). Moreover, others assume that the disability is the central identity and self-definition of the person with the disability. The word *salience* means "most noticeable" and, in the case of disability, salience also often means "different from the rest of us." Ascribing such salience and importance to the disability serves to heighten and exaggerate any differences between those with disabilities and those without disabilities (Goffman, 1963; Gordon, Minnes, & Holden, 1990; Schmelkin, 1988). The individual's other characteristics, such as age, sex, educational level, and personality qualities, are neither acknowledged nor understood. The individual becomes his or her disability (Horne, 1988). Two feminist disability scholars, Fine and Asch (1988b), summarized:

> To date almost all research on disabled [*sic*] men and women seems simply to assume the irrelevance of gender, race, ethnicity, sexual ori-

entation, or social status. Having a disability presumably eclipses these dimensions of social experience. Even sensitive students of disability . . . have focused on disability as a unitary concept and have taken it to be the "master" status but apparently the exclusive status for disabled [*sic*] people. (p. 3)

Olkin (1999) described how the salience of her adaptive device, in the view of others, completely overshadows any of her other personal characteristics. When meeting an individual for the first time in her scooter and then meeting the same individual for a second time when she is using crutches, the individual does not remember meeting her. She stated, "I got encoded in their memory as a scooter, and they would sure remember a scooter, if they saw it again. But they don't remember *me*. One year my son's teacher, having met me on my scooter, kept trying to clarify at our second meeting (I was on foot) exactly what my relationship to my son was. I finally understood her confusion, and said, "I'm his mother."

Irving Zola, a polio survivor, recalled his surprise at being mistaken for other men with disabilities—something like "all you PWDs look alike." Zola (1991) remembers his surprise and annoyance:

I use a cane, wear a long leg brace, and back support, walk stifflegged with a pronounced limp. All in all, I think of myself as fairly unusual in appearance and thus easily recognizable. And yet for years I have had the experience of being "mistaken" for someone else. Usually I was in a new place and a stranger would greet me as Tom, Dick, or Harry. After I explained that I was not he, they would usually apologize saying, "You look just like him." Inevitably, I would meet this Tom, Dick, or Harry and he would be inches shorter or taller, 40 pounds heavier or lighter, a double amputee on crutches, or a paraplegic in a wheelchair. I was continually annoyed and even puzzled how anyone would mistake "him" for the "unique me." What eventually dawned on me was that to many I was handicapped [*sic*] first and foremost. So much so that in the eyes of the "able-bodied," I and all the others "looked alike." (p. 158)

Others see the disability as the motivator for every thought and action that the PWD has or does. The disability, according to these individuals, must be the central identity of the PWD, and therefore PWODs mistakenly believe that the disability is foremost in the individual's comparison of himself or herself to others and also in choosing friends and associates. Counselors often consider the disability to be the "presenting problem" when meeting a PWD for the first time. This is an example of a professional service provider viewing the disability as the salient characteristic of the individual. Many PWDs report that they have to go to great lengths to convince counselors that the disability has nothing to do with the problem or issue they wish to discuss. Similarly, whenever a PWD is in a bad mood, becomes angry, or displays any negative behavior, many assume that such behavior is a result of the disability, that the person has not "accepted the disability" or is "in denial," or that the individual has "a chip on her shoulder."

Judith Heumann, the assistant secretary of the Office of Special Education and Rehabilitative Services, uses a wheelchair; she recounted the experience of attending a National Organization for Women (NOW) meeting. The focus of the meeting was to plan strategies to help women gain their rights (Thomson, 1997). Dr. Heumann summarized the impression others had gained of her: "When I come into a room full of feminists, all they see is a wheelchair" (p. 286). Rather than viewing Dr. Heumann as a woman committed to equal rights for girls and women, most of the NOW members saw her *only* as a person in a wheelchair. The disability was far more prominent than either her gender or her long history of accomplishments and government work. Further, an organization whose main focus is on the rights of individuals and equal access to opportunity could see no further than a wheelchair. The salience of the disability makes all social comparisons dependent on the disability. Rather than comparing individuals based on their value systems, their experiences, or their preferences, the salience of disability reduces all comparisons to the disability.

This salience or defining nature of the disability can become a self-identifier. Lucy Grealy (1997) had cancer and had had numerous surgeries to her face. She described herself: "I *was* my face. I *was* ugliness" (p. 19). A mother of a child with a disability related her decision not to have an abortion after prenatal testing revealed that her baby would have Down syndrome. The mother relates how the physicians considered her unborn child as nothing more than a disability. "I began thinking about how we understand who is fit and who is not. We didn't know our child yet. Yet, [the disability] was such a critical aspect of her identity before she was born" (National Public Radio, "Tomorrow's Children," May, 1998).

Attitude scales (Yuker, 1988) include statements such as "It is impossible for a disabled [*sic*] person to lead a normal life." The test-taker responds "true" or "false." Agreement with items like this one demonstrates the salience of the disability. Obviously, automatically assuming that anyone with any type of disability has an "abnormal" life shows that the test-taker assumes (1) the disability is the most important (or only) aspect of the individual, and (2) the disability is a negative and a deficit.

The media, for centuries, have powerfully reinforced the false concept of the salience of the disability. In literature, newspapers, television, and movies, the individual with a disability is shown as (1) having no life other than the disability; (2) existing in a negative light, as evil, weak, or simply pathetic; and (3) usually not being a member of a family. When the media does not portray PWDs as having families, jobs, community affiliations, and all the other types of relationships and achievements, the audience is left to conclude that the only important salient characteristic of the individual is his or her disability. Furthermore, as disability scholars who study the media and their portrayal of PWDs have discovered, most depictions of PWDs are negative (Byrd, 1979; Byrd et al., 1977; Byrd & Elliott, 1985, 1988; Byrd et al., 1986; Gartner & Joe, 1987; Longmore, 1985a, 1985b). In reality, after medical stabilization, the disability is only one aspect of the individual and sometimes a relatively minor part of the individual's self-concept. Most PWDs report that PWODs ascribe far more importance and salience to their disability than they themselves do, and furthermore, most PWODs ascribe more limitations to the disability than actually exist.

Spread or Overgeneralization

In this section, look for—

- The definition of spread and how spread affects PWDs
- How most PWDs view their disability as a single aspect of their identity
- How FDR understood the importance of controlling the effects of spread

Beatrice Wright, a pioneer in the psychology of disability, coined the term *spread* to describe the overgeneralization (by observers) of the effects of the disability. Another disability scholar (Livneh, 1982) called this the *negative halo effect*. Both describe the widespread discounting and underrating of *all* of the abilities of the individual with the disability. In simplest forms, it is shouting at the person who is blind because it is thought that he or she cannot hear. Such behavior seems laughable, but generalizing the effects of disability is commonplace and usually more insidious. Most PWDs think of their disability as an attribute, not as a problem. Moreover, the disability is only a single aspect of their identity. In contrast, many PWODs consider the disability to be the central, defining characteristic of the PWD. For example, a Washington, DC, lawyer and Congressional lobbyist stated, "People don't think you're smart if you limp." A woman of small stature (a dwarf) commented, "Most people associate my maturity with my size." It can be seen that all of these examples overgeneralize the effects of the disability (and no one is disputing that the disability does indeed have limitations) to totally unrelated aspects of the individuals. In addition, all of these overgeneralizations tend to be negative.

There are a few exceptions when the overgeneralizations are thought to be positive and flattering; this is called the "Tiny Tim" syndrome. Tiny Tim, the boy with a disability in Charles Dickens's *A Christmas Carol*, was very sweet and appreciative and wished everybody well. Dickens used the character of Tiny Tim to show by contrast how mean and miserly Scrooge was. Not only was Tiny Tim poor, but he had a disability. Scrooge, however, was wealthy and able-bodied, and he was the villain. Nowadays, the "Tiny Tim" syndrome is a derisive term to describe the idea that a disability automatically results in a sweet and saintly personality. Often we hear that PWDs are compassionate, wise, or insightful or are heroes or saints. These are examples of the Tiny Tim syndrome.

M. J. Bienvenu (1989) related a joke that communicates the tendency of PWODs to overgeneralize the effects of disability. "A Deaf person is having a difficult time vacuuming the carpet. He goes over the same spot of dirt repeatedly, to no avail. In a fit of frustration, he turns around and notices that the machine is unplugged." Bienvenu then explained why the joke is both uninformed and insulting: "This is a perfect example of humor that is not part of the Deaf culture. Of course, this would never happen in the first place, because a Deaf person would naturally feel the inactive motor and immediately respond appropriately . . . . The fact that the author does not address deaf people's keenly developed sense of sight and touch is rather significant" (p. 19). This joke also illustrates that false and negative stereotypes are readily apparent to PWDs. This joke was published in a book entitled *Hazards of Deafness* (Holcomb, 1977), certainly not a flattering (or accurate) title. Once again, PWODs think they understand the experience of disability (when they do not); PWODs misinterpret the disability experience in negative and insulting ways, and these types of misinterpretation can lead to false stereotypes—for example, the stereotype that Deaf people are easily frustrated. Deaf people do read this joke and laugh. However, it is not for the reason that the author intended.

Far more pervasive, insidious, and damaging is the "twisted body, twisted soul" concept of spread. This widely held view claims that the disability has somehow negatively affected the individual's personality or character, making the individual permanently bitter, angry, deviant, and hostile. A variation of this idea states that the PWD is angry and bitter, not directly because of the disability but because he or she has failed to "accept" the disability, thus "pathologizing" the PWD. Of course, it is others who are making the judgment of the person's character and then ascribing the causes or sources of these character failings.

Esso Leete (1991) has experienced schizophrenia for more than 20 years. She summarized the experience of being stigmatized by making a list.

You understand stigma firsthand when:

- Your college refuses to readmit you after discharge from the hospital because you now have a history of mental illness.
- You are denied a driver's license because you are naïve enough to answer the questionnaire truthfully.

- A general hospital emergency room physician brusquely explains, after reading in your chart the diagnosis of "residual schizophrenia," that your fever, nausea, and vomiting are "in your head."
- Your friends decide they need to develop other relationships on learning of your past troubles and treatment.
- Stigma is an ugly word, with ugly consequences (p. 19).

It should be noted that some of this treatment would now be illegal under the ADA.

A well-known example of an individual who had a disability and understood the results of others overgeneralizing his disability was President Franklin Roosevelt. Roosevelt contracted polio at age 39 and never walked again. Before and after the onset of his disability, he pursued a political career. However, after he contracted polio, he and his family went to great lengths to hide the disability (they had the financial resources). The American media, mostly print, cooperated by not photographing Roosevelt in his wheelchair or being carried in someone's arms. All of Roosevelt's assistive devices; architectural accommodations, such as ramps into government buildings; and the personal assistance rendered by his sons or members of the Secret Service were systematically hidden from the public view. Roosevelt and his political advisors thought that the American public and international leaders would not accord respect and trust to Roosevelt if they were reminded of his disability too often (Gallagher, 1985). Yet Roosevelt guided the United States through the Great Depression and World War II, becoming one of the most influential individuals of the 20th century. He was also a great advocate for PWDs, especially for those who had survived polio. Roosevelt's image on the dime is often thought to be the result of his work in easing the economic depression, something akin to "Brother, can you spare a dime?" In fact, Roosevelt's image on the dime is an allusion to his work in founding the March of Dimes, a fundraiser for polio research and services for people with polio.

Today, some in the Disability Rights Movement consider Roosevelt to have been a "closet crip," someone who hid his disability for his own convenience and advancement. Another view of Roosevelt and his disability is described by Hugh Sidey in the *Time* magazine article (April 28, 1997, p. 4), describing the erection of a monument in Washington, DC, to honor Roosevelt (Exhibit 3–4). Originally, the builders planned to eliminate Roosevelt's wheelchair from the sculpture, but many groups of PWDs protested strongly. The protesters argued that the disability was an inherent part of Roosevelt and, furthermore, it is no longer necessary to prove that the disability of polio was not, or is not, an obstacle to being president. Indeed, many political analysts, not disability analysts (Evans, 1998), consider Roosevelt's disability to have contributed to his national and world leadership achievements because polio forced Roosevelt, for the first time in his life, to interact with, and attempt to understand, the struggles of the "common man."

Exhibit 3-4

A Monumental Mistake:
The FDR Memorial Misses the Essence of the Man

They came humbly and quietly last week in wheelchairs and with leader dogs and a sign-language interpreter, hopeful paraplegic old men, and vigorous middle-age people except for their weakened limbs and dimmed eyes, and glowing youngsters with silence in their ears.

They were a coterie representing 50 million disabled Americans who were invited by the U.S. Park Service to preview the sprawling monument for Franklin Roosevelt to be dedicated May 2. The monument spreads out grandly on 7.5 acres along Washington's Tidal Basin, great blocks of ocher South Dakota granite carved with the soaring phrases of FDR's that brought this nation through economic collapse and war.

But in the $48 million monument there is no depiction of Roosevelt in the wheelchair he used for 24 years, nothing in the gardens and along the pathways to show his disability at a glance for those who remember and for children who never knew the personal struggle that shaped him.

The small vanguard of disabled people left the site saddened, believing to a person that the monument seemed lifeless, lacking the heroic vibrancy of FDR with his radiant smile, head back, steering himself into that destiny he saw beyond all adversity. "The essence of the man is missing," said wheelchair user Mike Deland, chairman of the National Organization on Disability.

And a handful of Gallaudet College students in sign language declared it incomplete history as they had learned it and said they would join a demonstration planned for the dedication day.

Mick Countee sensed the emptiness because after he broke his neck in a diving accident, while he was a Harvard student, his mother told him, "Son, if Franklin Roosevelt could be President, you can finish your education." Countee, a black [person], not only finished, but also went on to get a law degree from Georgetown and an MBA from Harvard. "Not a day went by," he said last week, "that I did not think of Roosevelt and Roy Campanella." Campanella was the Brooklyn Dodger catcher who was paralyzed in a car accident but never despaired in public.

Jim Dickson, the man organizing the demonstration, stood nearly sightless along the huge monument walls and imagined how a statue of Roosevelt in a wheelchair at the entrance would bring the stone to life. When Dickson was seventeen he was told by his doctor that he had juvenile macular degeneration and would soon be blind. As he walked with his parents out of the doctor's office, his mother told him, "If Franklin Roosevelt, who had polio and was in a wheelchair, could be President, then you can do what you want." He never forgot.

This cry for understanding from the disabled community is being heard. At least 16 Roosevelt family members now seek a design alteration. A demonstration at a New York foundry casting some of the sculptures halted a press conference. Another protest is planned around the office of monument designer Lawrence Halprin in San Francisco.

(continues)

Former Presidents Bush, Ford, and Carter have urged an additional sculpture to show Roosevelt in a wheelchair, and Bush has sent off a "Dear Bill" note to Clinton in hopes he can encourage a peace before Clinton gives the dedication address. Meanwhile every historian of consequence who has considered the issue has concluded that the monument is a tragic misreading of the spirit of FDR and a grave misstatement of history for the generations to come.

Contrast the way in which another famous individual, often in the media, has chosen to deal with his disability. Itzak Perlman, the world-famous violinist, has the same disability as FDR had; both had contracted polio and neither could walk unassisted. Perlman has pointedly insisted that his television appearances show him walking on to the stage on his crutches. Of course, Perlman has the option to hide or minimize his disability simply by appearing in a seated position playing the violin. Olkin (1999) described a result of this: "Itzak Perlman . . . said that when he began playing violin professionally all the stories about him described him as a man who had polio and also played the violin. It was only after he became one of the four premier violinists in the world did the stories switch to describing him as a premier violinist who also happened to have had polio" (pp. 88–89).

Roosevelt felt he could not afford to remind the American people of his disability, whereas Perlman has chosen to show his self-identity: a violinist who has had polio. This is not to say that one of these individuals is right and the other wrong. These two examples demonstrate the following:

1. The processes and rationales underlying the choice to disclose or not to disclose; certainly both Roosevelt and Perlman knew/know that their orthopaedic disabilities had no functional impairments for the chosen occupations, and yet each knew that the public would react to the disability and, furthermore, each needed the public to fulfill his occupational aspirations. Roosevelt needed people to vote for him and Perlman needs people to attend his concerts and buy his CDs.

2. The relationship both Roosevelt and Perlman had, or have, with their public is most often not a personal relationship. A teacher or a physician with a disability meets the individuals with whom he or she works and can, therefore, respond to concerns about the disability on a one-to-one basis; Roosevelt never met or talked to each of the American people on an individual basis, and Perlman meets and speaks with very few of the people who attend his concerts or buy his CDs.

3. The differing results and others' judgments of Perlman and Roosevelt choosing to disclose their disability or to hide their dis-

ability; for example, many in the Disability Rights Movement resent the fact that Roosevelt went to such lengths to hide his disability or, more correctly stated, the effects of his disability.

4. The capability of both these men to hide their disability simply because they are both gifted and famous; certainly the inability to walk and the use of crutches or a wheelchair is considered a visible disability. However, the juxtaposition of fame and media has enlarged the definition of "hidden" disability for those few who are gifted and famous. Furthermore, because most people do not have the choice, they are not criticized for choosing not to disclose.

A letter from Ann Landers titled "Angry in Montana," in which a woman in a wheelchair said she did not want to talk to the child in the grocery store about her disability or answer the child's questions, clearly shows Ann Landers's quickness to overgeneralize the effects of the disability. In reply, Landers tells the writer with a disability that she has not accepted her disability and the wheelchair. Never does Landers consider that it is the child, and his or her mother, who are rude, insensitive, and intrusive. This is an example of being a "forced representative." Perhaps the woman in the wheelchair does not have a lot of privacy. For example, maybe a personal care attendant must perform many functions for the woman. Therefore, privacy is precious and important to the woman. Perhaps the woman was in a hurry and did not have time to present a one-woman disability-awareness seminar. Perhaps the woman was in a bad mood after having had a hard day. Everyone, including a PWD, is entitled to have bad moods. Perhaps the woman simply did not like children. Landers does not consider for a moment that there is any explanation for the woman refusing to speak to the child other than her disability. The authors of the following letters written to protest Landers's reply to this woman clearly resent Landers's "twisted body, twisted soul" implication (Exhibit 3–5).

The letters are the rebuttals Ann Landers received, commenting on her response to "Angry in Montana." The first letter criticizes Landers, but the second writer, from Lansing, Michigan, states that, as a wheelchair user, she was disappointed when the mother of the curious child "snatches" him away. Perhaps Lansing misperceived the situation and the mother was simply teaching her son rules of courtesy and spoke to her son about "the funny chair" in a more private setting.

Exhibit 3–5

Ann Gets an Earful on Disability Response

Dear Ann: You goofed. Your reply to "Angry in Montana" about people with physical disabilities and the curiosity of "innocent" children was totally off the mark. "Montana" is right. It is NOT OK for children to ask questions about a physical disability. Just because it comes from a child's "natural curiosity" does not make it all right.

It is natural for a child to want to do away with a new baby who is getting entirely too much attention, but we won't allow it. We also will not allow jumping on the bed in muddy sneakers or taking Daddy's watch apart. When my grandson displayed a bit of "natural curiosity" and attempted to disengage the brake on my car, you'd better believe I lost no time letting him know it was NOT OK. There is no reason to indulge a child's inquisitiveness just because it is "natural."

Your out-of-the-blue statements that Angry in Montana has not come to terms with his disability and the suggestion that he "lighten up" were insensitive and condescending.
—Disappointed in You

Dear D.I.Y.: I appreciate your comment. Keep reading for others.

Lansing, Mich.: I have been confined to a wheelchair since 1957. When I first went to a restaurant back then, a child of about 4 years old came over and asked why I was in that "funny chair." Before I could respond, his mother snatched him away. The child looked startled and probably got the impression that whatever I had must be contagious. I realize the mother didn't want her child to be rude, but her response only made things worse. Times have changed for the better, thank the good Lord. And thanks, too, for those recently installed ramps that now make almost all buildings wheelchair accessible.

Assisted Suicide

> ### *In this section, look for—*
>
> - Support for assisted suicide is based on a combination of three factors:
>
>   1. The false ideas of pity and fear
>
>   2. The idea of individual autonomy and personal liberty
>
>   3. The economic savings allowed
>
> *(continues)*

> ■ The pitfalls of assisted suicide for PWDs
>
> 1. Abortion and infanticide of PWDs can be defended using the arguments for assisted suicide
>
> 2. Assisted suicide of PWDs can interact with other minority statuses of the individual
>
> 3. The "right" to die may become the "duty" to die

The Story of Larry McAfee, or There Is a Better Solution

One of the most widely publicized stories of an individual with a disability requesting assisted suicide is that of a 34-year-old man from Georgia, Larry McAfee. In 1989 McAfee was in a motorcycle accident that left him with quadriplegia and on a respirator. At the time of McAfee's injury, he was close to completing an engineering degree at Georgia Tech. After 3 months in a nursing home he called a lawyer asking for the legal right to commit suicide. McAfee's case went to the Georgia Supreme Court and the Court upheld McAfee's "right" to assisted suicide. After the court ruling, McAfee's situation had changed and he no longer wished to die; therefore, he "escaped" to a nursing home in Alabama because the Georgia court ruling applied only to the state of Georgia. By 1990 McAfee had become a disability rights activist and testified before the Georgia State Senate, stating "Medicaid and Medicare policies that do not work in the best interest of the disabled [*sic*] have caused me and those like me to become prisoners of bureaucracy" (Shapiro, 1997, p. 177). Until McAfee's case, Medicare and Medicaid only paid for treatment and services provided in a nursing home.

What changed McAfee's mind? Of course, it is impossible to entirely understand McAfee's situation. Nonetheless, leaving nursing homes and living in a group home that was fully accessible and provided 24-hour personal care attendant service was a beginning. To live in a group home in the community, it was necessary to change the funding requirements of Medicaid and Medicare. Shapiro summarized:

> From a disability rights point of view, the McAfee decision was better understood as the story of how this country fails miserably to care for severely disabled [*sic*] people. Instead of getting help to live on his own, McAfee was sentenced to indifferent nursing homes and hospitals and stripped of basic decision-making about his life. (1997, pp. 171–172)

Second, an individual stepped forward, making it clear that he supported McAfee's right to die, but he insisted that McAfee first consider all of his options. This individual, named Russ Fine, began to acquire assistive technology for McAfee, took him out for rides in a van, and investigated ways in which to circumnavigate Medicaid's funding requirements. A computer engineer in California, Bob Stockwell, saw a television report on McAfee and flew out to Georgia to set up a voice-activated computer that allowed him to turn the lights and television on and off, lock the doors, and regulate the thermostat. Stockwell also set up a computer system with which McAfee could make architectural drawings with a sonar beam directed from a strap on his head. It is interesting that Stockwell knew nothing or very little about disability but he was an expert in computers. After receiving this technology, McAfee no longer wished to die. McAfee now uses a wheelchair that is powered by his breaths. A respirator is built into the wheelchair. With his customized van and "sip and puff" wheelchair, McAfee has the freedom and independence to go almost anywhere he wants whenever he wants.

Incidentally, the play and subsequent movie, "Whose Life Is It Anyway?" about a young man who was paralyzed and attempted to commit suicide, takes place entirely within a hospital. To the general public this is not an important consideration. However, PWDs, many with the same disability, are dismayed that this man accepted suicide before he had attempted to live independently in the community. This same ill-informed perspective is found in the Clint Eastwood/Hilary Swank movie, "Million Dollar Baby," based on the short stories of F. X. Toole, where the boxing trainer (Eastwood) assists a young woman (Swank) to commit suicide. Therefore, most PWODs assume (falsely) that suicide is justifiable, while most PWDs understand that the character's desire for suicide is premature and totally uninformed.

Support for Assisted Suicide of PWDs

The voluntary self-elimination of PWDs aided by others has received attention in both the media and the American court system. The support for assisted suicide is a result of many factors. These factors are intertwined, often unvoiced, and difficult to assess. The first factor is the false ideas of pity and fear that lead to the inevitable conclusion that, if disability is such a tragedy, then it is simply humane to allow PWDs to die. However, as we have seen, PWODs, as a group, hold an inaccurate view of the disability experience. Lives with disabilities are often automatically considered to be "life unworthy of life." Furthermore, in the few widely publicized cases of assisted suicide for PWDs, no examination of the PWD's quality of life was undertaken. To cite a single example, in Larry McAfee's case, he asked for assistance in committing suicide at the time he was living in a nursing home (rather than at home with a personal care attendant), and he had not received any assistive technology. Indeed, after McAfee received these accommodations, he no longer wanted to die. Furthermore, McAfee was never asked if he wished to undergo counseling or psychotherapy. Shapiro (1997) stated, "To disabled [sic] people, however, Larry McAfee's case was not a simple right-to-die case. Instead, it was a chilling reminder of how a disabled [*sic*] life was dismissed—by doctors, judges, and the public—as a devalued life" (p. 171).

The second factor is the strong pressure to accord everyone autonomy and personal liberty. However, when a PWOD threatens suicide, an array of services is mobilized to *prevent* the suicide. In contrast, when a PWD asks for assistance in committing suicide, an array of services is mobilized to *facilitate* the suicide. One disability scholar pointed out: "It would be ironic if (at a time when millions of Americans lack adequate health care) the judiciary selected physician-assisted suicide as the one health care right that deserves constitutional status" (Fleischer & Zames, 2001, p. 134).

The third factor, the economic savings to society when PWDs commit suicide, is the most unpleasant and therefore it is rarely discussed openly. In spite of not being discussed publicly, some disability scholars consider this third argument to be the *only* reason for supporting assisted suicide of PWDs. Two disability scholars, Doris Zames Fleischer and Frieda Zames (2001), explained:

> Campaigners for a right-to-die movement in the 1990s Derek Humphry and Mary Clement state that "in the final analysis, economics, not the quest for broadened individual liberties or increased autonomy, will drive assisted suicide to the plateau of accepted practice. (pp. 139–140)

Ed Roberts, considered by many to be the founder of the Independent Living Movement, was a polio survivor who lived for decades by using a respirator. He succinctly stated his judgment of these assisted suicide cases: "It's not the respirator. It's the money."

Pitfalls of Assisted Suicide

Disability rights advocates claim that legally supported assisted suicide is simply legalized discrimination against PWDs. Perhaps alluding to the Nazi death trains that transported Jewish people to be murdered, Mark O'Brien, who uses an iron lung to breathe, stated: "We are people who hear the death train. We will not board that train willingly." Hockenberry (1995) said, "Pray to be normal no matter how impossible that seems is the sentimental message. The alternative is too horrible to contemplate" (p. 204).

Obviously O'Brien is an articulate, strong-willed individual. But what of other PWDs? What about those PWDs who are often termed "vulnerable?" Nat Henoff (1996) considered that the more vulnerable the individual, the more likely it was that he or she would be euthanized:

> It's a bitter irony (that a) quintessentially liberal judge (Ninth Circuit Judge Stephen Reinhardt) has opened the door wide not only to assisted suicide but also to euthanasia, because the majority of the resul-

tant dead will be the poor, the disabled, and other vulnerable people. Many of them will persuade themselves to die because they feel nobody thinks their lives are worth preserving. Or that keeping themselves alive will cost too much, thereby burdening their families and companions. (p. 12)

Most vulnerable are babies. Individuals who are elderly, women, or of racial/ethnic minorities (or any combination of these identities) and who also have disabilities are also vulnerable. There is a great deal written about euthanasia. For example, euthanasia has been practiced in the Netherlands since 1972, and in 1988 an estimate of euthanasia on newborn babies and infants up to 3 months old was published by the Royal Dutch Society of Medicine. It was reported that 300 babies each year are starved and dehydrated to death or denied lifesaving surgery. Ten babies with disabilities receive lethal injections each year. These babies experience birth trauma or have spina bifida or Down syndrome (Fenigsen, 1997). Peter Singer, the Princeton professor of philosophy, is an outspoken advocate of euthanasia of babies with disabilities, stating: "Killing unwanted infants or allowing them to die has been a normal practice in most societies throughout human history and prehistory" (p. 159).

One physician (Hendin, 2001) is clear in stating that state-supported infanticide, if legalized, would be far more widespread in the United States than in the Netherlands. "The Netherlands? With a homogenous, pretty much law-abiding citizenry, almost all of whom have medical coverage? And America, with many cultures represented, many marginalized people, tens of millions without health care insurance? As bad as it was *there*, in other words, it could be much, much worse *here*" (Fleischer & Zames, 2001, p. 144).

People in these vulnerable categories are well aware that they are more likely to be considered for euthanasia. It is no coincidence that in a 1996 *Washington Post* poll, 70% of African Americans opposed legalized assisted suicide and 58% of those termed "elderly" opposed legalized suicide. Indeed, members of minority groups with disabilities understand the long history of medical exploitation of people who are poor or institutionalized with either mental illness or mental retardation, especially children. However, without doubt, it is African Americans who have experienced the greatest degree of medical exploitation, including forced experimentations and forced sterilizations. Therefore, it is understandable that many racial and ethnic minorities with disabilities view assisted suicide and euthanasia with suspicion and, often, outright hostility. Stefan (2001), a legal scholar whose specialty is psychiatric disabilities, reports the following medical practice and demonstrates that the triple combination of disability, parental race, and perceived poverty resulted in the deaths of infants.

> Researchers at the University of Oklahoma decided to investigate the effects of treatment on the survival rates of infants born with spina bifida. To further their research, they divided infants born at the hospital

with spina bifida into two categories, those who would receive treatment and those who would not—obviously without the knowledge or consent of the parents of the children who did not receive treatment. The way the children were divided was based on the researchers' perceptions of the parents' ability to take care of their children, so the children of poor, minority parents did not receive treatment, and the children of more economically stable parents did. Virtually every one of the children who did not receive treatment died. Virtually every one of the children who did receive treatment lived. (p. 155)

When the facts surrounding this "research study" became known, the parents of the deaf children sued (*Johnson v. Thompson*, 1992). The court ruled that the parents did not have a case based on race because some of the babies from poor families were white. Additionally, the court ruled that there was no discrimination based on disability because some of the children with spina bifida did receive treatment. Therefore, the parents lost the case. Stefan concluded that this case was "one of the most crushing examples of the way in which the law's obsession with neat categories results in the denial of relief to people who are subject to multiple, intersecting forms of discrimination . . ." (p. 155).

This case also reveals the importance of informed choice (the parents of the babies who did not receive treatment were not told of this decision) and the fact that poor people and racial and ethnic minorities are often not given their rights.

Women will be more vulnerable to pressures for assisted suicide and the related "duty to die." In testimony before Congress, two disability activists spoke against the assisted suicide practices of Dr. Kevorkian:

If anyone doubts that women will be exploited and endangered by assisted suicide, the doubters should study Kevorkian's "clients." The first eight were all middle-aged or elderly women with chronic illnesses and disabilities. Many said they feared being a burden on others. An autopsy on one of them revealed no evidence of any physical illness. Women with disabilities are going to be the first to feel a "duty to die." (Fleischer & Zames, 2001, p. 139)

In the next chapter, we shall learn of more sources of prejudice and discrimination against PWDs. Keep in mind that prejudice and discrimination as experienced by anyone cannot be separated into these 10 neat and tidy categories. However, these 10 categories provide a structure to learn about the sources of negative judgments of PWDs.

In-Class Videos

- View the 19-minute video "disAbility Awareness" (1999) by Insight Media.

- View the 45-minute video "Understanding the Disabled: Dances with the Minotaur" by Insight Media. This video "examines issues of stereotyping and inaccessibility, confronts day-to-day issues" of those with disabilities, and "raises provocative questions about equality" (Insight Media, 2162 Broadway, New York, NY 10024-0621, 800-233-9910). Which of the three types of justice presented in this chapter is or are advocated in this video?

- View the 56-minute video "A New Sense of Place" released by Films for the Humanities and Sciences. The producers describe this video as profiling "individuals who have found a way to 'ramp' their way into the world. Among them is Grammy Award winner Evelyn Glennie, one of the world's leading solo percussionists and deaf since the age of 12; and NBC News correspondent John Hockenberry, partially paralyzed since the age of 19, who travels the world to report the news. Also featured in the program is a legally blind woman who is not only a district attorney but an accomplished athlete as well."

- View the 56-minute video "Without Barriers or Borders" by Films for the Humanities and Sciences. The producers state: "This program explores the burgeoning global movement for independent living. Among the efforts featured in this program are a group of disabled high school students from Russia, who learn confidence, teamwork, and communication skills through whitewater rafting; Japanese activists who are working to persuade their society to provide access to transportation and buildings; and a Cambodian clinic where over half the workers have disabilities."

- View the 54-minute film "Nazi Medicine: In the Shadow of the Reich" produced by Program Development Associates. The producers describe this video: "From 1933–1945, the medical profession in Nazi Germany suspended its conscience as it involved itself in unethical practices related to disability-diagnosis, human experimentation, euthanasia and sterilization. With the help of historical film clips, this documentary studies the process that led the medical profession in the Third Reich down the road to the genocide of people with disabilities and others they considered devalued minorities." Resource #NM899E

- View the 35-minute film "A World Without Bodies" produced by Program Development Associates. The producers describe this film: "Shot on location at Bernburg Psychiatric Institution, Germany, this video documents the Nazi Regime horror with respect to its treatment of people with disabilities. Beginning with an overview of Eugenics ideology, the filmmakers delved into the instruments of mass murder developed first on the bodies of people with disabilities and later transferred to concentration camps. Provides a haunting glimpse into the medical and social mindset that led to the systematic killing of more than 240,000 individuals, perceived as disabled." Resource #AWWB211E.

- View the 28-minute video "Making a Life: Opportunity, Not Disability" produced by Insight Media. The producers describe this video: "People with disabilities are often regarded only in terms of what they cannot do, rather than what they can do. In this video, social workers, special education teachers, employers, and those challenged by an ailment or accident discuss society's perceptions and how, when given the chance, people with disabilities rise to the challenges of life." #TAD2456

Learning Activities

Find examples in the media (films, literature, television, advertising) that communicate prejudice and stereotypes of PWDs. Share these with the class.

As a class, listen to the National Public Radio program "The Overdue Revolution" in the Disability History Project. This 45-minute program re-enacts the sit-in by PWDs of the Federal Building in San Francisco. Protesters forced the signing of the regulations of Section 504 of the Rehabilitation Act of 1973, which made discrimination against PWDs by universities, colleges, state governments, and hospitals and other agencies that received federal funding illegal. Many consider this 1977 sit-in to be the beginnings of a concerted disability rights movement.

Read the following books: *By Trust Betrayed, The Origins of Nazi Genocide,* and *Nazi Doctors: The Medical Killing and the Psychology of Genocide* on the Nazi mass murder of Germans with disabilities. Discuss in class the ways in which the following factors may have contributed to these deaths:

- The collectivistic concept of society, the German idea of "volk"
- The economic considerations of caring for PWDs
- The language used to describe Germans with disabilities: "life unworthy of life."

Read the following books, which discuss the fear of contagion: *The Colony* by John Tayman, *Polio and Its Aftermath* by Marc Shell, *Living with Polio* by Daniel J. Wilson, and *And the Band Played On* by Randy Shilts. *The Colony* tells of the leper colony in Hawaii; the two polio books relate the history of the polio epidemics, and *And The Band Played On* discusses the history of the AIDS epidemic. Compare and contrast the reactions of the public to these different types of epidemics. Has any progress been made?

Writing Experience

Write a paper that responds to one of the 11 "bullet" questions listed at the beginning of this chapter.

References

Abroms, K. I., & Hodera, T. L. (1979). Acceptance hierarchy of handicaps: Validation of Kirk's statement "Special education often begins where medicine stops." *Journal of Learning Disabilities, 12,* 15–20.

Albrecht, G. L. (1976). Socialization and the disability process. In G. Albrecht (Ed.), *The sociology of physical disability and rehabilitation* (pp. 3–38). Pittsburgh, PA: University of Pittsburgh.

Albrecht, G. L. (1992). The social meaning of impairment and interpretation of disability. In G. L. Albrecht (Ed.), *The disability business in America* (pp. 67–90). Newbury Park, CA: Sage.

Allport, G. W. (1954). *The nature of prejudice.* Reading, MA: Addison-Wesley.

Allport, G. W. (1958). *The nature of prejudice* (2nd ed.). Garden City, NY: Doubleday Anchor.

Allport, G. W. (1986). *The nature of prejudice* (25th anniversary ed.). Reading, MA: Addison-Wesley.

Americans with Disabilities Act of 1990, 42 U.S.C. § 12101 *et seq.*

Amundson, R. (2000). "Against normal functions." *Studies in the History and Philosophy of Biological and Biomedical Sciences, 31,* 33–53.

Anderson, G. R., & Glesnes-Anderson, V. A. (Eds.). (1987). *Health care ethics: A guide for decision makers.* Rockville, MD: Aspen.

Anthony, R. N., & Young, D. W. (1984). *Management control in nonprofit organizations* (3rd ed.). Homewood, IL: Richard D. Irwin.

Antonak, R. F. (1980). A hierarchy of attitudes toward exceptionality. *The Journal of Special Education, 14,* 231–241.

Antonak, R. F. (1985). Societal factors in disablement. *Rehabilitation Counseling Bulletin, 28,* 188–201.

Antonak, R. F. (1988). Methods to measure attitudes toward people who are disabled. In H. E. Yuker (Ed.), *Attitudes toward persons with disabilities* (pp. 109–126). New York: Springer.

Battin, M. P. (1986). Euthanasia. In D. Van De Veer & T. Regan (Eds.), *Health care ethics: An introduction* (pp. 58–97). Philadelphia: Temple University.

Bayles, M. D. (1987). The value of life. In D. Van De Veer & T. Regan (Eds.), *Health care ethics: An introduction* (pp. 265–289). Philadelphia: Temple University.

Beck, M. (1999). *Expecting Adam: A true story of birth, rebirth, and everyday magic.* New York: Times Books/Random House.

Belgrave, F. Z. (1984). The effectiveness of strategies for increasing social interaction with a physically disabled person. *Journal of Applied Social Psychology, 141,* 147–161.

Belgrave, F. Z., & Mills, J. (1981). Effect upon desire for social interaction with a physically disabled person of mentioning the disability in different contexts. *Journal of Applied Social Psychology, 11,* 44–57.

Berkowitz, E. D. (1987). *Disability policy: America's programs for the handicapped.* Cambridge: Cambridge University.

Berry, J. O. (1995). Employing people with disabilities: Impact on attitude and situation. *Rehabilitation Psychology, 40,* 211–222.

Berube, M. (1996). *Life as we know it: A father, a family, and an exceptional child.* New York: Pantheon Books.

Bettancourt, B. A., & Dorr, N. (1998). Cooperative interaction and intergroup bias: Effects of numerical representation and cross-cut role assignment. *Personality and Social Psychology Bulletin, 24,* 1276–1304.

Bickenbach, J. E. (1993). *Physical disability and social policy.* Toronto, Ontario: University of Toronto.

Bienvenu, M. J. (1989). Reflections of deaf culture in deaf humor. In C. J. Erring, R. C. Johnson, D. L. Smith, & B. D. Snider (Eds.), *The deaf way: Perspectives from the International Conference on Deaf Culture* (pp. 16–23). Washington, DC: Gallaudet University Press.

Biklen, D. (1986). Framed: Journalism's treatment of disability. *Social Policy, 16*(3), 45–51.

Biklen, D., & Bailey, L. (Eds.). (1981). *"Rudely stamp'd": Imaginal disability and prejudice.* Washington, DC: University Press of America.

Blood, I. M. (1997). The hearing aid effect: Challenges for counseling. *Journal of Rehabilitation, 63,* 59–63.

Bogdan, R. (1988). *Freak show: Presenting human oddities for amusement and profit.* Chicago: University of Chicago.

Bogdan, R., & Biklen, D. (1977). Handicapism. *Social Policy, March/April,* 14–19.

Bogdan, R., & Knoll, J. (1995). The sociology of disability. In E. L. Meyen & T. M. Skrtic (Eds.), *Special education and student disability* (pp. 677–711). Denver, CO: Love.

Bogdan, R., & Taylor, S. J. (1976). The judged, not the judges: An insider's view of mental retardation. *American Psychologist, 31,* 47–52.

Bogdan, R., & Taylor, S. J. (1982). *Inside out: The social meaning of mental retardation.* Toronto: University of Toronto.

Bowe, F. (1978). *Handicapping America: Barriers to disabled people.* New York: Harper & Row.

Bowe, F. (1980). *Rehabilitating America: Toward independence for disabled and elderly people.* New York: Harper & Row.

Bowe, F. (1990). Employment and people with disabilities: Challenges for the nineties. *OSERS News in Print, 3,* 2–6.

Bower, E. M. (Ed.). (1980). *The handicapped in literature: A psychosocial perspective.* Denver, CO: Love.

Brown, E. R. (1987). DRGs and the rationing of hospital care. In G. R. Anderson & V. A. Glesnes-Anderson (Eds.), *Health care ethics: A guide for decision makers* (pp. 69–90). Rockville, MD: Aspen.

Bryan, W. V. (1996). *In search of freedom: How people with disabilities have been disenfranchised from the mainstream of American society.* Springfield, IL: Charles C. Thomas.

Byrd, E. K. (1979). Magazine articles and disability. *American Rehabilitation, 4,* 18–20.

Byrd, E. K., & Elliott, T. R. (1985). Feature films and disability: A descriptive study. *Rehabilitation Psychology, 30,* 47–51.

Byrd, E. K., & Elliott, T. R. (1988). Media and disability: A discussion of the research. In H. E. Yuker (Ed.), *Attitudes toward persons with disabilities* (pp. 82–95). New York: Springer.

Byrd, E. K., Byrd, P. D., & Allen, C. (1977). Television programming and disability: A descriptive study. *Journal of Applied Rehabilitation Counseling, 8,* 28–32.

Byrd, E. K., Williamson, W., & Byrd, P. D. (1986). Literary characters who are disabled. *Rehabilitation Counseling Bulletin, 30,* 57–61.

Byrom, B. (2004). A pupil and a patient: Hospital-schools in progressive America. In S. Danforth & S. D. Taff (Eds.), *Crucial readings in special education* (pp. 25–37). Upper Saddle River, NJ: Pearson, Merrill, Prentice Hall.

Charlton, J. I. (1998). *Nothing about us without us: Disability oppression and empowerment.* Berkeley, CA: University of California.

Chirikos, T. N. (1989). Aggregate economic losses from disability in the United States: A preliminary assay. *The Milbank Quarterly, 67,* 59–61.

Chubon, R. A. (1994). *Social and psychological foundations of rehabilitation.* Springfield, IL: Charles C. Thomas.

Cole, S. S. (1984). Facing the challenge of sexual abuse in persons with disabilities. *Sexuality and Disability, 7,* 71–88.

Cole, S. S. (Ed.). (1991). Sexual exploitation of people with disabilities [Special issue]. *Sexuality and Disability, 9* (3).

Coleman, L. M. (1997). Stigma: An enigma demystified. In L. J. Davis (Ed.), *The disability studies reader* (pp. 216–231). New York: Routledge.

Cornwell, J. (1999). *Hitler's pope: The secret history of Pius XII.* New York: Viking Penguin.

Couser, G. T. (1997). *Recovering bodies: Illness, disability, and life writing.* Madison, WI: University of Wisconsin.

Covey, H. C. (1998). *Social perceptions of people with disabilities in history.* Springfield, IL: Charles C. Thomas.

Craine, L. S., Henson, C. E., Colliver, J. A., & McLeland, D. G. (1988). Prevalence of a history of sexual abuse among female psychiatric patients in a state hospital system. *Hospital and Community Psychiatry, 39,* 300–304.

Davis, L. J. (Ed.). (1997). *The disability studies reader.* New York: Routledge.

DeJong, G., & Batavia, A. I. (1990). The Americans with Disabilities Act and the current state of U.S. disability policy. *Journal of Disability Policy Studies, 1,* 65–75.

DeJong, G., & Lifchez, R. (1983). Physical disability and public policy. *Scientific American, 248,* 40–49.

Deshen, S. A. (1992). *Blind people: The private and public life of sightless Israelis.* Albany, NY: State University of New York.

Disadvantages. Available: www.nod.org. Retrieved June 29, 2004.

Eisenberg, M. G. (1982). Disability as stigma. In M. G. Eisenberg, C. Griggins, & R. J. Duval (Eds.), *Disabled people as second-class citizens* (pp. 1–11). New York: Springer.

Eisenberg, M. G., Griggins, C., & Duval, R. J. (Eds.). (1982). *Disabled people as second-class citizens.* New York: Springer.

Evans, H. (1998). *The American century.* New York: Alfred A. Knopf.

Fenigsen, R. (1997). Euthanasia of disabled infants is not morally acceptable (pp. 160–164). In B. Stalcup (Ed.), *The disabled.* San Diego, CA: Greenhaven.

Ferguson, P. M., Ferguson, D. L., & Taylor, S. J. (Eds.). (1991). *Interpreting disability: A qualitative reader.* New York: Columbia University.

Ferrans, C. W. (1987). Quality of life as a criterion for allocation of life-sustaining treatment: The case of hemodialysis. In G. R. Anderson & V. A. Glesnes-Anderson (Eds.), *Health care ethics: A guide for decision makers* (pp. 109–124). Rockville, MD: Aspen.

Fichten, C. S. (1986). Self, other, and situation-referent automatic thoughts: Interaction between people who have a physical disability and those who do not. *Cognitive Therapy and Research, 10,* 571–587.

Fichten, C. S., Robillard, K., Tagalakis, V., & Amsel, R. (1991). Causal interaction between college students with various disabilities and their nondisabled peers: The internal dialogue. *Rehabilitation Psychology, 36,* 3–20.

Fine, M., & Asch, A. (1988a). Disability beyond stigma: Social interaction, discrimination, and activism. *Journal of Social Issues, 44,* 3–21.

Fine, M., & Asch, A. (Eds.). (1988b). *Women with disabilities.* Philadelphia: Temple University.

Fleischer, D. Z., & Zames, F. (2001). *The disability rights movement: From charity to confrontation.* Philadelphia: Temple University.

Friedlander, H. (1995). *The origins of Nazi genocide: From euthanasia to the final solution.* Chapel Hill, NC: University of North Carolina.

Gallagher, H. G. (1985). *FDR's splendid deception.* New York: Dodd and Mead.

Gallagher, H. G. (1990). *By trust betrayed: Patients, physicians, and the license to kill in the Third Reich.* New York: Henry Holt.

Gartner, A., & Joe, T. (Eds.). (1987). *Images of the disabled, disabling images.* New York: Praeger.

Gellman, W. (1959). Roots of prejudice against the handicapped. *Journal of Rehabilitation, 40,* 115–123.

Goffman, E. (1963). *Stigma: Notes on the management of spoiled identity.* Englewood Cliffs, NJ: Prentice Hall.

Gordon, E. D., Minnes, P. M., & Holden, R. R. (1990). The structure of attitudes toward persons with a disability, when specific disability and context are considered. *Rehabilitation Psychology, 35,* 79–90.

Gouvier, W. D., Coon, R. C., Todd, M. E., & Fuller, K. H. (1994). Verbal interactions with individuals presenting with and without physical disability. *Rehabilitation Psychology, 39,* 263–268.

Gouvier, W. D., Steiner, D. D., Jackson, W. T., Schlater, D., & Rain, J. S. (1991). Employment discrimination against handicapped job candidates: An analog study of the effects of neurological causation, visibility of handicap, and public contact. *Rehabilitation Psychology, 36,* 121–129.

Gove, W. R. (1976). Social reaction theory and disability. In G. L. Albrecht (Ed.), *The sociology of physical disability and rehabilitation* (pp. 57–71). Pittsburgh, PA: University of Pittsburgh.

Grand, S. A., Bernier, J. E., & Strohmer, D. C. (1982). Attitudes toward disabled persons as a function of social context and specific disability. *Rehabilitation Psychology, 27.*

Grealy, L. (1997). Pony party. In K. Fries (Ed.), *Staring back: The disability experience from the inside out* (pp. 13–21). New York: Plume.

Hahn, H. (1987). Civil rights for disabled Americans: The foundation of a political agenda. In A. Garther & T. Joe (Eds.), *Images of the disabled, disabled images* (pp. 181–203). New York: Praeger.

Hahn, H. (1997). Advertising the acceptable employment image: Disability and capitalism. In L. J. Davis (Ed.), *The disability reader* (pp. 172–186). New York: Routledge.

Hahn, H. (2005). Academic debates and political advocacy: The U.S. disability movement. In G. E. May & M. B. Raske (Eds.), *Ending disability discrimination: Strategies for social workers* (pp. 1–24). Boston: Pearson.

Hannah, M. E., & Midlarsky, E. (1987). Differential impact of labels and behavioral descriptions on attitudes toward people with disabilities. *Rehabilitation Psychology, 32,* 227–238.

Harris, L. (1986). *The ICD survey II: Employing disabled Americans.* New York: Louis Harris.

Harris, L. (1994). *The ICD survey III: Employing disabled Americans.* New York: Louis Harris.

Harrison, J. (1987). *Severe physical disability: Responses to the challenges of care.* London: Cassell.

Hastorf, A. H., Wildfogel, J., & Cassman, T. (1979). Acknowledgment of handicap as a tactic in social interaction. *Journal of Personality and Social Psychology, 37*, 1790–1797.

Henderson, G., & Bryan, W. V. (1997). *Psychosocial aspects of disability* (2nd ed.). Springfield, IL: Charles C. Thomas.

Henoff, N. (1996, May 21). Class warfare to the death. *Village Voice*, 12.

Higgins, P. C. (1992). *Making disability: Exploring the social transformation of human variation.* Springfield, IL: Charles C. Thomas.

Hockenberry, J. (1995). *Moving violations: Warzones, wheelchairs, and declarations of independence.* New York: Hyperion.

Holcomb, R. (1977). *Hazards of deafness.* Northridge, CA: Joyce Media.

Holocaust foreshadowed in newspaper obituaries. (1999, July 30). *The Herald Journal*, p. 5.

Hormuth, S.E. (1990). *The ecology of the self: Relocation and self-concept change.* Cambridge, England: Cambridge University.

Horne, M. D. (1988). Modifying peer attitudes toward the handicapped: Procedures and research issues. *Attitudes toward persons with disabilities* (pp. 203–222). New York: Springer.

Hyler, S. E. (1988). DSM-III at the cinema: Madness in the movies. *Comprehensive Psychiatry, 29*, 195–206.

Hyler, S. E., Gabbard, G. O., & Schneider, I. (1991). Homicidal maniacs and narcissistic parasites: Stigmatization of mentally ill persons in the movies. *Hospital and Community Psychiatry, 42*, 1044–1048.

Ince, L. P. (Ed.). (1980). *Behavioral psychology in rehabilitation medicine: Clinical applications.* Baltimore: Williams & Wilkins.

Kleck, R. (1968). Physical stigma and nonverbal cues emitted in face-to-face interaction. *Human Relations, 21*, 19–28.

Kriegel, L. (1987). The cripple in literature. In A. Gartner & T. Joe (Eds.), *Images of the disabled, disabling images* (pp. 31–46). New York: Praeger.

Leete, E. (1991). The stigmatized patient. In P. J. Fink & A. Tasman (Eds.), *Stigma and mental illness* (pp. 17–25). Washington, DC: American Psychiatric Association Press.

Liachowitz, C. H. (1988). *Disability as a social construct: Legislative roots.* Philadelphia: University of Pennsylvania.

Livneh, H. (1982). On the origins of negative attitudes toward people with disabilities. *Rehabilitation Literature, 43*, 338–347.

Livneh, H. (1983). Application of smallest space analysis to the study of attitudes toward disabled persons. *Professional Psychology: Research and Practice, 14*, 406–413.

Livneh, H. (1991). On the origins of negative attitudes toward people with disabilities. In R. P. Marinelli & A. E. Dell Orto (Eds.), *The psychological and social impact of disability* (3rd ed., pp. 181–196). New York: Springer.

Longmore, P. K. (1985a). A note on the language and social identity of disabled people. *American Behavioral Scientist, 28*, 419–423.

Longmore, P. K. (1985b). Screening stereotypes. *Social Policy, 16*, 31–37.

Longmore, P. K. (2003). *Why I burned my book and other essays on disability.* Philadelphia: Temple University.

Mackelprang, R., & Salsgiver, R. (1999). *Disability: A diversity model approach in human service practice.* Pacific Grove, CA: Brooks/Cole.

McCarthy, H. (1982). Partnership as a method of enhancing attitudes and behaviors toward employment of disabled individuals. *Rehabilitation Counseling Bulletin, 26*, 119–132.

Mee, C. L. (1999). *A nearly normal life.* Boston: Little, Brown.

Michalko, R. (2002). *The difference disability makes.* Philadelphia: Temple University.

Mirzoeff, N. (1997). Blindness and art. In L. J. Davis (Ed.), *The disability studies reader* (pp. 382–398). New York: Routledge.

Moore, C. L., & Feist-Price, S. (1999). Societal attitudes and the civil rights of persons with disabilities. *Journal of Applied Rehabilitation Counseling, 30,* 19–24.

Morris, J. (1991). *Pride against prejudice: Transforming attitudes towards disability.* London: The Women's Press.

Murphy, R. (1987). *The body silent.* London: Dent.

National Disability Statistics and Policy Forum. (1995). *Working with disability: Employment statistics and policy.* Washington, DC: U.S. Government Printing Office. (ERIC Document Reproduction Service No. 1.21153:2)

National Organization on Disability (June 24, 2004). Press Release. "Landmark survey finds pervasive disadvantages." Washington, DC: NOD.

National Public Radio (May 4, 1998). The disability history project. "Inventing the Poster Child."

National Public Radio (May 4, 1998). The disability history project. "Tomorrow's Children."

Obermann, C. E. (1965). *A history of vocational rehabilitation in America.* Minneapolis, MN: T. S. Dennison.

Olkin, R. (1999). *What psychotherapists should know about disability.* New York: Guilford.

Pelka, F. (1997). *The ABC-CLIO companion to the disability rights movement.* Santa Barbara, CA: ABC-CLIO.

Perlman, L. B., & Kirk, F. S. (1991). Key disability and rehabilitation legislation. *Journal of Applied Rehabilitation Counseling, 22,* 21–27.

Pfeiffer, D. (2005). Changing the future of disability: The disability discrimination model. In G. E. May & M.S. Raske (Eds.), *Ending disability discrimination: Strategies for social workers* (pp. 82–98). Boston, MA: Allyn & Bacon.

Phillips, M. J. (1992). "Try harder": The experience of disability and the dilemma of normalization. In P. M. Ferguson, D. L. Ferguson, & S. J. Taylor (Eds.), *Interpreting disability: A qualitative reader* (pp. 213–227). New York: Columbia University.

Proctor, R. (1988). *Racial hygiene: Medicine under the Nazis.* Cambridge, MA: Harvard University.

Public Broadcasting Service. (1999). *Paralyzing fear: The story of polio in America.* Available: www.shoppbs.org. Retrieved August 2, 2007.

Putnam, M., Greenen, S., Powers, L., Saxton, M., Finney, S., & Dautel, P. (2003). Health and wellness: People with disabilities discuss barriers and facilitators to well-being. *Journal of Rehabilitation, 69,* 37–45.

Roessler, R., & Bolton, B. (1978). *Psychosocial adjustment to disability.* Baltimore: University Park Press.

Rossides, D. W. (1990). *Social stratification: The American class system in comparative perspective* (2nd ed.). Englewood Cliffs, NJ: Prentice Hall.

Safilios-Rothschild, C. (1970). *The sociology and social psychology of disability and rehabilitation.* New York: Random House.

Safran, S. P. (1998). The first century of disability portrayal in film: An analysis of the literature. *The Journal of Special Education, 31,* 467–479.

Schmelkin, L. P. (1988). Multidimensional perspectives in the perception of disabilities. In H. E. Yuker (Ed.), *Attitudes toward persons with disabilities* (pp. 127–137). New York: Springer.

Schmitt, S. M. (1999). Criminalizing the mentally ill. *Counseling Today, 1,* 26–27.

Schur, E. M. (1971). *Labeling deviant behavior: Its sociological implications.* New York: Harper and Row.

Schur, E. M. (1979). *Interpreting deviance.* New York: Harper and Row.

Scott, R. A. (1969). *The making of blind men: A study of adult socialization.* New York: Sage.

Shapiro, J. P. (1993). *No pity: People with disabilities forging a new civil rights movement.* New York: Times Book.

Shapiro, J. P. (1997). Assisted suicide devalues the lives of disabled people (pp. 170–178). In B. Stalcup (Ed.), *The disabled.* San Diego, CA: Greenhaven.

Shell, M. (2005). *Polio and its aftermath: The paralysis of culture.* Cambridge, MA: Harvard University.

Shilts, R. (1987). *And the band played on: Politics, people, and the AIDS epidemic.* New York: St. Martin's.

Sidey, H. (1997, April 28). A monumental mistake. *Time, 149*(17), 4.

Siller, J. (1976). Attitudes toward disability. In H. Rusalem & D. Malikin (Eds.), *Contemporary vocational rehabilitation* (pp. 67–79). New York: New York University.

Silvers, A. (1996). (In)equality, (ab)normality, and the Americans with Disabilities Act. *Journal of Medicine and Philosophy, 21,* 209–224.

Sobsey, D. (1994). *Violence and abuse in the lives of people with disabilities: The end of silent acceptance.* Baltimore: Brookes.

Sobsey, D., & Mansell, S. (1993). The prevention of sexual abuse of people with developmental disabilities. In M. Nagler (Ed.), *Perspectives on disability* (2nd ed., pp. 283–292). Palo Alto, CA: Health Markets Research.

Stefan, S. (2001). *Unequal rights: Discrimination against people with mental disabilities and the Americans with Disabilities Act.* Washington, DC: American Psychological Association.

Strohmer, D. C., Grand, S. A., & Purcell, M. J. (1984). Attitudes toward persons with a disability: An examination of demographic factors, social context, and specific disability. *Rehabilitation Psychology, 29,* 131–145.

Tayman, J. (2006). *The colony: The harrowing true story of the exiles of Molokai.* New York: Scribner.

Thomson, R. G. (1997). Feminist theory, the body, and the disabled figure. In L. J. Davis (Ed.), *The disability studies reader* (pp. 279–292). New York: Routledge.

Tucker, B. P., & Goldstein, B. A. (1991). *Legal rights of persons with disabilities: An analysis of federal law.* (ERIC Document Reproduction Service No. ED 332-453.) Horsham, PA: PRP Publications.

Turner, C. S. V., & Louis, K. S. (1996). Society's response to differences: A sociological perspective. *Remedial and Special Education, 17,* 134–141.

Tuttle, D. W. (1984). *Self-esteem and adjusting with blindness: The process of responding to life's demands.* Springfield, IL: Charles C. Thomas.

U.S. General Accounting Office. (1990). *Persons with disabilities: Reports on costs of accommodations* (Human Resources Division Report GAO/HRD 90-44BR). Gaithersburg, MD: Author.

Ulicny, G. R., White, G. W., Bradford, B., & Matthews, R. M. (1990). Consumer exploitation attendants: How often does it happen and can anything be done about it? *Rehabilitation Counseling Bulletin, 33,* 240–246.

Van De Veer, D., & Regan, T. (Eds.). (1987). *Health care ethics: An introduction.* Philadelphia: Temple University.

Vander Kolk, C. J. (1976a). Physiological measures as a means of accessing reactions to the disabled. *New Outlook for the Blind, 70,* 101–103.

Vander Kolk, C. J. (1976b). Physiological and self-reported reactions to the disabled and deviant. *Rehabilitation Psychology, 23,* 77–83.

Vash, C. L. (1981). *The psychology of disability.* New York: Springer.

Waxman, B. F. (1991). Hatred: The unacknowledged dimension in violence against disabled people. *Sexuality and Disability, 9,* 185–199.

Weisgerber, R. A. (1991). *Quality of life for persons with disabilities: Skill development and transitions across life stages.* Gaithersburg, MD: Aspen Publishers, Inc.

Wilson, D. J. (1990). *Living with polio: The epidemic and its survivors.* Chicago, IL: University of Chicago.

Wright, B. A. (1988). Attitudes and the fundamental negative bias: Conditions and corrections. In H. E. Yuker (Ed.), *Attitudes toward persons with disabilities* (pp. 3–21). New York: Springer.

Yuker, H. E. (Ed.), (1988). *Attitudes toward persons with disabilities.* New York: Springer.

Zola, I. K. (1982). *Missing pieces: A chronicle of living with a disability.* Philadelphia: Temple University.

Zola, I. K. (1985). Depictions of disability-metaphor, message, and media: A research and political agenda. *The Social Science Journal, 22,* 5–17.

Zola, I. K. (1991). Communication barriers between "the able-bodied" and "the handicapped." In R. P. Marinelli & A. E. Dell Orto (Eds.), *The psychological and social impact of disability* (pp. 157–164). New York: Springer.

Zola, I. K. (1992). "Any distinguishing features?" The portrayal of disability in the crime-mystery genre. In P. M. Ferguson, D. L. Ferguson, & S. J. Taylor (Eds.), *Interpreting disability: A qualitative reader* (pp. 233–250). New York: Columbia University.

Sources of Prejudice and Discrimination, Part 2

- What does the statement "Disability is a normative experience" mean?
- How are disability costs calculated?
- How did the Nazi regime justify the murder of Germans with disabilities?
- How can allowing PWDs their civil rights and full social integration result in a reduction of PWODs' fear of disablement?
- What are four societal responses to disability?
- Why do PWDs view charities and telethons as another form of victimization?
- What is justice?

Moral Accountability
for the Cause of the Disability

> **In this section, look for—**
>
> - The hierarchy of stigma based on the perceived cause of the disability
> - The relationship between primitive retributivism and the stigma directed toward PWDs
> - How the preventive medicine movement may contribute to blaming the PWD for his or her disability
> - The ethical issue of individuals who cause their own disabilities
> - The need to blame the PWDs for their disabilities

The perceived cause of the disability can influence the degree of stigma directed toward the individual (Auge & Herzlich, 1995; Bordieri & Drehmer, 1988; Couser, 1997; Kravetz, Katz, & Albez, 1994; Safilios-Rothschild, 1982; Shurka & Katz, 1976; Thorn, Hershenson, & Romney, 1994). Generally, disabilities acquired in "noble" and honorable endeavors such as combat injuries or industrial accidents are the least stigmatizing. Defending the nation and working are considered to be both noble and honorable. Higgins (1992) described the *way* in which American government "assist(s) most generously those who become disabled in the defense of the country, disabled veterans . . . . Disabled veterans have the strongest claim on our disability dollars" (p. 213). Other disability policy analysts (Berkowitz, 1987; Tanenbaum, 1986; Yelin, 1989) have demonstrated that veterans receive more disability benefits than civilians with the same disabilities. Berkowitz (1987) stated that veterans are "entitled to more generous benefits and their programs are older and better established than civilian programs" (p. 169). Indeed, the only candidate with a known physical disability who ran for the presidency of the United States (other than Franklin Roosevelt) was Robert Dole in 1996. Dole's disability was the result of wounds received in World War II. It should be noted that in 1962 Congress broadened the veterans programs to include those who served in peacetime. Moreover, the *lack* of stigma ascribed to the onset of the disability (and not the disability itself) often translates into more money and other benefits.

Those with congenital disabilities are stigmatized to a greater degree, and those with acquired disabilities are often perceived by others to be personally and morally responsible for the onset of the disability, to have somehow "caused" the disability or, at minimum, to have not taken steps to prevent the disability. And, in those cases in which the individual actually does possess a self-inflicted disability (such as a spinal cord injury incurred while riding a motorcycle without wearing a helmet and after drinking alcohol), the stigma is great. Much of the stigma directed toward individuals with mental illness is a result of society ascribing the responsibility for the illness to the individual's lifestyle choices or lack of character and self-control (Bordieri & Drehmer, 1988; Marantz, 1990; Murphy, 1998; Sontag, 1978; Thorn et al., 1994; Weiner, Perry, & Magnusson, 1988; Wilder, 1987; Zola, 1983). Often, society tends to hold people responsible for their emotional problems but not for their physical problems. Contrast society's perception of individuals with schizophrenia with the perception of individuals with diabetes. In the case of schizophrenia, the individual is held responsible for the illness, but in the case of diabetes, the individual is not held responsible and therefore is not stigmatized to the same degree. (In many cases, failure to comply with medical regimens such as taking medications may result, in part, from the individual's unconscious internalization of society's judgment that he or she should be able to control and manage the illness with simple willpower and strength of character.) Walster (1966) suggested that the human tendency to blame the individual for his or her disability is an attempt to protect ourselves from existential angst or acknowledging the randomness of disability. If we can believe the individual *caused* his or her disability, then we can comfort ourselves by saying, "We'll never cause ourselves a disability."

Jenny Morris (1991), who acquired paraplegia after jumping over a fence to save a small child, was stunned to learn that the hospital nurses thought that she had acquired her disability as a result of a suicide attempt. It took Morris a bit of time to understand that the nurses, by jumping to the conclusion of a suicide attempt, were trying to distance themselves from Morris's disability. The nurses could say to themselves: "I would never attempt suicide. So, I'm safe from acquiring a disability."

> I didn't fully realize it then, but [after my accident], I became someone whose physical condition others feared—too awful for many people to contemplate. They therefore used a variety of defense mechanisms to prevent themselves from having to identify with my reality. These defense mechanisms all took the form of people separating themselves off from me. Sometimes this was achieved by believing that I had somehow brought my paralysis upon myself—as when the hospital nurses assumed that I had attempted suicide and thrown myself off the wall. Often it was the denial of the pain I was experiencing—it's very difficult to acknowledge another's physical pain, especially when there is nothing you can do about it. (p. 3)

Wendell (1997) describes the way in which we blame others for their pain to distance ourselves from the possibility that we ourselves might experience long-term pain.

If someone tells me she is in pain, she reminds me of the existence of pain, the imperfection and fragility of the body, the possibility of my own, the *inevitability* of it. The less willing I am to accept all these, the less I want to know about her pain. If I cannot avoid it in her presence, I will avoid her. I may even blame her for it. I may tell myself that she *could have* avoided it, in order to go on believing that I *can* avoid it. I want to believe that I am not like her: I cling to the differences. (p. 268)

Read the letter from "Smoking Mad" (Exhibit 4–1). Notice that Ann Landers agrees with the writer.

Attitudes about the perceived cause or blame for the disability (and not only the disability itself) result in reduced opportunities for PWDs. Researchers (Bordieri & Drehmer, 1988; Thorn et al., 1994; Weiner et al., 1988) proved that individuals who were judged to be responsible for their disability were offered not as many job interviews or as many actual jobs or offers of assistance as were those individuals who were not held accountable

Exhibit 4–1

> **Dear Ann Landers:** Some months ago, I was diagnosed with a disease that my doctor said would be aggravated by cigarettes, even though the disease itself was not caused by smoking. For me, this was a no-brainer—give up smoking.
>
> Several of my co-workers smoke, but not at work, because it is not allowed in our building. One of these co-workers recently had surgery to replace veins in his legs. He was advised by his surgeon to quit smoking, but continues to puff away. Another co-worker had a quadruple bypass, but continues to smoke a pack-and-a-half a day. A third co-worker developed a cancerous growth on his tongue, but continues to smoke like a chimney.
>
> These people share my group insurance, and frankly, I am mad as hell. As my premiums go up, I am tempted to tell the bookkeeper to attach my increases to the bills of the smokers. It is not fair that we should all be penalized by people too selfish to get their own insurance, who instead insist on raising our premiums by continuing with their destructive behavior.
>
> I know there is probably no solution other than for insurance companies to drop the policies of people who continue to smoke against medical advice, but I really needed to vent my anger in a public way.
> —Smoking Mad in Minnesota
>
> **Dear Mad in Minn.:** You came to the right place. I am pleased to give you space in which to vent your anger. We now know that smoking is more than just a filthy habit, it is an addiction. I have only one close friend who smokes, and she has the decency to excuse herself when she feels the need to light up. Need I say, I appreciate it.

for their disability. These well-designed experiments proved that perceived cause of disability is a factor in the degree of prejudice and discrimination the PWD experiences (Fig. 4–1).

PWODs have always been more interested in the cause of an individual's disability than the impact of the disability on the individual's life. This is seen in children's first question to strangers with disabilities: "How did you get this way?" Adults usually do not verbalize the question of "How did you get this way?" but they, like children, are more interested in the cause and/or onset of the disability than in the management of the disability.

Moral accountability for the onset of the disability often translates into responsibility or blame. When reading the history of the treatment of PWDs, it is clear that many, if not most, societies considered disabilities to be caused by some sort of sin or wrongdoing by the person with the disability or his or her parents or ancestors. Blaming the individual for his or her disability is an erroneous belief that has persisted for centuries in all types of societies. In this day and age of science, connecting disability with sin or ill fortune seems absurd. Today, for many disabilities, both the etiology (cause) and the pathogenesis (source) are known. Moreover, many disabilities are known to be hereditary or, at minimum, to be more common among first-degree relatives, and, therefore, it would be foolish to blame the individual for his or her disability. For example, many mental illnesses are hereditary, and often several individuals within the same family have the same mental illness. In spite of this, the desire to establish responsibility for the disability appears to be strong.

The natural result of holding *someone* responsible for the disability is to hold that same person totally responsible for the treatment and care of the disability. The rationale is, whoever created the situation should also

Figure 4–1 Stigma associated with type of onset.

deal with it. Therefore, the individual and his or her family should manage the disability and not subject others (who are totally blameless) to requests for assistance, accommodations, resources, or rights. Whether the source of the disability is ascribed to ill fortune, the anger of the gods, or bad luck, the disability is thought to be an individual responsibility.

Bickenbach (1993) wrote a powerful description of two strongly held ideas about disability: (1) the individual (or his or her parents or ancestors) is responsible for the disability, and (2) because the individual with a disability is evil, it is "our duty" to isolate that individual. He added, "In a nutshell, primitive retributivism is the view that people who are manifestly defective are living out a just punishment for sins, vices, or other moral faults, known or unknown, that have been inflicted by some powerful and moral force. At most, in this view, these manifest sinners are entitled to our pity; but it is our duty to dissociate ourselves from them" (p. 189). In contrast, one of the participants in the National Public Radio Disability History Project explained, "It simply isn't useful [for a PWD] to be the symbol of a theological puzzle" (NPR, 1998).

Bickenbach's short summary also shows how beliefs about etiology often lead to treatment strategies. Note that we are speaking about *beliefs* about etiology and not about *known* etiology. In Biblical times, outward signs such as blindness or a mobility impairment were thought to be signs of inward evil (Bickenbach, 1993). Today in some cultures the idea that disabilities are somehow "God-ordained" still persists, and attempts to treat the disability or reduce its effects are resisted because it is believed that if God ordains the disability, God would not approve of any human attempt to alleviate it.

Also note that this primitive retributivism limits the responsibilities of society and any resulting guilt for not allowing PWDs their civil rights and for isolating them. Bickenbach's (1993) clear-cut statement helps us to see how convenient and guilt-absolving it is to blame the individual for his or her disability. One man clearly understood the stigma directed toward the perceived morality of the disability when he stated, "I wish I had cancer instead of AIDS. I could stand the treatment and the pain and my hair falling out. And I'm going to die anyway. But at least, my family wouldn't reject me. I could go home" (D. Morris, 1998, p. 212). PWDs whose disabilities are visible are often approached by strangers with this question: "What did you do to yourself?"

Today, we can see the same dynamic of searching for the cause and the blame for the disability. Mothers who have babies with congenital disabilities are often asked about their pregnancies and what they did and what they did not do. Most mothers of babies without disabilities are not asked about their pregnancies. Autism in children was thought to be caused by parents who were remote and cold, usually the mother. Now, autism is known to be a genetic biological disorder (Films for the Humanities and Sciences, 1999). Individuals with psychiatric disabilities, such as mental illness, are often perceived to be weak, to be lacking in self-control and character, and to have been unable to do something that would have prevented the onset of mental illness. A mother of an adult daughter with mental illness told of her reaction for being blamed for her daughter's disability:

> The psychiatrist says, "There is this thing called 'expressed emotion.'" Here I am sobbing my heart out, right? She [the daughter] is going into the hospital and she is not safe and he said, "And you need to stop doing this expressed emotion or you are going to alienate this kid." And I looked at him and I said, "Don't you go there!" I said, "Don't you dare blame this victim because I won't have it!" How dare he watch me sob my heart out about this kid that isn't safe and say, "You need to stop doing expressed emotion." (Karp, 2001, p. 168)

In contrast, no one with diabetes is accused of being weak and lacking in self-control. Yet, in both diabetes and mental illness, there is an organ of the body that is malfunctioning.

A noted disability scholar stated, "Indeed, while obesity is not generally considered to be a disability, it is a condition which is highly stigmatized since the notion exists that obese people must be, to some extent, weak and irresponsible people" (Safilios-Rothschild, 1982, p. 43). Today, people who are obese still experience a great deal of prejudice and stigma, in spite of the fact that research has shown (since 1982, when Safilios-Rothschild made the aforementioned statement) that body shape and size are primarily a result of hereditary and genetic factors. Yet simply because people *believe* that individuals are responsible for their condition, they stigmatize them.

Susan Sontag (1978) clearly outlined how society tends to transform illness into moral character in her two books that deal with cancer, tuberculosis, and AIDS. Sontag wrote: "Psychological theories of illness are a powerful means of placing the blame upon the ill. Patients who are instructed that they have, unwittingly, caused their disease are also being made to feel that they have deserved it" (pp. 55–56).

Accountability for the cause of the disability is influenced by social, cultural, and political factors. In individualistic, capitalistic societies, such as the United States, lack of disability is viewed "as a form of individual emancipation" (Cockerham, 1998, p. 95). Some PWDs have felt that PWODs consider it un-American to have a disability. Robert Murphy (1987), an anthropology professor, explained: "Most handicapped people, myself included, sense that others resent them for this reason: we are subverters of an American Ideal" (p. 143). Zola (1991) echoed this idea: "The United States is a nation built on the premise that there is no mountain which cannot be leveled, no river untamed, no force of nature unharnessed. It should thus be no great surprise we similarly claim that there is no disease that cannot be cured" (p. 159). Marks (1999) adds, "Healthcare is pursued with such moral zeal that ill health and disability become difficult to integrate within conceptions of community and humanity" (p. 175).

Lack of disability is also viewed as a form of efficiency, relieving society of the responsibility and expense of rehabilitation. Read the account (Miller, 1988) in Chapter 8 of the mother who gave birth to a baby with a congenital disability. She felt that she had "failed . . . society." Cockerham (1998) explained the relationship between differing political systems and accountability for both the cause and treatment of disability:

> Marxist scholars like Howard Waitzkin and Vicente Navarro claim that an emphasis on individual responsibility for leading a healthy life excuses the larger society from direct accountability in health matters. Waitzkin (1991) maintains that capitalism puts the burden of being healthy squarely on the individual, rather than seeking collective solutions to health problems. The emphasis in capitalist societies on healthy lifestyles is seen as an effort to displace the responsibility for health from the social system and its health sector down to individuals. (p. 99)

The preventive medicine movement may actually contribute to the societal response of holding individuals responsible for their illnesses and disabilities (Marantz, 1990). Because it can be empirically shown that preventive measures can *reduce* the incidence of illness and disability, there are many individuals who would then (erroneously) conclude that these preventive measures can *eliminate* all illness and disability (Wang, 1993). For example, frequent routine medical examinations can (and do) detect asymptomatic (without symptoms) chronic health conditions and disabilities or the predisposing factors of disabilities. If left undiagnosed and untreated, these disabilities and chronic health conditions are exacerbated and often result in secondary conditions, further complications, and pervasive functional impairments. Conditions such as diabetes and high blood pressure do not manifest any symptoms, and the individual has no way of knowing that he or she has the condition other than undergoing medical examination. Diabetes, if left untreated, can lead to blindness and lower limb amputation. High blood pressure is an antecedent to strokes. Therefore, submitting to routine medical examinations is both sensible and cost-effective. Should society hold individuals who refuse to undergo medical examinations responsible for their disabilities?

Similarly, the emergence of such concepts as "emotional resilience" also can lead to the erroneous conclusion that individuals with mental illness or other psychiatric disabilities could have prevented their disability. Psychologists (Hayes, Barlow, & Nelson-Gray, 1999) have outlined the role of prevention (or prophylaxis) in avoiding the onset of psychiatric disabilities: "[Prevention programs] are designed to create competencies and coping skills that are prophylactic" (p. 76). In spite of the fact that proponents of preventive medicine and emotional resilience acknowledge the significant role of prevention, they also understand that most individuals are not to blame for their disabilities and illnesses (Marantz, 1990).

What about those cases in which the individual is truly responsible for the onset of the disability? In rehabilitation counseling, the term "thrills and chills" is used to describe individuals who have a desire or need for danger, intense experiences, novelty, and stimulation. Often, these are the people who enjoy outdoor physical activities and engage in such sports as hang gliding, sky diving, mountain climbing, and other dangerous and exhilarating activities. In the first chapter, we learned about traumatic brain injury (TBI) and learned that, overwhelmingly, the greatest proportion of people with TBI are males between the ages of 19 and 24. TBI, more than any other type of disability, has an onset associated with the use of alcohol, and the time of day of the onset is most often between midnight and 5:00 A.M. Individuals with TBI are often described as "thrills and chills" types. Another example of a disability whose onset is well known is fetal alcohol syndrome (FAS). FAS has resulted in many babies' being born with learning disabilities, hearing losses, and other congenital deficits. Women are now advised to totally abstain from alcohol throughout the course of their pregnancies.

What about thrill-seekers who knowingly disregard safety procedures? What about pregnant women who choose to drink alcohol? What about people who refuse to wear helmets or seatbelts? Are these not lifestyle choices and therefore personal, private, and privileged? What about the use of alcohol during dangerous activities? These are extreme and clear-cut examples, and certainly most people have agreed that these types of choices should be actively discouraged or even declared illegal simply because (1) the evidence clearly points to a cause-and-effect relationship between these choices and injury and death, and (2) the individual who chooses to be "irresponsible" may also harm others in addition to himself or herself. So, the notions of "risk" and "error" are straightforward in the aforementioned cases.

Nonetheless, two other significant circumstances in which risk and error are clearly present merit attention. First, almost everybody engages in some types of behaviors, or, more accurately, does not engage in other behaviors, that put them at risk for a disability, injury, or illness. And, because we choose to do or not to do certain things, we raise insurance premiums, consume scarce medical resources, and drive up the costs of disability (Ann Landers, October 6, 1999). Indeed, the costs of most disabilities are paid out of the public purse (insurance or taxes). Everybody, or almost everybody, believes in wisdom, moderation, health maintenance, and prevention of risk (Fox, 1997; Sherrill, 1997). In spite of this, we still smoke, overeat, and refuse to exercise or floss our teeth. The question is this: At what point are individuals allowed to make choices that have a high probability of ending in disability, injury, or illness? Are individuals expected to change their entire personality and lifestyle simply to avoid illness, injury, or disability?

The second situation that involves the principle of responsibility for the onset of disability is the result of medical technology. Should prospective parents who know that their unborn child will have a disability allow the baby to be born? The availability of technology has expanded the definition of moral accountability for disability. What if the question was "Should prospective parents who know that their unborn child will have *severe* and *multiple* disabilities choose to continue the pregnancy and deliver the baby?" (Hubbard, 1997). Who decides what "severe" and "multiple" are? Will the parents bear all the costs of caring for the baby, or will insurance and government dollars be used ("Scholar Under Fire," 1999)? If the parents choose to have the baby, will the child always be considered, by society, as an avoidable mistake? (Note: Technology is a two-edged sword for PWDs. On the one hand, assistive technology provides independence and a higher quality of life, while on the other hand, technology may be used to end the lives of PWDs.)

Medical technology has given society the ability to eliminate entire groups of disabilities by preventing the birth of all babies with certain types of disabilities. Mundy (2003) explained:

> What I wonder is whether they'll be able to eliminate the deaf gene. Maybe they'll be able to pluck out the deaf gene. Maybe there will be no more deaf people. It isn't out of the question. Members of another disabled group were taken by surprise when the gene that causes their condition was discovered. Now, a child with achondroplasia, or disproportionately short arms and legs—also known as dwarfism—can be identified in utero. And, if the parents don't want a child with dwarfism, the fetus can be aborted. The community of "little people" which has its own association, its own Website and a strong tradition in Hollywood, and a powerful fellowship, has been left contemplating its children destroyed, its numbers dwindling, its existing members consigned to a narrowing life of freakishness and isolation. Such a fate could—it's possible—befall the deaf. (p. 84)

In Chapter 3, we learned of the Dutch government–sponsored euthanasia programs of newborn infants with a disability. Fenigsen (1997) quoted a Dutch professor's assessment of one of the long-term results of infant euthanasia: "The killing of handicapped children . . . denotes the end, or the beginning of the end, of care for the mentally retarded" (p. 163). In other words, the government will address the "issue" of mental retardation by eliminating people with this disability, rather than by providing services. Dutch parents of a child with a disability have reported being told, "What? Is that child still alive?" "How can one love such a child?" "Nowadays such a being need not be born at all," and "Such a thing should have been given an injection."

Another framework in which to conceptualize disability considers the cause for the disability and the responsibility for dealing with the disability in four forms:

1. The individual is responsible for the onset of the disability, and the individual is also responsible for dealing with the disability.

2. The individual is responsible for the onset of the disability; however, the individual is not responsible for dealing with the disability.

3. The individual is responsible neither for the onset of the disability nor for dealing with the disability.

4. The individual is not responsible for the onset of the disability, but the individual is responsible for dealing with the disability.

It can readily be seen that the second statement reflects the Biomedical Model of disability in that the individual is held responsible for somehow causing the disability (or, at minimum, not preventing the disability), but the "cure" or amelioration of disability is best left to trained medical professionals. Obviously, most PWDs consider the last statement to most closely identify their conceptualization of responsibility for the cause of and the response to the disability.

These are difficult, and perhaps unanswerable, questions. Nonetheless, it can be stated that there is a human tendency to want to establish fault, blame, accountability, or responsibility for the onset of the disability. Even with our scientific knowledge and technical expertise, we fall prey to the same questions with which people thousands of years ago grappled. Perhaps we confuse "how" with "why." We don't always know "how," but we often do. Science and medicine can answer many questions of "how." Science does not answer questions of "why." The "why" of disability is a question that religion/spirituality/philosophy attempts to answer.

Moral Accountability for the Management of the Disability

> ### In this section, look for—
>
> - The explanation of the statement "Disability is a normative experience"
> - The results when PWDs do not "follow the rules"
> - The rules of having a disability
> - Who is a Tiny Tim, according to the Disability Rights Movement?

Disability is a normative experience (Auge & Herzlich, 1995). This means that there are rules and expectations of PWDs; certain behaviors and attitudes are obligatory, and rule breakers experience severe consequences

(Bishop, 1980; Crewe, 1980; Druss, 1995; Leinhardt & Pallay, 1982). Indeed, PWDs who choose not to comply experience the consequences of greater prejudice and discrimination and, in extreme cases, are abandoned medically and socially. However, those who learn the rules, live the rules, and believe in the rules are rewarded (Lehr & Brinckerhoff, 1996). As with most rules, it is the people in power who make the rules and, in this case, often it is people without disabilities who make the rules about managing the disability. These rules, in large part, are a result of the lingering effects of the Biomedical Model and society's fear of acquiring a disability.

Zola (1991) observed that PWDs who are "successful mainstream adapters" (p. 160) are most often accepted by PWODs as spokespersons for all PWDs. Zola stated, "Moreover, almost every 'successful' handicapped [*sic*] person, as well as every 'success' I have met (including myself), usually regards, as a key element, the self-conception: 'I never think of myself as handicapped [*sic*]'" (p. 160).

Indeed, many in the Disability Rights Movement use the derisive term "Tiny Tim" to describe a PWD "who is eager to please the nondisabled people in his or her life, or mainstream society in general, by ignoring slights to his or her rights and dignity and acting the part of the cheerful 'handicapped' person" (Pelka, 1997, p. 305). Evident in this statement are (1) an understanding that to have a disability is a normative role—the words "acting the part" are used, (2) the rules are made by those in power (PWODs) and not by those who have the knowledge and experience of the disability (PWDs), and (3) one of the most important rules is to be cheerful and another rule is to ignore prejudice and discrimination. The term "Tiny Tim" is derived from Charles Dickens's character who is sweet and cheerful. To be seen as a Tiny Tim by PWDs is to be seen as someone who, to make life easier for himself or herself, does not advance the cause of PWDs.

Society has set the standards of evaluation of dealing with disability without much knowledge or experience about the disability. It is easy to see how lack of capability, loss of function, or side effects of medication can be erroneously viewed by others as breaking the rules of managing disability.

What are the rules? PWDs are to face their disability with as much courage and optimism as possible. Self-mastery, emotional robustness, and resilience are all required (Fowler & Wadsworth, 1991). The individual should demonstrate the motivation and desire to recover or, at minimum, to regain as many capabilities as possible. Active and independent management of the disability are expected, rather than giving the impression of a passive victim. Individuals who adhere to medical regimens, who appear to "adapt" well to the situation, and who request only those necessary accommodations and assistance are subjected to less stigma than those individuals who appear to not manage their disability well.

Even children with disabilities know and understand the "rules." Mee (1999), in his memoir that tells of contracting polio in the 1950s, stated, "Every boy and girl at Sherman Hospital knew this was what was expected, this was the story and the character that needed to be enacted. These were not lessons that had to be learned over a long life; they were so deeply, pervasively embedded in the culture that they were instantly available to any kid in a hospital bed" (p. 88).

PWDs are also expected to make others comfortable with their disabilities. The unwritten rules mandate that the person with a disability initiate the subject of his or her disability; disclose the etiology and any limitations; and finally and most important, communicate to others that he or she is comfortable with the disability. All of the information must be delivered at the beginning of each new interaction and must be delivered in a fun, upbeat, and semi-indirect manner (Belgrave, 1984; Belgrave & Mills, 1981). Robert Murphy, an anthropology professor, had a spinal tumor that paralyzed him. He clearly understood that his disability required him to comfort PWODs:

> As the price for normal relations, PWDs must comfort others about their condition. They cannot show fear, sorrow, depression, sexuality, or anger, for this disturbs the able-bodied. The unsound of limb are permitted only to laugh. The rest of the emotions, including anger and the expression of hostility, must be bottled up, repressed, and allowed to simmer or be released in the backstage of the home . . . . As for the rest of the world, I must sustain their faith in their own immunity by looking resolutely cheery. Have a nice day! (Murphy, 1987, p. 108)

In May 1997 Mattel brought out a doll in a wheelchair who was intended to be a friend to the Barbie doll. The doll's name was "Share a Smile Becky." Parents of children with disabilities also understand the importance of these rules.

> Despite their need, the parents sense there are rules for this game of social integration. Most of the time they feel they should initiate contact, explaining the disability to newcomers and readily appreciating inclusion. Part of their consciousness is always censoring what they share lest they lose their "admission" to the ordinary world. They find an emotional closet in which to store their feelings. The closet is opened only with a few tested friends or in moments of reckless bravery. (Curry, 1995, p. 29)

Yet the PWD is compelled to maintain a balance between active management of the disability, including a highly developed knowledge about the disability, and passive submission to professional treatment plans and decisions. Thus, the rules for managing disability are somewhat contradictory. Some PWDs feel that there are only two roles open to them, either the "pathetic crip" or the "super crip" (Morris, 1991). Of course, each is an extreme and each is an opposite of the other. The "pathetic crip" role reinforces the power and privilege of PWODs, and the "super crip" role assures PWODs that having a disability is not that bad. Neither role allows the PWD to be an ordinary person.

Most of the time society expects PWDs to appear in control of both the disability and the emotional reaction to the disability (which, of course, includes the emotional reactions of PWODs to their disabilities). Occasionally, however, society expects and demands that PWDs relinquish their control, their status, and their roles to become compliant patients. At these times, the PWD's highly developed knowledge of the disability and accommodations is often viewed by professionals as irrelevant and unnecessary. Part of the responsibility (and skill) of the PWD includes the ability to determine when and where to show assertive independence and when and where to show passive compliance.

One of the most difficult disability ethical issues concerns individuals with mental illness who refuse to take medications to control the symptoms. Should "society" force these individuals to adhere to a medical regimen? If these individuals do not take their medications, they may hurt others, hurt themselves, lose their jobs, alienate their families, or become homeless. The scientific and medical advances of psychotropic drugs have led to new ethical issues. However, perhaps these new antipsychotic medications do not present a new ethical issue because before their advent, individuals with mental illness were physically restrained. Indeed, psychotropic drugs are often referred to as "chemical straitjackets." Nonetheless, "forced medication" and other types of coerced treatment do raise the issue of "society's" right to force an individual to manage his or her disability.

The Inferred Emotional Consequence of the Disability, or Difficult Does Not Mean Tragic

In this section, look for—

- Distressed identification
- The "requirements of mourning"
- The three factors of which PWODs are often unaware:
  1. The disability is a familiar part of the individual's self-concept
  2. The individual has learned how to deal with the disability
  3. The individual feels that there are valuable aspects of the disability

Often termed *distressed identification*, inferred emotional responses usually refer to the fact that most PWODs automatically assume that an individual's disability must be the worst thing that ever happened to the person, an unending, devastating personal tragedy (Thompson, 1982). Certainly, many disabilities are difficult to manage, and the world is not designed for PWDs, but nonetheless, difficult does not automatically translate to bad or tragic. Another way in which distressed identification is expressed is the belief that the PWD must be of no worth to himself or herself or anyone else. Early pioneers in the study and measurement of attitudes toward PWDs, Dembo, Leviton, and Wright (1956) asserted that PWODs expect PWDs to suffer because their suffering proves that their "losses" are valuable. Wright (1960) termed this need that PWDs have a "requirement for mourning" (p. 64). Livneh (1991) explained the reason why PWODs need or want PWDs to suffer: "The nondisabled [*sic*] individual has a need to safeguard his or her values, by wanting the disabled [*sic*] to suffer, and show the appropriate grieving, so as to protect one's own values of the importance of a functioning body. Any attempt on the disabled [*sic*] person's part to deny or reject the 'suffering role' is met with negative attitude" (p. 184).

According to these scholars, when the PWD does not appear to suffer, then PWODs devalue the PWD because he or she has violated one of the rules of having a disability: the person should suffer. In the National Public Radio Disability History Project (1998), a mother of a child with a disability told of the prenatal testing that showed that her baby would be born with a severe disability. The expectant parents began to seek out more information to make an informed choice. "When we started to talk with parents of children with disabilities, we learned it's not the end of the world. It made the doctor seem judgmental, that disability is possibly the worse thing that can happen to you. We learned that this is not so."

In research studies, PWDs have been asked, using several different types of questions: if the possibility of a "cure" for their disability existed, would they accept it? Most do not automatically say "yes." Some say "no," and others put conditions on their "yes" response. For example, many of the participants responded "yes" if the fantasy cure would not take too long or be too involved. Most people would be surprised to learn that many expectant parents who are deaf want their baby to be deaf. Rather than viewing deafness as a tragic flaw, they see deafness as part of their identity, and most parents want children who are like themselves. Many people who are deaf refuse cochlear implants, which would restore some hearing (Lane, 1993).

True–false questions on scales used to measure attitudes of PWODs toward PWDs measure the test-taker's degree of distressed identification of the disability experience. The following are examples of these types of questions: "Most disabled people do not feel that they are as good as other people"; "Most disabled people feel sorry for themselves"; "Disabled people are often grouchy"; "It must be pretty degrading to a blind person to depend so much on others"; "A blind person can never really be happy";

"Disabled people are more easily upset than other people"; and "Most disabled persons worry a great deal." These questions reveal the inferred emotional consequences of inferiority, grouchiness, feelings of degradation, unhappiness, and worry, none of which are positive and pleasant emotions.

In the video "My Body Is Not Who I Am," a woman with a leg amputation recounts her experience with a physician who, for years, prescribed the tranquilizer Valium for her. All the woman had to do was to telephone the physician's office and the Valium prescription would be renewed, in spite of the fact that the doctor did not see or talk to the woman for years. In the video, the woman explains her view of why the physician gave her tranquilizers. According to her, he simply thought of her disability as so overwhelmingly tragic that the only way in which she could deal with it was to be chemically tranquilized. (It is also of interest to note that it is the woman who decided to terminate the use of Valium and not the physician.)

Individuals who are not blind often conceptualize total blindness as continual darkness and blackness. Congenital, total blindness is relatively rare, but nonetheless, total blindness is not darkness. In much the same way, individuals who are not deaf conceptualize total deafness as complete silence. Not only is the experience of the disability misinterpreted (usually in an exaggerated, negative way), but also the individual's reaction to the disability is misunderstood. Rarely do people consider three important aspects of the disability experience: (1) the disability is a familiar part of the person's self-concept, (2) the individual has learned how to deal with the disability and often feels a sense of mastery and accomplishment, and (3) the individual often feels that he or she has gained invaluable insights and growth because of the disability experience (Wright, 1988).

Dr. Geerat Vermeij, an evolutionary biologist and professor at the University of California at Davis, has been blind since early childhood. He wrote a book entitled *Privileged Hands* (1997), and in the chapter "A Glow of Yellow" he describes the experience of blindness. Moreover, he discusses how sighted people view blindness:

> Yet opinion polls almost unanimously portray blindness as the most feared of human conditions. Sight is *perceived* as the means by which we gain the bulk of our information about one another and about our surroundings. Accordingly, educators have built curricula almost entirely on a foundation of visual learning. For this reason, blind people are widely regarded as being incapable of learning or interacting fully with others. Skeptics despair that blind people cannot see facial expressions, cannot witness a baby's first tentative steps, cannot respond to a smile, cannot see how others behave. Without such quintessentially visual experiences, the argument goes, the blind are denied a basic dimension of what it means to be human. Naively, [they] fear or loathe blindness. (p. 16)

A straightforward description of deaf–blindness is found in Koestler's (1976) description by an English businessman who became deaf and blind after a car accident. The man says that blindness is not total darkness and deafness is not total silence.

> What is it actually like to be deaf-blind? I can only tell you what it is like for me. What it's like for a person who has never seen or heard, I do not know. First, it is neither "dark" nor "silent." If you were to go out into a London fog—one of the thick yellow variety—then close your eyes, you would see what I see. A dull, flesh-colored opacity. So much for literal "darkness" . . .
>
> Nor is my world "silent" (most of us wish it were so!). You have all put a shell to your ear as children and "listened to the waves." You may at times—when dropping off to sleep perhaps—have "heard" the clang of a bell in your ear, a sound like the shunting of railway wagons, or a shrill whistle, or the wind moaning round the eaves on Christmas Eve. All these have I perpetually. They have become part of the background. Cracklings, squeaking, rumblings—what I hear is the machinery of my being working. The blood rushing through my veins, and little cracklings of nerves and muscles as they expand and contract. In short, my hearing has "turned inwards." (p. 452)

The individual who infers that another's disability is an unending tragedy communicates this attitude clearly. In the video "My Body Is Not Who I Am," a young man in a wheelchair who fell while rock climbing expresses resentment toward his father, who sat at his hospital bedside and said, "If only this had happened to me." The son feels resentment years after he has left the hospital, probably because the father was saying, "This was the worst thing that could have happened to you." Ed Roberts, founder of the Rolling Quads and the former director of the State of California Office of Rehabilitation, had a doctor who said it was too bad the high fever of the polio did not kill him.

Ascribing "unbearable" and "suffering" to PWDs could be fatal for those with severe and multiple disabilities. Harriet McBryde Johnson (2003), a disability rights lawyer, was born with a muscle-wasting disease. She describes herself: "At this stage of my life, I'm Karen Carpenter thin, flesh mostly vanished, a jumble of bones in a floppy bag of skin. . . . Now my right side is two deep canyons. To keep myself upright, I lean forward, rest my rib cage on my lap, plant my elbows beside my knees. Since my backbone found its own natural shape, I've been entirely comfortable in my skin. I am in the first generation to survive to such decrepitude. Because antibiotics were available, we didn't die from the childhood pneumonias that often come with weakened respiratory systems" (p. 52). Johnson writes about a visit to Princeton University in an article entitled "Should I Have Been Killed at Birth: The Case for My Life." The purpose of the visit is the debate a professor, Dr. Peter Singer, who advocates abortion or euthanasia of newborn babies with certain types of disabilities, including the type that Johnson has. In fact, Singer advocates the killing of anyone, at any age, with certain types of severe disabilities. Much of the debate focuses on Singer's attempts to force Johnson to say that her life is miserable because of the disability. Here is Johnson's reaction:

> It's right out of the telethon. I expected something more sophisticated from a professional thinker. I respond: "As a little girl playing on the beach, I was already aware that some people felt sorry for me, that I wasn't frolicking with the same level of frenzy as other children. This annoyed me, and still does." (p. 53)

At the end of the article, Johnson concluded:

> But like the protagonist in a classical drama, Singer has his flaw. It is his unexamined assumption that disabled [*sic*] people are inherently "worse off," that we "suffer," that we have lesser "prospects of a happy life." Because of this all-too-common prejudice, and his rare courage in taking it to its logical conclusion, catastrophe looms. (p. 54)

Other PWDs have reported that friends and family offered to assist them in committing suicide. Doctors have advised parents of newborns with severe and multiple disabilities to either withhold treatment or allow the baby to die. These are extreme examples of inferring negative consequences (to the point of being unbearable) to the disability. Other examples include the enabling of alcohol and substance abuse because others, including professional caregivers, consider the disability to be so devastating that the PWD "deserves something" to help him or her cope.

Another woman, in an attempt to inform PWODs, stated, "Putting on my artificial leg is no more distressing to me than you putting on your socks" (DeLoach & Greer, 1981). Naturally, it takes more effort and time to put on a prosthesis than socks, but the woman was trying to communicate that it is not an emotionally sad task. In much the same way, a father who contracted polio as a boy and wore leg braces from that time on was not viewed by his children as either tragic or an object of pity. Indeed, when this father died, the mortician asked the six adult children if they wanted the leg braces on their father. The children replied "yes," saying that to bury their father without his leg braces would be like burying their mother without her glasses. The braces were a part of their father and, furthermore, were not viewed as a symbol of sadness. In fact, the children reported that the braces were a reminder of happy times. Their father sat on the bed, morning and evening, to put the braces on and off, and each of the six children received a turn sitting on the bed talking one-on-one with their dad.

In Safran's (1998) comprehensive review of the portrayal of disability in film, he concluded that the movie-going public, from the advent of filmmaking, has considered disabilities to be dramatic and out of the ordinary. Such fascination with disabilities, and a little fear, has sold a lot of theater tickets, making disabilities profitable dramatic and commercial devices.

It is true that (1) most disabilities are difficult (including the prejudice and lack of accommodations) and (2) PWDs are more aware of assistive devices and coping mechanisms used by other PWDs simply because they themselves use them. PWDs know what to look for. This is a lot like someone who wears contact lenses being aware of others who wear contact lenses. Those who wear artificial limbs are usually aware of others who wear prostheses; those who wear hearing aids are more aware of others who use hearing aids, and so on. However, the use of these assistive devices/prostheses is not inherently sad and demeaning to PWDs. Of course, people who use these devices are often aware of the emotional reaction of others, and if they have the capability to conceal the use of these devices, the users usually will do so.

Helen Keller presents an example of someone who did use prosthetic devices but others rarely were aware of it. Helen Keller was a beautiful woman who cared about her appearance and carefully arranged her wardrobe, makeup, and hair. As a result of an infection during her infancy, Helen Keller was deaf and blind. Reporters who interviewed and photographed her throughout her long life often commented on her beautiful blue eyes. Not one reporter questioned if they were glass eyes. Both her eyes had been surgically removed because one of them "bulged" or protruded and Helen Keller wanted to be attractive. Up until the surgery, she allowed photographers to take pictures of her from only one side so as to hide the unattractive eye. But Helen Keller opted for artificial eyes when she began her lecture tours. This was a cosmetic, rather than therapeutic, surgery because the removal of her eyes did not make any difference, either good or bad, in her vision. It was a source of amusement to Helen Keller (and probably everybody who had some knowledge and understanding of blindness) that the media commented on her beautiful blue eyes, and no one ever entertained the idea that the beautiful eyes might be artificial.

Society's Emphasis on Health, Fitness, and Beauty

> ### In this section, look for—
> - The advantages of beauty
> - The elements of beauty: health, sexuality, symmetry, and physical fitness

We worship beauty. Beauty, health, and independence are all judged to be valued and attainable with the prerequisite effort. Goffman (1963), in his classic book *Stigma: Notes on the Management of Spoiled Identity*, included athletic ability in describing a "normal" male. As would be expected, the man's age, marital status, race, ethnicity, sexual orientation, religious affiliation, educational attainment, and employment status are described. Moreover, the last part of the description talks about the male's physical appearance and his athletic record.

> In an important sense, there is only one complete unblushing male in America: a young, married, white, urban, northern heterosexual Protestant father of college education, fully employed, of good complexion, weight, and height, and a recent record in sports. Any male who fails to qualify in any of these ways is likely to view himself—during moments at least—as unworthy, incomplete, and inferior. (p. 128)

It is true that individuals who are attractive and independent and appear healthy reap the rewards that society can provide. While both unattractive men and women are disadvantaged because of their lack of beauty, it is well known that it is unattractive women who experience the greatest disadvantage. It is accepted that attractive people earn more money over their lifetimes, receive more social benefits, and experience less rejection and isolation than those who are not good-looking.

It is debatable, however, that beauty and attractiveness can result from individual effort. To promulgate this idea is insulting to those who are not attractive because the message is (1) you're ugly, and (2) it's your fault. Also, because "a woman's beauty is seen as a reflection of a male partner's social status" (Asch & Fine, 1997, p. 244), a married woman who is judged to be unattractive is devalued in three ways: (1) you're ugly, (2) it's your fault, and (3) your husband/mate must be a loser to have settled for you. Furthermore, a woman with a disability is rarely considered to be a "trophy wife."

Most advantaged groups of people are unaware of their privileges, their automatic acceptance, and the advantages that their status brings, and beautiful people are no exception. Beautiful people probably assume that they will have a lifetime partner, perhaps have children, and have an extended family. From birth, beautiful people enjoy many advantages that unattractive people do not.

Mothers give more attention and care to (and are less likely to neglect or abuse) their beautiful babies. Beautiful people do not experience as much punishment and discipline throughout their lives as do unattractive people. Indeed, police, judges, and juries are more lenient toward attractive adults of both sexes. As children, beautiful people were the teacher's pet and the parents' favorite child, and other children realized that beautiful children had the automatic approval and protection of adults. Beautiful people know that job interviews will be fairly easy to obtain, and when they get a job, they will be paid higher starting salaries, and they will be promoted faster. They will not be assigned to the "back room"; they will deal with the customers/

clients/patrons. Beautiful people understand that they will not be requested to present as many credentials and achievements to prospective employers simply because beautiful people are automatically considered by others to be intelligent and confident. Beautiful people probably prefer to present themselves in person rather than sending a letter or résumé or speaking to someone over the telephone. Others are anxious to do favors for beautiful people.

Research at Harvard University found that people "brake for beauty." Experiments in which a beautiful woman and a plain woman had flat tires and were standing by the side of the road waiting for help found that far more people stopped for the beautiful woman (Etcoff, 1999).

Beautiful people know that people enjoy talking to them, prolonging the conversation, laughing, joking, and occasionally touching them. Even young babies prefer beautiful people! Beautiful people understand that others like to be associated with them—as colleagues, as friends, as family members, as classmates. For a beautiful person, belonging to a group is effortless and automatic. If the individual is attractive, others will seek him or her out and make sure that the beautiful person is included. Life is not that difficult when you're beautiful.

Beautiful people know that there are many people who are not attractive and beautiful, and they are also vaguely aware that unattractive people do not receive all the social and occupational rewards that they do. However, unattractive people know that beauty is skin deep, but they also know that skin deep is all that is necessary to ensure a life full of privileges.

Beauty is important (Schur, 1983). In fact, it continues to become more important. Unattractive people appear to be falling further behind.

> The importance of attractiveness has increased dramatically in the United States in this century . . . . For nearly every decade since 1930, physical appearance has increased in importance for men and women about equally, corresponding with the rise in television, fashion, magazines, advertising, and other media depictions of attractive models. For example, the importance attached to good looks in a marriage partner on a scale of 0 to 3 increased between 1939 and 1996 from 1.50 to 2.11 for men and 0.94 to 1.67 for women . . . . The sex difference so far remains invariant, however. The gap between men and women is no more nor less than it was in the late 1930s. (Buss, 1999, p. 145)

The impression that beauty is an unattainable ideal is substantiated by research (Langlois & Roggman, 1990). Researchers found that participants judged computer-generated faces to be more attractive than photographs of real people who were beautiful. Computer-generated faces are completely symmetrical, having eliminated all irregularities; however, these computer-generated images are not pictures of actual people. Indeed, even the most beautiful people cannot "compete" with computer-generated composites, proving that individuals with less symmetrical features are considered less attractive. The media have the power to make everybody disappointed with his or her body and appearance.

An Associated Press article dated October 1999 was entitled "Egg Salesman Defends Web Venture" (Wilson, 1999). The article told of a former photographer for *Playboy* magazine, Ron Harris, who plans to purchase ovarian eggs from models and then sell these eggs to prospective parents. The article states Harris's motives: "The egg auction is an opportunity for parents to give their children a head start in a society that worships beauty" (p. 1). Harris stated, "I've been around beautiful women my whole life and I think they have power most of us will never understand" (p. 1). Harris's Web site began accepting bids on Monday morning, and by noon the site had received 5 million hits. The highest bid for an ovarian egg was $42,000. Each model decides how long she will allow the bidding to continue and what price she will accept. Harris's commission is 20% of the sale price. The Web site states, "This site simply mirrors our current society, in that beauty always goes to the highest bidder" (p. 10).

To summarize: (1) Beautiful people do receive more privileges and advantages based solely on their appearance; (2) beauty, because of the media, is becoming even more important than ever before; (3) in some ways, beauty is an unattainable ideal because people are never completely symmetrical; and (4) there is the widespread notion that beauty is the result of individual effort. It is interesting to note that the media are expanding the definition of beauty to include older people. The media have the power to define beauty and also have consciously decided to respond to the aging of the American population. However, the beautiful older women and men shown in the media are not typical-looking older men and women, just as the beautiful younger women and men are not typical-looking younger people.

People who are unattractive, especially women, are often assumed to be isolated, unfulfilled, and even tortured (Imrie, 1996). Other, more extreme characteristics ascribed to people who are unattractive are *monstrosity* and *deviance*. Indeed, later in this chapter we will learn that many consider facial disfigurements to be the disability that experiences the greatest degree of stigma, in spite of the fact that there are few functional limitations. However, people who are unattractive, with or without disabilities, are often viewed as inferior.

What is beauty? We have seen that one component of beauty is symmetry. Other elements of beauty are health, sexuality, and physical fitness. Many people with disabilities are not viewed as being symmetrical, healthy, sexy, or physically fit (Bogdan & Taylor, 1987; Macgregor, 1951). Further, we have seen that many quality-of-life issues are a direct function of a person's attractiveness. Indeed, many prospective employers have told qualified job candidates with disabilities that they cannot hire them because their appearance would be distressing to customers, coworkers, or supervisors. Viewing the video "Facial Disfigurement," it can be seen that none of these individuals experience functional limitations but each is greatly limited by others' reactions to his or her appearance.

Fear of Acquiring a Disability, or Existential Angst, or "There But for the Grace of God Go I"

In this section, look for—

- The definition of "existential angst"
- Why disability challenges our concepts of a fair world and mastery and control over our bodies
- The definition of TAB
- Two ways to reduce existential angst

Marc Shell (2005) relates the following story about a mother's response to disability:

> I thought of Tom, who through war, lost an arm, and bravely keeping it secret from his mother in order to spare her pain for a while at least, he telephoned her when he docked in New York to say that he would be home for Christmas.
>
> "But could I bring a friend of mine with me?" he added. "He's crippled, Mother. He lost an arm."
>
> Without a moment's hesitation, her voice came back across the wires, cutting deep into Tom's heart. "Oh no, Tom. Not at Christmas. It would spoil all the happy plans I have made for us." (p. 217)

Obviously, the son had some idea of how his mother would respond to the loss of an arm or he would not have concocted the story about his friend.

The onset of a disability challenges our sense of control and *seems* contrary to the natural order. Yet we *know* that disabilities are an inherent, ordinary part of the natural order. We like to believe that we totally control both our destinies and our bodies. We also like to believe that we can overcome anything. None of this is true. Nonetheless, these are deeply held beliefs. We can control many aspects of our bodies and lives, and we can overcome many circumstances. However, no one has total control. We also like to believe that science, medicine, and physicians can protect us from disability or chronic illness.

"Disability is a symbol of vulnerability, fallibility, weakness, dependence, and failure to master our bodies" (Bickenbach, 1993, p. 82). PWDs carry this negative and distress-inducing symbol—the disability—with them. In the video "Don't Go to Your Room," one of the participants states, "We confront the other person with what he/she would like to deny or ignore." For many PWODs, seeing someone with a disability reminds them that "I could become *like that*."

Disability seems to be random and without purpose and occurs with "unbearable unpredictability" (Auge & Herzlich, 1995, p. 166). The onset of a disability seems to transgress some nonexistent laws of justice and fairness and appears to demonstrate human inequality because not everyone has a disability. Lack of justice, human inequality, and unpredictability are unpleasant to contemplate, yet everyone is vulnerable to acquiring a disability. It is difficult for those without disabilities to assign meaning to the disability when it occurs unexpectedly, brings with it a host of secondary losses, reduces the individual's sense of control and independence, and may bring a lifetime of pain. For some, the concept of disability is synonymous with mutilation, deformity, and disfigurement. The onset of a disability may also bring many financial and social costs. Although not inherent in the disability itself, the onset of a disability automatically assigns an individual to the category of "disabled," which usually means a sudden reduction in status and identity. And, the important questions can never really be answered with certainty: "Why him or her?"; "Why here?"; or "Why now?" Medical diagnoses and etiologies are of some help, but the answers to the truly important question of "why" cannot be found in medicine or science.

Fear of acquiring a disability is sometimes referred to as the "existential angst of disability." *Angst* is the German word for fear, and existentialism is a school of philosophy that holds that human life is fraught with peril, to which everyone is subject. The human condition, according to existential philosophers, is full of unexpected and unwanted circumstances that have the potential to threaten our well-being. Disability is one of these unexpected circumstances, although existentialists usually worry more about death. For an existentialist, every moment as a person without a disability may be the person's last moment without a disability.

Alex Valdez, on the PBS video "Look Who's Laughing," is a comedian who is blind. Valdez summarizes the audience's first reaction to him: "They don't know what to do with a blind guy on stage. They don't know whether to laugh or cry. They're too preoccupied with how they're feeling." Valdez's last statement concisely describes the existential angst of the audience. Rather than concentrate on the comedian on stage who is telling jokes, the audience members are dealing with their individual reactions to blindness.

Much of the fear, anxiety, and painful reminders of the possibility of acquiring a disability can be easily dealt with by simply avoiding contact with PWDs. When a PWOD meets a PWD, the PWOD often questions his or her own identity as a person totally in control of life. Rather than deal with unpleasant feelings brought on by seeing a PWD, others can simply stay away or, if necessary, institutionalize PWDs so as not to be subjected to their presence. Of course, PWDs are aware of the effect of their disability and they use "in-group" words to describe PWODs, such as TABs (temporarily able-bodied), normies, or ABs (able-bodied). Certainly, the term *TABs* points to the possibility or eventuality of most individuals' acquiring a disability and also plays on the TABs' fear of acquiring disabilities. Lucy Grealy (1997), a teenager with facial disfigurements resulting from sarcoma (cancer), found some satisfaction in her "macabre status." Grealy had a part-time job at a horse stable that provided birthday parties, or pony parties, for children from upper-class families:

> While the eyes of these perfectly formed children swiftly and deftly bored into the deepest part of me, the glances from their parents provided me with an exotic sense of power as I watched them inexpertly pretend not to notice me. After I passed around the swing sets and looped around to pick up the next child waiting near the picnic table littered with cake plates, juice bottles, and party favors, I'd stand confrontationally, like some Dickensian ghost, imagining that my presence served as an uneasy reminder of what might happen. What had happened to me was any parent's nightmare, and I allowed myself to believe that I was dangerous to them. The parents obliged me: they brushed past me, around me, sometimes even smiled at me . . . . They were uncomfortable because of my face. I ignored the deep hurt by allowing the side of me that was desperate for any kind of definition to staunchly act out, if not exactly relish, this macabre status. (p. 19)

Paul Longmore (2003) succinctly captures the relationship between anxiety and stigmatization: "Disability happens around us more often than we generally recognize or care to notice, and we harbor unspoken anxieties about the possibility of disablement to us, or to someone close to us. What we fear, we often stigmatize and shun" (p. 2003).

We have been discussing the concept of existential angst as an individual response. However, "collective neurosis" refers to the anxiety and fear of disability experienced by large groups, especially those in power. Collective neurosis often results in segregation and isolation for PWDs.

Costs of Existential Angst to PWODs

If PWODs could see that they, or someone they love, could acquire a disability, they would probably become advocates for providing resources and civil rights for PWDs (Wendell, 1997). Indeed, one of the pleasures of watching charity telethons is the misguided and inaccurate assumption that the PWDs shown have nothing to do with us. Existential angst separates PWODs from what Wendell termed "their future selves" (p. 266). PWODs never tire of denying the possibility of disability.

Kleege (2006), a university professor who is blind, worries about the "Normals" and feels like "they need a lot of help."

There is more than one way to be a human being . . . . On the surface, it seems a pretty innocuous statement, but in fact, it's quite revolutionary. It forces people to question everything they take for granted as normal. It's a message that needs to be spoken of still . . . . We say it by forcing our way into their notice, into their world.

I worried about a lot of them so much, the Normals I know. If some of them never became disabled . . . it will be a bad business. If they could just let go of the fear, I think. I have the fear, too. I'm afraid of losing my hearing. But I know that if or when it happens, I'll make do somehow. Making do is not such a foreign concept to me. For the Normals, making do is dreadful even to contemplate. What would life be without a leg, without eyesight, without hearing, they worry. Life would be life . . . I say. Flawed and limited in some ways, rich and various in others.

I don't enjoy feeling like we [PWDs] exist to offer illuminating insights to the Normals. But in my more generous moments (few and far between as they are), I feel it's something worth doing. They [Normals] need a lot of help. (Kleege, 2006, p. 182)

Fear of acquiring a disability, or existential angst, is a powerful negative emotion. Ironically, two methods to reduce (not eliminate) existential angst would be (1) accord PWDs their civil rights and necessary accommodations, and (2) allow PWDs full social integration. In other words, the solution to existential angst is to see disability for what it truly is—a societal concern rather than an individual concern. If we choose to view disability as an individual condition, which humans have done for most of history, then we "construct" disability as a terrible reality. If, however, we choose to view disability as a societal concern, we construct disability as a part of life, which we can negotiate *as a group*. If PWDs were accorded their rights, provided reasonable accommodations, and allowed full equal-status social relationships, the prospect of acquiring a disability would probably not be so anxiety-provoking for PWODs.

Individuals Who Acquire Disabilities Later in Life Have Internalized Many of the Negative Stereotypes of Disabilities

Dr. Fredrick Schroeder, former commissioner of the Rehabilitation Services Administration, became blind at age 16. Dr. Schroeder (1997) commented on his own negative stereotypes of blindness: "I assumed that my life as a blind person would be very limited, isolated, and dependent. I had limited expectations of myself. With blindness did not come any insights into blindness. I attributed to myself all the stereotypes that society holds of blind people. I needed someone to stretch my expectations. I needed someone with a perspective wider than my own. I needed hope."

Holding false and unrealistic beliefs about disabilities limits any individual's view of the world, but if the person should acquire a disability, then he or she literally becomes the object of his or her own prejudice and narrow views. Dr. Schroeder's experiences are valuable because he has insight into the needless self-limitations that his own pervasive, unrealistic, and narrow beliefs inflicted on himself. He reports, "As I was lying in my hospital bed, I thought, 'I can still talk, so I guess I will be a radio disc jockey or a psychologist.'" At that point in his life, Dr. Schroeder had very limited views of what people who are blind can do. (That's not to say that there is anything wrong with being a disc jockey or a psychologist. However, as a 16-year-old boy, Dr. Schroeder needed to consider a wide range of occupational options, which he obviously did because he did not become a psychologist or a disc jockey.)

The tenacity with which he held to his limiting and stereotypical views can be seen in another experience Dr. Schroeder related:

> My rehabilitation counselor was Bob Nessler and he was blind. I remember Bob asked me if I wanted a cup of coffee. I said "yes." He got his white cane and we crossed Van Ness Boulevard (in San Francisco) and went into a coffee shop. (I knew that there was coffee in the rehab office.) I was shocked. I had had mobility and orientation training, but I thought blind people only went where they absolutely had to go. Bob Nessler changed my life and he helped me to see that as a blind person I would live a normal life. He did it without making a speech, making me read a book, but the way in which he lived his life. He took me to a coffee shop for a cup of coffee.

Even after completing his orientation and mobility (O & M) training, Dr. Schroeder still retained his narrow and limiting views of the way in which people who are blind should live. But since Dr. Schroeder was blind, these prejudices and stereotypes were now self-limiting and self-imposed.

Hierarchy of Stigma

A "hierarchy of stigma" is associated with the four main categories of disabilities (Antonak, 1980; Charlton, 1998; Deal, 2003; Furnham & Pendred, 1983; Harasymiw, Horne, & Lewis, 1976; Henderson & Bryan, 1997; Horne & Ricciardo, 1988; Jones et al., 1984; Jones, 1974; Olshansky, 1965; Tringo, 1970). In ascending order, this is the hierarchy of stigma: Individuals with physical disabilities have the least amount of stigma directed toward them;

individuals with cognitive disabilities have more stigma; individuals with intellectual disabilities experience even more stigma; and, finally, those with psychiatric disabilities experience the greatest degree of stigma (Fig. 4–2). While there is no disagreement on which disabilities elicit the least stigma, there is some disagreement on which disabilities elicit the greatest degree of stigma. Longmore (2003) states that there is "a complex interaction among such factors as visibility, severity, mode of functioning, and proximity to the face and head" (p. 146). Esses and Beaufoy (1994) found three "key cognitive elements: stereotypes about various types of disability, symbolic beliefs that PWDs may promote or threaten one's values, and control over the occurrence of the disability" (p. 62). Other researchers (Harper, 1999; Janicki, 1970) found facial disfigurements to be ranked lowest in preference scales, and Corrigan and Penn (1999) consider psychiatric disabilities to be the target of the greatest stigma.

This hierarchy of stigma has implications for individuals with disabilities and societal implications. The general history of services and benefits to people with disabilities follows the hierarchy of stigma. Those with physical disabilities received services and benefits first, those with cognitive and intellectual disabilities received services next, and those with psychiatric disabilities received services last. Lawmakers and policymakers are subject to society's judgments and evaluations, and it is understandable that the history of disability services closely parallels the hierarchy of stigma toward disability. The hierarchy of stigma, in part, determined which people would be institutionalized and which people would be allowed to live in the community. (Note: Disability rights activists do not use the word "institutionalized"; instead they use the word "incarcerated.")

Researchers who attempt to empirically prove and quantify this hierarchy study the reactions of employers to hypothetical employees with different types of disability and their willingness to hire these individuals. These types of studies have also used children without disabilities, showing the pictures of children with various types of disabilities and asking

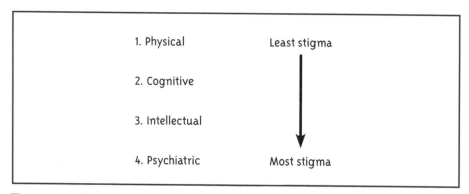

1. Physical   Least stigma

2. Cognitive

3. Intellectual

4. Psychiatric   Most stigma

Figure 4–2 The hierarchy of stigma of disability categories.

them which child would they like to have as a friend (Richardson & Ronald, 1977). Other researchers have had college students respond to surveys asking if they would date or develop friendships, work, or become romantically involved with individuals with various types of disabilities (Bell & Klein, 2001). Therefore, we can see that the hierarchy of stigma toward certain types of disabilities also determines the type of social life PWDs will enjoy. Clearly, most aspects of a PWD's life are directly affected by this hierarchy. Taken to the extreme of eugenics, we have seen the way in which those people whose disabilities elicited the greatest prejudice were killed in Nazi Germany. An article entitled "Where Do We Draw the Line? Surviving Eugenics in a Technological World" (Wolbring, 2001, p. 46) draws attention to these life-and-death decisions, all based on the hierarchy of disability.

After 30 years, little has changed (Thomas, 2000). Regardless of the legislative process, such as the Americans with Disabilities Act (ADA) and the Disability Rights Movement, the same hierarchy of stigma influences American life. Tringo conducted the first study in 1970 and Thomas replicated Tringo's study in 2000, finding the same results. PWDs also accept this hierarchy. Shakespeare, Gillespie-Sells, and Davies (1996) stated, "There is a real hierarchy of what is acceptable appearance within the disabled community: what is beautiful, what is ugly. At the top is someone who sits in a wheelchair but looks perfect. I have a friend who has cerebral palsy; she always says cerebral palsy is the dreg. They drool and have a speech impairment, movement problems, that kind of thing. On the high end of the scale is the person with a polio disability because physically they look okay. It's something we have to work on" (p. 71). Wolbring (2001) suggests that some PWDs advocate eugenics for PWDs with other types of disabilities. "Deaf people, blind people and dwarves may denounce eugenic practices for their own impairment characteristics, but not for others. In resisting the tide of eugenic practices, it is tempting for different groups to see only their own salvation in distancing themselves from others—'Not for me, but them'" (p. 46).

Burch (2007) considers the beginnings of Deaf beauty pageants to have been a combination of a reaction to the eugenics movement in the United States and a result of wishing to distance Deaf people from other PWDs:

> Deaf people have long accepted the hierarchy of "handicaps" expressed by early eugenists and have rejected such negative classifications for their own population. Deaf leaders and advocates consistently focused on their "normal" intelligence and ability to work—their "able-bodiness"—in public relations campaigns and in expressions to each other. Yet mainstream society commonly perceived deaf people as similar, if not identical, with "defectives" like feebleminded people, undercutting community members' citizenship status. As eugenic ideology intensified during the twentieth century, Deaf activists sought to

preserve and protect their society by distancing themselves from other disabled [*sic*] people and emphasizing their commonality with mainstream, middle-class society. Deaf beauty contests exemplify this strategy. Women's beauty, as projected by the Deaf media and pageants, enforced the notion of normalcy in two ways: sense of commonality with (able-bodied) others, and the sense that beauty specifically suggests healthiness and vitality. The issues of "passing" (as able-bodied), normalcy, and beauty strongly inform the popularity of Deaf beauty pageants. (2007, p. 243)

Those with physical disabilities experience the least degree of stigma and prejudice, probably because these types of disabilities are the easiest to understand. The cause, the onset, the course, and the limitations are easier for most people to comprehend. Simply stated, physical disabilities do not have the degree of ambiguity that other types of disabilities do. Indeed, many people consider physical disabilities to be the only type of disability. The following quotation explains the greater acceptance of people with blindness than of people with other types of disabilities:

Possibly it is because the unimpaired can easily imagine and sympathize with their plight; unlike mental illness, for example, the state of blindness involves little stigma. Possibly it is because blindness has existed since the beginning of history, so that the blind have had more time to secure a place for themselves as legitimate objects of aid from the state. The very fact that their impairment is less disabling than others gives the blind advantages in political organization. (Berkowitz, 1987, p. 168)

Because of a longer history and greater acceptance by society, people with physical disabilities have been able to receive more professional services and benefits and also have had a longer history of political advocacy for themselves. Just about everyone can identify with a person with a physical disability (Goodyear, 1983; Gordon, Minnes, & Holden, 1990). The prospect of acquiring a physical disability or having a loved one with a physical disability seems (and actually is) possible. In contrast, the prospect of acquiring an intellectual, cognitive, or psychiatric disability is rarely considered by PWODs. The media also follow the hierarchy of stigma, in that advertising media most often show people with physical disabilities, most often people in wheelchairs. Rarely would people with other types of disabilities, for example, someone with Down syndrome, be shown.

Cognitive disabilities, which include learning disabilities and some types of traumatic brain injuries, are subjected to more stigma and prejudice than are physical disabilities. These types of disabilities appear ambiguous to others because the cause, the course, and the limitations are not clear-cut or well quantified. Even clinicians differ in their diagnoses and treatment plans for individuals with cognitive disabilities. In some environments, cognitive disabilities might be considered "hidden" or "invisible" disabilities because the individual can choose to conceal the disability in those settings where cognitive skills are not required. Choosing not to disclose the cognitive disability may result in others' attributing negative motives to the individual. For example, if others are not aware that the individual has a learning disability, they may think the person is lazy, unmotivated, or oppositional, when the reality is that the person does not understand, cannot remember, or is unable to filter out extraneous stimuli in order to concentrate.

Individuals with intellectual disabilities, which include mental retardation, autism, and developmental disabilities, experience more stigma and prejudice than those with physical or cognitive disabilities, probably because the limitations of these types of disabilities are so great and affect many areas of the individual's life. And, as we learned in Chapter 1, today's labor market and economy are moving toward service jobs and jobs in technology. For individuals with intellectual disabilities, the changing labor market is redefining their disability. People with intellectual disabilities often appear to be ambiguous and unpredictable or somewhat frightening to the general public. Their disability and its limitations often arouse feelings of discomfort, especially because others feel they do not know how to interact with people with intellectual disabilities. In addition, "appropriate support systems with mental . . . disabilities are the most complex and necessarily professionalized and technical" (Charlton, 1998, p. 97). Not only are mental disabilities difficult to understand, but, as Charlton observed, the treatment of individuals with these types of disabilities is also difficult to understand.

Throughout history, individuals with intellectual disabilities were often not thought of as being completely "human." Intellectual functioning was considered to be the defining feature of humans, and if a person lacked this capacity, then he or she was often considered to be subhuman.

The types of disability against which the greatest degree of prejudice and discrimination is shown are psychiatric disabilities. Psychiatric disabilities are usually thought to include mental illness, alcohol abuse, and substance abuse. The two letters to Ann Landers in Chapter 3 are from people who have psychiatric disabilities. The writers describe the prejudice and discrimination they feel from others. The fact that these letters were not written by people with physical disabilities, people with cognitive disabilities, or people with intellectual disabilities shows us that these types of disabilities have been accepted by the general public as legitimate disabilities. In contrast, individuals with psychiatric disabilities are not fully accepted as having a disability. Often, these individuals are somehow "blamed" for having the disability, as not being "strong enough" to have avoided the onset of the disability. In the video "Depression and Manic Depression" by Aquarius Productions, one of the participants makes this comment: "There is no shame in recognizing that the brain gets sick." This statement very clearly summarizes that there is "shame" in having a psychiatric disability and that the shame is undeserved. No one would say, "There is no shame in recognizing that the heart (pancreas, eyes, ears, or any other organ) gets sick" because there is not the degree of stigma directed toward physical disabilities as there is toward psychiatric disabilities. Donna Orrin, who has bipolar disorder, currently owns her own business and holds a master's of social work degree. She also provides training for mental health professions. Orrin (1999) presents a clear-cut result of the hierarchy of stigma from her experiences of hospitalization: "It is ironic that, if you go to a hospital for physical care, you have your own phone and your own room. But if you are in a state hospital for mental illness, you get one phone for 30 women, in the hallway, with no privacy. We had to line up for a chance to use the phone" (Mackelprang & Salsgiver, 1999, pp. 181–182).

Most people have little understanding of psychiatric disabilities. Psychiatric disabilities appear to be both ambiguous and dangerous; people with these types of disabilities have been portrayed for centuries by the media as violent and hostile. Also, perception, in contrast to actuality, plays a large part in the amount of stigma toward people with disabilities. For example, many cognitive disabilities are often *perceived* to be psychiatric disabilities and, of course, then the stigma directed toward psychiatric disabilities is misdirected toward individuals who have cognitive disabilities.

This hierarchy of stigma is a useful model. However, reality is often more complicated than this simple model, and no one model can ever totally represent what a person experiences. For example, many individuals have more than one disability, and it is safe to state the degree of stigma directed toward these individuals probably is a result of the disability that is most visible or has the greatest number of limitations. Individuals who belong to more than one "minority" group, such as an older African American lesbian with a disability, will experience prejudice, stigma, and discrimination from many sources, and she may not be able to determine the exact source of this evaluation and treatment. Is it racism? Is it ageism? Is it homophobia? Is it sexism? Is it handicapism? Is it all of them? Three of them? Two of them?

Perceived social class is also an important factor. Individuals who are thought to be of higher social classes and who have a disability are perceived more positively than those people with disabilities who are thought to be of a lower social class. Parents of children in wheelchairs often decorate the wheelchair very colorfully to attract children to their child. In much the same way, adults with disabilities know that they will have a greater chance of being accepted if they can present themselves as well educated and of a high social status. Those PWDs who have some sort of ability that is highly valued by society will experience greater acceptance than someone else who does not have a socially valued role or capability but has the same disability. For example, a lawyer spoke in *Time* magazine about her experience with depression and about the kinship she felt with the homeless people on the street, many of whom the lawyer thought had mental illness. The lawyer appeared in a national news magazine precisely because she was a graduate of an Ivy League law school; was employed in a high-paying job; and had experienced institutionalization, medication regimens, and other treatment plans. With whom did the lawyer identify most—the other lawyers or the homeless people on the street? She identified with the homeless people because, according to her perception, they were living the 24-hour-a-day experience of mental illness that she was. She was a lawyer for only 8 to 10 hours a day.

The old joke that a rich person is considered to be eccentric but a poor person who exhibits the same behaviors is considered to be mentally ill reflects the influence that perceived social class exerts on the degree of prejudice and discrimination directed toward the individual. Some of the logic behind the old joke might also refer to the functional definition of disability. Rich people do not have to get up in the morning and go to work; therefore, their mental illness may seem more benign. Rich people not only have fewer functional demands, but they also have more resources with which to hide their mental illness, which, at minimum, would prolong the prediagnosis period. Rich people also have the resources to shield themselves from stress, a known exacerbator of mental illness.

The posters of famous and gifted people with disabilities demonstrate the role the perceived social class of the PWD plays in the degree of stigma or prejudice directed toward him or her. Posters of Beethoven and Einstein, with the question, "Did you know he had a disability?" are designed to help people reevaluate their attitudes toward PWDs. As would be expected, the impact of these posters has been difficult to determine, but many PWDs are offended by these posters because they seem to imply that for a PWD to be accepted, he or she must accomplish some superhuman, heroic task, akin to what Beethoven and Einstein did. Certainly, the poster creators needed to use PWDs who were readily identifiable. Celebrities with disabilities today also may present an unrealistic picture of the experience of most PWDs. Nonetheless, most PWDs do not accomplish world-famous acts (nor do most PWODs), and they feel resentful that these posters present only those PWDs who are rich, famous, and extremely gifted. Often, PWDs use the derisive term "super crips" or "overcomers" to describe the famous individuals with disabilities. Furthermore, most PWODs are more comfortable with PWDs who are "overcomers."

"Society" also includes PWDs, and PWDs often are not accepting of *other* people with disabilities. Coleman (1997) explained: "Moreover, even among stigmatized people, relative comparisons are made, and people are reassured by the fact that there is someone else who is worse off" (p. 218). For example, in the video "Don't Go to Your Room," a woman in a wheelchair remarks, "Walking is not all it's cracked up to be. A lot of walking people are depressed or alcoholic." Some PWDs may feel that they are exceptions to the rule, and they therefore can feel prejudice and discrimination toward other PWDs and yet not consider that this is incongruent. These PWDs consider themselves to have worked harder or somehow done something extraordinary that separates them from other PWDs.

Three Societal Responses to Disability

In this section, look for—

- Charity
- Preferential treatment
- Compensation

We do not allow PWDs to be ordinary citizens with civil rights and protection under the law when PWODs make them recipients of charity. Most PWDs want to rely on themselves (by working) or on the government (by ensuring civil rights). Indeed, in the 1930s, the slogan of The League of the Physically Handicapped was "We Don't Want Tin Cups. We Want Jobs" (Longmore, 2003, p. 69).

The education of deaf children illustrates the relationship between civil rights and charity. It was not until 1975, with the passage of the Education for All Handicapped Children Act (later renamed the Individuals with Disabilities Education Act), that the education of deaf children came under federal supervision. Until 1975, the education of deaf children was provided in a haphazard way, largely by charities. It is safe to say that most deaf children received very little education, and most of that was vocational and religious in nature. "Charity supports a society which is based on the unequal distribution of wealth, and where tax concessions offered to donors rather than redistribution of resources maintain an unequal status quo. Charities tend to exist because of socially constructed dependence in a society which fails to address the needs of citizens with disabilities . . . . It does represent a *reparative* intent. Just because an act may emerge as a way of resolving negative unconscious conflict does not mean that this act may not also have valuable outcomes" (Marks, 1999, p. 167).

Many PWDs have had experiences such as this:

I was in Kansas City, doing Christmas shopping. This old man came up to me and looked at me and said, "Do you need money for Christmas?" I'm a lawyer and I'm working for the government EPA. Nearly every adult with a disability that I knew had a story about being given unsolicited money as donations. As a little kid, absolutely. I would be walking down the street with my mother (and people gave me money). (National Public Radio, Disability History Project, Inventing the Poster Child, 1998)

Charity Telethons, or "Elephants Running in the Forest"

In this section, look for—

Charities:

- Exaggerate and sensationalize disabilities
- Make PWDs objects of pity
- Are considered by many PWDs to be a type of victimization
- Relieve the government of the responsibility to provide services for PWDs
- Require PWDs to submit to the benefactor's definition of them
- Are polarizing
- Create artificial factions among disability groups
- Are businesses, and many PWODs "live off" PWDs
- Reinforce the power relationship between PWODs and PWDs
- Focus on eradication of the disability rather than quality-of-life concerns

Charities

In the National Public Radio Disability History Project ("Inventing the Poster Child," 1998) charity telethons are compared to "elephants running in the forest." This statement is meant to convey the powerful fascination that charity telethons hold for the public. Perhaps this statement also expresses the difficulty, if not impossibility, of asking Americans to examine deeply ingrained assumptions of kindness and charity. Can elephants running in the forest be stopped?

Charity and fundraising exaggerate and sensationalize disability to solicit money. Exaggeration and sensationalism of the disability can lead to segregation and isolation for PWDs. Many PWDs feel that any money raised is not worth the costs to their self-concept.

Joshua Malinga (of Disabled Peoples International/Disabled Peoples South Africa) stated:

> Charities play a negative social role. They seek to control us. Charities are not interested in empowerment and integration. They support segregation. In fact, once we have integration and equalization of opportunity, these charities will begin to die. Their institutional interests lie with segregation, ours with integration. (Charlton, 1998, p. 92)

Mee (1999), a polio survivor, believes that PWODs view telethons to vicariously "experience" a disability: "I think it is intact people who like to experience the feelings of sorrow and loss and bitterness over and over again—and who always ask injured people about those feelings, to conjure them up and experience them vicariously" (p. 36).

The roots of televised charity telethons lie in the March of Dimes, a charity founded by Franklin Roosevelt, to raise money for polio. As Marks (1999) stated, there are some positive outcomes of charity. Many people with polio, including children, had their hospitalization, treatment, and equipment paid for by the March of Dimes. Additionally, all of the research work of both Sabin and Salk, the discoverers of the polio vaccine, was funded by the March of Dimes. Nonetheless, many polio survivors and their families assert that the American government should have provided public support for both the treatment of polio and the research to eradicate it, rather than depending on sporadic private donations.

Marc Shell (2005) explained: "'Crippledom' was a good thing for the March of Dimes. It furthered money collection and a cure. It allowed telethon masters to use us polios (survivors) as distinctively dehumanized and deformed money collection props.... Polio survivors were likewise defiantly *commodified*.... This exploitative practice ... seems to make the public sector both weak and unnecessary" (p. 145). "Commodified" means that the poster children were considered to be products, commodities, or objects. It is interesting that one of the greatest politicians of the 20th century, Franklin Roosevelt, who established the National Foundation for Infantile Paralysis and its successor, the March of Dimes, never supported government assistance for polio.

Charity, or benevolence or goodwill, is demeaning and insulting to the recipient and is simply another type of victimization. Certainly the benefactor functions from a position of superiority, and, furthermore, charity is dependent on the goodwill of the benefactor (Alder, Wright, & Ulicny, 1991). Stated another way, benevolence is dependent on the generosity and kindness of the benefactor. The benefactor may or may not decide to give. Furthermore, the benefactor is free to ration both the amount and the timing of the charity. For example, when money is acquired through charitable fundraising, it is never possible to accurately predict the amount of money that will be available. People may or may not decide to give. On an individual level, if a personal care attendant does not want to feed his employer, the employer (person with the disability) cannot do much about it. Parents of children who require special education often have had to resort to all sorts of fundraising, such as bake sales. Parents whose children do not have disabilities are not required to bake brownies to ensure that their children receive appropriate public education. These children have the automatic right to education. Furthermore, if parents whose children do not have disabilities had to raise funds to pay for their children's public education, they would probably discontinue asking for charity and start advocating for their rights from the government. Often the public considers education for children with disabilities to be a conditional gift, or charity, rather than an automatic right.

Individuals with disabilities have been protesting telethons since the 1970s. In 1976 and 1979, a disability rights group, Disabled in Action, picketed the United Cerebral Palsy Association, calling their telethons "demeaning and paternalistic shows which celebrate and encourage pity" (Pelka, 1997, p. 302). One of the most well-known charities for PWDs is Jerry Lewis's Labor Day marathon television program for raising funds for muscular dystrophy. Since 1991, a group calling themselves Jerry's Orphans has picketed local television stations that carry the program. Incidentally, Jerry's Orphans was founded by two former Muscular Dystrophy Association poster children, Mike Ervin and Cris Matthews.

Because the provision of charity is under the control of the benefactor, often the benefactor thinks that he or she knows what the recipient needs and wants. This is an example of paternalism. Rather than viewing people with disabilities as experts in their own needs, charitable people provide what they think people with disabilities need (even when their ideas are totally wrong). Since the 1970s, many disability advocacy groups require that members of their governing board be PWDs. Two groups were unwilling to change the structure of their boards to allow PWDs to serve. These two were the Muscular Dystrophy Association and the March of Dimes.

The most straightforward example of this is an article that appeared in the September 2, 1990, issue of *Parade* magazine, written by Jerry Lewis, who does not have muscular dystrophy. Lewis wrote, "I know the courage it takes to get on the court with other cripples [*sic*] and play wheelchair basketball." Lewis pretended to write from the point of view of a person with a disability. "I'd like to play basketball like normal, healthy, vital and energetic people . . . . When I sit back and think more rationally, I realize my life is half, so I must learn to do things halfway. I just have to learn to try to be good at being half a person" (Pelka, 1997, p. 301). An Associated Press article (Torriero, September 3, 2006) related: "Led by a former muscular dystrophy poster boy from Chicago, the activists scored what they call their 'big triumph' last November as protesters in wheelchairs ambushed Lewis in an appearance at the Harold Washington Library Center in Chicago . . . . Despite the protestors' urgings, the telethon has not changed its ways and has not promoted accessibility for the disabled [*sic*], better housing and employment possibilities, activists say." Lewis's conclusion about the protesters: "I paid for the wheelchairs." This is a clear-cut example of paternalism because Lewis is implying that the protestors have no right to criticize any aspect of the telethon because Lewis paid for benefits.

Also, if the person is to receive help, he or she must submit to the benefactor's definition of him or her, almost to the point of "playing the part." Essentially, the benefactor has inordinate power over the charity receiver. An adult survivor of polio stated, "Those telethons featuring a semimaniacal Jerry Lewis are responded to by men and women who think they are *charitable*. Those well-meaning Shriners interviewed at halftime during the East–West football games they sponsor—let me remind you of the game's motto: 'Strong legs run so that weak legs can walk'—do not believe that they have tampered with our reality" (Kriegel, 1982, p. 82).

Children who grew up believing that they needed charity were often "programmed" with learned helplessness. The message of charity, especially to a child, is "someone has to *give* this to you because you are not capable of *earning* it." Indeed, many adults in the Disability Rights Movement feel resentment about the harmful effects of having been recipients of charity as children. They feel that they have paid a very high price for every dollar received.

Charity is polarizing—it is very clear who is the giver and who is the receiver. Generous people give to poor, pitiful, downtrodden, and unfortunate people. We have seen that, as a result of the increasing rates of disability, many Americans are, and will be, in the ranks of persons with disabilities. Defenders of charity will state, "No one, with or without a disability, is completely independent and everyone needs help at one time or another." This is true, but people with disabilities are *continuously* in the position of accepting charity. Also, PWODs are more often the recipients of invisible and anonymous charity that maintains their dignity and privacy and does not require expressions of gratitude. Poster children, telethons, and neighborhood fund drives are considered by many in the Disability Rights Movement to be modern-day freak shows.

Charity to people with disabilities has had a pervasive and insidious effect on our society. It is impossible to establish equal social status relationships, in the workplace or in social situations, when one group is always the benefactor and the other group is always the beneficiary. Morris (1991) stated, "Charities need to present disability in such a way as to encourage people to part with their money. The portrayal of a strong disabled [*sic*] person going about his/her life, and enjoying it, is not going to bring in any money" (p. 108). If the media portray people with disabilities as objects of charity, these individuals will have difficulty in establishing intimate, familial relationships with people who do not have disabilities. Scott-Parker (as cited in Morris, 1991) viewed charities as objectifying PWDs. She stated,

"As a study of advertising and disabled put it, charities tend to commission [advertising campaigns] as though they owned their particular 'model' of disabled [*sic*] person, in much the same way that Ford owns Fiesta cars. The charity is assumed to have a similar expert authority, enhanced by unimpeachable motives, and can therefore present its product to the market in any way it sees fit" (Morris, 1991, p. 109).

Charities are businesses. A few charities are big businesses, and many professional, salaried people "live off" charity in that their jobs, their salaries, and their professional identities are dependent on (1) the existence of pitiful, unfortunate people, and (2) the generosity of others. Albrecht, in his book *The Disability Business* (1992), presented a chart (p. 171) that lists nine large American charities, their 1986 dollar figure, and percentages of these four categories: (1) their total intake, (2) the cost of overhead, (3) the cost of fundraising activities, and (4) the total payout. Those organizations listed on this chart that seek to assist PWDs are March of Dimes, the American Cancer Society, the American Lung Society, the National Easter Seal Society, and Disabled American Veterans. Albrecht's graphic representation of these charitable organizations shows that overhead costs, which include the salaries of professional workers, vary. For example, the organization World Hunger Year spent 30% of its funds on overhead and paid out only 43% to its recipients. In contrast, the American Cancer Society used only 7% for overhead and paid out 87% to its recipients. Albrecht included the column of "fundraising costs" to distinguish between those administrative costs, which include salaries, from those costs that are necessary to raise the funds.

Charity given to one group and not to other groups can create factions within the disability community. Factionalizing the disability community can undermine efforts of advocating for civil rights and raising public awareness. The most clear-cut example of this is televised telethons that raise huge amounts of money for a single type of disability. One writer has termed this "brand awareness" in terms of types of disabilities (Campbell, as cited in Morris, 1991, p. 110). Anne Finger (1993) observed, "[B]ut each individual charity must compete with other charities for the 'charitable dollar.' Thus, charity advertising aims at simultaneously creating an image of 'its' disease or impairment and of that particular charity as the custodian/savior/earthly representation of all those with that dreaded impairment" (p. 29). Further, benefactors probably do not fully value the objects of their charity. There are no expectations of the recipients other than to be appropriately grateful. Liachowitz (1988) summarized: "Thus, the many handicapped [*sic*] people whose physical disorder is permanent remain in a position of indebtedness—a position that probably accounts for at least some portion of their socially conferred devaluation" (p. 11).

Also, the clear message of much charitable fundraising is that the disability must be eradicated. Rarely is any consideration given to improving the quality of life for those who have the disability. Occasionally, some large-scale charity drives pay for research that supports prenatal testing that likely will result in abortions. One mother told of her son Robbie being asked to be in the March of Dimes charity drives:

> "I'm sorry," I explain, "but I don't feel comfortable telling my son that he is doing this to prevent other children like him. We're trying to help him understand where he fits into a world that is often more confused than he is about his problem. I can't put him out there as something to 'prevent.' This poster thing also seems to use these kids to collect money, yet you tell me none of it goes toward addressing their problems now. That feels sort of dishonest."
>
> I realize that I have given away potential "celebrity" status for Robbie by declining their invitation. I have also risked being labeled an ungrateful parent. But I think I have been true to what I really want for him. Free lunches and pictures in the newspaper are not going to help push his wheelchair into a community that sees him as something that should not have happened. (Toombs, Barnard, & Carson, 1995, pp. 32–33)

The argument can also be made that it is the benefactor who "needs" the charity more than the beneficiary. Recipients of charity must be grateful for whatever they can get. (Often benefactors are irritated if the recipients are not appropriately and sufficiently grateful.) This simply reinforces the power relationship between those with disabilities and those without disabilities. Being charitable comes from a position of superiority, and gratitude comes from a position of inferiority. Charity can "objectify" the recipients. Society "needs" objects of charity. The objectifying of people with disabilities is clearly seen in the poster children. (There are never "poster adults" because adults have the ability to fight the objectification, and the public's sympathy would not be as aroused as it is for sweet, innocent, lovable children. However, according to Shapiro [1993], some adults resent having been poster children.) Everybody feels good when they give to "Jerry's kids." Charity allows the benefactor to defend his or her privileges to himself or herself and to the public (Allport, 1986). However, on closer scrutiny, people with disabilities want the rights and responsibilities of citizens, not charity. It is no coincidence that Labor Day (the same day that the Jerry Lewis muscular dystrophy telethon is held) was chosen for the "Onarollathon." The "Onarollathon," sponsored by Disability Talk Radio, raised funds for the Literacy Volunteers of America, an organization that helps adults learn to read. Radio host Greg Smith, who has muscular dystrophy, stated, "I know in my heart that our community, people with disabilities, care about important social issues, beyond those that directly impact us. We are a part of a powerful civil rights movement that can create positive change, which is why we are joining forces to help advance another great cause. On this particular weekend when people with disabilities are depicted as hopeless objects of pity, we want to deliver the message that we are important builders of this society."

Do the ends justify the means? Do the millions of dollars raised justify the results for PWDs? Most PWDs would say no.

Preferential Treatment

Like charity, preferential treatment is demeaning and insulting to the individual it is designed to help. Like charity, preferential treatment is also often thought to be a positive response. Preferential treatment for people with disabilities can include such things as showing hiring preferences and promotion preferences, lowering standards, granting admission to schools solely on the basis of disability, and applying differing standards.

The ADA does not mandate preferential treatment for people with disabilities. It does not require the hiring, promotion, or admission of unqualified people, nor does the ADA mandate quotas in jobs or schools. The ADA does mandate accommodations and provision of opportunities to compete for qualified people with disabilities.

Proponents of preferential treatment accurately point out that there is not equal competition in acquiring jobs and education and, therefore, preferential treatment is necessary to "level the playing field." Advocates of preferential treatment for groups who have experienced inequities remind us that historically there have been groups of individuals who have received preferential treatment, such as White Anglo-Saxons without disabilities. However, opponents assert that there are better ways to provide equal opportunity and it is unreasonable to correct an inequitable system by simply substituting another group to provide preferential treatment to.

Preferential treatment and charity are thought, perhaps at an unconscious level, to be an appropriate compensation, or redress, for the well-documented history of prejudice and discrimination experienced by people with disabilities. Past discrimination can never be fully redressed or compensated. Most people with disabilities do not want, or need, preferential treatment; furthermore, the *public perception* of preferential treatment may further undermine the position of people with disabilities. If the public thinks that people receive "freebies" and "perks" simply because they are members of a designated group, resentment and factional rivalry will result. The perception of preferential treatment often results in cries of reverse discrimination. Further, there are those who would say, "I am not personally responsible for the prejudice and discrimination experienced by people with disabilities, so why should I have to make amends?"

Preferential treatment communicates, in a not very subtle way, that PWDs really are not capable of competing with others who do not have disabilities. The individual is being told that he or she truly is inferior and does not have the ability to be successful on his or her own merit. Preferential treatment for people with disabilities is a fairly common occurrence and, in the long run, usually does not have positive results for the individual. Eventually, standards are upheld; honest feedback is given; and the individual must, at a later date, be judged according to widely accepted standards. For example, someone who is admitted to medical school because he or she is a member of a certain group (disability, gender, or racial/ethnic group) must graduate from medical school. Simply thinking in terms of the individual, it does this individual little good, and perhaps much harm, to have standards lowered so that he or she be allowed to enter medical school only to be "flunked out" later.

Preferential treatment of a person with a disability often results in excusing the individual from widely held standards or expectations. Such indulgence and exemption from standards are seen in ideas such as, "Children with disabilities should not be disciplined" or, at minimum, "Parents of children with disabilities should be less strict than other parents." Even as adults, PWDs may be sheltered or protected from life's demands, such as working or managing the disability. In the next chapter, we will discuss the high rates of substance abuse among PWDs, and we will learn that one of the factors is the enabling behavior of PWODs who, out of pity or something else, assist PWDs in obtaining drugs or knowingly choose to ignore the PWD's substance abuse. Such enabling is another form of preferential treatment based on the premise that PWDs should not be held to standards. Preferential treatment of PWDs does not lead to positive results either for the PWDs or for society as a whole.

Compensation and Benefits

Compensation to PWDs includes pensions, insurance benefits such as workers' compensation and Social Security Disability Insurance (SSDI), and private insurance benefits. Implicit in the assumption of compensation is the idea that no further expectations are required of the individual and, because he or she has documented or proved that he or she has a disability, the individual will receive a monthly check. Also, the idea that the individual has somehow earned the right to benefits is also part of the rationale behind compensating PWDs. The Supplemental Security Income (SSI) program, created in 1972, is another form of compensation to PWDs, but it is not based on the premise that the individual has worked and thus "paid into the system." Instead, SSI is a sort of "safety net" for people who have failed to qualify for SSDI because they have not worked. SSI also has a "needs test" that requires the applicant to prove financial need. However, SSDI, workers' compensation insurance, private insurance funds, and military veterans' benefits for disability all consider that the individual has "contributed" to the system and therefore is eligible for benefits. Most compensation schemes do not include individuals with congenital disabilities simply because it is thought that these people never had the opportunity to contribute. (Of course, these congenital disabilities must be sufficiently severe that the individual is unable to work.)

The public purse pays individuals who have acquired disabilities through participating in socially valued activities such as work or war and for whom there is no possibility of returning to work. Often, "in-kind" benefits, such as Medicare and Medicaid, or subsidized housing are included in the benefits. For some PWDs, affordable medical care and medications and vouchers "documenting" a disability may be complicated, but after the disability has been proved, the compensator (government, military, or private insurance company) pays the PWD. Society then feels that it has fulfilled its responsibility to PWDs, and the PWD knows that he or she has contributed to some sort of "scheme," which has provided the benefits and therefore does not consider the benefits to be charity. Some have conceptualized the relationship between compensator and compensatee as "We'll send you a check if you keep out of our sight" and "I get a check every month simply because I have a label (disability)." There is some truth to this.

First, compensation schemes often have built-in financial disincentives that make it difficult for the individual to return to work even if accommodations for the disability are provided. Simply stated, the PWD, if he or she were to become employed, would lose the financial benefits. Therefore, there is no economic advantage to accepting minimum wage jobs, especially for individuals who have high costs associated with the management of the disability and/or individuals who have many dependents. Thus, the PWD is caught in a double bind: He or she cannot "afford" to work and, furthermore, he or she is stereotyped as lazy and unmotivated. Policymakers are working to dismantle this system of disincentives, developing strategies that will allow PWDs to work and still guarantee their benefits, especially their medical benefits. The government has the difficult task of providing for those who truly need assistance and, at the same time, not sabotaging a work-based society.

Second, there are those people who "milk the system." This means that these individuals are capable of working, but they prefer to receive benefits. The most extreme examples of these types of people are seen on television newsmagazine programs where private detectives with video cameras "catch" people with severe back injuries, which supposedly prevent them from working, performing all sorts of recreational activities, such as skiing, painting the house, or hang gliding. Naturally, the public is outraged that there are people who would take advantage of the system. (Television viewers choose to watch these types of programs that may present a one-sided and distorted view of disability issues.) However, most experts consider individuals who fake disabilities (malingerers) to be relatively rare.

Another shortcoming of compensation systems is the difficulty in the determination or diagnosis of a disability. Some applicants are skilled in seeking out those physicians who have a reputation for defining disability very broadly, and insurance companies and government agencies seek to offset this strategy by requesting second opinions from physicians who have reputations for rarely giving disability diagnoses. The determination of disability process can become both complicated and adversarial.

The system of public disability insurance has developed in a patchwork manner because (1) most public insurance programs, with the exception of programs for federal employees, are administered by the states, and there is wide variation in both the definition of disability and in the amounts of compensation from state to state, and (2) the desire to care for those who truly need assistance often conflicts with the need to keep as many individuals in the labor market as possible.

Liachowitz (1988) recounted that during the American Revolutionary War of 1776, both soldiers and sailors who were judged to be "invalids" were required to stay on active duty if they were "found to be capable of doing guard or garrison duty . . . or doing any other duty on board the navy or any department thereof, shall be liable to be so employed" (p. 25). Also, "invalid" sailors and soldiers were required to teach various subjects to young soldiers and sailors. Early in American history, military veterans with disabilities were encouraged (or required) to return to work because the military had broadly defined work to include noncombat jobs and because the military recognized the value of these "invalid" sailors and soldiers. Ironically, the word "invalid" means without value. Implicit in this requirement was the assumption that these veterans were capable of making valuable contributions.

Civil Rights for PWDs

> ### In this section, look for—
>
> - The antecedents of the Disability Rights Movement
> - A discussion of the idea that civil rights for Americans are not based on monetary considerations

The three responses to PWDs of (1) charity, (2) preferential treatment, and (3) compensation are all based on the inherent inferiority of the individual. That is to say, for an individual to receive charity, preferential treatment, or compensation, he or she must first be declared inferior, subordinate, and needy. Of course, most would be quick to add that the inferiority of the individual is the result of a process of nature (the onset of the disability) for which the individual is not personally responsible. In spite of this, inferiority is the basis of the entitlement.

Furthermore, each of these three responses is viewed as a corrective, virtuous, and benevolent action of the larger society. Rarely do proponents of these types of programs consider that self-empowerment, self-determination, and dignity are not possible for PWDs in these types of systems.

In addition, much of the discussion of any response toward Americans with disabilities very quickly arrives at the money question. Costs of workplace and transportation accommodations, costs of care and treatment, and all the other costs can be, and are, calculated. In contrast, the national discussion preceding the passage of the Civil Rights Act of 1964 rarely, if ever, mentioned money or costs. For example, the Civil Rights Act assisted in the desegregation of public schools (building on *Brown v. Board of Education*). Such desegregation must have been expensive, yet there was little, if any, discussion of putting a dollar figure on the right of American children, regardless of their skin color, to integrated education.

Civil rights for Americans are not accorded on the basis of monetary cost, although the ADA does take into consideration the costs to employers of accommodations. Civil rights for PWDs, as outlined in the ADA, are accorded on the basis of American citizenship. Ensuring, by the power of the law, that all important benefits and opportunities of citizenship are extended to PWDs shifts the responsibility for disability issues from the individual to the American nation. The "problem" of disability, as the ADA states clearly and at length, is society's prejudicial attitudes and actions. Therefore, the solution for the "disability problem" is the responsibility of the American nation, and the first step is the passage of national legislation. Parallel with the rationale behind the Civil Rights Act of 1964, the intent of the ADA is to eradicate prejudice, discrimination, segregation, and reduced opportunities for PWDs.

Civil rights for anyone are individually empowering because these rights are an automatic entitlement and legally protected. The individual does not have to depend on the goodwill of others to receive benefits. The ADA, or any other legislation, cannot redress past injustices. However, the ADA states that the status quo (in 1990) was not going to continue, meaning a certain group of American citizens had been intentionally excluded from employment, education, housing, transportation, public buildings, and telecommunications. Further, the responsibility for this disenfranchisement was the collective responsibility of the American people, both for allowing it and for stopping it. Centuries of discrimination and prejudice cannot be redressed, but discrimination and prejudice against PWDs can be stopped.

What Is Justice?

> **In this section, look for—**
>
> - Why standardization is important if everyone is to receive the same treatment
>
> *(continues)*

- Why the standard of evaluation has been White, middle-class males without disabilities
- The argument that accommodations cannot be provided for PWDs because everyone else does not receive these accommodations
- The definition of a meritocracy
- The relationship between Social Darwinism and meritocracies
- Why a "disability-blind" society is not necessarily good
- How a society determines which needs are legitimate and which needs are not
- The concept of "equal outcome"

Basically, there are three types of justice: (1) everybody receives equal treatment, (2) everybody receives what he or she has earned, and (3) everybody receives what he or she needs.

Everybody Receives Equal Treatment

The "everybody receives equal treatment" philosophy of justice is based on accurate standards and guidelines that are upheld for everyone. The word *equal is* used in this case to mean "the same." Standardization is important if everyone is to receive equal treatment. For a long time, the standard of evaluation in the United States, according to many authors, was the White, middle-class male without disabilities. Naturally, not everyone who applied for entrance to schools, jobs, or anything else met all these criteria. In fact, it is debatable whether the numerical majority ever comprised individuals who met all these criteria. Despite this, the rationale was not that everyone or even the majority of people were White, middle-class males without disabilities, but that everyone should *compete* with this group. Therefore, testing and evaluation procedures were validated on norm groups composed of individuals who met the criteria (White, middle-class males without disabilities). Application, admission, promotion, tenure, and termination policies were developed with this standard of evaluation group in mind. Administrative policies could be clear, straightforward, and without exception. Another advantage was the applicability of the standards and rules to *everyone*. All of these examples are termed "institutional" policies, and until recently, these institutional policies were not often questioned or challenged. The idea of equal treatment for everybody appeared to be justice. This type of justice chooses equal opportunity but also understands that there will not be equal outcomes. For example, everybody is free to apply to Harvard, but not all applicants are accepted.

When teachers or employers argue that they cannot provide certain accommodations for PWDs because they "cannot provide the same thing for everybody else," they are invoking the "everybody receives equal treatment" view of justice. Of course, not all students need (or want) their textbooks in Braille. But, if we follow the "everyone receives equal, meaning same, treatment" logic, then the student who is blind cannot have Braille textbooks because the other students do not have Braille textbooks. Ed Roberts, founder of the Independent Living Movement and a polio survivor, was repeatedly refused high school graduation because he had not taken two courses: physical education (PE) and Driver's Ed. Roberts was quadriplegic. Roberts's experience provides an absurd example of holding everyone to the standards.

Everybody Receives What He or She Has Earned

In the view of justice that everybody receives what he or she has earned, everything is earned, including rewards and penalties. This type of society is called a "meritocracy." Some people are clearly "superior" because of intelligence, motivation, skills, or other personal characteristics, and they should be able to enjoy more freedom, more justice, and more rights. Conversely, some people are "inferior" because they lack the requisite personal characteristics to earn their rewards. Further, regardless of the situation in which either of these two types of people (superior or inferior) are placed, the inferior will fail and the superior will rise to the top.

Much of the rationale for this view of justice is derived from Darwinism and Social Darwinism, both of which were based on "survival of the fittest." Social Darwinism was also based on "success of the fittest." Any attempts at "distributive justice" (reallocation of rights and resources) will fail because, as stated before, some people are inferior and some people are superior. If we give the inferior people rights or welfare assistance, they would not know what to do with them and they would end up squandering both. Thus, the inequities in the system are deserved. The superior people do not have to feel guilty about their privileges or feel sorry about the plight of the inferior people. The inferior people should not be jealous of the rights and privileges of the superior people because they could have the same rights and privileges if they would only exert the effort. Social inequities are totally irrelevant to government policy.

Under this type of justice, PWDs are thought to have acquired their disabilities through just plain bad luck, but it is *their* bad luck. Disabilities are seen as deviance and inferiority because this type of justice assumes that the world is a predictable and moral place. If superior people consider their superiority to be justly earned, then they also consider others' inferiority to be justly deserved. Sanctimonious pity is enough for PWDs, and in some societies, such as Nazi Germany, PWDs, because of their (perceived) total lack of merit, were efficiently murdered.

Naturally, when outlined in such a straightforward way, this type of justice makes us uncomfortable, violating our values of compassion and equal opportunity for all. Further, a meritocracy depends on accurate definition and measurement of merit. The most astute authorities cannot agree on what "merit" is. "Inferiority" must also be defined and, in the case of PWDs, much (if not all) of the inferiority is the result of society's handicapping, prejudice, and discrimination.

Everybody Receives What He or She Needs

The view of justice that everybody receives what he or she needs takes individual differences into consideration and also believes that by allowing individuals rights and opportunities, the group as a whole benefits. Of the three types of justice discussed here, the ADA is based on the premise that justice is ensuring that everybody has what he or she needs. The long list of court litigation of ADA issues demonstrates that this type of justice can be complicated and difficult to enact. How does a society determine which needs are legitimate and which needs are not?

Such a view of justice may appear contrary to those who argue that the United States should be "disability-blind" (or "color-blind" or "gender-blind"). Inherent in this view is the idea that there are some groups that have stronger claims for resources, including PWDs. This can result in many groups making claims for resources and accommodations. Where do we stop? But, if we accept that there are biological and functional realities to the experience of disability, then accommodations are both necessary and legitimate. It is expensive to live with a disability. PWDs do require more resources to maintain a reasonable quality of life. Further, as we have learned in this chapter, if society gives PWDs their civil rights and necessary accommodations, society will benefit economically. In addition, and perhaps more important, there are benefits to having a diverse society.

This view of justice is linked with the "equal outcome" concept, meaning that if everyone were to receive what he or she needs from infancy, all types of people would succeed in gaining the rewards of society. Everyone would be earning the same reward, at the same standards, but with differing accommodations. All types of people would graduate from Harvard, become movie stars, and become President of the United States.

In-Class Videos

- View the video "Face First" by Mike Grundmann of Fanlight Productions. In this video, several individuals discuss societal reaction to their disability. Discuss the common issues with which each of these individuals must deal. Include a discussion of the relationships between facial disfigurement and the lack of functional limitations. Which of the sources of stigma apply in this type of disability?

- View the 28-minute video "Images in Media," available from Films for the Humanities and Sciences (P.O. Box 2053, Princeton, NJ 08543-2053, www.films.com). "The pictures in our heads that define who we are and help us neatly categorize others are increasingly shaped by the newspaper, magazine, film, and TV images that bombard our senses . . . . This program is a behind-the-scenes look at the media's image-makers from the first photographers to today's Madison Avenue wizards, and asks some disturbing questions about the self-selected few who hold a distorted mirror up to our society." Discuss how the media's idea of beauty might be viewed by PWDs.

- View the 51-minute video "Children of Gaia: Living with Physical Challenges" by Films for the Humanities and Sciences. "Powerful personal narratives, plus a history of human deformity traced from ancient times through World War II, create a comprehensive and balanced picture of those whose lives have been altered by undeveloped limbs, facial disfigurement, or dwarfism" (producer's description). Discuss the sources of prejudice and discrimination shown in this video.

- View the 19-minute video "Fetal Alcohol Syndrome and Other Drug Use During Pregnancy" by Films for the Humanities and Sciences. The producers describe this video: "This program profiles an eight-year-old boy born with FAS (fetal alcohol syndrome), showing how alcohol enters the bloodstream of the fetus. It describes the common features of children with FAS and their learning disabilities. The program also illustrates in detail how cocaine affects the fetus."

- View the 35-minute video "Breathing Lessons: The Life and Work of Mark O'Brien" produced by Fanlight Productions. The producers describe this video: "Mark O'Brien, a journalist and polio survivor, contracted polio in childhood, and spent much of his life in an iron lung. For more than forty years, he fought against illnesses, bureaucracy and society's conflicting perceptions of disability, to lead an independent life. Incorporating the vivid imagery of O'Brien's poetry, and his candid, wry, and often profound reflections on work, sex, death, and God, this provocative film asks: what makes a life worth living?" Note: This film won the Academy Award for Best Short Documentary. Order No. HN-180.

- View two videos: "Sound & Fury: A Film About the Communication Wars of the Deaf" (55 minutes) and "Sound & Fury: Six Years Later." Both videos are available from Aquarius Health Care Videos. The producers describe the first "Sound & Fury": "This film takes viewers inside the seldom seen world of the deaf to witness a painful family struggle over a controversial medical technology called the cochlear implant. Some of the family members celebrate the implant as a long overdue cure for deafness while others fear it will destroy their language and way of life. Illuminates the ongoing struggle for identity among deaf people today." Product #A-DISSOUND. The video "Sound & Fury: Six Years Later" follows the Artinian family after their daughter receives a cochlear implant. Product #A-DISSOUND6D.

Learning Activities

1. Read *Expecting Adam: A True Story of Birth, Rebirth, and Everyday Magic* (1999) by Martha Beck. This is a memoir of a woman and her husband who learn that the child they are expecting has Down syndrome. Much of the book relates how the Harvard community—both students and faculty—regarded the opportunity to earn an Ivy League graduate degree (which Beck gives up) as more important than the birth of a baby with Down syndrome.

2. Write a paper that explains this statement: If PWDs are accorded (1) civil rights, (2) full social integration, (3) all necessary treatment and assistive technology, and (4) capable and ethical personal care attendants (if needed), PWODs would lose many of their own fears of acquiring a disability.

3. Read *Our Guys* (1998) by Bernard Lefkowitz. This book tells the true story of the 1989 Glen Ridge (New Jersey) rape case in which a group of teenage athletes lured a girl who was mentally retarded into a basement and gang raped her with a broomstick and baseball bat. Write a short paper on the different levels of status and prestige ascribed to the male athletes and to the girl. Discuss your perceptions of the boys' justification of their crime and the town's reaction to the crime. Why is the title of the book *Our Guys?* Why isn't the title *Our Girl?*

4. Read the bestseller *The Broken Cord* (1993) by Michael Dorris. Dorris, a Native American anthropologist, adopted a son with fetal alcohol syndrome (FAS). Before becoming the father of a child with a congenital disability, Dorris was opposed to forced sterilization and advocated for reproductive rights for everyone. Indeed, Dorris's professional work had, up to this point, centered on the genocide of Native American people. However, coping with the FAS of his son, Dorris was tempted to advocate the very practices that he had so vehemently opposed, such as forced sterilization for pregnant women who refuse to stop drinking. Write a paper outlining the changes in Dorris's thinking.

5. As a class, listen to "Inventing the Poster Child" in National Public Radio's Disability History Project. Discuss the advantages and disadvantages of charity and, especially, charity telethons.

Writing Experience

Write a paper that responds to one of the seven "bullet" questions listed at the beginning of this chapter.

References

Albrecht, G. L. (1992). *The disability business: Rehabilitation in America.* Newbury Park, CA: Sage.

Alder, A. B., Wright, B. A., & Ulicny, G. R. (1991). Fundraising portrayals of people with disabilities: Donations and attitudes. *Rehabilitation Psychology, 36,* 231–240.

Allport, G. W. (1986). *The nature of prejudice* (25th anniversary ed.). Reading, MA: Addison-Wesley.

Antonak, R. F. (1980). A hierarchy of attitudes toward exceptionality. *The Journal of Special Education, 14,* 231–241.

Asch, A., & Fine, M. (1997). Nurturance, sexuality, and women with disabilities: The example of women and literature. In L. J. Davis (Ed.), *The disability studies reader* (pp. 241–259). New York: Routledge.

Auge, M., & Herzlich, C. (Eds.). (1995). *The meaning of illness: Anthropology, history, and sociology.* Luxembourg: Harwood Academic Publishers.

Belgrave, F. Z. (1984). The effectiveness of strategies for increasing social interaction with a physically disabled person. *Journal of Applied Social Psychology, 14,* 147–161.

Belgrave, F. Z., & Mills, J. (1981). Effect upon desire for social interaction with a physically disabled person of mentioning the disability in different contexts. *Journal of Applied Social Psychology, 40,* 211–222.

Bell, B. S., & Klein, K. J. (2001). Effects of disability, gender, and job level on ratings of job applicants. *Rehabilitation Psychology, 46,* 229–246.

Berkowitz, E. D. (1987). *Disability policy: America's programs for the handicapped.* Cambridge, England: Cambridge University.

Bickenbach, J. E. (1993). *Physical disability and social policy.* Toronto: University of Toronto.

Bishop, D. S. (Ed.). (1980). *Behavioral problems and the disabled: Assessment and management.* Baltimore: Williams & Wilkins.

Bogdan, R., & Taylor, S. (1987). Toward a sociology of acceptance: The other side of the study of deviance. *Social Policy, Fall,* 34–39.

Bordieri, J. E., & Drehmer, D. E. (1988). Causal attribution and hiring recommendations for disabled job applicants. *Rehabilitation Psychology, 33,* 239–247.

Bowe, F. (1990). Employment and people with disabilities: Challenges for the nineties. *OSERS News in Print, 3,* 2–6.

Bruggemann, B. J., & Burch, S. (Eds.) (2007). *Women and deafness: Double visions:* Washington, DC: Gallaudet University.

Burch, S. (2007). "Beautiful though deaf": The Deaf American beauty pageants. In B. J. Bruggemann & S. Burch (Eds.), *Women and deafness: Double visions* (pp. 242–261). Washington, DC: Gallaudet University.

Buss, D. M. (1999). *Evolutionary psychology: The new science of the mind*. Boston: Allyn & Bacon.

Charlton, J. I. (1998). *Nothing about us without us: Disability oppression and empowerment*. Berkeley, CA: University of California.

Cockerham, W. C. (1998). *Medical sociology* (7th ed.). Upper Saddle River, NJ: Prentice Hall.

Coleman, L. M. (1997). Stigma: An enigma demystified. In L. J. Davis (Ed.), *The disability studies reader* (pp. 216–231). New York: Routledge.

Corrigan, P. W., & Penn, D. L. (1999). Lessons from social psychology on discrediting psychiatric stigma. *American Psychologist, 54*, 765–776.

Couser, G. T. (1997). *Recovering bodies: Illness, disability, and life writing*. Madison, WI: University of Wisconsin.

Crewe, N. M. (1980). The difficult patient. In D. S. Bishop (Ed.), *Behavior problems and the disabled: Assessment and management* (pp. 98–119). Baltimore: Williams & Wilkins.

Curry, R. L. (1995). The exceptional family: Walking the edge of tragedy and transformation (pp. 24–57). In S. K. Toombs, D. Barnard, & R. A. Carson (Eds.), *Chronic illness: From chronic illness to policy*. Bloomington, IN: University of Indiana.

Deal, M. (2003). Disabled people's attitudes toward other impairment groups. A hierarchy of impairment. *Disability and Society, 18*, 897–910.

DeLoach, C., & Greer, B. G. (1981). *Adjustment to severe disability: A metamorphosis*. New York: McGraw-Hill.

Dembo, T., Leviton, G. L., & Wright, B. A. (1956). Adjustment to misfortune: A problem of social-psychological rehabilitation. *Artificial Limbs, 3*, 4–62.

Druss, R. G. (1995). *The psychology of illness: In sickness and in health*. Washington, DC: American Psychiatric Press.

Esses, V. M., & Beaufoy, S. L. (1994). Determinants of attitudes toward people with disabilities. *Journal of Social Behavior and Personality, 9*, 43–64.

Etcoff, N. (1999). *Survival of the prettiest: The science of beauty*. Cambridge, MA: Harvard University Press.

Fiedler, L. (1978). *Freaks: Myths and images of the secret self*. New York: Simon & Schuster.

Fenigsen, R. (1997). Euthanasia of disabled infants is not morally acceptable (pp. 160–164). In B. Stalcup (Ed.), *The disabled*. San Diego, CA: Greenhaven.

Films for the Humanities and Sciences. (1999). *Autism. The child who couldn't play* [Film]. (Available from Films for the Humanities and Sciences, P.O. Box 2053, Princeton, NJ 08543-2053, 800-257-5126; www.films.com)

Finger, A. (1993). Toward a theory of radical disability photography. *Disability Rag, November*, 29–31.

Fowler, C. A., & Wadsworth, J. S. (1991). Individualism and equality: Critical values in North American culture and the impact on disability. *Journal of Applied Rehabilitation Counseling, 22*, 19–23.

Fox, K. R. (Ed.). (1997). *The physical self: From motivation to well-being*. Champaign, IL: Human Kinetics.

Furnham, A., & Pendred, J. (1983). Attitudes toward the mentally and physically disabled. *British Journal of Medical Psychology, 56*, 179–187.

Goffman, E. (1963). *Stigma: Notes on the management of spoiled identity*. Englewood Cliffs, NJ: Prentice Hall.

Goodyear, R. K. (1983). Patterns of counselors' attitudes toward disability groups. *Rehabilitation Counseling Bulletin, 26*, 181–184.

Gordon, E. D., Minnes, P. M., & Holden, R. R. (1990). The structure of attitudes towards persons with a disability when specific disability and context are concerned. *Rehabilitation Psychology, 35*, 79–90.

Grealy, L. (1999). Pony parties. In K. Fries (Ed.), *Staring back: The disability experience from the inside out* (pp. 13–21). New York: Plume.

Harasymiw, S. J., Home, M. D., & Lewis, S. C. (1976). A longitudinal study of disability group acceptance. *Rehabilitation Literature, 37*, 98–102.

Harper, D. C. (1999). Social psychology of difference: Stigma, spread, and stereotypes in childhood. *Rehabilitation Psychology, 44*, 133–144.

Hayes, S. C., Barlow, D. H., & Nelson-Gray, R. G. (1999). *The scientist-practitioner: Research and accountability in the age of managed care* (2nd ed.). Needham Heights, MA: Allyn & Bacon.

Henderson, G., & Bryan, W. V. (1997). *Psychosocial aspects of disability* (2nd ed.). Springfield, IL: Charles C. Thomas.

Higgins, P. C. (1992). *Making disability: Exploring the social transformation of human variation.* Springfield, IL: Charles C. Thomas.

Horne, M. D., & Ricciardo, J. L. (1988). Hierarchy of response to handicaps. *Psychological Reports, 62*, 83–86.

Hubbard, R. (1997). Abortion and disability: Who should and who should not inhabit the world? In L. J. Davis (Ed.), *The disability studies reader* (pp. 187–200). New York: Routledge.

Imrie, R. (1996). *Disability and the city: International perspectives.* New York: St. Martin's Press.

Janicki, M. P. (1970). Attitudes of health professionals toward twelve disabilities. *Perceptual and Motor Skills, 30*, 77–78.

Johnson, H. B. (2003, February 16). Should I have been killed at birth? The case for my life. *The New York Times Magazine, 50*, 52–56, 74.

Jones, E. E., Farina, A., Hastorf, A. H., Markus, H., Miller, D. T., & Scott, R. A. (1984). *Social stigma: The psychology of marked relationships.* New York: W. H. Freeman.

Jones, R. L. (1974). The hierarchical structure of attitudes toward the exceptional. *Exceptional Children, 40*, 430–435.

Karp, D. A. (2001). *The burden of sympathy: How families cope with mental illness.* Oxford, UK: Oxford University.

Kleege, G. (2006). *Blind rage: Letters to Helen Keller.* Washington, DC: Gallaudet University.

Koestler, F. A. (1976). *The unseen minority: A social history of blindness in America.* New York: David McKay.

Kravetz, S., Katz, S., & Albez, D. (1994). Attitudes toward Israeli war veterans with disabilities: Combat versus noncombat military service and responsibility for the disability. *Rehabilitation Counseling Bulletin, 37*, 371–379.

Kriegel, L. (1982). Claiming the self: The cripple as American male. In M. G. Eisenberg, C. Griggins, & R. J. Duval (Eds.), *Disabled people as second-class citizens* (pp. 52–63). New York: Springer.

Landers, A. (1999, October 6). Smokers raise insurance for all. *The Herald Journal*, p. 15.

Lane, H. (1993). Cochlear implants: Their cultural and historical meaning. In J. V. Van Cleve (Ed.), *Deaf history unveiled: Interpretations from the new scholarship* (pp. 272–291). Washington, DC: Gallaudet University Press.

Langlois, J. H., & Roggman, L. A. (1990). Attractive faces are only average. *Psychological Science, 1,* 115–121.

Lehr, D. H., & Brinckerhoff, J. (1996). Bases of practice for young children with disabilities who challenge the system. In D. H. Lehr & F. Brown (Eds.), *People with disabilities who challenge the system* (pp. 3–22). Baltimore: Brookes.

Leinhardt, G., & Pallay, A. (1982). Restrictive educational settings: Exile or haven. *Review of Educational Research, 52,* 557–558.

Liachowitz, C. H. (1988). *Disability as a social construct: Legislative roots.* Philadelphia: University of Pennsylvania.

Livneh, H. (1991). On the origins of negative attitudes toward people with disabilities. In R. P. Marinelli & A. E. Dell Otto (Eds.), *The psychological and social impact of disability* (3rd ed., pp. 181–196). New York: Springer.

Longmore, P. K. (2003). *Why I burned my book and other essays on disability.* Philadelphia: Temple University.

Macgregor, F. C. (1951). Some psycho-social problems associated with facial deformities. *American Social Review, 16,* 629–638.

Mackelprang, R., & Salsgiver, R. (1999). *Disability: A diversity approach in human service practice.* Pacific Grove, CA: Brookes/Cole.

Marantz, P. R. (1990). Blaming the victim: The negative consequences of preventive medicine. *American Journal of Public Health, 80,* 1185–1187.

Marks, D. (1999). *Disability: Controversial debates and psychosocial perspectives.* London: Routledge.

Mee, C. L. (1999). *A nearly normal life.* Boston: Little, Brown.

Miller, J. (1988). Personal statement: Mechanisms for coping with the disability of a child—A mother's perspective. In P. W. Power, A. E. Dell Otto, & M. B. Gibbons (Eds.), *Family interventions throughout chronic illness and disability* (pp. 136–147). New York: Springer.

Morris, D. B. (1998). *Illness and culture in the postmodern age.* Berkeley: University of California.

Morris, J. (1991). *Pride against prejudice: Transforming attitudes to disability.* Philadelphia: New Society.

Mundy, L. (2003). A world of their own (pp. 68–87). In O. Sacks (Ed.), *The best science writing 2003.* New York: Harper Collins.

Murphy, M. A. (1998). Rejection, stigma, and hope. *Psychiatric Rehabilitation Journal, 22,* 185–189.

Murphy, R. F. (1987). *The body silent.* New York: Henry Holt.

National Public Radio (1998, May). *The Disability History Project: Tomorrow's Children.*

Olshansky, S. (1965). Stigma: Its meaning and its problems for vocational rehabilitation agencies. *Rehabilitation Literature, 26,* 71–72.

Pelka, F. (1997). *The ABC-CLIO companion to the disability rights movement.* Santa Barbara, CA: ABC-CLIO.

Richardson, S. A., & Ronald, L. (1977). The effect of a physically handicapped interviewer on children's expression of values toward handicap. *Rehabilitation Psychology, 24,* 111–128.

Safilios-Rothschild, C. (1982). Social and psychological parameters of friendship and intimacy for disabled people. In M. G. Eisenberg, C. Griggins, & R. J. Duval (Eds.), *Disabled people as second-class citizens* (pp. 40–51). New York: Springer.

Safran, S. P. (1998). The first century of disability portrayal in film: An analysis of the literature. *The Journal of Special Education, 31,* 467–479.

Scholar under fire for views on infanticide. (1999, October 2). *The Herald Journal,* pp. 2, 4.

Schroeder, F. (1997, March). Presentation given at the Annual Training Conference of the National Council on Rehabilitation Education/Rehabilitation Services Administration and Council of State Administrators of Vocational Rehabilitation, Washington, DC.

Schur, E. M. (1983). *Labeling women deviant: Gender, stigma, and social control.* Philadelphia: Temple University.

Shakespeare, T., Gillespie-Sells, K., & Davies, D. (1996). *The sexual politics of disability: Untold stories.* London: Caswell.

Shapiro, J. P. (1993). *No pity: People with disabilities forging a new civil rights movement.* New York: Times Book.

Shell, M. (2005). *Polio and its aftermath.* Cambridge, MA: Harvard University Press.

Sherrill, C. (1997). Disability, identity, and involvement in sport and exercise. In K. R. Fox (Ed.), *The physical self: From motivation to well-being* (pp. 257–286). Champaign, IL: Human Kinetics.

Shurka, E., & Katz, J. (1976). Evaluations of persons with disability: The influence of disability context and personal responsibility for the disability. *Rehabilitation Psychology, 23,* 65–71.

Sontag, S. (1978). *Illness as metaphor.* New York: Farrar, Strauss, & Giroux.

Tanenbaum, S. J. (1986). *Engineering disability: Public policy and compensatory technology.* Philadelphia: Temple University.

Thomas, A. (2000). Stability of Tringo's hierarchy of preference toward disability groups: Thirty years later. *Psychological Reports, 86,* 1155–1156.

Thompson, T. (1982). Gaze toward the avoidance of the handicapped: A field experiment. *Journal of Nonverbal Behavior, 6,* 188–196.

Thorn, K. R., Hershenson, D. B., & Romney, A. K. (1994). Causal attribution factors in conceptions of disability. *Rehabilitation Counseling Bulletin, 37,* 315–331.

Toombs, S. K., Barnard, D., & Carson, R. A. (Eds.). (1995). *Chronic illness: From experience to policy.* Bloomington, IN: University of Indiana.

Torriero, E. A. (2006, September 3). Disabled activists don't deter Jerry Lewis. Associated Press.

Tringo, J. L. (1970). The hierarchy of preference toward disability groups. *The Journal of Special Education, 4,* 295–306.

Vermeij, G. (1997). *Privileged hands: A scientific life.* New York: Freeman.

Waitzkin, W. C. (1991). *The politics of medical encounters: How patients and doctors deal with social problems.* New Haven, CT: Yale University.

Walster, E. (1966). Assignment of responsibility for an accident. *Journal of Personality and Social Psychology, 3,* 73–79.

Wang, C. (1993). Culture, meaning, and disability: Injury prevention campaigns and the production of stigma. In M. Nagler (Ed.), *Perspectives on disability* (2nd ed., pp. 77–90). Palo Alto, CA: Health Markets Research.

Weiner, B., Perry, R. P., & Magnusson, J. (1988). An attributional analysis of reactions to stigmas. *Journal of Personality and Social Psychology, 55,* 738–748.

Wendell, S. (1997). Toward a feminist theory of disability. In L. J. Davis (Ed.), *The disability studies reader* (pp. 260–278). New York: Routledge.

Wilder, D. (1987). Personal responsibility for illness. In D. Van De Veer & T. Regan (Eds.), *Health care ethics: An introduction* (pp. 326–358). Philadelphia: Temple University.

Wilson, J. (1999, October 20). Egg salesman defends web venture. *The Herald Journal,* pp. 1, 10.

Wolbring, G. (2001). Where do we draw the line? Surviving eugenics in a technological world. In M. Priestley (Ed.), *Disability and life course.* Cambridge, UK: Cambridge University.

Wright, B. A. (1960). *Physical disability: A psychological approach* (1st ed.). New York: Harper-Collins.

Wright, B. A. (1988). Attitudes and the fundamental negative bias: Conditions and corrections. In H. E. Yuker (Ed.), *Attitudes toward persons with disabilities* (pp. 3–21). New York: Springer.

Yelin, E. (1989). Disabled concern: The social context of the work-disability problem. *The Milbank Quarterly, 67,* 114–165.

Zola, I. K. (1983). *Socio-medical inquiries: Recollections, reflections, and reconsiderations.* Philadelphia: Temple University.

Zola, I. K. (1991). Communication barriers between "the able-bodied" and "the handicapped." In R. P. Marinelli & A. E. Dell Orto (Eds.), *The psychological and social impact of disability* (pp. 157–164). New York: Springer.

Suggested Readings

Antonak, R. F., & Livneh, H. (1988). *The measurement of attitudes toward people with disabilities.* Springfield, IL: Charles C. Thomas.

Bordieri, J. E. (1993). Self-blame attributions for disability and perceived client involvement in the vocational rehabilitation process. *Journal of Applied Rehabilitation Counseling, 24*(2), 3–7.

Dorris, M. (1989). *The broken cord.* New York: Harper.

Eisenberg, M. G. (1982). Disability as stigma. In M. G. Eisenberg, C. Griggins, & R. J. Duval (Eds.), *Disabled people as second-class citizens* (pp. 1–11). New York: Springer.

Eisenberg, M. G., Griggins, C., & Duval, R. J. (Eds.). (1982). *Disabled people as second-class citizens.* New York: Springer.

Harris, L. (1987). *The ICD survey IL: Employing disabled Americans.* New York: Louis Harris.

Harris, L. (1994). *The ICD survey III: Employing disabled Americans.* New York: Louis Harris.

Harrison, J. (1987). *Severe physical disability: Responses to the challenges of care.* London: Cassell.

Watson, J. D. (1984). Talking about the best kept secret: Sexual abuse and children with disabilities. *Exceptional Parent, 14*(6), 15–20.

Whitney, C. R. (1993, January 19). Disabled Germans fear they'll be the next target. *The New York Times,* p. A3.

The Effects of Prejudice and Discrimination

- Are disabilities perceived as difference or are disabilities perceived as deviance?
- Are PWDs "differently challenged"?
- Does society teach PWDs to think of themselves as inferior?
- Why have PWDs experienced more prejudice and discrimination than any other group in history?
- What is the difference between institutional handicapism and social handicapism?
- Can well-intentioned people be handicapping?
- What does the following sentence mean? "The world is designed to further the purposes of PWODs."
- Do factors inherent in the disability itself lead to prejudice and discrimination?
- Why has the contact theory not worked in reducing prejudice and discrimination?
- Why are simulation exercises ineffective and offensive to PWDs?
- How do PWODs (and society) pay for their prejudice and discrimination against PWDs?

Are Disabilities Viewed as Difference or as Deviance?

> **In this section, look for—**
>
> - How difference and diversity are considered to be positive
> - How deviance is considered to be negative
> - How, in reality, difference, diversity, and deviance do not have an inherent value
> - How the label of deviance is based on society's fears, anxieties, and false assumptions
> - How society treats those who are considered to be deviant by morally excluding them
> - The relationship between stigmatization and deviancy
> - Why the Biomedical Model of disability has contributed to defining PWDs as deviant

Many differences among people are considered to be desirable, enriching, valuable, and strengthening to the larger group. We often use the positive word "diversity" to describe these valued differences. These types of differences and diversities usually do not have a hierarchical component. In other words, individuals who are diverse or have differences are considered to be equal to everyone else. Inherent in this notion of equality is the lack of a standard of evaluation or a widely accepted concept of a "norm." In Chapter 1, we discussed the concept of normalcy as a standard of evaluation and concluded that normality was defined and measured/evaluated/assessed by the group in power.

If there is any hierarchical component applied to people who are different or diverse, these people are most often considered to be superior. Indeed, much of the media today plays on our fascination with people we consider to be unlike ourselves. For example, we like to see and hear about film stars and political figures, mostly because they are different from us. Society considers their differences to be desirable, enriching, and strengthening to the larger group. Such diversity and difference are considered to be positive, and although a relatively small portion of the larger society will ever attain such diversity or difference, we still admire and respect these few people who are different. These differences and diversity often translate into power and authority, which is conferred by society, and most people usually like to align themselves with power and authority.

Deviance, however, is considered to be socially undesirable and weakening to the larger group, and people who are labeled deviant are automatically considered to be inferior. People usually do not aspire to become labeled "deviant"; indeed, most individuals work very hard to avoid this label. Jenny Morris (1991) explained the way in which these attitudes affected her: "It is very undermining to recognize that people look at me and see an existence, an experience, which they would do everything to avoid for themselves" (p. 15). People who exhibit differences that are labeled "deviant" are not considered to be assets to the larger group. Indeed, often "deviants" are thought of as "drains" or "burdens" to the group or, at minimum, as not having much to contribute. Society tends to avoid, isolate, reject, and segregate people who are labeled as deviants. Also, "deviants" are often feared and evoke hostile reactions. We often think of deviants as undeserving; "consequently harming them appears acceptable, appropriate, or just" (Opotow, 1990, p. 1).

Friedson (1965) stated that a disability "is an imputation of difference from others; more particularly an imputation of undesirable difference. By definition, then, a person who is said to be handicapped [sic] is so defined because he [sic] deviates from what he himself or others believe to be normal or appropriate" (p. 72). Higgins (1992), in his book *Making Disability: Exploring the Social Transformation of Human Variation*, described the relationship between disability labels/identities and societal norms: "Differences reside in the different persons rather than in relation to norms embedded in prevailing institutions. It is also presumed that the status quo is natural and good" (p. 230). Lerita Coleman (1997) used the term "stigmatization" to describe society's tendency to ascribe deviancy to PWDs: "To further clarify the definition of stigma, one must differentiate between 'undesired differentness' that is likely to lead to feelings of stigmatization and actual forms of stigmatization. *It appears that stigmatization occurs only when the social control component is imposed, or when the undesired differentness leads to some restriction in physical and social mobility and access to opportunities that allow an individual to develop his or her potential* [italics added]" (p. 227).

Any attribute can be labeled deviant. Age, racial/ethnic group, nationality, income level, religion, political affiliation, sexual orientation, and gender are all examples of attributes that have been, and to some extent still are, labeled as deviant (Goffman, 1963). However, with all of these examples of types of attributes, the deviancy and stigmatization ascribed to individuals who fit these categories have not been as widespread and pervasive as the deviancy and stigmatization ascribed to PWDs. Reviewing the list of often-stigmatized attributes, we can see that there are environments in which they can escape these negative judgments. For example, individuals of certain races or nationalities are not stigmatized in their native country or in their homes with family members who, most likely, share the same racial/ethnic/cultural identity. For PWDs, there are few such environments.

Lennard Davis (1997) used the word "undesirable" instead of "deviance." In the following excerpt from his book *The Disability Studies Reader*, Davis described the tendency to "lump" all people considered to be deviant, or undesirable, into one category: "The problem for people with disabilities was that eugenicists tended to group together all allegedly 'undesirable' traits. So, for example, criminals, the poor, and people with disabilities might be mentioned in the same breath. A leading figure defined the 'unfit' as follows: 'the habitual criminal, the professional tramp, the tuberculous, the insane, the mentally defective, the alcoholic, the diseased from birth or from excess'" (p. 17).

The only factor that people with disabilities have in common with the other types of individuals listed is the deviance and inferiority ascribed to them by the larger society. Davis (1997) judged the results of "lumping" PWDs with these other types of people: "The loose association between what we would now call disability and criminal activity . . . sexual license, and so on established a legacy that the people with disabilities are still having trouble living down . . . . The conflation of disability with depravity expressed itself in the formulation of 'defective class'" (p. 18).

Of course, the accurate definition of <u>deviance is simply *differing from a norm*</u>. Chapter 1 presented two important ideas: (1) technically, the concepts of deviance, difference, and norms do not have an inherent value component—all of these concepts are neutral; they can be either good or bad, and (2) defining groups in power develops norms. When these two concepts are taken into consideration, it can be seen that deviance can also mean valuable, extraordinary, superior, and desirable. In addition, simply because societal norms have been in place for literally centuries, it is often easy to leap to the conclusion that these norms are both immutable (unchanging) and completely valid and appropriate. When we pause to think about societal norms, without which judgments of differences and deviance would be impossible, we can see that norms and standards do evolve and change, and often <u>these standards and norms are arbitrary because they are based on the fears, anxieties, and false assumptions of the defining group</u> (Schur, 1971, 1979, 1983).

Deviance, therefore, is not within the individual; rather, <u>deviance is a judgment of the dominant, defining segment of society</u> (Gellman, 1959; Goffman, 1963, 1997). Without social comparison, there can be no judgment of deviance. Stated in another way, both deviance and normalcy are defined in relation to each other; thus, <u>sociologists consider deviance-labeling to be an interactionist theory</u>. One sociologist (Becker, 1963) clearly explained:

> Social groups create deviance by making the rules whose infraction constitutes defiance, and by applying these rules to particular people and labeling them as outsiders. From this point of view, deviance is not a quality of the person . . . but rather a consequence of the application by others of rules and sanctions to an "offender." The deviant is one to whom that label has been successfully applied. (p. 9)

Most, if not all, deviance is forced on the individual. Certainly the individual does not choose to carry this label or to be subjected to the resulting prejudice and discrimination. Often his or her family and marriage partner are labeled "deviant by association" even when these family members do not exhibit the "deviant" characteristics. Indeed, most individuals considered by others to be deviant do not think of themselves in this way. Furthermore, occasionally, individuals who are stigmatized in this way are not aware of their forced status of being viewed as deviant. In the last section of this book, we will discuss the importance of "a personal awakening, a discovery that the responsibility for being stigmatized does not lie with oneself" (Davis, 1997, p. 223).

Many PWODs mistakenly believe that PWDs want to be "normal." Jenny Morris explained: "One of the most oppressive features of the prejudice which disabled [*sic*] people experience is the assumption that we want to be other than we are, that is, we want to be normal. . . . Do we only have value, even to ourselves, in direct relation to how closely we can imitate 'normal' appearance, function, belief, and behavior? The only way in which it seems we can gain acceptance is to emulate normality . . . . [T]he pressures on us to aspire to be 'normal' are huge—friends and family all conspire from the kindest and highest of intentions to ensure that we make the wrong choice" (p. 35). Nadine LaSpina, a polio survivor, describes her pride in being an individual with a disability, despite some of the difficulties:

> I'm proud of being Italian. There are things I am ashamed of, like the existence of the Mafia—but these things do not stop me from embracing my Italian-ness. I love being a woman, but I hate going through menopause. But I wouldn't want a sex-change operation just because of menopause. Certainly the pain and physical limitations of disability are not wonderful, yet that identity is who I am. And I am proud of it."
> (Fleischer & Zames, 2001, p. 202)

LaSpina's viewpoint echoes Morris's statement—"I can value my disability, while not denying the difficulties associated with it"—and asserts that PWDs are "thrown on the defensive of trying to prove that our lives are worth living by denying that disability sometimes involves being sick, in pain, or generally experiencing an awful time" (p. 71).

Deviance also implies shame, holding the "deviant" individual responsible both for his or her own devaluation and for many of society's problems. PWDs historically have been viewed as scapegoats. "People with disabilities have represented a convenient group to blame for a number of problems" (Covey, 1998, p. 12). Thus, the Biomedical Model of disability has contributed to the tendency to label PWDs as deviants simply because this model considers the "problem" to be totally within the individual. Rather than acknowledging society's judgments and evaluations as the "problem," the Biomedical Model holds that the disability (and the individual who experiences the disability) is the "problem." Therefore, society is not required to change; it is the individual with the disability who has to be "fixed" to "fit in." Of course, for most individuals with disabilities, the disability is both permanent and visible, thus making it impossible for the individual to "fit in." Rob Imrie (1996) explained how assumptions of the Biomedical Model have resulted in stigmatization and deviance-labeling and architectural inaccessibility for PWDs: "And because the physical or built environment remains a given in the medical theorization of disability, there has been a tendency for disabled [*sic*] people to be stigmatized, or the association of disability with stigma wholly reinforces the notion of disability as an individually derived problem" (p. 39). Therefore, because the Biomedical Model views the PWD as the problem, it was thought that there is no need for the physical environment to change.

In the National Public Radio's Disability History Project, a mother of a child with a disability expressed the hope that "people with disabilities will no longer be alien from our affections" (National Public Radio, 1998, Tomorrow's Children). By using the words "alien" she expressed the idea that society considers PWDs to be deviants and outsiders, and the word "affections" captures the idea that society, as a whole, has not felt much empathy or concern for PWDs. At worst, society has often thought of PWDs as less than human. Prejudice and discrimination can seem rational when people are labeled as deviants, such as those with disabilities, especially people who are thought to have brought the deviance on themselves (as PWDS are often thought to have caused their disability). "Moral exclusion can occur in degrees from overt evil to passive unconcern" (Opotow, 1990, p. 13). For PWDs, overt evil has included abuse and murder, and the passive unconcern is found in inaccessible environments. Leytens et al. (2000) explained that when societies "regard out-groups as less human" (p. 194) or lacking "the human essence," discrimination results.

There is a lack of interest in lives we consider different from the mainstream; we simply prefer that PWDs remain silent and invisible. However, we do tend to either exclude PWDs from our attention or render them hypervisible in sensationalized, exaggerated media portrayals. Society distances itself from those it considers to be deviant. It is interesting that the Mental Health Bell, the symbol of the National Mental Health Association, was forged out of metal melted down from chains, shackles, and restraints that had been used to restrain people with psychiatric disabilities (New York ABLE, 2000). The similarity of the Mental Health Bell to the Liberty Bell, a symbol of American independence, was not unintentional.

Society often does not recognize the prejudice and discrimination against PWDs. Fleischer and Zames (2001) explained:

> Unkind words against homosexuals, African Americans, Hispanics, and other minorities at least prompt rebuke from people who, though not members of these stigmatized groups, still recognize the prejudice. But prejudice against individuals with disabilities commonly goes un-

detected by a general public too unaware of its own feelings to recognize what has been said or written as prejudicial." (p. xv)

This lack of awareness is probably the result of a combination of factors, which includes: (1) the Biomedical Model of disability, which has "excused" society from responsibility toward citizens with disabilities; (2) the feelings of vulnerability and existential questioning that disabilities arouse in PWODs; and (3) the widespread myth that disability is a private, family concern.

PWDs do have actual differences from people who do not have disabilities, although the differences are not as great as most PWODs consider them to be. Stefan (2001), a legal scholar, demonstrated that physical differences are relevant and important and, further, individuals with these differences (such as disabilities) have the right to government resources. Stefan argued that women and men in the United States have had different rights and resources provided to them based on their gender differences and this has never been considered as inequality: "Women get pregnant, give birth, live longer, and are, on average, shorter and lighter. These differences, although relevant in a variety of ways, do not necessarily justify disadvantageous treatment, even when no comparison appears available. Thus, gross underfunding of breast cancer research was denounced as discrimination against women without showing that more research was being funded for breast cancer in men" (p. 113). Stefan argued that Americans with disabilities have legitimate rights to government resources as a result of the needs of their disabilities; further, these rights should not be considered preferential treatment.

Occasionally, PWDs are not aware of their "deviant" status. Children with disabilities who have grown up in a loving and accepting home know they have a disability and that they are different from other children, but it is not until they begin activities outside the home, such as school, that these children understand the meaning their disability has for others. At home, the disability was difference but it was not stigma, inferiority, shame, or deviance (Eisenberg, Griggins, & Duval, 1982). The first day of school for these children often is unpleasantly surprising when they realize that others think of their disability as inferiority and as shameful. Adults who acquire a disability later in life often are unpleasantly surprised (or shocked) when they discover that they are viewed as objects of pity and inferiority (Eisenberg, 1982). Before the onset of the disability, they were individuals of status who enjoyed the respect of others. After the onset, the PWD is treated as an inferior, childlike person who is to be avoided.

Obviously, the attitudes and behaviors toward PWDs are being labeled as prejudice and discrimination. PWDs are integrating into the wider culture; services are being offered and PWDs are forming a group identity to gain their civil rights. The number of barriers and inaccessible environments is decreasing; ossified federal legislation, such as Social Security laws, is changing to allow PWDs the financial freedom to work. PWDs are refusing to be excluded from American life.

Disability Should be Considered as Diversity

The disability experience should be viewed as a valued type of diversity with the potential to enrich and strengthen the broader culture. Harriet McBryde Johnson succinctly captured this idea by stating, "We have something the world needs." Every human is required to understand and accept his or her body. Individuals without disabilities may mistakenly (or wishfully) think that they have complete control over their bodies. PWDs could teach us a great deal about accepting our humanity. Disability can happen to anyone and it is not the worst thing possible. Life with a disability can be satisfying, rich, and happy.

Are PWDs "Differently Challenged"?

In this section, look for—

- Why the expression "differently challenged" is trivializing and demeaning to PWDs

In the past, have PWDs been labeled as different or deviant? Are PWDs considered to be different or deviant today? Disability scholars have shown that PWDs were, and continue to be, labeled as deviant. Most PWDs consider it incorrect to use the expression "differently challenged" for individuals with disabilities. Difference, as we have seen, is a positive term, and many PWDs do not consider their treatment by PWODs to be positive. The use of the word "differently" denies and trivializes the history (and the current experience) of PWDs being labeled deviant and inferior.

Cheryl Wade (1997) wrote a poem entitled *I Am Not One of The*. The first line is "I am not one of the physically challenged" and another line is "I am not one of the differently abled." Wade organized the stanzas of the poem around each of the trivializing and ill-informed labels that PWODs ascribe to the disability experience. Indeed, the title of the poem clearly shows the poem's purpose and the author's insistence that she be allowed to define and describe herself and her disability experience.

Do Disabilities Always Lead to Social Inferiority?

In this section, look for—

■ The examples from history and the present-day media that confer second-class citizenship on PWDs

People considered to be inferior do not have freedom, dignity, or security (Henderson & Bryan, 1997). People who are considered inferior are often labeled as "second-class citizens" (Eisenberg et al., 1982), meaning that legal, institutionalized practices contribute to their lack of opportunity and segregation. Disability scholars have documented the inferior status of PWDs (Hillyer, 1993; Murphy, 1998). Liachowitz (1988) succinctly stated, "The laws that deal with handicapped [*sic*] people reflect . . . the views that biological deficiency confers social deficiency and that handicapped people [*sic*] deserve . . . a place outside the mainstream of society" (p. 1).

The following are a few examples of prejudice and discrimination.

■ A 1997 Associated Press article entitled "Handicapped [*sic*] Used as Guinea Pigs" revealed that Sweden forcibly sterilized 60,000 people with disabilities between the years 1935 and 1976, and hundreds of institutionalized Swedes who were mentally retarded were fed daily diets of candy to provide scientists the opportunity to prove the cause-and-effect relationship between eating sugar and tooth decay.

■ A Louis Harris poll, conducted in 1987, found that the unemployment rate of people with disabilities is the highest of any demographic group in the United States. Furthermore, a Harris poll in 1994 (4 years after the passage of the Americans with Disabilities Act [ADA]) found no improvement in the rate of employment among people with disabilities compared to 1987. Two thirds of individuals with disabilities are unemployed, and of those who do work, only 11% have full-time jobs. This high rate of unemployment and underemployment persists in spite of the fact that most individuals with disabilities report that they want to work (Hahn, 1997; Trupin, Sebesta, Yelin, & LaPlante, 1997).

■ Medical researchers (Lerner & Belts, 2005) stated that the medical profession is not meeting the needs of PWDs, citing "worrisome" differences between the medical care provided to PWODs and the care provided to PWDs. "Fifteen years since the passage of the ADA, people with physical disabilities still find that both the access to and quality of care provided to them lags significantly behind that for people who do not have such disabilities. Insurance isn't the issue either. Even with health insurance, people with disabilities are often unable to get needed care. In spring 2000, a national survey commissioned by the National Organization on Disability of people age 16 and older with and without disabilities found worrisome disparities. Fully 28% of insured people with disabilities reported that they need particular therapies, equipment or medications that were not covered by their health plans, compared to 7% of those without disabilities. Nineteen percent of disabled persons [*sic*] reported that they needed medical care within the previous year but didn't get it, compared with 6% of nondisabled people" (p. 20).

- It is often questioned if fetuses with disabilities should be allowed to live. Hubbard (1997) stated, "No one these days openly suggests that certain kinds of people should be killed; they just should not be born" (p. 198).

- The "why bother?" concept is based on the assumption that the individual's disabilities are so severe and multiple "that treatment would make no difference or that the extra expenditures would not be worthwhile or cost-effective" (Lehr & Brinkerhoff, 1996, p. 10). These authors cite examples in which "[p]arents have been told, directly or indirectly, 'What difference would it make if Barry could see better with glasses? He can't understand what he sees anyway.' 'Why bother continuing to work on oral motor development? The tube feeding is going fine'" (pp. 10–11). Extreme examples of the "why bother?" syndrome are the "Baby Doe" cases in which infants with severe disabilities were denied lifesaving medical treatment because of physicians' predictions about their lack of quality of life. In contrast, infants without disabilities, or with less severe disabilities, were automatically provided with these lifesaving treatments (Anderson, 1987).

- People with disabilities are far more often the targets of crime, physical abuse, and sexual abuse (Cole, 1984, 1993; Craine, Henson, Colliver, & McLelan, 1988; Sobsey & Doe, 1991; Ulicny, White, Bradford, & Matthews, 1990; Waxman, 1991). For example, Sobsey (1994) reported that studies from many countries, such as the United States, the United Kingdom, and Australia, "suggest that child abuse, beatings, and rape are common occurrences in the lives of many, probably most, people with developmental disabilities" (cited in Pelka, 1997, p. 260). "[The damaged merchandise myth] provides the offender with a rationalization not only for the choice of victim but also may alleviate any guilt or inhibition about exploiting the disabled [*sic*] person" (Sobsey & Mansell, 1993, pp. 289–290).

- "It is estimated that only about 20 percent of private practicing dentists are willing to accept patients with minimal disabilities. This failure of the dental profession to treat PWDs persists in spite of the fact that both the prevalence and severity of dental disease are significantly increased in the disabled [*sic*] population. In many instances, the disability itself either contributes directly to oral disease or greatly exaggerates an existing condition . . . . Accordingly, frequently the treatment regimen indicated for the management of these cases also may be a causative factor in dental disease. Perhaps the most notorious of treatments directly causing oral disease is the resultant gingival hyperplasia seen following the administration of the anticonvulsant dilantin or the antihypertensive nifedpine . . . . The drug is capable of producing an overgrowth of gingival soft tissue to the extent that the crowns of all teeth will be nearly submerged by the overgrowth. Obviously, the condition presents a formidable obstacle to chewing and speaking, not to mention the negative aesthetic aspects. Similarly, many sedatives and psychotropic medications, besides containing sugars in a liquid medium that contribute to tooth decay, also have effects that dramatically reduce the flow of saliva. This lack of salivary flow, or xerostomia, reduces the natural tooth-cleansing effect of saliva . . . . The American Dental Association does not require dental schools to teach students how to manage and provide dental treatment for the disabled [*sic*] patient" (Bennett, 1998, pp. 20–21).

- According to Buss (1999), children with congenital disabilities such as spina bifida, fibrocystic disease, cleft palate, or Down syndrome are "abandoned" (p. 206) more often than children born without disabilities. Buss defined abandonment as institutionalization and adoption. Children with congenital disabilities who are not abandoned "are abused at considerably higher rates" (p. 206). Buss offered a hypothesis to explain this abuse and neglect. Titled the "healthy baby syndrome," this hypothesis states "that the health status of the child affects the degree of positive maternal behavior" (p. 206).

- PWDs are bombarded with negative images of themselves, of which most people without disabilities are unaware. Captain Hook, the Hunchback of Notre Dame, and Mr. Magoo are demeaning and offensive (Bower, 1980; Byrd & Elliott, 1988; Gartner & Joe, 1987; Kriegel, 1982; Longmore, 1985; Safran, 1998; Zola, 1992). Those without disabilities probably are totally unaware of such media or the lifelong effects these can have on the self-concepts of people with disabilities. Those without disabilities might argue, "Don't be so hypersensitive. It's just a children's cartoon." These same individuals, however, would not want their own racial/ ethnic group or religious group portrayed with such triviality and condescension.

- Until recently it was legal to forcibly sterilize individuals with certain kinds of disabilities. Indeed, in 1931 there were 30 states in the United States that had compulsory-sterilization laws. Individuals who were labeled "insane," "feeble-minded," "epileptic," and "other diseased and degenerate persons" were subjected to sterilization. Many states still have eugenic-sterilization laws today (Hubbard, 1997).

 The Deaf Culture labels society's refusal to accommodate people who are deaf to be "communication abuse" or "communication violence." This communication violence includes refusing to provide education for children in a language they can understand such as American Sign Language (ASL), the inability of many people to communicate with their nonsigning family members, and lack of TTYs (teletypewriters) at public phone booths. One of the most extreme examples of communication violence is the lack of TTYs for 911 emergency phone lines, which has resulted in the deaths of many individuals who are deaf (Jankowski, 1997).

- Many individuals with disabilities have not been allowed to participate in the religious life of their community or to practice their faith as a result of attitudinal and physical barriers. Rachel Hurst (1998), European Regional Chairperson of Disability, stated, "Religions too have disempowered disabled [sic] people . . . denying them access to the priesthood . . . . The leper is always at the gate of the church—never inside" (p. 15). Dr. Judith Heumann, former Assistant Secretary for the Office of Special Education and Rehabilitative Services and a polio survivor, spoke about the inaccessibility of Jewish synagogues.

> When the environment is made accessible, people have to start going out and becoming more independent, doing things they never did before. A simple example of this occurred in a synagogue that I attended when I lived in Berkeley. The bema, an area where people go to do readings and worship, was not accessible. One day, I told the rabbi, "The bema is not accessible." Two weeks later it was accessible. The rabbi said, "OK, now it's accessible and you have to come up and do some of the things that other people do." I thought, "Oh my God, I've never been trained!" I didn't even know how to participate because I hadn't learned the things that a person needs to learn in order to participate. (Heumann, 1999, p. 53)

The National Organization on Disability (NOD) has begun a program entitled "Accessible Congregations Campaign." To join the campaign, an accessible congregation must commit to the following three principles:

1. In our congregation, people with disabilities are valued as individuals, having been created in the image of God.
2. Our congregation is endeavoring to remove barriers or architecture, communications, and attitudes that exclude people with disabilities from full and active participation.
3. People, with and without disabilities, are encouraged to practice their faith and use their gifts in worship, service, study, and leadership.

- Before the passage of the Air Carrier Act of 1986, people in wheelchairs were prohibited from flying or they were required to bring an attendant—and to pay for the attendant's fare. In addition, before the ADA, most airports did not have wheelchair-accessible restrooms.

- Holzbauer and Berven (1996) reported these experiences: "In Cologne, Germany, Frank Weber, a wheelchair user, entered a department store to buy a concert ticket. Three neo-Nazis, wearing swastikas, leather jackets, and boots surrounded and began insulting him, saying: 'They must have forgotten you in Dachau.' (This refers to the practice of 60 years earlier of imprisoning people with disabilities along with Jews, Communists, and Gypsies in concentration camps) . . . . Another German, Gunther Schirmer, had lost his leg in a car accident in 1979. He had learned to ride a tricycle. One afternoon . . . his wife saw boys harassing her husband, spitting on him and saying repeatedly, 'You live off our taxes. You'd have been gassed under Hitler.' . . . Shortly after this incident, Gunther Schirmer committed suicide. He wrote to his wife that people with disabilities do not have a chance in this world and that he would now personally 'destroy the cripple" (p. 480). The title of an article (Whitney, 1993) that appeared in *The New York Times* illustrates that for many Germans (those with disabilities and their family members), the Holocaust is not forgotten. The title is "Disabled [*sic*] Germans Fear They'll Be the Next Target."

- From Fries (1997): "It is hereby prohibited for any person who is diseased, maimed, mutilated, or deformed in any way so as to be an unsightly and disgusting object to expose himself to public view" (1911 City of Chicago Ordinance). According to Imrie (1996), these types of ordinances are still on the books in Columbus, Ohio, and Omaha, Nebraska.

People who are considered to be inferior, which often includes PWDs, are avoided, segregated, and marginalized. "Able-bodied" is considered to be better than "disabled." Independence is better than dependence. Integration is better than segregation. Active is better than passive. Making contributions is better than receiving charity. Respect is better than pity.

Of course, there are exceptions to these broad generalities. The age, sex, perceived social class, and other characteristics of the individual with the disability contribute to the status ascribed to him or her. We will discuss these later.

Handicapism

In this section, look for—

- The definition of handicapism
- The definition of institutional handicapism
- The definition of social handicapism

Handicapism has been defined as the assumptions and practices that promote the unequal treatment of people because of apparent or assumed physical, mental, or behavioral differences. The clearest and most complete definition of *institutional handicapism* can be found in the Findings section of the ADA (presented in Chapter 2). Handicapism occurs in both the social and physical environment, although handicapism is more visible in the physical environment. For example, the availability of elevators and ramps is easy to see because they are part of the physical environment. Equal-status relationships between PWDs and PWODs are part of the social environment and are more difficult to discern. It is, therefore, easier to counter handicapism in the physical environment than handicapism in the social environment. Both the term "handicapism" and the *public awareness of* handicapism are relatively recent developments. In contrast, handicapism itself has persisted in most societies of the world for centuries.

Some of the impetus for the Disability Rights Movement and other organized efforts to combat handicapism is derived from the parallel movements of civil rights and women's rights. As racial and ethnic minorities and women began to organize and empower themselves to advocate for their rights as American citizens, PWDs began to develop a group identity and sought to learn from the Civil Rights and Women's Rights Movements and to also build on their successes. Naturally, a first step in such an undertaking is to increase public awareness of the disenfranchisement of PWDs in all facets of life. This chapter will focus on social handicapism, which is the automatic devaluing and marginalization of PWDs in relationships.

In the not-too-distant past, the majority considered the assumed inferiority of racial and ethnic minority individuals and women to be biological. This spurious, but widely held, assumption was supported by so-called science and research. Bickenbach (1993), making reference to Gould's (1981) book *The Mismeasure of Man*, stated, "Theories of human races based on dubious techniques of craniometry and phrenology, and theories of criminal morphology, such as Cesare Lombroso's infamous theory of the 'criminal type' are some of Gould's examples of how science can come to the aid of racism, sexism, and other prejudices" (p. 190).

If inferiority is biological, then society is not obligated to confer rights on inferior groups of people, nor is society to be blamed for its unequal treatment of these people who are biologically inferior. Further, these people who are biologically inferior cannot, and should not, fight or resist the unequal treatment. It is now well understood and acknowledged that the inferior status (and not the innate, inherent inferiority) of racial groups and women was solely the result of prejudice and discrimination of the broader culture. There is nothing inherently, or biologically, inferior about racial minorities or women.

PWDs, in very much the same way, have also been the objects of widely held views of biological inferiority (Anthony, 1984). The resulting legal disenfranchisement and marginalization of PWDs were also much like the experience of racial and ethnic groups and women. Because the inferiority was thought to be biological, then societies were not obligated to accord rights, privileges, and obligations to PWDs and, furthermore, PWDs should not protest this treatment. The American government, at all levels, supported the assumption of the biological inferiority of PWDs, and, as has been stated, PWDs often internalize the prevailing attitudes of the larger society around them, including society's attitudes toward PWDs. Therefore, many PWDs assumed themselves to be biologically inferior.

In the past, PWODs have had the power to define who had a disability; define what types of services PWDs received; and control the environment, both physical and social. The power to categorize, label, and define is legally conferred by governments; and, in the case of PWDs, the people who understood the experience best and knew their needs were not allowed a voice in the labels and categories conferred on them. Majority and minority status were once theoretically based on numbers, meaning that the majority was the numerical majority. In practice, however, majority and minority status were based on power and not on numbers. A clear-cut example of this is American slavery. On a single plantation, there often were more slaves than slaveholders. But, majority status was based on power, and the single slaveholder was considered to be the majority. Bickenbach (1993), a Canadian disability scholar, discussed the relationship between the power of the majority to categorize and label the physical realities of disabilities. "Of course, in the case of persons with disabilities it would have to be agreed that disabilities are not entirely arbitrary social or political constructions by those who have the power to label and categorize people. If this were true, then people in power could simply 're-label' or 're-categorize' people. Disabilities do have physical and mental realities. Disabilities are biological facts" (p. 177).

Certainly, there are physical and biological realities to disability. The ADA acknowledges the biological facts of disability when it mandates accommodations. However, as we have seen, these biological realities are not inferiority and, furthermore, accommodations would greatly reduce (if not eliminate) the effects of the biomedical aspects of disability. Indeed, we have discussed such disabilities as facial disfigurements, dwarfism, and even obesity, which have no, or almost no, functional limitations, and we have also observed the prejudice, discrimination, and isolation that society confers on individuals with these types of disabilities. Of course, there are disabilities that do have functional limitations, which does not mean inferiority. However, most of these limitations could be eliminated with accommodations. (No one would advocate hiring bus drivers who are blind.) Reread the examples of Sharon L. and the woman in Weinberg's research study in Chapter 2. Each of these examples clearly illustrates that it was not the functional limitations (or biological reality) of their disability that "handicapped" them. Rather, the lack of accommodations was the true handicap. PWDs know that asking for accommodations often results in stigma, categorization, and prejudice.

The false idea of the biological inferiority of PWDs persists. In contrast, the widespread acceptance of the idea of the biological inferiority of racial and ethnic groups and women has ended. In the case of disability, the concept of biological inferiority will be difficult to dispel. When PWODs focus on the disability and its limitations rather than on the person and his or her abilities, it is often an attempt to ascribe biological inferiority to the individual. Society has ascribed inferiority and difference where there is neither.

The Handicapism of Well-Intentioned People

> **In this section, look for—**
> ■ Ways in which well-intentioned people can be handicapping to PWDs

Well-intentioned people who view themselves as neither prejudiced nor discriminatory often promote handicapism. Most of the time, these people are not aware of their handicapism. Nonetheless, it is handicapism, and handicapism results in the disenfranchisement and marginalization of PWDs. The results of their handicapism conflict with their good intentions. Most of these individuals would be quick to assist someone with a disability and also profess to believe in the equality of PWDs; they are well-intentioned people. However, by focusing solely on the disability and its limitations and not viewing the PWD as a unique individual who has strengths, abilities, and skills that far outnumber the limitations of the disabilities, they are engaging in handicapism. Such a narrow focus often is an unconscious attempt to determine and ascribe biological inferiority to the PWD. Proponents of the contact theory and simulation exercises are well-intentioned people who practice handicapism.

Reading the experience of Jenny Morris earlier in this chapter, we can see that her family and friends "conspire from the kindest and highest of intentions to ensure that we make the wrong choices." Furthermore, Morris uses the word "pressures" to describe the effects this has on her. Morris's family and friends want her to be "normal" in spite of the fact that she has a disability. This is an example of unintentional handicapism—behaviors and attitudes arise from kindness, but the results of this encouragement are harmful. If we were to substitute any other minority status, such as race, ethnicity, or gender, we can see that it would be absurd to encourage individuals to be something that they are not. Additionally, the clear message behind these ideas is that it is better to be something else—a PWOD.

In the following excerpt, notice that the PWD is willing to sacrifice competence to avoid prejudice. Medical competence and skill in one's physician may seem to be the single, greatest criterion. Nonetheless, for this individual, who feels that she is required to choose between competence and lack of prejudice, being viewed as a complete person and having a physician who views their relationship as a partnership is more important than medical skill.

> Right now I have a very nice doctor who's like really good in terms of trying to work with me. She's just not as competent as I would like . . . there are some doctors who might be better, but what they do to me emotionally it's not worth it. . . . [I]t always feels like I'm walking a tightrope . . . . I'd love to find somebody that's both a really good doctor and who's not prejudiced against me . . . who can really see me for, for [me]. (Putnam et al., 2003, p. 41)

The World Is Designed to Further the Purposes of PWODs

American society has considered the needs of PWDs to be either unimportant or invisible. Many options available to PWODs are closed to PWDs. The Deaf Culture has a slogan: "It's our world, too." This slogan expresses the right of all PWDs to full social, economic, educational, vocational, and political integration. It may appear to be obvious, but we can ask, "Why do PWDs feel it necessary to remind PWODs that 'it's our world, too'?"

Certainly, it is obvious that the world is inconvenient and physically inaccessible for many PWDs, not as a result of the disability itself, but as a result of the absence of accommodations. The lack of ramps and elevators, sign language interpreters, and a vast array of other accommodations renders the world an inconvenient place for PWDs.

The Biomedical Model of disability regards the PWD as responsible for "adapting" to the environment and does not consider PWODs to have any obligation to modify or change. The Biomedical Model probably played a large part in the indifference of the public to provide accommodations. When PWDs claim the world as also belonging to them, they are asserting their right to accommodations. The Deaf Culture provides an easily understood example. Because most hearing people have hands, they have the capability to learn sign language, and, indeed, it would be easier for people who can hear to learn sign language than for most people who are congenitally deaf to learn to speak or to read lips. We saw that on Martha's Vineyard many hearing residents learned sign language. This example illustrates the need for PWODs to make accommodations rather than simply expecting PWDs to adapt to an indifferent social and physical environment. Individuals with disabilities, because of the lack of accommodations and inaccessible environments, must plan their activities in advance, build in extra time, have a back-up plan, and demonstrate an unfailing sense of humor. For example, most Americans do not need to plan their schedules based on the availability of a public bathroom. For many PWDs, there can be no last-minute or spontaneous changes in plans. Therefore, we can see that the lack of accommodations and inaccessible environments unnecessarily constrict the choices and options available to PWDs.

Often, inaccessible environments and the lack of appropriate technology and personal assistance services result in helplessness; dependence; isolation; and narrow, constricted lives for PWDs. Without accommodations (and civil rights), Americans with disabilities cannot succeed and indeed have difficulty simply surviving. Yet, society often views the dependence and isolation to be the result of the disabilities when these conditions are, in fact, a result of society's failures. For example, many PWDs report feelings similar to these individuals:

> "When I got my electric cart, my life started all over again." Another said, "I've always had cerebral palsy. But . . . I have before the chair and after the chair . . . . I got this chair and I thought 'Whoa. I can hit the road wherever I want to.' And I have more energy and a lot more fun." (Putnam et al., 2003, p. 42)

The polio epidemics in the 20th century clearly show the way in which the lack of accommodations added to the difficulties of the disease. Thousands of polio survivors were children with orthopedic disabilities; nonetheless, many of these children were not allowed to attend public schools.

The few polio survivors who did attend (only after their parents had fought with school officials) received few accommodations.

> There were many teachers who did not know how to work with students with disabilities, had no desire to learn, and openly displayed their displeasure. For example, Jennifer Williams's second-grade teacher "just couldn't relate to a child with a handicap [*sic*]." This teacher was always hard on the young girl and refused to believe she was any different. As Williams remembers, "[S]he would always say things like, 'They're doing it, so you have to do it too. You know we can't play favorites.'" And Wanda Peterson's sixth-grade teacher would talk about her in front of the class. The teacher would declare, without naming Peterson, "Some people in this room think they are so great because they aren't supposed to run in P.E." The teacher also made her move her desk away from everyone else's . . . . The attitudes and actions of teachers could make all the difference in the class. Those who were supportive helped polio survivors to fit in as best they could and to excel where they were able. The worst helped make school a living hell. (Wilson, 1990, pp. 187–188)

Lack of accommodations and an inaccessible environment often eliminate basic rights of citizenship for PWDs.

> This particular discrimination, of course, has had a profound effect on the lives of disabled [*sic*] people. It has a psychological effect, among other things, but it also prevents [PWDs] from participating in society actively, getting jobs, paying taxes . . . . This lack of mobility in many cases even affects the participation in the fundamental democratic process, the right to vote. Without transportation, in many cases, it is impossible even to cast your ballot in election, something which means that, at least in part, disabled [*sic*] people are excluded far more or just as much from the process as black people were by closed polls and poll taxes. (Fleischer & Zames, 2001, p. 69)

Wheelchair athletics has captured the attention of America and has substantially increased the quality of life for these athletes. Nonetheless, before the 1980s, the term "wheelchair athletes" would have seemed a contradiction in terms. Wheelchair sports resulted from assistive technology. Indeed, there were no wheelchair athletics until the sports wheelchair was invented in the 1980s. Today, sports wheelchairs are so specialized that each sport has its own chair that meets the demands of that particular sport. Some sports wheelchairs have three, four, five, or six wheels. In fact, it was World War II veterans who pushed for better wheelchairs (and other adaptive technology, such as hand controls for cars). As we have seen, World War II veterans with physical disabilities had much better survival rates (than the veterans of previous wars) and longer life spans as a result of the introduction of antibiotics. More important, probably because of the large numbers of veterans with disabilities and the fact that the American nation felt an obligation to acknowledge soldiers' sacrifices, the entire field of assistive technology for PWDs was expanded. Compare the lives of today's wheelchair athletes with individuals with the same types of disabilities who, 100 years ago, lived (and died) in institutions and back bedrooms.

Accommodations often are provided only after legislation has mandated them. In our discussion of the Americans with Disabilities Act we saw that movie theaters, concert halls, and restaurants became accessible to PWDs only after the ADA made the lack of accessibility illegal. It was not the free market, the profit motive, or humanitarian concerns that opened theaters to Americans with disabilities; it was the force of law and the threat of legal action. In addition to the reluctant provision of accommodations, PWDs are expected to be grateful for such accommodations.

Even more important than physical accessibility is the fact that disability public policy, educational services (including goals and curricula), and rehabilitation services, in the past, were designed and executed by PWODs. As a subordinate group, PWDs have been controlled by PWODs. Without any experience of disability or knowledge of the needs or use of accommodations, PWODs have asserted the right to determine the resources and services that PWDs receive. As PWDs have become more empowered, they have begun to claim the right to determine their own needs, policies, and goals.

For example, Patricia Deegan, in her work describing her recovery from mental illness (1991), described how rehabilitation programs designed by PWODs often impede and handicap the PWD. Deegan stated, "Too often, rehabilitation programs are structured in such a way as to work against this process of recovery. These programs tend to have rigid guidelines for acceptance. They tend to have linear program designs in which a person must enter at point 'A' and move through a series of consecutive steps to arrive at point 'B.' Failure at any point along the way will require that participants return to entry level" (p. 51).

Brenda Premo, director of the California Department of Rehabilitation, is legally blind. She tells of this experience:

> One time my mother got called into the principal's office because I wouldn't use big-print books. Instead of just bringing me in and chatting with me, the principal brought my mother in. In the meeting, my mother turned to me and said, "Sweetheart, why don't you want to use big-print books?" I said, "Mom, it's like this; I've got four academic classes and all the teachers assign several chapters to read. In large-print books, chapters are in volumes. So if I have four academic classes and I have to have three volumes each, I need a wagon to take my books home." I told her I needed a magnifier, a $1.50 magnifier, but nobody asked me. (Mackelprang & Salsgiver, 1999, p. 141)

Ms. Premo's experience in junior high school makes it clear that simple accommodations are often the best (the $1.50 magnifying glass) and that professionals may not think to simply ask the PWD what would fulfill his or her needs.

A long list of programs and accommodations to assist PWDs, developed by PWODs, which in reality does not assist and often keeps PWDs marginalized, could be presented. Indeed, in almost every first-person narrative, the individual with the disability tells of "professionals" who have, with the best of intentions, withheld accommodations or provided what they considered to be accommodations but actually made the PWD's functioning more difficult. Both the goals and the accommodations needed to reach them should be decided by the individuals who understand the disability experience. Therefore, the Disability Rights Movement is claiming its right to develop the programs and accommodations for PWDs.

The Contact Theory

> ### In this section, look for—
>
> - Why (initially) the contact theory failed
> - The four conditions necessary for contact to reduce prejudice

The contact theory was first developed during the 1950s and 1960s as a method to integrate racial and ethnic minorities on a fully equal basis and to facilitate a racially pluralistic society (Allport, 1954, 1958, 1986; Amir, 1969). In the beginning, it was thought that contact of any kind between the majority and minority individuals was sufficient to decrease prejudice, stigma, and discrimination. Contact was defined as direct, one-on-one interaction. Simply stated, it was theorized that contact would lead to attitude change, and attitude change would foster behavioral changes (Yuker, 1965, 1983, 1988, 1994; Yuker & Block, 1986; Yuker & Hurley, 1987; Yuker, Block, & Young, 1970). Contact of any kind was thought to be a solution to the centuries of isolation and segregation that led to misinformation, stereotypes, and prejudice.

A few years later, the contact theory was expanded to include people with disabilities (Yuker, Block, & Young, 1970). Clearly, both racial/ethnic minorities and PWDs had experienced centuries of institutionalized segregation. Thus, it was thought that by allowing and encouraging PWODs to interact with PWDs, the prejudice and discrimination demonstrated toward PWDs would decrease (Donaldson, 1980; Elliott, Frank, Corcoran,

Beardon, & Byrd, 1990; Evans, 1976; Fichten, Robillard, Judd, & Amsel, 1989). When discussing racial/ethnic/cultural/linguistic minority individuals, their right to move within the larger communities is termed "integration," while in discussing PWDs, this right is often termed "mainstreaming," "full social integration," or "inclusion." Nonetheless, the rationale and the methods of the contact theory were basically the same for both types of groups.

It is surprising that, for both types of groups, the initial research suggested that the contact between members of majority groups and members of minority groups did not decrease prejudice and discrimination; rather, it *increased* it (Yuker, 1988). For example, when children with disabilities were mainstreamed into regular classrooms with children who did not have disabilities, the amount of playtime at home in the neighborhood between children with disabilities and children without disabilities actually decreased (Woods & Carrow, 1959). It seemed that the contact theory actually *reinforced* prejudice and discrimination. Indeed, many of these interactions were unpleasant, tense, and frustrating and were ended as quickly as possible (Anthony, 1972).

The researchers then sought to define "contact" in a more rigorous way. Cook (1978) summed up the literature on the research dealing with racial/ethnic minorities by stating, "Attitude change favorable to a disliked group will result from equal social status contact with stereotype-disconfirming persons from that group, provided that the contact is cooperative and of such a nature as to reveal the individual characteristics of the person contacted, and that it takes place in a situation characterized by social norms favoring equality and egalitarian association among the participating groups" (pp. 97–98).

Another sociologist (Duckitt, 1992) stated, "The conclusion that only certain kinds of contact actually reduce prejudice has been clearly confirmed. In fact, it has become increasingly apparent that contact does not reduce prejudice nearly as easily as had been hoped" (p. 144). Therefore, it was determined that the following conditions must be present for contact situations to decrease prejudice and have positive outcomes:

1. Equal social status relationships are necessary, which is not the situation when the PWD is clearly perceived to be inferior (Dembo, Leviton, & Wright, 1975). This explains, in part, why professionals who serve PWDs and, therefore, experience a great deal of contact often hold negative stereotypes of PWDs (Bell, 1962; Berkowitz, 1984; Blood & Blood, 1982; Brodwin & Gardner, 1978; Chubon, 1982; Fuchs, Fuchs, Dailey, & Power, 1985; Gaier, Linkowski, & Jaques, 1968; Garske & Thomas, 1990; Home, 1988; Janicki, 1970; Krauft, Rubin, Cook, & Bozarth, 1976; Larrivee & Cook, 1979; Palmerton & Frumkin, 1969). Indeed, Yuker (1994) stated, "Virtually all helpers perceive themselves as superior to people who need help" (p. 16). Disability scholars have suggested that it is very pow-

erful (in reducing prejudice) if the PWD has a status superior to the PWOD's in the contact (Anthony, 1972; Olkin, 1999).

2. The contact occurs under "natural" and voluntary conditions (Sigelman, Spanhel, & Lorenzen, 1979). This probably explains why the schoolchildren without disabilities did not play at home with their classmates who had disabilities (Woods & Carrow, 1959). Indeed, "incidental, involuntary, tension-laden contact is likely to increase prejudice" (Simpson & Yinger, 1985, p. 396).

3. The contact should facilitate viewing the PWD as an individual, rather than as a member of a group, thus disallowing negative stereotypes of PWDs (Jaques, Linkowski, & Seika, 1970; Langer, Bashner, & Chanowitz, 1985; Thomas, Foreman, & Remenyi, 1985; Yuker, 1988). This explains why superficial and casual interactions do not lead to a reduction in prejudice. In these superficial types of interaction, negative stereotypes are actually reinforced (Langer, Fiske, Taylor, & Chanowitz, 1976).

4. Both individuals have the same goal. Such mutual goals reduce prejudice, especially if the goal cannot be achieved without the active cooperation of both individuals (Deutsch, 1949).

Reading this list of conditions, it can be seen that none of these can be legislated by law or mandated by policy. As with any minority group, PWDs can be allowed in schools and jobs and, at the same time, can be isolated and segregated. Such laws as the ADA are, of course, necessary and positive influences, but they are simply *a starting point*. True integration is built on the four conditions listed here. Further, if the contact situations do not include these four conditions, the contact will not reduce prejudice and may, in fact, serve to *strengthen and reinforce* prejudice, with the individual mistakenly thinking that he or she now has more "sophisticated" knowledge about PWDs. In the following section, we will discuss each of these four conditions in more detail.

Equal Social Status Contact

In this section, look for—

- The two components necessary for equal social status relationships: similarities and equal resources
- Why true similarities are not readily apparent
- When two individuals do not bring equal resources to the relationship, the relationship is considered to be stressful and unbalanced

Contact, sometimes referred to as "exposure" or "interaction," includes marriage, family relationships, friendships, work colleagues, teacher/student relationships, schoolmates, and professional helping relationships such as doctor/patient relationships. Not all of these types of relationships involve equal social status; for example, teacher/student relationships and professional helping relationships usually place the PWD in an inferior position (as a student or patient). The contact theory defines contact as more than simple propinquity (Comer & Piliavin, 1972). Contact between PWDs and PWODs must include equal social status for both individuals if the contact is to lead to a reduction in prejudice and formation of more realistic attitudes. Indeed, Yuker (1983) presented an excellent review and interpretation of 274 studies that investigated the effect of the contact theory. Yuker made a strong point that in most of these studies the variable of contact was very loosely and ambiguously defined. For example, some studies simply asked the PWODs if they had contact with a PWD; in other studies, the "contact" was watching a video of a PWD. Yuker concluded, "We should no longer waste time studying and discussing the effects of experience or contact in general. The precise nature and duration of the contact and the nature of the interpersonal relationships involved must be specified before conclusions can be drawn" (p. 100). Moreover, Yuker and his associates found that when research studies included equal social status and common goals and were of a voluntary nature, these studies were more likely to find a significant reduction in prejudice on the part of PWODs. However, in many studies attempting to measure the effect of "contact," the contact was only observational tours of residential institutions for individuals with mental retardation or people with mental illness. Indeed, many college courses use these types of "tours" as part of course curricula and these tours or observations are a class requirement (Baker, Baker, & McDaniel, 1975). As would be expected, there was no reduction in prejudice among the tourists, and, in some cases, there was an increase in prejudice. Rabkin (1972) explained this increase in prejudice: "Tours of institutions, like tours of zoos, may arouse feelings of pity or revulsion, but almost never stimulate a sense of respect and empathy regarding the inmates; it is only when roles are transformed and patients are given 'normal' role assignments that they seem like you or me" (p. 163).

How do two people form equal social status relationships? Experts report that two conditions must be present: (1) similarities and (2) equal resources. Briefly stated, relationships are formed when people have something in common and both individuals bring equal resources such as power, prestige, material resources, and emotional resources, including consideration for and understanding of others. Of course, in the beginning stages of any relationship, the similarities are only *perceived* similarities and the resources are only *perceived* to be equal. As the relationship progresses and builds, the individuals find that true similarities are shared values, goals, and experiences and, therefore, true similarities are not quickly apparent. In any relationship with equal social status, physical appearance and first impressions are important in the initial stages. However, as the relationship builds, personality, character, values, and goals become more important than superficial, readily visible characteristics (Safilios-Rothschild, 1970). Physical appearance becomes less important; nonetheless, the difficulty is in maintaining the relationship beyond the point where these visible characteristics are important, long enough to allow more relevant characteristics to be demonstrated. Whether a job interview or a first date, we all understand that physical appearance has great significance, and we also know that getting past this initial stage will allow us to demonstrate relevant characteristics. Furthermore, these types of contact create a great deal of interaction strain. In much the same way, the PWD knows that the disability causes discomfort to the PWOD and therefore he or she must work harder to advance the relationship beyond the first-impression stage (Kleck, 1966; Kleck, Ono, & Hastorf, 1966).

The second condition on which long-standing relationships are built is that of *equal* resources of each partner, keeping in mind that equal resources do not necessarily mean the *same* resources. Relationships in which one partner has more resources are often termed "asymmetrical" or "unbalanced." Asymmetrical relationships are considered to be stressful; the partner with the greater resources is resentful that he or she brings more to the relationship, and the partner with fewer resources becomes resentful that he or she is always in an inferior position and may fear abandonment. Resources are both visible and invisible. For example, money and prestige are easy to see, while emotional resources can only be discovered as the relationship progresses. Some resources, such as power, are both visible and invisible.

Similarities and equal resources are necessary components for any long-standing social relationship in which the partners consider themselves to be equal. Equal social status relationships between a PWD and a PWOD are no exception, although these components are more complicated when one partner has a disability. It is not the disability itself that makes these types of equal social status relationships more complex; rather, it is the perceptions and attitudes of others toward the disability. For example, when one marriage partner has a disability, the partner without a disability is often thought to be a "saint" or a "loser." These derisive and insulting judgments reflect the widely held attitude that PWDs have few resources (including social status) and that PWDs cannot contribute anything but must always be the recipients of their partners' care and compassion. If the PWOD is thought to be a "loser," then the relationship is a balanced relationship (because it is automatically assumed that the PWD is also a "loser"). However, if the PWOD is thought to be a "saint," then the relationship is not balanced.

Remarkably, the idea that a PWD and a PWOD can have an equal social status relationship of any type—friendship, work colleague, romantic, marriage—wherein both bring resources to the relationship and thus both benefit is rarely considered. Further, the concept of shared similarities of the two individuals is often overlooked because, as we learned in Chapter 4, others mistakenly believe that the disability is the most salient (defining) characteristic of the PWD. This erroneous assumption leads to the equally erroneous conclusion that PWODs and PWDs cannot share common values, goals, and experiences because one partner has a disability. In the video "My Body Is Not Who I Am," a man in a wheelchair tells us that he is often asked if he has a girlfriend, and when he answers "yes," he is then asked if his girlfriend has a disability. While rude and intrusive, these questions also illustrate the widely held belief that equal social status relationships between PWODs and PWDs are not possible because the PWD is perceived to be (1) dissimilar to PWODs and (2) not bringing equal resources to the relationship.

The Contact Must Be Natural and Voluntary

Having a marriage partner, family member, or a child with a disability is usually not voluntary. (In the case of the marriage partner, it would be voluntary if the individual had the disability before the marriage.) Nonetheless, for the contact theory to reduce prejudice in nonfamilial associations, the relationship between the PWD and the PWOD must be perceived as both natural and voluntary. Assigning PWODs to PWDs for tutoring, mentoring, and "best buddies" is neither voluntary nor natural. Both PWODs and PWDs clearly understand that the "relationship" is "coerced" and time limited. The motivation to move beyond the initial stages of the relationship is reduced because both individuals understand that, under typical conditions, they would not associate with each other. These types of contact have the potential to succeed if the relationship evolves beyond the involuntary (assigned) stage.

Many schools have "best buddies" programs in which a student without a disability is assigned to a student with mental retardation. The student without the disability assists his or her "best buddy" with schoolwork and negotiating the school day and engages in social activities with him or her. Because of the disability of mental retardation, the PWD may not understand that the PWOD is simply fulfilling some type of requirement and once this is accomplished, the PWOD will no longer be a "best buddy."

The Contact Should Facilitate Viewing the PWD As an Individual

Once the relationship has progressed beyond the initial stages, the disability should no longer be the focus. This is not to say that the disability is denied or ignored, only that the disability is no longer the defining or most important aspect of the relationship. Other specific, more relevant characteristics form the basis of the contact. The contact must facilitate the PWOD in viewing the PWD as more than a stereotype, label, or diagnosis (Parenti, Beaufils, & Paicheler, 1987). As the salience of the disability is reduced, the interaction strain felt by the PWOD is also reduced (Amsel & Fichten, 1988; Fichten, Robillard, Judd, & Amsel, 1989; Genskow & Maglione, 1965; Makas, 1993). Yuker (1965) summarized the results of viewing the PWD as an individual. (Note that the labels used to describe various types of individuals are 35 years old and are considered offensive and insulting today.) "If you have known a person over a period of time, you cannot help but think of him as an individual. You think of him as John or Dave, not as a cripple, a Negro, a Catholic, or a Jew. You may not like him, but if you don't like him you don't like him as an individual. Or, if you do like him, you like him as an individual. But the attitude is based on him as a person, not as a member of a particular group" (p. 16).

In this type of contact, the PWD is recategorized as an individual, not as "one of *those* people." Stereotyping and distancing, as we have learned in other chapters, serve (1) to communicate that these types of people are not like us, and (2) to present individuals as their categories. With contact, complex, long-held stereotypes are broken down when the PWOD learns that (1) "this PWD is more like me than I had thought," and (2) "this PWD doesn't act (or think) like I thought PWDs do."

Two Canadian disability scholars, Robert Bogdan and Steven Taylor (1992), conducted interviews with family members of people who had severe and multiple disabilities. Compiling 15 years of qualitative research, they found that those families who had warm and accepting relationships with their member with a disability (or more than one disability) viewed the PWD as a unique individual; indeed, the families described the PWD in positive terms, such as "she has sparkling eyes," "she has beautiful hair," and "he has a great smile." Bogdan and Taylor found that these accepting families often had nicknames for the PWD that were positive, conferred dignity, and described something unique about the individual. These families dressed and groomed the PWDs in age-appropriate, gender-appropriate, stylish clothes. Older men often had beards; the women had makeup and attractive hairdos. Bogdan and Taylor stated, "By paying attention to clothing style and color and appearance (hairstyle, nails, makeup, cleanliness, beards for men), they helped construct an identity . . . . Thus, the person is given . . . an identity as an individual" (p. 104). Further, these families spoke at length about the PWD's likes and dislikes in food, recreation, and music. Although Bogdan and Taylor's research focused only on family relationships and was limited to people who had severe and multiple disabilities, clearly one of the components of acceptance was ascribing individuality to the PWD.

The Contact Should Involve Cooperative Goals

The contact must include the contributions of the PWD, and these contributions must be viewed as valued and necessary for success. Some textbooks describe this as "reciprocating," in that both the PWD and the PWOD need the contribution and assistance of the other.

In summary, we can see that previous PWODs' contact or experience with PWDs may or may not reduce prejudice and foster realistic attitudes. Therefore, it is not only the quantity of previous experience with PWDs, it is the quality of the experience that makes the difference. Therefore, both quantity and quality are important. Attending a 1-day seminar on disability awareness, viewing a video, or reading a book (such as this one) are only *starting points*. Each of these methods is an excellent place to begin, but it must be followed up with one-on-one relationships with PWDs that incorporate the four components discussed in this section.

Perceptions of the Disability That May Be Associated With Prejudice

> **In this section, look for—**
> - Effects of the following factors:
>   1. The degree of visibility of the disability
>   2. Visibility/aesthetic qualities of the disability
>   3. Communication difficulties
>   4. Perceived cause of the disability
>   5. Perceived threat of the disability
>   6. Course of the disability

A disability scholar, Liora Pedhazur Schmelkin (1988), listed the above six factors as "six critical dimensions of stigma" (p. 129). Naturally, both the experience of a disability and the reactions of others to an individual with a disability are complex and interrelated. Nonetheless, to impose structure and gain a preliminary understanding of the stigma directed toward PWDs, disability scholars have devised categorization schemes, such as the one listed previously. Whatever categorization scheme is used, everyone agrees that stigma is multidimensional and any scheme must be considered only a starting point to understanding stigma. Second, the factors are only *perceptions* of PWODs and are not accurate judgments of either the disability itself or the individual with the disability. Third, the degree of stigma directed toward the PWD will affect the PWD's response to his or her disability. Sociologists and psychologists know that the judgments of others profoundly influence an individual's self-concept. In the case of PWDs, if there is a great deal of prejudice and discrimination against a certain type (or level of severity) of disability, it is likely that the individual with this type of disability will incorporate some of these negative judgments into his or her self-identity (Garske & Thomas, 1990; Siller, 1984; Wright, 1983, 1988).

The Degree of Visibility of the Disability

In this section, look for—

- The fact that lack of visibility does not mean absence of impairment
- How PWODs often attribute negative characteristics to PWDs with invisible disabilities
- How PWDs often will choose to hide the disability, even at the cost of necessary accommodations
- When PWDs must weigh the cost/benefit ratio of disclosure
- Read the letter sent to Ann Landers (Exhibit 5–1).

Exhibit 5–1

Dear Ann Landers: I am handicapped, but one would never know it by looking at me. I have had two back operations and four knee surgeries. If I do any walking or standing, even for a few minutes, I get very tired and must sit and rest.

Recently, I parked in the handicapped spot at the supermarket. I have a handicapped tag hanging on my rearview mirror. Before I could get out of the car, a "gentleman" walked up and said, "You certainly don't look handicapped to me. You should not be parking in that space." I looked at him and said, "And you, sir, look intelligent, but I guess looks can be deceiving."

If more people realized that some handicapped folks have physical disabilities that are not visible, life would be easier for all of us.

—Yes I Am in Palm Harbor, Fla.

Invisible disabilities include many health conditions, psychiatric disabilities, hearing impairments, and a vast range of other types of disabilities. Many times, it is not the disability itself that is visible; the accommodations the disability requires, such as hearing aids, wheelchairs, and note-takers in a college classroom for student(s) with learning disabilities, are what is apparent to others. There is no correlation between the degree of visibility and degree of impairment. Clearly, the Ann Landers letter illustrates that simply because a disability is not visible, it does not mean that there are not severe functional limitations.

Indeed, reactions to invisible disabilities reveal the lack of awareness of many PWODs of disabilities in general. It is not possible to discern if an individual has a disability from his or her appearance. Further, many PWODs attribute negative motives to (1) the functional limitations of the disability, or (2) the accommodations that the individual uses. We learned in Chapter 2 that ambiguity, of any kind, is often interpreted as negative (or hostile). Here are two examples. A young woman student in our department has a heart condition (she breathes from oxygen tanks at home each day from 5:00 P.M. to 8:00 A.M.). Naturally, this student must use the elevators. While waiting for an elevator or riding the elevator, strangers often approach her and say, "Are we feeling a little lazy today?" It is interesting that, at some point, this student's disability will become visible when she will be required to breathe oxygen from a tank 24 hours a day. The other example concerns the wife of a political candidate who has a progressive neuromuscular disability that affects her coordination and motor abilities. These types of conditions are often exacerbated by stress and fatigue, and episodes of heightened symptoms are impossible to predict. Therefore, when the individual is stressed and tired, symptoms may appear precisely when he or she needs and wants to make a good impression. At a fundraising cocktail party, the woman held her husband's arm because she was experiencing the heightened symptoms of loss of motor control. The next day, a newspaper article asked, "Do we want a governor who has a wife who gets falling-down drunk?" Adding to the irony was the fact that the wife had not had any alcohol because she understood the serious effects alcohol has for these kinds of disabilities.

Richard Cohen was a television news reporter when he was diagnosed with multiple sclerosis at age 25. He is married to the television personality Meredith Viera. Cohen (2004) describes how he has wrestled with the decision to disclose, including weighing "what is at stake":

> I learned a valuable lesson then and there. Honesty is not the best policy. Candor about health problems works in the confines of academia and maybe in the movies. Full disclosure does not work so well in the real world. Hard times in a competitive industry at a tough moment in history leave little room for dealing fairly with a serious illness. People with serious problems can be perceived as weak candidates for

employment in the dollars-and-cents world. The right thing to do has currency when nothing is at stake . . . . Don't tell nobody nuthin. . . . My stealth approach bothered me enough to write my private rulebook outlining when dishonesty went too far and when it was permissible. (pp. 54–55)

A woman with a psychiatric disability relates the way in which she "paces" the rate of disclosure: "It is difficult to build meaningful relationships while withholding information about one's identity that is so central to one's sense of self. The disclosure of such information, however, may very well abruptly end the relationship. I pace the disclosure out based on what is comfortable for me and what is comfortable for them" (Karp, 2001, p. 119).

A reporter for *Time* magazine who acquired a disability while covering the war in Iraq wrote an article entitled "How I Lost My Hand but Found Myself" (Weisskopf, 2006, p. 37). He tells of his decision not to hide his disability:

Before Iraq, the technology of arm prostheses hadn't changed much since World War II. The tiny population of amputees created little market incentive. Miguelez (the prosthetist) used the burst in demand from Walter Reed (Hospital) to lean on manufacturers for progress. Before long, he was outfitting Iraq war amputees with an electronic hand that opened and closed 2½ times faster and could be programmed to function at different speeds and grip strength.

The cosmetic arts also had improved. I received a silicone hand that was so lifelike it passed for real in social settings. But Pretty Boy, as I called it, kept tearing and afforded the precision of a boxing glove. It was too spongy to grasp anything small and too slippery to hold most objects for long.

Function was only part of the problem. The idea of trying to pass had begun to trouble me. It made me feel as if I had something to hide or to be ashamed of. When I started to go bald, I shaved my head. No comb-overs, transplants or toupees for me. So why try to conceal a handicap? I was proud of how I had lost my hand. The stump had a story to tell . . . . (p. 37)

But what about people who do not have a disability but fake one? Certainly, there are incentives to fake disabilities, such as to gain financial benefits or drugs or to gain exemption from criminal prosecution, work, or military duty. This is termed "malingering," and one of the criteria of this diagnosis is that the individual must be aware that he or she is trying to deceive others (in contrast to unconscious denial of the disability, in which the individual is not aware that he or she is attempting to deceive anyone). In a previous chapter, we read about college athletes who claimed nonexistent disabilities to receive "handicapped" parking tags. There are people who fake disabilities. At a large high school in Salt Lake City, 70% of the students taking the *Scholastic Aptitude Test* claimed a learning disability, requesting more time in which to complete the test. It would be rather remarkable if there were such a large number of individuals with documented, diagnosed learning disabilities in one school.

The letter to Ann Landers also illustrates that many individuals mistakenly think of legitimate accommodations for a disability as preferential treatment, and "handicapped" parking spaces are a particularly "hot button." (In the disability community, there are jokes about "handicapped parking stickers" being big sellers at garage sales.) Both people with visible disabilities and people with invisible disabilities are aware that others often resent the accommodations provided for the disability. As we have learned in previous chapters, under the ADA, when PWDs use accommodations, they are simply exercising their rights as American citizens.

Obviously, for individuals whose disability (or the accommodations or adaptive technology) is clearly visible, there is no decision about the costs of disclosure. In contrast, when an individual has a disability that can be hidden, he or she must weigh the costs and benefits of disclosure.

Choosing not to disclose an invisible disability is often termed "passing." Individuals with invisible disabilities can *decide when or to whom* to disclose. The option of choosing the point of disclosure allows the individual to display the relevant characteristics, such as work skills and work habits, before telling others about his or her disability. Often, individuals with invisible disabilities choose to never reveal their disability. As you may remember, the ADA does not mandate accommodations for the disability unless the individual discloses his or her disability. Therefore, one of the benefits of disclosure is the provision of accommodations.

Foremost among the benefits of choosing not to disclose an invisible disability is the ability to shed the "disabled image" and "disabled role." The disabled image has led to prejudice, discrimination, and stigma, and it is understandable when individuals refuse this devalued role.

Often, the individual who attempts to "pass" sacrifices functioning. Examples of this include individuals who decide not to wear their hearing aids in public (others may think they are rude and conceited, but in reality, they cannot hear), those wearing a prosthetic hand in public that is not very functional because they understand that the very useful hook is distressing to others, and those individuals wishing to keep their disability hidden by not taking medications or injections in the view of others. Exhibit 5–2 lists some of the costs/benefits of disclosure.

Reading the list of "costs" or disadvantages of not disclosing a disability, we can see that sometimes the truth (revealing the disability) is better than allowing others to "think the worst." For example, a gap of time (months or years) on a résumé as a result of a hospitalization may raise more questions than simply telling the job interviewer the truth. In the example

Exhibit 5-2

Benefits of Disclosure

1. Accommodations are provided.
2. The truth is often better than negative assumptions.

Costs of Nondisclosure

1. No accommodations are given.
2. Negative characteristics are attributed to the individual with the disability.
3. Others with the same disability who have disclosed consider the person who "passes" as disloyal.
4. It is stressful to hide something that is part of one's self-identity.
5. The individual has lost an opportunity to advocate and educate others about the disability.
6. There might be more problems if the disability is discovered by others.
7. The individual sacrifices the solidarity, support, and understanding of associating with other PWDs.

of the political candidate's wife, the truth about the disability was certainly better than the implications drawn by newspaper reporters. Also, the individual is aware that there is more societal stigma directed toward some disabilities than others. For example, an individual with an invisible disability of diabetes (a disability toward which society holds very little prejudice) may be more willing to disclose the disability than an individual with a psychiatric disability (a disability toward which society holds a great deal of prejudice). In addition, those who choose to hide their disability often are considered "disloyal" by others with the same disability. For example, many in the Disability Rights Movement label Franklin Roosevelt a "closet crip" because he hid and minimized his disability. Another cost is the stress of hiding both the disability and the accommodations or treatment of the disability. An individual may need time off from work during the day to attend Alcoholics Anonymous meetings and his coworkers may think that he or she is goofing off. Another example is that of an individual with a psychiatric disability who has chosen not to disclose the disability and then must listen to friends' jokes about "fruitcakes," "wackos," and "psychos" and remain silent.

Cynthia Rich (as cited in Morris's 1991 book *Pride Against Prejudice: Transforming Attitudes to Disability*) described two distinct types of "passing." The first type is that of a "consciously political tactic for carefully limited purposes," and for her, this type of passing does not have serious, pervasive, or long-term consequences for the individual. The second type of passing, in which the individual loses his or her own identity, has serious results.

> Passing—except as a consciously political tactic for carefully limited purposes—is one of the most serious threats to selfhood. We attempt, of course, to avoid the oppressor's hateful distortion to our identity and the real menace to our survival of his [*sic*] hatred. But, meanwhile, our identity is never acted out, can lose its substance, its meaning, even for ourselves. (p. 36)

It should be pointed out that others who have the same disability (or who have a great deal of experience with that type of disability) often are able to detect the disability, while most PWODs are not. Simply because these individuals are aware of the symptoms, limitations, treatments, and compensations of that particular disability, they can recognize the disability in others. They know what to look for. For example, people who wear contact lenses are usually aware of others who wear contact lenses, whereas most other people would not know. Individuals who have learning disabilities can often "pick up" on the adaptive techniques of others with learning disabilities simply because they know what to look for. People who wear prostheses are aware of others who wear similar prostheses. Others have no "expectation" or "awareness" of prostheses.

In today's age of technology and telecommunications, the concept of invisible disabilities has been changed. John Hockenberry, the news journalist in a wheelchair, worked in Los Angeles and did not tell his bosses in New York City that he had a disability. This is a single example that illustrates the changing definition of an invisible disability. Certainly, the people in Los Angeles saw the wheelchair, but Hockenberry decided that he wanted his bosses to see the quality of his work before disclosing his disability. (Hockenberry also "paid" for his refusal to disclose. He had no accessible bathroom at work.)

Looking at the Ann Landers letter, we can see that the writer chose to disclose the disability in the first paragraph, stressing both the disability and the functional limitations. (Perhaps this would not be considered true disclosure because it is an anonymous letter.) Nonetheless, it is thought-provoking to consider what Ann Landers's response and the reader response would have been if the writer had chosen not to disclose the type of disability and the resulting limitations but simply stated, "I am handicapped, but one would never know it by looking at me."

Other Factors That Influence the Perception of PWDs

> **In this section, look for—**
>
> - Perceived cause of the disability
> - Perceived social class and educational level of the PWD
> - The specific situation
> - Functional limitations of the disability

In discussing the perception of and response to PWDs, there are many factors—some are situational factors (Dunn, 1996); some are related to the PWD, such as his or her perceived social class, social prestige, and educational level (clinicians are less likely to give certain diagnoses, such as antisocial personality disorder, to individuals they believe to be of higher social status); some are related to the perceptions that others have of the disability; and finally, some factors are related to the disability itself (Gordon, Minnes, & Holden, 1990; Gouvier, Coon, Todd, & Fuller, 1994; Grand, Bernier, & Strohmer, 1982; Greenwood & Johnson, 1987; Harosymia, Home, & Lewis, 1976; Heinemann, Pellander, Vogelbusch, & Wojtek, 1981). Reading the list of factors listed earlier, we see that the word "perceived" precedes the first two listed. The perceptions of others can be inaccurate; nonetheless, they consider these perceptions to be reality. In Chapter 4 we learned that the disability or disabilities acquired in war or industrial accidents are considered to be "noble" disabilities and therefore have the least amount of stigma, individuals with congenital disabilities experience more prejudice, and disabilities that are thought to be self-inflicted have the greatest stigma. A student in our department was born with a displaced hip and has had several surgeries. Today, she walks with a limp. When she was a little girl, a rumor circulated around her church that her father had physically beaten her when she was a baby, causing the displaced hip. Not very long ago, many disabilities, such as autism and affective disorders, were thought (by many professionals and by the general public) to be caused by "refrigerator parents." Refrigerator parents were described as cold, distant, and rejecting. Thus, we can see that perceptions are not always accurate, and they influence the way in which the PWD (and in this case, her family) is viewed.

The functional limitations of the disability usually do not create many barriers between the PWD and others. However, such limitations as difficulty in communication, which people who are deaf or who have speech disorders experience, have the potential to create tension and frustration for both the PWD and the PWOD. These communication limitations can be overcome with the use of adaptive technology or interpreters, patience, and a willingness to talk with the PWD. It is safe to state that most PWODs exaggerate the extent and impact of the functional limitations of most disabilities.

"Disabled Heroes"

> **In this section, look for—**
>
> - The definition of a "disabled hero"
> - Three reasons why disabled heroes create more prejudice and discrimination against PWDs
>   1. Most PWODs do not understand the functional limitations of various disabilities and therefore have no basis on which to judge "heroism"
>   2. Disabled heroes have extraordinary resources available to them, which most people, with or without disabilities, do not have
>   3. The disabled hero perpetuates the myth that PWDs should "try harder"

Perceived social class, educational level, income, and occupational level do matter. Most of us do not like to admit that we are influenced by an individual's grooming, style of clothing, manners, and speaking ability. Nonetheless, individuals who are believed to be well educated, well mannered, and of high social status are accorded more respect. This holds true for PWDs (although it should be remembered that as a group, PWDs are far more likely to live in poverty, receive inferior educations, and be unemployed or underemployed). PWDs, like anyone else, realize that they will be more readily accepted if they appear in a position of authority and status.

All of us have seen the posters of "disabled heroes," in which individuals who have accomplished extraordinary achievements in science, the arts, athletics, or politics are pictured. Some examples include the physicist Stephen Hawking, American President Franklin Roosevelt, Helen Keller, the composer Beethoven, and Albert Einstein. Their accomplishments are remarkable for anyone, with or without a disability. These posters are intended to reduce the prejudice and discrimination against PWDs, but in reality they perpetuate more prejudice and discrimination simply because they give a false impression of a "typical" PWD and communicate, in a not very subtle way, that anyone can overcome a disability. It is easy to understand why many PWDs resent these disabled heroes.

Speaking of false impressions, there are highway billboards showing Erik Weihenmayer, the blind man who climbed Mount Everest. However, what is not advertised on billboards is Weihenmayer's failure to obtain a dishwasher's job in Cambridge, Massachusetts:

> Too big, too small, too fast, too hot, like a twisted version of the three bears—the story repeated itself again and again. I had thought somehow, that with my force of will, with my ingenuity, with my tenacity, I could eventually win people over and get what I wanted out of life. I hadn't realized there were doors that would remain locked in front of me. I wanted so badly to break through, to take a battering ram to them, to bash them into a million splinters, but the doors were locked too securely and their surfaces were impenetrable. I never got a dishwasher job in Cambridge, but I did choke down an important lesson, that people's perceptions of our limitations are more damaging than the limitations themselves, and it was the hardest lesson I ever had to swallow. (Weihenmayer, 2001, pp. 127–128)

Further, most PWODs are unaware of the functional limitations of disabilities and, therefore, are not in a position to evaluate the accomplishments of PWDs. For example, Wendell (1997) made the observation that athletes with amputations or spinal cord injuries do not have as many functional limitations as people with arthritis. Arthritis is a debilitating, painful, pervasive disability that affects many joints in the body, yet it is safe to state that most PWODs would consider a spinal cord injury or an amputation (or congenital limb deficiency) as more limiting than arthritis. However, it would be most unusual to see an athlete with severe arthritis.

These individuals who are considered to be disabled heroes have had remarkable resources available to them, including money, education, family support, innate talents, and intelligence, and, indeed, they are probably more famous for their accomplishments than they were/are for having a disability. For example, Helen Keller, who was deaf and blind, came from a prominent Southern family, was physically beautiful, and had personal friends such as Alexander Graham Bell, Mark Twain, Eleanor Roosevelt, and Albert Einstein. She graduated from Radcliffe College and occasionally lived on the financial support of admiring millionaires. But, by far, her greatest asset, not available to most people who are deaf and blind, was a companion/teacher who stayed with her for more than 49 years, Anne Sullivan (Hermann, 1998). (It is interesting to note that Keller's family often could not afford to pay Sullivan, but she remained with Helen Keller until her own death.) It is also interesting that Helen Keller's parents wrote to the Perkins Institute for the Blind after hearing about the successful education of a young woman, Laura Bridgman, who was deaf and blind. One of Laura Bridgman's teachers at the Perkins Institute was Anne Sullivan, and the Kellers were able to engage Anne Sullivan as the teacher/live-in companion for their daughter, Helen. Laura Bridgman lived most of her life at the Perkins Institute and died there; today there are few people who know who she was, and yet Helen Keller would not have been a celebrity and famous writer if it had not been for Laura Bridgman. (However, Charles Dickens met Laura Bridgman and modeled his fictional character "Little Nell" after her.)

Often the time of the onset of the disability has an impact on the accomplishments of the individual. For example, Christopher Reeve was able to develop his celebrity status before the onset of the disability, and Stephen Hawking received his education before the onset of amyotrophic lateral sclerosis (ALS). (The disability of ALS would not have prevented him from receiving a PhD, but most universities would not have had the accommodations necessary for Hawking, and, therefore, Hawking probably would not have been admitted.) Beethoven became deaf later in life, after he was a famous composer. The lives of these individuals would have been very different if their disabilities had been congenital or acquired early in life.

Finally, in the case of learning disabilities, it is difficult to know if these celebrities truly had a disability. Individuals of great achievement, such as Einstein, Edison, the Danish writer of fairy tales Hans Christian Andersen; the British prime minister Winston Churchill; and the Italian artist Leonardo da Vinci have been reported to have had a learning disability. However, most experts in learning disabilities do not think that any of these individuals had a learning disability. Of course, all of these individuals lived in a time when learning disabilities were not known about or diagnosed. Many of these assumptions are based on these individuals' handwriting, examples of misspelled words, and reports that they had problems in school. Huston (1987) summarized:

> Frequently, in books and articles on dyslexia, writers report a number of notable adults reputed to have had dyslexia. Repetition of these names has become almost a litany. These names are usually just listed in a series in books with rarely any explanation or evidence given why the person is considered to have been dyslexic. The few times any evidence is given it is scanty—often irrelevant or questionable . . . . Often there are more simple explanations for the difficulties these persons are said to have had. (pp. 151–152)

The Drawbacks To Having Disabled Heroes

> **In this section, look for—**
> - The two harmful prejudices perpetuated by "super crips"
> - The public wrongly believes that it is rare for PWDs to succeed
> - By focusing on individual achievements, the accomplishments of advocacy groups are ignored

Many PWDs use the derisive term "super crip" to label these disabled heroes. Indeed, many in the Disability Rights Movement regard super crips as perpetuating two harmful ideas/prejudices. First, by focusing only on the individual, the efforts and successes of the Disability Rights Movement, the passage of legislation such as the ADA, and the realities of the physical and attitudinal barriers that PWDs confront are ignored. The concept of a super crip concentrates on a remarkable individual and conveniently overlooks the accomplishments of disability advocates who facilitated the creation of the super crip. Once again, by focusing on *individuals*, society can reassure itself that the difficulties that PWDs encounter can be solved by individual effort. Second, posters and other advertisements of disabled heroes subtly plant the idea in the mind of the general public that *all* people with the same type of disability should be able to accomplish at the level of the super crip. However, for the "typical" PWD (whoever that might be) who does not have all the resources of the super crip, this is impossible. In spite of these realities, in the minds of the public, the super crip now becomes the standard by which *all* PWDs are judged. Covington (1997, as cited in Pelka, 1997) summarized:

> Super crip is usually a character struck down in the prime of life who fights to overcome insurmountable odds to succeed as a meaningful member of society. Through strength of will, perseverance, and hard work, the disabled individual achieves *a normal* life . . . . Too often, the news media treats an individual with disabilities who has attained success in his [*sic*] field or profession as though they [*sic*] were one-of-a-kind. While this one-of-a-kind aspect might make for a better story angle, it perpetuates in the mind of the general public how rare it is for the citizen with disabilities to succeed. (p. 292)

If the public thinks it knows *by name* the few PWDs who have succeeded, then it is also logical, although wrong, to think that most PWDs are failures. Irving Zola, the sociologist, college professor, and disability scholar, was a survivor of polio. He died in 1994 at the age of 59. Zola (1991) described the message and effects of "super crips."

> It is the . . . message that I have recently begun to abhor. It states that if a Franklin Delano Roosevelt or Wilma Rudolph could OVERCOME their handicap [*sic*], so could and should all the disabled [*sic*]. And if we fail, it's *our* problem, *our* personality, *our* weakness. And this further masks what chronic illness is all about. For our lives or even our adaptations do not center around one single activity or physical achievement but around many individual and complex ones. Our daily living is not filled with dramatic accomplishments but with mundane ones. And most of all, our physical difficulties are not temporary ones to be overcome once-and-for-all but ones we must face again and again for the rest of our lives. That's what chronic means! (p. 161)

J. Morris (1991) has stated that PWDs are only allowed two roles— "the pathetic crip and the Super Crip" (p. 100). Each is the opposite of the other; each is an extreme role. Both roles construct the disability as the individual's most salient identity, and neither allows the PWD to be an ordinary person. Neither the "pathetic crip" nor the "super crip" is considered to be an individual.

Christopher Reeve, the movie actor who acquired a spinal cord injury in a polo accident, died in 2006. Reeve was a controversial figure among PWDs. Reeve's appearance on an advertisement shown during the Super Bowl 2000 illustrates why many PWDs feel that super crips do not speak for most PWDs, and further, Reeve and other super crips may actually promote more stereotyping of PWDs. The advertisement was for Nuveen, a "wealth management" corporation (an investment company) that manages $71 billion in assets and trades on the New York Stock Exchange (Hersey, 2000). In 1999, Nuveen had record sales of $14.1 billion. The advertisement was not for any disability organization. In the advertisement Reeve, through the use of special effects, appears to be walking, wearing a tuxedo, presenting a hypothetical award for the "great strides" in AIDS, cancer, and spinal cord injury research. Christopher Reeve said that he did the commercial to raise public consciousness.

The disability community was outraged. First, Nuveen paid millions of dollars to air this commercial during the most expensive television time slot, the Super Bowl (January 23, 2000). Second, Nuveen blatantly used disability issues to promote its investment company, implying that a few rich people (like their customers) would fund research and eventually eliminate many kinds of disability (including spinal cord injuries). Laura Hersey, a writer with a disability, stated, "Nuveen was not advertising a product or service during this Super Bowl; it was selling an idea: that the very rich are good, powerful people who think deeply and through their thoughtful action, help society . . . . Nuveen's new ad latches onto and amplifies the idea of clobbering the problem of disability, by leveraging the accumulated funds of the upper classes. 'Invest well' means to pay now to eliminate physical differences which, otherwise, will haunt society later with complex, expensive legal and architectural demands." Ironically, most PWDs have monthly incomes that are far less than those of PWODs; therefore, Nuveen probably does not have many PWDs as customers. Charles Krauthammer, a physician who acquired a spinal cord injury 28 years ago, wrote an editorial for *Time* magazine (February 14, 2000, p. 100) (Exhibit 5–3). Krauthammer labels the Christopher Reeve Super Bowl advertisement as "disgracefully misleading" and "cruel." As a physician, Krauthammer understood.

Reeve is what Hersey terms a "baby crip." She said, "Four years post-injury, he still doesn't know what hit him, nor what lies ahead." Although Hersey does not use the term "super crip," she does mention Reeve's resources in dealing with his disability, which most PWDs do not have: "He still thinks that being disabled means you need two RNs attending you around the clock," and Reeve is "insulated by his wealth and celebrity." Reeve is insulting to other PWDs, giving television interviews in which he is critical of others with spinal cord injuries who are content to live their lives in a wheelchair. Further, he avoids associating with disability groups.

People with disabilities resent the assumption that he speaks for all PWDs. Hersey explained, "Reeve's message doesn't reflect how most disabled [sic] people live their lives. For most of us, things like work, personal relationships, having fun, and basic survival occupy far more of our attention and energy than any eventual cure. We come to terms with life as it is—complete with the disability and all its hazards, revelations, inconveniences, and adaptations. Many, though not all, come to value the crip life as a bold deviation from the boring norm . . . . For me, being disabled is part of life. I'm baffled when someone wants to talk cure with me. It's not something I seriously contemplate; I feel no connection. When someone insists on a cure as a prerequisite for my happiness, I am angry. What's wrong with being who I am?"

In many ways, Helen Keller was considered to be a super crip by the general public, and decades after her death, she is still remembered as having achieved remarkable accomplishments (for anyone, with or without a disability). Nonetheless, PWDs have raised questions about her contributions to the disability community. Moreover, there are Deaf advocates (Brueggemann & Burch, 2006; Kleege, 2007; Nielsen, 2006) who feel that Keller's notoriety and her personal beliefs harmed the community of Deaf people. Nielsen's (2006) article—entitled "Was Helen Keller Deaf?"—shows that Helen Keller did not form any relationships with the Deaf organizations, in spite of the fact that her method of communication, finger spelling, came from the Deaf. Nielsen summarized: "The newly created American Federation for the Blind (AFB) supplied both an income and a meaningful public life, becoming the center of her and Anne Sullivan Macey's life. Keller's employment with AFB cemented her public identification with the cause of blindness, removing her further from deafness, the Deaf community, and other causes, almost exclusively" (p. 27).

Exhibit 5-3

Charles Krauthammer

RESTORATION, REALITY AND CHRISTOPHER REEVE

"Paralyzed people fooled by a Super Bowl ad showing Christopher Reeve walking have been calling an advocacy group to find out how he was cured." —Associated Press, Feb. 1, 2000

I have long been reluctant to criticize Christopher Reeve. It is not easy attacking someone who suffered such a devastating injury and has carried on with spirit. Nor am I particularly keen to violate the Brotherhood of the Extremely Unlucky. (I injured my spinal cord when I was 22 and have been in a wheelchair ever since.)

But his Super Bowl ad was just too much. Why did he do it? To raise consciousness, he says. Convinced that a cure is imminent, he wants to share the good news with the largest possible audience. For 28 years I've been hearing that a cure is just a few years away. Being a doctor, I have discounted such nonsense. Most of the spinal-cord injured, however, are not doctors.

These are the facts. Yes, there is research into spinal-cord regeneration and, occasionally, there are some positive results in animal models. But the research is preliminary, at best suggestive. There remain enormous scientific obstacles even beyond the extremely problematic question of getting the neurons to regrow. Yes, this research will bear fruit one day. Unhappily, it is overwhelmingly likely that this day lies many years in the future.

Second, when that time does come, the principal beneficiaries will be the newly injured. People long injured—who've developed scar tissue at the site of the break and whose distal spinal cord (the part below the injury) often turns to mush as the old neurons die—will be the last people to be helped by this research, if they'll be helped at all. The "cure" will probably end up like the polio vaccine: preventing paralysis, not abolishing it.

Third, even in the unlikely event there is a cure for those presently paralyzed, it will at best be partial. The idea so dramatized in the Super Bowl commercial—that someone with a completely severed cord will actually walk—is very farfetched. Walking is a hugely complex motor and feedback activity. Look at how long it takes babies, who have totally intact nervous systems, to learn it. Look at how, despite decades of research to develop robots that walk, they remain primitive, often comical. Perhaps the long-injured will enjoy some partial return, some movement in the hands or chest or even legs. That would be a considerable boon. But it is far from the fantasy Reeve promotes; walking, i.e., restoration to preinjury status.

Reeve believes restoration is just around the corner. Fine. I have no quarrel with a man who wants to believe that. If he needs that to get through his day, who am I to disabuse him of his fantasies?

But Reeve insists on parading his fantasies in public with the express purpose of converting others to them. In his public pronouncements and now in his disgracefully

(continues)

misleading Super Bowl ad, he is evangelizing the imminent redemption. He goes so far as to criticize those who believe otherwise.

"The biggest problem, actually," he told *Good Morning America* the day after the commercial aired, "is people who've been in a chair for a very long time, because in order to survive psychologically they've had to accept 'O.K . . . I'm going to spend my life in a chair.' "

In Reeve's view, reality is a psychological crutch. His propaganda to that effect undermines those—particularly the young and newly injured—who are struggling to face reality, master it, and make a life for themselves from their wheelchairs.

Odder still is Reeve's belief that people in wheelchairs don't dream enough about getting out of them. (Hence the $2 million ad.) On the contrary. The problem is that some—again, the newly devastated young especially—dream about it too much.

When I was injured, I had a roommate in my four-bed ward who was making no effort to continue his education or plan for a new career. One day he told me why: "I'm going to wait seven years for a cure. Then I'm going to kill myself."

The false optimism Reeve is peddling is not just psychologically harmful, cruelly raising hopes. The harm is practical too. The newly paralyzed young might end up emulating Reeve, spending hours on end preparing their bodies to be ready to walk the day the miracle cure comes, much like the millenarians who abandon their homes and sell their worldly goods to await the Rapture on a mountaintop. These kids should instead be spending those hours reading, studying, and preparing themselves for the opportunities in the new world that high technology has for the first time in history made possible for the disabled.

They can have jobs and lives and careers. But they'll need to work very hard at it. And they'll need to start with precisely the psychological acceptance of reality that Reeve is so determined to undermine.

If I am wrong, the worst that can happen is that when the miracle comes, the non-believers will find themselves overtrained and overtoughened. But if Reeve is wrong, what will his dreamers be left with?

Keller was also an advocate of oralism and did not support the teaching of sign languages, thus hindering the education of Deaf children for decades. Touted as proof of the superiority of oralist teaching methods, Keller was used as a success story by oralist advocates. However, on her lecture tours, newspapers reported that no one in the audience could understand what Keller was saying when she spoke orally. Finally, Keller believed in both eugenics and euthanasia policies for babies and children with severe disabilities. Keller eventually changed her mind and reversed her stance; nonetheless, during the height of her fame, she spoke and wrote publicly in support of policies to prevent the birth of children with disabilities. Much has been written by Deaf advocates about Helen Keller, documenting her beliefs and activities, and it is not surprising that many Deaf advocates view Helen Keller with both suspicion and anger.

It is safe to say that most Americans do not know about the true disabled heroes. These disabled heroes are political activists who fought for the rights of all PWDs. Individuals with disabilities formed organizations such as Disabled in Action; they founded the Independent Living Movement; they fought for housing, transportation, and civil rights for PWDs. Parents of children with disabilities lobbied for a free, public education for their children. Others parked their wheelchairs in front of inaccessible buses, thus bringing public transportation to a halt in many major American cities. (They would have been taken to jail but the jails were not wheelchair accessible.) Activists have staged sit-ins in front of inaccessible restaurants and hotels. Individuals with disabilities forced the signing of the regulations of federal legislation by staging the longest sit-in (28 days) at a federal building. During this sit-in, phone service was cut off; one of the protesters was Deaf and simply signed through the window to an individual waiting outside, who then relayed the information to the media. Justin Dart is considered to be the father of the ADA. PWDs and their advocacy groups have worked to ensure the civil rights of Americans with disabilities, but most Americans would not recognize their names, and their pictures are not displayed on billboards along the freeway.

Aesthetic Qualities of the Disability

In this section, look for—

- The increased stigma directed toward individuals whose disability is perceived as "disfiguring"
- Often there are no functional limitations to a disfigurement
- In the past, there were only two alternatives for those with disfigurements
- Most PWDs whose disabilities are disfiguring have even less privacy than most other PWDs

It is clear that there is a great deal of stigma directed toward individuals whose disabilities are considered to be "maiming," "deforming," or "disfiguring." It is less clear, however, why there is increased prejudice. Disability scholars hypothesize that the anxiety and existential questioning that these types of disabilities evoke in others is at the root of this stigma. On viewing someone with a disfiguring disability, often we are reminded that disability and disfigurements can happen to anyone. Another source of stigma may be the overgeneralization and "spread" that is accorded to PW[...] stated, when we see someone who looks very different from our expecta- tions, or who is ugly, deformed, or maimed, we might assume that his or her personality and character are also very different or ugly, deformed, and maimed. Morris (1991) explained, "Our physical characteristics evoke such strong feelings that people often have to express them in some way. At the same time, they feel able to impose their feelings on us because we are not considered to be autonomous human beings" (p. 29). Perhaps another rea- son for violating the PWD's privacy is that the observer mistakenly thinks that the PWD is responsible for the strong feelings that the observer is feeling when, in reality, the observer is responsible for his or her own feel- ings and reactions.

Disfigurements illustrate the relationship between the disability itself and the handicapism of society. Most facial disfigurements, for example, have no functional limitations and yet they are considered to be disabilities and, moreover, one of the most handicapping disabilities. The handicaps and limitations have nothing to do with the disfigurement; rather, these handicaps are the result of society's reaction. As would be expected, there is debate today concerning the lengths to which PWDs should submit to eliminate or reduce disfigurements. Parents of children with Down syn- drome struggle with the decision of whether their children should undergo cosmetic plastic surgery. On the one hand, such surgery will not result in any functional restoration and there are risks involved in any surgery. On the other hand, many parents choose the surgery because they hope that their children will be less stigmatized. An English disability scholar (Marks, 1999) told of a man who had cosmetic surgery that decreased his functioning. "One speaker at the Sheffield MA Programme explained that he had been born with one thumb. This thumb was surgically removed in order to give his hands 'symmetry'" (p. 67). Individuals with these types of disfiguring disabilities experience even less privacy than do PWDs with other types of disabilities. JoAnne Rome was born without a left arm below the elbow and in the following excerpt, she discussed her lack of privacy.

> I used to believe I owed an explanation to whomever demanded one. I felt fearful, intimidated, ashamed, out of control, and outraged, yet "what happened to your arm?" was not a question that I could choose to answer or not. I was a freak, an outsider, an "other" and the world made it very clear that I owed them an explanation. I was also a little girl who was chased home from school with taunts of "Captain Hook!" ringing in my ears, the object of whispers, stares and laughter. (Morris, 1991, p. 28)

We have discussed the various ways in which the reactions of PWODs to an individual with a disability may become part of the PWD's self- concept. People with a disfiguring disability understand that they are not the disfigurement and may be forced to isolate themselves from others to maintain this self-identity. One woman called her facial scars "my mask," therefore making it not part of her self-identity, and felt she could be herself only at home. Molly McIntosh was burned as a child and has scars on her face and the upper part of her body. She stated:

> I have horrible scars on my face. What I mean by that is that people react to them with horror. Forty years ago, when I was in my twenties, and also when I was a child, I so hated the way that I looked. I tried not to think about it but every time I went out in the street I would be reminded about how I looked because of the way people reacted to me. As I walked down the street and someone was coming towards me, they would look and then drop their eyes or move their heads, as if the horror was too much. But then they could never, ever resist looking again. I used to have bets with myself about the second look. I would promise myself a treat if they didn't look again, but they always did. (J. Morris, 1991, p. 24)

In contrast, in Chapter 3 we discussed how Lucy Grealy stated, "I *was* my face. I *was* ugliness." Throughout her lifetime, she underwent 30 surgeries that were intended to reconstruct her face. Lucy Grealy eventually committed suicide. The account (Goffman, 1963) of a 37-year-old man "whose face is grossly disfigured" (p. 118) and who runs a successful real estate business provides an example of a third way to reduce the discomfort of others. The man states, "When I have an appointment with a new contact, I try to manage to be standing at a distance and facing the door, so the person entering will have more time to see me and get adjusted to my appearance before we start talking" (p. 118). Notice how the man carefully "manages" and positions himself and, at the same time, appears to be acting naturally and casually. Also notice that these strategies are not necessary after the first meeting.

In the past, there were only two ways for individuals with disfiguring disabilities to live. Most simply secluded themselves at home, thereby avoiding a lifetime of being objects of revulsion and rejection. A few chose to display themselves in freak shows and circuses, choosing to use people's horror and fascination as a moneymaker (Bogdan, 1988).

Impression Management

> **In this section, look for—**
>
> - Disability-specific impression management
> - An answer to the question, "Should PWDs be concerned with reducing interaction strain?" Or, stated differently, "Whose problem is it that PWODs are uncomfortable around PWDs?"
> - How even the most socially adept PWDs experience more rejection than most PWODs

Most everybody, with or without a disability, engages in some type of impression management. We wear appropriate clothing, are well groomed, speak appropriately, and practice good manners. Especially when interacting with people we do not know very well and we wish to favorably impress, we invest a great deal of time and effort in impression management. First dates and job interviews are classic examples of these types of situations, in that we wish to impress an individual who does not know us very well; furthermore, there is always the possibility that we will be rejected.

PWDs are aware that their disability creates discomfort in others; therefore, impression management for them becomes even more complicated. In fact, many PWDs use disability-specific impression-management techniques in an effort to reduce the tension felt by others (Belgrave, 1984; Belgrave & Mills, 1981; Kleck, 1966; Kleck et al., 1966, 1968). These techniques do not assist the individual's functioning and, in fact, actually may jeopardize his or her functioning. The sole purpose of these impression-management techniques is to reduce discomfort in others. Such impression-management techniques are criticized by many in the Disability Rights Movement because activists believe that the discomfort felt by PWODs is an issue with which PWODs should deal, and that it is not the responsibility of PWDs to become "court jesters" or "Tiny Tims." Some impression-management techniques are so costly to PWDs, in terms of time and physical pain, that they decide to abandon these attempts.

In spite of this controversy, many PWDs do actively engage in impression-management techniques to cope with the reactions of others. Some general techniques are the use of humor, the skillful introduction of the topic of the disability, and tactfully correcting PWODs when they make a mistake. Disability-specific techniques include a person who is blind maintaining "eye contact" with those who are speaking and turning on the lights at night. Individuals who are deaf have undergone years of speech training to have a more pleasant-sounding voice, and individuals with motor difficulties are subjected to "gait-training" to appear more "normal" to others. Other types of impression management include wearing prostheses for their cosmetic value rather than for their functional use. For anyone, the total impression conveyed is made up of many small, individual elements, and it is this overall impression that is important. Nonetheless, it is safe to state that for many PWDs, impression management is a greater challenge than it is for PWODs. One of my students who is blind, in a class discussion on impression management, reminded us that it is difficult for a person who is blind to know when it is dark outside and, therefore, she is not quite sure when to turn the lights on. This student told us that many times visitors had driven to her house, saw her house in total darkness, and drove away, thinking that she was not home. She also said that when she does turn on the lights, it may be days before she remembers to turn them off. Michalko (2002) described impression management as "actions required of the visually impaired . . . that are primarily responses to the sighted person's needs, and have little purpose from a non-visual perspective" (p. 137). "Adapting to the images of the 'sighted world' does not restore sight, it simply acts as demonstration: it demonstrates a blind person's commitment to participating in humanity . . ." (p. 139).

Franklin Roosevelt was a master at impression management. For example, he developed a type of "walk" in which he used a cane and a man walked on each side of him. (Often these men were his sons.) The three men had devised a carefully rehearsed act, at Roosevelt's request, to talk and laugh as they walked, appearing relaxed. In reality, all three were exerting themselves, carefully shifting Roosevelt's weight with each step and taking turns lifting him. (Roosevelt was lifting his legs with his body muscles because he had no hip muscles.) It was hard work, but it appeared that Roosevelt was walking on his own. Another example of Roosevelt's impression-management techniques was the navy blue cape that he wore. The public mistakenly thought this cape to be part of his "style," much as his cigarette holder was. In reality, it is easier to wear a cape rather than a coat when using a wheelchair; therefore the cape was an accommodation to Roosevelt's disability.

Simulation Exercises

In this section, look for—

■ What simulation exercises are designed to accomplish

■ Why simulation exercises fail to accomplish these purposes

   i. How can a congenital disability, such as blindness, be simulated?

(continues)

2. Is "forced empathy" possible?

3. Is it possible to simulate a significant aspect of an individual's self-concept?

4. Simulation exercises may evoke feelings of dependence among the simulators.

5. Simulation exercises may lead simulators to mistakenly believe that they now have a complete understanding of disability.

6. No other minority group (such as racial/ethnic groups) would allow others to simulate their experience.

- Often, simulation exercises increase prejudice and discrimination

- Simulations are often assaults on the self-esteem of PWDs

Simulation exercises are designed to give those without disabilities insight into the experience of disability (Baesler, 1995; Fichten, Compton, & Amsel, 1985). Individuals wear blindfolds to simulate blindness and use wheelchairs and other devices to simulate other types of disabilities, and often students in drug or alcohol abuse counseling classes are required to forgo one type of food or drink for 2 or 3 weeks (often chocolate, coffee, or beer). Other types of simulation include the following:

All Thumbs (physical disabilities, group activity)

Materials: masking tape, raisins, nuts, pudding.

Activity: Sometimes people with physical disabilities don't have good muscle control. With masking tape, tape together the fingers of the participant's weaker hand, leaving only the thumb free. Give each participant a cup of raisins or a dish of pudding to eat using only that hand. Divide participants into pairs. Let one in each pair feed the other a dish of pudding. Trade places.

Discussion: How did you feel during these experiments? Did you find ways to overcome the problems of eating when you had less control of your hands? How does it feel to be fed by someone else?

Thick Hands

Materials: thick socks, shirts, sweaters, shoes, beads, string, and ruler.

Activity: Some people have trouble with fine motor coordination. This is because their muscles are weaker and they need more time and practice to learn how to move. To help participants understand

this condition, have them put a pair of thick socks on each hand
and try to tie shoes, button a shirt, and string beads. Tie a ruler
between the students' ankles so that their legs are stiff and apart
from each other. Have them walk down the hall and back, slowly.
Discussion: How would you feel if people laughed or stared at you or
imitated the way you walked? (Brew-Parrish, 2004).

However, it is now known that these exercises are useless and they
may actually increase prejudice and discrimination toward PWDs (Kiger,
1992; Olkin, 1999; Pfeiffer, 1989; Wright, 1975). Imagine how a PWOD in
the first exercise would feel. For most adults, the idea of being spoon-fed
appears demeaning; however, PWDs remind us that PWODs do not feel
embarrassed when the barber or beautician cuts their hair.

Allport (1954, 1958, 1986), in his classic work *The Nature of Prejudice*,
discussed the usefulness of role-playing techniques in which a member of
the dominant group takes on the role of an individual of a minority group.
In Allport's examples, the groups are racial/ethnic groups. Allport explained
that the White person is "required to act out the roles of other people—of
employees, of students, of Negro servants, he [sic] learned through such
'psychodrama' what it feels like to be in another's shoes. He [sic] also gains
insight regarding his own motives, his anxieties, his projections" (Allport,
1986, p. 491). Indeed, Allport used the expression "forced empathy" to describe the purpose of these simulations.

Is it possible to simulate a disability? Simulation exercises, regardless
of how carefully designed, cannot allow a PWOD to assume the identity
of a PWD. The fatigue, pain, and social isolation cannot be simulated
(Marks, 1999). John Hockenberry spent more than 10 years with National
Public Radio as a reporter, Middle East correspondent, and program host.
As you read Hockenberry's description of paralysis, including the uniqueness (like a fingerprint), consider whether the experience of paralysis can
be simulated.

"Paralyzed from the waist down" describes so little of the experiences
of a spinal-cord injury that most crips used it as a kind of shorthand
joke. In my case, I am paralyzed from the nipples down. When people
learn this they are shocked to realize that there is no international
checkpoint at the waist. It is an arbitrary demarcation. In actual fact,
relatively few people are paralyzed from the waist down. Everyone has
their particular line separating sensation from numbness. Each line of
separation is invisible to the eye. In some people the aspects of temperature and pressure and muscle control are separate. Some spinal-cord
injured people can feel pressure but not temperature in some parts of
their body and vice versa. There are people with almost total sensation
but with no motor control . . . a partially damaged fiber-optic cable
. . . picture, but no sound . . . bad reception. All these metaphors aid
understanding, but none is precise. The trace of each paraplegic and

quadriplegic's sensory border zone is as unique as a fingerprint. Each person has a different answer to the question: What does paralysis feel like? (Hockenberry, 1996, p. 97)

As discussed before, most PWDs consider their disability to be a valued part of their self-identity, are proud of their mastery of the disability, and have developed many idiosyncratic responses and accommodations. None of these self-defining characteristics can be simulated. Voluntarily giving up coffee, chocolate, or beer may allow an individual to see how difficult such self-control can be, but the experience cannot begin to parallel the experience of recovery from alcohol and/or drug abuse. Furthermore, how can a PWOD simulate a congenital disability, such as blindness, deafness, or a limb deficiency?

However, it is possible to glimpse some of the prejudice and discrimination PWDs encounter. If a person is required to use a wheelchair for 24 hours, he or she can understand the frustration of nonaccessible restrooms, water fountains, and doorways. Nonetheless, the simulator knows that the simulation is of short duration (Sawyer & Clark, 1980).

Most important, simulation exercises reinforce and strengthen prejudice against PWDs because simulations often evoke feelings of dependence, hopelessness, and discouragement in the simulator. People who are blind or deaf or who use a wheelchair are skilled in mastering their environment; people who wear a blindfold or earmuffs or use a wheelchair for a simulation exercise, however, experience 24 hours of frustration, dependence, and hopelessness. Using a wheelchair requires strength and technique, both of which require time to develop. The experience of blindness would be very different if an individual did not know how to read Braille. However, learning Braille is a difficult and time-consuming process. Wandering around the corridors of a university building with a blindfold would probably give the simulator a discouraging and frustrating view of blindness because Braille is used on doors and elevators. (In addition, people who are blind have had orientation and mobility [O & M] training.) Further, the simulator mistakenly may think that he or she now has "expert knowledge" of the disability experience. However, it is not knowledge of disability that has been acquired, but rather the myth that PWDs feel helpless, dependent, and discouraged all the time.

Lifchez and Wade (1982) described simulation exercises and their unexpected results:

Workshops where one temporarily "tries on" a disability constitute attempts to give ... an entry into the subjective experience of the disability. Trying on a disability offers ... a sense of the physical issues involved, but it often backfires, as it can generate so much anxiety.... Trying on fails to offer ... any sense of the way in which the environment affects, feeds, and is sustained by social and cultural prejudices and expectation. (p. 91)

Marks (1999) pointed out shortcomings of simulation exercises. "Rather than listening to what disabled [sic] people are saying, simulation may pander to voyeuristic excitement and give non-disabled people a very distorted and reductive kind of 'empathy,' a cavalier fantasy that an experience has been understood, or an increase in pity for the person with a disability" (p. 134).

Kiger (1992) undertook a review of 60 studies of simulation exercises and found that none had any positive effect on the attitudes of PWODs toward the disability experience. There are other issues in using simulation exercises; one of these issues concerns the response of PWDs to PWODs attempting to "imitate" them. Olkin (1999), a polio survivor who uses a wheelchair, summarized her feelings about simulation exercises: "I find it rude for people to 'imitate' me as a way of understanding my minority status. It implies that only through direct experience can one come to understand 'minority status,' as if the word of people with disabilities isn't good enough. For no other minority status do we direct students to use imitation as a means of enlightenment" (p. 330).

Experiential learning is valuable, and most disability scholars advocate the use of such learning methods to help PWODs understand the experience of disability. Indeed, if done correctly, experiential learning activities can decrease the heightened sensitivity and interaction strain PWODs often feel in the presence of PWDs. Beatrice Wright required her university students to undertake a semester-long advocacy project, such as overseeing the accessibility of a public playground or generating a list of public entertainment facilities that are not accessible to PWDs and then developing a plan to facilitate change. Other projects included listing negative, condescending portrayals of PWDs in the media (McCarthy, 1993). Olkin (1999) used other types of experiential learning, including having her students use assistive devices, such as TTY telephones, and requiring students to go to the Department of Rehabilitation office and learn how to fill out an application form. (TTY telephones, used by people who are deaf, have a keyboard and a screen. The two "callers" type to each other.) Both these professors/scholars emphasize that these types of learning activities need to be preceded and followed by the appropriate information and discussion. In an article in *The Disability Rag*, an outspoken magazine written by and for PWDs, the author (who is a polio survivor and whose husband is blind) recounts:

> My daughter Tara had come home from school in tears. It was Disability Simulation Day at Greenwood High (School). Blindfolded students were being led around by sighted students, others were bumping into walls. The students were terrified of their newly created disabilities. Some had told Tara they thought persons with disabilities had horrible lives; a few thought they would be better off dead.
>
> I contacted the school's psychology teacher once and tried to get Disability Simulation Day stopped. It was a lost cause. She (the

teacher) liked having Disability Simulation Day featured in the local newspaper, and saw no need for me or my husband—or anyone from our local independent living center—to come to her classroom to talk with students.

I am baffled as to why nondisabled people see a need to simulate a disability. Across our nation in February, we celebrate Black History Month. Is it necessary for people with white skin to paint their faces black to better understand this minority? (Brew-Parrish, 2004)

Some individuals with disabilities advocate the use of simulation exercises but only if a PWD guides the exercise. While the PWD who acts as a guide can offer interpretation and greater understanding of the experience, many PWDs consider all simulation exercises to be useless and demeaning to individuals who experience disability 24 hours a day, 7 days a week.

The Costs of Handicapism for PWODs and Society

Thus far, we have discussed the costs of prejudice and discrimination against PWDs (handicapism) only in terms of PWDs. Indeed, the costs to PWODs, and society in general, are rarely considered. Nonetheless, whether acknowledged or not, there are consequences and costs to the dominant group—PWODs. Society pays for its prejudice against PWDs in three ways: (1) the economic costs; (2) the collective, and individual, fear of acquiring a disability; and (3) the narrow (and inaccurate) view of the world and human experience that PWODs have when they choose to ignore the disability experience. Perhaps there is an additional "cost" of prejudice—that of our moral ambivalence. A society (or individual) is morally ambivalent when the society (or individual) publicly *professes* one set of values and *acts* on another set of values. For example, our society professes that all people are created equal; however, as we have seen, PWDs have systematically been treated as second-class citizens. Handicapism is deeply rooted, legitimized, institutionalized, and individually internalized throughout American society. Moreover, society blames the victims, telling PWDs that their disabilities are the cause of the prejudice and discrimination. Believing this premise, many consider handicapism to be an inevitable and unavoidable outcome. In contrast, if we could understand that our prejudices and discrimination (and the resulting lack of accommodations) were both irrational and unjustified, then institutional changes could be made.

The Economic Costs of Prejudice and Discrimination, or "Do the Math"

Of course, it is impossible to generate an accurate dollar cost of what a society loses in wasted skills, lower production, and fewer customers to buy products. Nonetheless, economic costs are incurred in three ways: (1) the loss of productivity of PWDs, (2) the financial costs to compensate PWDs rather than to employ them, and (3) the loss of a customer base to buy products. The economic costs of keeping PWDs unemployed or underemployed do not begin to consider the social and emotional costs of unemployment to the PWD. Work for anyone, with or without a disability, brings financial security and economic empowerment, but there are other benefits, such as social relationships, the opportunity to learn and develop skills, and the chance to make a contribution. These types of benefits are not easily translated into dollar costs, but they may, in many respects, be more important than the financial benefits. Yet, PWDs continue to be denied entrance into the labor market.

Lest anyone think that government financial compensation, such as Social Security, allows PWDs a life of economic comfort and dignity, most Social Security benefits keep the individual below the poverty line. Who pays for the unemployment and underemployment of PWDs? The American taxpayer. The taxpayer pays in two ways: for the loss of productivity of PWDs and for the financial compensation required to keep PWDs unemployed. Sociologists (Simpson & Yinger, 1985) cited another cost: "That discrimination prevents the training and use of workers as their highest possible skill is shown not only in the failure to employ fully the trained carpenter or pilot or teacher if he or she belongs to the 'wrong groups,' but more particularly in the failure to train many individuals in the first place" (p. 161).

Hahn (1997) stated: "The concept of an 'industrial reserve army' seems to provide an explanation for the depressed economic position of men and women with disabilities. Available estimates indicate that approximately two-thirds of disabled [sic] persons in most industrialized nations are unemployed, a level that exceeds the unemployment rate among other deprived and disadvantaged groups" (p. 173).

Weisgerber (1991) reported, "These losses amounted to 6.9 percent of the gross national product in 1980," or "alternatively, as Chirikos pointed out, the losses can be characterized as a 'tax of about $800 levied on each and every American'" (p. 190). Because these are 1980 statistics and the rate of employment of PWDs has not improved, we can conclude that at the present time, each American pays more than $800.

Fear of Acquiring a Disability

If PWODs were to understand the disability experience more accurately, they would fear it less. Disability has been termed "the only open minority group," meaning that anyone, at any time, can become a member of the group by acquiring a disability. Rosemarie Garland Thomson concisely stated, "There is no 'we' and 'they' when it comes to disability" (1997, p. 297). Clearly, such assumptions as that PWDs are the "other" or "those people" and the belief that we will never acquire a disability defy logic. Disability is a universal concern. The existential angst, or fear of acquiring disability, is self-inflicted by PWODs' indifference to learning about the disability experience. We learned from Groce's book, *Everybody Here Spoke Sign Language*, that when a child was born deaf on Martha's Vineyard, the birth was not considered tragic nor were the baby's social or vocational opportunities automatically reduced as a result of the deafness. On Martha's Vineyard, because of the large number (relatively speaking) of residents who were deaf, everyone "spoke" sign language and people who were deaf were not considered to have a disability, to be different, or to be inferior. Deafness, to everyone, seemed natural and nothing to be feared. Hearing people who were "bilingual" might be regarded as an accommodation for people who are deaf, but certainly the bilingualism of everyone on Martha's Vineyard helped hearing people not to fear deafness. Wendell (1997) stated, "If disabled people [*sic*] and their knowledge were fully integrated into society, everybody's relation to his or her own body would be liberated" (p. 260). Dorothy Hermann (1998), after writing the biography of Helen Keller, wrote that she had learned that disability is "not inevitably accompanied by deformity, suffering, and limitations" and that disability was "not inevitably sacrifice and loss of freedom. Disability is not to be feared." (p. xxxiii). Accommodations for PWDs also assist PWODs. For example, the Americans with Disabilities Act requires standardizing admission requirements for schools and job functions for employment. Such standardization and widening of the pool of qualified applicants help both PWDs and PWODs. Employers and educational programs will now have a larger and more qualified pool from which to hire/admit, and all applicants, with or without a disability, will have clear, written job qualifications and admission standards.

A Narrow and Inaccurate Worldview

PWODs have designed a society based on the false assumption that there are few PWDs when, in fact, disability is both common and natural. Believing this assumption, PWODs rob themselves of the richness and diversity that PWDs could contribute if PWODs would allow them. A society is richer when it appreciates, understands, and respects a wide range of experiences, values, points of view, and self-identities. When society reduces (consciously or subconsciously) its level of tolerance for difference of any kind, its framework for viewing the world becomes both narrow and inaccurate. However, in times of change, boundaries between groups are less clear-cut. The rising movement of PWDs (and their families) to claim their civil rights and the higher rates of disability incidence have begun, and will continue, to blur the demarcations between PWODs and PWDs.

Franklin Roosevelt, one of the world's greatest leaders, who guided the United States through the worst financial crisis in history, the Great Depression, and oversaw the creation and deployment of the largest military and industrial force to win World War II, had a disability. Everyone knew that Roosevelt was a survivor of polio and could not walk, but they cooperated in minimizing and hiding the effects of the disability. Historians and biographers, in the past, judged Roosevelt to have made his world-changing accomplishments *in spite of* his disability. Now, Geoffrey Ward, in his book *A First Class Temperament: The Emergence of Franklin Roosevelt* (1989), advances the thesis that Roosevelt's disability experience *contributed to* his accomplishments. Ward stated that the experience of surviving polio "humanized" Roosevelt, changing him from "a superficial opportunist, self-centered lightweight who sacrificed old friends in the interest of personal advancement" (p. 74). Ward continued, "To win that battle (polio) . . . would demand of him qualities not conspicuously displayed so far in his largely charmed life: patience, application, recognition of his own limitations, a willingness to fail in front of others and try again" (p. 75). Ward's biography of Roosevelt makes it clear that it is not possible to understand Roosevelt or his achievements without understanding his experience with polio.

In-Class Videos

- View the 60-minute video "Deafblind: A World Without Sight and Sound" by Films for the Humanities and Sciences. The producers describe this video: "We think in words—without access to them, how does one construct thoughts? Adam and Mark are 12-year-old boys born deaf and blind. With no exposure to language, how do they communicate with their parents? This fascinating program provides a window into the world of those who are deafblind. Using special effects that simulate sensory deprivation and compensation, this video illustrates how deafblind people live."
- View the 70-minute PBS video "Understanding Learning Disabilities: How Difficult Can This Be?" by the F. A. T. City Workshop. This is an example of a simulation exercise; however, in this case, the experience of having a learning disability is realistically portrayed. Answer the following questions. After viewing this video, (1) do you have a better understanding of learning disabilities? (2) Do you think that the social environment can exacerbate learning disabilities? (3) Are there examples of negative motives attributed to individuals with learning disabilities? (4) Did some of the "students'" internalize society's negative image of them? (5) Do you think that people without learning disabilities need to be educated?
- View the video "Without Pity: A Film About Disabilities." This documentary, narrated by Christopher Reeve, introduces the audience to several people of different ages, professions, and disabilities. In this video, Reeve makes this comment: "Disabled people [sic] are tired of being invisible and are declaring their right to an equal chance at life." Available from Films for the Humanities and Sciences.
- View the 60-minute video "Ways To Move." The producers describe this video: "[It] contains three stories which explore the

debate between what has been called the medical model of disability (in which the disability is a challenge to be cured) and the independence model (in which the challenge is to make society more accessible). Viewers meet individuals who shatter stereotypes about disability: dancers who use wheelchairs as part of their choreography, researchers on the quest for a cure for paralysis, and a candidate running for Congress who happens to be disabled." Available from Program Development Resource.

- View the video "My Country." This video tells the stories of three people with disabilities and their hard-won success for equal rights under the law. Available from Aquarius Health Care Videos (5 Powderhouse Lane, P.O. Box 1159, Sherbon, MA 01770; telephone 508-651-2963; fax 508-650-4216; e-mail aqvideo@tiac.net, www.aquariusproductions.com.

- View the 50-minute video "The Ragin' Cajun: Oliver Sacks Investigates Usher Syndrome" by Films for the Humanities and Sciences. The producers describe this video: "The deaf-blind community in Seattle is extraordinarily vibrant, with a strong sense of pride and independence. That is why Danny Delcambre moved there. Deaf from birth, and steadily losing his sight, Danny suffers [*sic*] from Usher syndrome. The region in Louisiana he left behind has the highest concentration of Usher syndrome in the world. This program takes a sensitive look at this degenerative condition as neurologist/author Oliver Sacks and Danny explore the nature of Deaf Culture and the marvelous richness of American Sign Language, which includes a sophisticated touch-based variation called tactile signing. A BBC (British Broadcasting Company) production."

- View the 40-minute video "Signs of Life" by Films for the Humanities and Sciences. The producers describe this video: "People with hearing impairments have been a misunderstood minority for too long. This program blows away the stereotypes and should be required viewing for everyone, including the Deaf and hard-of-hearing."

- View the 30-minute video "The Right Future: Beyond Institutionalization" by Films for the Humanities and Sciences. The producers describe this video: "For people with developmental disabilities, misunderstanding, fear, and financial constraints historically have created barriers to successful community living. This documentary is a compelling profile of the Right Future project, a model program that integrates people with developmental disabilities into a supportive and welcoming community."

- View the 25-minute video "Ethics, Residents' Rights, and Dignity" by Insight Media (2162 Broadway, New York, NY 10024-0621, 800-233-9910, www.insight-media.com). The producers describe this video: "Legal issues and advances in technology make it imperative to consider ethics and residents' rights. This video explores the difference between law and ethics, details the rights of every resident, and helps viewers to determine standards of personal conduct for the workplace." Note: This video discusses issues of elderly people in residential care; however, there are many ethical issues that apply to PWDs in residential care.

- View the award-winning video "Fred's Story." This 27-minute video is described by the producers: "A charming older gentleman tells about the 40 years he spent inside Mansfield Training School, a Connecticut institution closed in 1990. Fred Calabrese tells of the unpleasant realities of decades of institutional life, then a move to his own apartment. Fred is a disturbingly honest but overwhelmingly charming speaker on his own behalf." Mr. Calabrese states, "He said he'd get me out when the time comes. Well, the time never came and I was there for 40 years." Available from Program Development Resource (P.O. Box 2038, Syracuse, NY 13220, 800-543-2119, fax 315-452-0710). This video comes with four discussion guides.

- View the 26-minute video "Waddie Welcome." The producers describe this video: "The many fascinating stories, the heartbreak, and the triumphs experienced by Waddie Welcome are presented by his circle of friends. They listened to his pleas, learned to communicate in his language, and used person-centered planning to enable Mr. Welcome to live with a family after a 10-year stay in a nursing home. This video signifies an effort to sustain justice and challenges us to redesign the responsiveness of community delivery systems." Available from Program Development Resource.

- View two 30-minute videos, "This Is YOUR Right." The producers describe these videos: "Imagine a news magazine type television program like 60 Minutes or 20/20. Then imagine the anchors, segments, field reporters, and commercials. Now imagine instead that the news magazine type show is called Human Rights TV, and the anchors and field reporters all have disabilities. If you can imagine all of this, you'll have a pretty good idea of what this humorous production is all about. The production includes funny commercials about fictitious products and services that are intended to lampoon situations that people with disabilities encounter in everyday life."

- View the 60-minute video "Ready To Live." Producers describe this video: "This program looks at ways adaptive technologies help people with disabilities to find independence. Included is a profile of the late Ed Roberts, a national disability rights activist, once called a 'helpless cripple,' who became one of the founders of the 'Independent Living Movement.' Other profiles include a world-class runner who used an advanced prosthetic leg, a former Bosnian soldier whose life was transformed by a pair of artificial hands, a woman who inspired a revolution in wheelchair design and construction." Available from Program Development Resource.

- View the 29-minute video "Self-Advocacy: Freedom, Equality, and Justice for All." The producers state: "Freedom, Equality, and Justice for All is a remarkable package of specific concrete strategies for promoting and strengthening self-advocacy. Learn the rich history of self-advocates, disability rights advocates, and the civil rights struggles. Viewers will have a stronger sense of empowerment and understand the importance of self-advocacy." Available from Program Development Resource.

- View the 23-minute video "A Little History Worth Knowing: Disability Down Through the Ages." The producers describe this video: "From ancient times to telethons, to today's burgeoning disability movement, A Little History Worth Knowing traces the often-overlooked history of people with disabilities. With a combination of hard-hitting facts and rare historical footage, the video looks at:

  1. stereotypes in films, TV, and other media
  2. the ongoing struggle for disability rights
  3. the effects of technology on people's ability to work and live independently
  4. historical stereotypes, including the 'medical model.'

  Although the video doesn't shy away from the abuses of the past (including Hitler's extermination of more than 200,000 people with disabilities), it ends with a hopeful look at the future as changing attitudes and advancing technology help people with disabilities to enter the global economy." This Irene M. Wood and Associates production is available from Program Development Resource. Phone: 800-543-2119.

- View the 48-minute video "Vital Signs: Crip Culture Talks Back" by David Mitchells and Sharon Snyder. The producers describe this video as an "edgy, raw documentary [that] explores the politics of disability through the performances, debates, and late-night conversations of activists at a recent national conference on Disability and the Arts. Including interviews with well-known disability rights advocates such as Cheryl Marie Wade, Mary Duffy, and Harland Hahn, Vital Signs conveys the intensity, variety, and vitality of the disability culture today." Available from Fanlight Productions (4196 Washington Street, Boston, MA 02131, 800-937-4113, www.fanlight.com).

- View the 24-minute video "Voices in a Deaf Theater." The producers describe this video: "This perceptive documentary follows a mixed cast of deaf and hearing actors as they prepare to stage *The Glass Menagerie*. As they rehearse, each group experiences a difficult but rewarding journey into the culture of the other. This outstanding video offers viewers a window into the Deaf world, with its rich culture and expressive language, as well as an opportunity to witness the way two groups, with a common goal but very different communication tools, can bridge their language barrier." A study guide is included. Available from Fanlight Productions.
- View the 60-minute video "My Country: Disability Rights" produced by Aquarius Health Care Videos. The producers describe the video: "By telling the stories of three people with disabilities and their struggle for equal rights under the law, this film draws a powerful parallel with the civil rights struggle of the 1960s." ISBN 1-58140-043-8.

Learning Activities

1. Read and discuss two or three issues of *The Ragged Edge: The Disability Experience in America*. Available from The Avocado Press, Box 145, Louisville, KY 40201; e-mail: circulation@ragged-edge -mag.com; Web site: www.avocadopress.com. This is the most widely circulated disability rights magazine.
2. Read and discuss two or three issues of *Mouth: Voice of the Disability Nation*. This is a very direct and straightforward publication written by those who have disabilities. Write to 4201 SW 30th Street, Topeka, KS 66614-3023.
3. Obtain the transcript from the NBC *Dateline* Sept. 9, 1997, program. This program, featuring John Hockenberry, showed prejudice and discrimination against PWDs in applying for jobs, trying to rent an apartment, and other situations. Hidden cameras were used to record apartment owners and store managers refusing to rent an apartment or give a job interview to people in wheelchairs. Available from Burrell's Information Services, Box 7, Livingston, NJ 07039. Ask for transcript Number 560.
4. Read the book *Blind Rage: Letters to Helen Keller* by G. Kleege (Washington, DC: Gallaudet University). On page 1, Kleege introduces herself and gives her reasons for writing the book.

> Dear Helen Keller,
>   Allow me to introduce myself. I am a writer and part-time English professor. I am American, married, middle-aged, middle-class. Like you, I am blind, though not deaf. But the most important thing you need to know about me,

and the reason for my letter, is that I grew up hating you . . . .
I hated you because you were always held up to me as a role
model, and one who set an impossibly high standard of cheer-
fulness in the face of adversity. "Why can't you be more like
Helen Keller?" people always said to me.

I am not alone in this. Many disabled people [*sic*] think
you did our cause a lot of harm. Your life story inscribes
the idea that disability is a personal tragedy to be overcome
through an individual's fortitude and pluck, rather than a set
of cultural practices and assumptions, affecting many individuals, that could be changed through collective action. (p. 1)

Ms. Kleege has the unique vantage of a professor of English and
a blind person. Because of this, she is able to ask questions about
Keller's writings, the play *The Miracle Worker*, and Keller's
adaptations to blindness and deafness.

5. Read the following books:
   - Freeburg, E. (2001). *The education of Laura Bridgman: The first
     deaf and blind person to learn language.* Cambridge, MA: Harvard
     University.
   - Gitter, E. (2001). *The imprisoned guest: Samuel Howe and Laura
     Bridgman, the first deaf-blind girl.* New York: Farrar, Straus &
     Giroux.

6. Anne Sullivan, Helen Keller's teacher (or Miracle Worker), learned
   how to teach Laura Bridgman, who was deaf–blind, by using finger-
   spelling. Helen Keller's parents heard of this success and hired Anne
   Sullivan to teach Helen. Laura Bridgman was one of the most famous women in the world. Newspapers and ladies' magazines wrote
   about her, and Charles Dickens modeled his character Little Nell
   on Bridgman. Laura Bridgman died in 1889 at age 59. Today, no
   one remembers Laura Bridgman and everyone remembers Helen
   Keller. What made the difference?

Writing Activity

Using one of the 11 "bullets" listed at the beginning of this chapter, write
a response paper.

References

Allport, G. W. (1954). *The nature of prejudice.* Reading, MA: Addison-Wesley.

Allport, G. W. (1958). *The nature of prejudice* (2nd ed.). Garden City, NY: Doubleday
Anchor.

Allport, G. W. (1986). *The nature of prejudice* (25th anniversary ed.). Reading, MA: Addison
Wesley.

Amir, Y. (1969). Contact hypothesis in ethnic relations. *Psychological Bulletin, 71*, 319–342.

Amsel, R., & Fichten, C. S. (1988). Effects of contact on thoughts about interaction with students who have a physical disability. *Journal of Rehabilitation, 54*, 61–65.

Anderson, G. R. (1987). Paternalism. In G. R. Anderson & V. A. Glesnes-Anderson (Eds.), *Health care ethics: A guide for decision makers* (pp. 177–191). Rockville, MD: Aspen.

Anthony, W. (1972). Societal rehabilitation: Changing society's attitudes toward the physically and mentally disabled. *Rehabilitation Psychology, 19*, 117–126.

Anthony, W. (1984). Social rehabilitation: Changing society's attitudes toward the physically and mentally disabled. In R. Marinelli & A. Dell Orto (Eds.), *The psychology and social impact of physical disability* (2nd ed., pp. 193–203). New York: Springer.

Baesler, E. J. (1995). Persuasive effects of an involving disability role play. *Journal of Applied Rehabilitation Counseling, 26*(2), 29–35.

Baker, F. M., Baker R. J., & McDaniel, R. S. (1975). Demoralizing practices in rehabilitation facilities. *Rehabilitation Literature, 36*, 112–115.

Becker, H. S. (Ed.). (1963). *Outsiders: Studies in the sociology of deviance.* New York: Free Press.

Belgrave, F. Z. (1984). The effectiveness of strategies for increasing social interaction with a physically disabled person. *Journal of Applied Social Psychology, 14*, 147–161.

Belgrave, F. Z., & Mills, J. (1981). Effect upon desire for social interaction with a physically disabled person of mentioning the disability in different contexts. *Journal of Applied Social Psychology, 11*, 44–57.

Bell, A. H. (1962). Attitudes of selected rehabilitation workers and other hospital employees toward the physically disabled. *Psychological Reports, 10*, 183–186.

Bennett, C.R. (1998). Dentistry and the disabled. *Rehab Team, January*, 20–24.

Berkowitz, E. D. (1984). Professionals as providers: Some thoughts on disability and ideology. *Rehabilitation Psychology, 29*, 211–216.

Bickenbach, J. E. (1993). *Physical disability and social policy.* Toronto: University of Toronto.

Blood, I. M., & Blood, G. W. (1982). Classroom teachers' impressions of normal-hearing and hearing-impaired children. *Perceptual and Motor Skills, 54*, 877–878.

Bogdan, R. (1988). *Freak show: Presenting human oddities for amusement and profit.* Chicago: University of Chicago Press.

Bogdan, R., & Taylor, S. J. (1992). The social construction of humanness: Relationships with severely disabled people. In P. M. Ferguson, D. L. Ferguson, & S. J. Taylor (Eds.). *Interpreting disability: A qualitative reader* (pp. 275–294). New York: Teachers College, Columbia University.

Bower, E. M. (Ed.). (1980). *The handicapped in literature: A psychosocial perspective.* Denver, CO: Love.

Brew-Parrish, V. (2004, August 9). The wrong message—still. *Ragged Edge. www.raggededge magzine.com/focus/wrongmessage04.html.*

Brodwin, M. G., & Gardner, G. (1978). Teacher attitudes toward the physically disabled. *Journal of Teaching and Learning, 3*(3), 40–45.

Brueggemann, B. J., & Burch, S. (Eds.). (2006). *Women and deafness: Double visions.* Washington, DC: Gallaudet University.

Buss, D. M. (1999). *Evolutionary psychology: The new science of the mind.* Boston: Allyn & Bacon.

Byrd, E. K., & Elliott, T. R. (1988). Media and disability: A discussion of the research. In H. E. Yuker (Ed.), *Attitudes toward persons with disabilities* (pp. 82–95). New York: Springer.

Chubon, R. A. (1982). An analysis of research dealing with the attitudes of professionals toward disability. *Journal of Rehabilitation, 48*, 25–30.

Cohen, R. (2004). *Blindsided: Living a life above illness: A reluctant memoir.* New York: HarperCollins.

Cole, S. S. (1984). Facing the challenge of sexual abuse of persons with disabilities. *Sexuality and Disability, 7,* 71–88.

Cole, S. S. (1993). Facing the challenges of sexual abuse in persons with disabilities. In M. Nagler (Ed.). *Perspectives on disability* (2nd ed., pp. 273–282). Palo Alto, CA: Health Markets Research.

Coleman, L. M. (1997). Stigma: An enigma demystified. In L. J. Davis (Ed.), *The disability studies reader* (pp. 216–231). New York: Routledge.

Comer, R. J., & Piliavin, J. A. (1972). The effects of physical deviance upon face-to-face interaction: The other side. *Journal of Personality and Social Psychology, 23,* 33–39.

Cook, S. W. (1978). Interpersonal and attitudinal outcomes in cooperating interracial groups. *Journal of Research in Developmental Education, 12,* 97–113.

Covey, H. C. (1998). *Social perceptions of people with disabilities in history.* Springfield, IL: Charles C. Thomas.

Covington, G. (1997). Super crip. In F. Pelka (Ed.), *The disability rights movement* (p. 92). Santa Barbara, CA: ABC-CLIO.

Craine, L. S., Henson, C. E., Colliver, J. A., & McLeland, D. G. (1988). Prevalence of a history of sexual abuse among female psychiatric patients in a state hospital system. *Hospital and Community Psychiatry, 39,* 300–304.

Davis, L. J. (Ed.). (1997). *The disability studies reader.* New York: Routledge.

Deegan, P. E. (1991). Recovery: The lived experience of rehabilitation. In R. P. Marinelli & A. E. Dell Orto (Eds.). *The psychological and social impact of disability* (3rd ed., pp. 47–54). New York: Springer.

Dembo, T., Leviton, G. L., & Wright, B. A. (1975). Adjustment to misfortune: A problem of social-psychological rehabilitation. *Rehabilitation Psychology, 2,* 1–100.

Deutsch, M. (1949). A theory of cooperation and competition. *Human Relations, 2,* 129–152.

Donaldson, J. (1980). Changing attitudes toward handicapped persons: A review and analysis of the research. *Exceptional Children, 46,* 504–514.

Duckitt, J. (1992). *The social psychology of prejudice.* New York: Praeger.

Dunn, M. (1996). Subscale development of the Rehabilitation Situations Inventory. *Rehabilitation Psychology, 41,* 255–264.

Eisenberg, M. G. (1982), Disability as stigma. In M. G. Eisenberg, C. Griggins, & R. J. Duval (Eds.), *Disabled people as second-class citizens* (pp. 1–11). New York: Springer.

Eisenberg, M. G., Griggins, C., & Duval, R. J. (Eds.). (1982). *Disabled people as second-class citizens.* New York: Springer.

Elliott, T. R., Frank, R. G., Corcoran, J., Beardon, L., & Byrd, E. K. (1990). Previous personal experience and reactions to depression and physical disability. *Rehabilitation Psychology, 35,* 111–119.

Evans, J. H. (1976). Changing attitudes toward disabled persons: An experimental study. *Rehabilitation Counseling Bulletin, 19,* 572–579.

Fichten, C. S., Compton, V., & Amsel, R. (1985). Imagined empathy and attributions concerning activity preferences of physically disabled college students. *Rehabilitation Psychology, 30,* 235–239.

Fichten, C. S., Robillard, K., Judd, D., & Amsel, R. (1989). College students with disabilities: Myths and realities. *Rehabilitation Psychology, 34,* 243–257.

Fleischer, D. Z., & Zames, F. (2001). *The disability rights movement: From charity to confrontation.* Philadelphia: Temple University.

Friedson, E. (1965). Disability as social deviance. In M. Sussman (Ed.), *Sociology and rehabilitation* (pp. 71–99). Washington, DC: American Sociology Association and the US Vocational Education Administration.

Fries, K. (Ed.). (1997). *Staring back: The disability experience from the inside out.* New York: Plume.

Fuchs, D., Fuchs, L. S., Dailey, A. M., & Power, M. H. (1985). The effects of examiners' personal familiarity and professional experience on handicapped children's test performance. *Journal of Educational Research, 78,* 141–146.

Gaier, E. L., Linkowski, D. C., & Jaques, M. E. (1968). Contact as a variable in the perception of disability. *The Journal of Social Psychology, 74,* 117–126.

Garske, G. G., & Thomas, K. R. (1990). The relationship of self-esteem and contact to attitudes of students in rehabilitation counseling toward persons with disabilities. *Rehabilitation Counseling Bulletin, 34,* 67–71.

Gartner, A., & Joe, T. (Eds.). (1987). *Images of the disabled, disabling images.* New York: Praeger.

Gellman, W. (1959). Roots of prejudice against the handicapped. *Journal of Rehabilitation, 40,* 115–123.

Genskow, J. K., & Maglione, F. D. (1965). Familiarity, dogmatism, and reported student attitudes toward the disabled. *The Journal of Social Psychology, 67,* 329–341.

Goffman, E. (1963). *Stigma: Notes on the management of spoiled identity.* Englewood Cliffs, NJ: Prentice-Hall.

Goffman, E. (1997). Selections from stigma. In L. J. Davis (Ed.), *The disability studies reader* (pp. 203–215). New York: Routledge.

Gordon, E. D., Minnes, P. M., & Holden, R. R. (1990). The structure of attitudes toward persons with a disability, when specific disability and context are considered. *Rehabilitation Psychology, 35,* 79–90.

Gould, S. (1981). *The mismeasure of man.* New York: Norton.

Gouvier, W. D., Coon, R. C., Todd, M. E., & Fuller, K. H. (1994). Verbal interactions with individuals presenting with and without physical disability. *Rehabilitation Psychology, 39,* 263–268.

Grand, S. A., Bernier, J. E., & Strohmer, D. C. (1982). Attitudes toward disabled persons as a function of social context and specific disability. *Rehabilitation Psychology, 27,* 165–174.

Greenwood, R., & Johnson, V. A. (1987). Employer perspectives on workers with disabilities. *Journal of Rehabilitation, 53*(3), 37–54.

Hahn, H. (1997). Advertising the acceptably employable image: Disability and capitalism. In L. J. Davis (Ed.), *The disability studies reader* (pp. 172–186). New York: Routledge.

Harosymia, S. J., Home, M. D., & Lewis, C. A. (1976). A longitudinal study of disability group acceptance. *Rehabilitation Literature, 37,* 98–102.

Heinemann, W., Pellander, F., Vogelbusch, A., & Wojtek, B. (1981). Meeting a deviant person: Subjective norms and affective reactions. *European Journal of Social Psychology, 11,* 1–25.

Henderson, G., & Bryan, W. V. (1997). *Psychosocial aspects of disability* (2nd ed.). Springfield, IL: Charles C. Thomas.

Hermann, D. (1998). *Helen Keller: A life.* New York: Knopf.

Hersey, L. (2000). *Commentary on the Super Bowl Ad: Quad Man Walking.* Available from Compuserve.com.

Heumann, J. (1999). Personal narrative. In R. Mackelprang & R. Salsgiver (Eds.), *Disability: A diversity model in human service practice* (pp. 51–54). Pacific Grove, CA: Brooks/Cole.

Higgins, P. C. (1992). *Making disability: Exploring the social transformation of human variation.* Springfield, IL: Charles C. Thomas.

Hillyer, B. (1993). *Feminism and disability.* Norman, OK: University of Oklahoma.

Hockenberry, J. (1995). *Moving violations: War zones, wheelchairs, and declarations of independence.* New York: Hyperion.

Holzbauer, J., & Berven, N. (1996). Disability harassment: A new term for a longstanding problem. *Journal of Counseling and Development, 74,* 478–483.

Home, M. D. (1988). Modifying peer attitudes toward the handicapped: Procedures and research issues. In H. E. Yuker (Ed.), *Attitudes toward persons with disabilities* (pp. 203–222). New York: Springer.

Hubbard, R. (1997). Abortion and disability: Who should live and inhabit the world? In L. J. Davis (Ed.), *The disability studies reader (pp. 187–200).* New York: Routledge.

Hurst, R. (1998). Forget pity or charity: Disability is a rights issue. *Disability International, 5*(3), 14–16.

Huston, A. M. (1987). *Common sense about dyslexia.* New York: Madison.

Imrie, R. (1996). *Disability in the city: International perspectives.* New York: St. Martin's Press.

Janicki, M. P. (1970). Attitudes of health professionals toward disabilities. *Perceptual and Motor Skills, 30,* 77–78.

Jankowski, K. A. (1997). *Deaf empowerment: Emergence, struggle, and rhetoric.* Washington, DC: Gallaudet University.

Jaques, M. E., Linkowski, D. C., & Seika, F. L. (1970). Cultural attitudes toward disability: Denmark, Greece, and the United States. *International Journal of Social Psychiatry, 16,* 54–62.

Johnson, H. B. (2003, February 16). Should I have been killed at birth? The case for my life. *The New York Times Magazine, 50,* 52–56, 74.

Karp, D. A. (2001). *The burden of sympathy: How families cope with mental illness.*

Kiger, G. (1992). Disability simulations: Logical, methodological, and ethical issues. *Disability, Handicap, & Society, 7,* 71–78.

Kleck, R. (1966). Emotional arousal in interactions with stigmatized persons. *Psychological Reports, 19,* 12–26.

Kleck, R. (1968). Physical stigma and nonverbal cues emitted in face-to-face interaction. *Human Relations, 21,* 19–28.

Kleck, R., Buck, P. L., Goller, W. L., London, R. S., Pfeiffer, J. R., & Vukcevic, D. P. (1968). Effect of stigmatizing conditions on the use of personal space. *Psychological Reports, 23,* 111–118.

Kleck, R., Ono, H., & Hastorf, A. H. (1966). The effects of physical deviance upon face-to-face interaction. *Human Relations, 19,* 425–436.

Kleege, G. (2006). *Blind rage: Letters to Helen Keller.* Washington, DC: Gallaudet University.

Krauft, C. C., Rubin, S. D., Cook, D. W., & Bozarth, J. D. (1976). Counselor attitudes towards disabled persons and client program completion: A pilot study. *Journal of Applied Rehabilitation Counseling, 7,* 72–77.

Krauthammer, C. (2000, February 14). Restoration, reality and Christopher Reeve. *Time, 155*(6), 100.

Kriegel, L. (1982). Claiming the self: The cripple as American male. In M. G. Eisenberg, C. Griggins, & R. J. Duval (Eds.), *Disabled people as second class citizens* (pp. 52–63). New York: Springer.

Langer, E. J., Bashner, R. S., & Chanowitz, B. (1985). Decreasing prejudice by increasing discrimination. *Journal of Personality and Social Psychology, 49,* 113–120.

Langer, E. J., Fiske, S., Taylor, S. E., & Chanowitz, B. (1976). Stigma, staring, and discomfort: A novel-stimulus hypothesis. *Journal of Experimental and Social Psychology, 12,* 451–463.

Larrivee, B., & Cook, L. (1979). Mainstreaming: A study of the variables affecting teacher attitude. *The Journal of Special Education, 13,* 315–324.

Lehr, D. H., & Brinkerhoff, J. (1996). Bases of practice for young children with disabilities who challenge the system. In D. H. Lehr & F. Brown (Eds.), *People with disabilities who challenge the system* (pp. 3–21). Baltimore: Brookes.

Lerner, W., & Belts, H. (2005, May 5). Striving for equity. *Modern Health Care, 35*(26), 20.

Leytens, J. P., Paladino, P. M., Rodriguez-Torres, R., Vaes, J., Demoulin, S., Rodriguez-Torres, A., & Gaunt, R. (2000). The emotional side of prejudice: The attribution of secondary emotions to ingroups and outgroups. *Personality and Social Psychology Review, 4,* 186–197.

Liachowitz, C. H. (1988). *Disability as a social construct: Legislative roots.* Philadelphia: University of Pennsylvania.

Lifchez, R., & Wade, C. (1982). What every architect should know. In M. G. Eisenberg, C. Griggins, & R. J. Duval (Eds.), *Disabled people as second class citizens* (pp. 88–102). New York: Springer.

Longmore, P. (1985). Screening stereotypes: Images of disabled people in television and motion pictures. *Social Policy, 16,* 31–38.

Louis Harris and Associates, Inc. (1986). *The ICD survey of disabled Americans: Bringing disabled Americans into the mainstream.* New York: Author.

Louis Harris and Associates, Inc. (1994). *N.O.D.L. Harris survey of disabled Americans.* Washington, DC: National Organization of Disability.

Mackelprang, R., & Salsgiver, R. (1999). *Disability: A diversity model approach in human service practice.* Pacific Grove, CA: Brooks Cole.

Makas, E. (1993). Getting in touch: The relationship between contact with and attitudes toward people with disabilities. In M. Nagler (Ed.), *Perspectives on disability* (2nd ed., pp. 121–136). Palo Alto, CA: Health Markets Research.

Marks, D. (1999). *Disability: Controversial debates and psychosocial perspectives.* London: Routledge.

McCarthy, H. (1993). Learning with Beatrice A. Wright: A breath of fresh air that uncovers the unique virtues and human flaws in us all. *Rehabilitation Education, 7,* 149–166.

Michalko, R. (2002). *What a difference disability makes.* Philadelphia: Temple University.

Morris, J. (1991). *Pride against prejudice: Transforming attitudes to disability.* Philadelphia: New Society.

Murphy, M. A. (1998). Rejection, stigma, and hope. *Psychiatric Rehabilitation Journal, 22,* 185–189.

National Public Radio (1998, May). *The Disability History Project: Tomorrow's Children.*

New York ABLE. (2000, January). *Chains and shackles replaced with programs and services.* 26M–27M.

Nielsen, K. E. (2006). Was Helen Keller deaf? Blindness, deafness, and multiple identities. In B. J. Brueggemann & S. Burch (Eds.), *Women and deafness: Double visions* (pp. 21–39). Washington, DC: Gallaudet University.

Olkin, R. (1999). *What psychotherapists should know about disability.* New York: Guilford.

Opotow, S. (1990). Moral exclusion and injustice: An introduction. *Journal of Social Issues, 46,* 1–20.

Palmerton, K. E., & Frumkin, R. M. (1969). Contact with disabled persons and intensity of counselors' attitudes. *Perceptual and Motor Skills, 28,* 434.

Parenti, J. F., Beaufils, B., & Paicheler, H. (1987). Stereotyping and intergroup perceptions of disabled and nondisabled children: A new perspective. *The Exceptional Child, 34*, 93–106.

Pelka, F. (Ed.). (1997). *The ABC-CLIO companion to the disability rights movement.* Santa Barbara, CA: ABCCLIO.

Pfeiffer, D. (1989). Disability simulation using a wheelchair simulation. *Journal of Post Secondary Education and Disability, 7*, 53–60.

Putnam, M., Greenen, S., Powers, L., Saxton, M., Finney, S., & Dautel, P. (2003). Health and wellness: People with disabilities discuss barriers and facilitators to well being. *Journal of Rehabilitation, 69*, 37–45.

Rabkin, J. G. (1972). Opinions about mental illness: A review of the literature. *Psychological Bulletin, 77*, 153–171.

Safilios-Rothschild, C. (1970). *The sociology and social psychology of disability and rehabilitation.* New York: Random House.

Safran, S. P. (1998). The first century of disability portrayal in film: An analysis of the literature. *The Journal of Special Education, 31*, 467–479.

Sawyer, H. W., & Clark, W. D. (1980). Disability simulation as a strategy for attitude change. *Journal of Applied Rehabilitation Counseling, 11*, 132–135.

Schmelkin, L. P. (1988). Multidimensional perspectives in the perception of disabilities. In H. E. Yuker (Ed.), *Attitudes toward persons with disabilities* (pp. 127–137). New York: Springer.

Schur, E. M. (1971). *Labeling deviant behavior: Its sociological implications.* New York: Harper and Row.

Schur, E. M. (1979). *Interpreting deviance.* New York: Harper and Row.

Schur, E. M. (1983). *Labeling women deviant: Gender, stigma, and social control.* Philadelphia: Temple University.

Sigelman, C. K., Spanhel, C. L., & Lorenzen, C. D. (1979). Community reaction to deinstitutionalization. *Journal of Rehabilitation, 45*, 52–54, 60.

Siller, J. (1984). The role of personality in attitude toward those with physical disabilities. In C. J. Golden (Ed.), *Current topics in rehabilitation psychology* (pp. 201–227). Orlando, FL: Grune & Stratton.

Simpson, G. E., & Yinger, J. M. (1985). *Racial and cultural minorities: An analysis of prejudice and discrimination* (5th ed.). New York: Plenum.

Sobsey, D. (1994). *Violence and abuse in the lives of people with disabilities: The end of silent acceptance.* Baltimore: Brookes.

Sobsey, D., & Doe, T. (1991). Patterns of sexual abuse and assault. *Sexuality and Disability, 9*, 243–260.

Sobsey, D., & Mansell, S. (1993). The prevention of sexual abuse of people with developmental disabilities. In M. Nagler (Ed.), *Perspectives on disability* (2nd ed., pp. 283–292). Palo Alto, CA: Health Markets Research.

Stefan, S. (2001). *Unequal rights: Discrimination against people with mental disabilities and the Americans with Disabilities Act.* Washington, DC: American Psychological Association.

Thomas, S. A., Foreman, P. E., & Remenyi, A. G. (1985). The effects of previous contact with physical disability upon Australian children's attitudes toward people with physical disabilities. *International Journal of Rehabilitation Research, 8*, 69–70.

Thomson, R. G. (1997). Integrating disability studies into the existing curriculum: The example of "Women and Literature" at Howard University. In L. J. Davis (Ed.). *The disability studies reader* (pp. 295–306). New York: Routledge.

Trupin, L., Sebesta, D. S., Yelin, E., & LaPlante, M. P. (1997). *Trends in labor force participation*. Disability Status Report No. 10. San Francisco, CA: University of California, Institute for Health and Aging.

Ulicny, G. R., White, G. W., Bradford, B., & Matthews, R. M. (1990). Consumer exploitation by attendants: How often does it happen and can anything be done about it? *Rehabilitation Counseling Bulletin, 33*, 240–246.

Wade, C. M. (1997). *Poems*. In L. J. Davis (Ed.), *The disability studies reader* (pp. 408–409). New York: Routledge.

Ward, G. C. (1989). *A first class temperament: The emergence of Franklin Roosevelt*. New York: Harper and Row.

Waxman, B. F. (1991). Hatred: The unacknowledged dimension in violence against disabled people. *Sexuality and Disability, 9*, 185–189.

Weihenmayer, E. (2001). *Touch the top of the world: A blind man's journey to climb farther than the eye can see*. New York: Dutton.

Weisgerber, R. A. (1991). *Quality of life for persons with disabilities*. Gaithersburg, MD: Aspen Publishers, Inc.

Wendell, S. (1997). Toward a feminist theory of disability. In L. J. Davis (Ed.), *The disability studies reader* (pp. 260–278). New York: Routledge.

Whitney, C. R. (1993, January 19). Disabled Germans fear they'll be the next target. *The New York Times*, p. A3.

Wilson, D. J. (1990). *Living with polio: The epidemic and its survivors*. Chicago, IL: University of Chicago.

Woods, F. J., & Carrow, M. A. (1959). Choice rejection status of speech defective children. *Exceptional Children, 25*, 279–283.

Wright, B. A. (1975). Sensitizing outsiders to the position of the insider. *Rehabilitation Psychology, 22*, 129–135.

Wright, B. A. (1983). *Physical disability: A psychosocial approach* (2nd ed.). New York: Harper and Row.

Wright, B. A. (1988). Attitudes and fundamental negative bias: Conditions and corrections. In H.E. Yuker (Ed.), *Attitudes toward persons with disabilities* (pp. 3–21). New York: Springer.

Yuker, H. E., & Block, J. R. (1986). *Research with the Attitude Toward Disabled Persons Scales: 1960–1985*. Hempstead, NJ: Hofstra University Center for the Study of Attitudes Toward Persons with Disabilities.

Yuker, H. E. (1965). Attitudes as determinants of behavior. *Journal of Rehabilitation, 31*, 15–16.

Yuker, H. E. (1983). The lack of a stable order of preference for disabilities: A response to Richardson and Ronald. *Rehabilitation Psychology, 28*, 93–103.

Yuker, H. E. (1988). The effects of contact on attitudes toward disabled person: Some empirical generalizations. In H. E. Yuker (Ed.). *Attitudes toward persons with disabilities* (pp. 262–274). New York: Springer.

Yuker, H. E. (1994). Variables that influence attitudes toward persons with disabilities: Conclusions from the data. *Journal of Social Behavior and Personality, 9*, 3–22.

Yuker, H. E., & Hurley, M. K. (1987). Contact with and attitudes toward persons with disabilities: The measure of intergroup contact. *Rehabilitation Psychology, 32*, 145–154.

Yuker, H. E., Block, J. R., & Young, J. H. (1970). *The measurement of attitudes toward disabled persons*. Albertson, NY: Human Resources Center.

Zola, I. K. (1991). Communication barriers between "the able-bodied" and "the handicapped." In R. P. Marinelli & A. E. Dell Orto (Eds.), *The psychological and social impact of disability* (3rd ed., pp. 157–180). New York: Springer.

Zola, I. K. (1992). "Any distinguishing features?" The portrayal of disability in the crime-mystery genre. In P. M. Ferguson, D. L. Ferguson, & S. J. Taylor (Eds.), *Interpreting disability: A qualitative reader* (pp. 233–250). New York: Columbia University.

Suggested Readings

Blood, I. M. (1997). The hearing aid effect. *Journal of Rehabilitation, 63*(4), 59–63.

Fichten, C. S., & Amsel, R. (1986). Trait attributions about college students with a physical disability: Circumplex analyses and methodological issues. *Journal of Applied Social Psychology, 16,* 401–427.

Fichten, C. S., Tagalakis, V., & Amsel, R. (1986). Effects of cognitive modeling, affect, and contact on attitudes, thoughts, and feelings toward college students with physical disabilities. *Journal of the Multihandicapped Person, 2,* 119–137.

Furnham, A., & Pendred, J. (1983). Attitudes toward the mentally and physically disabled. *British Journal of Medical Psychology, 56,* 179–187.

Gallagher, H. G. (1985). *FDR's splendid deception.* New York: Dodd & Mead.

Havranek, J. E. (1991). The social and individual costs of negative attitudes toward people with disabilities. *Journal of Applied Rehabilitation Counseling, 24,* 16–18.

Ladd, G. W., Munson, H. L., & Miller, J. K. (1984). Social integration of deaf adolescents in secondary level mainstreamed programs. *Exceptional Children, 50,* 420–428.

Livneh, H. (1983). Application of smallest space analysis to the study of attitudes toward disabled persons. *Professional Psychology: Research and Practice, 14,* 406–413.

Livneh, H., & Thomas, K. R. (1997). Psychosocial aspects of disability. *Rehabilitation Education, 11,* 173–183.

Millington, M. J., Strohmer, D. C., Reid, C. A., & Spengler, P. M. (1996). A preliminary investigation of the role of differential complexity and response style in measuring attitudes toward persons with disabilities. *Rehabilitation Psychology, 41,* 243–254.

Morgan, S. R. (1987). *Abuse and neglect of handicapped children.* Boston: Little, Brown.

Nosek, M. A., Zhu, Y., & Howland, C. A. (1992). The evolution of independent living programs. *Rehabilitation Counseling Bulletin, 35,* 174–189.

Obermann, C. E. (1965). *A history of vocational rehabilitation in America.* Minneapolis, MN: T. S. Dennison.

O'Connell, B. (1999). *Civil society: The underpinnings of American democracy.* Hanover, NJ: University Press of New England.

Olkin, R., & Howson, L. (1994). Attitudes toward and images of physical disability. *Journal of Social Behavior and Personality, 9,* 81–96.

Rees, L. M., Spreen, O., & Harnadek, M. (1991). Do attitudes toward persons with handicaps really shift over time? Comparison between 1975 and 1978. *Mental Retardation, 29,* 81–86.

Richardson, S. A. (1971). Children's values and friendships: A study of physical disability. *Journal of Health and Social Behavior, 12,* 253–259.

Sagatun, I. J. (1985). The effects of acknowledging a disability and initiating contact on interaction between disabled and nondisabled persons. *The Social Science Journal, 22*(4), 33–43.

Satcher, J., & Bookey-Dickey, K. (1992). Attitudes of human-resource management students towards persons with disabilities. *Rehabilitation Counseling Bulletin, 35,* 248–252.

Scheer, J., & Groce, N. (1988). Impairment as human constraint: Cross cultural and historical perspectives on variation. *Journal of Social Issues, 44,* 23–37.

Soder, M. (1990). Prejudice or ambivalence? Attitudes toward people with disabilities. *Disability, Handicap, & Society, 5,* 227–241.

Strauch, J. D. (1970). Social contact as a variable in the expressed attitudes of normal adolescents toward EMR pupils. *Exceptional Children, 36,* 495–500.

Strohmer, D. C., Grand, S. A., & Purcell, M. J. (1984). Attitudes toward persons with a disability: An examination of demographic factors, social context, and specific disability. *Rehabilitation Psychology, 29,* 131–145.

Strohmer, D. C., Leierer, S. J., Cochran, N. A., & Arokiasamy, C. V. (1996). The importance of counselor disability status. *Rehabilitation Counseling Bulletin, 40,* 96–115.

Vander Kolk, C. J. (1976). Physiological and self-reported reactions to the disabled and deviant. *Rehabilitation Psychology, 23,* 77–83.

Watson, F. (1930). *Civilization and the cripple.* London: John Bales, Sons, & Danielson.

Waxman, B. F. (1991). Hatred: The unacknowledged dimension in violence against disabled people. *Sexuality and Disability, 9,* 185–189.

Weinberg, N. (1978). Modifying social stereotypes of the physically disabled. *Rehabilitation Counseling Bulletin, 22,* 114–124.

Weinberg, N. (1978). Preschool children's perception of orthopedic disability. *Rehabilitation Counseling Bulletin, 21,* 183–189.

Weisskopf, M. (2006, October 2). How I lost my hand but found myself. *Time,* 28–37.

Wilson, D. J. (1990). *Living with polio: The epidemic and its survivors.* Chicago: University of Chicago.

Experiencing Prejudice and Discrimination

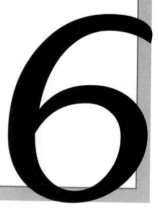

- What are the effects for PWDs of the following behaviors and attitudes?

  —Stereotyping

  —Role entrapment

  —Pity

  —Lowered expectations

  —Lack of privacy

  —Hypervisibility and overobservation

  —Solo status

  —Token status

  —Infantilization, paternalism, and "motherese"

  —Objectification

  —Being viewed as animals

  —Unnecessary dependence

  —Marginality

  —Lack of equal social status relationships

  —The media's portrayal of PWDs

  —Crime and abuse against PWDs

  —Second-class citizenship

- In what ways is handicapism like racism? In what ways is handicapism unlike racism?
- The way in which supposedly beneficent behaviors (such as charity, pity, and paternalism) often result in handicapism

Introduction

In this section, look for—

- The ways in which handicapism is socially sanctioned
- Handicapism does allow for a socially valued place for PWDs

Itzhak Perlman, the world-famous violinist and a survivor of polio, stated that PWDs experience two problems: (1) the environment that is not physically accessible, and (2) the attitudes of PWODs toward disability and PWDs. As difficult as these problems are, it can be seen that neither problem concerns the disability itself (or the individual with the disability). Indeed, one of the results of the Americans with Disabilities Act (ADA) has been the increased public awareness that many of the problems and obstacles experienced by PWDs result from their environments (both social and physical).

None of the behaviors and attitudes listed at the beginning of this chapter help create a socially valued and respected position for PWDs. PWDs are subjected to many types of negative and harmful responses from PWODs, in much the same manner as individuals who are members of racial/ethnic/cultural minority groups. Indeed, many of these behaviors, such as stereotyping, infantilizing, and withholding equal social status, are also experienced by individuals belonging to other types of minority groups. People allow degrading stereotypes for what (and whom) they do not understand and do not like. However, PWDs also encounter added prejudice and discrimination. For example, PWDs have less privacy than PWODs and are often considered to be dependent. These two conditions/characteristics are usually not part of the racial/ethnic minority individual's experience. In discussing the experience of PWDs, it is important to remember that (1) while the PWD considers the behaviors and attitudes of PWODs to be prejudicial and negative, often PWODs do not; (2) it is then logical to assume that many PWODs are unaware of their behaviors and the effects (or at least minimize and rationalize their attitudes and behaviors; many times, we operate on the assumption that if we are not aware of attitudes and behavior, then they cannot be important); (3) these types of behaviors and attitudes are found in all types of people, including professionals who provide services to PWDs, policymakers, and program administrators; and (4) many of these behaviors and attitudes are closely related to each other, although there are important differences among them. For example, the concepts of lack of privacy and hypervisibility are closely related, but there are also important differences between these two concepts.

Handicapism Is Socially Sanctioned and Continually Reinforced in American Culture

The following are examples of socially sanctioned handicapism: inaccessible environments; jokes about PWDs that go unchallenged; media outlets that sensationalize PWDs, exaggerate disability, and demonize PWDs; federal laws that are not funded, are underfunded, or place the burden of proof on PWDs; and the facile acceptance of abortion and assisted suicide for PWDs. Much of this handicapism is not recognized as prejudice and discrimination; however, the same types of treatment of any racial or ethnic group, religious group, or sexual orientation group would readily (and justifiably) be acknowledged as prejudice and discrimination.

Most PWDs Identify as Typical, Ordinary People

Carol Gill, a psychologist who is paraplegic, noted that most PWDs identify themselves as typical, ordinary people with the usual life concerns, such as family, career, and community life. Nonetheless, often PWDs are unpleasantly reminded that others may not see them as ordinary or typical people:

> Unless they have developed a political or cultural consciousness that centralizes difference, most disabled [*sic*] people identify as typical. Disabled [*sic*] people generally lack preparation to be continually conscious of minority status and its life consequences in the way that growing up in a marginalized racial/ethnic community informs community members about racism. Moreover, most disabled [*sic*] people think of themselves as ordinary because impairments recede in importance as they are integrated into daily routines. In our world, abnormal is normal. It can be repeatedly jolting for individuals who identify as ordinary to be persistently categorized as extraordinary or pathetic by those whom they regard as peers, even intimates. (Gill, 2001, p. 351)

"The Warrior in Me Gets Tired"

As we shall see, there are many institutional and interpersonal barriers in dealing with society's response to disability. Note that we are not discussing the management of the disability itself. These barriers and attitudes are persistent, unremitting, and found most everywhere. Support groups that are comprised of PWDs offer some respite from frustrating social, legal, and physical environments. PWDs (and their families) develop idiosyncratic coping mechanisms to confront and circumnavigate these barriers. Some PWDs become powerful advocates for PWDs, making improvements in the lives of everyone with a disability. Other PWDs may tire of the constant demands and stress. One PWD stated:

> There is a warrior in me, but that warrior gets tired. And the frustration of having every part of your life affected again and again by thoughtless people, by crooked bureaucrats . . . it's constant . . . . it takes so much out of you." (Putnam et al., 2003, pp 39–40)

Notice how the individual feels that every part of his or her life is affected. The word "warrior" may also communicate that this PWD feels at war with prejudice and discrimination. PWDs reject prejudice and discrimination, but they do not reject their disabilities.

Stereotyping

> ### In this section, look for—
> - The difference between a category and a stereotype
> - How PWDs can internalize society's false stereotypes
> - How seemingly positive stereotypes about PWDs are handicapping
> - The three factors that serve to maintain and reinforce false stereotypes

To be viewed as a person with a disability is to be both categorized and stereotyped. The person is no longer viewed as an individual. Stereotyping is defined as "an exaggerated belief associated with a category. Its function is to justify (rationalize) our conduct in relation to that category" (Allport, 1986, p. 191). Most stereotypes about PWDs are unsupported by fact. For example, we saw in Chapter 2 that PWODs have a tendency to sensation-alize the disability and to impute emotional reactions to disabilities that PWDs simply do not experience. Some examples of stereotypes that are unsupported by fact include the ideas that blindness is a dark pit and that PWDs do not have "normal" sexual feelings. It would, therefore, appear logical that PWDs would not adopt these stereotypes as self-identifiers. However, especially in the past, some of the stereotypes held by PWODs have been so pervasive and widespread that PWDs (and their families) have internalized these false stereotypes. Reread the story of Gunther Schirmer in Chapter 5. Tragically, Schirmer had taken society's prejudice and dis-crimination as his self-concept. Speaking of himself, he said he would "de-stroy the cripple." Schirmer committed suicide.

A stereotype is not a category; it is a *belief* about a category. Therefore, it is not prejudicial to recognize someone as having a disability. It is preju-dicial to assume that this one category (or any other one category) is the sole determinant of the individual's attitudes and behaviors. Categorization of people is sometimes necessary, although not as often as we think. The tendencies to overcategorize and to stereotype people in categories are the result of our need to simplify a vast array of different types of people and their individual characteristics and identities.

Stereotypes are usually negative and categorize people in subordinate positions. Of course, there is the *possibility* of positive stereotypes. For ex-ample, consider this stereotype: PWDs are compassionate and wise because their suffering has given them sensitivity and insight. On the surface, this appears to be a positive statement. However, this stereotype is false, and it is also negative. In much the same way as unintentional handicapism, posi-tive stereotypes may not be malicious in *intent* but their *results* are harmful to PWDs. All types of stereotyping (even those we think are positive) are detrimental for the following reasons: (1) stereotypes do not portray indi-viduals in the category as individuals, (2) stereotypes are polarizing because they make a clear demarcation between those in the category and those not in the category, and (3) stereotypes of any kind lead to behaviors and actions that limit and reduce the opportunities of people in that category. Using our example of a false stereotype of PWDs' being compassionate, we can see that many professions requiring assertive, competitive, win-at-all-costs behaviors (such as being a lawyer) would automatically be ruled out for a PWD because PWDs are thought to be too nice and compassionate. In Chapter 3 we learned that our culture, especially the media, reinforces and builds on our stereotypes. In short, stereotypes are socially supported.

Positive stereotypes are often difficult to recognize as false and limit-ing beliefs. Irving Zola in the National Public Radio Disability History Project (1998) remarked that the most troubling stereotypes about PWDs were positive ones. Zola spoke of two such positive stereotypes: (1) be-ing brave and courageous in the face of adversity and (2) being endowed with special gifts and qualities. Jenny Morris, the Englishwoman who is paraplegic, described her difficulty in recognizing positive statements as stereotypes:

> During the years following my accident, I have on countless occasions been told by both strangers and acquaintances how "wonderful" they think I am. It took a while to realize why this kind of remark provoked such anger in me. After all, those who say it seem to think that they are praising me for struggling against the difficulties which a physical disability brings. When I eventually unpeeled the layers of patronizing nonsense I realized that at the heart of such remarks lay the judgment that being disabled must be awful, indeed, intolerable. It is very undermining to recognize that people look at me and see an existence, an experience, which they would do everything to avoid for themselves. (Morris, 1991, p. 15)

Professionals also fall prey to stereotypes. In his autobiography, Henry Kisor, who became deaf at age 3, discussed standardized testing and diagnostic procedures and concluded that these professional tools are based on false stereotypes. For example, Kisor was offended by the mandatory psychological counseling that people who are deaf are required to undergo before they are allowed to receive speech therapy. Kisor submitted to the psychological counseling and therefore did receive speech training, but decades later, he found it insulting that "deaf experts" automatically assumed that he needed counseling. Kisor termed his practice of mandatory psychological counseling as "official stereotyping" (Kisor, 1990).

Stereotypes are not harmless because job, housing, educational, and social decisions are based on stereotypes (Allport, 1954, 1958). Also, legislation is based on deeply held assumptions that are often stereotypes. (Policymakers and legislators are exposed to the same media as everyone else.) Stereotypes circumscribe opportunities for individuals and handicap society as a whole. Stereotypes are resistant to the truth, probably as a result of these three factors: (1) constant reinforcement by the media, (2) the human need to simplify and organize people, and (3) the prejudice and discrimination that allow those in power to benefit and profit from the subordinate status of stereotyped groups.

More than 30 years ago, an article appeared in a scholarly rehabilitation journal that strongly argued that there is no one personality type associated with a certain disability (Shontz, 1977). For example, there is no "rheumatoid arthritis personality" or "paraplegia and quadriplegia personality." Well-written and comprehensive, much of the value of this article lies in its extensive listing of scholarly writings that have stereotyped individuals according to the type of disability they experience. As long ago as 1977, the listing of the stereotypes was amazingly long. For example, the list of personality attributes ascribed to patients with arthritis is lengthy. They have been said to have weak egos; to repress hostility; and to be compliant and subservient, potentially psychotic, depressed, dependent, conscientious, masochistic, emotionally labile, compulsive, introverted, conservative, perfectionistic, moody, nervous, worried, tense, overconcerned about personal appearance, and prone to express psychopathology in physical symptoms (Shontz, 1977, p. 339).

Shontz (1977) summarized much of the scholarly writing on various types of disabilities (in addition to rheumatoid arthritis) and concluded that "the recent literature provides no support for the hypothesis that particular disabilities are associated with particular personality characteristics or for the hypothesis that disability is a sufficient cause of maladjustment" (pp. 340–341). The Deaf have had many stereotypical psychological characteristics applied to them. Lane, Hoffmeister, and Bahan (1996) reviewed the scientific literature on the "psychology of the deaf" (there is no such thing as the "psychology of the deaf"), reading more than 350 journal articles and books. Lane et al. then developed a list of these characteristics and divided them into four columns: (1) social, (2) cognitive, (3) behavioral, and (4) emotional. There are 67 adjectives on the list. Lane and colleagues summarized:

> In general, people who are deaf are characterized as socially isolated, intellectually weak, behaviorally impulsive, and emotionally immature. The list of traits attributed to the Deaf is inconsistent: they are both *aggressive* and *submissive; naive, shrewd, detached, passionate, explosive, shy, stubborn and submissive, suspicious* and *trusting.* However, the list is consistently negative; nearly all of the traits ascribed, even many in pairs of opposites, are unfavorable. Clearly we must suspect that the "psychology of the deaf" consists of hearing people's stereotypes about others who are deaf. (p. 349)

Obviously, none of these stereotypes have been confirmed. Further, these examples demonstrate that stereotyping can occur in very sophisticated and scholarly settings. The perpetuation of these stereotypes was labeled "education," "science," "scholarship," and "research." In the not-too-distant past, university students memorized these disability stereotypes for exams. The better the students learned these stereotypes, the more successful they were in their "education." Physicians and psychologists, who are the products of their professional education, approach their patients with disabilities with these false stereotypes in mind. Furthermore, the continuing education and upgrading of skills required to maintain the licensure and certification of most clinicians is often accomplished through reading professional/scholarly journals. And, as we have seen, many of the professional journals have simply maintained and reinforced these false stereotypes of individuals with disabilities. The stereotypes held by physicians, psychologists, and other clinicians have negative consequences for their patients with disabilities. For example, individuals who are deaf experience longer lengths of stay in psychiatric hospitals than people who are not deaf; there is inappropriate placement of people who are deaf in institutions that care for individuals with mental retardation; and they face psychiatric misdiagnosis. Lane et al. (1996) attribute much of this to negative stereotypes of the Deaf. Stereotypes are not harmless.

Reread the description of the "arthritis personality" and ask yourself if you would like to go out on a date with this type of individual (not an individual with arthritis, but someone who has a weak ego; represses hostility; and is potentially psychotic, depressed, emotionally labile, moody, nervous, tense, and worried). Of course you would not—it would be the date from hell. People with arthritis are not like this, but if these stereotypes persist, it will be difficult for people with arthritis (or any other disability) to enjoy equal social status relationships.

For the individual who is the target of these stereotypes, it is often easier to accept the stereotypes than to fight them. We have learned that the "disability role" is a normative role, meaning that there are rules and expectations that describe how an individual should act. Obviously, the individual knows that these stereotypes are untrue and, indeed, much of the humor of the Disability Rights Movement makes fun of these stereotypes. Nonetheless, when the PWD acts according to these expectations and stereotypes, he or she is rewarded, and when the PWD violates the expectations of PWODs, often PWODs withhold the rewards and even punish the individual. Therefore, often it is simply easier for PWDs to accept the stereotype than to fight it. For those who have invisible disabilities and therefore have the option of disclosure, they may choose to keep the disability hidden. However, those with visible disabilities may react to stereotyping by attempting to downplay or minimize the disability or to conceal its effects. Many PWDs have consciously developed "presentation strategies" to comply with these stereotypes. Before the advent of disability rights groups, an individual with a disability understood that if he or she decided to fight the stereotypes, it would be a difficult (and probably losing) battle because these stereotypes have a history of centuries of development and have been subscribed to by millions of people. For a single individual contemplating these formidable odds, he or she may decide to focus his or her attention and energy elsewhere and simply comply with the stereotype. Also, it should be remembered that societal stereotypes were often held by family members of the PWD. Therefore, the PWD had few places of refuge where he or she could escape the stereotyping. Recall the letter to Ann Landers from "Angry in Montana" in Chapter 3. Angry in Montana, a woman in a wheelchair, did not want to answer a curious child's question about her disability. Ann Landers replies that "Angry in Montana" was unwilling to speak to the strange child because "Angry in Montana" has not accepted her disability. Ann Landers responded with punishment and blame. There are many PWDs who, unwillingly, answer strangers' questions simply because it is easier than fighting stereotypes.

Some PWDs internalize these stereotypes, and these false assumptions become a part of their self-concept. Simply because they have heard these stereotypes so often and from prestigious and authoritative sources, PWDs may accept them as truth. Before the Disability Rights Movement, when PWDs were often isolated, with little access to peers, role models, and leaders or authorities who had disabilities, PWDs had little basis on which to judge these false stereotypes. They simply accepted them as truth— truth about themselves. This situation was especially common for individuals with congenital disabilities or disabilities acquired early in life because young children unquestioningly accept the attitudes and viewpoints of the adults around them. PWDs who have experienced institutionalization are isolated from the broader culture and have no way to disprove these stereotypes; as a result, these PWDs internalize society's stereotypes. Society has effectively taught them to feel inferior.

Pity

In this section, look for—

- Pity can be fatal
- Pity comprises four (negative) components:
  1. A judgment of a PWD's life
  2. The idea that disability is a tragic catastrophe
  3. Pity is derived from a position of superiority
  4. Pity excludes respect for the individual
- Pity reinforces the power structure between PWODs and PWDs

The concept of pity was discussed in the section on charity and charity telethons in Chapter 4; nonetheless, pity merits attention here. Pity, like charity and paternalism, appears to be a positive and beneficent behavior; therefore the demeaning and exploitative results of pity are difficult for PWODs to understand. Those without disabilities, who rarely experience being pitied, struggle with the idea that pity has resulted in lack of opportunities for PWDs; social isolation and institutionalization of PWDs; reduced social and legislative change; and most important, the deaths of many PWDs. Remember, Jerry Lewis has stated that he would rather be dead than disabled (Barnartt, Shriner, & Scotch, 2001). Pity also makes it difficult for PWDs to achieve self-respect when pervasive, generalized pity communicates that they are only worthy of recognition for being (perceived as) inferior.

At its extreme, pity requires PWDs to defend and justify their lives. Further, pity forces PWDs to prove their quality of life. These are unnecessary burdens PWODs place on PWDs (and then expect PWDs to be grateful for the pity!). Dr. Peter Singer, a professor of philosophy at Princeton University, has written books and lectures on his ideas that some PWDs, especially those with severe and multiple disabilities, should be killed. An individual who debated Singer at Princeton summarized his views:

> In the lecture hall that afternoon, Singer lays it all out. The "illogic" of allowing abortion but not infanticide, of allowing withdrawal of life support but not active killing. Applying the basic assumptions of preference utilitarianism, he spins out his bone-chilling argument for letting parents kill disabled [sic] babies and replace them with nondisabled babies who have a greater chance of happiness. (Johnson, 2003, p. 53)

Mark O'Brien is in an iron lung, is a journalist, is a member of a group called Not Dead Yet, and was the subject of the 1997 Academy Award-winning documentary "Breathing Lessons." Fleischer and Zames (2001) wrote:

> It is tempting to pity a man in an iron lung. But pity has become a lethal weapon. On January 8, [1997], the Supreme Court heard arguments in favor of killing people like me—out of pity—to end our suffering. An iron lung has been my second skin since the 1955 polio epidemic. For forty years, people have said, "That poor thing—how he must suffer. He's terminally ill, you know." I'm not "suffering," "terminal," or even "ill." Don't waste your pity on me. I want to live. Every year, practitioners of mercy death kill thousands of people against our will—out of pity. If the Supreme Court declares mercy death legal, that's like declaring open season on people with disabilities. We're not contagious or dangerous. And we aren't affiliated with any political party. We are people who hear the death train. We will not board that train willingly.

Pity makes it possible to morally exclude PWDs without feeling guilty. PWODs often feel that their pity constitutes an interest in the lives of PWDs when, in fact, pity categorizes, distances, and polarizes PWDs. Further, pity makes it clear that PWODs are superior and PWDs are inferior. Pity makes it possible for society to refuse a fair share of the nation's resources for PWDs because, after all, society gives generously to charities. It is a small step from pity to exclusion, discrediting, and segregation. Pity is often invisible and indirect and most often is considered to be a positive, beneficent attitude, yet pity erects many barriers for PWDs.

Role Entrapment

Role entrapment occurs when the group in power, in this case PWODs, defines those roles minority individuals can and cannot assume. Role entrapment can be social or occupational and usually includes only inferior and undesirable roles. Often occupational role entrapment has been termed "occupational stereotyping." Individuals who are ethnic and racial minorities have long been aware of role entrapment; for example, years ago black men were expected to do certain jobs. Obviously, role entrapment is not self-imposed unless the minority individual comes to internalize the majority's view of himself or herself. Once again, as in categorization and stereotyping, the person is not viewed as an individual, and his or her strengths and abilities are never considered. It is a matter of "Your kind of people do [or do not] do these type of things." Here is an often-told riddle that relies on occupational role entrapment to confuse people: A young boy is injured in an automobile accident. The boy's father dies in the accident. He is taken to the hospital. The boy needs emergency surgery. The surgeon says, "I cannot operate on this boy. He is my son." The surgeon was not the boy's father (the father is dead). What relation was the surgeon to the injured boy?" Answers often include stepfather, adopted father, or grandfather. Very few people respond that the surgeon is the boy's mother. This is an example of gender occupational role entrapment, and as more and more women become physicians and surgeons, this riddle will probably no longer be told because without gender stereotyping, the answer is obvious.

As with stereotyping, often the PWD simply accepts the role entrapment rather than fight it. Since it is the group in power that makes the rules, they "reward" those minority people who "know their place," keep their aspirations and achievements at a modest level, and refrain from testing the limits of acceptance (Yuker, 1988). Individuals who attempt to assume roles that are not endorsed by the majority are called "uppity" and told that "they don't know their place." The entrapment may be more powerful for PWDs than for racial and ethnic groups because "society" often feels that they have provided many benefits to PWDs (charity, special services, etc.) and consider these attempts to escape role entrapment to be lack of gratitude. According to this viewpoint, PWDs should accept their inferior quality of life with gratitude and equanimity. Davis (1997) summed up this view: "[You PWDs should] accept our [PWODs'] construction of your life or give up your access to equal citizenship" (p. 167).

Social role entrapment occurs when PWDs are told that they should associate with their own kind. In the video "My Body Is Not Who I Am," the young man in the wheelchair tells of being asked if he has a girlfriend. When he replies "yes," the next question is, "Does she have a disability?" This is an example of social role entrapment. It is automatically assumed that PWDs have romantic/sexual relationships only with other PWDs. Social relationships in which one individual has a disability and the other does not have a disability are often automatically assumed to be asymmetrical. The most extreme example of social role entrapment is segregation and institutionalization.

Occupational role entrapment for PWDs has been so widespread as to gain derisive nicknames. The "Bulova Syndrome" refers to the tendency to place men in wheelchairs in watch repair. While the Bulova Watch Company should not be faulted because they were hiring PWDs when very few companies were, the Bulova Syndrome refers to a time when people with a certain disability (usually paraplegia) were often automatically "assigned" a life's occupation. Today, the nickname for role entrapment for PWDs, especially those with mental retardation, is "the five Fs." The "five Fs" are food, filth, flowers, filing, and folding. *Food* is work in fast-food restaurants; *filth* is janitorial and housekeeping work; *flowers* refers to work in yard maintenance and landscaping; *filing* is simple office work, and *folding* refers to work in laundry facilities. Men who were deaf were often placed in printing jobs because their disability was viewed as an asset because they could not hear the loud machinery. Women who were deaf and not homemakers were often placed in textile mills, and in the late 1960s, girls in residential schools who were deaf were trained for keypunch work or to be seamstresses; men who were blind often trained for photographic darkroom work (Sinick, 1969). At the Perkins School for the Blind, girls were trained to be typists or dictaphone users and boys were trained to be piano tuners (Holcomb, 1990). It is not an exaggeration to state that, first, most individuals with physical disabilities were placed in lower-level jobs requiring manual skills and, second, much of this role entrapment was a result of the false stereotypes that held that individuals with physical disabilities were intellectually incapable of managerial or professional-level jobs. (This is another example of spread.) Further, most of these jobs were low paying. For example, men who were deaf were rarely the managers of printing companies; they were allowed only to run the machinery and produce the printing products.

In the past, occupational role entrapment was often termed *occupational stereotyping*, and there is some indication that the tendency of professionals to relegate an individual to a job on the sole basis of his or her disability is decreasing. It should be noted that Hahn (1997) strongly asserted that relegating PWDs to lower-paid jobs has little to do with the disability itself; rather, it is the result of a capitalist system that needs workers willing to work for low wages for employers to maintain high profits. Simply stated, according to Hahn, keeping PWDs in low-level jobs maintains the social order. Occupational role entrapment began early in life for PWDs. The little education that children with disabilities received emphasized manual skills and vocational training. There were no "career days" at schools for children with disabilities, nor were there individual career/college planning sessions with the school counselor for these children. The type of disability determined the child's career. Sharon L., the medical social worker we met in Chapter 2, tells that she clearly remembers the day that the school counselor told her that she should become a professional artist. The counselor told Sharon that (1) she was good at art, (2) she would not have to be around people, and (3) no one would recognize her art as "disabled art." Probably the reason why this one day in Sharon's high school career is so indelibly etched in her memory is that she was surprised by the role entrapment that the counselor was attempting to enforce. Also, as we will see in the chapter on the individual's adjustment to disability (Chapter 9), "stigma recognition" is often shocking to the PWD. In many situations, PWDs are not aware of the stigma that others hold toward their disability. For example, what did the counselor mean by "disabled art," other than to imply that such art would be inferior to "nondisabled art"? Even individuals like Sharon, who have had their disabilities for many years, are unpleasantly surprised when confronted with prejudice, discrimination, and stigma. Disability scholars have labeled this experience "stigma recognition." As a teenager, Sharon was unaware that some school officials thought she would be forced to choose a profession that would not require interaction with people; after all, she had been attending high school, church, and community activities all her life. The high school counselor, probably out of good intentions, tried to guide Sharon to art. (This is an example of the handicapism of well-intentioned people.) There is nothing wrong with being an artist. The error lies in (1) someone else choosing Sharon's life work, and (2) choosing a profession based on how others *might* react to the disability.

When considering the situation of PWDs, we can indulge in the circular argument: Did the inferior education of children with disabilities lead to occupational role entrapment? Or, did the occupational role entrapment lead to inferior education for children with disabilities? The answer to each question is "yes." An extreme example of the practice of preparing children with disabilities for a life of occupational entrapment is presented in Margret A. Winzer's (1993) work *Education, Urbanization, and the Deaf Community: A Case Study of Toronto, 1870–1900*. Winzer makes two points: (1) "The Ontario institution tried to reproduce the factory conditions as a means of socializing its students and disciplining them to the rigidity and monotony of modern industrial labor" (p. 127), and (2) "these efforts were a mistake . . . . [T]hey limited the opportunities for deaf workers and made them easily expendable as technology changed" (p. 127). It does not sound like school was much fun for these children.

David Wright, a South African who is deaf and who now works as a university professor of literature in England, wrote an autobiography. He related his lifelong response to the role entrapment perpetuated in schools for children who are deaf:

> Since then, I have had an aversion to doing anything with my hands. To this day, I cannot draw, or tie up a parcel properly, if it comes to that . . . . But, for a long time, dating from my attendance at this school, if it was a school, I refused on principle to learn, or was deliberately bad at manipulatory skills like carpentry, painting, and so on. Schools of this type, where the teacher was usually untrained—they probably do not exist nowadays—took the line of least resistance and while teaching their deaf pupils a little speech and lip-reading, concentrated on instruction in handicrafts. This seemed to me, even then, to be equating deafness with stupidity; and I resented it. So much so that I took cleverness with the hands to be a badge of deafness, and I would not wear that badge. Instead of being taught to use my head, because I was deaf, I was being fobbed off with handicrafts. (Wright, 1994, p. 40)

Another way in which career options may be limited for PWDs is the idea that PWDs should "help their own kind." In the video "Irving King Jordan," the President of Gallaudet University, Dr. Jordan, reports that 20 years ago, entering students who were deaf usually had a career goal of teaching the deaf. Now, Jordan notes that students at Gallaudet prepare for all types of careers and professions.

The concept of "helping your own kind" probably arose from the assumption that PWDs could best understand other PWDs (Strohmer, Leierer, Cochran, & Arokiasamy, 1996). Also, the need to counter the paternalism of PWODs who worked with PWDs probably activated the desire for PWDs to be taught by other PWDs. However, we have learned that PWDs can, and do, hold false prejudicial views about individuals with other types of disabilities. Further, it would be impossible to match each individual with a counselor or teacher who has the same type of disability. This is to say nothing about limiting the career opportunities for PWDs. In addition, the "help your own kind" philosophy is blatantly holding disability to be the most salient characteristic of the individual.

Lowered Expectations, or "Let's Give Those Poor Disabled People a Break"

In this section, look for—

- How lowered expectations can result in fewer opportunities for PWDs
- Overprotection and sheltering and their results
- The difference between providing accommodations and lowering standards
- Misguided acts of perceived kindness

Related to both stereotyping and role entrapment of PWDs are inappropriate pessimism and the practice of automatically lowering expectations. Such a relaxing of standards communicates that PWDs should be excused or indulged and, furthermore, that PWDs are not considered capable of being judged against high standards. In the video "Tell Them I'm a Mermaid," one of the women, who is in a wheelchair, states, "All that lack of belief does something to you." Another PWD stated, "When people stop having expectations of you, you know they have given up on you." PWDs often report that they have been told, "You did pretty well for a (deaf person, a blind person, a PWD)," and subsequently they felt insulted and demeaned.

When widely held standards and expectations are lowered for PWDs, their credibility and competence is questioned. However, when PWDs do succeed, many PWODs are genuinely surprised, which is also insulting and demeaning. Praising a PWD for minor accomplishments is another way in which lowered expectations are expressed.

The provision of accommodations for the disability is often confused with lowering standards. Brenda Premo, the director of the California Department of Rehabilitation, who is legally blind, described this difference when she stated:

> I really appreciated the teachers in high school who would accommodate me but who had high expectations. They would ask me, "What can I do that would make this better for you?" but they wouldn't let me slide at all academically. There was a math teacher, an old gruff guy. He would accommodate me, but I had to achieve and I had to earn my grade. I always got B's from him but I respected him so much more than some other teachers who always gave me easy A's. The same thing happened in college. I always appreciated the teachers who expected the most out of me and I worked my hardest in their classes. I got the most out of them. (Mackelprang & Salsgiver, 1999, p. 142)

Behaviors and attitudes that (1) do not allow the PWD to be an equal partner, (2) communicate the message that he or she is not capable, and (3) reduce the range of opportunities open to the individual are harmful. Lowered expectations, which at first glance may appear to be kindness and generosity, harm the individual because he or she does not receive helpful and honest feedback. And, without honest feedback, an individual is kept in an inferior and dependent position. Praising the individual for small achievements (when the individual is capable of much more) is insulting and demeaning for the individual. Robert Scott (1969), in his book *The Making of Blind Men: A Study of Adult Socialization*, observed one additional result from lowered expectations: The individual begins to believe that the disability (in this case, blindness) is the cause of his or her incompetence. "Clients are rewarded by trivial things and praised for performing tasks in a mediocre fashion. This superficial and overgenerous reward system makes it impossible for most clients to assess their accomplishments accurately. Eventually, since anything they do is praised as outstanding, many of them come to believe that the underlying assumption must be that the blindness makes them incompetent" (p. 85).

PWDs are aware when standards are relaxed for them, which implicitly states, "You're never expected to be any good." Those who have lowered expectations of PWDs often do not allow PWDs opportunities for achievement. One woman with a disability experienced this when she said, "Even if you can, no one will let you." Often, overprotection and "sheltering" of the PWD are other forms of lowered expectations. Thus, the PWD falsely assumes that he or she is not reducing the PWD's independence and achievement; the PWOD thinks he or she is protecting the PWD. Lowered expectations of PWODs often result in failure to inform PWDs of available opportunities and the standards and requirements for gaining these opportunities. Frequently, educational opportunities, job openings, and social occasions are not considered relevant because PWODs are quick to judge such opportunities to be unobtainable and unrealistic for the individual with a disability. Lowered expectations often lead to lack of challenge and achievement for PWDs.

The following are examples of PWDs refusing the lowered expectations that are often thrust on them:

Erik Weihenmayer (2001), the blind man who climbed Mt. Everest, appeared on a popular daytime talk show. Weihenmayer wrote about his appearance:

> Throughout the rest of the segment, I squirmed in my seat. I should have been proud to be picked out as being "amazing and inspirational," but strangely, I felt more embarrassed and even a little sick. I was no more accomplished (than the other blind guests). I was simply a blind person who planned to climb a mountain and nothing more. But people sensationalize the lives of blind people when, often, all they did was exhibit a semblance of normalcy. I have been receiving these accolades my

whole life: give someone directions to my house—incredible. Make eye contact in a conversation—amazing. Each of us on the panel was being honored for our heroic tables, but the recognition spoke more loudly of low expectations than of accomplishment. (p. 167)

Chuck Close (1993), an artist who became paralyzed, wrote of the importance of selling one of his paintings to the Museum of Modern Art, which he considered to be the "Good Housekeeping seal of approval" in the art world.

After I got back to work, I didn't want all of a sudden to become known as the "handicapped artist." People around me were very reluctant at first to let me do interviews; they were very protective of me. I'd had a successful fifteen, twenty year-long career as an artist. Now all of a sudden not to be seen as an artist anymore, but as a "handicapped" artist was a risk. Would people think differently about what I had made? So that was the real fear. It was very important that the very first large painting I made when I got out of the hospital was bought by the Museum of Modern Art . . . not only important to me, but important to the art world, because it was sort of a Good Housekeeping seal of approval. The Museum of Modern Art is not in the business of buying handicapped art, you know, just to make someone feel better. (p. 24)

Harris (1992), a coordinator of a university program designed to provide services for students with disabilities, summarized the effects of lowered expectations: "Misguided acts of perceived kindness are a much harder construct to deal with than even overt negative discrimination. One of the reasons for this is generally neither party understands the pernicious effects of this behavior. It may be years before the person with the disability realizes that he/she has been victimized by inadequate preparation and a lack of necessary independence" (p. 208).

Failing to discipline children with disabilities and "mercy graduations" for schoolchildren with disabilities are examples of the lowered expectations of PWODs. Lowering expectations, excusing, indulging, and tolerating poor performance from PWDs are all forms of discrimination.

Lack of Privacy

> ### In this section, look for—
>
> - Reasons why PWDs experience less privacy than others
> - Explanations of why the "dehumanization" of assistive technology is appealing to many PWDs

WDs experience less privacy and anonymity than do PWODs. Goff-
963), speaking of a stigmatized person, described this lack of privacy:
present among normals nakedly exposes him [sic] to invasions of
" (p. 212). Some of this lack of privacy may result from the disability
itself. Individuals who are deaf and use sign language interpreters and individuals with visual impairments who often require readers or scribes are
examples of loss of privacy that are a result of the disability itself. Personal
care attendants dress PWDs, assist them in using the bathroom and using
suppositories and catheters, and assist with menstrual needs. Furthermore,
these types of losses in privacy are unavoidable. Such a continuous, daily
loss of privacy, in areas of life that are considered to be the most personal, is
difficult for most PWODs to understand. Sue Suter, former U.S. Commissioner of Rehabilitation and President of the World Institute on Disability
Services (1993), described the loss of privacy that many PWDs experience
when the services of a paid personal care attendant are necessary. Suter related the following anecdote of a PWD advocating before a state legislature:
". . . [O]ne consumer, named Terry Gutterman, made the issue understandable to legislators by simply asking them to 'Imagine giving the keys to your
house to 14 different people in a single year.'" Higgins (1980), in his book
Outsiders in a Hearing World, interviewed a married couple who uses sign
language. He explained: "When one deaf couple dines in a restaurant, they
imagine that they have drawn a curtain between themselves and the hearing people who stare at them" (and mimic their signing) (p. 128). PWDs
who must sustain this loss of privacy often regard privacy and anonymity as
precious resources to be carefully defended. Individuals who use sign language must occasionally guard against others "overseeing" (not overhear-
ing) them. For example, Groce (1985) related a story in her book *Everybody
Here Spoke Sign Language*. On the island of Martha's Vineyard, because a
large number of people were deaf, everybody knew and used sign language.
Groce interviewed a woman who remembered young teenage boys (hearing
and deaf) gathering at the general store to socialize and tell stories. Many
of these stories were sexually oriented; therefore, whenever anyone (hearing
or deaf) entered the store, the boys would have to turn around to hide their
signing. They did not want adults to oversee the jokes and stories. (The
fact that the woman was aware of the boys' attempts to hide their signing
indicates that the adults knew exactly what type of stories and jokes were
being told.)

Miller and Morgan (1980) spoke about the need for emotional privacy
in the context of marriage. Citing the change in attitudes of caregivers toward PWDs marrying, Miller and Morgan concluded that married PWDs
now have to deal with "overenthusiasm" for their marriage. While undeniably the result of good intentions, the intrusion of PWODs into the private,
personal spheres of an individual's life is another form of denying PWDs
privacy. "Emotional privacy is as important as physical privacy for a couple
who are severely disabled [sic] and physically dependent, and probably more
difficult to ensure" (p. 353).

Hospitalization, institutionalization, and resident schooling of PWDs all greatly decrease the PWD's opportunity for privacy. Living with large groups of people the individual has not chosen to live with, day after day, allows little chance for either private time or private space. Chubon and Moore (1982) studied individuals in a large rehabilitation center for spinal cord injuries. They observed that many people spent large amounts of time in bed with the blankets pulled over their heads. When they interviewed these individuals, they learned these patients were attempting to gain some seclusion and privacy. Chubon and Moore termed this behavior "cocooning."

Often, PWDs interpret and define privacy differently than PWODs (Lane, Hoffmeister, & Bahan, 1996). Beisser (1989), who contracted polio after graduating from medical school, was paralyzed from the neck down and placed in an iron lung. Dr. Beisser related that hospital caregivers asked permission before they touched his head. In contrast, caregivers poked, prodded, handled, and displayed the rest of his body without asking permission or giving prior warning. Beisser realized that everyone was very respectful of his head! Assistive technology, such as voice-activated computers and TDD (telecommunications device for the deaf) telephones, offers a measure of privacy to PWDs and thus eliminates the need for a family member or a personal care attendant to perform certain types of functions. Ironically, the very "dehumanization" of technology is appealing to PWDs. Technology, in contrast to people, always maintains confidentiality, does not get sick, and does not refuse to assist when irritated or in a bad mood, thus allowing the user more independence. Technology can, and does, break down and "crash," but technology is far more reliable than most people. Technology provides both independence and privacy to PWDs.

Hypervisibility and Overobservation

In this section, look for—

- The definitions of hypervisibility and overobservation
- The power relationship between the individual who is staring and the individual who is being stared at
- The effects of hypervisibility
- Having unintended meanings attributed to PWDs' actions

Individuals with visible disabilities also enjoy less privacy and anonymity and experience more hypervisibility and overobservation. The letters to Ann Landers from individuals in wheelchairs who are the target of curious children are examples of this reduced privacy. Kenneth Fries (1997) compiled a book of essays, poetry, and fiction written by PWDs, entitling the book *Staring Back*. There is a clear message in the fact that all the writers and artists, with their differing life histories and various types of disabilities, shared one experience in common: being stared at. Such hypervisibility is exhausting—emotionally, mentally, and physically. A woman who acquired a spinal cord injury at age 36 stated, "When I was first in a wheelchair, I was terrified that people were going to stare at me" (Mackelprang & Salsgiver,1999, p. 100). In American Sign Language, the sign for the word "stare" communicates both the intrusiveness and hostility felt by the Deaf. The sign is "the fingertips of both hands almost poking into one's own face" (Walker, 1986, p. 100). A student of mine, a middle-aged, former professor who is blind, was stopped by a young student at the doorway of my classroom. The student said, "I've been watching you walk down the street and seeing how many times you mess up." From a distance, my student's white cane made him hypervisible. Obviously, most people who do not have visible disabilities are not stopped by strangers and asked questions or told they had "messed up." Thomson (1997) perceptively noted the power differential between the person who is staring ("the spectator") and the person who is being stared at ("the spectacle"), stating, "One role is to look, judge, and act while the other role is to be gazed upon, measured, and passive" (p. 300). Read the letter from the mother of an infant with a disability (Exhibit 6–1).

For everyone, there are times when we wish to remain in the background or totally anonymous. For someone with a visible disability or someone who uses some sort of assistive technology (such as a hearing aid or wheelchair), remaining in the background is not possible. A woman with a disability explained: "Having a visible disability means always being noticed, standing out, being different *everywhere you go*." Indeed, she terms her disability "a blinking neon sign" (Olkin, 1999, pp. 80–81). Following is an example when anonymity would be desirable. A professor in a large class of 300 students states that attendance will not be taken and therefore will not affect students' grades. Almost every student can skip class, realizing that the professor has no way of knowing who is attending and who is not. Anonymity is not possible for the one student enrolled in the class who uses a wheelchair, or the one student who uses a sign language interpreter, or the one African American student.

For someone who is subjected to hypervisibility, life can become an unending public performance in which he or she is expected to exhibit positive behaviors and attitudes. In Chapter 4, we discussed that disability is a "normative" experience, meaning that there are rules, usually unwritten but strongly held, about how PWDs should behave. Coupled with these "rules of disability" is the general lack of knowledge about disabilities. Nonetheless, PWDs are aware that they are being scrutinized and often judged. The individual in the wheelchair who falls asleep during an important meeting is thought to be rude simply because it never enters the minds of others that

Exhibit 6-1

> **Dear Ann Landers:** I gave birth to my first child last April. "Crystal" was 12 weeks pre-mature and weighed less than 2 pounds. We were afraid that she would die or have se-vere handicaps, but we were blessed with good fortune as her only remaining require-ment is the extra oxygen she receives through a nasal tube worn 24 hours a day.
>
> Her doctors told us, "Don't let her alter your lifestyle." We took their advice and take Crystal everywhere. She's been to the mall, five restaurants, a small boat harbor, and the county fair.
>
> Because the nasal tube makes her look different, I have received a lot of unsolicited and rude comments. People ask, "What's wrong with her? Was she born that way? What's her problem?" I do not wish to discuss my daughter's medical condition with strangers, and considering the handicaps she might have had, my husband and I feel there's nothing wrong with Crystal at all.
>
> Ann, please alert the boneheads out there that if they see a child who is "different," to coo over the baby the way they would a "normal" child. The parents already know their child looks different, and they love the child anyway. The anguish they have al-ready gone through doesn't need to be rehashed to satisfy a stranger's curiosity. A kind word would make a world of difference.
> —Grateful Mom in Buffalo, NY
>
> **Dear Buffalo Mom:** Thank you for speaking up about an intensely personal matter. You have performed a valuable service by sharing your problem with millions of readers today. Many of them will see themselves and be reminded of your letter when they see a child who is "different."

this PWD must take large doses of medication to control muscle spasms, which make him or her sleepy. With hypervisibility, everything the PWD does takes on added meaning, and this added meaning is often the result of negative inferences. Public performance, with the subsequent judgment of others, is stressful and anxiety-provoking. The individual is not allowed to relax and "just hang out." Some individuals can escape hypervisibility by returning "home" or someplace where there are a lot of other people who look like themselves. These people have a place where they can "blend in." Often, PWDs do not have this haven or sanctuary. Frequently, the PWD feels alienated and different from even his or her own family. Many PWDs cannot shed their hypervisibility and simply be a person, not for an evening, not for a weekend, not for the Christmas holidays.

Much of the attention directed toward PWDs is well-intentioned and not planned to annoy or inconvenience anyone. Unintended or not, atten-tion that is not wanted or attention that is directed solely toward the disabil-ity, rather than the person, is both irritating and inconvenient. Intrusive and insulting questions that would never be asked of PWODs are often asked of

PWDs. In the video "My Body Is Not Who I Am," an adult woman with a disability remarks, "It's like I am a child. People can ask me anything they want. I have no boundaries." In that same video, a single young man (in a wheelchair) tells that he is often asked by strangers if he has a girlfriend. He always replies, "Of course I do. Why do you ask?" This question is insulting and intrusive on at least two counts: (1) It is a question that would not be asked of an adult man without a disability because romantic relationships are considered to be private, and (2) it conveys the questioner's stereotypical, prejudicial view of PWDs as sexually neutered (not desiring or capable of intimate relationships) and unattractive to the opposite sex. His response of "why do you ask?" shows some irritation at being asked such a demeaning question. The young man goes on to say that after he answers "yes," some questioners continue to ask, "Does your girlfriend have a disability?" Murphy and colleagues (1988) described hypervisibility in this way: "noticed by everyone and acknowledged by nobody" (p. 239). Stated differently, PWDs are subjected to staring and intrusive questions; but at the same time, PWDs are not considered to be individuals with identities other than the disability. Therefore, PWDs are "acknowledged by nobody" because they are often not involved in ordinary social situations.

Read the letter to Ann Landers in Exhibit 6–2.

Two circumstances may account for the different responses of Grateful Mom in Buffalo, New York, and S. R. in Meraux, Louisiana. Grateful Mom was dealing with adults who were strangers, while S. R. was responding to children who may have been friends of her own children, people with whom she had a relationship. It is probably safe to say that the curiosity and fascination of complete strangers has more potential to insult and irritate PWDs than the interest of people with whom they are acquainted. Second, PWDs often report that children are more honest and forthright in their interest than are adults, who often display subtle (and sometimes not so subtle) hypocrisy about the disability. Further, children have not yet acquired the stereotypes and myths about disabilities; therefore, their questions are free of demeaning, preconceived ideas. Susan Wendell (1997) summarized the experience of being an object of curiosity: "Visibly disabled [sic] women report that curiosity about medical diagnoses, physical appearance and the sexual and other intimate aspects of disability is more common than willingness to listen and to understand the experience of disability" (p. 267).

Such intrusions of privacy also affect the partners and family members of PWDs. Most people on family outings do not enjoy being approached by strangers and being forced to deal with others' misinformed and negative attitudes toward disability. Lefley (1991) summarized: "Generalization of stigma to families is an additional source of psychological risk" (p. 127). In an empirical research study that focused on the brothers and sisters of a child with a disability entitled, "Experiences of Siblings of Children with Physical Disabilities," the authors summarized one of the findings: "The

Exhibit 6-2

Dear Ann Landers: I was interested in the letter from "Upfront in Vermont," who taught children to ask questions rather than just state people are different. As a person who has had a disability since birth, I was especially pleased that you printed it. Growing up, I was hurt far more by people who gawked and made comments among themselves than by those who asked me questions.

My right arm ends just below the elbow, and when I see children looking at it curiously, or if they ask what happened, I explain that God makes each of us different. Some people have brown hair, some blond; some people are tall, some are short; some people have two hands, some may have only one. But each of us is special in our way. Sometimes, the children touch my arm or want to know how I can drive with one hand. I never take offense to their questions. I simply hope they learn that we can all be and do whatever we want. It's about ability, not disability.

Some parents are embarrassed when their child asks a question, but I believe children should feel free to ask questions so long as they do so politely. How else are they to learn? I was worried that my daughter would be upset by other children's reactions to my arm. Now, at age 6, she answers questions, saying, "That is how God made her and my mom can do anything."
—S. R., Meraux, LA

Dear S.R.: What a wonderfully positive attitude! Some people would see the cup as half empty, but in your case, it is overflowing. Thanks for writing.

---

siblings [of a child with a disability] took the view that the behaviour of strangers was certainly open to improvement. They thought that people should be better informed, should behave more 'naturally,' show more respect, and certainly refrain from staring" (Cate & Loots, 2000, p. 403). Lee Martin (2000) wrote about his childhood with his father, who had lost both hands in a farm machine accident and wore hooks: "I had never gotten used to the attention those hooks drew, the furtive glances from people trying not to be rude, the out-and-out stares from others who were so surprised to see the prostheses they couldn't begin to mask their curiosity" (p. 114). It is interesting that, throughout the years, Martin never became accustomed to the stares directed at his father.

Wilson (1990) read many first-person accounts of individuals who had survived polio and noted the difficulty that polio survivors experienced because of hypervisibility and staring. Wilson focused on the emotional reactions of the polio survivor.

Going out in public for the first time was a big step psychologically and emotionally and one every polio survivor needed to talk about if he or she was to have a social life, or go to school or work. For example, Jan Little remembers that in her community, "being in a wheelchair carried a fair amount of shame." After her parents took her to a local concert, one of their neighbors chastised them for "taking a child like that out in public." Arnold Beisser remembers that it was a "major step" to go out in public after having been isolated for years in a hospital. On one of Hugh Gallagher's initial forays into the outside world a young girl "crossed herself as we passed." Gallagher was shocked, especially when "she said a prayer that she wouldn't be like me." (p. 179)

In another book about individuals with polio, a man, Leroy, enjoyed photography as a hobby and continued with his hobby while at Warm Springs Rehabilitation Hospital in Georgia:

There was Leroy who must spend the rest of his life flat on his back. Sometimes the curious ones would make so bold as to stand directly above him. Without a word, they would stand and stare.

Photography has long been Leroy's hobby and he decided that a splendid opportunity has come to get unusual shots. Slightly concealed in his clothing so that no one would suspect, he planted his candid camera. Now let the curious ones come!

Slowly as before, they approached his cot. Now they stood beside him. Now they were bending over to *really* get a look. Eyes were opened wide. The jaw had dropped a bit. Then *click* went the camera. And bewildered, nonplussed onlookers fled speedily away.

What a collection Leroy must have now. (Lee, 1948)

An African American male with a disability commented on the additive effects of his gender, his race, and his disability:

I've gotten used to the stares . . . . it's like—and especially if it's a young African American male in a wheelchair. I can almost read their minds. Gang member. Drug dealer. It's all negative. It's always negative. (Putnam et al., 2003, p. 43)

Often, PWDs do not want to be ignored; however, instead of asking intrusive, personal questions, it is more appropriate to engage in simple "small talk." Sports, weather, current events, and other innocuous subjects are good starting places for developing a relationship or chatting with any individual we do not know. As one PWD summarized, "At least PWDs in circuses and freak shows got paid."

Solo Status

> **In this section, look for—**
> - The definition of solo status
> - What it means to:
>   1. Be a forced representative
>   2. Be in an unending public performance
>   3. Have no role models

Related to lack of privacy and hypervisibility is solo status. Solo status is when an individual is the only person with a particular visible characteristic; in many settings, there may be only one PWD. Solo status often constrains PWDs to become "forced representatives." Regardless of whether an individual has the desire or inclination, he or she now becomes the spokesperson for the disability group. At any time or place, the individual is expected to speak for individuals who have the same disability or to present extemporaneous educational and entertaining lectures. Being a solo, for whatever reason—gender (the only woman), race (the only African American), nationality (the only American), profession (the only professor)—adds another duty to the individual's list of jobs. Whenever a committee needs (1) a woman, (2) an African American, (3) an American, or (4) a PWD, there will be no question who will be asked! Goffman (1963) explained: "A new career is likely to be thrust upon him, that of representing his category" (p. 26). At the committee meeting, the members will turn to the solo and ask, "How do women (African Americans, Americans, professors, or PWDs) feel about this issue?" It is automatically assumed that the forced representative will know. If this occurs frequently, it can be burdensome for the PWD (Olkin, 1999). When an individual states, "I am not the poster boy (or girl)" for whatever disability the individual has, he or she is refusing the forced representative role.

In addition to being a forced representative and feeling isolated, the solo may be viewed as his or her category rather than as an individual. The solo is often viewed as "the disabled," "the deaf," and so on. Everything the solo does and says takes on unintended meaning simply because the solo has, in the eyes of others, become the group he or she is thought to represent. Olkin (1999) explained: "One's failings or mistakes also can be misinterpreted as representative of the group. Thus, the person with a visible disability is always an ambassador from the disability community on assignment to the able-bodied (AB) world" (p. 82). Ironically, occasionally solos do not subscribe to the identity that the larger group has given them. Once again, it is not the *actual* identity or characteristics of the individual that determines his or her treatment, but the *perceived* identity.

Often solos do not have access to informal communication networks, such as office gossip; they have no role models or mentors. Informal communication, role models, and colleagues are all sources of professional development and emotional support. Much of the helpful (and interesting) information at school and work is derived from informal sources. In addition, professional development can be facilitated by coworkers and mentors who can "clue the new person in." However, the one individual who is perceived as different, the solo, the PWD, will be accorded all his or her rights under the ADA but often will not be viewed as a peer by coworkers. The solo may sit alone at lunches and on coffee breaks and will not be "in" on the office gossip. The importance of role models for PWDs can be seen in the experience of Dr. Schroeder, whom we met in Chapter 4. Although he had received orientation and mobility (O & M) training, Schroeder wrongly assumed that people who were blind went to only those places in the community that were necessary, such as work or school. As you remember, his rehabilitation counselor, who was also blind, asked Schroeder if he would like to go out for a cup of coffee. The two of them then went to a coffee shop, crossing busy streets in downtown San Francisco. This short outing for a cup of coffee was a life-changing experience for Schroeder. His rehabilitation counselor was a role model who helped Schroeder to understand (1) how to make better use of his O & M training, and (2) that his life as a person who is blind did not have to be isolated and lacking in social contact. As a young man who had experienced the onset of blindness, Schroeder was given high-quality professional services to assist him in dealing with the disability, but he also needed a role model, an individual who was blind who could *show* (not *tell*) Schroeder ways in which to expand his world. When an individual is a solo, he or she has no access to role models. The fact that Schroeder remembers this single cup of coffee years later attests to the importance of role models.

Harilyn Rousso, a woman with cerebral palsy, tells of the importance of role models in her book *Disabled, Female, and Proud!* (1993):

> When I was about twenty-two, I had an unexpected, important experience. I worked one summer for a prominent woman economist who happened to have cerebral palsy. I can't tell you my surprise when I met her at the job interview. It was a bit like looking at myself in the mirror. Betty had a powerful effect on me. I was impressed that a woman with cerebral palsy, not a very socially acceptable disability in our culture, could become so successful in her career, particularly in a "man's field," anti-trust economics. I was even more impressed that she was married . . . . It never occurred to me that I had any alternative, that I could have *both* a career and a romantic life. Betty's lifestyle, her successful marriage to an interesting, dynamic man made me question for the first time the negative assumptions that I had made about my social potential. (p. 2)

As can be seen, meeting and working with this economist occurred at an age, 22 years old, when Ms. Rousso could take advantage of an expanded view of both work and romantic options available to her. We can also see that Ms. Rousso identified with her employer because she states, "It was a bit like looking at myself in a mirror."

Poster Children

The invention of poster children (or poster boys and girls) began with polio. As you recall, polio was first called "infantile paralysis" because most of those who contracted the disease (until the epidemics of the 20th century) were children or infants (Gallagher, 1985; Shell, 2005; Wilson, 1990). Polio was also the beginning of a new type of charity—"handicapitalism," the antecedents of the modern telethons. Handicapitalism is the large-scale solicitation of funds for both the treatment and the eradication of a certain disability or disease, using celebrities and the modern media. President Franklin Roosevelt was the celebrity for polio, while today there are many celebrities who choose to solicit charity for different types of disabilities. Poster children and polio seemed to be a natural combination: Here was a disability that struck randomly and predominantly affected innocent children who in no way could be considered at fault for their disability. Poster children and handicapitalism also seemed a natural combination. Innocent children who were paralyzed elicited a great deal of sympathy and pity (far more than adults with the same disability). Of course, the most important element of charity telethons is pity. One PWD stated, "The larger the lump in the throat, the larger the check." Another definition of a poster boy or poster girl is someone who is seen only as a disability and not as an individual.

Token Status

> ### In this section, look for—
> - The definition of token status
> - Why tokens are not acknowledged for their achievements and talents

Token status refers to being viewed as having received rewards and privileges as a result of membership in a certain category. When we discussed the ADA in Chapter 2, we learned that this law does not mandate hiring for jobs or entrance into schools of anyone with a disability who is not qualified.

In spite of this, many PWODs think that PWDs have special privileges or exemptions from qualifications. On a personal level, being perceived as a token is both demeaning and frustrating. On a national level, these misperceptions can affect both legislation and policy. It would make no economic sense to hire someone who is not qualified, although he or she belongs to a minority group or has a disability. Further, the law does not mandate that companies hire, or schools admit, individuals from any particular group. The law does require that application and hiring processes be open to all.

As would be expected, when an individual is considered to be a token (for membership in any type of group), years of hard work, preparation, study, and sacrifice are disregarded and ignored. The individual is thought to have received his or her position because he or she is a member of some "disadvantaged group." Further, the token's talents, abilities, skills, intelligence, and work habits are also unacknowledged. Thus, the token fully understands that if he or she were not a member of "some disadvantaged group," his or her accomplishments would be recognized and acknowledged as *individual* achievements. Certainly, the token realizes that it is his or her membership in the group that results in being perceived as a token. It is clear that being viewed as a token is the result of the mistaken stereotypes of the token's associates.

In the video "Look Who's Laughing," a comedian with a disability relates that he was told by another comedian, who did not have a disability, that he was "lucky" to have a disability. Implied in this statement is the idea that the comedian with a disability did not have the qualification to be a comedian, which is to be funny, but that his disability helped him to get comedy jobs. Another comedian states, "You can get only so far on any type of gimmick [speaking of her disability]. You need talent."

Paternalism

> *In this section, look for—*
>
> - Why the practice of paternalism is common when serving PWDs
> - When paternalism is justified
> - When paternalism is not justified
> - What "limited paternalism" and "paternalism by permission" mean
> - The principle of informed choice
> - The principle of self-determination

Paternalism has been defined as "acting upon one's own idea of what is best for another person without consulting that other person" (Marchewka, cited in Anderson, 1987, p. 177). Sissela Bok (1979) defined paternalism as "to guide and even coerce people in order to protect them and serve their best interests, as a father might his children. He must keep them out of harm's way, by force if necessary" (p. 215). Both these definitions emphasize that the individuals for whom this guidance, protection, and service are provided are, at best, not consulted, and, at worse, coerced. Therefore, an individual's autonomy has been violated. However, the concept of a father implies someone who (1) has the best interests of the child in mind and would not want to harm his child, and (2) is more knowledgeable and qualified than his child. The "child," or patient, or client is considered to be vulnerable and in need of guidance. It is not difficult to determine that paternalism is a product of the Biomedical Model of disability. As you will remember, the Biomedical Model relies on the expert knowledge of physicians and other health care providers.

Of course, there are situations in which paternalism is both appropriate and desirable, and therefore society provides the power and resources for paternalism to be enforced. For individuals with severe mental retardation who do not have the ability to understand the nature, extent, and ramifications of important decisions, paternalism is desirable. Indeed, Anderson (1987) stated:

> Some might argue that because of cognitive impairment, the incompetent or severely mentally retarded [sic] have no right to the truth as they have no "true liberty." This leads to a logical difficulty: if people have no liberty, it is not possible to abridge that liberty, and therefore it is not paternalistic to choose for them; in fact it is not possible to be paternalistic. (pp. 183–184)

Paternalism is justified when it is thought that the individual may make decisions that would cause harm to himself or herself. (Another obvious example is that of children and their parents.) Often, professionals ask the question, "How serious are the potential consequences of the individual's making his or her own decisions?" However, many PWDs feel that paternalism has been overused. In the video "Don't Go to Your Room," one woman with a physical disability states, "I have the right to control my body," and another woman remarks, "We have the right to control all aspects of our lives." A third PWD states, "Let me define who I am and what I want to do with my life." Such statements as these reflect a long history of needless paternalism toward PWDs.

The unethical use of paternalism is readily apparent when decisions are made for individuals who have the capability to make their own decisions. A woman who has experienced schizophrenia for 20 years related her experiences with paternalism: "You are given insulin coma therapy and ECT [electroconvulsive therapy] without being consulted or informed because your psychiatrist and your family assume you are too ill to understand" (Leete, 1991, p. 19). Ruth Morris has a degenerating physical disability. She worries that as her condition deteriorates, physicians may make paternalistic decisions about the quality of her life. Further, she knows that physicians have the power to enforce their decisions, regardless of how wrong or patronizing:

> The neurosurgeon told me that he was only interested in quality of life and that in no way would he be looking to prolong my life if he didn't feel the quality would be acceptable. However, neither he nor anyone else has asked me what criteria I would use in judging what was an acceptable quality of life. I am very worried that if I get admitted unconscious or without the power of speech, he will make a decision based on his judgment and his criteria about what is an acceptable quality of life. (Morris, 1991, p. 62)

Here is another example of paternalism: "Upon retirement, the head of the Spastic Society of Britain was asked if he could envision the day when a person with spasticity would head that charity. 'That'd be like putting dogs and cats in charge of the Humane Society,' he quipped" (Pelka, 1997, p. 3; quoted from the November/December 1993 issue of *Mouth: The Voice of Disability Rights*). Incidentally, this short story also illustrates other concepts that we have discussed in this book: (1) the use of improper language ("The Spastic Society"), (2) comparing PWDs to animals, (3) the use of humor to stereotype and devalue PWDs, and (4) the harm that so-called "charities" perpetuate on people they claim to help. Not so quickly discernible is the unintentional misuse of paternalism for individuals who are not capable of making decisions (and for whom society therefore deems paternalism to be appropriate), but these important decisions are based on false stereotypes, inaccurate information about the PWD, or both. We have seen that highly trained professionals hold many false stereotypes of PWDs, and in those cases where paternalism is both necessary and desirable, it is important to ensure that these judgments and choices, made on the behalf of another person, are based on accurate and complete knowledge of the individual. Many disability rights advocates have argued that an individual's worst behavior, regardless of how infrequently that behavior occurred, determined the individual's placement and treatment plans.

Thus, there are types of abuse of paternalism. The first, and most clear-cut, is enforcing paternalism when the individual can make decisions for himself or herself. The second, and less obvious, is enforcing paternalism when the individual cannot make decisions but unintentionally basing decisions on inaccurate information, false stereotypes, or both. Indeed, unjustified paternalism has resulted in restrictive and humiliating treatment for PWDs.

Why have PWDs been subjected to so much paternalism? First, the normative role of a PWD demands dependency, compliance, and passive acceptance of treatment, benefits, and rehabilitation. The power is in the hands of the physicians and counselors who, if they chose, could withhold treatment and benefits if a PWD questions or challenges their decisions. Second, the overgeneralization or perceived spread concerning the effects of the disability often contributes to the mistaken idea that a PWD does not have the mental capacity to make decisions on his or her own behalf. Third, the (unnecessary) need to protect and shelter the PWD may lead some service providers to withhold information from the PWD. Fourth, simply as a result of the nature of the living and treatment environments, many PWDs experience daily, lifelong contact with care providers. These types of settings, rather than any characteristic or need of the client, promote and encourage the paternalism. Fifth, some service providers may be paternalistic simply for the convenience and ease of the institution/hospital/agency. These service providers often feel that "things just go more smoothly when the client/patient does what he or she is told to do." (This last example may not be true paternalism because paternalism implies beneficence or consideration of the individual's best interests.)

Overall, the greatest motivation for paternalism is kindness. There is a fine line between paternalism and beneficence, both on an individual level and on a societal level. We have seen the way in which misguided acts of kindness may be interpreted as paternalism. Nonetheless, it is important to judge the behavior by its results. For example, charity, especially telethons, is considered paternalism by PWDs. Hahn (2005) clarifies the relationship between paternalism and charity and the long-term results: "Because of historical traditions that had defined disabled [sic] people as the 'deserving poor,' the disability movement was enmeshed in a legacy of charity. Most nondisabled observers claimed that they were sympathetic to disabled [sic] people, even if they did not actively support their objectives. Paternalism implies that benefits for disabled [sic] people are motivated by private philanthropy instead of government decision making" (p. 7). Hahn concludes that paternalism and charity prevented opportunities for PWDs and "a healthy debate concerning disability policies" (p. 7). Several disability reformers, such as Samuel Gridley Howe, Alexander Graham Bell, and Helen Keller, are considered by many to have actually limited the opportunities and civil rights for PWDs. On an individual level, it is somewhat easier to understand how the need to be helpful and kind can result in paternalism.

What are the ways in which paternalism is promoted? As mentioned earlier, withholding important information about the disability, about treatment options and their consequences, or about alternative placements is a common form of paternalism. Forcing PWDs to undergo treatments, such as cochlear implants for individuals who are deaf or forced sterilization of people with mental retardation, is another type of paternalism. Paternalism is often directed toward "the hateful client" (Purtilo, 1991, p. 29), especially individuals who are perceived as difficult or demanding. Occasionally, paternalism is deemed to be justified because the resulting decisions will be "better for all concerned." Often, the "all concerned" means family members of the PWD. However, parents of children with disabilities have often felt they have been manipulated by professionals. Paternalism on the behalf of PWDs is often considered to be appropriate when a PWD wishes to undertake a particular activity and his or her caregiver considers the activity to be unobtainable or impractical. As can be seen, there is a very thin line between paternalism and coercion. Today, there is a heightened sensitivity about the risks of paternalism. As would be expected, several methods to reduce the risk of abusing paternalism have been devised. Concepts such as "limited paternalism" are often implemented with individuals who have the capability to make some decisions but are incapable of making other decisions. Therefore, instead of completely controlling the individual's life, it may be necessary, for example, to make financial decisions for the individual, but he or she can guide and control all other aspects of his or her life. However, "paternalism by permission" can be justified. When a patient acknowledges that the health professional is in a better position to decide on a course of action, a patient may actually exercise autonomy by appointing the health professional as a decision maker. The patient must explicitly acknowledge that he or she chooses to follow the professional's judgment (Purtilo, 1991, p. 29). Inherent in these two concepts is the idea that a certain degree of paternalism may be necessary, but the need for total control and complete paternalism may be rare.

Two other movements, both supported by federal legislation, designed to minimize paternalism are (1) informed choice, in which the client is given all available information about the disability, the various treatment plans and options, and their consequences, and (2) self-determination, in which the individual has the right to make decisions about his or her treatment, living arrangements, job placement, and social networks. Often, self-determination is called empowerment. Both of these movements acknowledge that the individual is the expert in his or her own needs and desires.

Indeed, PWDs have had to *fight* for their rights, whereas all others are automatically *given* their rights. The right to control their own lives has often been denied (needlessly) to PWDs.

Infantilization

In this section, look for—

- The definition of infantilization
- The definition of "motherese"
- Which types of people are subjected to motherese

PWDs have often been viewed as "eternal children," in need of control, management, and spiritual guidance (Imrie, 1996). Wolfensberger (1981) explained: "Adults [with disabilities] may be cast into the roles of eternal children by being encouraged to play children's games and to follow children's school schedules rather than adult work schedules; by children's decoration and children's clothing; by funding of services for adults coming from departments charged with serving children; and by such names as 'day care center' for day programs for adults" (p. 205). Thus, it can be seen that infantilization is practiced both on an individual level and on an institutional level.

Sharon L., a medical social worker with a congenital bone disease that has resulted in her small stature, stated, "It is difficult to cross that border from childhood to adulthood." Sharon has developed "presentation strategies" to offset the tendency of others to, as she states, "associate my maturity with my size." For example, when she speaks on the telephone, her voice sounds like the voice of a child; therefore, she "uses big words" so as to "sound" like an adult. Charities have often used "poster kids" and, indeed, some celebrities have demonstrated a tendency not only to infantilize people with a certain type of disability, but also to claim a paternalistic relationship. For example, Jerry Lewis terms individuals with muscular dystrophy (MD) as "Jerry's Kids." It is safe to say that most people with MD do not consider themselves either to be children or to belong to Jerry Lewis.

One woman with a disability talked about her difficulty in crossing the border from childhood to adulthood:

> With one extremely painful exception, as long as I was in the protective custody of family life or college, scheduled and lived without exercising my rights as an adult citizen, the forces of society were kindly and unruffling. It was after college, business schools and innumerable stretches as a volunteer worker on community projects that I was often bogged down by the medieval prejudices and superstitions of the business world. Looking for a job was like standing before a firing squad. Employers were shocked that I had the gall to apply for a job. (Goffman, 1963, p. 34)

Another example of infantilization is seen in the remark made by a woman in the video "My Body Is Not Who I Am." She states, "It's as if I am a child and I have no boundaries." PWDs are often spoken to in a speech pattern that has been labeled "motherese" (Gouvier, Coon, Todd, & Fuller, 1994). Other authors label this type of speech pattern as "child-directed speech" (Warren-Leubecker & Bohannon, 1989). Motherese "involves exaggerated prosodic inflections and other characteristics such as the use of diminutives in naming (e.g., Bobby rather than Bob) and shortened phrase and sentence length . . . greater redundancy and higher usage of questions and concrete referents" (Gouvier et al., p. 264). *Prosodic* refers to singsong speech. Gouvier and his colleagues surreptitiously audiotaped conversations of bookstore employees giving directions to customers in wheelchairs and customers who had no visible disability. Employees speaking to customers in wheelchairs used more words, more repetition, and more questions than when these employees were speaking to customers without a visible disability. Incidentally, none of these fake customers had a disability of any kind (they simply used the wheelchair for the purpose of the experiment) and all were university students. Furthermore, each student played both roles; he or she would use the wheelchair one time and then on another day walk into the bookstore. These students reported that when they used the wheelchair, they sensed "a reverse discrimination in which people actually seemed 'nicer' to them than when they approached in the walking condition" (p. 267). Gouvier and his colleagues concluded, "This study offers clear behavioral validation that people do speak differently to individuals with disabilities, and that some of these differences parallel those observed in the way people speak to their infant children, pets, and other individuals of lower social standing" (p. 266).

We can hear motherese spoken when a nurse asks someone, "How are we feeling today?" or "Did we eat all our dinner?" Terms of endearment such as "honey" or "sweetheart" used when addressing adult strangers are another indication of "motherese." PWDs are often addressed in this insulting and degrading manner. Indeed, adults in institutions were/are often deprived of some small pleasure as a form of punishment. "If you don't do your physical therapy, you won't get dessert" and "If you don't take your medication, you won't be allowed to watch television." These are all examples of motherese. J. Morris (1991) related a story of "motherese" that was clearly abusive.

> Mary Lawson felt that she must be nice to the people who were helping her with the most intimate tasks otherwise they would refuse to do them, or do them in such a way that caused her pain and humiliation. "I want them to help me so I've got to somehow make them like me." One night she was being lifted into bed by two care assistants when she noticed that her shoes were still on. When she said, "Could you take my shoes off?" the care assistant responded by telling her to say "please." As Mary said, "I don't know whether the humiliation and anger I felt at saying "please" was worth the benefit of having my shoes taken off." (p. 32)

Incidentally, personal care attendants are employees of the individual with the disability and most of us do not tell our bosses to say "please" when they ask us to do our job.

PWDs are subjected to intrusive touching by strangers. In our society, adults usually do not touch other adults they do not know. Other than a handshake, in which both individuals must cooperate, a stranger touching another adult is usually considered to be intrusive. PWDs are patted on the head and hugged, and their assistive devices (such as wheelchairs) are moved. All of these behaviors are viewed as intrusive and infantilizing by PWDs.

There is a complex relationship between infantilization, paternalism, dependence, and the Biomedical Model of disability. PWDs are often thought to be sexually neutered and to not be capable of working and making contributions to society; both of these characteristics we usually attribute to children. Furthermore, PWDs are expected to comply with the rules made by PWODs, again a characteristic of childhood in that a child is expected to obey his or her "elders and superiors." Indeed, Ludwig and Adams (1968) undertook a study in a large rehabilitation center to assess the relationship between patient dependency and subordination and patient rehabilitation success rate. The authors stated, "The role of a patient has been likened to that of children by many . . . . What is held in common, of course, among these . . . social positions is the lack of independence, the necessity of accepting a subordinate position and submitting to others" (p. 227). Their study, which included 406 PWDs, "hypothesized that persons whose normal role relationships and social position contained elements of dependency or subordination would be more inclined to successfully perform such a role and complete treatment. Persons in dependent age status, females, Negroes, the unemployed . . . were found more likely to complete recommended services, thus supporting the general hypothesis" (p. 235).

This study was completed 40 years ago. Nonetheless, the straightforward and clearly stated hypothesis (and the entire purpose of the study) sought to demonstrate that "childlike" patients were more successful in their rehabilitation. Hypothesizing that PWDs who were women, African Americans, or unemployed would be more submissive clearly shows that these types of individuals, with or without disabilities, also are not accorded full adult status in our society.

Viewing PWDs as Objects

> **In this section, look for—**
> - The history and purpose of freak shows
> - Present-day freak shows

The long history of freak shows and circuses in which PWDs were put on display for the entertainment of others provides a clear definition of the objectification of PWDs. Nervous curiosity and fascination with people who are viewed not as being human, but rather as objects, continue today. However, the media, such as movies and television, have replaced most of the freak shows and circuses. It was thought that there were moral lessons to be learned by viewing these "freaks" and, indeed, these individuals who were put on display were thought to be symbols of evil, disease, and sin. Pelka (1997) described these "sideshows":

> The Catholic Church, during the Middle Ages in Europe, sponsored traveling exhibitions of disabled [*sic*] people, while families exhibited their disabled [*sic*] members for a fee or sold them to royalty at court. By Victorian times, these forms of "entertainment" had evolved into carnival sideshows or "dime museums," where the public paid to see "armless and legless wonders," "giants," "dwarfs," "seal boys," "living skeletons," and "pinheads." Such exhibits were particularly popular in small-town America. (p. 127)

Ironically, many, if not most, of these individuals experienced no functional limitations. It was simply their appearance that made them "freaks."

Circuses and freak shows were often viewed by PWDs as sources of income when there were not many opportunities for employment and integration with the general population (Thompson, 1996). Furthermore, these PWDs who worked in circuses and freak shows felt a sense of acceptance and understanding by living, working, and traveling with other people who knew what it meant to be labeled a "freak." There was a dark and brutal side to these traveling circuses, and many PWDs were abused and exploited simply because the operators of these circuses and freak shows knew very well that there were few places to which the PWD could escape (Bogdan, 1988). Clearly, these PWDs were exploited and objectified for the entertainment of avid audiences with the express purpose of making money for others.

Deborah Marks (1999) read many first-person narratives of PWDs who worked as "freaks" in circuses and sideshows and came to the conclusion that many of these PWDs felt that their jobs helped them to "exact revenge." These PWDs derived some sort of satisfaction and power from creating discomfort in their audience,

> ... ultimately consoling themselves with the thought that they were exacting some revenge on a hostile, insensitive world of ignorant suckers by exploiting their vulgarity and credulity, and rather effortlessly taking their money. At the same time, we should not be surprised by another state of mind, perhaps coexisting and competing with cynicism. In the narratives of freaks who retrospectively interpreted their lives in terms of the progress of their careers, we see evidence of the effort to give coherence and meaning to life by seeing it in terms of volition and unfolding purpose rather than oppression and victimization. (Marks, 1999, p. 32)

The efforts to raise awareness and funds for the education of PWDs often included prestigious authorities, such as physicians and teachers, "displaying" a PWD and showing the audience what the PWD could do. Basically, these types of demonstrations consisted of a teacher putting a PWD "through his or her paces." Thus, physicians and teachers used PWDs as objects, albeit under the guise of advancing education and medical science. Helen Keller, an honors graduate of Radcliffe College, performed in vaudeville twice a day for 4 years, much to Helen's mother's disappointment, who had claimed that her daughter would "go on stage over my dead body" (Hermann, 1998). After the act, the audience was allowed to ask Ms. Keller questions. Ms. Keller said that she enjoyed acting in vaudeville, but it also solved her financial problems. Before her vaudeville days, and after, Ms. Keller relied on the charity of millionaire philanthropists and income from lecturing. She did view herself as a "spectacle." She wrote of herself and her fellow actors, "for the sake of many for whom fate is unkind . . . . I can conceive that in time the spectacle might have grown stale" (Hermann, 1998, p. 223).

Paul Higgins, a disability scholar, forthrightly depicts telethons and other charitable fundraising activities as modern-day freak shows. Higgins (1992) explained, "Fund raisers still exhibit disabled [*sic*] people for 'profit.' Audiences marvel at the accomplishments of the disabled [*sic*] people who are presented to tug at our heartstrings—and our purse strings" (p. 94).

Today, PWDs feel viewed as objects when they state, "I was *something* to stare at," or "I was interesting to people and that's dehumanizing" (as in the video "My Body Is Not Who I Am"). A woman who was born with spina bifida described an unforgettable experience of objectification. "I was barely human. One time, as a 14-year-old, I was paraded in front of a whole class of doctors so they could see my "abnormal gait." I was wearing only my panties. They would never have done that to a nondisabled girl but it was OK to parade me almost naked. The crazy thing is, it wasn't until years later that I realized they had dehumanized me" (Mackelprang & Salsgiver, 1999, p. 39).

Two ideas are immediately apparent from reading this adult's memory of the treatment she received as a teenager. First, the woman has become aware that the doctors could have had the same quality of training and demonstration while, at the same time, according the girl some measure of respect and dignity (i.e., allowing her to wear more clothing). Second, rather than being overly sensitive and hypervigilant for any evidence of prejudice and discrimination, the 14-year-old willingly complied with the doctors' requests and, amazingly, only comes to an awareness of this disrespectful treatment years later. Mee (1999) reported the same experience:

> Dr. Blount, proud of his work, kept inviting me back to Milwaukee whenever he brought together a group of doctors from around the world, to put me on the stage in the medical theater. I would arrive early, strip, and put on a little loincloth, like a diaper. This, in itself, was a disagreeable experience. I was, in any case, an embarrassable adolescent boy. But to be reduced to an object, as these days, finally,

everybody knows, is profoundly diminishing. In fact, I was reduced to something even less than an object: I was a specimen. (p. 175)

An extreme example of objectification of PWDs is a practice called "dwarf tossing." Patrons at bars or clubs pay a fee to throw a person who is a dwarf onto a padded surface. Dwarf tossing is a competition, with those who throw the person the farthest or the most accurately winning the "game" (Higgins, 1992, p. 94).

The perpetrators of crime against PWDs and sexual abuse of PWDs often defend themselves by stating that they did not view their victims as people. Reading David Hevey's (1997) essay *The Enfreakment of Photography*, we learn that modern-day photography has exploited PWDs. A line from the first paragraph states, "I ask the reader to join me on a journey into oppressive disability imagery" (p. 332). PWDs report that they feel objectified when PWODs, including their own families, "put them on a pedestal." While this might be admiration and may be thought to be a positive experience for the individual with the disability, it is both distancing and objectifying.

Viewing PWDs as Animals

In this section, look for—

- Ways in which society views PWDs as less than human
- The four dimensions of ascribing humanness to PWDs, according to Bogdan and Taylor (1987)

You will remember that in Chapter 1 when we discussed the concept of normalcy we read the following statement of Wolfensberger (1972): "Normalcy is often confused with humanity" (p. 205). Implied in this statement is the corresponding idea that disability is not associated with humanity. Davis (1997) stated, "To have a disability is to be an animal" (p. 20). A brief listing of the derisive names applied to PWDs illustrates Wolfensberger's statement: Joseph Merrick, the 19th century Englishman with neurofibromatosis, was called the "Elephant Man"; a woman who was born without several fingers on either hand is called "Lobster Claws"; freak shows exhibited "Jo-Jo, the Dog-faced Boy" and "Lionel, the Lion-faced Man"; Samuel D. Parks, a dwarf without legs, was billed as "Hopp, the Frog Boy"; a native of New Guinea, Prince Randian, had no arms or legs and was billed as the "Snake Man" and the "Caterpillar Man" (Pelka, 1997); and a man with mental retardation is called "Monkey Boy." Mackelprang and Salsgiver (1999) proposed that "disabilities suggest to people humankind's imperfections and dissimilarities to God while illuminating humankind's relationship to the imperfect animal kingdom" (pp. 37–38). In 1998 in Utah, a manager of a large grocery store referred to and addressed an employee who bagged groceries (and who was mentally retarded) as "Monkey Boy." When the bagger was out in the parking lot gathering up shopping carts, the manager would use the loudspeaker to call the bagger back into the store, addressing him as "Monkey Boy." The bagger's parents sued the grocery store chain (Mims, 1998).

People who used sign language were called "ape-like." A teacher at the Pennsylvania School for the Deaf observed in 1873 that sign language was "being decried, denounced, and ridiculed . . . as a set of monkey-like grimaces and antics" (Pettingill, 1873, cited in Baynton, 1997). Furthermore, the ability to speak was often "the constituting force of humanity" (Nelson & Berens, 1997, p. 52), and therefore people who were deaf and did not speak were not considered to be human "in the relentlessly aural world of early modern England . . . [where] civilization was possible only through *spoken* [italics added] language" (Nelson & Berens, 1997, p. 52). St. Augustine denied church membership to individuals who were deaf, including the right to communion or the other sacraments, based on the assumption that they could not confess their sins.

Ree (1999) emphasized that it was not only novels and plays that have declared deaf people to be less than human, but also scholarly works of science, philosophy, and anthropology:

> Such stories and parables about the inhumanity, irrationality, stupidity and depravity of the dumb (mute) are numerous and quite well attested, and for centuries they have been circulated as if they were plain and unassailable facts. And yet, the accounts cannot possibly be true, not even metaphorically and approximately . . . . There are numerous fictions about mutism, but they are to be found not in works of imaginative literature, but in the archives of natural history and philosophical anthropology. (p. 93)

Commenting on the experiences of Joseph Merrick, Darke (1993) made the observation that English Victorian society dehumanized and objectified PWDs "rather than representing abnormality/disability as human and valid in itself" (p. 340). Darke remarked that PWDs were thought of as "potential exhibits in what was a cross between a zoo and a museum" (p. 339). What are typically viewed in a museum? Objects. What are typically viewed in a zoo? Animals. Goffman (1963), speaking about all types of stigmatized people, stated, "[They] are not quite human" (p. 3).

A famous deaf actor, Bernard Bragg, provided another example of viewing PWDs as less than human, perhaps on a subconscious level. Bragg was approached by a producer of documentaries who wished to make a film on language and asked Bragg to write and star in a segment on sign language. On asking about the other segments of the proposed film and learning that the other parts of the film would present communication among whales and chimpanzees, Bragg refused to participate. The film producer was surprised and perplexed, not understanding how insulting such associations are (Bragg, 1989).

It is well known that people who live in institutions are often not thought to be fully human by their caregivers (Livneh, 1980). Criminals often choose PWDs as their targets because they often do not think of PWDs as "people" and therefore these criminals do not experience guilt and remorse for their crimes. Also, the myth that PWDs are insensitive or indifferent to pain increases the likelihood that they will be abused. Sobsey, in his book *Violence and Abuse in the Lives of People with Disabilities: The End of Silent Acceptance* (1994), conceives of the dehumanization of people with disabilities who live in institutions to take three forms. He labels these forms "1) conceptual dehumanization, 2) ecobehavioral dehumanization, and 3) reactive dehumanization" (p. 311). Conceptual dehumanization includes "attitudes, expectations, beliefs, labels and language"; ecobehavioral dehumanization includes segregating people, putting them into uniforms, thus robbing them of their humanity and individuality, humiliating them, and denying them the necessities of life"; reactive dehumanization occurs when "the behaviors and appearance of people who are dehumanized deteriorate to conform to their societal status" (pp. 311–312). Sobsey sees dehumanization of people with disabilities to be a circular process. In other words, the more they are treated as less than human, the more they conform to these expectations. Other examples of not viewing PWDs as fully human include scientists and researchers who have, in the past, used PWDs as research subjects. Of course, it is not unethical to use people as research subjects; however, PWDs have often been used in unethical medical experiments simply because PWODs would have refused to participate (and had the power to enforce that refusal). For instance, in the 1960s in Sweden, individuals with mental retardation were fed high-sugar diets to establish a causal link between sugar and tooth decay. The headlines of the news stories that reported these experiments included the words "guinea pigs" and "laboratory rats" to describe the subjects of these studies.

Wolfensberger and Tullman (1982) described ways in which society views children with disabilities as animals:

> If a group of children is [unconsciously] viewed as animals, then they may be segregated in a special class that is given an animal name—often even the name of animals that are seen as expressive of the devalued children's identity. Thus, a class for retarded children may be called "The Turtles." The animal kingdom may serve as an analogue for or source of service measures for that group of people. (pp. 134–135)

Two disability scholars, Robert Bogdan and Steven Taylor, wrote *The Social Construction of Humanness: Relationships with Severely Disabled People* (1989), in which they describe 15 years of qualitative research. Bogdan and

Taylor interviewed more than 100 family members and caregivers of individuals with severe and multiple disabilities. They describe the PWDs in their study in this way: "Some scholars and professionals would argue that [our research subjects] lack the characteristics of a human being . . . . The severely and profoundly retarded people in our study have often been the target of the indictment 'vegetable'" (p. 279). Bogdan and Taylor analyzed the interviews and found four dimensions of humanness: (1) ascribing thinking to PWDs, (2) seeing individuality and personality in the PWD, (3) viewing the PWD as reciprocating and contributing to the family, and (4) defining a social place for the PWD and thinking of the PWD as an integral part of the family. This research presents a monumental shift in the way in which PWODs view individuals with severe and multiple disabilities.

Technology and neonatal medical science have added another dimension to the question of ascribing humanity to PWDs. Such questions of humanity now apply to unborn babies. Now that it is possible, in some cases, to determine the presence of severe and multiple disabilities in unborn children, should these babies be born? (Fletcher, 1979; Frohock, 1986).

Bogdan and Taylor concluded, "We [PWODs] can show that they [PWDs] are human by proving we are capable of showing humanity to them" (p. 29).

Unnecessary Dependence

> **In this section, look for—**
>
> - How PWDs define dependence differently
> - How PWODs often misinterpret adaptive coping responses of PWDs to be dependence
> - How PWODs often promote unnecessary dependence for PWDs

The idea of independence/dependence is probably defined a little differently by everyone. In other words, independence/dependence is very idiosyncratically defined. Nonetheless, we can broadly state that independence means having control over one's life and one's decisions, which includes (1) control of the resources necessary to care for oneself; (2) the choice of affiliation with other people, in families, in friendships, and in colleague groups; and (3) the freedom to make choices for oneself (Chesler & Chesney, 1988). For anyone, with or without a disability, the resources necessary to care for oneself include economic empowerment (which usually means a job); in addition, for PWDs, included in the resources necessary to care for oneself may be medical care, complete information about the disability, assistive technology, personal care attendants, and the services of other types of caregivers (Crewe & Zola, 1983; Deegan, 1992). Physical independence is relatively easy to describe and define; emotional independence is more difficult to define. However, Anne Finger (1991) observed that some types of physical dependence are acceptable to PWODs, while others are not. She uses the examples of using a car (acceptable to PWODs) and using a wheelchair (unacceptable to PWODs). A second set of examples includes going to a hairstylist for a haircut (acceptable to PWODs) and having an attendant wash your face (not acceptable to PWODs). For instance, what one person describes as emotional independence, another might describe as loneliness and isolation.

Of course, no one, with or without a disability, is completely independent. Everyone depends on someone else to some extent; however, most of us would agree that the greater the degree of independence an individual experiences, the more options he or she enjoys. Indeed, independence is considered to be one of the *sine qua non* of quality of life.

It is safe to state that our "value system distrusts and devalues dependence in other people and vulnerability in general" (Wendell, 1997, p. 261). PWDs are often viewed as both dependent and vulnerable.

PWDs often define and interpret dependence/independence differently. Whereas independence is valued and needless dependence is avoided, PWDs do not "glorify independence" (Wright, 1960). Control and consent are important components of independence. Indeed, what is thought to be independence, for many PWDs, is neither possible nor a great need. A professional artist who needs the services of a personal care attendant explained:

> My attendant is an extension of my body. It takes a very emotionally strong as well as spiritually strong person to understand that and not resent it. If I don't direct the person, then I'm dependent on that person. Then I'm not autonomous and ultimately it's harder on the attendant. I made it very clear that I'm not making decisions for *them*, only for myself. (Panzarino, as cited in Rousso, 1993, p. 111)

Notice the way in which Panzarino redefines the concept of autonomy (or independence). Most people who have had no experience with personal care attendants would assume that being fed, bathed, and dressed by a paid attendant would make an individual feel dependent and helpless. In contrast, when Ms. Panzarino is directing the attendant, she feels "autonomous" and in control. Notice also that she is aware that when she does not remain independent and directive, it makes the attendant's job harder. Ms. Panzarino also explains that it is possible for an individual to become "overly dependent" on an attendant.

Leonard Kriegel, in his book *Falling into Life* (1991), details how learning to fall was a turning point in the recovery of his independence. When he was 11 years old, Kriegel contracted polio and his legs were paralyzed. To learn how to walk in his braces, it was necessary to learn how to fall "properly" and to get back on his feet. The physical therapists taught these skills to all the patients, but Kriegel would not allow himself to fall, explaining, "The prospect of letting go was precisely what terrified me. That the other boys in the ward had no trouble falling added to my shame and terror. I knew there was virtually no chance of injury when I fell, but the knowledge simply made me more ashamed of a cowardice that was as monumental as it was unexplainable" (pp. 10–11).

For Kriegel, falling down meant a loss of independence and succumbing to failure. When he does learn to fall, he writes in almost biblical language of how learning to deliberately and autonomously sacrifice his independence by falling is the beginning of learning how to control his body: "I dropped. I did not crash. I dropped. I did not collapse. I dropped. I did not plummet. I felt myself enveloped by a curiously gentle moment in my life. In that sliver of time before I was kissed by the mat, I could sense my shame and fear drain from my soul, and I knew that my sense of my own cowardice would soon follow. In falling, I had given myself a new life, a new start" (p. 8). Kriegel, at age 11, had redefined independence.

In the American culture, independence is both highly valued and narrowly defined. Naturally, PWDs value independence and autonomy and also know that they have a right to independence. They simply redefine these concepts. Also, they manipulate both their personal environment and the disability to achieve independence. However, PWDs cannot manipulate all of the physical environment or the attitudes of PWODs. Obviously, for some PWDs, there are activities that they will not be able to do, regardless of how much they "try harder" (Phillips, 1991). PWODs may unwittingly curtail the independence of PWDs in an attempt to be helpful. For example, encouraging the use of prostheses that serve no functional purpose, but instead are uncomfortable and confining, diminishes the independence of the PWD.

Often PWODs misinterpret assertive and independent behaviors of PWDs. For example, the use of certain assistive devices to conserve energy (an individual using a wheelchair or scooter when he or she is capable of walking but wants to conserve his or her energy for something more important), the side effects of medication (falling asleep in public places), and all sorts of strategies to complete activities of daily living (such as keeping the clean dishes in the refrigerator) are sometimes viewed, erroneously, by PWODs as maladaptive and dependent behaviors. When PWDs ask for accommodations or assistance, for example, they are often seen as being dependent and passive. Does it make sense for a very highly paid corporate attorney to spend 2½ hours in the morning dressing himself or herself, finishing exhausted, or should a personal care attendant be hired? Obviously, the attorney is capable of dressing himself or herself, but how rational is the decision to do as much for oneself as possible in this particular case? At other times, when PWDs resist or refuse assistance, they are seen as rude and ungrateful. Unwanted assistance may be viewed by PWDs as attempts to control them. Certainly, because PWODs have so little understanding of the experience of disability, it is difficult for them to judge the degree of independence a PWD has.

Society can, and does, impose unnecessary dependence on PWDs. Certainly, the Biomedical Model of disability has never encouraged PWDs to be active, assertive, or independent (Zola, 1972). Medical and human service bureaucracies are often dehumanizing, expecting passive compliance from patients/clients. The services provided are intended to assist the individual; however, the expectations of passive compliance promote needless dependence and prevent the individual from making his or her own choices and decisions. Residential schooling, institutionalization, and prolonged hospitalizations also contribute to promoting needless dependence. Decision making is a learned skill that individuals learn in small incremental steps. For example, children in kindergarten make their daily clothing choices, and young adults choose marriage partners and careers. In between kindergarten and young adulthood, there are many choices and decisions, appropriate to the individual's age. For individuals who have lived in institutions and have not been allowed to make decisions of when they will sleep, when they will eat, or what they will eat, typical adult independence can seem overwhelming.

Society institutionalizes dependence for PWDs. By giving children with disabilities inferior education, by making policies and regulations that incorporate financial disincentives that make it difficult for PWDs to go to work, and by refusing to provide accommodations, society has institutionalized unnecessary dependence for PWDs.

The unwillingness to provide accommodations (as mandated by the ADA) can be recognized in thoughtless comments such as "Don't these people lip read?" It can be seen in a sign with a picture of a wheelchair that states "Ring for assistance" or in signs that direct wheelchair users to use the delivery entrance. Another example of reluctance to provide accommodations is reflected in efforts to determine if PWDs will attend specific events. As we have already learned, it is both irrelevant and illegal to provide physical accessibility *only* after it has been determined that PWDs will need them. Certainly, it is clear from these examples that the independence of PWDs has been needlessly limited. It is surprising that most individuals would consider these examples to be adequate accommodations for PWDs. Imrie (1996) summarized: "Mobility [is] liberty for the human body" (p. 18). Facilities, both public and private, that are accessible to PWODs and are necessary for day-to-day living are unavailable to PWDs. This is an example of institutionalizing needless dependence for PWDs.

A court interpreter for the New York State Supreme Court (English/Spanish) who is blind told how difficult it was to ask for accommodations when she was new on the job. (She had threatened a lawsuit to be considered for the job and was therefore unwilling to appear demanding.)

Having Braille indicators on the elevators would have made my life easier, but I didn't ask for them because I felt I shouldn't make any special demands. Now, eight years later, I feel a lot more comfortable asking for what I need, but I feel silly demanding changes in the elevator at this point, when I have been using them as they are for so long. I guess asking for help is not yet as easy for me as I would like it to be. But it is an issue that all of us as disabled [*sic*] people need to keep struggling with—to make sure we get what we need. (Crespo, 1993, p. 98)

Dependence is also fostered by the false stereotype that PWDs can never contribute. According to this stereotype, all assistance and contribution is one-way—all given to the PWD, with the PWD never being acknowledged as a benefactor or a contributor. Looking back to Chapter 4 and the example of Greg Smith and his Onarollathon fundraiser for Literacy Volunteers of America, we can see that PWDs, like everyone else, like to contribute to the community and to their families. Smith planned his fundraiser to coincide with the Labor Day Jerry Lewis telethon to make a strong point that PWDs participate in community service.

Marginality

Everyone wants to know where he or she "belongs" in the world. The concept of marginality was originally discussed in relation to members of racial and ethnic minority groups (Stonequist, 1937). The condition of marginality occurs when an individual, because of his or her membership in a devalued group (sometimes referred to as "defining status"), is not allowed to participate fully in the life of the community according to his or her interests and abilities. Stonequist posited that because racial and ethnic minority individuals were barred from full participation in the life of society, these individuals are "caught" between two groups—the dominant, powerful majority group and their own minority group. Gist and Dworkin (1972) described a marginal person as "one who lives in two worlds, in both of which he [*sic*] is more or less a stranger" (p. 10).

The solution to remedying the condition of marginality seems simple—the individual should choose his or her identity in one of the two groups. This is not possible because the power of definition is held by the dominant group. In other words, it does not matter how the individual defines himself or herself because the individual's position is determined by how the dominant group defines him or her. Therefore, the defining characteristic must be visible. The theory of marginality holds that (1) the majority group will not allow the minority individual entrance, stating that the individual has no legitimate claim to this status, and (2) the minority individual does not want to identify with his or her minority group because of the subordinate status. Therefore, the individual belongs to neither group and lacks a strong identification with any one group. Minority group individuals know far more about the majority group than the reverse. To survive, minority group members, including PWDs, must know about the majority culture. In contrast, majority group members often have little interest in or need to know about the minority group. Indeed, PWODs, unless they have had a family member with a disability, usually have not been interested in learning about the experiences and perspectives of PWDs.

Some aspects of marginality can be applied to individuals with disabilities, while others cannot. Charles Mee, a survivor of polio, wrote of one of his first realizations of his own marginality. He described marginality perfectly: "This world seemed too foreign to me, and at the same time so familiar" (p. 131). Notice how, as a teenager, the only way in which he can describe this realization is to compare his situation with that of a racial minority.

> I spent many hours in the living room, watching Ed Sullivan's *Toast of the Town* and Sid Caesar's *Your Show of Shows* and *Ozzie and Harriet* and *I Love Lucy.*
>
> These shows, and their commercials, made me dizzy with their vision of a world so wholesome, intact, healthy, vigorous, upbeat, smooth-skinned, smiling, sleek, plump; with all the unattainable girls in swimming suits, each one of them incredibly sexy even as they were evidently not thinking about sex or anything other than purity, purity of soap and purity of complexion and purity of thought, the purity of a perfect Ipana toothpaste smile; clean people, good people, winning people, with their milk shakes and hamburgers and French fries, bobby sox and swirling skirts and snug sweaters, their pep and vigor. This world seemed too foreign to me, and at the same time so familiar: actually, in many confusing ways, this vision of the close-knit, happy family, secure in the possession of the basic consumer durables, described my life. But at the same time, in some way I couldn't put my finger on, I knew this was not my world at all. I thought: Oh, I think I know how *Negroes* feel. I thought: These people on television could be from the moon. (Mee, 1999, p. 131)

In 1948, a disability scholar (Barker, cited in Goffman, 1997) stated that PWDs "live on a social-psychological frontier constantly facing new situations" (p. 215). Disability scholars use words such as "marginality" and "frontier" to describe the experience and identity of PWDs. An individual who is deaf and blind communicated his sense of marginality when he stated, "I see myself within the world, against the world, but not really part of the world" (Petty, 1979, p. 10).

In the case of visible disabilities, the PWD is often denied membership in the dominant culture (Hannaford, 1985). However, the concept of marginality includes the necessity of two cultures, between which the

PWD can be caught. Until recently, there was no disability culture with which a PWD could identify. Indeed, much of the literature on the marginality of racial/ethnic minority individuals speaks about the loss of minority cultures because individuals have decided to take on the identity of the dominant group or, at minimum, to have their children and grandchildren take on this identity. Again, until very recently, there has been no disability culture to lose or to retain. Nonetheless, many PWDs do feel "caught." For example, the title of Higgins's (1980) book, *Outsiders in a Hearing World*, clearly communicates the alienation of the Deaf. Any kind of marginality, it can be argued, must be based on clear-cut demarcations between majority and minority. It is doubtful if there is such a standardized, widely understood demarcation, other than a few types of disabilities, such as deafness.

The term "status inconsistency" describes the experience of the person who is marginal. Status inconsistency refers to the ambivalence, self-hatred, and heightened sensitivity to insult and threat that, supposedly, the marginal person experiences. Rather than viewing these individuals as bicultural, adaptable, and flexible, social scientists and scholars viewed them as being "pulled in two directions" or having internalized the negative views of the dominant group toward their own group. Thus, the dominant group has effectively "taught" minority individuals to feel inferior.

Margins and frontiers (or borders) sound like physical places, but in sociological/psychological references, margins and frontiers are most often used as metaphors. However, when we read the autobiographical accounts of PWDs, there are often references to "I lived in another country" (Cohen, 2004; Murphy, 1980). Robert Murphy (1990), a professor of anthropology at Columbia University, became paralyzed as a result of a tumor of the spinal cord, from which he eventually died. Murphy used his academic field of anthropology to understand and describe his experience of disability. He describes the feeling of marginality as going on a long trip (or sojourn) and leaving his native culture.

> Just as an anthropologist gets a better perspective on his culture through long and deep study of a radically different one, my extended sojourn in disability has given me, like it or not, a measure of my estrangement far beyond the yield of any trip. I now stand somewhat apart from American culture, making me in many ways a stranger. And with this estrangement has come a greater urge to penetrate the veneer of cultural differences and reach an understanding of the underlying unity of all human experience. (pp. 102–103)

When Anne Finger (1991), a polio survivor, attended her first support group with other polio survivors, she said, "It was as if I was living all my life in a foreign country, speaking a language which was not mine." Until that first support meeting, which she attended when she was an adult, we are left to conclude that Finger felt that everyone around her was speaking a foreign language. Nonetheless, there may be some "status inconsistency" because Finger said, "I wanted to be able to embrace this community. And I wanted to be able to walk away from it, too. I want to be able to return to the world in which I more or less passed for able" (pp. 16–17).

Simpson and Yinger (1985), two sociologists, stated:

> Other authors emphasize the personal instability that they believe is likely to characterize persons who lack a strong feeling of identification with one group. Minority-group members who feel torn between association with the group in which they are categorically placed by prejudice and their feelings of identification with the dominant society may lack some of the security that comes from stable and acceptable group relationships. (p. 124)

Whether the psychopathology, psychological strain, personality disorganization, ambivalence, and lack of identity (none of which is a positive trait) must always be present in the marginal person is somewhat unclear. The "scientific" theory of the marginal person may have added to the prejudice and discrimination against minority individuals.

Most PWODs experience a certain level of acceptance and respect and are allowed to function within a relatively wide comfort zone. (Physical accessibility of the environment also contributes to the privileges of PWODs.) According to Young (1990), marginalization is the "most dangerous" (p. 54) form of discrimination for PWDs because marginalization removes PWDs from social life, and inferior education and lack of accommodations remove PWDs from economic life. Further, marginal people, including PWDs, must submit to "the invasive authority of social service providers and other public and private administrators who enforce the rules with which the marginal must comply, and otherwise exercise power over the conditions of their lives" (p. 54).

Sociologists describe individuals who experience status inconsistency as people who have acquired many of the achievements and statuses of the dominant group but, nonetheless, are still identified as being a member of a minority group. Therefore, PWDs with high occupational positions, high incomes, high levels of education, and prestige are aware that, notwithstanding these accomplishments, they are readily perceived as members of a devalued group. Therefore, when these PWDs are among strangers, the strangers have no way (usually) of knowing the *achieved status* (the education, money, prestige) but only see the PWD's *ascribed status* (as a PWD).

In summary, PWDs must negotiate a relationship with a world that ignores, devalues, and rejects them. Further, the PWD may be open to attack from both sides—from PWODs and PWDs. If the PWD tries to "pass" as not having a disability, other PWDs may think of him or her as a "closet crip." If the PWD appears to be overly eager to please PWODs and "grateful for any crumbs" (Pelka, 1997, p. 305), other PWDs may call him or her a "Tiny Tim."

Equal Social Status Relationships

> **In this section, look for—**
> - Differing levels of social distance
> - The way in which dating is, for PWDs, Mount Everest

Friendships, family relationships, and loving and sexual relationships are quality-of-life issues. Most people seek out and develop these types of equal social status associations. However, the segregation, isolation, and institutionalization of PWDs have created physical distance between PWDs and PWODs, which in turn has created social distance. Moreover, the stereotyping, role entrapment, lowered expectations, solo status, infantilization, paternalism, objectification, and unnecessary dependence that PWDs experience work together to make equal social status relationships difficult to initiate and maintain.

Social distance is defined by sociologists as "the degree of intimacy which group norms allow between any two individuals" (Poole, 1927, p. 115). Theories of social distance were originally developed to describe relationships between individuals of differing racial, ethnic, cultural, and religious groups. Bogardus (1928) devised a numerical scale that listed six degrees of social distance. These include allowing members of a certain group (6) to visit my country, (5) to gain citizenship in my country, (4) to gain employment in my occupation, (3) to live on my street as neighbors, (2) to join my club as personal friends, and (1) to have close kinship by marriage. This order, from least intimate to most intimate, describes the degree of social relationship desired or allowed.

Olkin (1999) has also quantified social distance when speaking of PWDs, stating,

> For people with disabilities, dating is Mount Everest. Disability discrimination is most felt in the romantic realm. Studies of attitudes toward disability repeatedly show that people's attitudes become more and more negative as the relationship with the person with the disability gets closer. Those who indicate that they would be fine with the idea of a neighbor with a disability draw the line at their children dating a person with a disability, and most people indicate that they would not marry a person with a disability. (p. 223)

Mount Everest may not be a numerical rating, but it does communicate the difficulty of dating for PWDs. Many PWDs report that going out for an evening of fun with a group of men and women is relatively easy for a

PWD. As long as specific couples are not identified (i.e., John is with Mary), PWODs are willing to go out with PWDs. However, it is much more difficult for a PWD to arrange a one-on-one date with a PWOD.

Other measures of social distance include the progressive steps of speaking with an acquaintance, speaking with a work colleague, having a member of a family marry this type of individual, and marrying this type of individual oneself. While these measures of social distance may be somewhat outdated (and were originally developed for racial/ethnic minority relationships), there are several ways in which they apply to PWDs. As we have discussed, perceived characteristics of PWDs, such as intelligence, social class, and level of education, influence the judgment of others. Those PWDs who are thought to be of higher social class, with more education, will probably experience less social distance than PWDs who are thought to not possess these characteristics. Therefore, there is an interplay of both the disability status and other types of desired characteristics.

However, it is safe to state that most PWDs experience more difficulty in establishing all types of equal social status relationships (DeLoach, 1994; Fisher & Galler, 1988). The widely held idea that PWDs are not able to contribute and must always be passive recipients contributes to this difficulty. On an impersonal level, we have seen how the idea that PWDs are incapable of making contributions has led to their high underemployment and unemployment rates. In spite of this widely held myth, PWDs have made important contributions as workers during labor shortages and world wars. On a personal level, this false idea has led to the unquestioned assumptions that PWDs must overachieve to be considered equal. Often, others, including professionals, automatically assume that a child with a disability is an unwanted burden to his or her parents, never considering that a child with a disability is more likely a source of joy to the parents.

Intimate, loving relationships are even more difficult (than friendships or workplace colleagues) for PWDs to achieve as a result of two widespread ideas: (1) PWDs are not interested in or capable of intimate and loving relationships, and (2) an intimate relationship between a PWD and a PWOD must be asymmetrical, or unbalanced, with the PWOD holding the position of power.

Many PWODs think that the onset of a disability means the end of all sexuality for the individual. For those with congenital disabilities, it is often thought that the individual will experience neither sexuality nor intimate, loving relationships. In the video "Tell Them I'm a Mermaid," one woman stated that when she acquired her disability, a psychologist told her that "romance would mean less, work would mean more, and religion a lot more." We can readily recognize the psychologist's statement as paternalizing, but we can also see how, in a very concise way, the psychologist neatly assigned values to the important parts of this woman's life. Romance is assigned the lowest value. The sexuality of PWDs is often misunderstood (Lesh & Marshall, 1984). At times, PWDs, such as those with mental retardation or mental illness, are viewed as sexually dangerous and threatening;

at other times, PWDs are seen as sexually unattractiv
times, PWDs are viewed as uninterested or incapable. I
are true, but all these ideas consider PWDs to have som
adjustment (Olkin & Howson, 1994; Rousso, 1981).

Intimate relationships between a PWD and a PW
asymmetrical and stressful because the PWD is often thought to be a burden.
Several scholars have written on the perceptions of PWODs who choose to
marry a PWD or to engage in any long-term relationship with a PWD.
Asch and Fine (1997) reported that others view the PWOD "as a saint or a
loser" or someone who was forced into a "default position" (p. 247). Toombs
(1995), a professor of English with multiple sclerosis, relates that many
people have said to her, "How *lucky* you are to have your husband" (p. 16).
Unbalanced relationships of any kind, in which one individual is seen as
the contributor and the other as the passive recipient, are stressful for both
partners. The contributor (saint) might become resentful and the recipient
(burden) may feel insecure, fearing that his or her partner will leave. De-
Loach and Greer (1981) devoted several pages of their book *Adjustment to
Severe Physical Disability: A Metamorphosis* to discussing individuals who are
sexually attracted to PWDs.

> The "walking wounded" ... [are] those persons who have been so
> deeply hurt in a previous relationship with a "normal" person that they
> seek out persons who seem unlikely to injure them again .... The
> "would-be dictators" are persons who are so insecure that they feel the
> need to dominate another human being. Such persons seek out disabled
> persons [*sic*] because they feel superior to those with physical limita-
> tions .... The "unsolicited missionaries" are persons who develop a
> relationship with disabled [*sic*] persons in order to save them .... The
> "gallant gesturers" are persons who discount the disabled [*sic*] as sexual
> beings, and thus view any liaison with them as a basis for self-congrat-
> ulation. (pp. 95–96)

These scholars underscore the imbalance that is automatically assumed in relationships between PWDs and PWODs. In each of DeLoach
and Greer's examples, the PWOD is using his or her partner to meet his or
her own needs.

PWDs have often internalized this view of relationships and have
made comments such as, "There is a tendency for PWDs to feel grateful
when someone loves them or pays attention to them." Another PWD says,
"We are perceived as burdens" (Nordqvist, 1980). Abby Kovalsky stated, "I
joined a dating service a year and a half ago. All I hear from the agency is
that anyone who reads my profile and then sees my photo is basically not
willing to meet someone with my disability" (Mackelprang & Salsgiver,
1999, p. 17). Equally distancing is the perception (held by PWODs) that
PWDs are either "saints" or "heroes." One woman with a disability state
"I have a lot of people who respect me, but I have no friends."

Naturally, there are difficulties related to the disability itself when initiating and establishing relationships between PWDs and PWODs (Perduta-Fulginiti, 1996). Scheer (1993) quoted a man: "On the romantic side, women have a tendency to move away from me . . . . It's like 'see ya later.' I mean, it's easy to find someone to say, 'Okay, let's go out,' but when it comes to the romantic side of it, they're not quite sure what to do, what to expect. Too, it's hard to approach someone when you're in a wheelchair, as opposed to the way it was before. I mean, what do you say? Can I buy you a drink, and, by the way, would you help me with mine?" (p. 9).

Ironically, research shows that married people enjoy better health, probably as a result of eating better; having emotional support; and having someone to monitor one's health, including such behaviors as regular exercise, seat belt use, and undergoing routine medical examinations.

The Media's Portrayal of PWDs

In this section, look for—

- The mass media has not changed its portrayal of PWDs for hundreds of years

- The mass media portrays other minorities more accurately and respectfully

- The depiction of PWDs in media is a type of socially sanctioned discrimination

- Disability is seen as a symbol (most often for negative characteristics)

The first response to thinking about the portrayal of PWDs in movies, books, and television programs might be as follows: "It's only entertainment, and, besides, nobody thinks that television or movies depict reality. Lighten up." Nonetheless, the ongoing negative and inaccurate depiction of PWDs can lead to a lack of opportunities and civil rights for PWDs. The lives of PWDs are influenced by the way in which the culture represents disability in its media (Hahn, 1998a, 1988b). Many scholars consider the depiction of PWDs in the media to be "hostile fantasies" (Longmore,). 134). Furthermore, most consumers of media do not take the time ct that these negative portrayals of PWDs say nothing about PWDs ther, are excellent encapsulations of the attitudes PWODs hold of . Indeed, these distorted images say more about the writers than PWDs.

Charles Dickens wrote 16 major literary works, of which 14 had a character with a disability (Byrd & Elliott, 1988). Dickens visited Laura Bridgman in 1842 in Boston and "waxed lyrical in his 'American Notes' over the 'fair young creature' whose face shone 'radiant with intelligence and pleasure,' a face much like his own Little Nell, a kind of allegory" (Angier, 2001, p. 13). You will remember that we discussed Laura Bridgman in Chapter 5. She was a girl who was deaf–blind and was taught by Anne Sullivan. Anne Sullivan later became the teacher of Helen Keller. Many great novelists used characters with disabilities, and often these PWDs were bitter and self-pitying. Certainly, inaccurate representations of PWDs were found in the media before the introduction of film and television. Therefore, the mass media did not invent prejudice and discrimination against PWDs; the mass media simply made it available to far larger audiences (Norden, 1994).

When movies were first introduced, individuals in racial and ethnic minority groups were portrayed in racist, very simplified, negative, exaggerated, sensationalized, and demeaning ways. These individuals were often the villain, often did not have families or other social statuses, and did not have jobs or professions other than to serve White people. The race of the character was not a secondary characteristic; the character *was* his or her race and little more. Often the minority person served as some type of metaphor or allegory (and so it was unnecessary to endow the person with a personality). Of course, these racist depictions said nothing about racial minority individuals and everything about the White filmmakers. The media now represents racial and ethnic minority individuals in more accurate and complete ways. In contrast, Klobas (1988) concludes that the image of disability represented in film and television has not changed much since the inception of these forms of entertainment.

PWDs are portrayed in exaggerated, sensationalized, and demeaning ways. Women who are blind are often passive and victimized in movies, whereas men who are blind have been endowed with special gifts and wisdom (Safran, 1998). Other PWDs often represent evil, anger, sin, or internal aberration (Byrd & Elliott, 1985; Longmore, 1985; McBrien, 1997). "Captain Hook and Richard III plot and scheme in order to gain vengeance on a world each sees as responsible for his wounds" (Marks, 1999, p. 167).

Disability elicits an emotional response, and writers play on this ignorance and fear to sell tickets and make a profit. The portrayal of disability often heightens comedy or melodrama. J. Morris summarized:

> Disability is used as a metaphor, as a code for the message that the non-disabled writer wishes to convey. In doing this, the writer draws on the prejudice, ignorance, and fear that generally exist toward disabled [*sic*] people, knowing that to portray a character with a humped back, with a missing leg, with facial scars will evoke certain feelings in the reader or the audience. The disability is used to

induce a sense of unease, the more the cultural stereotype is rein-forced." (Morris, 1991, p. 93)

Leonard Kriegel stated:

The world of the crippled and disabled [*sic*] is strange and dark, and it is held up to judgment by those who live in fear of it. The cripple [*sic*] is the creature who has been deprived of his ability to create a self . . . . He is the other, if for no other reason than that only by being the other will he be allowed to presume upon the "normals." He must accept definition from outside the boundaries of his own existence." (Kriegel, 1987, p. 66)

This negative and inaccurate portrayal of PWDs in the media is slowly changing to show PWDs as ordinary people. A *New York Times* article (Navarro, 2007, May 17) quotes the actor Robert David Hall, a double amputee who plays a coroner on the popular television series *CSI*: "It used to be that if you were disabled and on television, they'd play soft piano behind you. The thing I love about *CSI* is that I'm just Dr. Robbins." The author of the *New York Times* article, Mireya Navarro, suggests three catalysts for these changes. First, the absolute number of PWDs has provided strength in numbers. "The most recent population survey, in 2002, showed the disabled [*sic*] population to be the country's largest minority: 51 million, or 18 per-cent of all Americans." Second, by providing PWDs with civil rights, there are more PWDs visible in society. Navarro concludes: "With increased ac-cess has come visibility. The public image of the disabled [*sic*] is increasingly informed by actual experience of disability rather than the imagined un-derstanding of it." Third, the increasing numbers of actors with disabilities in the Screen Actors Guild have advocated for more stories that include characters with disabilities and, moreover, hiring actors with disabilities to play these characters. Navarro concludes: "The heart-wrenching movie of the week and fund-raising telethons striving for cures have given way to amputees rock climbing on reality shows like *The Amazing Race* and doing the jive on *Dancing with the Stars*. Sitcoms and crime shows have jumped on the bandwagon, too: An actor who is a paraplegic, for instance, depicts a member of the casino surveillance team on *Las Vegas*."

Effect of the Media on PWDs

Many PWDs, or their families, have spoken about the effect the media has on the individual with a disability when he or she first receives the diagnosis:

The physical therapist said, "Oh well, it's dwarfism" and she went on about his (her baby son) being a dwarf. She didn't see my reaction was to just fall backwards, because to me dwarfism or being a dwarf was the troll under the bridge in Three Billy Goats Gruff. (Albon, 1984, p. 351)

Donna Orrin holds a master's of social work and provides training for mental health professionals. She wrote of her reaction when she received the diagnosis of bipolar disorder:

At that time, I was not involved at all in the community mental health [CMH] system; I didn't even know that there was such a thing as CMH. I hardly knew anyone with mental illness. My education about mental illness consisted of the book, *One Flew Over the Cuckoo's Nest*, which was really bad news. I felt all alone, and I believed there were a lot of really bad things wrong with me. (Mackelprang & Salsgiver, 1999, p. 181)

Rod Michalko (2002) wrote about his experiences watching television and movies, paying particular attention to the characters who were blind:

In my teens, I saw blind people on television and in the movies and sometimes came across a blind character in a book. They were all portrayed as victims of a misfortune . . . . When I saw blind people in the movies or on television and even when I saw the "real" blind ones, I saw incompetence, sadness, and poverty. And I saw misfortune. Whether my perception was accurate or not is irrelevant; that's just what I saw. What I did not see when I saw these blind people is just as significant as what I did see: I did not see me. Still, when I saw them, I experienced a nebulous fear that I later understood was the fear of seeing myself. (p. 24)

PWDs are made the "other" by the media. This is now changing with the introduction of television programs (on the Learning and Discovery channels) that portray the lives and families of people with disabilities in a more realistic way. The mass media has great potential to teach and shape public attitudes about disability and the people who experience them.

Crime and Abuse of People With Disabilities

In this section, look for—
- Different thresholds of belief and intervention
- Mutual forgiving, excusing, or "not knowing"
- Structured normality of violence against PWDs

The prevalence of violence and crime against PWDs is higher than in the general population. One survey found that noninstitutionalized women with disabilities were twice as likely to experience physical violence as were nondisabled women (Albrecht, Seelman, & Bury, 2001; Chang et al., 2003; McFarlane et al., 2001). Other national surveys have also found physical and sexual abuse of people to be double the national rates for those without disabilities (National Research Council, 1996; Saxton et al., 2006) These statistics do not reveal the full extent of the violence and abuse because it has also been found that people with disabilities, especially those with severe mental retardation, experience abuse at a younger age, are abused for longer periods of time, and report larger numbers of perpetrators. Moreover, many PWDs do not report the abuse, or when they do come forward, they are not taken seriously. Michelle McCarthy (2000) summarized: "Among disabled [*sic*] people there are more girls who are abused than boys, and girls are less often believed than boys." In this study, 32% of the cases of abuse of women with mental retardation were not taken seriously enough to be reported to service managers, whereas the figure for men with mental retardation who reported abuse was 7%. McCarthy termed these discrepancies "different thresholds of belief and intervention" (p. 146).

What is abuse of people with disabilities? As with anyone else, it is physical and sexual abuse, robbery, stealing money, abuse of children and pets, and threats of physical harm. However, there are many types of abuse and violence that are specific to people with disabilities, including medication manipulation or withholding; equipment destruction; neglecting to provide needed services, such as feeding or toileting; personal care attendants who come to work drunk or high; rough handling; or deliberately dropping the PWD. A personal care attendant has a great deal of power over his or her employer—access to the individual's home, credit cards, and body. Indeed, many PWDs submit to the abuse because of fear of losing the attendant. One person said, "I just put up with it." A man told of this experience:

> He and I got into the verbal altercation . . . so he thought he put me in my place by throwing me upon the back of the chair, then letting me hang there. I'm on a ventilator . . . . I had already been off for an hour and a half, and I was getting winded . . . . [H]e just kept screaming at me, (forced me) to apologize to him . . . hardly able to breathe, and I'm supposed to apologize to some guy. He really scared the hell out of me. (Saxton et al., 2006, p. 4)

Why is abuse and violence toward PWDs so prevalent? The power differential between the abuser and the victim is very large when the victim has a disability and is therefore unable to avoid the abuse or escape. Some individuals with mental retardation may not realize that what is being done to them is abuse. The abuser enjoys the feeling of control and power over someone who is weak and often chooses victims who cannot defend themselves. Sobsey's (1994) study revealed that individuals with severe mental disabilities were raped far more often than persons with mild mental disabilities.

Lack of privacy and the visibility of the disability put PWDs at higher risk (Powers et al., 2002). For example, in hospitals, institutions, and residential schools there are no locks on the bedroom doors. These types of care settings can be very closed environments without much oversight or supervision. The large number of strangers with whom PWDs must interact on a daily basis poses more risks; for example, bus drivers know the individual's schedule and where he or she lives. Often, PWDs are subjected to multiple caregivers during the course of the day, and many times caregivers are alone with PWDs. In or out of an institution, it is easy to isolate a PWD and make it difficult to solicit help.

Institutions and other caregiving settings now require criminal background checks for all their employees and demand full reporting of any abuse, neglect, or violence. In the past, paid attendants in public institutions rarely committed an abusive act just once; most abusers had chronic, long-term patterns of abuse and violence (Zavirsek, 2002). When allegations were investigated, it was often found that many staff members knew of the abuse but chose to ignore or excuse it. If the abuse was discovered, the abuser would leave that particular institution and quickly find work at another care setting to continue his or her pattern of abuse and violence. Criminal background checks have greatly decreased abuse and violence in public care settings.

Prejudice and discrimination against PWDs assist perpetrators in avoiding guilt or remorse. Myths such as that PWDs are insensitive to pain, PWDs are less than human, and PWDs are not sexual beings may make it difficult for abusers to feel empathy for their victims. Personal care attendants have often excused their abuse by citing their low wages, the high stress and physical demands of their jobs, and the feeling that "I have a right to something." Unpaid family caregivers often feel even more license to commit abuse and violence against the individual with a disability. This has been called the "structured normality of abuse against PWDs."

In one focus group, men with disabilities saw little or no value in reporting abuse to the police, saying, "The cops won't do anything" (Saxton et al., 2006, p. 7). Often, the victim is blamed or, at minimum, not believed. PWDs are told that they need more medication, that they somehow provoked the violence, or that they fabricated the story. Accommodations are not available when PWDs do report crimes. One Deaf woman reported a rape to the police. When she asked for a sign language interpreter, the police replied that finding an interpreter would take too much time and insisted that she write everything. The woman was shaking but nevertheless attempted to write a full account of her rape.

PWDs, especially those with severe disabilities, are not accorded much respect, credibility, or prestige, and, because of this, the legal system is not always quick to prosecute. Even when prosecuted for crimes against PWDs, perpetrators received lighter and shorter sentences than perpetrators of crimes against PWODs. The low social status of PWDs is reflected in the legal system.

Second-Class Citizenship (for Which Americans Must Assume Collective Responsibility)

As a conclusion to these six chapters, a list of the ways in which PWDs experience second-class citizenship seems to be in order.

- PWODs are the standard of evaluation, beauty, and good. For example, PWDs are rarely part of norm groups used in standardized testing. Thus, PWODs are both the norm and the ideal to which individuals should strive.
- Their sense of "otherness" is perpetuated; their sense of "differentness" is exaggerated.
- PWDs are "pathologized" so that PWODs can legitimize and rationalize their treatment of them.
- They are pressured to hide or minimize their identity as PWDs.
- They have a long history of segregation, isolation, and marginalization. When PWDs are institutionalized, the institutions are administered for the convenience of PWODs. When the public does not see PWDs, their absence is not noticed.
- They are consistently undervalued and demeaned.
- They are denied their dignity.
- They must fight for their rights, while PWODs are automatically given their rights. For example, school entrance for children with disabilities was often conditional rather than automatic.
- They are given secondary, inferior facilities (schools, housing, transportation, public buildings, telecommunications).
- Other minority groups (such as racial and ethnic groups, women, and gays and lesbians) do not recognize their members with disabilities.
- When they are given accommodations (which is their right under federal law), they are expected to be grateful.
- They are underemployed and unemployed (when most express a desire to work). They are also first to be laid off in times of economic distress.
- PWODs create and reinforce unnecessary dependency, including financial disincentives for not working and physically inaccessible facilities.

- They are more likely to be poorer than the general population.
- Their abilities and capabilities are underestimated.
- They are less educated than the general population.
- The physical and psychological experience of PWDs is not acknowledged and shared (Wendell, 1997).
- They are considered to be sexually maladjusted, including neutered, incapable of or uninterested in sex, undersexed, or oversexed.
- The contributions and accomplishments of PWDs are not acknowledged. (Sharon L.'s high school counselor told her that no one would know that Sharon's art was "disabled art." Geerat Vermeij refused to participate in "Handicapped Science Fairs.")
- Their history is ignored; people, including PWDs, do not have access to this history.
- They are given charity and pity rather than their rights as citizens.
- They are less likely to be married or to be a part of a family.
- Their mobility is obstructed.
- They experience abuse and are targets of crime far more often than the general population.
- They are the targets of harassment and hate crimes.
- They are not assigned positions of authority.
- Others, without much knowledge of the disability experience, make decisions for them and, in some cases, define the disability experience.
- PWDs provide jobs for PWODs, and therefore PWDs are a source of income.
- When PWDs advocate for their rights, others become angry.
- They are at high risk for substance abuse.
- They must assume the burden of proof when they experience prejudice and discrimination. Moreover, until recently, the maintenance of this system of inequality was both legally and socially acceptable. Discrimination must be proved on a case-by-case basis.

Comparing Handicapism to Racism

In this section, look for—

- The results of handicapism and racism
- The sources of handicapism and of racism
- Methods to combat racism and handicapism
- The Civil Rights Movement and the Disability Rights Movement

Some people identify as racial/ethnic/cultural minorities and have disabilities. We also know that the combination of race and disability puts an individual at risk for prejudice and discrimination from at least two different sources. Having stated this, for the sake of this discussion, let us consider racism and handicapism as two separate concepts (although they are not). Also, we are not thinking about an individual's cultural identification, only about the prejudice and discrimination of the majority cultural group.

Many disability scholars (Hahn, 2005; Pfeiffer, 2005) consider the prejudice and discrimination directed toward PWDs to be similar to that experienced by racial/ethnic/cultural/linguistic groups. EEPC Commissioner Paul S. Miller considers the *results* of racism and handicapism to be parallel:

> In my mind, there is no difference between being asked to be sent to segregated schools because you are black or being sent to colonies because you have mental retardation and society believes that you will be better off with your own kind. There's no difference between being asked to leave a restaurant because you are black or because you use a wheelchair and you're considered a fire hazard. There's no difference between being denied the right to vote because you are black or because of an inaccessible polling place. And yes, there's no difference between being denied the right to a job or to a promotion because you are black or because you are blind or deaf. All of it's discrimination. No such thing as separate but equal. (cf. Fleischer & Zames, 2001, p. 111)

While the *results* of racism and handicapism are similar, some disability scholars consider the *sources* of racism and handicapism to be comparable, while other experts do not. Pfeiffer (2005) used Vander Zanden's (1972) five criteria of racial/ethnic minority groups and concluded that PWDs meet all five criteria. These criteria are as follows (cf. Pfeiffer, 2005, p. 27):

1. As a group and individually, the members face prejudice, discrimination, segregation, or persecution, or a combination.
2. As a group, it has a trait that is viewed negatively by the dominant group.
3. The group has a collective awareness of itself and its problems.
4. Membership is involuntary, usually from birth.
5. Members practice endogamy or intragroup marriage.

Wendell (1997) and J. Morris (1991), two feminist disability scholars, consider handicapism to have the same source as sexism and racism—the false idea of corporeal (physical) inferiority. This would be like calling a woman "male impaired," or calling a Black person "White impaired," or calling a blind person "vision impaired."

Crowe (1996) argued that there are fundamentally differing sources of racism and handicapism: "Whilst there is nothing 'inherently' negative about sexuality, sex, or skin colour, as these are neutral factors, disability can be unpleasant and difficult" (p. 58). In other words, if all the handicapism were eliminated, it would still be difficult to have a disability. So, in the last sentence of the preceding paragraph, Crowe might say that it is wrong to call a woman "male impaired" and a Black person "White impaired," but it is correct to refer to the blind person as "vision impaired." Further, it is difficult to understand the way in which Pfeiffer considers PWDs to meet Vander Zanden's last two criteria—having the characteristic from birth, and practicing intragroup marriage. These five criteria would apply to the Deaf Culture but probably no other disability group.

One undisputed parallel between racism and handicapism concerns the ways in which both are combated. The Disability Rights Movement learned from the Civil Rights Movement of African Americans. Judith Heumann, who headed the sit-in of the HEW building in San Francisco, stated: "We staged demonstrations. We learned from African Americans. I had to give Joe Califano [HEW Secretary] something he could not handle. Put people with disabilities in his office. That would make him feel uncomfortable . . . . We took the power back by a sit-in. We were in there for almost a month" (National Public Radio, Disability History Project, Overdue Revolution, 1988). It should be noted that the Black Panthers assisted the disability activists in this sit-in.

By viewing disability rights as a civil rights issue, monetary concerns could not be an issue. Civil rights must be provided to Americans regardless of the cost involved. Of course, considerations such as the most cost-effective way to implement these civil rights laws are justifiable. Nonetheless, budgetary constraints cannot interfere with the justice of civil rights. Disability and people with disabilities were no longer considered to be only a medical/health concern. People with disabilities are American citizens.

Court cases, sit-ins, and demonstrations were methods that African Americans had used successfully, and various disability organizations and coalitions used these methods. Much of the language for disability rights law was taken directly from the Civil Rights Act of 1964, including the American with Disabilities Act (ADA) and Sections 504, 505, 506, 507, and 508 of the 1973 Rehabilitation Act, which mandated accommodations and accessibility for PWDs. In 1978, Frank Bowe, who was director of the American Coalition of Citizens with Disabilities wrote:

Why did it [the signing of the Section 504 regulations] happen? For a long time I had trouble answering that question because so many different factors and influences seemed to have combined to make it happen. Then, sometime later in 1977, I happened to be reading a book about the black civil rights movement, and I found the answer to that question . . . . This advisor [to Martin Luther King] said, 'People think that revolutions begin with injustices. They don't. A revolution begins with hope.' (cf. Fleischer & Zames, 2001, p. 55)

In-Class Videos

- View the 13-minute, open-captioned video "Disabled Women: Visions and Voices." The producers describe this video: "Women from around the world passionately share their concerns and success! Their stories demonstrate the diversity and commonality of women's issues." This video comes with a 35-page discussion guide. Available from Program Development Resource (P.O. Box 2038, Syracuse, NY 13220, 800-543-2119, fax 315-452-0710).

- View the 56-minute video "Look Who's Laughing." The producers describe this video as a "funny and compelling documentary about the lives, experiences, and humor of six working comedians who have various types of disabilities. Shot at comedy clubs across the country, 'Look Who's Laughing' spotlights some of the most talented and truly funny comics working today." Look for examples of stereotyping, role entrapment, lowered expectations, lack of privacy, hypervisibility, infantilization, objectification, marginality, and lack of equal social status relationships. Available from Program Development Resource.

- View the 31-minute video "CASA: The Community Attendant Services Act." The producers state: "Mike Auberger, Director of Denver-based Atlantis Community and one of the key leaders of American Disabled for Attendant Programs Today (ADAPT), provides insights into ADAPT which has been labeled 'the radical arm of the disability movement,' the CASA bill, and the advocacy movement in the U.S. today." Available from Program Development Resource.

- View the 60-minute video "Redesigning the Human Machine." The producers describe this video: "This program explores the use of technological advances. Virtual reality is being used as a learning tool for children with disabilities, as assistive technology for Parkinson's disease patients, and as a form of empowerment for people with disabilities. The program also examines the potential use of robotics to assist people with limited mobility and cochlear implants for the hearing impaired." Available from Program Development Resource.

- View the 57-minute video "If I Can't Do It . . ." by Walter Brock. This is a presentation of the Independent Television Service, with funding provided by the Corporation for Public Broadcasting. It was shown on the PBS series *P.O.V.* The producers describe this video: "Born with cerebral palsy in an isolated Kentucky cabin,

Arthur Campbell spent his first thirty-eight years sheltered by his overprotective parents at home. 'I watched a lot of television,' he says, 'and I never saw a program about anyone whose life is like mine.' Today, he lives independently and is an advocate and activist for disability rights. Witty, stubborn, and often exasperating, Campbell is neither a hero nor a saint, but a complex individual working to fulfill his dreams by seizing control of his own existence and living on his own terms." Available from Fanlight Productions (4196 Washington Street, Boston, MA 02131, 800-937-4113, www.fanlight.com).

- View the 16-minute video "Shaking Off Stereotypes." The producers state: "'Shaking Off Stereotypes' will help people with disabilities and others recognize that we are all unique individuals with something to contribute. It is an entertaining story about a woman wheelchair user who discovers her own self-worth in spite of the everyday stereotypical situations she encounters." Available from Program Development Resource.

- View the 57-minute video "When Billy Broke His Head . . . And Other Tales of Wonder" produced by Fanlight Productions. The producers describe this video: "Billy Golfus, an award-winning journalist, became brain-injured in a motor scooter accident ten years ago. But this video, as he says, 'ain't exactly your inspirational cripple story.' In this irreverent, first-person road movie, he meets disabled people [sic] around the country, and witnesses the strength and anger that is forging a new civil rights movement for disabled Americans." Order No. HN-136.

- View the 56-minute DVD "Unforgotten: 25 Years After Willowbrook" produced by Program Development Associates. The producers describe this DVD: "Critically acclaimed, award winning documentary about the infamous Willowbrook State School for the developmentally disabled. Using a stolen key, Geraldo Rivera entered Willowbrook with a film crew in 1972, and his historic exposé of its horrific conditions shocked all of America and led to widespread reform in the treatment of people with disabilities. Narrated by Danny Aiello." Resource #UNFV299E.

Learning Activities

Choose one of the 19 bulleted attitudes and/or behaviors listed at the beginning of this chapter and write a paper that (1) describes the behavior or attitude and (2) explains their effects and results.

Writing Experiences

Using any of the 19 bullet experiences listed at the beginning of this chapter, write a paper describing and giving examples of this experience.

References

Albon, J. (1984). *Little People of America: The social dimensions of dwarfism.* New York: Praeger.

Albrecht, G. L., Seelman, K. D., & Bury, M. (Eds.). (2001). *Handbook of disability studies.* Thousand Oaks, CA: Sage.

Allport, G. W. (1954). *The nature of prejudice.* Reading, MA: Addison-Wesley.

Allport, G. W. (1958). *The nature of prejudice* (2nd ed.). Garden City, NY: Doubleday Anchor.

Allport, G. W. (1986). *The nature of prejudice* (25th anniversary ed.). Reading, MA: Addison-Wesley.

Anderson, G. R. (1987). Paternalism. In G. R. Anderson & V. A. Glesnes-Anderson (Eds.), *Health care ethics: A guide for decision makers* (pp. 177–191). Rockville, MD: Aspen.

Angier, N. (2001, May 27). Before the miracle. *New York Times Book Review*, pp. 12–13.

Asch, A., & Fine, M. (1997). Nurturance, sexuality, and women with disabilities: The example of women and literature. In L. J. Davis (Ed.), *The disability studies reader* (pp. 241–259). New York: Routledge.

Barnartt, S., Schriner, K., & Scotch, R. (2001). Advocacy and political action. In G. L. Albrecht, K. D. Seelman, & M. Bury (Eds.), *Handbook of disability studies* (pp. 430–449). Thousand Oaks, CA: Sage.

Baynton, D. (1997). A silent exile on this earth: The metaphorical construction of deafness in the nineteenth century. In L. J. Davis (Ed.), *The disability studies reader* (pp. 128–150). New York: Routledge.

Bogardus, E. S. (1928). *Immigration and race attitudes.* Lexington, MA: D. C. Heath.

Bogdan, R. (1988). *Freak show: Presenting human oddities for amusement and profit.* Chicago: University of Chicago.

Bogdan, R., & Taylor, S. J. (1987, Fall). Toward a sociology of acceptance: The other side of the study of deviance. *Social Policy*, pp. 34–39.

Bogdan, R., & Taylor, S. J. (1989). Relationships with severely disabled people: The social construction of humanness. *Social Problems, 36*(1).

Bok, S. (1979). *Lying: Moral choice in public and private life.* New York: Vintage.

Bragg, B. (1989). *Lessons in laughter: The autobiography of a Deaf actor. As signed to Eugene Bergman.* Washington, DC: Gallaudet University.

Buzzer, A. (1989). *Flying without wings: Personal reflections on being disabled.* New York: Doubleday.

Byrd, E. K. (1989). A study of specific characteristics of characters with disability in film. *Journal of Applied Rehabilitation Counseling, 20,* 43–45.

Byrd, E. K., & Elliott, T. R. (1985). Feature film and disability: A descriptive study. *Rehabilitation Psychology, 30,* 47–51.

Byrd, E. K., & Elliott, T. R. (1988). Disability in full-length films: Frequency and quality of films over an 11 year span. *International Journal of Rehabilitation Research, 11,* 143–148.

Cate, I. M. P., & Loots, G. M. P. (2000). Experiences of siblings of children with physical disabilities: An empirical investigation. *Disability and Rehabilitation, 22,* 399–408.

Chang, J. C., Martin, S. L., Moracco, K. E., Dulli, L., Scandlin, D., Loucks-Sorrel, M. B., et al. (2003). Helping women with disabilities and domestic violence: Strategies, limitations, and challenges of domestic violence programs and services. *Journal of Women's Health, 12,* 699–708.

Chesler, M. A., & Chesney, B. K. (1988). Self-help groups: Empowerment attitudes and behaviors of disabled and chronically ill persons. In H. E. Yuker (Ed.) *Attitudes toward individuals with disabilities* (pp. 230–244). New York: Springer.

Chubon, R. A., & Moore, C. T. (1982). The cocoon syndrome: A coping mechanism of spinal cord injured persons. *Rehabilitation Psychology, 27,* 87–96.

Cohen, R. (2004). *Blindsided: Living a life above illness—A reluctant memoir.* New York: Harper Collins.

Crespo, A. (1993). Alice Crespo, court interpreter. In H. Rousso (Ed.). *Disabled, female, and proud!* (pp. 95–104). Westport, CT: Bergin & Garvey.

Crewe, N. M., & Zola, I. K. (1983). *Independent living for physically disabled people.* San Francisco: Jossey-Bass.

Crowe, L. (1996). Including all our lives: Renewing the social model of disability. In C. Barnes & G. Mercer (Eds.), *Exploring the divide: Illness and disability.* Leeds, UK: Leeds Disability Press.

Darke, E. (1993). The Elephant Man: An analysis from a disabled perspective. *Disability and Society, 9,* 327–343.

Davis, L. J. (Ed.). (1997). *The disability studies reader.* New York: Routledge.

Deegan, P. E. (1992). The independent living movement and people with psychiatric disabilities: Taking back control over our own lives. *Psychosocial Rehabilitation Journal, 15*(3), 3–19.

DeLoach, C. P. (1994). Attitudes toward disability: Impact on sexual development and forging of intimate relationships. *Journal of Applied Rehabilitation Counseling, 25,* 18–25.

DeLoach, C., & Greer, B. G. (1981). *Adjustment to severe physical disability: A metamorphosis.* New York: McGraw-Hill.

Finger, A. (1991). *Past due: A story of disability, pregnancy, and birth.* Seattle, WA: Seal Press.

Fisher, B., & Galler, R. (1988). Friendship and fairness: How disability affects friendship between women. In M. Fine & A. Asch (Eds.), *Women with disabilities: Essays in psychology, culture, and politics* (pp. 172–194). Philadelphia: Temple University.

Fleischer, D. Z., & Zames, F. (2001). *The disability rights movement: From charity to confrontation.* Philadelphia: Temple University.

Fletcher, J. F. (1979). *Humanhood: Essays in biomedical ethics.* Buffalo, NY: Prometheus.

Fries, K. (Ed.). (1997). *Staring back: The disability experience from the inside out.* New York: Plume.

Frohock, F. M. (1986). *Special care: Medical decisions at the beginning of life.* Chicago: University of Chicago Press.

Gallagher, H. (1985). *FDR's splendid deception.* New York: Dodd, Mead.

Gill, C. J. (2001). Divided understandings: The social experience of disability. In G. L. Albrecht, K. D. Seelman, & M. Bury (Eds.), *The handbook of disability studies* (pp. 351–373). Thousand Oaks, CA: Sage.

Gist, N. R., & Dworkin, A. G. (1972). *The blending of the races: Marginality and identity in a world perspective.* New York: Wiley Interscience.

Goffman, E. (1963). *Stigma: Notes on the management of spoiled identity.* Englewood Cliffs, NJ: Prentice-Hall.

Goffman, E. (1997). Selection from Stigma. In L. J. Davis (Ed.), *The disability studies reader* (pp. 203–215). New York: Routledge.

Gouvier, W. D., Coon, R. C., Todd, M. E., & Fuller, K. H. (1994). Verbal interactions with individuals presenting with and without physical disability. *Rehabilitation Psychology, 39,* 263–268.

Groce, N. E. (1985). *Everybody here spoke sign language: Hereditary deafness on Martha's Vineyard.* Cambridge, MA: Harvard University Press.

Hahn, H. (1988a). Can disability be beautiful? *Social Policy, 18*, 26–32.

Hahn, H. (1988b). The politics of physical differences: Disability and discrimination. *Journal of Social Issues, 44*, 39–47.

Hahn, H. (1997). Advertising the acceptably employable image: Disability and capitalism. In L. J. Davis (Ed.), *The disability studies reader* (pp. 172–186). New York: Routledge.

Hahn, H. (2005). Academic debates and political advocacy: The U.S. disability movement. In G. E. May & M. B. Raske (Eds.), *Ending disability discrimination: Strategies for social workers* (pp. 1–24). Boston: Pearson.

Hannaford, S. (1985). *Living outside inside: A disabled woman's experience—Towards a social and political perspective.* Berkeley, CA: Canterbury Press.

Harris, R. W. (1992). Musings from 20 years of hard-earned experience. *Rehabilitation Education, 6*, 207–211.

Hermann, D. (1998). *Helen Keller: A life.* New York: Alfred A. Knopf.

Hevey, D. (1997). The enfreakment of photography. In L. J. Davis (Ed.), *The disability studies reader* (pp. 332–347). New York: Routledge.

Higgins, P. C. (1980). *Outsiders in a hearing world: A sociology of deafness.* Newbury Park, CA: Sage.

Higgins, P. C. (1992). *Making disability: Exploring the social transformation of human variation.* Springfield, IL: Charles C .Thomas.

Holcomb, L. P. (1990). Disabled women: A new issue in education. In M. Nagler (Ed.), *Perspectives on disability* (pp. 381–388). Palo Alto, CA: Health Markets Research.

Imrie, R. (1996). *Disability and the city: International perspectives.* New York: St. Martin's Press.

Johnson, H. M. (2003, February 16). Should I have been killed at birth? A case for my life. *The New York Times Magazine*, pp. 50–55.

Kisor, H. (1990). *What's that pig outdoors? A memoir of deafness.* New York: Hill and Wang.

Klobas, L. (1988). *Disability drama in television and film.* Jefferson, NC: McFarlan.

Kriegel, L. (1987). The cripple in literature. In A. Gartner & T. Joe (Eds.), *Images of the disabled, disabling images.* New York: Praeger.

Kriegel, L. (1991). *Falling into life.* San Francisco: North Point.

Lane, H., Hoffmeister, R., & Bahan, B. (1996). *A journey into the deaf-world.* San Diego, CA: Dawn Sign Press.

Lee, A. (1948). *My soul more bent.* Minneapolis, MN: Augsburg College.

Leete, E. (1991). The stigmatized patient. In P. J. Fink & A. Tasman (Eds.). *Stigma and mental illness* (pp. 17–25). Washington, DC: American Psychiatric Association Press.

Lefley, H. P. (1991). The stigmatized family. In P. J. Fink & A. Tasman (Eds.), *Stigma and mental illness* (pp. 127–138). Washington, DC: American Psychiatric Association Press.

Lesh, K., & Marshall, C. (1984). Rehabilitation: Focus on women with disabilities. *Journal of Applied Rehabilitation Counseling, 15*, 18–21.

Livneh, H. (1980). Disability and monstrosity: Further comments. *Rehabilitation Literature, 41*, 280–283.

Longmore, P. K. (1985). Screening stereotypes: Images of disabled people. *Social Policy, 16*, 31–37.

Longmore, P. K. (2003). *Why I burned my book and other essays on disability.* Philadelphia: Temple University.

Ludwig, E. G., & Adams, S. D. (1968). Patient cooperation in a rehabilitation center: Assumption of the client role. *Journal of Health and Social Behavior, 9*, 328–336.

Mackelprang, R., & Salsgiver, R. (1999). *Disability: A diversity model approach in human service practice.* Pacific Grove, CA: Brooks/Cole.

Marks, D. (1999). *Disability: Controversial debates and psychosocial perspectives.* London: Routledge.

Martin, L. (2000). *From our house: A memoir.* New York: Dutton.

McBrien, M. (1997). "Maybe you'd rather die than be me." *DIA Activist, January,* 3.

McCarthy, M. (1999). Consent, abuse, and choices: Women with intellectual disabilities and sexuality. In R. Traustadottir & K. Johnson (Eds.), *Women with intellectual disabilities: Finding a place in the world.* London/Philadelphia: Jessica Kingsley Publishers.

McFarlane, J., Hughes, R. B., Nosek, M. A., Groff, J. Y., Swedlend, N., & Mullen, P. D. (2001). Abuse Assessment Screen-Disability (AAS-D): Measuring frequency, type, and perpetrator of abuse toward women with physical disabilities. *Journal of Women's Health & Gender-Based Medicine, 10,* 861–866.

Mee, C. L. (1999). *A nearly normal life.* Boston: Little, Brown.

Michalko, R. (2002). *The difference disability makes.* Philadelphia: Temple University.

Miller, S., & Morgan, M. (1980). Marriage matters: For people with disabilities, too. *Sexuality and Disability, 3,* 203–211.

Mims, B. (1998, January 24). Mentally disabled worker files $10M suit charging Smith's co-workers ridiculed him. *Salt Lake Tribute,* pp. B1, B5.

Morris, J. (1991). *Pride against prejudice: Transforming attitudes to disability.* Philadelphia: New Society.

Murphy, R. (1980). *The body silent.* New York: W. W. Norton.

Murphy, R. F., Scheer, J., Murphy, Y., & Mack, R. (1988). Physical disability and social liminality: A study in the rituals of adversity. *Social Science and Medicine, 26,* 235–242.

National Public Radio. (1998, May). Disability History Project. "The Overdue Revolution."

National Research Council. (1996). *Understanding violence against women.* Washington, DC: National Academy Press.

Navarro, M. (2007, May 17). Clearly, frankly, unabashedly disabled. *New York Times.*

Nelson, J. L., & Berens, B. S. (1997). Spoken daggers, deaf ears, and silent mouths: Fantasies of deafness in early modern England. In L. J. David (Ed.). *Disability studies reader* (pp. 52–74). New York: Routledge.

Norden, M. F. (1994). *The cinema of isolation: A history of disabilities in the movies.* New Brunswick, NJ: Rutgers University.

Nordqvist, I. (1980). Sexual counseling for disabled persons. *Sexuality and Disability, 3,* 193–198.

Olkin, R. (1999). *What psychotherapists should know about disability.* New York: Guilford.

Olkin, R., & Howson, L. J. (1994). Attitudes toward and images of physical disability. *Social Behavior and Psychology, 9,* 81–96.

Panzarino, C. (1993). Connie Panzarino: Art therapist. In H. Rousso (Ed.), *Disabled, female, and proud!* (pp. 107–118). Westport, CT: Bergin & Garvey.

Pelka, F. (1997). *The ABC-CLIO companion to the disability rights movement.* Santa Barbara, CA: ABC-CLIO.

Perduta-Fulginiti, P. S. (1996). Impact of bowel and bladder dysfunction on sexuality and self esteem. In D. M. Krotoski, M. A. Nosek, & M. A. Turk (Eds.), *Women with physical disabilities: Achieving and maintaining health and well-being* (pp. 287–298). Baltimore: Brookes.

Petty, D. (1979). What is it like to be deaf-blind? *Consumers Contemporary, 1,* 10–11.

Pfeiffer, D. (2005). The conceptualization of disability. In G. E. May & M. B. Raske (Eds.), *Ending disability discrimination: Strategies for social workers* (pp. 25–44). Boston: Pearson.

Phillips, M. J. (1991). "Try harder": The experience of disability and the dilemma of normalization. In P. M. Ferguson, D. L. Ferguson, & S. J. Taylor (Eds.), *Interpreting disability: A qualitative reader* (pp. 213–227). New York: Columbia University Teachers College Press.

Poole, W. C., Jr. (1927). Social distance and personal distance. *Journal of Applied Sociology, 11*, 114–120.

Powers, L. E., Curry, M. A., Oschwalk, M., Maley, S., Saxton, M., & Eckels, K. (2002). Barriers and strategies in addressing abuse: Survey of disabled women's experiences. *Journal of Rehabilitation, 68*, 4–13.

Purtilo, R. B. (1991). Ethical issues in teamwork: The context of rehabilitation. In R. P. Marinelli & A. E. Dell Orto (Eds.), *The psychological and social impact of disability* (3rd ed., pp. 18–31). New York: Springer.

Putnam, M., Greenen, S., Powers, L., Saxton, M., Finney, S., & Dautel, P. (2003). Health and wellness: People with disabilities discuss barriers and facilitators to well being. *Journal of Rehabilitation, 69*, 37–45.

Ree, J. (1999). *I see a voice: A philosophical history of language, deafness, and the senses.* New York: Harper Collins.

Rousso, H. (1981). Disabled people are sexual, too. *The Exceptional Parent, 11*, 21–25.

Rousso, H. (1993). *Disabled, female, and proud!* Westport, CT: Bergin & Garvey.

Safran, S. P. (1998). The first century of disability portrayal in film: An analysis of the literature. *The Journal of Special Education, 31*, 467–479.

Saxton, M., Curry, M. A., McNeff, E., Limont, M., Powers, L., & Benson, J. (2006). We're all little John Waynes: A study of disabled men's experience of abuse by personal assistants. *Journal of Rehabilitation, 72*, 3–13.

Scheer, M. J. (1993). *Living in the state of stuck: How technology impacts the lives of people with disabilities.* Cambridge, MA: Brookline.

Scott, R. (1969). *The making of blind men: A study of adult socialization.* New York: Russell Sage Foundation.

Shell, M. (2005). *Polio and its aftermath: The paralysis of culture.* Cambridge, MA: Harvard University.

Shontz, F. (1977). Physical disability and personality: Theory and recent research. In J. Stubbins (Ed.), *Social and psychological aspects of disability: A handbook for practitioners* (pp. 333–353). Baltimore: University Park Press.

Simpson, G. E., & Yinger, J. M. (1985). *Racial and cultural minorities: An analysis of prejudice and discrimination* (5th ed.). New York: Plenum.

Sinick, D. (1969). Training, job placement, and follow-up. In D. Malikin & H. Rusalem (Eds.). *Vocational rehabilitation of the disabled: An overview* (pp. 129–153). New York: New York University Press.

Smith, J. K., & Plimpton, G. (1993). *Chronicles of courage: Very special artists.* New York: Random House.

Sobsey, D. (1994). *Violence and abuse in the lives of people with disabilities: The end of silent acceptance.* Baltimore: Brookes.

Stefan, S. P. (1998). The first century of disability portrayal in film: An analysis of the literature. *The Journal of Special Education, 31*, 467–479.

Stonequist, E. V. (1937). *The marginal man: A study in personality and culture conflict.* New York: Charles Scribners.

Strohmer, D. C., Leierer, S. J., Cochran, N. A., & Arokiasamy, C. V. (1996). The importance of counselor disability status. *Rehabilitation Counseling Bulletin, 40*, 96–115.

Suter, S. (1993, August 16). *Women with disabilities: How to become a boat rocker in life.* Paper presented at the Ethics in Rehabilitation Conference, New Zealand Rehabilitation Organization, Dunedin.

Thomson, R. G. (1996). *Freakery: Cultural spectacles of the extraordinary body.* New York: New York University.

Thomson, R. G. (1997). Integrating disability studies into the existing curriculum: The example of "women and literature" at Howard University. In L. J. Davis (Ed.), *The disability studies reader* (pp. 296–311). New York: Routledge.

Toombs, S. K. (1995). Sufficient unto the day: A life with multiple sclerosis. In S. K. Toombs, D. Barnard, & R. A. Carson (Eds.), *Chronic illness: From experience to policy* (pp. 2–23). Bloomington: University of Indiana

Vander Zanden, J. (1972). *American minority relations* (3rd ed.) New York: Ronald Press.

Walker, L. A. (1986). *A loss for words: The story of deafness in a family.* New York: Harper.

Warren-Leubecker, A., & Bohannon, J. N. (1989). Pragmatics: Language in social contexts. In J. Berko-Gleason (Ed.), *The development of language* (pp. 327–368). Columbus, OH: Merrill.

Weihenmayer, E. (2001). *Touch the top of the world: A blind man's journey to climb farther than the eye can see.* New York: Dutton.

Wendell, S. (1997). Toward a feminist theory of disability. In L. J. Davis (Ed.), *The disability studies reader* (pp. 260–278). New York: Routledge.

Wilson, D. J. (1990). *Living with polio: The epidemic and its survivors.* Chicago: University of Chicago.

Winzer, M. A. (1993). Education, urbanization, and the Deaf community: A case study of Toronto, 1870–1900. In J. V. Van Cleve (Ed.), *Deaf history unveiled: Interpretations of the new scholarship* (pp. 127–145). Washington, DC: Gallaudet University.

Wolfensberger, W. (1972). *The principle of normalization in human services.* Toronto, Canada: National Institute on Mental Retardation.

Wolfensberger, W. (1981). The extermination of handicapped people in World War II Germany. *Mental Retardation, Vol. 1–7.*

Wolfensberger, W., & Tullman, S. (1982). A brief outline of the principle of normalization. *Rehabilitation Psychology, 27*(3), 131–145.

Wright, B. A. (1960). *Physical disability: A psychological approach.* New York: Harper & Row.

Wright, B. A. (1983). *Physical disability: A psychosocial approach* (2nd ed.). New York: Harper & Row.

Wright, D. (1994). *Deafness: An autobiography.* New York: Harper Perennial.

Young, I. (1990). *Justice and the politics of difference.* Princeton, NJ: Princeton University.

Yuker, H. E. (Ed.). (1988). *Attitudes toward persons with disabilities.* New York: Springer.

Zavirsek, D. (2002). Pictures and silences: Memories of sexual abuse of disabled people. *Journal of Social Welfare, 11*, 270–285.

Zola, I. K. (1972). Medicine as an institution of social control. *Sociological Review, 20*, 487–504.

The Individual and Disability

The Individual's Response to Disability

- Why would many PWDs choose not to eliminate their disability if they could?
- Is there a real difference between the terms "acceptance of disability" and "response to disability"?
- How does an individual's ethnic/racial/cultural/linguistic identification influence his or her response to a disability?
- When discussing an individual's response to a disability, why is it important to consider the individual's environment?
- Of the three types of response to disability—affective, cognitive, and behavioral—which is the most difficult to measure?
- Why is the PWD's subjective judgment of his or her disability often more important than the objective medical diagnosis?
- What are the four components of Beatrice Wright's "cognitive restructuring" model?
- What is the difference between coping strategies and defense mechanisms?
- What is a somatization disorder?
- What are some possible secondary gains of a disability?
- What is psychogenic pain? Why is it necessary to establish a temporal relationship between environmental stimuli and onset of pain?
- Why would anyone malinger?

- What are possible problems in measuring adjustment to disability?
- What are the advantages of the stage theory of adaptation/ response?
- What are the three types of denial?
- Why is denial often considered to be therapeutic?
- How is transcendence defined?
- Why is transcendence in conflict with the Biomedical Model of disability?
- What are some cautions in implementing the stage theory?

The three major divisions of this book are (1) the definition of disability, (2) society and disability, and (3) the individual and disability. These convenient, easily understood demarcations are a starting point to learning about the disability. However, these divisions are not actually experienced by anyone, nor do they represent reality. For instance, it is important to learn about the various definitions of disability—what a disability is and what a disability is not. So far we have learned that there are four definitions of disability: clinical, legal, cultural, and personal. This final section of the book will discuss the personal definitions of disability. However, definitions of disability are closely tied to society's perception of disability and, furthermore, the individual's experience with a disability involves both the definition of disability and society's response to his or her disability (Antonak & Livneh, 1991; DeLoach & Greer, 1981; Dembo, Leviton, & Wright, 1956; Wright, 1991). These interrelationships are complex and idiosyncratic (specific to each individual) (Heinemann & Shontz, 1984; Roessler & Bolton, 1978). No one with a disability thinks of his or her disability in these three divisions; indeed, to the individual there can be no neat, three-division paradigm to the disability experience. Nonetheless, it does make sense to discuss some basic issues to gain a preliminary understanding but with the knowledge that these basic issues are only a starting point and that some aspects of the disability experience apply only to specific individuals. Disability happens to one person at a time.

Perhaps the title of this chapter should be "The Individual's Response to *Acquired* Disability" because an individual with a congenital disability, or a disability acquired during infancy, has incorporated the disability into his or her identity. Individuals with congenital disabilities have no memory of not having the disability. Nonetheless, there are adjustment demands for these individuals—not to a new identity, but to stigma recognition. Very often, children with disabilities do not know until they enter school that their disabilities are perceived as inferiority and deviance. These children understand that (1) they have a disability and (2) the disability requires management, treatment, and/or accommodations, but they may not have experienced prejudice and discrimination. Therefore, a child with a disability must learn to adjust to and negotiate a prejudiced and discriminating environment.

For these reasons, this section of the book will use many first-person narratives (individuals telling us what they have experienced and learned). Can the disability experience be understood by someone who has not lived it? Probably not, but PWODs can begin to learn about the disability. However, most PWDs have not written about their experiences and, thus, their experiences with disability are unrecorded (Couser, 1997; Frank, 1991, 1995; Hawkins, 1993). Some of these narratives have found publishers because the authors are seen as "super crips," people with extraordinary resources or celebrity. Indeed, most of those who have written about disability experience have been White, upper-class, highly educated individuals (Ballin, 1930; Beisser, 1989; Brookes, 1995; Callahan, 1989; Cohen, 1994; Hull, 1991; Keller, 1990; Kisor, 1990; Kriegel, 1991; Murphy, 1987; Padden & Humphries, 1988; Price, 1994; Schaller, 1991; Sienkiewicz-Mercer & Kaplan, 1989; Spradley & Spradley, 1985; Zola, 1982). Also, on the one hand, first-person accounts carry the weight of someone who has lived the experience, giving us an immediate and direct look at disability (Kleinman, 1988; Mairs, 1997). On the other hand, every disability account must, of necessity, speak about individual circumstances. Nonetheless, there are some universal aspects of the disability experience, and furthermore, we can learn from the idiosyncratic aspects of these narratives (see Appendix 7–A for a listing of published narratives).

View From the Outside
Versus Life on the Inside

In this section, look for—

- How PWODs assume that all PWDs would eliminate their disability if they could

- How most PWDs

    —Consider their disability to be an integral part of their identity

    —Are proud of their mastery of the disability

    —Consider their disability to have positive options

- How PWODs assume that the onset/acquisition/diagnosis of every disability is distressful to the individual

Myths Held by PWODs

Outsiders (meaning those who do not have a disability) often think they understand how PWDs feel about their disability. Naturally, such conceptions are based on an outsider's point of view; it is difficult to imagine the life of someone else. Moreover, rarely do PWODs question their own assumptions. (We learned in Part II that most PWODs sensationalize and misunderstand disability, thinking that all disabilities are an unending source of tragedy and grief for the individual.) One misconception, widely and strongly held, is that if the PWD were offered a way to eliminate the disability, he or she would enthusiastically accept it. Rarely do PWODs consider the possibility that the disability is an integral part of the PWD's self-identity or that the PWD might be proud of the mastery and control that he or she has gained over the disability. Many of the first-person accounts of disability reveal that the individual would *not* choose to eliminate the disability (Davis, 1995). The most straightforward example is that of cochlear implants for individuals who are deaf. Cochlear implants are comprised of electrodes that are surgically placed in the inner ear to stimulate the nerve cells along a pathway to the auditory region of the brain. Designed to improve the individual's speech perception and oral communication, the cochlear implant has not been unanimously accepted by the Deaf community. First, it should be stated that not all cochlear implants are successful. But, even more important, the Deaf Culture feels that, as one scholar wrote, "in America, the recognition of the status of the Deaf community, fueled by the civil rights movement, is leading to greater acceptance of people who are deaf. The interest of the child who is deaf and his [*sic*] parents may best be served by accepting that he is Deaf, with an elaborate culture and linguistic heritage that can enrich his parents' life as well as his own. We should heed the advice of the teenager who was deaf who, when reprimanded by her mother for not wearing the processor of her cochlear prosthesis, hurled back bitterly: 'I'm deaf. Let me be deaf'" (Lane, 1992, p. 238).

In learning about how the individual experiences his or her disability, it seems appropriate to begin by making the point that most PWDs consider their disability to be an integral part of their identity—not their sole identity, or even the most important part of the identity, but an important part (Higgins, 1980). It therefore follows that PWDs would not eliminate the disability if they could. Cochlear implants, very much favored by people who are not deaf, including parents of children who are deaf and physicians, are sometimes refused by the Deaf.

Other first-person accounts describe PWDs who think of their disability part of their identity and have no wish to eliminate it. In Rousso's book led, *Female, and Proud!* (1993), Rousso interviews Barbara Cole-Appel, nan paralyzed in an automobile accident. Cole-Appel told of a friend isked her if she would rather win a $30 million lottery or regain the use r legs. (Neither winning the lottery nor regaining the use of her legs ctually possible.) Cole-Appel responded, "I decided that I would rather have the $30 million because losing the use of my legs has not inhibited me other than walking, as far as I'm concerned. Not being able to walk is something I have learned to live with. It's no longer something that I have to be able to do in order to feel complete" (p. 41).

In the video "Irving King Jordan," the interviewer asks Dr. Jordan, President of Gallaudet College, twice about the disadvantages of being deaf. Dr. Jordan replied, "If there are 1,000 differences (between hearing and being deaf), 998 are good opportunities and 2 are bad." In the video "Don't Go to Your Room," a woman states, "I believe that I've had wonderful experiences because of my disability." Another woman states, "I present my disability as a strength."

Disability also involves impairment, sometimes the loss of valued activities, and sometimes pain; it often makes time demands on the individual and most often includes the prejudice and discrimination of the larger society. Nonetheless, the onset/acquisition/diagnosis of a disability is not automatically distressing to everyone. Shontz (1991) summarized:

> Though many efforts have been made to correlate disability with overall personality maladjustment, no systematic evidence has yet been published to show that reactions involving psychiatric disturbance occur any more frequently with a truly representative sample of people with disabilities than within the general population . . . . The personality resources of an individual may be strengthened, not weakened, when the stresses that disability imposes are successfully managed. (p. 108)

We have seen in Part II that the tendency of PWODs to view all disability as devastating and overwhelming tragedy has resulted in abortion, murder, and institutionalization of PWDs.

Acceptance of Disability or Response to Disability

In this section, look for—

- Four reasons why "response" to disability is now the preferred term

  1. It is not the disability itself, but the meaning the individual ascribes to it

  2. There are many other types of acceptance, not simply psychological acceptance

(continued)

3. The word "response" does not pathologize the disability experience

4. The individual copes with and responds to a disability throughout his or her life

Disability scholars have used the terms *adjustment, adaptation,* or *acceptance* of disability to describe the end result of coping with a disability and successfully integrating the disability into the individual's life and identity (Lindemann, 1981; Linkowski & Dunn, 1974; Livneh, 1986a, 1986b; Moos, 1984). In the early stages of scholarship, adjustment to disability was conceptualized as a series of stages through which the individual passed, ending with acceptance of the disability. The current model of coping with a disability uses the term *the individual's response to disability* (Livneh & Antonak, 1997). The word *response* is more accurate because it communicates more fully that (1) it is not disability itself, but the meaning that the individual ascribes to the disability that will determine the response to the disability; (2) there are many types of responses or adjustments to disability in addition to the psychological adjustment, including occupational and social adjustment or response; (3) the words *adjustment, adaptation,* and *acceptance* pathologize the experience of a disability, meaning a disability is automatically assumed to be an undesirable state (we would not say that a person adjusts to being a woman or a person of color); and (4) the individual copes with disability and makes adjustments throughout his or her lifetime, including those with stable disabilities, and therefore *acceptance* is not a one-time event (Kendall & Buys, 1998; Schlossberg, 1981; Wortman & Silver, 1989). In this chapter, the expressions "response/reaction" and "adaptation/acceptance/adjustment" will be used but with the awareness that "response/reaction" is the more accurate term.

In this section, we shall discuss the individual's response to disability in terms of the American culture. At times, references will be made to other cultures because an individual's cultural/linguistic/ethnic identity affects the way in which the individual views and treats the disability. Further, behavioral manifestations of responding to a disability can only be interpreted with knowledge of the individual's cultural identity. What is considered to be "acceptance of disability" in one culture may not apply in another culture. Moreover, we have learned that disability itself is culturally defined her, symptom recognition is also culturally and socially deter or example, someone with a large family to support them and who a physically demanding job may not recognize his or her chronic n as a disability. Obviously, in this case, the individual's economic situation does not allow him or her to recognize (much less respond to) subjective discomfort. Also, the individual's perception of etiology is shaped by his or her cultural identification. For example, someone from a culture that is deterministic and fatalistic may feel that his or her automobile accident was "meant to happen" and not the result of anything that individual did or did not do. In contrast, an individual who identifies with the American culture may view the same automobile accident as his or her fault and thus engage in self-blame (Bordieri, 1993).

Carolyn Vash (1981), another disability scholar, introduced the concept of "transcendence," which is a step beyond acceptance or adjustment to disability. Transcendence of a disability is a combination of refusing to idealize normality (lack of disability), adopting a spiritual/philosophical orientation to the disability, and "embracing the experience" (p. 135). Inherent in the concept of transcendence are the questions, "What can I learn from this disability? and "What positive options are available?" The disability is seen as a catalyst for the individual to grow and develop, with the individual feeling that he or she is a "better" person for having experienced a disability. According to Vash, when an individual has achieved transcendence, he or she views the disability as a tool, an asset, and an opportunity.

Consideration of the Individual's Environment

Shontz (1977) emphasized that reacting to a disability is not only a response to a physical, intellectual, cognitive, or psychiatric impairment; it also includes other factors in the individual's environment. Factors such as economic security, educational level, family support, and availability of treatment influence the disability experience. Therefore, Shontz argued that clinicians and researchers should consider the individual's environmental resources, rather than simply focusing on the psychodynamics of the PWD.

The factors that have not been fully addressed in the individual's response to the disability concern the degree of prejudice; discrimination toward the type and severity of disability; and whether the individual is also subject to prejudice or discrimination because of other perceived identities, such as belonging to other cultural/ethnic/racial groups, being a woman, being older, or having a different sexual orientation (Corbett & Bregante, 1993; Fine & Asch, 1988; Marinelli & Dell Orto, 1991; Marks, 1999; Stefan, 2001; Wendell, 1997). The degree of stigma and prejudice the individual experiences will influence his or her response to example, people who are gay and also who have a disability way to describe their doubly stigmatized status: "I want t closet, but the doorway isn't wide enough for my wheelch

What Is a "Good" Response to a Disability?

> **In this section, look for—**
> - The three categories of response to disability: behavioral, cognitive, affective
> - Which is easiest to define and measure?

There is a vast range in the definitions of disability, there is great variability in the severity or degree of disability, and PWDs have many environmental factors and varying types of psychological/emotional coping abilities. Added to this combination of disability variables are the differing levels of stigma directed toward specific disabilities. In Chapter 4 we learned about the hierarchy of stigma toward disabilities; the clinical picture of an individual's adjustment to a psychiatric disability would not be complete without recognizing that psychiatric disabilities are the most stigmatizing disabilities in our society. Having stated the great variability of the experience of disability, it is nonetheless possible to list some general attributes, behaviors, and manifestations of a "good" response to disability.

Generally speaking, response to a disability can be divided into three categories: cognitive, behavioral, and affective. *Cognitive* means how one chooses to view (or to think about) the disability. A positive or good cognitive response to disability includes redefining reality rather than ignoring it or denying it. *Behavioral* responses to disability include active mastery of the disability; compliance with treatment regimens; seeking out social support; returning to work; and, for many PWDs, actively fighting against the stigma and prejudice of society. *Affective* response means how the individual feels about the disability and how he or she manages emotions. Of course, the individual does not view his or her coping responses as neatly divided into these three categories. Behavioral acceptance/response to disability is relatively easy to operationally define and measure. Cognitive and affective responses are more difficult to measure. These types of assessments are made either by interviewing the PWD and/or family members or via paper-and-pencil psychological instruments. Of course, extreme and severe affective/emotional responses such as total denial of the disability, externalized anger and aggression, abuse of alcohol and/or drugs, family conflict and dissolution, and self-blame are readily observable. However, most affective responses are less extreme and, therefore, are less obvious and more difficult to measure and assess.

Cognitive Restructuring

In this section, look for—

- Beatrice Wright's theory of cognitive restructuring
  1. Enlargement of the scope of values
  2. Subordination of the physique
  3. Containment of disability effects
  4. Transformation from comparative values to asset values

Beatrice Wright (1960) pioneered the study of the individual's response to *physical* disability, working with veterans of World War II. Her theory of cognitive restructuring described how the individual with a disability can redefine reality. Wright's cognitive restructuring has four points:

1. Enlargement of the scope of values. The PWD subscribes to values that are not in conflict with the disability. A clear-cut illustration of this is the large number of professors, editors, and writers with physical disabilities who have devoted their lives to intellectual pursuits that are not affected by the physical disability. Psychological theories describe well-adjusted individuals as being able to generate many options and responses to the demands of their environment. This capability is also termed "having more cards to play." The PWD who is able to enlarge his or her value system will have more options and choices.

2. Subordination of the physique. The individual does not think of his or her body as a symbol of worth, desirability, or competence. The title of the video "My Body Is Not Who I Am" illustrates subordination of the physique. Later, we shall discuss the importance of body image.

3. Containment of disability effects. The individual does not deny the disability but *contains* or limits the effects, realizing that there are other activities that he or she can do. Rather than thinking that his or her life has no value or meaning, the individual finds meaning in other areas.

4. Transformation from comparative to asset values. Rather than comparing oneself to others who do not have disabilities or thinking only in terms of the limitations and losses of the disabilities, the individual focuses attention on his or her assets.

The literature on the individual's response to disability describes an individual with a positive response as someone who is flexible, demonstrates active mastery, rallies social support, and is capable of tolerating a degree of ambiguity. On acquiring a disability, normality (which is the absence of ambiguity because it is familiar to the individual) is gone. For most people, the experience of acquiring a disability, especially a severe disability or multiple disabilities, is a novel situation, one with which he or she has not had any experience. One of the first responses of a PWD is a desire to return to normality—that is to say, the individual's idiosyncratic conception of normality. A positive response does not view normality as the absence or cure of the disability; it conceptualizes normality as the reinstatement of the individual's identity, family, social system, home, status, income, professional identity, and sexuality (after the medical stabilization of the disability). The extent to which the individual is able to regain these aspects of his or her life will determine his or her response to the disability. An individual who is considered to have a positive response is judged to have a realistic view of the disability—is aware of the limitations but not exaggerating them (Yoshida, 1993).

As would be expected, it is easier to judge/assess the behavioral manifestations of response to disability than the affective or cognitive responses. Behavioral responses can be observed, measured, and quantified. In contrast, clinicians must rely on the self-report of the PWD to obtain some understanding of affective or cognitive responses. Behavioral responses such as complying with treatment and rehabilitation regimens, increasing activity levels, seeking out social support, and returning to work are relatively easy to operationally define and measure. The degree of emotional stress, physical pain, hope, and optimism for the future, however, are difficult to define and measure. Nonetheless, it is these subjective responses to disability that influence the individual's help-seeking behaviors and response to the disability. These assessments are made either by interviewing the PWD and/or family members or via paper-and-pencil psychological instruments. Well-planned, goal-directed activity and stress reduction are considered necessary for a positive response. Naturally, extreme and severe affective/emotional responses such as denial of the disability, externalized anger or aggression, abuse of alcohol and/or drugs, family conflict and dissolution, and self-blame are readily observable. However, it is safe to say that most affective/emotional responses are less extreme and therefore less obvious.

What Is a Poor Response to a Disability?

> **In this section, look for—**
> - The indicators of a "poor" response to disability
> - The difference between coping skills and defense mechanisms

An individual may perceive his or her disability as (1) loss of status, (2) loss of social support, (3) loss of functioning, and (4) loss of control, thinking that he or she will be isolated, dependent, and a burden on others. Further, in the American culture, the PWD may feel that he or she has somehow violated his or her duty to *not* acquire a disability.

Other studies of individuals with various types of disability have described poor response to disability as including unnecessary dependence on others, social isolation resulting from "shame" about the disability, feelings of helplessness, negative body image and self-esteem, anger and aggression toward others, longstanding feelings of dissatisfaction, high levels of stress, hypersensitivity to criticism, passivity, developmental immaturity, exhibiting an external locus of control, hypermorality, internalized anger and depression, holding unrealistic hopes of a cure, relying on defense mechanisms such as rigidity, holding on to the past, emotional lability (widely fluctuating moods, temperamental, easily upset), resignation (giving up), and humorlessness (Livneh & Antonak, 1997; Marshak & Seligman, 1993). Coupled with these poor responses is the lack of a realistic plan for dealing with the disability.

Coping strategies are different from defense mechanisms. Coping strategies are considered to be goal-directed, positive steps such as rallying social support, obtaining treatment and rehabilitation, redefining life goals, and seeking information. In contrast, defense mechanisms are an effort to avoid anxiety and reality, and, most often, the individual is not aware that he or she is using them. Examples of defense mechanisms are regression (preoccupied with the past when the individual did not have the disability or returning to a less mature pattern of behavior), projection (attributing one's own feelings to someone else), displacement (blaming others), withdrawal (socially isolated and unable to form therapeutic alliances with service providers), denial (at certain stages in the adjustment period, denial is considered to be therapeutic), and depersonalization (detached from self). Professional caregivers *reinforce* coping strategies but *challenge* the use of defense mechanisms.

Secondary Gains, Malingering, and Psychogenic Pain Disorder

In this section, look for—

- Reasons why an individual would seek secondary gains
- The difference between malingering and somatization disorders
- The importance of a temporal relationship between the onset of pain and environmental stimuli

Four responses to disability are considered to be counterproductive: (1) maintaining secondary gains, (2) somatization, (3) malingering, and (4) psychogenic pain disorder. Although relatively rare and often confused with adaptive responses, the symptoms of the disability itself, or both, clear distinctions characterize these responses. Furthermore, in all four of these responses, physicians must first rule out valid physical, cognitive, or psychiatric disorders.

Secondary gains that may result from a disability include financial compensation; freedom from responsibility (such as working or family obligations); receiving pity, attention, and care from others; free time; and freedom from evaluation. Seeking secondary gains is a self-protection strategy (of which the individual may or may not be aware). The individual who seeks secondary gains maintains his or her dependence, seeking environmental supports when they are not necessary, trying to maintain the sick role as long as possible. As would be expected, it is difficult to make an accurate distinction between adaptive, coping responses to the realities of a disability and secondary gain seeking. Nonetheless, seeking secondary gains is viewed as an avoidance behavior.

In somatization, the individual reports symptoms of long duration that have caused serious impairment in his or her life. However, there is no organic basis for these symptoms or, stated differently, the individual has functional symptoms without organic cause (American Psychiatric Association, 1994). The distinguishing feature of somatoform disorders is the fact that the individual is not consciously aware that he or she has produced the symptoms or is faking the symptoms. Somatization is "a process in which emotional and/or psychosocial stress is expressed in physical symptoms, precedes the development of these disorders and accounts for a large number of patients seeking medical care for symptoms that have no organic cause" (Spelic, 1997, p. 30). With such cases, there is a great deal of frustration on the part of medical service providers and on the part of the patient. Individuals with somatization disorder use medical resources frequently, having had many diagnostic procedures and visited many physicians (sometimes termed "doctor shopping"). Often, patients are perceived as manipulators. On the other side, patients are defensive because they sense the resentment, distrust, and irritation of medical care providers. Patients feel overwhelmed, helpless, and inadequate. Recently, with the emerging awareness of the frequency of childhood sexual abuse, somatization has been hypothesized, at times, to be an adaptive strategy on the part of the child. Illness and pain may have provided the child an escape from sexual abuse, starting a pattern that continues into adulthood. Indeed, many physicians now screen for childhood abuse when they suspect that a patient has somatization disorder. The difficulty of somatization disorder is that often individuals with invisible chronic diseases (especially autoimmune diseases), such as multiple sclerosis, lupus, chronic fatigue syndrome, and Crohn's disease, are thought to be engaging in somatization when, in reality, their pain, fatigue, numbness, and muscle weakness are real. For example, "on average, from the first onset of symptoms to diagnosis of multiple sclerosis, an individual will endure 40 baffling months" (Donoghue & Siegel, 1992). Therefore, in addition to experiencing the symptoms of a real disease without treatment, the individual has also endured the distrust of medical care providers.

Malingering is deliberate. According to the *Diagnostic and Statistical Manual of Mental Disorders–Fourth Edition* (*DSM-IV*) of the American Psychiatric Association (1994), "The essential feature of malingering is the intentional production of false or grossly exaggerated physical or psychological symptoms, motivated by external incentives such as avoiding military duty, avoiding work, obtaining financial compensation, evading criminal prosecution, or obtaining drugs" (p. 683). Like somatization, there are symptoms without organic causes (or the symptoms are "grossly exaggerated"). Unlike somatization, in malingering the individual is not experiencing some underlying emotional conflict and he or she is aware that he or she is faking. When malingering is suspected, clinicians look for incentives to fake, such as receiving workers' compensation benefits or an insurance settlement. However, often malingering is difficult to detect because the individual is medically knowledgeable and sophisticated.

Psychogenic pain disorder (the *DSM-IV* has changed the name to "pain disorder associated with psychological factors") is pain that "causes significant clinical distress or impairment in social, occupational, or other important areas of functioning" (*DSM-IV*, 1994, p. 461). The symptoms of pain are not intentionally produced or feigned, but psychological factors are thought to play an important part in the onset, severity, exaggeration, or maintenance of the pain. Therefore, when psychogenic pain disorder is suspected, physicians look for a temporal relationship between the psychological factors and the onset or exaggeration of the pain. Stated another way, the physician attempts to establish if a psychological stimulus precedes the onset of the pain. This is often difficult to establish because the patient often is not aware of the distressing nature of the psychological stimulus. For example, a college student may not think that final exam week is stressful. However, if the physician is able to establish a temporal relationship—that is to say, if the student's physical pain begins every final exam week—then it is reasonable to suspect that the stress of final examinations is responsible for the onset of the pain.

Although relatively rare and often confused with legitimate symptoms and/or coping strategies, these four responses to disability are counterproductive.

Problems in Measuring an Individual's Response to a Disability

---

In this section, look for—

- 10 difficulties in measuring response to disability:
  1. Most measurements are unidimensional.
  2. Most measurements do not include the stigma of society.
  3. There has been little longitudinal research.
  4. Most measurements have been on people with physical disabilities.
  5. For some disabilities, it is difficult to distinguish between response to the disability and symptoms of the disability.
  6. Many of the research instruments are psychological instruments that render diagnoses of exclusion.
  7. Much of the research is based on self-report.
  8. Many of the research instruments report little or no reliability or validity studies.
  9. Some disability scholars argue that response to disability should be measured by disability-specific instruments.
  10. Most research studies do not take into account the individual's level of premorbid (predisability) functioning.

Research Is Only as Good as the Model on Which It Is Based

The research that has sought to understand the individual's adaptation/response to a disability has been grounded in the Biomedical Model. As you remember, the Biomedical Model posits that the "problem" lies entirely within the individual and, therefore, the responsibility for resolution/adaptation lies with that individual. Psychological instruments that have been used to assess a person's adjustment to a disability have not attempted to assess (1) the availability of resources to the individual, (2) the degree of stigma directed toward the type of disability that the individual experiences, or (3) the functions that are affected by the disability. The Biomedical Model deals with the treatment and rehabilitation of PWDs and does not usually consider such interventions as changing the social and physical environments. In a book titled *Medical Statistics* (Feinstein & Chapman, 2002), the authors assert that a great deal of research "has been done with biases that destroy the scientific credibility of the results" (p. 3).

Disability scholars (Anson, Stanwyck, & Krause, 1993; Krause, 1998a, 1998b; Krause & Anson, 1997; Krause, Coker, Charlifue, & Whiteneck, 1999) have begun to incorporate measures such as the *Life Situations Questionnaire* (LSQ; Krause, 1998b) and the *Reciprocal Support Scale* (RSS; Krause & Anson, 1997) in their studies of the ways in which individuals respond to disabilities. The LSQ and the RSS ask questions about the individual's finances, career opportunities, living circumstances (whether he or she lives in an institution or at home), level of education, and degree of social interaction and emotional support. The environmental and functional models of disability are the bases of these types of questionnaires. Instruments such as these are used *in addition to* instruments that assess the individual's emotional response to the disability. As would be expected, by incorporating three models of disability—Biomedical, Functional, and Environmental—a more complete and accurate picture of the individual's response to the disability can be obtained.

Research Is Only as Good as the Instruments Used

Up until the publication of Linkowski's (1971, 1987) *The Acceptance of Disability Scale*, acceptance of disability was usually measured using psychological instruments such as the *Minnesota Multiphasic Personality Inventory–Second Edition* (MMPI-2; Butcher, Dahlstrom, Graham, Tellegen, & Kaemmer, 1989) or the *California Psychological Inventory* (CPI; Gough, 1957). Using these types of instruments has two disadvantages. First, many of these instruments were "designed to assess personality characteristics indicative of psychological abnormality . . . . Each of the nine scales on which the MMPI is scored consists of items that distinguish between responses of a specified psychiatric patient group and a control group of normal people" (Aiken, 1997, p. 317).

These instruments were designed for use in psychiatric hospitals to assess and diagnose pathology and psychological disorder, and when psychopathology is not found, a diagnosis of exclusion is rendered. In other words, the person is "normal" (whatever that means). Such a diagnosis of exclusion does not provide information on the individual's adaptive functioning and psychological growth. The diagnosis simply declares that psychopathology was looked for and none was found. No one would want to brag about high scores on the MMPI!

Second, these psychological inventories are comprised of scales such as Hypochondriasis (the MMPI and the *Basic Personality Inventory*) and Somatoform Disorders (Scale H of the *Millon Clinical Multiaxial Inventory*; Millon, Millon, Davis, & Grossman, 1981), which do not adequately describe the disability experience. Many PWDs are healthy, not sick; furthermore, concerns with body functioning, which the psychological instrument would score as pathology, would reflect active, adaptive management of the disability. For example, an individual with diabetes probably thinks about his or her body more than someone without diabetes. Other scales, such as the *Edwards Personal Preference Scale* (Edwards, 1959), have Independence scales. Independence, for many PWDs, has been redefined; therefore, their scores on these types of scales would not truly reflect their experience and certainly would not be indicative of psychopathology. For example, someone who depends on a respirator to breathe carefully devises back-up systems and emergency responses. However, such plans and considerations should be viewed as positive, productive adaptive responses to the disability and not as pathological dependence.

These psychological instruments also depend on self-report, and, for this reason, several of these instruments have validity scales that can detect quite accurately when the examinee is not being truthful. Stated simply, there are two basic ways in which a person can answer dishonestly. The first is intentional deception, in which the person deliberately attempts to make himself or herself appear better ("faking good") or attempts to make himself or herself appear worse ("faking bad"). The second type of dishonesty is unintentional and termed "response sets." The individual is not aware that he or she is giving distorted answers.

Psychometrists and psychologists agree that the results of psychological instruments are valid only when test-takers understand that "they have nothing to gain by failing to answer thoughtfully and truthfully" (Aiken, 1997, p. 308). Yet, many service programs for PWDs, such as vocational rehabilitation, are eligibility programs, meaning that the individual must demonstrate the presence of a disability. For this reason, there would be a tendency to "fake bad" to establish eligibility for services and benefits. The best-case scenario of the examinee having nothing to gain by failing to answer thoughtfully and truthfully probably rarely exists.

For individuals who are deaf and use American Sign Language (ASL) as their first language, tests and measurements given in English will yield questionable, if not useless, results. Anyone tested in his or her second language is at a great disadvantage. Pollard, DeMatteo, Lentz, and Rediess (2007) summarized:

> ASL is the primary sign language used by deaf individuals in the United States and Canada. Its structural properties, increasingly well documented by researchers, differ markedly from those of English (Fischer & van der Hulst, 2003). Psychologists unfamiliar with the unique properties of ASL, its differences from English, and the compromised Eng-

lish reading abilities of many deaf people may inappropriately use English-based measures in cognitive, personality, and neuropsychological assessments of deaf individuals, which may yield invalid results. (p.11)

Livneh and Antonak (1997) presented a review of the 10 available instruments that measure psychosocial adaptation to disability. The authors concluded their review by noting "the considerable variability" in the theoretical orientations of the developers of these instruments and the concomitant variation in the operational definitions of psychosocial adaptation to chronic illness and disability.

For instance, psychosocial adaptation (or maladaptation) has been operationalized as (a) the presence of new and distressing physical, behavioral, and psychosomatic complaints (*General Health Questionnaire, Millon Behavioral Health Inventory* [Goldberg, 1972], and *Sickness Impact Profile* [Millon, Green, & Meager, 1979]); (b) the alteration of vocational and avocational productivity (*Psychosocial Adjustment to Illness Scale* [Derogatis, 1976]); (c) reduction in performance of domestic activities or daily living skills (*Psychosocial Adjustment to Illness Scale* [Derogatis, 1976] and *Sickness Impact Profile* [Bergner et al., 1976]); (d) coping style (*Millon Behavioral Health Inventory*); (e) degree of disability acceptance (*The Acceptance of Disability Scale* and *Acceptance of Loss Scale* [Osuji, 1975]); (f) pathological dimensions of personality that influence the course of disability or the efficacy of treatment (*Millon Behavioral Health Inventory*); (g) impact on interpersonal relations, communication, and sexual behavior (*Psychosocial Adjustment to Illness Scale* and *Sickness Impact Profile*); and (h) emotional and psychological distress, as manifested in anxiety, shock, guilt, depression, anger, hostility, and denial (*Heinemann and Shontz Q–Sort* and *Reactions to Impairment and Disability Inventory* [Heinemann & Shontz, 1984, 1985]). (Livneh & Antonak, 1997, p. 63)

The Few Instruments That Measure Acceptance of Disability Are Designed for *Physical* Disabilities

Paper-and-pencil instruments are derived from theory. Linkowski's (1987) *The Acceptance of Disability Scale* (AD) provides an easily understood example in that Linkowski operationalized Wright's theory of cognitive restructuring. However, as we have seen, Wright's theory applies only to *physical* disabilities and does not consider the response of individuals who have intellectual, cognitive, or psychiatric disabilities. (Linkowski reports that he is in the process of changing and adapting the AD scale.) Both Wright and Linkowski are considered to be pioneers, having developed their theory and instrument in the 1960s. Nonetheless, there are few, if any, instruments currently available to assess the response of an individual to an intellectual, cognitive, or psychiatric disability.

Most Often, There Is No Premorbid Empirical Measure of the Individual's Psychological Functioning

Many disability scholars have posited that the single most important variable in responding to the disability is the individual's premorbid psychological functioning. (It should be noted that the thesis of this book holds that environmental variables are also important.) Psychological functioning thought to be related to a positive response to a disability includes such factors as high levels of stress and tension control, excellent problem-solving and decision-making abilities, high levels of assertiveness and goal direction, capability of mobilizing a social-support system, accurate and positive appraisal abilities, high levels of emotional control, high levels of self-esteem, well-developed cognitive flexibility, high levels of self-insight, and a well-developed sense of humor (Linkowski & Dunn, 1974).

However, measurements of the individual's psychological functioning prior to the onset/diagnosis of the disability rarely exist. Therefore, there is no "baseline" to which to refer. Of course, this can be *inferred* by reading the individual's history, by asking the individual himself or herself, or by relying on the reports of family members and other significant people in the PWD's life. Nevertheless, such inferences lack empirical precision and quantification.

Another issue in the psychodynamic functioning of the individual before the onset/diagnosis of a disability concerns the confounding of psychological functioning with environmental resources. For example, research has shown that individuals with higher levels of education and income tend to accept disabilities better. Intuitively, this makes sense because the individual has more options at his or her disposal, and these options act as stress moderators (for anyone—with or without a disability). The problem arises when trying to separate the individual's psychological functioning from the resources in his or her environment. The individual's functional demands also affect his or her emotional acceptance or response to the disability. For example, generally speaking, it is acknowledged that older people tend to accept disability better. However, it is not entirely understood *why* this relationship between age and acceptance has been found. Is it because older individuals have had more experience in dealing with life situations and therefore possess more emotional/psychological resources with which to respond? Or is it because older individuals usually have fewer functional demands, such as working or child care? Elderly people are usually "excused" from work or child care. Or, perhaps it is easier for an individual to accept his or her disability if all of his or her agemates have disabilities and/

or functional limitations; the elderly individual may have reduced expectations concerning his or her quality of life.

Some Disability Scholars Advocate Disability-Specific Instruments

In contrast to general instruments that measure psychosocial response/adaptation to disability, such as *The Acceptance of Disability Scale* (Linkowski, 1971), there are 11 instruments that measure adaptation to eight specific disabilities: hearing impairment, arthritis, spinal cord injuries, visual impairment, cancer, diabetes, traumatic brain injury, and seizure disorders. For example, the *Communication Profile for the Hearing Impaired* (Demorest & Erdman, 1987) measures the communication skills and personal adjustment and asks questions about the environment of individuals with hearing impairments. The *Arthritis Impact Measurement Scale* (Meenan, Gertman, Mason, & Dunaif, 1980) elicits information on the individual's mobility, social activity, and ability to perform household activities and activities of daily living, and the *Washington Psychosocial Seizure Disorder Inventory* (Dodrill, Batzel, Queisser, & Tempkin, 1980) seeks to measure overall psychological and social functioning but also assesses financial status, management of medications, vocational adjustment, and adjustment to seizures. Certainly, these instruments would have a great deal of face validity for the test-takers. Even more important, these disability-specific instruments assess function and environment in addition to the individual's response. Therefore, three models of disability—medical, functional, and environmental—are used to more completely assess the individual's response.

Often, It Is Difficult To Distinguish Between Symptoms of the Disability and the Individual's Response to Disability

It is important, albeit difficult, to separate symptoms of the disability from the individual's response to the disability. For example, depression is a disability-triggered, organically based manifestation of several disabilities, including spinal cord injury, multiple sclerosis, and traumatic brain injury. Garland and Zis (1991) suggested that affective disorders in people with multiple sclerosis, such as depression, result from structural lesions (wounds) in the neurological system. Instruments such as the *Beck Depression Inventory* and the *Minnesota Multiphasic Personality Inventory* can determine the presence and degree of depression in the individual; however, these instruments cannot distinguish between depression that is a direct *result* of the disability and depression that is a *response* to the disability. Naugle (1991) addressed the reaction of denial of deficit as a "psychological sequelae" of disability or, in other words, denial as an emotional response to a disability. However, Naugle clearly distinguished denial-as-an-emotional-response from another type of denial—"'anosognosia' associated with and directly attributed to a focal cortical lesion" (p. 139). Obviously, the psychologist or psychometrist who is administering and interpreting these instruments should be knowledgeable about disabilities and their symptoms, course, and outcome in addition to adaptation/response theories. If not, the results of these instruments could be misinterpreted.

Most Research on Adaptation to Disability Has Not Been Longitudinal

Overwhelmingly, the majority of research investigating the adaptation/reaction to disability has gathered data at one point in time (Shontz, 1975). There are exceptions to this, such as Krause and colleagues' longitudinal studies (data gathered from the same people at several points in time) with people with spinal cord injuries (Krause, 1997, 1998a, 1998b). Longitudinal studies, using participants with or without disabilities, are expensive and difficult to implement. As would be expected, participants tend to drop out of studies; therefore, in most longitudinal studies, the size of the sample becomes smaller and smaller. Longitudinal studies have the potential to assess growth and development in adaptation, to assess the interaction of the various psychosocial developmental stages with the disability, and to measure the impact of legislation such as the Americans with Disabilities Act on the lives of PWDs. Not only has most research on adaptation to disability gathered data only at one point in time, but often the data were collected relatively soon after the onset/diagnosis of the disability. Because patients in hospitals or residents of institutions are more accessible to researchers, PWDs were often "recruited" into studies that are purported to measure their adaptation to disability.

Acceptance of Disability Instruments Does Not Always Translate to Other Cultures

For any psychological instrument to be translated into another language, there must be cultural equivalence on the psychological concepts measured between the two languages. In other words, translating *The Acceptance of Disability Scale* into another language, such as Spanish, from the English in which Linkowski originally developed it requires that the construct of acceptance of disability be defined in much the same way in the American cultures as in the Hispanic cultures (Smart, 1993; Smart & Smart, 1991, 1992a, 1992b, 1993a, 1993b, 1994a, 1994b, 1995a, 1995b, 1995c, 1995d, 1995e, 1996). You will remember that earlier in the book we learned that being a PWD is a "normative" role. In other words, there are rules (norms) that govern the "correct" or "socially acceptable" way in which to have a disability. Moreover, this normative role is culturally defined and, therefore, the role of a PWD may be different in an Asian culture than it is in a Hispanic culture.

Using the Hispanic cultures and the Spanish language as an example, it can be seen that the broad concept of acceptance/response to disability is probably viewed and defined differently in Hispanic cultures than it is in North American cultures. Hispanic cultural values, such as familism, well-defined sex roles, and religious beliefs influence how Hispanics with disabilities respond to and accept a disability. However, if a Hispanic individual were to be administered a Spanish translation of *The Acceptance of Disability Scale* (the author did translate this instrument into Spanish; Linkowski, 1971), his or her responses might spuriously indicate low acceptance of disability. Such cultural distortions have been found in other psychological instruments, such as the *Minnesota Multiphasic Personality Inventory* (Butcher & Garcia, 1978; Butcher & Pancheri, 1976; Darlington, 1971; Greene, 1987; Velasquez & Callahan, 1991). Simply stated, regardless of how accurate and elegant a foreign language translation may be (the words of the test), the psychological concepts of the instrument must be equivalent in both cultures to present an accurate clinical picture.

The Stage Model of Adaptation to Disability

In this section, look for—

- How not all disabilities have a traumatic, acute onset/diagnosis
- How, for most disabilities, the individual is not able to engage in anticipatory adjustment
- How "difficult" does not always mean "tragic"
- How the stage model does not apply to deteriorating conditions
- How it is helpful to have some broad guidelines in predicting the course and outcome of the adjustment/response process

The stage theory of adaptation/response to disability provides some helpful guidelines in understanding and predicting the course and outcome of the individual's response process. This process is a gradual assimilation of an altered identity and is a continuous, ongoing process, not a one-time event (Livneh, 1986a, 1986b). Arnold Beisser (1989), the physician who contracted polio on his way to report for military duty, termed his response to the effects of polio to be like a marriage because he and his disability were in a long-term but ever-changing relationship. Fred Davis studied 14 young patients with polio and their families in Baltimore, Maryland, in the 1950s. Davis's study clearly showed how slowly the families and the individuals with polio adjusted to the idea of residual disability and a lengthy rehabilitation. Most of the families had expected a fairly short time in rehabilitation with no resulting disability (Wilson, 1990). Parents of a baby who was diagnosed with dwarfism reported that each time they attended support meetings they came home and took Pepto Bismol:

> Paul said, "Why don't you come over to our house after the meeting. We're going to have dessert in the evening." I remember sitting on the couch. These people had all their furniture cut down. Well, we had the best time. We got up ready to go and when we stood, that's when it hit me. Because when we were sitting, everyone was the same. But when we stood up, these people were down below my waist. Our heads were spinning and our stomachs were churning and we went home. We ended up being involved, and going to other meetings that they had because we felt that it was important for Joey to have that exposure at that time, if he was indeed a dwarf, which is a permanent condition. These people were real people in different professions and a lot of members were a big help during that time. But we used to have to take Pepto Bismol when we got home, because even though we'd had a good time; it was the reality of it all. And I think that's what's good. I think that's good for parents, to be hit with the reality. You find you're enjoying it, but when you go home, you suffer the effects of that reality—that my child is not going to grow. He's really going to stay small. (Albon, 1989, p. 357)

Responding to a disability is a continuous process and a reorientation of personal priorities and relationships. Not all disabilities have a sudden, acute, traumatic onset. For example, disabilities such as diabetes and lupus have an insidious onset, and therefore it is more accurate to speak ⎫e time of diagnosis rather than the time of onset (Moos, 1984). Mov-⎫hrough these stages requires goal-directed changes in attitude and be-⎫r, but this does not imply that the onset/diagnosis of every disability ⎫ught to be tragic. The stage theory is based on theories of adapta-⎫ loss, especially Kübler-Ross's theories of acceptance of one's death ⎫r-Ross, 1969). The value of these theories to individuals (and their ⎫) facing loss and death cannot be underestimated. However, there are two differences in the stage theory for death/loss and the stage theory of adaptation to disability. First, in many losses, or with regard to one's impending death, there is a period of anticipatory adjustment that allows the individual to both behaviorally and emotionally prepare for the loss before the loss actually happens. Such an anticipatory period rarely occurs for a PWD. (Exceptions to this would include situations such as individuals who have time to prepare for a therapeutic amputation.) Second, in losses such as divorce or death, the individual experiencing the loss usually does not experience prejudice, stigma, and discrimination from society and, therefore, these stage theories do not consider the added stress of prejudice and discrimination. Indeed, many PWDs report that their greatest difficulty is not in dealing with the disability, but in confronting prejudice and discrimination. However, the stage theory of adaptation/response to disability remains silent on the prejudice and discrimination of society.

The stage theory of adaptation/response to disability probably does not apply as well to individuals who have gradually deteriorating conditions, especially elderly individuals. For example, people who experience the onset/diagnosis of a chronic, degenerating disability, such as arthritis or old-age deafness, typically do not go through the initial shock stage, nor would such individuals tend to experience long-term depression or mourning. These stages are neither inevitable nor universal (Olkin, 1999).

The Stages of Response in Disability

> **In this section, look for—**
>
> - Shock
> - Defensive retreat
> - Depression or mourning
> - Personal questioning
> - Adaptation, change, and integration

Shock or Initial Impact

Robert Perkins, in his book *Talking to Angels: A Life Spent* (1996), described the shock of the diagnosis/onset of his m

In the spring of 1968, I was nineteen and a freshman at I lege. I was soon to leave school, without even passing "GO the year, to start a journey. A journey I have yet to complete .... To have the wind knocked out of you, hard, at nineteen. To give you the feeling of it, I'd hit you on the side of the head, when you were not expecting it, with a flat board or a piece or rubber tubing. The shock of the thing! (pp. 5, 15)

In this stage, the individual's thinking is often disorganized, and he or she may be feeling overwhelmed and confused. Rereading Perkins's description, we can see the total unexpectedness and the devastating impact. First, he relates the abruptness of the onset as not being able to pass "GO." Then he describes the devastating impact in physical terms: being hit on the side of the head. Individuals in this stage of initial shock often feel that more is happening to them than they can understand or absorb. They are unable to think or feel. The combination of the suddenness of the onset and the significant changes often leads to shock.

An artist, Chuck Close (1993), described the sudden and thorough onset of his paralysis:

I was at Gracie Mansion in New York giving an award to someone. I suddenly had a tremendous pain in my chest that went through my back and my arms. I thought it was a heart attack. I went across the street to Doctors Hospital where, within a very a short time, I was totally paralyzed from the neck down. It was several days before they figured out what had happened, which was that an occluded or collapsed spinal artery had cut off the flow of blood to my spine and knocked out nerves all over my body. Virtually everything from the shoulders down was affected. (p. 17)

Another individual (Frese, 1997) describes the onset of schizophrenia:

I cannot tell you how difficult it is for a person to accept the fact that he or she is schizophrenic. Since the time when we were very young we have all been conditioned to accept that if something is crazy or insane, its worth to us is automatically dismissed .... The nature of this disorder is that it affects the chemistry that controls your cognitive processes. It affects your belief system .... It is exceedingly difficult for you to admit to yourself that the mind does not function properly. It fools you. (pp. 145–146)

From Frese's excerpt, we can see that society's prejudices and myths exerted a powerful influence on his reaction to his disability and on his self-esteem. The onset of Close's and Frese's disabilities was sudden and unpredictable and the functional limitations were great. It is interesting to compare the cause of Frese's schizophrenia ("the chemistry that controls your cognitive processes") with the cause of Close's paralysis ("an occluded or collapsed spinal artery"). Although the causes of both disabilities are physical, it is only in Frese's account that prejudice and discrimination are mentioned.

It is not only the diagnosis/onset of a disability that precedes this type of shock. For some individuals, it is a particular point in the treatment or rehabilitation process that has idiosyncratic, shocking meaning. For example, one individual with a progressive neurological disease stated, "Going into the wheelchair was awful!" Another individual stated, "Going into the assisted living center was the worst day of my life. I will never forget it."

Jack Hofsiss experienced the shock of a "life that has been unalterably changed and played around with" when he returned home from the hospital. Hofsiss was paralyzed after a diving accident in a swimming pool:

> Still, in no way was I prepared for returning home. The hardest part is those first two or three months after you get back home. When you're in the hospital, the anonymity of the space allows you to keep at a distance the fact that your life has been unalterably changed and played around with. But when you get home, you're surrounded by all the things of daily life before the accident: Then you walk into the kitchen to get yourself a cup of coffee or a glass of milk. No longer. That's where the serious adjusting takes place. (Hofsiss & Laffey, 1993, p. 81)

Defensive Retreat or Denial

As the word "defensive" implies, this stage is often considered to be a therapeutic, adaptive strategy on the part of the PWD. Denial can take three basic forms: (1) denial of the presence of the disability, (2) denial of the implications of the disability, or (3) denial of the permanence of the disability. Denial allows the individual to maintain his or her self-identity (Langer, 1994; Stewart, 1994). An individual who denies the implications of the disability may think "I'm the same as I always was" or may think "I'll soon be walking" or "I don't need to change any of my plans" or "Everything will be like it was before." The individual understands that he or she has the disability but minimizes and downplays the effects of the disability and often tries to live in his or her "predisability world." (Franklin Roosevelt denied the implications of his disability because he maintained that some day he would be able to walk.) When an individual denies the permanence of the disability, he or she may feel that the disability will disappear or "Soon, I'll be my old self again." Denial of the presence of the disability is rare; denial of the implications or the permanence of the disability is more common. Families of PWDs frequently engage in denial when they view the disability as not changing the PWD's life or insist that the PWD will "return to normal." For example, a wife asks physicians, "When will he walk out of here?" (M. Dunn, 1996). Chuck Close (1993), the artist who became paralyzed, remembered the medical stabilization process as "calm and not as scary" as the day when the permanence of his paralysis became apparent:

> But my recollection was that it [medical stabilization] was quite calm and not as scary as when the deadening reality of the kind of day-in and day-out existence of not being able to move really set in. On the tenth, eleventh, twelfth day you haven't moved a muscle from shoulders on down, and people are rolling you and over and back, attaching tubes and things, *that's* when you think, "Oh, it's never going to get any better than this." That's when it really gets scary. (p. 17)

For individuals with amputations, the stage of denial is often complicated and compounded by phantom limb pain.

Defensive retreat or denial can prevent what is called "emotional flooding" and allows the individual to gradually assimilate both the permanence and the full implications of the disability. Individuals in this stage, in an attempt to guard against the trauma, may refuse to accept information, insist that there has been a mistake, or seek out other service providers. Richard Cohen, who was diagnosed with multiple sclerosis at age 25, expressed denial in this way: "My radar screen was blank, not even plugged in and turned on" (2004, p. 13). Deegan (1991), in *Recovery: The Lived Experience of Rehabilitation*, described denial:

> Needless to say, we didn't believe our doctors and social workers. In fact, we adamantly denied and raged against these bleak prophesies for our lives. We felt it was all just a mistake, a bad dream, a temporary set-back in our lives. We just knew that in a week or two, things would get back to normal again. We felt our teenage world was still there, just waiting for us to return to it. Our denial was an important stage in our recovery. It was a normal reaction to an overwhelming situation. It was our way of surviving those first awful months. (p. 48)

Obviously, the individual in denial does not have any motivation (or understanding) to learn to live with the disability. For this reason, denial, or defensive retreat, is considered to be therapeutic if it does not continue too long. Service providers often counter denial with the concept of "dosage of information" (Naugle, 1991). Dosage of information refers to carefully determining exactly how much information can be tolerated. Timing of information is also important. Naugle summarized, "Equally important is the concept of dosage. If the individual is overwhelmed with information, that material is less likely to be accepted. Failure to recognize and accommodate an individual's tolerance level for distressing information may have the effect of interfering with participation in any treatment regimen. Smaller 'doses' of information allow the individual to assimilate that information at a more controlled, self-determined rate" (p. 147). Often, there is a rhythm of adaptation in which the individual, and his or her family, are allowed some necessary respite through the use of denial.

Toombs (1995), a professor of English with multiple sclerosis, clearly describes the way in which she uses denial as a tool:

> Now that my disease is actively progressive, I must face this fear more often . . . . There are thoughts that come unbidden in the night to re-awaken my deepest anxieties. There is no way for me to look at them in the face and remain intact. I must push them back. Back into the recesses of my consciousness. It is an act of will. I must think only of the new. Of this day. Of this moment. Of what I have. Of what I can do. Of what gives me joy. Please, let me think only of this. Sufficient unto the day is the evil thereof. (p. 22)

Of course, in Freudian terms the clinical diagnosis of denial includes the element that the individual is unaware that he or she is engaging in denial, and we can see that Toombs very deliberately and consciously uses denial to filter out unacceptable information. One of the ways in which Toombs supplements the protective factors of denial is to focus on positive aspects of her life. She is allowing only those interpretations of reality that are within her adaptive capabilities.

Bayton (1995) uses a slightly different type of denial, in which negative information is ignored. By conceptualizing negative information as related to only a *part* of himself, his self-esteem remains intact:

> Negative information is filtered out to the extent that it is trivial, or short-term in its implications. More significant information, with greater potential impact on the person, is brought into awareness. Or information that reflects badly on the self may be identified with a particular *part* of the self, but be prevented from influencing one's self-concept in a global fashion. This part of the self can then be interpreted as distance from one's "core" or "essential" nature, further minimizing the impact of negative information on self-esteem. (pp. 45–46)

Richard Cohen (2004) wrote about his therapeutic uses of denial that continued for years. Cohen referred to his denial as "a child-like response" (p. 33) and stated that "[s]erious sickness is a large reality sandwich for a skinny young man to swallow" (p. 19).

> For months I had lived in the house of denial. Now, in one moment, it had given way. It had been a flimsy structure, built on wishful thinking, but it had sheltered me from the weight of a reality that I could not bear to confront. Ignorance had been my ally; I had not even asked many questions of the doctors. Silence was an odd tactic for a journalist who, by trade, is all questions all the time. But I did not want to know too many facts. Facts would lead to truth and truth had been unacceptable. I was facing facts now. I had to admit to myself that I had MS.

Years would pass, however, before I easily and openly acknowledged my illness. Knowledge came slowly, too. (p. 22)

Denial can be used repeatedly, as the following excerpt demonstrates:

When I got up at last . . . and had learned to walk again, one day I took a hand glass and went to a long mirror to look at myself, and I went alone. I didn't want anyone . . . to know how I felt when I saw myself for the first time. The person in the mirror *couldn't* be me. I felt inside like a healthy, ordinary, lucky person. Over and over I forgot what I saw in the mirror. (Goffman, 1963, p. 7)

Denial, if continued too long, can be counterproductive and impede the response to the disability. Louis Sternburg contracted polio and was in an iron lung.

Louis Sternburg asked his physician when he was going to walk out of the respiratory center. After a long, painful pause, the doctor told him that not only would he never walk again, he would also probably never breathe again without assistance. Sternburg heard himself scream, "You sonofabitch, you're lying!" (Wilson, 1990, p. 94)

Until relatively recently, PWDs were often encouraged by both caregivers and their families to deny the disability and to never discuss it. After medical stabilization, they were encouraged to "get on with their lives" as though they had no disability. Furthermore, they were advised not to dwell on "what might have been." They were encouraged to focus their energies on their physical rehabilitation and to repress or deny their feelings and emotions about their experiences. There was sometimes a hidden cost in terms of both physical and psychological well-being (Wilson, 1990, pp. 200–201). Marc Shell (2005) stated, "My own father did not speak with me directly about my having had polio" (p. 84). Veterans of World War II and the Korean War who returned home with disabilities were given medical care and physical therapy, but no one questioned the lack of psychological rehabilitation. These soldiers were told to "forget" about their disabilities.

Depression or Mourning

Denial is often considered to be past-oriented, in that the individual is trying to retain his or her former identity. Depression is considered to be future-oriented because the individual now struggles with questions of an uncertain future and an uncertain identity (Austin, 1990; Johnson, 1993; Powers, 1993). Often, the PWD feels that "my family would be better off without me." In this stage, the PWD often does not have the energy or

motivation to invest in a rehabilitation program. The individual often with-
draws from others and has trouble sleeping, eating, and concentrating.

A man with a spinal cord injury described the grieving process: "If
someone is stuck in the grieving process . . . it's like an adjustment to a
death. The only thing is, for an injury or disability, it's not as easy to adjust
as with a death because with a death, the person's no longer there. With a
disability, you have a constant reminder. So, sometimes it takes even longer
to grieve and adjust. A lot of people turn to alcohol and drugs, which is a
way of going through denial. As long as you're smashed, you can forget
about your disability" (Scherer, 1993, p. 115).

It is often typical (or "normal") for the PWD to experience cycles of
loss of hope, apathy, and deep depression. Also associated with depression
are feelings of guilt and self-blame. As the grief subsides, the individual is
able to acknowledge that he or she feels better. Grieving is experienced by
family members. One mother described her grief over a daughter with "so
much potential" who was diagnosed with a mental illness:

> The problems with my daughter were like a black hole inside of me
> into which everything else had been drawn. My grief and pain were
> so intense sometimes that I barely got through the day. It felt like a
> mourning process as if I were dealing with the loss of the daughter
> I had loved for 18 years and for whom there was so much potential.
> (Marsh, 1992, p. 10)

The Difference Between Grieving a Disability and Society's "Requirement To Mourn"

Grieving a disability, by the individual and his or her family, is a valid reaction toward a disability and, like the other stages in responding to a disability, grieving can be an important step to self-mastery. Grieving is an
idiosyncratic acknowledgment of specific losses, including future plans and
goals. However, the "requirement to mourn" (Wright, 1983) is imposed by
society to maintain the superiority of PWODs. After all, if PWODs believe (mistakenly) that disability is always a tragic misfortune, then it makes
sense to expect PWDs to live in a constant state of suffering and grief. The
combination of the false perceptions of disability as tragedy and constant
grieving serves to make lack of disability (or "normality") appear valuable,
desirable, and superior. Jenny Morris (1991) expressed her views on society's
"requirement to mourn": "Not all of us view our disability as the unmiti-
gated disaster and diminishment that seems expected of us" (p. 187).

Grieving and loss are also culturally defined. To cite a single example,
researchers have found in societies that consider men superior to women
that a congenital disability of a male infant is considered a greater loss than
the birth of female with the same disability. Also, in these types of societies,

the probability of marriage for a man with a disability is greater than for a woman with the same type (and severity) of disability. This greater opportunity for marriage results from the fact that the woman with a disability is considered to be doubly disadvantaged—by her gender and the disability—while the man is thought to have only a single disadvantage, the disability (Westbrook, Legge, & Pennay, 1993).

Self-blame, or some other type of responsibility attribution in which the individual holds himself or herself to have acquired the disability through irresponsibility, negligence, or carelessness, has been found to hinder the acceptance process. Further, there is a strong societal insistence on determining causality, accountability, and blame for disability. As we have seen, society wants an explanation of the cause of the disability and, even more important, to be reassured that the disability is not some random event that might someday affect them. If others can believe that the PWD caused his or her own disability (and that they would never be so foolish or negligent to cause themselves a disability), they can remain confident that they are exempt from disability. Therefore, perhaps the PWD may overcome feelings of self-blame, but his or her family and friends might consider the PWD to be guilty of self-inflicting a disability. Blame for the disability serves two purposes: (1) it relieves everyone of responsibility for the disability because the "individual did this to himself/herself," and (2) it allows others to believe (falsely) that disability will never happen to them. Establishing blame, especially blaming the PWD, perpetuates the myth that the body can be controlled completely. Carolyn Vash talked about the power that blame can assume:

> Accidents, in which an official designation of responsibility is made, are simply the most obvious case. To believe that a permanent disability resulted from a momentary, foolish act of one's own may strongly affect reaction to the disability itself—at least until the feelings of self-blame are resolved. Blaming someone else may have an even stronger impact. Keith, who lost a leg when the motorcycle he was riding collided with a truck, became consumed with hatred toward the truck driver, especially after the courts found him not at fault. Fred, shot in the spine accidentally by his younger brother, believes both of their lives would have been better if their parents had permitted him to express the anger he felt. (Vash, 1981, p. 11)

We have also seen that the perceived onset of the disability determines, in part, the degree of stigma directed toward the individual. Looking at the examples of Keith and Fred, we can speculate that if their disabilities had been the result of war injuries, perhaps both the societal stigma and their own self-blame and anger would have been reduced.

Arthur Frank (1991) discussed the relationship between his disability and randomness: "As soon as cancer happened to me, it ceased to be random." Frank continues that although he understood that many people are diagnosed with cancer, "I could not resist asking, 'Why me?' As a bodily process, cancer 'just happened to me.' The explanations I like best are fairly medical" (Frank, 1991, p. 87). Commenting on Frank's assessment of the cause of his cancer, Michalko (2002) explained:

> Medicine does have its charm. Its explanations of phenomena such as cancer are far more attractive than those to be found in religious ideas involving the omission or commission of acts, which lead to guilt and self-blame. Medicine's neutral physiological depiction of cancer leads us away from such self-blame to the more comforting, "just happened." There is nothing that we did or did not do that causes cancer; it "just happens." (p. 35)

In contrast, if there is any self-blame in congenital disabilities, it is typically the parents who experience such feelings. Wilson (1990), who reviewed dozens of first-person accounts of polio survivors, found that the parents of these survivors often felt guilty for not protecting their children from the virus. These parents endlessly replayed the events leading up to their children's illness, trying to determine where and how their children were exposed. Charles Mee (1999) was a teenager on a family car trip from Chicago to visit his older sister at the University of Colorado when he became ill with the polio virus. In an effort to pinpoint the location in which he contracted polio, Mee tried to remember every public restroom he used on the trip.

Leonard Kriegel also contracted polio as a child. When his mother visited him in the hospital for the first time, Kriegel saw how frightened she looked and watched her "make her frightened way across the room. I yelled, 'Momma, I'm sorry.' She had the unconscious grace to cry. And I cried with her, relieved that I had won forgiveness" (pp. 13–14).

The individual with a congenital disability is often relieved of asking and answering the question "Why me?" Rod Michalko (2002) was born with a type of degenerating blindness. He concludes:

> I have nothing to do with the onset of my blindness since I have no role to play in the configuration of my genetic makeup. My blindness is caused by flawed genes and not by a flawed self or any other kind of self for that matter. (p. 33)

Regression

Closely tied to the stage of depression, regression occurs when the PWD simply gives up or regresses to an earlier, less mature, stage of life. Deegan (1991) described regression in herself and a fellow resident:

> Our denial gave way to despair and anguish. We both gave up. Giving up was the solution for us. It numbed the pain of our despair because

we stopped asking "Why? and How will I go on?" .... Giving up meant that for 14 years he sat in the day rooms of institutions gazing at soap operas, watching others live their lives. For months I sat in a chair in my family's living room, smoking cigarettes and waiting until it was 8:00 P.M. so that I could go back to bed. At this time, even the simplest of tasks were overwhelming. I remember being asked to come in to the kitchen to help knead some bread dough. I got up, went in to the kitchen and looked at the dough for what seemed to be an eternity. Then I walked back to my chair and wept. The task seemed overwhelming to me. (p. 49)

Cohen (2004) described his experience with regression after he heard his diagnosis on the telephone: "After the phone was returned to the cradle, immediately I wished I could be also (returned to the cradle). This would be a great time to be an infant again, to be picked up and rocked" (p. 18).

Another type of regression occurs when the individual romanticizes and idealizes "normality" or his or her premorbid identity. A lot like reminiscing about the "good old days," which may or may not have been so good, the individual nostalgically idealizes the memories of himself or herself without a disability. Charles Mee, the writer who contracted polio as a teenager, deeply resented his father's regression. Mee (1999) wrote:

For the rest of his life after I had polio, my father carried a picture of me in his wallet that he had taken at the halftime of a football game. I was sitting on the grass with my teammates while the coach talked to us. My father had come around to the side of the group, and as I turned to look at him, he took the picture: an adolescent boy in the vigor of youth, a strong jaw and neck, a crewcut, massive shoulders with the football pads .... I always took the fact that he carried that picture with him as a sign of disappointment in me, and it filled me with rage .... The photograph was still on a table not far from his bed when he died at the age of ninety-four. (p. 170)

Personal Questioning, Anger, or Both

In the personal questioning or anger stage, the individual may ask, "Why did God allow this to happen to me?" The onset of a disability seems unfair. Anger is often a combination of feelings of helplessness, frustration, fear, and irritability. Other types of personal questioning may take the form of the PWD "replaying" the accident or prediagnosis period in an attempt to find ways in which the disability could have been avoided. In trying to find the reason or meaning (which are not the same as the cause), the individual may lose trust in the world and in his or her value systems. For some individuals, this type of questioning is both lonely and futile. The responsibility or cause of the disability often becomes self-blame for the individual; for some individuals, holding themselves responsible for the disability is the price they pay for maintaining their belief that the world is not a random and unpredictable place.

If carried on for too long, compulsive, obsessive questioning and search for cause and meaning can delay the treatment and rehabilitation process. Helping the individual to understand the difference between the cause (responsibility) for the disability and the meaning and purpose can be therapeutic. Often, the individual's religious, spiritual, or philosophical belief systems can be implemented to help the individual clarify his or her beliefs about the purposes of his or her disability. Mee (1999), a survivor of polio, had the following conversation with a Jesuit priest.

> [Mee said,] "I've lost my faith. I no longer believe in God."
>
> "I see," the priest said. And then he made a mistake. Instead of honoring my thoughts and feelings—instead of gently exploring the anger that had taken me to this place I was in—he decided to bully me, to intimidate me back into the church with his superior reasoning. (p. 202)

Mee tells what the priest did wrong, which was not honoring his thoughts and feelings, and also states what the priest should have done, which was to gently explore the anger. Later, he related the way in which he kept his anger hidden, "keeping up the outward appearance of a well-balanced, emotionally stable all-American boy. The façade, however, was maintained by sheer will, for underneath was a seething cauldron of repressed emotion in which the 'damaged' and 'wounded' boy repressed the urge 'to kill'" (Wilson, 1990, p. 84).

Family members may feel anger that their loved one has a disability and may question and challenge God about the unfairness of the disability. In a published case study of a girl with a disability who had five adult siblings, the authors reported: "Two of the five siblings expressed anger at God. One sister said, 'When you see her lying in pain, you get angry at God, it's not fair. Sometimes I get cross at K because she died.' It was exhausting emotionally. Because we thought how much more does she have to endure? It seemed so cruel" (Rodger & Tooth, 2004, p. 63).

A man with a spinal cord injury spoke of "anger that just sits there and grows." He said, "I wish I'd had counseling regularly . . . on a fairly regular basis. I'm not sure what would've come out of it, but if you see someone enough, eventually you're going to say something. Try to bring things out, some of the anger, and things like that. That was something that was never done, and that anger just sits in there and grows" (Scherer, 1993, p. 160).

Erik Weihenmayer (2001) became increasingly blind during his adolescence. He also became increasingly angry. In this excerpt, Weihenmayer describes the way in which he focuses his anger at his assistive technology (the cane) and his orientation and mobility instructor, Mrs. Mundy;

ironically both the cane and the instructor would eventually expand his world. However, in recalling his teenage anger, Weihenmayer understands what the cane and Mrs. Mundy represented.

> Until this point, my anger flowed at the world like water from a sprinkler, spraying in too many directions to be dangerous, but in my brief meeting with Mrs. Mundy, I had found a target, a perfect candidate on whom to focus the force of my rage. I hated my cane almost as much as I was learning to hate Mrs. Mundy. In my mind they both represented the vast gulf that existed between me and everyone else. No matter how hard I tried, I'd never be able to bridge that insurmountable expanse. (p. 49)

Overwhelming feelings that worthwhile goals may no longer be possible are common. Anger can be directed toward others. Tuttle (1984) relates this example:

> I went to my club for lunch and sat opposite a woman whom I had known slightly for a long time, and who, in my opinion, had made very little use of her life. Her presence filled me with such anger and jealousy because she was keeping her sight while I was losing mine, that I could barely speak civilly to her. (p. 178)

One individual found spiritual growth in dealing with his anger: "I needed to grow in working with my anger. And this experience of being disabled has made me face and go through, and get angry, learn how to use my own anger . . . . Definitely spiritual" (Boswell, Knight, & Hamer, 2001, p. 21).

Integration and Acceptance

The individual reaches the integration and acceptance stage when he or she (1) understands and accepts the reality and implications of the disability, (2) establishes new values and goals that do not conflict with the disability, and (3) explores and uses his or her strengths and abilities. Often, integration and growth necessitate changes in the environment such as assistive technology, changes in role functioning, and assuming responsibility for the management of the disability. Weihenmayer (2001) discussed his initial acceptance of his blindness:

> Ironically, as I relinquished my grip on sight, I sank into bitter relief. I had not a clue how I would survive as a blind person, how I would cook a meal, walk around, read a book, but trying to live as a sighted person was becoming more painful than blindness could ever be, and

the uncertainty of what each tomorrow would bring was almost more terrifying. I knew nothing about blindness. I had no action plan. While I couldn't see well enough to . . . see an equation on the blackboard, I also couldn't accept myself as being blind. But one thing I knew: compared to this in-between world, total blindness couldn't be any worse, or any more terrifying. (p. 47)

Patricia Deegan (1991), who has a mental illness, spoke of her acceptance of her disability in much the same way as Weihenmayer:

In fact, our recovery is marked by an ever-deepening acceptance of our limitations. But, rather than being an occasion for despair, we find that our personal limitations are the ground from which spring our own unique possibilities. This is the paradox of recovery, that is, in accepting what we cannot do or be, we begin to discover who we can be and what we can do. (p. 50)

Transcendence

In this section, look for—

■ The way in which the concept of transcendence is in direct conflict with the Biomedical Model of disability

■ Dimensions of transcendence

■ Finding meaning and purpose in the disability

■ Reevaluating goals and identities

■ Discovering personal strengths

■ Finding positive aspects of the disability

■ Taking pride in the mastery of the disability

■ Seeking out new experiences

■ Assisting other PWDs

Carolyn Vash (1981) has termed the final stage "transcendence," in which the individual feels that the disability is an opportunity for growth and learning. This stage is never complete; life continues to make demands and challenges of everyone. Reed (1991) defined transcendence as follows: "There is a universal human desire for transcendence and connectedness. Transcendence is defined as a level of awareness that exceeds ordinary, physical boundaries and limitations, yet allows the individual to achieve new perspectives and experiences. Awareness of self-transcendence refers to the developmental maturity whereby there is an expansion of self-boundaries and an orientation toward broadened life perspectives and purposes" (p. 64). PWDs, on reaching this stage, often begin advocacy and support work with other PWDs and their families. Further, they view their advocacy, service, and political activity as a means of bringing meaning and purpose to their own disability experience.

In the past, such an integration and growth perspective toward a disability was thought to be some sort of denial, detachment, or inability to accept the realities of a disability. As we read these first-person accounts, we shall see that these individuals have achieved transcendence *because* of their disability and not *in spite of* their disability. These individuals manage their disability, develop and implement highly effective coping abilities, and experience positive outcomes and increased empowerment. They have incorporated the disability into their self-perception and consider the disability to be a source of potential.

Reading the first-person accounts of PWDs and considering the various dimensions of transcendence, it will become clear that much of transcendence is in direct conflict with the Biomedical Model of disability and the societal view that disability is an unending tragedy and a mark of inferiority. In these false conceptualizations of disability (typically held by PWODs), all disabilities should be eliminated (if the means were available) and all PWDs must want a cure. We can readily see results of such faulty thinking. If PWDs are truly miserable and helpless (and, without doubt, it is expensive to provide a reasonable quality of life for PWDs), then elimination of disability through abortion and assisted suicide seems more reasonable and, perhaps, humane.

In contrast, transcendence of disability is a more holistic view (in contrast to the Biomedical Model) and considers the individual and his or her strengths and assets, the religious/spiritual/philosophical identity of the individual, and the provision of civil rights and accommodations. In the Chapter 9 we shall answer the question, "What do PWDs want?" Much of that discussion will parallel these ideas of transcendence. However, this chapter is focusing on the *individual's* response to disability and Chapter 9 will discuss PWDs as a *group*. Nonetheless, many of these concepts are parallel, for both individuals and groups. In Chapter 9 it can be seen that by accommodating PWDs and incorporating their views, history, and experiences into the wider cultural life of the nation, PWODs will benefit greatly.

Finding Meaning and Purpose in the Disability

Many PWDs state that *because* of their disability they have richer, more satisfying lives. Their disabilities have transformed their lives, giving them a broader view of life. One woman ascribed religious and spiritual purposes: "My reactions came as a result of believing that this is probably not a freak accident that I became a quadriplegic. But, it has some purpose of the world I live in, and that I am not just here . . . because there's some reason or purpose that God intended to fulfill through a disability" (Boswell, Knight, & Hamer, 2001, p. 23).

Some PWDs state they have formed lasting and deep friendships, have become more compassionate toward others, and have a clearer view of what is really important in life. In the video "Harbor of Hope" (Aquarius) an individual speaks of his disability: "I found a new doorway into a room that's full of stuff." Another person states, "The whole experience of disability has been life enhancing. I have met people I would have never met. I have certainly grown and my ideas have undergone changes. I don't feel afraid of death." Weisskopf (2006, October 2), a journalist who lost his arm while covering the war in Iraq, titled his cover article in *Time Magazine*, "How I Lost My Arm and Found Myself." Weisskopf's experiences, and his skillful retelling, emphasize that he feels that he has gained more than he has lost.

In the book *A Life in Science* (1999), the authors described Stephen Hawking's disability, the assistive technology that has allowed Hawking to continue working, and the fact that his disability "seemed to act as a spur, focusing his intellect and energy."

> Many would argue that his liberation from the routine chores of life has enabled him to make greater progress than if he were able-bodied. In 1963, Hawking, just 21 years old, working in Cambridge on his Ph.D. in physics, was told that he had two and a half years to live as a result of ALS, a degenerative motor neuron disease that causes atrophy of muscles throughout the body. Inexplicably, however, Hawking continues to thrive beyond any reasonable expectation. With a voice synthesizer, provided after his 1985 tracheotomy resulting from his bout with pneumonia, and a small personal computer mounted on his wheelchair, his ability to lecture and to collaborate with other physicists, as well as to publish books and articles, have not been compromised. For Hawking, the knowledge that he had a severe disability seemed to act as a spur, focusing his intellect and his energy on his study of cosmology: "Before my condition had been diagnosed, I had been very bored with life. There had not seemed to be anything worth doing. But shortly after I came out of hospital, I dreamt that I was going to be executed. I suddenly realized that there were a lot of worthwhile things I could do if I were reprieved." (White & Gribbin, 1999, p. viii)

Survivors of polio often "believed that their disability made a substantive improvement in their lives" (Wilson, 1990, p. 14). In the book *Living with Polio: The Epidemic and Its Survivors*, Wilson read dozens of first-person accounts of individuals who had contracted polio. Two accounts illustrate the way in which polio changed the direction of the lives of these individuals.

> In high school in rural southern Wisconsin, Jan Little participated in forensics and debate, which didn't require standing and walking. "Roger and Bill, my debate partners, managed to carry me up and down stairways in schools all over southeastern Wisconsin and only dropped me a little one time." (p. 186)

> Robert Owen recalls that before polio struck when he was twelve, he was constantly in trouble, and fought to and from school. In addition to fighting, he also "loved to play football and things like that." He remembers that prior to polio, he "had only read about three books in my whole life." After he returned to school, following a year of rehabilitation, he focused on his studies. Owen is convinced that if he hadn't had polio, he probably would not have become a physician. (p. 202)

Others have discussed the way in which their disability reoriented them to different interests and goals. The director of the movie *The Elephant Man*, Jack Hofsiss, became quadriplegic in a diving accident in a swimming pool. The accident occurred after *The Elephant Man* was made and Hofsiss sees a connection between his disability and his work on the movie.

> It's odd, but I'm beginning to see a greater unity in my life. I came to terms with the worst experience of my life, which was this accident, and the best experience of my life, which was the pure, sweet sense of satisfaction that *The Elephant Man* gave me—the sweetness of working on that piece of material and being responsible for a large number of people knowing about that man and what he was like and how much we had to learn from him. (Hofsiss & Laffey, 1993, pp. 86–87)

Another individual begins his assessment of his disability with the exact words of Jack Hofsiss, "It's odd." Randy Souders views his disability (and the necessary recovery process) as rescuing him from a life in a "mediocre position in a mediocre little ad agency."

> It's odd. If I had a crystal ball to see what would have happened had I not had the injury, I don't see myself having done what I've done at all. I would probably have a mediocre position in a mediocre little ad agency and be like the rest of society—up to my ears in debt, just trying to get by—and frustrated that I didn't go for something that would have truly inspired me all along . . . . I don't know that I would have dedicated myself to art. Art was a vital part of my recovery from my injury. I found myself in a situation of being the same person in a new body, one that didn't work, along with the loss of self-esteem and self-confidence and all the things that come along with a traumatic injury.

Once I realized that I still had a chance at being creative and of value through my artwork, I just really focused in on that that. It was a real part of my recovery. (Smith & Plimpton, 1993, p. 153)

Perhaps the most well-known individual with a disability was President Franklin D. Roosevelt. Roosevelt contracted polio at age 39 and never walked again. Alter (2006), in his book on FDR, states, "Roosevelt reinvented the American presidency through bold policy innovations, brilliant speeches and broadcasts and a person connected with the American people which has not been equaled since." How was FDR able to accomplish all this? Alter views the way in which Roosevelt "embodied hope to a people consumed by despair." He gives much of the credit for this ineffable confidence to Roosevelt's earlier struggle with a disability relatively few Americans were aware he had. Through his agonizing triumph over polio and the bond he discovered with fellow sufferers, Alter writes, "Roosevelt discovered traits that would prove instrumental to the presidency—a theatrical bonhomie, mental suppleness and an empathy . . . that had not characterized his early career" (Widmer, 2006, p. 15). In other words, historians credit Roosevelt's great political successes to the lessons he learned in responding to polio.

Reevaluating Goals and Priorities

The disability and the resulting recovery process can provide the opportunity for individuals to consider their strengths and needs and allow them the time and space to redefine who they are. Some PWDs have reported that they found the goodness in themselves and in others (McColl et al., 2000). Another individual explained: "I found that by being alone—it just sort of sorted itself. It's about looking at yourself—need to put things in balance—I had to re-evaluate my whole life" (Faull et al., 2004, p. 134). Two authors summarized the way in which better perspectives and priorities can be developed: "A catastrophic event [such as a disability] generally results in disintegration of existing patterns, which in turn offers the opportunity for constructive reintegration" (Marsh & Lefly, 1996, p. 3). One woman with a mental illness felt that the recovery process was instrumental in changing her priorities. Note that she refers to her self-image several times in this short excerpt. "The illness itself has not had any good effects, but the process of getting healthier has, especially on my spirituality, my self-image, my character, and personal qualities. Now I have a greater sense of serenity, self-liking, wonder at the world, and caring for myself and others" (Marsh & Lefly, 1996, p. 10).

A psychologist (D. Dunn, 1996) interviewed 138 individuals who had experienced amputations, asking each of them if they had found a "silver lining" in their disability. Dunn categorized their responses into five categories, one of which was "Redefined event/reappraised life." One respondent stated, "All good has come out of it. I found God through it. It has given me purpose. It makes me special." Another stated, "I think I've become a much better person—more humble, more considerate and less selfish. I now know that I am not perfect." A third respondent said, "I was very much a 'wallflower' and since I can no longer blend in, I've become more outgoing." Each of these respondents speaks of having developed positive personality attributes.

A woman of an adult son with a mental illness speaks of her son's willpower and her own "stubbornness," which, if not the result of the disability, certainly strengthened their ability to deal with mental illness:

> My son has great willpower. He has graduated from college, also got his master's degree and has been working as a chemist for the past two years. My son has been hospitalized six times (four of which were court commitments) and he has been homeless. Through my stubbornness we rescued him from the streets. He is now so well and enjoying life. It gives me gratification that I never gave up hope. (Marsh & Lefly, 1996)

A polio survivor told of her awareness of and compassion for others:

> But now, far away from the hospital experience, I can evaluate what I have learned. For it wasn't only suffering: it was learning through suffering. I know my awareness of people has deepened and increased, that those who are close to me can count on me to turn all mind and heart and attention to their problem. I could not have learned *that* dashing all over a tennis court. (Goffman, 1963, p. 11)

In the video "My Body Is Not Who I Am," Leslie Rosen says that her disability has made her feel comfortable with her body and that "most people in society do not." Others stated that they were able to slow down and appreciate the world around them.

A movie prop man who was diagnosed with multiple sclerosis described the way in which he "had to start from square one" and the results:

> Before my disability, I was a superficial person, caught up with competitiveness and machismo. The disability gave me the opportunity to find out who I really am. I had to start from square one to become a member of a community that from time immemorial has been discriminated against and viewed as defective by mainstream society. Transferred to a world of disability culture, I developed deep and meaningful relationships with people in the disability rights movement . . . . They encouraged me to feel attractive and creative and powerful in my way. I don't have to be angry or full of self-pity anymore. (Fleischer & Zames, 2001, p. 202)

Disability can also allow individuals to appraise their life situations and make improvements and other types of changes. An Englishwoman wrote about the positive changes she made and the irony of having others view her disability as a negative experience:

> I feel that most of the people I know think my life has gotten immeasurably worse since I had the diagnosis of multiple sclerosis. In fact, it's better. I'm not denying the difficulties, but being told that I had this illness made me rethink what I was doing. I was able to get out of a very repressive relationship and to live with my mother and my daughter—which is wonderful, it's what I've always wanted. And not having to go to work every day is also wonderful, it's so liberating. The writing that I am doing now, I would never have done if I hadn't been told that I had MS. And yet, if I told my able-bodied friends that my life has improved they would think I was mad [insane], which makes me feel sad. (Morris, 1991, p. 38)

Other individuals have described the use of humor. Nick Vujicic is a 23-year-old Australian who was born without arms or legs. In a speech in Laguna Beach, California, in July 2006 (Basheda, 2006) his sense of humor was evident; nonetheless Vujicic was clear in stating, "I'm not here to say I understand your pain." His parents began a church in Australia, and the membership of the church mourned when he was born. Vujicic remembers reading a Bible scripture in Sunday School that said that all people were created in the image of God. His response was, "Yeah, right." When people ask what happened to him, he uses a one-word reply: "CIGARETTES!" At the end of the speech, Vujicic remarks, "If you run fast, I'm gonna get someone to throw me at you."

In New Zealand, researchers described the use of humor, especially making fun of oneself, by PWDs:

> Notably the ability to laugh at oneself and with others about experiences and situations [was important]. A dominant characteristic of humor described was that it was "in-house" or "black," and in some way at the expense of the teller. Stories often told of a catastrophic experience in which humor was used to make more bearable and acceptable as an aspect of normal life. Humor such as this was seen to indicate an ability to view oneself from the outside and to see oneself in the context of a wider picture. Moreover, it [humor] was considered to reflect the New Zealand cultural norm of understatement, together with an awareness of life which is precious and enjoyable. (Faull et al., 2004, p. 137)

Humor can also defuse and desensationalize disability:

> On several occasions the siblings mentioned humor as a coping mechanism within the family context. Jokes about "spastics" and "epilepsy"

became avenues for tension release within the safe bounds of home, where everyone had a shared understanding of the funny and the serious sides of the jokes. One sibling talked about epileptic jokes and said, ". . . We all just laughed, it was part of our lives. We could laugh, it wasn't that it was too shocking or cruel." (Rodger & Tooth, 2004, p. 61)

It should be noted that the humor is "in-group" humor, told by PWDs themselves and with audiences who know the PWD and understand the disability. None of this humor would be appropriate for PWODs to use.

Discovering Strengths

The PWD, by understanding his or her needs, values, and strengths, can decide on goals and the accommodations and compensations needed (Estroff, 1995). By conceptualizing, initiating action plans, and maintaining motivation, the PWD is able to move forward. The disability can also offer strengths and assets. For example, the golfer Casey Martin stated that his disability has been an asset because "I have expertise in adapting to change" (McCarthy, 2003, p. 203). Erik Weihenmayer (2001) seems to believe that an easy life is not exciting, challenging, or rewarding: "After sixteen years of blindness, one thing I've learned is that life is never meant to be easy; exciting, challenging, rewarding from time to time, but never easy. Ironically, when I finally accepted this reality, that's when life got easy" (p. 282).

In a Canadian study conducted with individuals with traumatic-onset disabilities, two individuals stated that they felt physically invincible since the acquisition of their disability. "One said that he felt invincible because he had seen what his body could survive, and the other said that she thought she would live longer than she might have predicted before the accident, because of changes to her lifestyle" (McColl et al., 2000, p. 561). Another individual stated, "I do believe that I am as good as all those wobblies who walk around on two legs" (Faull et al., 2004, p. 136).

Many PWDs have ascribed sacred meaning to their disability and consider their spirituality to be a strength that results in "a feeling of well-being that God knew their needs and empowered them to cope in difficult times" (Kaye & Raghavan, 2002, pp. 237–238). Indeed, a number of researchers have found spirituality to be a primary resource among PWDs. Fitzgerald (1997) summarized: Spirituality is ". . . both a grand project and an everyday task, referring simultaneously to a process of coming to terms with both the finite and the infinite—the losses and limitations that accompany a disability and the possibilities for a meaningful life and relationship with the world and a higher power. Such a spiritual understanding would overcome the negative themes in traditional theology, such as the notion of disability as punishment, as a tribute to the power of God, as a defect or imperfection, as glorification of suffering or as the object of charity."

A woman with a congenital limb deficiency discusses her spirituality and its relationship to her disability. At first she accepts society's prejudicial views as a self-identifier and abuses alcohol. (Note: A koan in Zen Buddhism is a paradox that is used to meditate on to gain enlightenment.)

> Being disabled is a deep wound, a source of pain. But like all wounds, it is also a gift. As Eastern wisdom has always known, it is hard to tell good luck from bad luck . . . . Having one arm is an endless koan. It is what it is, which is unknowable, and it attracts a lot of ideas, stories, and images. Caught up in the negative story, I felt ashamed, incomplete, and not okay. I drank to die. Later on, caught up in a more positive story, I felt pride and a sense of identity . . . . In a way, I have gone back to the innocence of a baby. When little babies encounter my arm—the arm that ends just below the elbow—it is seen as just another interesting shape to explore and put into their mouths. There is nothing scary or creepy or taboo about it . . . Not labeling what appears as either a deficit or an asset, perfect or imperfect, beautiful or ugly, but wondering openly without conclusion, without trying to get somewhere else. In such open being there is freedom and possibility for the new, even in the midst of what we call imperfection or limitation. I don't mean that the injustices or painful circumstances disappear, but they no longer bind us in the way in the way they did.

Assisting Other PWDs

Many PWDs volunteer in peer-support groups or become active in advocacy and disability rights groups. Some may choose to become professional providers of services to other PWDs and their families. A mother of a man with a psychiatric disability describes her son:

> Well, he is the most kind, wonderful human being—probably because of all he has been through. He volunteers at our local crisis unit. Patients will go in because he is there. Other families request him to speak to their mentally ill loved one. Because of Clozapine (an antipsychotic medication), he is in an MSW (master's of social work) program at our university, and he wants to work with severely mentally ill patients when he graduates. Our mental health center said they want him to work there. (Marsh & Lefly, 1996)

In the video "Harbor of Hope" (Aquarius), an individual decides very quickly, on diagnosis, to assist others. "My doctor told me that I had a brain tumor. I remember that day like yesterday. I remember promising myself in one split second that I would do everything in my power to help myself and others." Indeed, this individual may consider the relationship between helping oneself and helping others to be mutually beneficial and reciprocal.

A Vietnam veteran and a U.S. senator, Max Cleland is also a triple amputee. In his autobiography, *Strong at Broken Places*, he describes the way in which he acquired his disabilities in 1968: "Then I saw the grenade. It was where the chopper had lifted off. It must be mine, I thought. I bent down to pick up the grenade. A blinding explosion threw me backwards." Cleland served in the Georgia State Senate and wrote the state law for disability accessibility to public buildings. Today, he sits on the Senate Armed Services Committee. Obviously, Max Cleland's advocacy for PWDs is at a high level with a great deal of national visibility; nonetheless, it was his disabilities that led him to a career in politics and public service.

Advantages of the Stage Theory

In this section, look for—

- How the theory facilitates the selection of the most suitable forms of treatment
- How the theory emphasizes the need for both short-term treatment and long-term support
- How the theory allows the PWD to understand his or her own feelings and reactions
- How common variables can be tailored to the individual PWD
- How the theory helps to validate and normalize the PWD's intense and often contradictory emotions
- How the theory recognizes that adjustment/response is a process and not a one-time event

---

Educating the PWD and his or her family about these stages helps to "normalize" and "universalize" the experience of adaptation/response. When the PWD and his or her family learn that other individuals experience the same types of feelings, the PWD will not feel as isolated. It is strengthening to an individual to know that others understand his or her experience. The individual feels validated and is able to put his or her feelings in context. Proponents of the stage theory maintain that these types of responses of PWDs (and their families) are neither pathological nor dysfunctional. These stages can be steps to self-mastery. Occasionally, however, if the responses are prolonged or associated with major impairment, then interventions can be implemented.

The stage theory also assists service providers in understanding th process of response/adaptation and, in so doing, helps service providers to choose the best treatment goals (Livneh, 1986b). Tailoring concrete short-term goals compatible with the stage of adaptation/response can provide a task-oriented approach that does not overwhelm the individual. Conceptualizing the adaptation/response to a disability as a process can also assist service providers in encouraging and supporting the individual to progress to the next stage while not permitting coping mechanisms of one stage to become long-term habits. Caregivers cannot counter maladaptive responses and behaviors unless they understand the demands of each stage. Case management, in which many different professionals provide services to a single individual, is facilitated when there is agreement and understanding concerning the stage in which the PWD is operating. This agreement among members of the treatment team will ensure that all treatment will be coordinated. Furthermore, educating and supporting PWDs and their families can assist in maintaining family equilibrium and help families to avoid making major life changes until they are further along in the process.

Understanding the stages of adaptation/response assists family members in their efforts to support the PWD. For example, family members can be educated about the importance of noncritical acceptance of the PWD's denial. Family members learn that confronting or arguing with the PWD is counterproductive. Another example concerns the individual who is in the anger stage. Often, this anger is expressed toward the most accessible people—family members or care providers. Helping family and caregivers to understand that the anger of the PWD is an attempt to regain balance and control will reduce their stress and help to eliminate compassion fatigue and burnout. Therefore, if caregivers and family members understand the stages of adaptation, it is less likely that the PWD will become socially isolated. The stage theory promotes hope and optimism and provides a starting point for assisting the PWD. Deegan (1991) stated, "Hope is contagious" (p. 53).

Often professional caregivers minimize or purposely avoid certain stages of the adaptation/response process. For example, some professionals are not comfortable with individuals who are experiencing the anger stage (Clanton, Rude, & Taylor, 1992). By understanding the stage theory and developing an awareness of their own responses to certain stages, professional caregivers can develop alternative treatment strategies, such as refer ring PWDs to other caregivers.

Assisting PWDs to understand the stages of allow them to draw on their strengths and capabili & Antonak, 1990). Of course, such an understandi lectual understanding; it is a deep, therapeutic conc term process. Often, PWDs join support groups wi experienced the same disability. Because group mei

ges in the adaptation/response process, members often learn from
eriences of others. These self-help groups can do much to promote
intain hope. Further, group members know that others understand
periences.

Cautions in Implementing the Stage Theory

> **In this section, look for—**
>
> - Some stage theories that are specific to the disability, such as therapeutic amputations
> - How, in some disabilities, the stages progress not in a linear fashion but in a curvilinear fashion
> - How each stage encompasses a wide variety of behavioral characteristics
> - How the stage theory does not consider the prejudice and discrimination of others and how these affect the adjustment/response process
> - How individuals can recycle through the stages, repeat a stage, or skip a stage
> - How disability is not a single event but a process

The stage theory of adaptation/response to disability faces some criticism, even to the point of terming the stage theory "social oppression" (Kendall & Buys, 1998, p. 17). The idea that *every* PWD, and his or her family, regardless of the type or severity of disability, experiences a predictable, orderly, sequential, linear, hierarchical progression through these stages has never been suggested by the proponents of the theory. Nor has the wide variability in behavioral characteristics of each stage been disputed. One critique does, however, have merit. Kendall and Buys argued, "Stage models of adjustment also normalize responses such as denial and distress following acquired disability, which may lead rehabilitation workers to expect, or even encourage, such responses" (p. 17). Nonetheless, proponents of the stage model have noted the following:

> The process of adaptation is not irreversible. Individuals who experience a chronic illness or sustain a permanent disability may regress to an earlier phase or skip one or more phases of psychosocial adaptation.

Phases of adaptation comprise nondiscrete and categorically overlapping reactions. These reactions may fluctuate and blend with one another, providing for the experience of more than one reaction at a time. Attempts to specify the duration of each phase, or of the entire adaptation response, are futile at best. (Livneh & Antonak, 1997, p. 19)

Therefore, it is difficult to understand the criticism that rehabilitation workers, and other care providers, might encourage certain responses such as denial or distress. The stage theory provides *only* guidelines and acknowledges that PWDs do not proceed through these stages in a one-time-only, sequential, time-dated process. PWDs whose disability has been medically stabilized may recycle through these stages as the demands and stresses of developmental tasks and other life transitions arise.

The stage theory does propose a linear process, but it also acknowledges that, for some disabilities, the response/adaptation process is a curvilinear process. Many individuals with chronic, degenerating disabilities and chronic illnesses are thought to experience a curvilinear response, with a positive response in the beginning (when the symptoms and pain are not very great), a negative response in middle age (when the symptoms and pain increase), and a positive response in older age (when the individual has few functional demands).

There are a few disabilities for which the stage theory has been specifically adapted. For instance, the stage theory has been applied to individuals with amputations and congenital limb deficiencies. Individuals who undergo a surgical (therapeutic) amputation experience four phases: (1) realization that the loss of a limb is imminent; (2) early postoperative hospitalization; (3) in-hospital rehabilitation, in which the individual receives such treatments as the fitting of a prosthesis; and (4) home rehabilitation, in which the individual returns to his or her "normal" life (Bradway, Malone, Racy, Leal, & Poole, 1984).

The stage theory advocates viewing the person as someone with resources and capabilities. By acknowledging various stages, PWDs can understand their own feelings better and the feelings of family members. For example, clients (with or without disabilities) tend to terminate counseling/psychotherapy when they feel they are not "getting better." Recognizing and understanding that "you might feel worse before you feel better" may help clients to continue in counseling. Caregivers (both professional and family members) will be less likely to withdraw support if they understand that some of the typical stages a PWD experiences are often unpleasant. Rereading Patricia Deegan's *Recovery*, we can see that her family members never withdrew their support and encouragement, in spite of the fact that she sat on the couch all day. Arnold Beisser, the physician who contracted polio, described his relationship with his disability as like a marriage, especially when he realized that there was no final and complete stage to accepting his disability.

The argument that the stage theory promotes the idea that a disability is an undesirable state ("pathologizing" disability) has not been validated by research or by anecdotal evidence. Powers (1993) explained:

> The topic of disability-related grief is also associated with sensitivity and controversy when considered in relation to current positive perspectives of disability. Theories that postulate the existence of grief or chronic sorrow in response to a disability are sometimes regarded as promulgating the notion that disability is an inherently tragic event with an enduring negative impact on families. Yet . . . it can be through the validation and processing of grief that many family members shift their perspectives of disability from tragedy to challenge and opportunity. (p. 120)

An excellent summarization on the need for counseling support (and the dangers of not providing it) is provided by a PWD who said, "People in this condition need mental rehabilitation more than anything else. Because that is 90 percent of physical rehabilitation. [Rehabilitation doesn't] want to face that because it's too expensive. So you adapt. You develop coping mechanisms and some of them, like drinking, are not good ones. If way back then they had given us good coping mechanisms, a lot of problems could have been prevented" (Scherer, 1993, pp. 159–160).

In-Class Videos

- View the 33-minute video "Parenting and Disabilities: 24/7" produced by Fanlight Productions. The producers describe this video:
  - "For 18 years, Rob and Betsy Holl have taken care of their profoundly disabled [sic] daughter at home, with no help. Now middle-aged, exhausted by the constant stress of juggling Megan's unrelenting needs with the demands of raising their other child and hanging onto their jobs, they feel that they have hit the wall."
  - "Marsha Desso and Larry Kessler's son Stuart was born autistic in 1957. As a violent young man, he was restrained in state hospitals and jails, but today his elderly parents care for him at work with the assistance of a state-funded caregiver. But the state is cutting back, and Stuart's care budget is in growing jeopardy.
  - "When state institutions for people with severe developmental disabilities were closed down throughout the United States, few families mourned their loss. But it didn't take long to discover that the promised alternatives—programs to care for family members at home and in the community—were neglected and underfunded. Today, thousands of exhausted parents are providing all day, every day, care for a developmentally disabled loved one, while simultaneously battling for the help and resources they need." Order No. JF-438.

- View the 50-minute video "King Gimp" produced by Films for the Humanities. The producers describe this video: "Dan Keplinger was born with cerebral palsy. Filmed over thirteen years, this special classroom version by the Academy Award-winning King Gimp producers chronicles Dan's life from his years in a special school to his college graduation. A frank, uplifting epic of triumph over adversity, the program is also the portrait of an artist's birth, since it was Dan's discovery of painting and drawing that freed his spirit of expression from the prison of his body. His ongoing career as a successful painter attests to his victory over nearly insurmountable obstacles both physical and societal." #JMR30375.

In-Class Learning Activity

- Dr. Donald Linkowski, formerly a professor of rehabilitation at George Washington University, developed *The Acceptance of Disability Scale* (AD) in 1969. Linkowski has given permission to reprint this scale in the book (Appendix 7–B), with two provisos: (1) he is aware that the more accurate term is "response" to disability, and (2) he is in the process of making revisions. Nonetheless, *The Acceptance of Disability Scale* can be a useful learning tool for students (in addition to the original purpose of assessing an individual's acceptance of disability).

  You will remember that Linkowski derived this instrument from Beatrice Wright's theory of cognitive restructuring. Wright's theory has four components:

  1. Enlargement of the scope of values
  2. Subordination of the physique
  3. Containment of disability effects
  4. Transformation from comparative values to asset values (instead of viewing the limitations, viewing the assets the individual has).

  As you read and answer the questions of the AD scale (see Appendix 7–B), determine which of the four components Linkowski based each question on.

Learning Activities

1. Using one of the 19 "bullets" listed at the beginning of this chapter, write a response paper.
2. Read any of the following first-person accounts of disability. Look for these points:

   - Is the author White, middle-class, and highly educated?

- What is the disability? Is it a physical, intellectual, cognitive, or psychiatric disability?
- Is the disability part of the author's identity?
- Are there any extraordinary environmental resources?
- Are there examples of Beatrice Wright's cognitive restructuring coping mechanisms?
- Is there evidence (or lack of evidence) of the stage theory of acceptance/response to disability?

References

Aiken, L. R. (1997). *Psychological testing and assessment* (9th ed.). Needham Heights, MA: Allyn & Bacon.

Albon, J. (1989). Families with dwarf children. In S. C. Hey, G. Kiger, & D. Evans (Eds.), *The changing world of impaired and disabled people in society* (pp. 350–358). Salem, OR: The Society for Disability Studies and Willamette University.

Alter, J. (2006). *The defining moment: FDR's hundred days and the triumph of hope.* New York: Simon & Schuster.

American Psychiatric Association. (1994). *Diagnostic and statistical manual of mental disorders* (4th ed.). Washington, DC: Author.

Anson, C. A., Stanwyck, D. J., & Krause, J. S. (1993). Social support and health status in spinal cord injury. *International Journal of Paraplegia, 31,* 632–638.

Antonak, R. F., & Livneh, H. (1991). A hierarchy of reactions to disability. *International Journal of Rehabilitation Research, 14,* 13–24.

Austin, J. K. (1990). Assessment of coping mechanisms used by parents and children with chronic illness. *Maternal and Child Nursing, 15,* 98–102.

Ballin, A. (1930). *The deaf mute howls.* Los Angeles: Grafton.

Basheda, L. (2006, July). No arms, no legs—no worries. *Orange County Register, 1,* 7.

Bayton, D. (1995). Chronic illness and the dynamics of hoping. In S. K. Toombs, D. Barnard, & R. A. Carson (Eds.), *Chronic illness and the dynamics of hoping* (pp. 38–57). Bloomington: University of Indiana.

Beisser, A. (1989). *Flying without wings: Personal reflections on being disabled.* New York: Doubleday.

Bergner, M., Bobbitt, R. A., Kressel, S., Pollard, W. E., Gilson, B. S., & Morris, J. R. (1976). The *Sickness Impact Scale* Profile: Conceptual formulation and methodology for the development of a health status measure. *International Journal of Health Services, 6,* 393–415.

Bordieri, J. E. (1993). Self-blame attributions for disability and perceived client involvement in the vocational rehabilitation process. *Journal of Applied Rehabilitation Counseling, 24*(2), 3–6.

Boswell, B., Knight, S., & Hamer, M. (2001). Disability and spirituality: A reciprocal relationship with implications for the rehabilitation process. *Journal of Rehabilitation, 67,* 20–25.

Bradway, J. K., Malone, J. M., Racy, J., Leal, J. M., & Poole, J. (1984). Psychological adaptation to amputation: An overview. *Orthotics and Prosthetics, 38,* 46–50.

Brookes, T. (1995). *Catching my breath: An asthmatic explores his illness.* New York: Vintage.

Butcher, J. N., & Garcia, R. E. (1978). Cross-national application of psychological tests. *Personnel and Guidance Journal, 56,* 472–475.

Butcher, J. N., & Pancheri, P. (1976). *A handbook of cross-national MMPI research.* Minneapolis, MN: University of Minnesota.

Callahan, J. (1989). *Don't worry, he won't get far on foot.* New York: Random House.

Clanton, L. D., Rude, S. S., & Taylor, C. (1992). Learned resourcefulness as a moderator of burnout in a sample of rehabilitation providers. *Rehabilitation Psychology, 37,* 131–140.

Close, C. (1993). In J. K. Smith & G. Plimpton (Eds.), *Chronicles of courage: Very special artists.* New York: Random House.

Cohen, L. H. (1994). *Train go sorry: Inside a Deaf world.* Boston: Houghton Mifflin.

Cohen, R. M. (2004). *Blindsided: Living a life above illness: A reluctant memoir.* New York: HarperCollins.

Corbett, J. O., & Bregante, J. L. (1993). Disabled lesbians: Multicultural realities. In M. Nagler (Ed.). *Perspectives on disability* (pp. 261–271). Palo Alto, CA: Health Markets Research.

Couser, G. T. (1997). *Recovering bodies: Illness, disability, and life writing.* Madison, WI: University of Wisconsin.

Darlington, R. B. (1971). Another look at "cultural fairness." *Journal of Educational Measurement, 9,* 71–82.

Davis, L. J. (1995). *Enforcing normalcy: Disability, deafness, and the body.* London: Verso.

Deegan, P. E. (1991). Recovery: The lived experience of rehabilitation. In R. P. Marinelli & A. E. Dell Orto (Eds.), *The psychological and social impact of disability* (3rd ed.) (pp. 47–45). New York: Springer.

DeLoach, C., & Greer, B. G. (1981). *Adjustment to severe physical disability: A metamorphosis.* New York: McGraw-Hill.

Dembo, T., Leviton, G. L., & Wright, B. A. (1956). Adjustment to misfortune—A problem of social psychological rehabilitation. *Artificial Limbs, 3*(2), 4–62.

Demorest, M. E., & Erdman, S. A. (1987). Development of the Communication Profile for the Hearing Impaired. *Journal of Speech and Hearing Disorders, 52,* 129–143.

Derogatis, L. R. (1986). The Psychosocial Adjustment to Illness Scale (PAIS). *Journal of Psychosomatic Research, 30,* 77–91.

Dodrill, C. B., Batzel, L. W., Quisser, H. R., & Temkin, N. R. (1980). An objective method for the assessment of psychological and social problems among epileptics. *Epilepsia, 21,* 123–135.

Donoghue, P. J., & Siegel, M. E. (1992). *Sick and tired of feeling sick and tired: Living with invisible chronic illness.* New York: Norton.

Dunn, D. S. (1996). Well-being following amputation: Salutary effects of positive meaning, optimism, and control. *Rehabilitation Psychology, 41,* 285–302.

Dunn, M. (1996). Subscale development of the Rehabilitation Situations Inventory. *Rehabilitation Psychology, 41,* 255–264.

Edwards, A. L. (1959). *Edwards personal preference scale.* New York: Harcourt Assessment.

Estroff, S. E. (1995). Whose story is it anyway? Authority, voice, and responsibility in narratives of chronic illness. In S. K. Toombs, D. Barnard, & R. A. Carson (Eds.), *Chronic illness: From experience to policy* (pp. 77–102). Bloomington, IN: University of Indiana.

Faull, K., Hills, M. D., Cochrane, G., Gray, J., Hunt, McKenzie, M., & Winter, L. (2004). Investigation of health perspectives of those with physical disabilities: The role of spirituality as a determinant of health. *Disability and Rehabilitation, 26,* 129–144.

Feinstein, A.R., & Chapman, H. (2002). *Principles of medical statistics*. Boca Raton, FL: CRC Press.

Fine, M., & Asch, A. (1988). Introduction: Beyond pedestals. In M. Fine & A. Asch (Eds.), *Women with disabilities: Essays in psychology, culture, and politics* (pp. 1–37). Philadelphia: Temple University.

Fischer, S. D., & van der Hulst, H. (2003). Sign language structures. In M. Marschmark & P. E. Spencer (Eds.). *Oxford handbook of deaf studies, language, and education* (pp. 319–331). New York: Oxford University Press.

Fitzgerald, J. (1997). Reclaiming the whole self: Self, spirit, and society. *Disability and Rehabilitation, 19*, 407–413.

Fleischer, D. Z., & Zames, F. (2001). *The disability rights movement: From charity to confrontation*. Philadelphia: Temple University.

Frank, A. W. (1991). *At the will of the body: Reflections on illness*. Boston: Houghton Mifflin.

Frank, A. W. (1995). *The wounded storyteller: Body, illness, and ethics*. Chicago: University of Chicago.

Frese, F. (1997). Twelve aspects of coping for persons with serious and persistent mental illness. In L. Spaniol, C. Gagne, & M. Hoehler (Eds.), *Psychological and social aspects of psychiatric disability*. Boston: Center for Psychiatric Rehabilitation, Boston University.

Garland, F. J., & Zis, A. P. (1991). Multiple sclerosis and affective disorders. *Canadian Journal of Psychiatry, 36*, 112–117.

Goffman, E. (1963). *Stigma: Notes on a spoiled identity*. Englewood Cliffs, NJ: Prentice Hall.

Goldberg, D. P. (1972). *The detection of psychiatric illness by questionnaire*. London: Oxford University Press.

Gough, H. G. (1957). *California psychological inventory*. Mountain View, CA: Consulting Psychologists Press.

Greene, R. L. (1987). Ethnicity and MMPI performance: A review. *Journal of Consulting and Clinical Psychology, 55*, 497–512.

Hawkins, A. H. (1993). *Reconstructing illness: Studies in pathography*. West Lafayette, IN: Purdue University.

Heinemann, A. W., & Shontz, F. C. (1984). Adjustment following disability: Representative case studies. *Rehabilitation Counseling Bulletin, 58*, 3–14.

Heinemann, A. W., & Shontz, F. C. (1985). Methods of studying persons. *Counseling Psychologist, 13*, 111–125.

Higgins, P. C. (1980). *Outsiders in a hearing world: A sociology of Deafness*. Newbury Park, CA: Sage.

Hofsiss, J., & Laffey, M. (1993). Jack Hofsiss and Maureen Laffey (pp. 78–87). In J. K. Smith & G. Plimpton (Eds.), *Chronicles of courage: Very special artists*. New York. Random House.

Hull, J. M. (1991). *Touching the rock: The experience of blindness*. New York: Pantheon.

Johnson, D. L. (1993). Grieving is the pits. In G. H. S. Singer & L. E. Powers (Eds.), *Families, disability, and empowerment: Active coping skills and strategies for family interventions* (pp. 151–154). Baltimore: Brookes.

Kaye, J., & Raghavan, S. K. (2002). Spirituality in disability and illness. *Journal of Religion and Health, 41*, 231–242.

Keller, H. (1990). *The story of my life*. New York: Bantam.

Kendall, E., & Buys, N. (1998). An integrated model of psychosocial adjustment following acquired disability. *Journal of Rehabilitation, 64*(3), 16–21.

Kübler-Ross, E. (1969). *On death and dying*. New York: Macmillan.

Kisor, H. (1990). *What's that pig outdoors? A memoir of deafness.* New York: Hill and Wang.

Kleinman, A. (1988). *The illness narratives: Suffering, healing, and the human condition.* New York: Basic Books.

Krause, J. S. (1997). Adjustment after spinal cord injury: A nine-year longitudinal study (1985–1994). *Archives of Physical Medicine and Rehabilitation, 78,* 651–657.

Krause, J. S. (1998a). Changes in adjustment after spinal cord injury: A 20-year longitudinal study. *Rehabilitation Psychology, 43,* 41–55.

Krause, J. S. (1998b). Dimensions of subjective well-being after spinal cord injury: An empirical analysis by gender and race/ethnicity. *Archives of Physical Medicine and Rehabilitation, 79,* 900–909.

Krause, J. S., & Anson, C. A. (1997). Adjustment after spinal cord injury: Relationship to participation in employment or educational activities. *Rehabilitation Counseling Bulletin, 40,* 202–214.

Krause, J. S., Coker, J., Charlifue, S., & Whiteneck, G. G. (1999). Depression and subjective well being among 97 American Indians with spinal cord injury: A descriptive study. *Rehabilitation Psychology, 44,* 354–372.

Kriegel, L. (1991). *Falling into life.* San Francisco: North Point.

Lane, H. (1992). *The mask of benevolence: Bio-power and the Deaf community.* New York: Knopf.

Langer, K. G. (1994). Depression and denial in psychotherapy of persons with disabilities. *American Journal of Psychotherapy, 48,* 181–194.

Lindemann, J. I. (Ed.). (1981). *Psychological and behavioral aspects of physical disability.* New York: Plenum.

Linkowski, D. C. (1971). A scale to measure acceptance of disability. *Rehabilitation Counseling Bulletin, 14,* 236–244.

Linkowski, D. C. (1987). *The acceptance of disability scale.* Washington, DC: The George Washington University Medical Center, Department of Psychiatry and Behavioral Sciences, The Rehabilitation Research and Training Center (originally published in 1971).

Linkowski, D. C., & Dunn, M. A. (1974). Self-concept and acceptance of disability. *Rehabilitation Counseling Bulletin, 17,* 28–32.

Livneh, H. (1986a). A unified approach to existing models of adaptation to disability—I. A model of adaptation. *Journal of Applied Rehabilitation Counseling, 17*(1), 5–16, 56.

Livneh, H. (1986b). A unified approach to existing models of adaptation to disability—II. Intervention strategies. *Journal of Applied Rehabilitation Counseling, 17*(2), 6–10.

Livneh, H., & Antonak, R. F. (1990). Reactions to disability: An empirical investigation of their nature and structure. *Journal of Applied Rehabilitation Counseling, 21*(4), 13–21.

Livneh, H., & Antonak, R. F. (1997). *Psychosocial adaptation to chronic illness and disability.* Gaithersburg, MD: Aspen.

Mairs, N. (1997). Foreword. In G. T. Couser (Ed.), *Recovering bodies: Illness, disability, and life writing* (pp. ix–xiii). Madison, WI: University of Wisconsin.

Marks, D. (1999). *Disability: Controversial debates and psychosocial perspectives.* London: Routledge.

Marsh, D. T., & Lefly, H. P. (1996). The family experience of mental illness: Evidence for resilience. *Psychiatric Rehabilitation, 20*(2), 3–13.

Marsh, D. T. (1992). *Families and mental illness: New directions in professional practice.* New York: Praeger.

Marshak, L. E., & Seligman, M. (1993). *Counseling persons with physical disabilities: Theoretical and clinical perspectives.* Austin, TX: PRO-ED.

Martinelli, R. P., & Dell Orto, A. E. (1991). *The psychological and social impact of disability* (3rd ed.). New York: Springer.

McCarthy, H. (2003). The disability rights movement: Experiences and perspectives of selected leaders in the disability community. *Rehabilitation Counseling Bulletin, 46,* 209–223.

McColl, M. A., Bickenbach, J., Johnston, J., Nishihama, S., Schumaker, M., Smith, K., et al. (2000). Spiritual issues associated with traumatic-onset disability.

Mee, C. L. (1999). *A nearly normal life: A memoir.* Boston: Little, Brown.

Meenan, R. F., Gertman, P. M., & Mason, J. H. (1980). Measuring health status in arthritis: The Arthritis Impact and Measurement Scales. *Arthritis and Rheumatism, 23,* 146–152.

Michalko, R. (2002). *The difference disability makes.* Philadelphia: Temple University.

Millon, T., Green, C. J., & Maegher, R. B., Jr. (1979). The MBHI: A new inventory for the psychodiagnostician in medical settings. *Professional Psychology, 10,* 529–539.

Millon, T., Millon, C., Davis, R., & Grossman, S. (1981). *The Millon clinical multiaxial inventory.* Minneapolis: National Computer Systems.

Moos, R. H. (Ed.). (1984). *Coping with physical illness. Volume 2: New perspectives.* New York: Plenum.

Morris, J. (1991). *Pride against prejudice: Transforming attitudes to disability.* Philadelphia: New Society.

Murphy, R. (1987). *The body silent.* New York: Henry Holt.

Naugle, R. I. (1991). Denial in rehabilitation: Its genesis, consequences, and clinical management. In R. P. Marinelli & A. E. Dell Otto (Eds.), *The psychological and social impact of disability* (3rd ed.) (pp. 139–151). New York: Springer.

Olkin, R. (1999). *What psychotherapists should know about disability.* New York: Guilford.

Osuji, O. N. (1975). "Acceptance of loss"—quantification of the concept. *Rehabilitation Digest, 6,* 3–8.

Padden, C., & Humphries, T. (1988). *Deaf in America: Voices from a culture.* Cambridge, MA: Harvard University Press.

Perkins, R. (1996). *Talking to angels: A life spent in high latitudes.* Boston: Beacon.

Pollard, R. Q., DeMatteo, A., Lentz, E., & Rediess, S. (2007). A prose recall test using stories in American Sign Language. *Rehabilitation Psychology, 52,* 11–24.

Powers, L. E. (1993). Disability and grief: From tragedy to challenge. In G. H. S. Singer & L. E. Powers (Eds.), *Families, disability, and empowerment: Active coping skills and strategies for family interventions* (pp. 119–149). Baltimore: Brookes.

Price, R. (1994). *A whole new life: An illness and a healing.* New York: Atheneum.

Reed, P. G. (1991). Toward a nursing theory of self-transcendence: Deductive reformulation using developmental theories. *Advances in Nursing Science, 13(4),* 64–77.

Rodger, S., & Tooth, L. (2004). Adult siblings' perceptions of family life and loss: A pilot case study. *Journal of Developmental and Physical Disabilities, 16,* 53–71.

Roessler, R., & Bolton, B. (1978). *Psychosocial adjustment to disability.* Baltimore: University Park Press.

Rousso, H. (1993). *Disabled, female, and proud! Stories of ten women with disabilities.* Westport, CT: Bergin & Garvey.

Schaller, S. (1991). *A man without words.* New York: Summit.

Scherer, M. S. (1993). *Living in the state of stuck: How technologies affect the lives of people with disabilities.* Cambridge, MA: Brookline.

Schlossberg, N. K. (1981). A model for analyzing human adaptation to transition. *The Counseling Psychologist, 9,* 2–18.

Shell, M. (2005). *Polio and its aftermath: The culture of paralysis.* Cambridge, MA: Harvard University.

Shontz, F. C. (1975). *The psychological aspects of physical illness and disability.* New York: Macmillan.

Shontz, F. C. (1977). Physical disability and personality: Theory and research. In R. P. Marinelli & A. E. Dell Otto (Eds.), *The psychological and social impact of physical disability* (pp. 105–129). New York: Springer.

Shontz, F. C. (1991). Six principles relating to disability and psychological adjustment. In R. P. Marinelli & A. E. Dell Orto (Eds.), *The psychological and social impact of disability* (3rd ed.) (pp. 107–110). New York: Springer.

Sienkiewicz-Mercer, R., & Kaplan, S. B. (1989). *I raise my eyes to say yes.* Boston: Houghton-Mifflin.

Smart, J. F. (1993). Level of acculturation of Mexican Americans with disabilities and acceptance of disability. *Rehabilitation Counseling Bulletin, 36,* 199–211.

Smart, J. F., & Smart, D. W. (1991). Acceptance of disability and the Mexican American culture. *Rehabilitation Counseling Bulletin, 34,* 356–367.

Smart, J. F., & Smart, D. W. (1992a). Cultural issues in the rehabilitation of Hispanics. *Journal of Rehabilitation, 58,* 29–37.

Smart, J. F., & Smart, D. W. (1992b). Curriculum changes in multicultural rehabilitation. *Rehabilitation Education, 6,* 105–122.

Smart, J. F., & Smart, D. W. (1993a). Acculturation, biculturism, and the rehabilitation of Mexican Americans. *Journal of Applied Rehabilitation Counseling, 24,* 46–51.

Smart, J. F., & Smart, D. W. (1993b). The rehabilitation of Hispanics with disabilities: Sociocultural constraints. *Rehabilitation Education, 7,* 167–184.

Smart, J. F., & Smart, D. W. (1994a). The rehabilitation of Hispanics experiencing acculturative stress: Implications for practice. *The Journal of Rehabilitation, 60*(4), 8–12.

Smart, J. F., & Smart, D. W. (1994b). Rehabilitation of Hispanics: Implications for training and education. *Rehabilitation Education, 8,* 360–369.

Smart, J. F., & Smart, D. W. (1995a). Acculturative stress: The experience of Hispanic immigrants. *The Counseling Psychologist, 23,* 25–42.

Smart, J. F., & Smart, D. W. (1995b). Acculturative stress of Hispanics: Loss and challenge. *Journal of Counseling and Development, 73,* 390–396.

Smart, J. F., & Smart, D. W. (1995c). Response to Leal-Idrogo's "Further thoughts." *Journal of Rehabilitation, 61,* 24–25.

Smart, J. F., & Smart, D. W. (1995d). The use of translators/interpreters in rehabilitation. *Journal of Rehabilitation, 61,* 14–20.

Smart, J. F., & Smart, D. W. (1995e). Vocational evaluation of Hispanic clients with disabilities. *Directions in Rehabilitation Counseling, 6,* 1–12.

Smart, J. F., & Smart, D. W. (1996). The rehabilitation of Hispanics: Topics of interest to educators. *Rehabilitation Education, 10,* 171–184.

Smith, J. K., & Plimpton, G. (1993). *Chronicles of courage: Very special artists.* New York: Random House.

Spelic, S. S. (1997, Winter). Somatization and hypochondriasis. *Treatment Today,* pp. 30–34.

Spradley, R., & Spradley, J. (1985). *Deaf like me* (2nd ed.). Washington, DC: Gallaudet University.

Stefan, S. (2001). *Unequal rights: Discrimination against people with mental disabilities and the Americans with Disabilities Act.* Washington, DC: American Psychological Association.

Stewart, J. R. (1994). Denial of disabling conditions and specific interventions in the rehabilitation counseling setting. *Journal of Applied Rehabilitation Counseling, 25*(3), 7–15.

Toombs, S. K. (1995). Sufficient unto the day: A life with multiple sclerosis. In S. K. Toombs, D. Barnard, & R. A. Carson (Eds.), *Chronic illness: From experience to policy.* (pp. 2–23). Bloomington, IN: University of Indiana.

Tuttle, D. W. (1984). *Self-esteem and adjusting with blindness: The process of responding to life's demands.* Springfield, IL: Charles C. Thomas.

Vash, C. L. (1981). *The psychology of disability.* New York: Springer.

Velasquez, R. J., & Callahan, W. J. (1991). Psychological testing of Hispanic Americans in clinical settings: Overview and issues. In K. F. Geisinger (Ed.), *Psychological testing of Hispanics* (pp. 253–256). Washington, DC: American Psychological Association.

Weihenmayer, E. (2001). *Touch the top of the world: A blind man's journey to climb farther than the eye can see.* New York: Dutton.

Weisskopf, M. (2006, October 2). How I lost my hand but found myself. *Time Magazine,* 28–37.

Wendell, S. (1997). Toward a feminist theory of disability. In L. J. Davis (Ed.), *Disability Studies Reader* (pp. 260–278). New York: Routledge.

Westbrook, M. T., Legge, V., & Pennay, M. (1993). Attitudes towards disabilities in a multicultural society. *Social Science & Medicine, 36,* 615–623.

White, M., & Gribbin, J. (1999). *A life in science.* New York: Penguin.

Widmer, T. (2006, May 7). Magic man: How Franklin D. Roosevelt brought America back from the brink. *New York Times Book Review.*

Wilson, D. J. (1990). *Living with polio: The epidemic and its survivors.* Chicago, IL: University of Chicago.

Wortman, C. B., & Silver, R. C. (1989). The myths of coping with loss. *Journal of Consulting and Clinical Psychology, 57,* 349–357.

Wright, B. (1983). *Physical Disability—A psychosocial approach.* New York: Harper and Row.

Wright, B. A. (1960). *Physical disability: A psychological approach.* New York: Harper and Row.

Wright, B. A. (1991). Labeling: The need for greater person-environment individuation. In C. R. Snyder & D. R. Forsythe (Eds.), *Handbook of social and clinical psychology* (pp. 469–487). Elmsford, NY: Pergamon.

Yoshida, K. K. (1993). Reshaping of self: A pendular reconstruction of self and identity among adults with traumatic spinal cord injury. *Sociology of Health and Illness, 15,* 217–245.

Zola, I. K. (1982). *Missing pieces: A chronicle of living with a disability.* Philadelphia: Temple University.

Appendix 7—A

First-Person Narratives of People with Disabilities

Bailin, A. (1930). *The deaf mute howls.* Los Angeles: Grafton.

Beisser, A. R. (1989). *Flying without wings: Personal reflections on being disabled.* New York: Doubleday.

Black, K. (1996). *In the shadow of polio.* White Plains, NY: Addison Wesley Longman.

Brookes, T. (1995). *Catching my breath: An asthmatic explores his illness.* New York: Vintage.

Callahan, J. (1989). *Don't worry, he won't get far on foot.* New York: Random House.

Cohen, L. H. (1994). *Train go sorry: Inside a Deaf world.* Boston: Houghton Mifflin.

Cohen, R. M. (2004). *Blindsided: Living a life above illness—A reluctant memoir.* New York: HarperCollins.

Fries, K. (Ed.). (1997). *Staring back: The disability experience from the inside out.* New York: Plume.

Gallagher, H. G. (1985). *FDR's splendid deception.* New York: Dodd and Mead.

Hannaford, S. (1985). *Living outside inside: A disabled woman's experience. Towards a social and political perspective.* Berkeley, CA: Canterbury Press.

Hockenberry, J. (1995). *Moving violations: War zones, wheelchairs, and declarations of independence.* New York: Hyperion.

Hull, J. M. (1991). *Touching the rock: The experience of blindness.* New York: Pantheon.

Keller, H. (1903). *The story of my life.* New York: Doubleday.

Kisor, H. (1990). *What's that pig outdoors? A memoir of deafness.* New York: Hill and Wang.

Mee, C. L. (1999). *A nearly normal life.* Boston: Little, Brown.

Merker, H. (1994). *Listening.* New York: HarperCollins.

Murphy, R. (1987). *The body silent.* New York: Henry Holt.

Perkins, R. (1996). *Talking to angels: A life spent in high latitudes.* Boston: Beacon.

Price, R. (1994). *A whole new life: An illness and a healing.* New York: Atheneum.

Rousso, H. (1993). *Disabled, female, and proud!* Westport, CT: Bergin & Garvey.

Schaller, S. (1991). *A man without words.* New York: Summit.

Scott, R. (1969). *The making of blind men: A study of adult socialization.* New York: Russell Sage Foundation.

Sidransky, R. (1990). *In silence: Growing up in a deaf world.* New York: St. Martin's Press.

Sienkiewicz-Mercer, R., & Kaplan, S. B. (1989). *I raise my eyes to say yes.* Boston: Houghton Mifflin.

Vermeij, G. (1997). *Privileged hands: A scientific life.* New York: Freeman.

Weihenmayer, E. (2001). *Touch the top of the world: A blind man's journey to climb farther than the eye can see.* New York: Dutton.

White, M., & Gribbin, J. (1999). *A life in science.* New York: Penguin.

Wright, D. (1994). *Deafness: An autobiography.* New York: Harper Collins.

Zola, I. K. (1982). *Missing pieces: A chronicle of living with a disability.* Philadelphia: Temple University.

Appendix 7–B

Acceptance of Disability Scale*

READ EACH STATEMENT AND PUT AN "X" IN THE SPACE INDICATING HOW MUCH YOU AGREE OR DISAGREE WITH EACH STATEMENT.

1. A physical disability may limit a person in some ways, but this does not mean he or she should give up and do nothing with his or her life.

   _____ I disagree very much.　　　　_____ I agree a little.
   _____ I disagree pretty much.　　　_____ I agree pretty much.
   _____ I disagree a little.　　　　　_____ I agree very much.

2. Because of my disability, I feel miserable much of the time.

   _____ I disagree very much.　　　　_____ I agree a little.
   _____ I disagree pretty much.　　　_____ I agree pretty much.
   _____ I disagree a little.　　　　　_____ I agree very much.

3. More than anything else, I wish I didn't have this disability.

   _____ I disagree very much.　　　　_____ I agree a little.
   _____ I disagree pretty much.　　　_____ I agree pretty much.
   _____ I disagree a little.　　　　　_____ I agree very much.

4. Disability or not, I'm going to make good in life.

   _____ I disagree very much.　　　　_____ I agree a little.
   _____ I disagree pretty much.　　　_____ I agree pretty much.
   _____ I disagree a little.　　　　　_____ I agree very much.

Source: Courtesy of Donald C. Linkowski, PhD, CRC.

5. Good physical appearance and physical ability are the most important things in life.

_____ I disagree very much.   _____ I agree a little.
_____ I disagree pretty much.   _____ I agree pretty much.
_____ I disagree a little.   _____ I agree very much.

6. My disability prevents me from doing just about everything I really want to do and from becoming the kind of person I want to be.

_____ I disagree very much.   _____ I agree a little.
_____ I disagree pretty much.   _____ I agree pretty much.
_____ I disagree a little.   _____ I agree very much.

7. I can see the progress I am making in rehabilitation, and it makes me feel like an adequate person in spite of the limitations of my disability.

_____ I disagree very much.   _____ I agree a little.
_____ I disagree pretty much.   _____ I agree pretty much.
_____ I disagree a little.   _____ I agree very much.

8. It makes me feel very bad to see all the things nondisabled people can do which I cannot.

_____ I disagree very much.   _____ I agree a little.
_____ I disagree pretty much.   _____ I agree pretty much.
_____ I disagree a little.   _____ I agree very much.

9. My disability affects those aspects of life which I care most about.

_____ I disagree very much.   _____ I agree a little.
_____ I disagree pretty much.   _____ I agree pretty much.
_____ I disagree a little.   _____ I agree very much.

10. Though I am disabled, my life is full.

_____ I disagree very much.   _____ I agree a little.
_____ I disagree pretty much.   _____ I agree pretty much.
_____ I disagree a little.   _____ I agree very much.

11. If a person is not entirely physically able, he or she is that much less a person.

_____ I disagree very much.   _____ I agree a little.
_____ I disagree pretty much.   _____ I agree pretty much.
_____ I disagree a little.   _____ I agree very much.

12. A person with a disability is restricted in certain ways, but there is still much he or she is able to do.

_____ I disagree very much.   _____ I agree a little.
_____ I disagree pretty much.   _____ I agree pretty much.
_____ I disagree a little.   _____ I agree very much.

13. There are many more important things in life than physical ability and appearance.

_____ I disagree very much.   _____ I agree a little.
_____ I disagree pretty much.   _____ I agree pretty much.
_____ I disagree a little.   _____ I agree very much.

14. There are times I completely forget that I am physically disabled.

_____ I disagree very much.   _____ I agree a little.
_____ I disagree pretty much.   _____ I agree pretty much.
_____ I disagree a little.   _____ I agree very much.

15. You need a good and whole body to have a good mind

_____ I disagree very much.   _____ I agree a little.
_____ I disagree pretty much.   _____ I agree pretty much.
_____ I disagree a little.   _____ I agree very much.

16. There are many things a person with my disability is able to do.

_____ I disagree very much.   _____ I agree a little.
_____ I disagree pretty much.   _____ I agree pretty much.
_____ I disagree a little.   _____ I agree very much.

17. Since my disability interferes with just about everything I try to do, it is foremost in my mind practically all the time.

_____ I disagree very much.   _____ I agree a little.
_____ I disagree pretty much.   _____ I agree pretty much.
_____ I disagree a little.   _____ I agree very much.

18. If I didn't have my disability, I think I would be a much better person.

_____ I disagree very much.   _____ I agree a little.
_____ I disagree pretty much.   _____ I agree pretty much.
_____ I disagree a little.   _____ I agree very much.

19. My disability, in itself, affects me more than any other characteristic about me.

_____ I disagree very much.   _____ I agree a little.
_____ I disagree pretty much.   _____ I agree pretty much.
_____ I disagree a little.   _____ I agree very much.

20. The kind of person I am and my accomplishments in life are less important than those of nondisabled persons.

_____ I disagree very much.   _____ I agree a little.
_____ I disagree pretty much.   _____ I agree pretty much.
_____ I disagree a little.   _____ I agree very much.

21. I know what I can't do because of my disability, and I feel that I can live a full and normal life.

_____ I disagree very much.   _____ I agree a little.
_____ I disagree pretty much.   _____ I agree pretty much.
_____ I disagree a little.   _____ I agree very much.

22. Though I can see the progress I am making in rehabilitation, this is not very important since I can never be normal.

_____ I disagree very much.   _____ I agree a little.
_____ I disagree pretty much.   _____ I agree pretty much.
_____ I disagree a little.   _____ I agree very much.

23. In just about everything, my disability is annoying to me so that I can't enjoy anything.

_____ I disagree very much.   _____ I agree a little.
_____ I disagree pretty much.   _____ I agree pretty much.
_____ I disagree a little.   _____ I agree very much.

24. How a person conducts himself or herself in life is much more important than physical appearance and ability.

_____ I disagree very much.   _____ I agree a little.
_____ I disagree pretty much.   _____ I agree pretty much.
_____ I disagree a little.   _____ I agree very much.

25. A person with my disability is unable to enjoy very much in life.

_____ I disagree very much.   _____ I agree a little.
_____ I disagree pretty much.   _____ I agree pretty much.
_____ I disagree a little.   _____ I agree very much.

26. The most important thing in this world is to be physically normal.

_____ I disagree very much.   _____ I agree a little.
_____ I disagree pretty much.   _____ I agree pretty much.
_____ I disagree a little.   _____ I agree very much.

27. A person with a disability finds it especially difficult to expand his or her interests and range of abilities.

_____ I disagree very much.   _____ I agree a little.
_____ I disagree pretty much.   _____ I agree pretty much.
_____ I disagree a little.   _____ I agree very much.

28. I believe that physical wholeness and appearance make a person what he or she is.

_____ I disagree very much.   _____ I agree a little.
_____ I disagree pretty much.   _____ I agree pretty much.
_____ I disagree a little.   _____ I agree very much.

29. A physical disability affects a person's mental ability.

_____ I disagree very much.   _____ I agree a little.
_____ I disagree pretty much.   _____ I agree pretty much.
_____ I disagree a little.   _____ I agree very much.

30. With my condition, I know just what I can and cannot do.

_____ I disagree very much.   _____ I agree a little.
_____ I disagree pretty much.   _____ I agree pretty much.
_____ I disagree a little.   _____ I agree very much.

31. Almost every area of life is closed to me because of my disability.

_____ I disagree very much.   _____ I agree a little.
_____ I disagree pretty much.   _____ I agree pretty much.
_____ I disagree a little.   _____ I agree very much.

32. Because of my disability, I have little to offer other people.

_____ I disagree very much.   _____ I agree a little.
_____ I disagree pretty much.   _____ I agree pretty much.
_____ I disagree a little.   _____ I agree very much.

33. Besides the many physical things I am unable to do, there are many other things I am unable to do.

_____ I disagree very much.   _____ I agree a little.
_____ I disagree pretty much.   _____ I agree pretty much.
_____ I disagree a little.   _____ I agree very much.

34. Personal characteristics such as honesty and a willingness to work hard are much more important than physical appearance and ability.

_____ I disagree very much.   _____ I agree a little.
_____ I disagree pretty much.   _____ I agree pretty much.
_____ I disagree a little.   _____ I agree very much.

35. I get very annoyed with the way some people offer to help me.

    _____ I disagree very much.   _____ I agree a little.
    _____ I disagree pretty much.   _____ I agree pretty much.
    _____ I disagree a little.   _____ I agree very much.

36. With my disability, there isn't a single area of life that is not affected in some major way.

    _____ I disagree very much.   _____ I agree a little.
    _____ I disagree pretty much.   _____ I agree pretty much.
    _____ I disagree a little.   _____ I agree very much.

37. Though I can see that disabled people are able to do well in many ways, still they can never lead normal lives.

    _____ I disagree very much.   _____ I agree a little.
    _____ I disagree pretty much.   _____ I agree pretty much.
    _____ I disagree a little.   _____ I agree very much.

38. A disability, such as mine, is the worst possible thing that can happen to a person.

    _____ I disagree very much.   _____ I agree a little.
    _____ I disagree pretty much.   _____ I agree pretty much.
    _____ I disagree a little.   _____ I agree very much.

39. No matter how hard I try or what I accomplish, I could never be as good a person as one without my disability.

    _____ I disagree very much.   _____ I agree a little.
    _____ I disagree pretty much.   _____ I agree pretty much.
    _____ I disagree a little.   _____ I agree very much.

40. There is practically nothing a person in my condition is able to do and really enjoy it.

    _____ I disagree very much.   _____ I agree a little.
    _____ I disagree pretty much.   _____ I agree pretty much.
    _____ I disagree a little.   _____ I agree very much.

41. Because of my disability, I am unable to enjoy social relationships as much as I could if I were not disabled.

    _____ I disagree very much.   _____ I agree a little.
    _____ I disagree pretty much.   _____ I agree pretty much.
    _____ I disagree a little.   _____ I agree very much.

42. There are more important things in life than those my physical disability prevents me from doing.

_____ I disagree very much.   _____ I agree a little.
_____ I disagree pretty much.   _____ I agree pretty much.
_____ I disagree a little.   _____ I agree very much.

43. I want very much to do things that my disability prevents me from doing.

_____ I disagree very much.   _____ I agree a little.
_____ I disagree pretty much.   _____ I agree pretty much.
_____ I disagree a little.   _____ I agree very much.

44. Because of my disability, other people's lives have more meaning than my own.

_____ I disagree very much.   _____ I agree a little.
_____ I disagree pretty much.   _____ I agree pretty much.
_____ I disagree a little.   _____ I agree very much.

45. Oftentimes, when I think of my disability, it makes me feel so sad and upset that I am unable to think of or do anything else.

_____ I disagree very much.   _____ I agree a little.
_____ I disagree pretty much.   _____ I agree pretty much.
_____ I disagree a little.   _____ I agree very much.

46. A disability changes one's life completely. It causes one to think differently about everything.

_____ I disagree very much.   _____ I agree a little.
_____ I disagree pretty much.   _____ I agree pretty much.
_____ I disagree a little.   _____ I agree very much.

47. I feel that I should be as able as the next person, even in areas where my disability prevents me.

_____ I disagree very much.   _____ I agree a little.
_____ I disagree pretty much.   _____ I agree pretty much.
_____ I disagree a little.   _____ I agree very much.

48. Life is full of so many things that I sometimes forget for brief periods of time that I am disabled.

_____ I disagree very much.   _____ I agree a little.
_____ I disagree pretty much.   _____ I agree pretty much.
_____ I disagree a little.   _____ I agree very much.

49. Because of my disability, I can never do most things that normal people can do.

    _____ I disagree very much.   _____ I agree a little.
    _____ I disagree pretty much.   _____ I agree pretty much.
    _____ I disagree a little.   _____ I agree very much.

50. I feel satisfied with my abilities, and my disability doesn't bother me too much.

    _____ I disagree very much.   _____ I agree a little.
    _____ I disagree pretty much.   _____ I agree pretty much.
    _____ I disagree a little.   _____ I agree very much.

The Onset and Diagnosis of the Disability

- Why is psychoeducation often therapeutic?
- Do you agree that parental response to a baby with a congenital disability is often not validated by society?
- What are low-incidence disabilities?
- What are some of the atypical experiences of children with disabilities?
- Do CODAs (children of Deaf adults) assume responsibilities beyond their capabilities?
- What is prelingual deafness?
- Why do many in the Deaf Culture advocate residential schooling for children who are deaf?
- Do cochlear implants make deafness an elective disability?
- Why is the distinction between time of onset and time of diagnosis sometimes important?
- For individuals with acquired disabilities, why do their prejudices often become self-identifiers?
- Explain this statement: Many disabilities and chronic illnesses of children are low-incidence disabilities.
- Why is the time of onset of schizophrenia so disabling?
- Why is the role of women traditionally one of "caring for vulnerable people"?
- Why have few rehabilitation services been provided for elderly people with disabilities?

- Why is old age itself often considered to be a disability?
- Why do elderly people often respond positively to the onset of the disability?
- In what ways is the acquisition of a disability thought to be more timely, both socially and chronologically?
- What are the differences between insidious-onset disabilities and acute-onset disabilities?
- What is the impact of a long prediagnosis period on the individual?

Factors That Affect the Impact of the Onset of Disability

In this section, look for—

- The three broad categories of variables that affect the individual's response/adaptation to disability
—Factors in the disability
—Factors in the environment
—Factors in the individual

Carolyn Vash (1981), a disability scholar, constructed a model that assists in understanding the factors (or variables) that affect an individual's response to a disability. The broad categories are (1) factors in the disability itself, (2) factors in the environment, and (3) factors in the individual. Factors in the environment include the degree of family support and acceptance (Cook & Ferritor, 1985; Danek, 1988; Danek & Lawrence, 1985; Darling & Baxter, 1996; Eisenberg, Sutkin, & Jansen, 1984; Huberty, 1980; Perlesz, Kinsella, & Crowe, 1999; Power & Dell Orto, 1980), the availability of self-help and mutual support groups, the assistive technology that is available, the quality of professional services rendered, and the individual's income level. As can be seen, most of these factors in the environment are tangible, measurable elements.

In contrast, factors in the individual are often difficult to measure. These factors include the individual's previous experience with PWDs, the individual's premorbid (before the onset of the disability) coping skills (Affleck, Tennen, Pfeifer, & Fifield, 1987), problem-solving and decision-making abilities, challenge orientation, level of emotional control, cognitive appraisal skills, levels of self-esteem and self-confidence, and the individual's religious/spiritual/philosophical belief system. Reviewing this list of factors, it can be seen that all of these pose difficulties in measurement and clinical assessment. However, the individual's marital status (PWDs who are married or have a partner usually respond better to a disability), the individual's level of education (PWDs who are highly educated usually respond better to a disability), and the individual's work history and transferability of skills (PWDs who have a long and varied work history usually respond better to a disability) are factors that can be more easily measured and assessed.

This chapter will focus on the onset of the disability itself, including time of onset and type of onset. Following is a listing of all these factors. Each factor will be discussed in some detail in this chapter and in the next chapter. Remember, as we discussed previously, this model is an oversimplification of reality. For example, many PWDs have more than one disability, and, furthermore, it is not the disability itself that influences the way in which the individual views the disability; it is the meaning the individual ascribes to the disability. Therefore, each disability is an idiosyncratic experience; moreover, there is no one "personality type" associated with a particular disability. Nonetheless, there are some general guidelines in understanding specific types of disabilities. Indeed, knowledge and understanding of specific disabilities and their impact on individuals is one of the main functions of mutual support and self-help groups (Chilman, Nunnally, & Cox, 1988; Goodheart & Lansing, 1997; Kriegsman & Celotta, 1981). In these types of groups, individuals with the same disability (and their families) meet together to discuss all of the factors listed in Exhibit 8–1 (Drotar, Crawford, & Bush, 1984). This is what is termed *psychoeducation*, and psychoeducation alone—just learning about the disability itself from others who have experienced the same disability—is therapeutic (Pearson & Sternberg, 1986; Power & Rogers, 1979). Psychoeducation can do much to eliminate anxiety and ambiguity and create a feeling of universality, or the feeling that "someone else is experiencing the same thing I am."

Exhibit 8–1 contains a list of all 10 factors. Two factors will be discussed in this chapter.

Exhibit 8–1

Factors in the Disability That Influence an Individual's Response to Disability

Time of onset	Degree of stigma
Type of onset	The course of the disability—stable, progressive, episodic
Functions impaired	Prognosis of the disability
Severity of disability	Treatment required
Visibility of the disability	
Degree, if any, of disfigurement	

Time of Onset

In this section, look for—

- Time of onset—congenital or acquired
- Some aspects of congenital disabilities:

—Often involve treatment considerations of the parents and siblings of the PWD

—The individual has no memory of not having a disability

—There is no premorbid functioning with which the individual compares himself or herself

—The parents must make treatment/habilitation choices

—Individuals with congenital disabilities often have atypical childhood experiences

—Society attributes less stigma to congenital disabilities (than to acquired disabilities)

Basically, the time of onset of a disability is divided into two categories: congenital and acquired. Congenital disabilities are, by definition, those disabilities that exist at or before birth as a result of hereditary or environmental factors. Some disabilities are *only* congenital, such as Down syndrome, muscular dystrophy, cerebral palsy, spina bifida, and achondroplasia (dwarfism) (Batshaw, 1998; Bernbaum & Batshaw, 1998). Other disabilities, such as blindness, deafness, and mental retardation, can be either congenital or acquired later in life. You will remember that we learned in Chapter 4 that the type of onset of the disability influences the degree of stigma directed toward the individual. Generally speaking, congenital disabilities elicit less prejudice and stigma than do acquired disabilities. (This lack of stigma may be a result of the fact that individuals are usually not held responsible for the cause of a disability with which they are born.) Of course, disabilities acquired for "noble purposes," such as war, are viewed with less stigma than congenital disabilities. Also, keep in mind that we are discussing "perceived" onset because, in many cases, others do not actually know if the disability is congenital or acquired.

Generally, the earlier the age of onset, the better the response and adjustment (Alfano, Nielsen, & Fink, 1993; Krause, 1992; Krause & Crew, 1991; Schulz & Decker, 1985; Woodrich & Patterson, 1983). While this is not always true, it has been found that, for example, children with congenital limb deficiencies adjust better than children with acquired amputations, and children whose diabetes is diagnosed early adapt better than those who are diagnosed with diabetes later in life. This may be a result of several factors: (1) children's cognitive and affective resiliency and flexibility; (2) the fact that there are no premorbid identity or functional losses; (3) children have not internalized society's prejudices and discriminations about disability; and (4) children have not fully developed their body image. Children can be resilient and accepting of disability, able to learn medical self-management techniques and other adaptive strategies that are appropriate to their developmental level. For example, using a dialysis machine or hearing aids or putting on a prosthesis, for most children, is not a distressing and emotionally fraught experience. For these children, the adaptive strategies are part of daily living. Also, these children have no nondisability identity. Geri Jewell, a comedienne, explained, "It's not like I wake up every morning and say, 'Oh my goodness, I have cerebral palsy!' I was born like this." Many individuals with congenital disabilities state: "For me, abnormal is normal!" Finally, it is safe to say that the older the individual is when he or she acquires the disability, the more he or she acquires the prejudices, stereotypes, and attitudes of the tragic, limited view of life with a disability. Of course, there are some exceptions to this. For example, individuals who have a family member with a disability would have a more accurate view of life with a disability. In addition, a child with a disability will not confront, on a daily basis, all the prejudices and discrimination against disabilities until he or she enters school.

Brenda Premo, born with a degenerating type of blindness, describes what she considers to be the advantages of a congenital disability:

> The fact that I was born with my visual disability has had advantages. I have what my eye doctor calls "compensating skills." My brain has compensated and fills in the pictures of what I cannot see with my eyes. For example, I remember where steps are if I have been on them before. I see the steps because the brain is filling in what the eyes can't see. Sometimes I make mistakes, so I have to be careful, but my brain gives me the picture. It's easier for me than for someone who is blinded later in life. (Mackelprang & Salsgiver, 1999, p. 140)

Ruth Tollifson (1997) was born without her right hand and half her right arm. From this excerpt we can see that Tollifson has an unusual reaction to her congenital disability:

> I remember the first time I actually looked closely at my arm, without looking away. I was twenty-five years old at the time, in therapy, sobering up from a near-suicidal nosedive into substance abuse. It was a terrifying moment. I was drenched in sweat, literally. But amazingly enough, I found that the arm I was seeing was not some loathsome, ridiculous, scary object I had imagined, but something else entirely, a world I had never seen before. (p. 106)

A student of mine related in a class discussion the difference (for him) between congenital blindness and acquired blindness. My student was born blind and attended the Utah School for the Deaf and Blind and is, therefore, trained in orientation and mobility (O & M) and knows Braille very well. He was asked to speak to an older woman who was slowly losing her sight. My student felt that he could offer little help because he had no idea of what it is like to lose one's vision. The woman had had a highly successful career as a nurse/administrator, which her degenerating vision caused her to give up. While both my student and the woman were blind, my student felt that he could offer little assistance. With most disabilities there is a great deal of difference between congenital onset and an acquired onset, making the experience of the same disability very dissimilar.

Parents of Children With Congenital Disabilities

> ### In this section, look for—
>
> - How knowledge or perception of the cause of the disability is important in determining how the family deals with the disability

When a baby is born with a congenital disability, it is the parents who respond/adjust to the disability (Lindenberg, 1980; Olshansky, 1962; Patterson, 1988; Powers, 1993). Often, the parents grieve over the loss of the baby that they had imagined, the baby without a disability (Collins-Moore, 1984; Featherstone, 1980; Mitsos, 1972). At the same time that parents are grieving for the "loss of one baby," they must care for and provide treatment for the "baby that remains" (Powers, 1993, p. 121). Furthermore, although the onset/diagnosis of the disability occurred at the time of birth (or before), the symptoms, manifestations, or medical crises that occur later may create additional losses for the parents. Often, the unpredictability of the course of the disability, or even the prospect of the baby's death, makes the response/adjusting process difficult and unpredictable for parents and siblings (Frantz, 1981). As we learned in Chapter 1, there are more congenital disabilities than ever before because of the advances in neonatal medicine. Many adults with disabilities report that the doctors, and their parents, did not expect them to live (when they were infants) and, moreover, doctors were not quite sure of the type of medical treatment to provide for them (Knoll, 1992, 1996). In addition, many adolescents who had congenital disabilities or acquired disabilities early in life were not provided with either sex education or career counseling/exploration services because no one thought these children would survive to adulthood. Therefore, both sex education and career counseling were considered to be irrelevant for these teenagers (Ireys & Burr, 1984). However, many did (and do) survive to adulthood.

As we discussed in Chapter 7, there is a stage theory of response/ adaptation to disability. The stage theory holds that there are predictable, "normal" stages of responding; however, this theory is most often thought of in terms of the individual who is experiencing the disability. In the case of congenital disabilities, the parents and siblings (and perhaps grandparents) progress through these stages (Austin, 1990; Damrosch & Perry, 1989; Sutkin, 1984). Parental response/adaptation to a congenital disability in their baby is often not validated or even "normed" by society. That is to say, others, such as relatives or neighbors, may not understand the grief, anger, or questioning experienced by the parents (Harper, 1999; Singer & Irvin, 1989; Singer, Powers, & Olson, 1996). Reread the letter from "Grateful Mom in Buffalo" in Chapter 6.

Parental guilt plays a role in the adjustment/adaptation response (Downey, Silver, & Wortman, 1990; Heller, Rafman, Zvagulis, & Pless, 1985). You will remember that in Chapter 7 we learned that many PWDs engage in self-blame and guilt for the onset of the disability (Young, 1974). With congenital disabilities, it is the parents who attribute the cause of the disability to something they did or did not do (Nixon, 1993). Often, parents, especially mothers, feel responsible for the disability. One father did not assist his wife in caring for their newborn baby with a disability because he held his wife responsible for the baby's disability (Nixon, 1993). Genetically based disabilities elicit guilt in both the mother and the father. Friends and neighbors may ask what the mother did or did not do during the pregnancy, thus unintentionally blaming the mother for the disability. Parents also blame themselves when they are not able to "help" the child (Cummings, 1976). The role of a parent is to protect the helpless infant, and when a baby is born with a disability, the parents may feel that they failed to protect the child from harm. Often, parents feel directly or indirectly blamed by medical professionals, either for the cause of their child's disability or for the management of their child's disability (Wasow & Wilder, 1983). We also learned that self-blame is the price some individuals pay for devising an etiology for the disability. Rather than viewing the infant's disability as a random event, parents blame themselves and thus alleviate the stress of an unknown etiology. Parents can blame each other and, in so doing, place stress on the marital relationship with comments such as "This came from your side of the family." Older brothers and sisters often think that they "did" (or did not do) something to cause the disability. According to the National Public Radio Disability History Project (Tomorrow's Children, May, 1998), often extended family members look at the newborn with a congenital disability and say, "This should have been caught." Parents who know about the disability before the birth and choose not to have an abortion may be seen as irresponsible and selfish. Because of the combination of the capability to test for several types of disability before the birth of the child and the belief, held by some, that disability should be avoided at all costs, the parents may be blamed for refusing an abortion. In addition, the "superparent" ideals of doing everything possible for the child or of being 100% responsible for the child often lead to parental guilt when these unrealistic and self-imposed expectations cannot be met.

Families who have an infant with a congenital disability must deal with all the typical family demands and at the same time begin to negotiate a host of disability-related concerns (Singer & Powers, 1993; Turnbull & Turnbull, 1991). Parents must learn about the disability itself and must also learn to deal with a complex medical system. These parents are faced with a staggering amount of technical and medical information (Spaniol, Zipple, & Fitzgerald, 1985). Reread the excerpt in Chapter 7 that tells of the parents, who, on returning from peer support groups meetings, took Pepto Bismol. Further, some of the information and treatment recommendations are contradictory. For the first time for many families, they are required to contact and elicit the assistance of governmental agencies (Summers, Behr, & Turnbull, 1989). Simply moving through the medical and legal service systems can be bewildering. The parents are faced with these changes and tasks while experiencing the shock and grief many experience at the birth of a child with a disability (Head, Head, & Head, 1985; Rolland, 1994). In addition, many of their familiar social supports may have disappeared (Dell Orto, 1988). Friends and relatives often distance themselves from the parents who have a child with a disability; therefore, exactly when the parents need support, stability, and instrumental assistance, they slowly begin to understand that their familial and social networks are no longer there (Santelli, Turnbull, Lerner, & Marquis, 1993). Often, both parents are sleep-deprived, the mother has just finished a physically stressful pregnancy, or both. In addition, there may be older siblings that require care and support in their adjustment process (Graliker, Fishler, & Koch, 1962; Keydel, 1988). Often, one of the parents (usually the mother) must quit his or her job to provide care to the infant, further straining the family's financial status. Many parents feel overwhelmed (Fewell, 1986; Pearson & Sternberg, 1986).

One mother told of her experience, "There are heavy demands for a highly functional, two-parent family that is financially stable. However, many families that have children with disabilities do not enjoy these advantages. The increasing number of single parents (most often, mothers) and the mobility of the U.S. population make it far more common for the family of a child with a congenital disability to be a single mother without extended family nearby."

Another mother (Miller, 1988) did not feel that she experienced the "typical" stages of adjustment: "I had read many times about the grief surrounding the birth of a child with defects [sic], but the literature had not seemed to apply to me. My life certainly included denial, anger, bargaining, depression, and acceptance. But for me these were not milestones on a timeline, but were aspects of every day, sometimes every hour. Furthermore, there was little grief attached to the 'expected baby.' The grief was tied up with the whole mental picture I had for myself, my family, and our future. Feeling I had failed myself, Kurt [her husband], Beth [the baby], the family, and even society itself, what I really had lost was my whole sense of self-esteem" (p. 145). Baby Beth's mother seems to be caught up with both grief and self-blame. Another mother related: "Later, the words which have already reverberated in my head are pronounced by the neurologist: cerebral palsy. As he reviews the findings, a door slowly shuts. While there will be no miracle, neither will Robbie die soon. As we leave the clinic carrying our reprieved son, the ghost of Robbie-might-have-been begins to drift away" (Curry, 1995, p. 26). Note the way in which the mother expresses her growing awareness of her baby's disability: a door slowly closing and a ghost drifting away.

Grief over a disability is closely related to the individual's and his or her family's perception of loss and of normality. With the birth of a child with a congenital disability, many families may believe that their high standards can no longer be maintained. According to Rolland (1994):

> Families with strong beliefs in high achievement and perfectionism tend to equate normality with the optimal, to define normality or successful family functioning in terms of ideal or problem-free circumstances. Families that define normality in this way are prone to apply (disability) standards that are inappropriate because the kind of control they are accustomed to is impossible in this situation . . . . The fact that life cycle goals may take longer or need revision may require some modification in beliefs about what is normal and healthy. Sustaining hope, particularly in situations of long-term adversity, demands an ability to embrace a flexible and broad definition of normality. (p. 135)

However, the birth of a child with a congenital disability often results in a great deal of family cohesion, strong family bonds, and a high level of competence. The stress and demands of a baby with a disability can provide the opportunity for the family to change and grow in constructive ways.

Parents often must make decisions concerning medical care, living arrangements, and the type of education for their child with a disability, all of which have long-range ramifications for both the child and the family (Greenberg, 1980). For many community services, such as schools, children with severe congenital disabilities are "peripheral" to their basic mission (Sailor, Kleinhammer-Tramill, Skrtic, & Oas, 1996, p. 329), or insurance policies may not pay for noninstitutional care, or the prevailing professional opinion advocates a certain type of treatment or education. Faced with an array of needs—a complicated structure of services and payment requirements—parents make decisions. Occasionally, as would be expected, these children grow up and later question or resent the decisions made by the parent(s). Remember the man in the video "My Body Is Not Who I Am" who stated, "I resented my parents jumping at the requests of the doctors." This man had undergone many "corrective" surgeries during his childhood. Today, there are elderly parents with middle-aged children who have been in institutions for decades. These parents feel themselves unjustly maligned when they are asked why they allowed their children to "be put into an institution." These parents remind us that when their children were born, there were no special education classes in the neighborhood schools, no home nursing care, no respite care, nor the array of community and home services available today. Moreover, if the disability was or is a low-incidence disability, such as deaf–blindness, there were (and are) still fewer services. For example, if the parents lived in a rural area and their child had a severe disability, the physician may have had no experience in treating people with this disability. In sum, these parents felt they had no choice.

Couser (1997) stated, "The prevailing norms of the modern American family presume the absence of a disability" (p. 252). For example, most television comedies or dramas that feature families do not show families that have a member with a disability. Television programs portray families with gay parents, biracial families, and single-parent families. This makes sense because these types of families are representative of typical American life and viewers can relate to these imaginary TV families. Nonetheless, there are few, if any, families on television who have a member with a disability.

Not all families are Euro-American and middle-class (Brown, 1997). Westbrook and Legge (1993) conducted a study in Australia that provides a glimpse of the difference in familial coping with children with disabilities. Westbrook and Legge sought to learn the perceptions and attitudes of families toward children with disabilities because, as they stated, "The family's perception of the cause and meaning of the disability is communicated to the child and also influences the experiences which are provided for the child and the life roles that he or she is expected to achieve" (p. 176). The researchers studied six communities in Australia, labeling two of the communities "individualistic" and four of the communities "collectivistic." The collectivistic communities were the Arab, Chinese, Greek, and Italian groups, and the individualistic communities were Anglo-Australian and German groups. Westbrook and Legge found the following:

> In all four collectivistic communities, there were significant differences [when compared with the individualistic communities] in believing that it is a greater tragedy to have a son with a disability and that it is desirable to conceal the existence of a child with a disability. However, they considered that such a child places less strain on the parents' marriage than do Anglo-Australians. Giving birth to a disabled [sic] child was considered more shameful in the Greek and Chinese communities. In these and the Arabic communities there was a stronger belief that disability in a family reduces relatives' marital chances. (p. 183)

> There was significantly less expectation within the Italian, Greek, Arabic, and Chinese communities that children with disabilities would attend school, accompany their families on social outings, or behave like other children. (p. 182)

This is a single study, and as the authors themselves concluded, there are few studies that seek to examine cultural differences in family attitudes toward children with disabilities. Nonetheless, the questions they asked merit consideration because questions such as these underscore the importance of considering the family's cultural values before automatically assuming that the family responds to the child with a disability in the same way that Euro-American, middle-class families do.

Atypical Childhood Experiences

> ## In this section, look for—
>
> - How the atypical childhood experiences of individuals with congenital disabilities may include the following:
>   —Prolonged hospitalizations
>   —Early socialization into the role of patient
>   —Overprotection
>   —Relaxation of discipline
>   —A large number of adults with whom to relate
>   —Abuse, neglect, and abandonment

Individuals with some types of congenital disabilities often have atypical childhood experiences. Repeated hospitalizations; frequent surgeries and other types of medical treatments; and, occasionally, residential schooling are experiences that children with certain types of congenital disabilities (and disabilities acquired early in life) undergo. Thus, the infant or young child is completely socialized into the role of patient. These are not the typical childhood experiences; however, as the child is experiencing many of them, he or she is often not aware that his or her life is unusual. Nonetheless, most adults with congenital disabilities view their childhoods, in retrospect, as unique and different from the experiences of most children. Children without disabilities usually have very little contact with physicians. In contrast, children with disabilities are thoroughly socialized into the world of medical professionals.

One of the most commonly reported experiences of children with congenital disabilities is the overprotection of their mothers. Linda Pelletier, a woman with cerebral palsy, told of two experiences of overprotection. The first is somewhat humorous. "One of the complications of this birth trauma was that I was more susceptible to respiratory infection . . . . [my mother] was afraid to allow me to go outdoors for fear of my getting a chill . . . . One of my most vivid recollections is going to see fireworks on the Fourth of July. I was sitting in a car with the windows rolled up, wearing ski pants, thermal underwear, and a winter coat. I became nauseous and almost fainted before the fireworks were even over" (Pelletier, 1988, p. 55).

In contrast, Ms. Pelletier labels her mother's overprotectiveness as "destructive" in the second description.

> My mother's overprotection was also a destructive element in my development. She assumed complete care of all of my physical needs. This meant that I was lifted in and out of bed, onto the toilet, and in and out of our car. I was bathed, dressed, groomed and fed without my lifting a finger to help myself. I realize now that it would have been extremely difficult for her to sit by passively and watch me struggle to perform these basic activities of daily living. Although my mother meant well by catering to me in this way, it retarded my physical development because I was never given the opportunity to work on doing these essential tasks. Such a relationship caused me to be completely dependent upon my parents. (Pelletier, 1988, p. 58)

Often, children with congenital disabilities are not disciplined, or standards of behavior are lowered for them. Parents, caregivers, and teachers often tolerate inappropriate behavior, explaining they don't "have the heart" to discipline children with disabilities. Remember, this is related to the concept of sympathy and pity for PWDs or "let's give these poor PWDs a break" that we discussed earlier in Chapter 6. Read the following statement in which a young child begins to suspect that he is sick when the discipline is relaxed. "I know I'm very sick . . . because everyone treats me differently. Before I became ill, my parents never let me get away with bad behavior. Now, I can even hit my little sister without being punished" (Whitt, 1984, p. 77).

Overprotection and relaxation of discipline can result in a lack of mastery, competence, and self-confidence and can often isolate the child. Those behaviors and attitudes, begun in earliest infancy, often continue until the individual reaches adulthood. Thus, often children with congenital disabilities are needlessly handicapped. One of my students is blind. In a class discussion, this student told of a friend of hers who was also blind. The woman, who was born blind, was never allowed in the backyard or the basement of her home. She simply had no concept of these areas of her house, or of any house. Often, the overprotection of children who are congenitally blind is discovered when they begin school. Occasionally, these children cannot do the most basic tasks because family members have relieved these children of responsibilities such as dressing themselves or placing a telephone call.

Many adults who were born with congenital disabilities have expressed gratitude and some degree of amazement that their parents were able to demand services and accommodations for them. Parents demanded that their children be allowed to attend public school, often when they themselves did not have much education, and family members required that the child with the disability accomplish as much as possible. These adult PWDs credit much of their success to their parents and families. Erik Weihenmayer climbed Mt. Everest and he is blind. He relates an experience in which his mother insisted that Eric, as a young child, be permitted to enter school:

> I don't know how my mother found the strength to oppose the world. Maybe it's simply a mother's primal instinct to nurture and defend her child. She was as unprepared as the administrators sitting across from us. Somehow, though, she believed in me. I was just a little boy with my ink-smudged nose pressed against the page. I had nothing yet to prove myself, so how she saw strength, opportunity, and promise, while other people saw problems, obstacles, and limits, I'll never know for sure. (Weihenmayer, 2001, p. 14)

One clear-cut exception is the case of children with learning disabilities (LD) and/or attention-deficit disorder (usually boys) who are overpunished. Parents, relatives, and teachers attribute their inability to focus, sit still, control impulses, complete tasks on time, and respond to multiple requests at one time as defiance and willful lack of cooperation. Because of misunderstanding or lack of a diagnosis, these children are subjected to a great deal of punishment and negative feedback. Indeed, many experts on LD attribute the high rate of school dropout for children with LD to their wish to escape the punishment and humiliation of school.

Abuse and Neglect of Children With Congenital Disabilities

Parental depression, caregiver stress, or both can lead to abuse or neglect of the infant or child with a congenital disability. Stressors that are thought to lead to abuse and neglect include "(1) regular loss of sleep because of caregiving demands, (2) the child's severe medical problems, (3) the child's severe behavior problems, (4) the child's unusual appearance, and (5) adversity in the family combined with caregiving responsibilities" (Singer, 1996, p. 25). The more support the parents have in providing care for an infant, the smaller the probability of abuse and neglect occurring. Such support includes linking parents with self-help groups in which they can meet with "veteran" parents who have a child with the same type of disability, providing respite care, in-home health care for complicated medical procedures, financial subsidies, and supportive counseling. Two generations ago, all these types of support were usually provided by extended family members. With the changing demographics of America, such as divorce and geographic mobility, these types of support are now provided by professional caregivers.

A Large Number of Adults With Whom to Relate

Simply because the world of medical care is populated by adults, many children with congenital disabilities are in the care of a large number of different adults. Children probably do not form long-term relationships with many of these caregivers because (1) there are too many of these caregivers, (2) these relationships are often transient in nature, (3) the caregivers must obey hospital and agency rules, and (4) most caregivers are motivated by pay. A secretary at a residential school for children who are deaf reported, "They have so many people to relate to. They go to bed with one houseparent and wake up with another one, and then numerous adults engage them all day long, they must deal with various administrators and different security officers throughout their lives here . . ." (Evans & Falk, 1986, p. 100).

There are risks for children who are exposed to a great many adults, including (1) the lack of ability to develop healthy reciprocal, empathic feelings (attachment bonds) and (2) vulnerability to physical and/or sexual abuse. Rutter (1989) found that young children in institutions/hospitals typically encounter 50–80 caregivers before reaching school age.

In the PBS video "Paralyzing Fear," a woman told of a night in the hospital when she was a little girl with polio. The little girl was crying because she was homesick and missed her family. The nurse came in and told her if she did not stop crying, she would unplug her respirator. The little girl stopped crying that night, but she wept, as an adult, when she recounted the experience. When an adult is exposed to many different caregivers, he or she usually has the ability to question and challenge the treatment or the lack of treatment. However, children with disabilities are powerless and must submit to adults. Indeed, many adults report that it is only in retrospect that they understand the power that adult caregivers wielded over them when they were children.

The child who lives at home and attends community schools has daily reminders that, because of the disability, he or she is different from other children. Medical treatments, assistive devices, and doctors' appointments serve to remind the child that he or she is different. If the course of the disability is episodic, life threatening, or both, medical treatments can be unexpected emergencies that require aggressive treatment. At these points, the child understands that hospitalization/treatment is more important than school attendance.

Children with disabilities are at risk for emotional maladaptation, including behavioral problems, low self-esteem, and poor resolution of developmental tasks (Breslau, 1982; Breslau & Marshall, 1985; Heller et al., 1985). These researchers found that (1) central nervous system involvement in the disability (i.e., mental retardation) was associated with greater psychosocial problems, and (2) the family's coping responses affect the child's response.

Hearing Children of Parents Who Are Deaf

> ## In this section, look for—
>
> - Children of Deaf Adults (CODAs)
>
>   —How hearing children of parents who are deaf act as interpreters
>
>   —The argument that CODAs find themselves "caught" between the Deaf world and the hearing world
>
>   —How some CODAs feel that they have been "deprived" of a "normal" childhood

There is another situation in which a disability is present from the individual's birth; however, the disability is not the individual's disability, but rather the disability of his or her parents. Children of deaf adults (or CODAs) are children who are born hearing to two parents who are both deaf. Naturally, the CODAs grow up bilingual, learning both sign language and spoken language. CODAs, unlike parents of deaf children, assume that Deafness is "normal," have a way in which to communicate with their parents, and do not feel that their parents should try to enter the hearing world. (In contrast, hearing parents of a child who is deaf assume that deafness is an abnormality and deficit and have no way in which to communicate with their child because not all hearing parents learn sign language. They want their child to become part of the hearing world.)

One child in the family, usually the oldest daughter, assumes the role of "designated interpreter." Thus, it can be seen that age is an important factor in choosing the designated interpreter, but gender is even more important (it is usually the oldest *female* child, even when there is an older son). The role of the designated interpreter requires sacrifice and the need to consider the parents' needs, often before his or her own needs. However, the role of the designated interpreter offers power not usually accorded to children (Couser, 1997). Because CODAs must speak for their parents, they are required to assume adultlike roles in assisting their parents in dealing with the adult hearing world, often when these CODAs are very young children. Many CODAs, in retrospect, view the responsibilities they assumed as children as beyond their capabilities. Paul Preston wrote a book titled *Mother Father Deaf: Living Between Sound and Silence* (1994). Preston described the power and responsibility of being a CODA, "Although the negative associations of diminished identity and status were true for several women and men, a few other informants stressed that interpreting provided them with a much greater degree of visibility and control . . . . Rather than being a passive and objective translation, interpreting could be understood as authoritative and dynamic cultural brokering" (p. 102).

Ruth Sidransky spoke of "never quite fitting into either [the Deaf world or the hearing world], never knowing who I was" (p. 95). In her book, *In Silence: Growing Up Hearing in a Deaf World* (1990), Sidransky related her own experience and that of other CODAs. Note her use of such words as "sucked into," "buried," and "invisible."

> There were those of us who were sucked into a silence we carried with us always. There were those of us defiantly proud of our parents yet secretly ashamed of their garish sounds. There were those of us who, as soon as we were able, left home and abandoned our parents to grow old alone in withering silence. There were those of us who ignored our deaf parents, never quite learning to sign well enough to tell them what was in our hearts and minds. There were those of us who deliberately turned our heads when our parents raised their arms and hands to speak to us. And there were those of us who loved our parents with passion. We were the ones who buried the silence within. We abandoned our dreams and took care of our deaf mothers and fathers. They were our children, and we were their parents. We, the children, were invisible. (p. 96)

Lou Ann Walker, a CODA, wrote about her embarrassment over her parents' writing. Notice that she is in third grade and correcting her parents' written English. She wrote, "Mom and Dad's sentences sounded as if a foreigner had written them, as if English weren't their native tongue at all—and of course, it wasn't really. Still, I was to find out later their writing was far superior to most done by deaf adults—even deaf college graduates. Back then, a proud and self-conscious third grader correcting her parents' letters, I was filled with a mixture of pleasure and embarrassment—pleasure because I was useful to my parents, embarrassment because they couldn't do what I thought all other parents did with ease" (1986, p. 81).

CODAs protect their parents from the hearing world. Couser (1997) summarized Walker's feelings about protecting her parents. "On the one hand, she takes pride in her competence as a mediator and in her ability to shield her vulnerable parents from thoughtless and sometimes hostile hearing people. She is candid about the quite literal 'gaze' of the hearing world . . . . On the other hand, she makes clear the cost of providing such protection. When she censors, rather than passes on, rude remarks from hearing people, she becomes the receptacle of animosity directed at her parents; she contains both the hostility of the hearing world and the resentment it stirs in her. So, in interpreting for her parents, she absorbs much of the friction between the worlds" (p. 254).

CODAs often feel that they have been deprived of a normal childhood, a childhood in which parents protect children. Ruth Sidransky (1990) wrote of how her own needs were denied: "I didn't dare hear myself. It meant breaking an unforgivable taboo; to hear myself could only diminish my capacities to hear others who needed me. My mother said, 'I am helpless.' My father said, 'Take care of us.' I did not ask, 'Who will take care of me?' I was alone, walled in their silence and mine. Incommunicado. Blank" (p. 153).

Sidransky also wrote: "I did not recognize that this . . . was an abuse of my childhood. No one was to blame for this abuse. It was simply so" (p. 243). Other CODAs feel that they have had an advantaged childhood because they have grown up bilingual and bicultural and learned to empathize with others (Filer & Filer, 2000). Nonetheless, most CODAs deal with two conflicting sets of identity: (1) deaf and hearing and (2) parent to his or her parents and child to his or her parents. Support groups for CODAs help them sort these issues out (Preston, 1994). Regardless of how they view their childhood or the way in which they established their identities, CODAs are a unique group of individuals. Indeed, there is "coda-talk," a combination of spoken English and sign language, reflecting the bilingual language heritage of CODAs. The use of coda-talk is controversial; some CODAs feel that it trivializes sign language. However, those CODAs who do use coda-talk consider it to be (1) in-group communication, (2) identity reinforcement, and (3) self-help.

Prelingual Deafness

In this section look for—

- Prelingual deafness

  —Individual does not have speech abilities

  —Individual does not have a memory of sound or language

- Differences between a deaf child born to hearing parents and a deaf child born to deaf parents

Time of onset is an important factor in deafness; however, time of onset is thought of not as either congenital or acquired, but rather as prelingual deafness or postlingual deafness. Prelingual deafness refers to deafness acquired before the development of speech, and postlingual deafness refers to deafness acquired after the development of speech. (Of course, prelingual deafness can also be congenital deafness.) An example of an individual with prelingual deafness is Helen Keller. She was not born deaf or blind, but at the age of 19 months she developed what was then called "brain fever." Most physicians today think that the baby Helen Keller had either scarlet fever or meningitis. After her recovery, she was both deaf and blind with few, if any, memories of vision or hearing.

The earlier in life a child acquires deafness, the more likely he or she is to identify with the Deaf Culture. Gershon (as cited in Edwards, 1997) used the term "permanent exile" to describe all people who are deaf because they are exiled from the hearing world and used the term "immigrant" to describe individuals who become deaf later in life. These individuals are immigrants to the Deaf Culture because "they never lose their hearing accent." Those who grow up deaf are natives of the Deaf Culture (Edwards, 1997, p. 42).

Individuals with prelingual deafness have no memory of sound, of language, or of being able to hear and to speak. Congenital deafness also involves another element that most congenital disabilities do not—whether or not the parents are also deaf. Harlan Lane (1996) describes the reaction of parents who are deaf to the birth of a deaf child: "In general . . . many members of the DEAF-WORLD would prefer to have a Deaf child to having a hearing child, those whose happiness at the advent of a Deaf child is tinged with sadness (after all, that child will face many extra challenges) commonly overcome their reservations quickly. If you belong to a hearing culture, you may find such Deaf preferences hard to understand" (pp. 24–25). It is difficult to understand the Deaf Culture without knowledge of the tragic and horrific history of the oralist movement and residential schools.

Lane explains why parents who are deaf often want deaf children:

> The birth of a Deaf baby in a Deaf household signifies that the Deaf heritage of the family will be secure. Deaf families with many Deaf members are commonly proud of their genealogy.
>
> In other words, when a Deaf infant of Deaf parents is diagnosed as Deaf, the joy of the parents reflects the fact that most Deaf parents, like parents generally, look forward to having children who are a reflection of themselves . . . . Deaf parents bring their Deaf baby home to a nurturing environment in which communication is naturally dependent on visual, not aural (hearing) cues. Almost all use the signed language of the DEAF-WORLD to interact with their child. Their home is already functioning as an environment conducive to using vision as the main means of learning and communication . . . . Like the hearing

child born to a well-functioning hearing family, the Deaf infant in a Deaf family . . . is immediately exposed to a world suited to maximizing his or her social, emotional, psychological, cognitive, and linguistic development. (pp. 25–26)

Some couples in which both partners are deaf have undergone genetic testing when they are expecting a baby to ascertain the "risk" of having a hearing infant (Mackelprang & Salsgiver, 1999). Deaf parents of a baby who is deaf realize that their baby's physician and other medical care providers view the deafness as a negative situation and as a condition that must be ameliorated as quickly as possible. Many parents who are deaf appreciate the concern of the physician but resist the physician's attempts to pathologize the deafness of their baby or to subject the baby to hearing aids and other prostheses. Obviously the physicians often view disability from the Biomedical Model, and deaf parents of children who are deaf view it from the Environmental Model.

However, most children who are deaf, whether the time of onset is congenital, prelingual, or postlingual, are children of hearing parents. Indeed, 80% of all congenitally deaf babies are born to hearing parents; further, the diagnosis of deafness usually occurs months or years after birth. Most often, the child is isolated within his or her own family because of the lack of communication. Both the parents and the child are frustrated.

People who are deaf, like most PWDs, have been handicapped by medical and educational professionals who have advocated treatment and education that have not been in their best interests. Nonetheless, the Deaf have been subjected to more professional misjudgment, paternalism, and control than any other disability group. For example, for years, most educators of the Deaf (who usually were not deaf themselves) advocated the oralism method, in which children were not allowed to use sign language and instead were required to speak. (Alexander Graham Bell was the most famous advocate of oralism.) Oralism was impossible for many, and, for most children who were deaf, oralism provided years of frustration and failure. At the same time, these children were not allowed to learn and use sign language. (In some schools, children were required to sit on their hands or had their hands tied so they could not use their hands to sign.) Lipreading was taught, in spite of the fact that lipreading is not very accurate. Training or educating children who were deaf in oralism and lipreading was an attempt to reduce discomfort in people without disabilities and force the Deaf to fit into a hearing world, without making any demands on the hearing world. In so doing, children who were deaf were deprived of a language and a culture. Today, the Deaf Culture actively fights against these types of attempts by hearing physicians and educators to "make deaf people fit in."

The debate over cochlear implants often makes deafness appear to be an "elective disability." Although the technology of the implants has improved and the acceptance of the implants by Deaf families has increased, there are still those who refuse them. This illustrates the difficulties in viewing Deafness as a culture rather than as a disability group. Societies go to great lengths to preserve languages and cultures and understand the great loss when languages die. Cochlear implants have the potential to greatly reduce the use of sign languages. As we have learned, the Deaf Culture has sought to refuse the pathology, inferiority, and handicapping attitudes of PWODs. However, does society have an obligation to pay for accommodations and specialized education when deafness can be ameliorated? Tucker (1998) explains the dilemma facing the Deaf Culture:

> The primary argument against deliberately seeking to produce deaf children is that it violates the child's own autonomy and narrows the scope of her choices when she grows up; in other words, it violates her right to an "open future." Insisting that children who are deaf be raised in a Deaf cultural community denies those children the right to choose for themselves to accept or reject the larger hearing world.
>
> When most deafness becomes correctable, which for many people has already occurred and for others may well happen in the near future, an individual who chooses not to correct his or her deafness (or the deafness of his or her child) will lack the moral right to demand that others pay for costly accommodations to compensate for the lack of hearing of that individual. In this age of budget crises and cries for tax reform, when there is talk of, and some action with respect to, the need to cut funding for welfare, Medicaid, Social Security, federally supported food banks, and other social welfare programs, it is unrealistic, at best, to expect society to fund expenditures that could be eliminated. (Tucker, 1998, p. 8)

Congenital Blindness or Blindness Acquired in Infancy

In this section, look for—

- Individuals with congenital blindness:

    —Have no visual experience with concepts such as color, shape, distance, or proportion

    —Are not able to learn by observation

People who are born blind or become blind early in life have no visual experiences with concepts such as colors, distance, depth, or proportion. Falvo (1991) explained:

[Individuals who have congenital blindness] because of their lack of visual experience in their environment, such as the observation of tasks or behavior of others . . . must learn by other means concepts that sighted individuals often take for granted. This adaptive learning of tasks then becomes a natural part of their developmental process so that the adjustment to visual limitations is incorporated into their self-perception and daily activities as a normal part of growing up. Individuals who lose their vision later in life have the advantage of being able to draw on visual experiences in the environment as a frame of reference for physical concepts, but they may find it more difficult to accept their blindness than those who have never had vision. (p. 255)

Residential Schools

In this section, look for—

- Mainstreaming children in the community school is not always better than placing the child in a residential school
- For children in residential schools, "school is family"
- Negative aspects of residential schools, which include:
  - —Quality of education can be poor
  - —Bureaucracy and regulations can lead to regimentation
  - —Abuse and molestation can occur
  - —Lack of social skills may result
  - —Children are not socialized into their parents' world

Some children, especially those who are blind, deaf, or both, attend residential schools. Up until the 1960s, residential schooling was the only educational option for children who were deaf, blind, or both; indeed, before the 1960s, 80% of all children in the United States who were deaf attended residential schools (Lane, Hoffmeister, & Bahan, 1996). Residential schools offered education from preschool through high school and sometimes adult education. Since the 1960s, mainstreaming or inclusion into community schools has been facilitated by (1) providing sign language interpreters, (2) using "itinerant" teachers (teachers who teach at several different schools), and (3) providing self-contained classrooms for children who were deaf. Nonetheless, most children with severe hearing loss attend residential schools. Fifty-nine percent of all profoundly deaf and 41% of all severely deaf children attend residential schools (Karchmer & Trybus, 1977).

Thus, at an early age, children who attend residential schools are separated from their families, and many of these children are "homesick" for the school when they are at home for the holidays. In essence, school is their family. Residential education offers these children communication skills and socialization (Meadow-Orlans, 1996). Children in these types of schools, because everyone is deaf, blind, or both, participate in all school activities, including student body offices, athletics, and debate (opportunities they probably would not be afforded if they were mainstreamed in a community school). Other advantages of residential schooling include the availability of role models—teachers who are deaf, other students, and alumni of the school. Indeed, many individuals with congenital deafness or blindness have reported that their parents had very low educational and vocational expectations of them. It was the role models at residential schools who encouraged these individuals to fulfill their potential. Individuals in the Deaf Culture have campaigned against the closing of residential schools for deaf children. Dr. Geerat Vermeij, an evolutionary biologist/paleontologist/professor at the University of California, Davis, has been blind since infancy. Dr. Vermeij argued for mainstreaming in local schools but also advocated that the child receive a solid foundation in learning certain skills in a separate classroom before being allowed to attend class with sighted children.

> The ideal situation, it seems to me, is for a blind child to attend a local school. At first, full attention should be devoted to learning the essential skills—Braille, independent travel, getting to know one's physical and social surroundings—in a class wholly dedicated to that purpose. Gradually, blind children should be eased into class with their sighted peers, with time being set aside to hone and expand the fundamental skills of blindness. Whatever the right solution is for any particular child, the goal of providing the necessary techniques as well as the self-confidence and social adaptations to live and compete successfully in sighted society must remain clearly fixed at center stage. (Vermeij, 1997, p. 36)

Mainstreaming children in the community school is not always better than residential schooling. In a community school, the quality of education and accommodations for the disability may not be very good, and a child may simply "attend" school rather than receive an education. In the case of children who are deaf, sign language interpreters often have poor skills and, even more frequently, are not trained in the subject matter they are interpreting (such as chemistry). In addition, many children need to ride a bus for as long as 2 hours each way to attend a community school, thus consuming a large part of each school day. Also, there are no interpreters for casual, social encounters with hearing classmates. Therefore, the educational placement of children with deafness or blindness is complicated. Added to the complexity is the lack of coordination between medical services and educational services. For example, physicians who treat babies who are deaf often are not trained in or aware of available educational programs. Further, parents may receive conflicting advice from medical caregivers and educational professionals.

As would be expected, the quality of residential schools varies. Some of the negative aspects include the following:

- The quality of education at some schools was or is very poor; indeed, some schools concentrate on vocational education, especially in the manual trades. For example, in the past, the majority of graduates of residential schools for the Deaf did not continue on to college. (This is also a result of lack of accommodations at colleges/universities.)

- The bureaucracy, rules, and regulations often lead to regimentation. One graduate of a residential school spoke of the "damned bells" (Evans & Falk, 1986). This individual was referring to the fact that every minute of the day was controlled by the bells and a set, unchanging, monotonous schedule was enforced. This organization of every detail of daily life can inhibit children's sense of self-mastery, independence, individuality, creativity, and initiative.

- Any bureaucracy may respond more to the administrators' needs and convenience than to the needs of the students. For example, one book I read had a schedule of a residential school for the Deaf. The children were allowed to go home for Thanksgiving only for the Thursday and Friday of Thanksgiving.

- Families assume that they are placing their children in a safe, secure environment when, in reality, abuse of children may occur in residential schools. Indeed, one houseparent stated, "You have to break deaf kids when they're young." This houseparent whipped the children with a large leather belt when they "misbehaved" (Evans & Falk, 1986, p. 100). These beatings were administered for relatively minor infractions. Another type of abuse is discussed in this statement: "A top administrator estimates that one-third of all students were 'abused and molested' children" (Evans & Falk, 1986, p. 99).

- Children may become dependent because all their basic needs of life are met. Indeed, there is a risk of "learned helplessness," or overcompliance, when the child is required to yield self-mastery or never learned self-mastery in the first place.

- Children educated in residential schools usually experience less privacy and may have difficulty in adjusting to being alone; they also may be unprepared to take risks. Indeed, those in the Disability Rights Movement speak of the "dignity of risk," whereby an individual is allowed, and encouraged, to take risks, even with the possibility of failure. The dignity of risk is better than over-protection.

- The assumption that children can "practice" social behaviors in a supportive learning environment is not always true. Wolfensberger and Tullman (1991) argue that residential schools can be "culture-alien," and thus residential education can contribute to a child's lack of social skills and ability to live outside the school. Wolfensberger noted, "The skills, habits, and relationships that are prerequisites for a meaningful life in open society are difficult to acquire in settings that are culture-alien, that lack familiar cues, reduce opportunity, suggest or impose alien or devalued roles, and so on."

- Goffman's 1963 book discussed institutions and residential schools in this way: "The process starts with the 'mortification of the self.' From the moment of entry into the institution, the patient is subjected to series of 'degradation rituals' designed to produce docility and submissiveness. The old self is removed and a standardized, institutionalized alternative is provided. A process of stripping, washing, and re-clothing removes almost all remembrances of their former life and produces a new identity. Permission is required to undertake even ordinary activities. The institution then engages in a 'reorganization of the self' by supplying a new patient identity with appropriate social props such as standardized clothing and set routines. A 'privilege system' is operated to reward appropriate behavior and punish wrongdoing so that inmates identify with the 'organization's goals and fate'" (Barnes, Mercer, & Shakespeare, 1999, p. 45). Goffman's description makes residential schools for children who are blind, deaf, or both sound like prison or the Marines!

- Regardless of how excellent the education, a residential school is not a home. Children educated in residential schools are often not socialized into their parents' world, including such aspects as siblings, extended family, racial/ethnic/cultural identification, and religion.

Who decides a D/deaf child's identity? Most deaf babies are born to hearing parents who typically have no knowledge or understanding of deafness, American Sign Language, or the Deaf Culture. Deaf adults who know all about deafness are strangers to the family (Gulati, 2003).

It should be noted that we are not discussing institutions, such as those institutions that care for individuals with severe mental retardation or individuals with severe mental illness. These types of institutions typically do not offer education as residential schools do.

The Cost of Residential Schools to PWODs

By failing to provide quality accommodations and adequate education in the community schools to children with disabilities, society "pays" for this segregation. First, our tolerance for diversity and difference is, unnecessarily, reduced, and second, society reinforces the existential angst and fear of acquiring a disability. In other words, if, as children, everyone were educated and socialized with children with disabilities, PWODs would understand the experience of disability more realistically and not fear it. Wendell (1997) clearly explained: "The public world is the world of strength, the positive [valued] body, performance and production, the able-bodied and youth. Wellness, illness, rest, recovery, pain, and death and the negative [devalued] body are private, hidden, and often neglected" (p. 266).

Although Wendell was not speaking of residential schools, she made the point that by not acknowledging or trying to understand the disability experience (by relegating PWDs to a "private, hidden" world), PWODs harm themselves.

Acquired Disabilities

> **In this section, look for—**
> - Aspects of acquired disabilities
> - The distinction between diagnosis and onset
> - How the PWD may have internalized prejudices about disability
> - How the individual may have a well-defined social role and status
> - How, often, there is a literal overnight change

When we discussed congenital disabilities, we read that Geri Jewell said, "It's not like I wake up every morning and say, 'Oh my goodness, I have cerebral palsy!' I was born like this." Christopher Reeve, the actor who had a spinal cord injury, said in a television interview that on awakening every morning, he is surprised to find that he has quadriplegia. Obviously, the individual's disability identity, or lack of disability identity, differs in those with congenital disabilities and those with acquired disabilities.

It is important to make a distinction between onset and diagnosis. In many disabilities, the onset and the diagnosis occur at the same time;

however, in some congenital and acquired disabilities the time of the onset and the time of the diagnosis are different (Donoghue & Siegel, 1992; Gordon, Lewis, & Wong, 1994; Maloney, 1985; Strauss, 1981; White & Lubkin, 1998). For example, deafness can be congenital, yet it often is not diagnosed until the infant is older; therefore, the time of onset (birth) and time of diagnosis are different. (The average age of diagnosing congenital deafness is 15 months.) In the case of some types of acquired disabilities, such as diabetes, macular degeneration, and schizophrenia, the time of onset is unknown (the onset is considered to be "insidious") and it is the time of diagnosis that is referenced (although, in these types of disabilities, the genetic predisposition to develop these disabilities is present at birth). Nonetheless, for many disabilities, such as spinal cord injuries, traumatic brain injuries, and amputations, the time of onset and time of diagnosis are the same. In these types of disabilities, the onset is considered to be "acute."

Acquired Disabilities and Prejudice and Discrimination

An individual who acquires a disability later in life has often internalized prejudices and discrimination about the disability. For an individual who has not had much experience with or knowledge of PWDs, he or she has been subjected to the prejudicial stereotypes and inaccurate views of disability. PWDs are often thought to be victims of tragic circumstances, socially isolated, without any quality of life and with few choices. Kevin Shirley, who acquired a traumatic brain injury at age 30, remarked, "Before I became disabled, I used to feel sorry for disabled [*sic*] people. I would feel sorry for them and do what I could to avoid them" (Mackelprang & Salsgiver, 1999, p. 205). If an individual has internalized these inaccurate assumptions and prejudices and then acquires a disability himself or herself, these prejudices, stereotypes, and attitudes now become *self-perceptions* (Glueckauf & Quittner, 1984). Reread Dr. Schroeder's comments in Chapter 4. Note the limited career options he thinks he has (as a 16-year-old who has become blind) and his remark, "With blindness did not come any insights into blindness."

Karen Pendleton acquired a spinal cord injury at age 36. In the following excerpt she explains how little she knew about disability, even after she sustained her spinal cord injury:

> It seems weird now, but it took me a while to become really accepting of others with disabilities. A really good eye-opener for me was a college course I took on the psychological aspects of disability. I took the class thinking I would know everything and get an easy A. But I really learned a lot in the class about other disabilities. Since then, I've learned a lot from other people with disabilities. I'm much more accepting of

people with disabilities and of myself with a disability. (Mackelprang & Salsgiver, 1999, p. 99)

Lifelong attitudes and beliefs can be difficult to change, and, furthermore, most individuals never consider the possibility that one day they might have a disability, or they consider the possibility to be very remote. As we have stated before, disability is the only "open" minority group, meaning that anyone can "join" the minority at any time. Nonetheless, most people deny the possibility that they might acquire (or discover) a disability, and, moreover, most people unquestioningly accept the widely held stereotypes of what life must be with a disability. Then, in some cases, overnight, these prejudices become self-perceptions. It is "safer" to hold prejudices and stereotyped attitudes about racial/ethnic/cultural groups, religious groups, sexual orientation groups, or political groups because, in all likelihood, prejudiced individuals will never become a member of one of these groups.

An Acquired Disability Often Requires a Change of Identity

While not all acquired disabilities are considered to have a traumatic onset, such as the result of an accident, injury, or violence, most acquired disabilities are unpredictable and occur without warning. Because of this lack of warning, the individual has not been allowed to engage in anticipatory preparation. Many of life's transition points can be anticipated, including the natural results of aging, widowhood, retirement, the death of one's parents, and sudden loss of a job/career. Instrumental preparations include financial arrangements, such as retirement plans and insurance policies. Perhaps even more helpful are the emotional preparations for life's transitions. Many of life's transitions require a change in self-identity, and changes in self-identity are stressful. Transitions include a new beginning and a simultaneous ending. In addition, many life transitions are viewed as universal (they happen to everybody sooner or later). However, the onset of a disability is not thought of as happening, especially in the earlier years of life.

An acquired disability may seem like the loss of identity, status, and independence. Individuals who acquire a disability in midlife often have earned a place of status and prestige in the community and are people with well-developed self-concepts. Individuals in midlife often feel that this will be a period of life to enjoy. Because of this well-established identity, the disability can seem to be an overwhelming loss. Karen Pendleton, who acquired a spinal cord injury at age 36, spoke about her change in identity. Notice the way in which she speaks of herself before the onset of the disability in the third person and how she "buried" the old Karen. The word "buried" communicates the total change in identity—she is implying that the old Karen is dead. "Over time, I figured out that old Karen was no more. It's like I had to bury her and get to know the Karen that was left here. I found that I like the new Karen a lot better than the old one! . . . Now all I have left is me" (Mackelprang & Salsgiver, 1999, p. 98). We can see that Ms. Pendleton feels that she has sustained a loss, but she views it as a positive loss.

In 1976 Robert Murphy was diagnosed with a spinal cord tumor when he was 52 years old. A professor of anthropology at Columbia University, Murphy wrote a book entitled *The Body Silent* (Murphy, 1987). Murphy was an articulate man who was trained in foreign cultures. He described receiving the diagnosis of his disability as entering a country stranger and more foreign than any country in Africa or the Amazon. Murphy echoes the journalist Richard Cohen (2004) by describing his diagnosis period as a "journey into a strange land. That place would be exotic and rude" (p. 17).

Cohen said that he had had no training, education, or experience in dealing with the onset of a disability; nothing in his earlier life had prepared him for a disability. He felt that the label "winner" had been replaced with the label "damaged goods" (Cohen, 2004, p. 27).

The acquisition and onset of a disability can alter an individual's sense of the future and, in some instances, the individual's sense of the past. Deegan, who was diagnosed with schizophrenia, explained:

> We experienced time as a betrayer. Time did not heal us. Our pasts deserted us, and we could not return to who we had been. Our futures appeared to us to be barren, lifeless places in which no dream could be planted and grow into a reality. As for the present, it was a numbing succession of meaningless days and nights in a world in which we had no place, no use, and no reason to be." (Deegan, 1991, p. 49)

The reaction to the diagnosis or the onset differs. Some individuals dealing with a diagnosis feel that they have an entirely new identity, whereas others consider themselves to be the same person as before (with the exception of the disability). In the following excerpt, the 24-year-old who woke up one morning with polio felt that she was a stranger to herself:

> Something happened and I became a stranger. I was a greater stranger to myself than anyone. Even my dreams did not know me. They did not know what they ought to let me do—and when I went to dances or parties in (my dreams), there was always an odd provision or limitation—not spoken of or mentioned, but there just the same. I suddenly had the very confusion and mental and emotional conflict of a lady leading a double life. It was unreal and it puzzled me, and I could not help dwelling on it. (Goffman, 1963, p. 35)

Other PWDs state that they did not experience a radical shift in identity on the acquisition/onset of the disability. Michalko (2002) is clear: "You are who you always were. You haven't changed" (p. 7). Jenny Morris has a spinal cord injury and describes initial terror and the way in which she decided on her identity:

> At the time, lying there in hospital, my terror was not about the disability as such, but that I might have destroyed the structure of my life. However, this terror did not last long. I resolved that the structure I had built would remain unchanged. All that had happened was that I would now be doing things from a sitting position. I needed to sort things out in order to be able to do this. (Morris, 1991, p. 4)

Family and friends also react to an acquired disability. These associates often change the way in which they view the PWD, feeling that he or she has sustained a loss of identity and belonging. However, the individual often knows that he or she is the same person as before the acquisition of the disability but is also aware of the ways in which others do not relate to him or her (Crewe, 1997). Reread the letter from Mr. Mitchell in Chapter 3 when he talks about the reactions of his friends to his blindness.

The Developmental Stage of Acquisition

> **In this section, look for—**
> - Developmental stages
> - Required age-appropriate mastery of tasks
> - How development theories are silent on the topic of disability
> - How PWDs must negotiate the development tasks of each stage in addition to managing the disability

Developmental stages are usually defined as predictable phases that require certain responses from the individual. Basically, a child develops from requiring full support to being an adult with complete autonomy, with the individual mastering the tasks of each stage before moving on to the next stage. In other words, certain achievements are expected at each stage; indeed, there are "age-appropriate" tasks (or demands) that must be mastered. Each level of growth and development requires readjustment. Further, psychologists theorize that the successful, or unsuccessful, completion of these developmental tasks has a lifelong impact on the individual. Of course, these developmental stages do not proceed exactly on schedule for any individual; nonetheless, developmental stages provide a framework in which to view the phases of life.

The beginning or successful completion of a developmental stage is often marked with a rite of passage. We celebrate, hold observances, wear specific clothes (such as graduation robes and wedding dresses), receive gifts (the gold watch at retirement), give showers, give speeches, participate in religious ceremonies, send out announcements, send flowers, eat cake and ice cream, and in general go to great lengths and expense to move an individual from one social status to another. These rites of passage ensure that society changes its perception of the individual and that the individual changes perceptions of himself or herself. Rites of passage are one way in which society enforces its cultural beliefs; to be specific, rites of passage communicate that these social statuses are both positive and significant (Turner, 1979). There are no rites of passage when an individual acquires a disability, probably because disability is seen as tragic and out of the ordinary. Society has not endowed disability with a social category or identity. In spite of this lack of rites, many PWDs divide their lives into two categories: before the disability and after the disability. Marc Shell (2005) reviewed dozens of first-person accounts of polio and discovered that some polio survivors divided their lives into two parts—before polio and after polio—while others conceptualized the polio experience as a type of graduation. "A few polio-authors present themselves as having two lives—BP and AP—before polio and after polio. For others, the moment of poliomyelitic 'rebirth' is marked off as if the individual had graduated from something like a university or a 'school'" (p. 22).

There is little, if any, social role guidance for the disability experience (Agich, 1995), and there is no valued social category for disability. The absence of role guidance (and role models) exaggerates the difficulties of receiving a diagnosis. One 24-year-old woman explained:

> But suddenly, I woke up one morning and found that I could not stand. I had had polio and polio was as simple as that. I was like a very young child who had been dropped into a big, black hole . . . . The education, the lectures, and the parental training which I had received for twenty-four years didn't seem to make me the person who could do anything for me now. (Goffman, 1963, p. 35)

Before we begin our discussion of these developmental stages and their corresponding tasks, it should be noted that psychologists, such as Erikson (1963) and Havighurst (1951), devised their theories without much attention or awareness of disability issues. Nonetheless, individuals with disabilities must negotiate all the developmental stages that PWODs are required to negotiate. In addition, PWDs must respond to and manage the disability and society's prejudices and discrimination.

The acquisition of a disability, at any age or developmental stage of life, may signal the loss of universal and normative tasks. It may be necessary to alter, delay, or give up the developmental tasks of the next stage. Children with disabilities often see their older siblings successfully (and happily) negotiating developmental stages and expect that they, too, will have these experiences. Therefore, each developmental stage reached by siblings without disabilities can result in grieving for the child with a disability and for the entire family. In spite of this, it is becoming more and more common to allow children and young adults opportunities and experiences that were previously considered beyond their capabilities.

Infancy and Preschool Children

In infancy, the most important developmental task is that of establishing trust with the world. According to Erikson (1968), this trust is established primarily through the infant's relationship with the mother or other primary caregiver. For the infant with a disability, this may be difficult if he or she is hospitalized for long periods and is cared for by a host of different professionals (Bendell, 1984). In this situation, caregivers change with every 8-hour shift, and a trusting relationship with the mother is difficult to develop. Even when the infant with a disability is cared for at home, the parents may be depressed, withdrawn, exhausted, and resentful and, therefore, find it difficult to care for and relate to their baby. Of course, this type of parental withdrawal does not always occur.

A preschool child masters his or her environment by (1) learning sex roles (e.g., little children know whether they are a boy or a girl), (2) gaining some independence from the mother (feeding and dressing himself or herself), and (3) learning to communicate. Children with cognitive or intellectual disabilities are often unable to master some of these tasks, and children with hearing impairments may not learn to communicate. Children with motor impairments may not learn as much independence. Overprotection by family members may needlessly limit the child's independence. At this age, the preschooler's parents may not allow him or her to explore the environment. Reread the excerpts of Linda Pelletier and her appraisal of the effects of childhood overprotection on her adult life. Many disabilities (and chronic illnesses) of children are relatively rare (also called "low-incidence disabilities"). Table 8.1 shows some selected conditions that are present in fewer than 1% of children. In spite of the fact that medical advances, such as neonatal medicine, have resulted in more babies' surviving with a disability, these types of disabilities are relatively rare.

Patterson (1988) explained:

> Unlike adults, where the type of chronic illnesses [disabilities] are few in number but are prevalent, each of the hundreds of different conditions in children is relatively rare . . . . Except for a few common disorders such as mild asthma, the prevalence of any single condition is less than 1 per 100 children. This low incidence rate of many types of disabilities in children means that many families must seek treatment

Table 8–1

Estimated Prevalence of Low-Incidence Conditions in Children

Condition	Estimated prevalence per 1,000 children
Congenital heart disease	7.0
Seizure disorders	3.5
Cerebral palsy	2.5
Arthritis	2.2
Diabetes mellitus	1.8
Cleft lip/palate	1.5
Down syndrome	1.1
Blindness	0.6
Sickle cell disease	0.5
Cystic fibrosis	0.3
Deafness	0.1
Duchenne muscular dystrophy (males)	0.1

Note. The data in this table are from *The Future of Children*, a publication of the David and Lucile Packard Foundation.

in large metropolitan hospitals. Frequent travel, or perhaps moving the family residence, may be necessary in order to obtain treatment and services for the child with a disability.

School-Age Children

School-age children begin to learn what Erikson terms "industry," meaning that children learn to start and complete schoolwork. For young children, the completion of schoolwork is a major developmental task. School-age children also begin to emotionally separate from the family and develop peer relationships. Therefore, a disability that separates a child from peers can have a profound impact on the child's developmental progress. Disabilities that interrupt schooling or are visible (especially disfiguring disabilities) can make it difficult for the child to build peer relationships. There is stigma in attending "special" classes. Also, disabilities, such as cognitive or intellectual disabilities, that interfere with the child's self-concept as a competent student can make school, and any school-related activity, unpleasant and frustrating. Children with undiagnosed learning disabilities are often subjected to a great deal of punishment and criticism.

The actor Mia Farrow, in her memoir, *What Falls Away*, described the way in which the onset of her disability ended her childhood. "I was nine years old when my childhood ended." She contracted polio in 1954 at the age of 9.

Degenerating sensory loss is often discovered in the classroom. Eric Weihenmayer described his realization of his degenerating vision (and the difficulty of accepting this fact). "While I couldn't see well enough to . . . see an equation on the blackboard, I also couldn't accept myself as being blind" (2001, p. 47).

David Wright, a poet in England, lost his auditory nerve from an illness when he was 7 years old:

> Wright recalls that at first he did not realize what had happened: "How was I to know? Nobody told me." He had to "deduce the fact of deafness through a process of reasoning." He heard guns, motorbikes, lorries [trucks], crowds and drills by touch: "There can't be much I miss of the normal orchestration of urban existence." He could appreciate music too, resting his finger on a piano or a loudspeaker. And in a room with a wooden floor he would listen to drum and string instruments through his feet. (Wright, 1994, p. 22)

Brenda Premo was born with a type of degenerating blindness. In this excerpt, she describes the way in which she assumes that all of the other schoolchildren's vision was like hers.

> The first time I remember understanding that my vision was different from other people was in the second or third grade when I realized other students could read the blackboard. Before then, I couldn't understand why the teacher would bother to write on the board. When it dawned upon me that other kids could read the board and I couldn't, it was one of those "aha" moments in my life. It was a new discovery. (Mackelprang & Salsgiver, 1999, p. 140)

Adolescence

The tasks of adolescence include (1) emotionally separating from parents and family; (2) beginning to develop occupational identity; (3) establishing intimate, romantic relationships; (4) establishing an adult identity; and (5) establishing a strong sexual identity. Adolescents with disabilities must forge their new identity as an adult, discovering their identity, their values, and their career choices. In addition, they must integrate the disability into this new adult identity. Often, there are few role models for these teenagers. Friends and peers, and the companionship and feedback they provide, are important to teenagers. Disabilities that are disfiguring, or are visible, often make peer relationships difficult. One female teenager with a therapeutic leg amputation (as a result of cancer) stated, "I know young men, especially, really pay a lot of attention to looks and physical attractiveness. I wonder—will a boy accept me just the way I am? You hear them talking about how a girl's really built, or how she looks in a bathing suit and I hope they understand that they just amputated my leg, they didn't take my heart and soul and personality. I don't know if they'll ever accept me" (Darling, cited in Blumberg, Lewis, & Susman, 1984, p. 141).

As we can see in this statement, the treatment of illness and disabilities can be disfiguring. Gaining weight (a frequent side effect of medication), having tremors or spasticity, wearing hearing aids, or using a wheelchair can make teenagers self-conscious at a time in their life when they want to be attractive and fit in. Disabilities with unpredictable episodes of symptom manifestation can undermine the teenager's social confidence. Robert J. Neumann wrote about the effects of rheumatoid arthritis on his relationship, or lack of relationship, with girls:

> During my high school days, my social life was virtually nonexistent. Because I received physical therapy at home in the afternoon and because my stamina was poor in any event, I only attended school until about 1 p.m. This eliminated any possibility of interacting with peers in extracurricular activities . . . . Meanwhile, I unsuspectingly continued to . . . dream of the day I would start college and the active love life I had fantasized about for so long. Finally the big day arrived. Armed with a body of knowledge about women derived solely from TV, James Bond movies, and the *Playboy* magazines my younger brother smuggled in, I arrived at a small Midwestern college . . . . It took only a short while before I noticed my actual accomplishments with women were falling far short, not only of my expectations but also of the experiences of my friends . . . . [T]here was no need for me to call on social-sexual skills I had never learned. (1988, p. 159)

Seizure disorders and epilepsy are unpredictable in that the individual cannot predict the time, frequency, or level of intensity of the seizures. Livneh and Antonak (1997) summarized, "Psychosocial adaptation to epilepsy appears to have a complex curvilinear relationships with age of the individual, with increased risk of psychosocial maladaptation among adolescents and reduced risk among children and adults. The same conclusion appears to apply to the relationship between psychosocial adaptation and age at onset of epilepsy" (p. 302).

Teenagers typically experience more independence and freedom than younger children because they are capable of performing more functions. For example, learning to drive a car is a very important milestone and a step toward more freedom and independence. The child with epilepsy or mental retardation probably will never be able to drive a car. For a teenager, this is more than a functional loss—it is a loss of independence and "normality."

Every other 16-year-old is getting a driver's license. With the passage of the Americans with Disabilities Act (ADA), teenagers with disabilities are now afforded more than educational and career options. Before the ADA, these teenagers were often automatically excluded from high school career days or from interviews with visiting college and university representatives.

Teenagers are concerned about their future. When a teenager acquires a disability, such concerns are intensified: "Will I be able to have a baby?" "Will I be able to go to college?" "What kind of a career will I have?" and "Will anybody want to marry me?" are often asked (Bregman & Castles, 1988; Farrell & Hutter, 1984; Hahn, 1993; Houser & Seligman, 1991).

Schizophrenia is considered to be very disabling, in part because of its time of onset. The symptoms of schizophrenia usually begin during late adolescence or in one's early 20s. Therefore, exactly when the individual is confronting lifelong questions of occupational choice, educational issues, and choices in partners, he or she becomes ill. Schizophrenia would not be such a disabling illness if the typical time of onset were, for example, during the elderly years. The treatment of schizophrenia often requires long periods of hospitalizations and medications with many visible side effects, making it difficult for the teenager to fit in with his or her peers.

Spinal cord injuries often occur during the teenage years. More than 50% of individuals with spinal cord injuries acquired them between the ages of 15 and 24, and more than 80% of persons with spinal cord injuries are male (Livneh & Antonak, 1997). Most spinal cord injuries are caused by car accidents, falls, and stab and gunshot wounds.

Early Adulthood

The development tasks of young adulthood include establishing a family and beginning a career. The diagnosis or onset of a disability during young adulthood coincides with the peak years of career development and of assuming many social and economic responsibilities. "These factors maximize medical, social, and psychological problems that evolve and continue to grow over an extended period of time" (O'Brien, 1993, p. 24). One PWD recalled the diagnosis of his multiple sclerosis at age 25 as limiting his choices. He states, "Anyone's early years out of school and in the world are all about empowerment. Confidence in the future suddenly was neutralized (Cohen, 2004, pp. 26–27).

Sex and establishing intimate relationships are especially important in early adulthood. Many PWDs have internalized society's attitudes toward disability and, because of this, incorrectly think that no one would wish to date them. Society may teach PWDs to think of themselves as "damaged goods" (Wilson, 1990). Also, the risk of being turned down or ridiculed is often so great that the individual simply stays home or, at best, socializes in groups.

We have seen that there have been long-held beliefs that sexuality disappears with the onset of a disability, and these myths are difficult to eliminate. When we viewed the video "My Body is Not Who I Am," we met Tim, the man who acquired a spinal cord injury while climbing. Tim told of his physician talking to him in the hospital for 30 minutes about sex, marriage, and having a family (before his medical stabilization was completed). Years after his injury and hospitalization, Tim is grateful that the doctor initiated the discussion and answered many of Tim's unasked questions. Other PWDs have expressed disappointment in physicians and other medical caregivers who did not discuss sexual and physical intimacy. In one survey conducted with individuals with spinal cord injuries and traumatic brain injuries (Putnam et al., 2003), the participants were asked to describe wellness factors in dealing with their disability and those aspects that did not promote wellness. The authors summarized:

> Participants also expressed aggravation at physicians who do not provide specific health and wellness issues relevant to their conditions. One woman said, "And I'm tired of people dancing around the information that we need to know. For instance, very specifically about sexual dysfunction . . . why not tell us? Are we not all adults? Do most of us not have husbands and wives? Do we not have sex? Why can't you talk to us in plain English about things that are affecting us?"

Responding to the onset of a disability in early adulthood often includes not only the individual, but also his or her marriage partner. For example, the time of onset for multiple sclerosis usually occurs during the prime working years and, for a woman, during the childbearing years (Mairs, 1996). Therefore, the rehabilitation of individuals with this disability often includes family counseling to provide support to the spouse and children. Livneh and Antonak (1997) described the spouses of individuals with multiple sclerosis: "Spouses felt trapped, overwhelmed, and resentful" (p. 319). Disabilities that are acquired during the early years of marriage often require extensive assistance and custodial care of the partner with the disability. A wife of a man with a psychiatric disability summarized the experience by saying: "I feel like I've lost a partner and gained a problem child" (Mannion, 1996, p. 22). This type of custodial care may undermine the sexual relationship and render the partner with the disability sexually unattractive. Medications may interfere with sexual functioning (Schover & Jensen, 1988). Further, a parent–child relationship can evolve when one partner acquires a disability. The partner without the disability becomes a parent to the partner with the disability. Issues of power and control in a marriage are complicated when one partner is a custodial caregiver to the other ("If you don't agree with me about decorating the living room, I won't bathe or feed you"). It is surprising that many insurance policies do not cover marriage therapy for individuals with disabilities.

Nonetheless, families have great restorative powers 1996). Disability can provide the family with opportuni tive change. Family bonds can be strengthened. Family n pride in their mastery of the disability and report greater de compassion, spirituality, and personal strength. One family member sum marized, "I can now say that, like that old aluminum foil ad, I am 'oven tempered for flexible strength'" (Marsh & Lefly, 1996, p. 18). A study of caregivers whose spouses had multiple sclerosis showed that caregiver husbands and wives reported loving their spouse more than spouses in the normed sample (Perrone, Gordon, & Tschopp, 2006).

Family caregivers of an individual with a psychiatric disability are often required to assume an extra burden—that of being implicitly or explicitly blamed for the disability. Families with a member with a psychiatric disability may feel blamed, shamed, and unsupported (Mannion, Mueser, & Soloman, 1994). One man reported that his in-laws blamed him for his wife's depression (Mannion, Mueser, & Soloman, 1994). Most spouse caregivers have been women, probably because of the longer life spans of women and the traditional roles assigned to women. However, many chronic illnesses are more prevalent among women; therefore, it is becoming more common for the caretaker spouse to be the husband. Researchers report that the problems of male caregivers may be different than the problems of female caregivers (Perrone, Gordon, & Tschopp, 2006). Men typically have fewer outside supports than women in similar roles and may not be as skilled at role flexibility as women.

Disabilities, acquired at any age, are financially stressful. For a young couple trying to establish a household, disability expenses can be devastating. Treatment and adaptive technology are expensive, and many times, as the individual ages with the disability, these types of costs continue to rise. Medical crises and unexpected technology breakdowns can make budgeting difficult. Putnam et al. (2003) interviewed individuals with spinal cord injuries, cerebral palsy, polio, and amputations in Portland, Oregon; Houston, Texas; and San Francisco, asking which factors contributed to their wellness and sense of well-being and which factors decreased their sense of well-being. The authors described one often-mentioned concern:

> Many spoke about fears related to financing new equipment when their current devices needed replacing. Others relayed concerns about ongoing maintenance expenses. One participant said, "Once my scooter gives up, what am I going to do? Once my van goes toes up, what am I going to do?" So, it's not so much . . . about obtaining the assistive devices the first time, but replacing them. Because once my scooter gives up, how do I walk? (p. 42)

Pace-of-life issues are part of any marriage; one partner may be energetic, be hardworking, and enjoy activity and achievement, while the other may be relaxed, laid-back, and content to "kick back." However, with some disabilities, such as multiple sclerosis or rheumatoid arthritis, fatigue and pain are common symptoms. Individuals with these types of disabilities learn to conserve their energy (Rustad, 1984). The spouse without a disability may not totally understand these symptoms or may resent the partner with the disability, feeling that life is not as fun as before. Symptom exacerbation is often unpredictable, and therefore scheduling for family activities is difficult. In addition, the partner with the disability often must spend considerable time treating or managing the disability.

The loss of job and career can be devastating. Hillyer wrote: "Weekdays when I see other young women leaving for or returning from home I feel quite apart from the outside world. Whatever activities you take up, like painting, aren't the same. Nobody can convince you it's the same as being active within a normal work situation" (1993, p. 16). Another PWD explained the way in which her job loss affected her:

> I felt dreadful when I had to give up work. It was the most shattering experience I had had because going out to work you felt a part of society, you were contributing, you were earning your own money. You also had your friends that you went to work with, and then suddenly you were cut off. You were in the house alone. Also, of course, financially you are worse off. You were lonely, you felt useless, on the scrap heap, finished, and it really was a bad time. (Campling, 1981, p. 115)

Middle Adulthood

Since most individuals have established strong identities by middle adulthood, adjusting to the new identity as a PWD may pose certain questions. Middle adulthood is a time of peak achievement and career achievement. Indeed, many individuals in this period of life have reached their life goals and have gained some measure of status and prestige. Individuals now look forward to reaping the benefits of careful planning, hard work, and progressive success. In addition, marital happiness often increases in middle adulthood with the departure of the grown-up children from home. At this age, many individuals have resolved, or are in the process of working on, questions on the personal meaning of life. In short, middle adulthood is a time of life when personal satisfaction and feelings of mastery are greatest. Preparation for retirement also begins in this stage of life, and individuals begin to anticipate disengagement from the world of work.

The onset of a disability, for a man or a woman, during the middle adulthood years may prove to be interpreted as a loss of identity, status, and economic security. Because the individual in middle adulthood has established a strong, secure identity and a (perceived) place in society, a disability may appear to be an overwhelming shift in identity. Peak earning years may be lost, and the years that individuals looked forward to now may appear lost. Individuals with disabilities acquired earlier in life, such as arthritis or diabetes, may not have exhibited many symptoms, but with the advent of the aging process in the middle adulthood years, these symptoms frequently exacerbate and functioning now becomes impaired. Perhaps physical disabilities are easier to accept for individuals in this age range, ages 25–65 years, because they have begun to subordinate the importance of their physical body and their physical appearance. This is a developmental task of all individuals in this stage of life.

Middle adulthood is a time when many individuals are involved in the care of elderly parents with disabilities. Most of this care is provided by women, for both their own parents and the parents of their husband. Singer (1996) stated, "Currently, a woman can expect to spend more years caring for a parent than looking after dependent children" (p. 13). Such caregiving demands on women are difficult because these women most often work outside the home and therefore have multiple role demands (Elliott, Shewchuk, & Richards, 1999; Vash, 1982). Indeed, Singer (1996) labeled the traditional caregiving responsibilities of women as "the role of women as sources of support for vulnerable people" (p. 13). Rather than enjoying the benefits of more time and money to themselves and freedom from the responsibility of raising children, women in middle adulthood frequently find themselves providing long-term care for elderly parents.

As Fine and Asch (1988) pointed out, women with disabilities are more likely to be cared for by strangers, while men with disabilities are more likely to be cared for by female family members. There are demographic explanations for this: (1) some women have never been married; (2) some women are divorced or widowed; and (3) women tend to marry older men. However, caring for family members has been viewed as a female gender role. Ties of obligation and love "represent a defining aspect of femininity. Nurturing and connecting with others . . . evoke feminine associations. Many informants spoke of needing to be adaptable, invisible, and even subordinate . . . . These characteristics coincide with the generally tentative or inferior status traditionally available to women and, as such, contrast with the more fixed, visible, and dominant roles available to men" (Preston, 1994, p. 101).

Age 65 and Older

Despite the fact that disability onset is positively correlated with age, very few services have traditionally been provided to older PWDs. Until recently there were few existing programs to meet the needs of elderly PWDs. This is a reflection of the functional model of disability in that paid employment is the only function considered. In other words, rehabilitation has been focused on job placement and vocational skill development because such services are regarded as "investments" that would be paid back when PWDs go to work, get off public assistance, and start paying taxes. Elderly PWDs are not of working age and therefore are not considered to be able to "make a contribution to society" (Ouellette & Leja, 1988; Rubin & Rubin, 1988). Often, old age itself is seen as a disability. Of course, there is a loss of physical and cognitive functioning associated with aging, and there is also prejudice and discrimination directed toward elderly individuals (Blackburn, 1988; Hersen & Van Hasselt, 1990; Mitchell & Kemp, 1996). Stein and Cutler (1998) remarked on the physical effects of aging: "The normal wear and tear on the body takes its toll on the individual. Eyesight becomes weaker, hearing more difficult, range of movement in joints becomes limited, the muscles are not as strong, and the blood vessels begin to lose elasticity" (p. 204). The increased life span of Americans puts them at greater risk (and longer risk) for acquiring a disability (Wilkins & Cott, 1993). Added to these physical changes are the losses and stresses of isolation from family, decreased income, vulnerability to crime, and a lack of usefulness to a society that stresses youth and physical fitness.

The acquisition of a disability during old age appears to be more timely in both social and chronological time (Rolland, 1994). Loss occurs at any age, of course, but as people grow older they experience more losses, more frequently, and these losses have a cumulative effect (Lawton, 1996). Indeed, the loss of energy for general functioning often leads to social isolation; the person simply does not have the energy to socialize (Smith & Kampfe, 1997). Therefore, reduced activity and mobility, and occasionally reduced cognitive ability, are viewed as part of old age. Further, the incidence of various stressful conditions often adds up cumulatively, reaching their peak as the individual ages (Schienle & Eiler, 1984). The major developmental task for individuals in the elderly stages of life is adaptation to loss. Erikson, and other developmental psychologists, viewed old age (older than the age of 65) as a time to avoid ego despair and disengagement from life's activities and relationships. Nonetheless, it should not be assumed that growing old means inevitable loss or that the normative physiological changes of aging *always* result in disabilities (Schienle & Eiler, 1984). In addition to these physical losses, the elderly individual must deal with the ageism of a society that values youth, productivity, independence, achievement, and competition. Frequently, the knowledge and experience of elderly people are considered to be obsolete because of the fast pace of technological change. Much like PWDs, elderly people today may be viewed as "burdens" or "drains" because they no longer contribute to the economy (Zola, 1988). Another manifestation of society's ageism is the fact that hypochondriasis is overdiagnosed in people who are elderly. (This is not to say that there are not elderly hypochondriacs who use their physical complaints to exert control; it is to say that medical professionals overdiagnose hypochondriasis.) It is logical for people of advanced age to be preoccupied with their bodies. Also, just as PWDs often incorporate society's handicapism into their self-identity, many elderly people accept ageism as a self-identifier (Young & Olsen, 1991).

There are two types of elderly people with disabilities: (1) those who acquired a disability early in life (Trieschmann, 1987) and (2) those who acquire a disability later in life (Verbrugge, 1989). Disabilities acquired in old age may have an acute onset (such as a heart attack or a broken hip) or may have an insidious onset (such as diabetes or Parkinson's disease). Acute-onset disabilities often move the individual quickly into old age. Insidious-onset disabilities, however, manifest symptoms that are difficult to distinguish from the natural changes of aging. To further complicate the picture, in some old–age-onset disabilities, the individual's cognitive abilities and personality fade away (Lubkin & Larsen, 1998).

Individuals who are elderly may have acquired disabilities earlier in their life. The aging process often interacts with the disability to produce complications or more severe decline in functioning. For example, individuals who acquired a spinal cord injury early in life experience greater loss of energy, strength, stamina, mobility, and flexibility at an earlier age than do their age-mates without a spinal cord injury. Growing older with a disability is often associated with an earlier decline in functioning. Nonetheless, growing older with a disability requires that the individual negotiate all the tasks of old age and, at the same time, manage the disability. Some disability scholars have theorized that living an adult life with a disability assists the individual in adjusting to the demands of old age.

Elderly people often feel that they have not been accorded any input into the design of agencies and programs intended to serve them (Szymanski & Trueba, 1994; Zarit & Zarit, 1984). This also parallels the disability experience, in that many programs for PWDs are developed and administered by PWODs. Also, elderly people are frequently reluctant to accept services from government agencies, viewing such services as "charity" or some sort of admission of failure or lack of control. Seeking psychotherapy or counseling may be stigmatizing to these individuals (Chilman, Nunnally, & Cox, 1988). Because during their adult lives very few people received such services and the people receiving psychotherapy were experiencing severe problems, elderly people today often avoid counseling, viewing supportive counseling to be unnecessary.

Despite the previous discussion, PWDs who are elderly are thought to respond to disability more positively than PWDs who are young adults. This positive response is thought to be a function of the following factors: (1) disability is often seen as "normative" for old age (everyone else one's own age has some sort of a disability); (2) elderly people often have fewer functional demands, such as a career or taking care of children; (3) elderly people have had a lifetime of transition and changes and have developed effective idiosyncratic ways in which to deal with them; and (4) elderly people are often less concerned with body image. Indeed, the onset of a disability may appear relatively minor to someone who has lived a successful and long life.

Type of Onset

Thinking only of *onset* of disability (and not the time of *diagnosis*), we can conceptualize time of onset as falling within two broad categories: insidious onset and acute onset. An acute onset refers to a disability that has a sharp, definite beginning point (sometimes termed "clinical presentation"), and an insidious onset refers to a disability that begins in a subtle, stealthy manner. A spinal cord injury would be considered to have an acute onset, while diabetes is thought to have an insidious onset. Further, with many insidious-onset disabilities, it is the time of diagnosis that is referenced because no one can really accurately pinpoint the actual time of onset. (Although, to be truly accurate, with many mental illnesses, the onset can be considered to be both acute and insidious. For example, the onset of schizophrenia is considered to be acute in that the individual has an intensification of symptoms that greatly impairs the individual's functioning and usually requires immediate hospitalization. Therefore, the onset is considered to be an acute emergency, requiring immediate treatment, but it is acknowledged that the onset was also insidious, meaning that symptoms, in reality, did not appear "out of the blue.")

Acute-Onset Disabilities

Acute-onset disabilities are considered to be medical emergencies; the individual is often required to disengage from his or her typical life activities, such as school, work, and family obligations, and the treatment of the disability becomes top priority (Verbrugge & Jette, 1994). There is a sharp, decisive turning point for the individual, his or her family, and professional service providers. Rapid mobilization of medical, individual, and family resources is required (Chilman, Nunnally, & Cox, 1988; Lesak, 1986). Acute-onset disabilities, as would be expected, usually are a shock. Such events as accidents, disease presentation, or the birth of a baby with a congenital disability are unexpected, allowing no time for anticipatory and preparatory reaction. In the case of amputations, individuals with cancer or diabetes who were required to undergo a therapeutic amputation and who had only a few days' advance notice responded better to the amputation than did those individuals who experienced traumatic amputations. This makes intuitive sense because time for acceptance, even a few days, helps individuals to respond to the loss of a body part. (Most amputations are therapeutic amputations.) In contrast, individuals with traumatic amputations experience more problems with acceptance. In one sentence, a man tells of his acute-onset spinal cord injury with the accompanying feelings of suddenness, unexpectedness, and the need to deal with a medical diagnosis: "I was 22, a recent college graduate, and all of a sudden, I'm a T8 bilateral paraplegic, whatever the hell that is!" (Crewe, 1997, p. 32). This man, Roy, had gone on a graduation trip to the American West with friends. The driver fell asleep at the wheel and rolled the van. Roy was the only one seriously hurt.

Insidious-Onset Disabilities

Insidious-onset disabilities include such conditions as multiple sclerosis, diabetes, and rheumatoid arthritis. No one can definitively state the time of onset, not professional care providers nor the individual himself or herself. More support is usually given for acute-onset disabilities because friends and family can clearly understand a sharp, sudden (often traumatic) onset. Insidious-onset disabilities appear to be more ambiguous than acute-onset disabilities. Frequently, individuals with insidious-onset disabilities (that have been diagnosed) must seek emergency medical care, undergo hospitalization, and disengage from their major life activities. For example, the diagnosis of depression or diabetes often requires that the individual go to the hospital for immediate treatment. Many people who experience insidious-onset disabilities speak about "something being not quite right for a long time," probably speaking of warning signs or prodromal symptoms, which at the time were not understood or acknowledged (Viney & Westbrook, 1982).

Implications and Cautions

Viewing onset of disability from this simple dichotomy leads to these implications:

1. We are not discussing *course* of the disability; only the beginning.
2. We also are not discussing the *cause* of the disability, only the onset.
3. We are not talking about the *visibility* of the disability; both acute-onset disabilities and insidious-onset disabilities can be either invisible or visible.
4. Those with insidious-onset disabilities are less likely to seek treatment than those with acute-onset disabilities.
5. An unknown time of onset (an insidious onset) can be stressful.

6. A diagnosis leads to family support.
7. For many psychiatric disabilities, knowing the onset of the disability can help in arriving at an accurate diagnosis.

Therefore, physicians will ask, "When did you first start having problems?" and "What happened next?" Many psychiatric and cognitive disabilities have similar symptoms but different types of onset; therefore, it is necessary to establish the type of onset to make the right diagnosis. Ziporyn (1992) stated: "Symptoms associated with more than one disease can underlie years of misdiagnosis" (p. 104). Parkinson's disease and a stroke have many of the same symptoms; however, the first disability is an insidious-onset disability and the second is an acute-onset disability. Head injuries have an acute onset, while dementia has an insidious onset; yet, they share many of the same symptoms. Therefore, physicians will ask, "Have you been in a car accident or bumped your head in the last few weeks?" If the answer is "yes," then further probing for the presence of a head injury is warranted.

The Impact of a Long Prediagnosis Period

> **In this section, look for—**
>
> - The impact of prolonged uncertainty
> - How individuals are given less support and validation
> - How individuals are often labeled with negative diagnoses
> - How people need diagnoses to receive services

Many disabilities with an insidious onset, such as multiple sclerosis, lupus, thyroid disease, Crohn's disease, and a host of autoimmune diseases, have a long prediagnosis period. When the diagnosis is finally made, the individual is torn between relief at having a name for the symptoms that he or she has been experiencing and the shock of having a serious disability. There is a simple and straightforward explanation for their symptoms (Ziporyn, 1992). However, the diagnosis can be a devastating disability (Donoghue & Siegel, 1992). Nonetheless, the diagnosis ends "a frightening array of possibilities" (Goodheart & Lansing, 1997).

These types of disabilities often present with the following symptoms: muscle weakness, fatigue, pain, sleep disturbances, numbness, and/or vision disturbance, all of which impair the individual's functioning but are also easily dismissed by physicians. Therefore, the individual undergoes an exhaustive, long diagnostic period while dealing with the symptoms. Even more important, the individual is often diagnosed as having psychological problems, drug abuse, or alcoholism. According to Donoghue and Siegel (1992), on average, from the first onset of symptoms to diagnosis of multiple sclerosis, an individual will endure 40 months of prediagnosis.

Rereading the definitions of secondary gains and hypochondriasis, we can see how easy it is for both professionals and family members to think that the individual is engaging in trying to obtain secondary gains or is being a hypochondriac (Davidhizar, 1994). The doctor says, "The tests show nothing. There is nothing wrong with you." Friends and family often stop being supportive (and may, in fact, resent the individual for being such a "wimp") (Friedberg & Jason, 1998). However, those with less ambiguous disabilities and chronic illness are given support and validation, including medical care, time off from work, time to rest, flowers, cards, and the general solicitude of others. Further adding to the stress of the unknown problem are the negative labels given to the person. Physicians may accuse the individual of "doctor shopping," when in reality the individual is trying to seek help for the debilitating symptoms. These individuals may be told to buy a new hat, take a vacation, have the fillings in their teeth replaced, take herbs and vitamins, or see a psychologist. Occasionally, spouses and other family members are aware of the effects of the symptoms on the individual, but their observations are discounted or dismissed by physicians. The cyclic or intermittent nature of some symptoms makes it difficult for others to understand their severity. After all, at times the individual seems "like himself [or herself]." However, because the individual has no medical diagnosis, he or she may overcompensate and overexert himself or herself during times of symptom remission. Indeed, "many energy depleting conditions have no visible manifestations, [but] they are nevertheless incapacitating" (Kohler, Schweikert-Stary, & Lubkin, 1998, p. 129).

For many, the time of diagnosis is a relief from the stress of not understanding the symptoms that the individual is experiencing. One expert in families with a member who has a mental illness terms the time of diagnosis as an "epiphany." She states:

> After long periods of chaos and confusion, the nature of the problem suddenly seems clear. Family members, sometimes equally go for months or years of feeling anger, fear, confusion, and concern about a loved one's oppressive behaviors without being able to name them as illness. The point at which a person's troublesome behavior is transformed into a disease, via the pronouncements of medical experts, is typically a moment of epiphany. Such a moment of epiphany is, however, only the beginning of an ongoing interpretive process . . . . (Karp, 2001, p. 49)

A college professor with multiple sclerosis described the unforgettable day of her diagnosis: "Every [person with] multiple sclerosis can remember the moment of diagnosis. It is one of those events which can be forever recalled in the most exquisite detail" (Toombs, 1995, p. 4). A woman with a husband with mental illness described her reaction to receiving her husband's diagnosis:

> I'll tell you one of the best days of my life was when I got a phone call from the hospital telling me what they decided was wrong with my husband, and they couldn't understand why I was so excited or happy. (Karp, 2001, p. 50)

An Englishwoman, Clare, received a diagnosis of multiple sclerosis; after this diagnosis, friends told Clare that they had previously thought she was simply lazy:

> One interesting piece of information that came to light after I told people that I had MS was the opinions that they and others had had of me. I guess that I was both hurt and mildly angry to discover that I had been seen as a lazy and work-shy person . . . . I was just left feeling betrayed by friends of many years. (Morris, 1991)

Lack of a Diagnosis Does Not Mean Absence of Impairment

It is not uncommon for the individual who has an insidious-onset disability (which has not been diagnosed) to begin to wonder if he or she is "crazy." The pain, fatigue, and muscle weakness often work together to drastically change the individual's functioning and activities. Accordingly, these individuals devise coping devices, such as spending the entire weekend in bed to be able to go to work on Monday morning. Kohler, Schweikert-Stary, and Lubkin (1998) included an account of a woman with arthritis who found it difficult to accept her fatigue. She said, "It's hard to justify my fatigue to friends and relatives; my husband often asks, 'Why are you so tired?' It took an article in the *National Arthritis News* to finally help me to convince myself and him that my fatigue was real, physiologically, as well as emotionally" (p. 129).

Often, these individuals become "medical detectives," learning as much as possible about their symptoms and the best way in which to communicate the seriousness of these symptoms to physicians. As would be expected, some of these individuals become depressed (which, in itself can lead to loss of energy). Without a diagnosis, without family support and validation, and with the symptoms and functional loss, these individuals often report their emotional responses to feel like riding a roller coaster. The emotional roller coaster feels like helplessness, lack of control, and unpredictability. Furthermore, others (physicians, family members, and employers) perceive the individual as fully functional and, because of this, do not change their expectations of the individual. Donoghue and Siegel, in their book *Sick and Tired of Feeling Sick and Tired*, referred to a study that examined the psychological impact of multiple sclerosis. To the researchers' surprise, the group of participants who reported the greatest distress and depression were men (with multiple sclerosis) who had few physical impairments. Indeed, these men were more depressed than others with more severe physical and functional impairments. The researchers determined that the ambiguity and stress of the prediagnosis period was associated with their depression. Many of these men reported low feelings of self-worth and the need to constantly defend and explain themselves to skeptical physicians and family members. These stressors, ambiguity and the skepticism of others, in this one study, were more depressing than physical impairments.

Tosca Appel (1988) wrote of her prediagnosis period before she was found to have multiple sclerosis. Her young age (11 years) may have contributed to some of the misdiagnoses since the typical age of onset for multiple sclerosis is about age 20. Note (1) that none of these symptoms were invisible, (2) the number of misdiagnoses, (3) the severity of the first symptom (her parents took her to the emergency room of the hospital), (4) the prolonged prediagnosis period, and (5) the negative labels given to her.

> I was 11 years, 9 months old when my first symptom appeared. My first attack of MS took the form of a lack of motor coordination of my right hand. I was unable to hold utensils and my hand was turned inward; my parents in their concern rushed me to the emergency room of the hospital. The intern who saw me at the emergency room told my parents, without any exam, that I had a brain tumor . . . . I was admitted to the hospital, where I stayed for 12 days. Ten days after the initial attack the symptoms abated . . . . The doctors had put the blame of the attack on a bad case of nerves . . . . My second attack occurred when I was 16 years old and in the 11th grade . . . . One day . . . my history teacher asked me a question. I stood up to answer and my speech came out all garbled. I was unable to string the words into a sentence. I was even unable to utter words. All that came out were sounds. I clutched my throat to help the words come out easier . . . . I remembered the teacher's look. He looked at me in utter surprise and a little bit helplessly . . . . Again, my parents rushed me to the emergency room where another intern did his initial workup on me . . . . The intern, in his wisdom, thought this behavior was an attention-getter. He thought I was faking the whole thing. (pp. 253–254)

In-Class Videos

- Two videos illustrate the dichotomy between either describing d/Deafness as a disability or describing d/Deafness as a culture. View these videos: "Sound and Fury" and "Sound and Fury: Six

Years Later." Both films show the struggle of one family deciding whether to provide cochlear implants to their deaf children. Two cousins of Long Island, New York, are deaf. Heather, age 6½, has deaf parents and Peter, age 1½, has hearing parents. The grandparents and both sets of parents are faced with the decision to either improve the hearing of the children or raise the children as members of the Deaf Culture. This first film was a 2001 Academy Award nominee for Best Documentary feature. The second "Sound and Fury" film shows Heather 6 years later, and the family discusses the decision they made.

■ View the 26-minute video "Multiple Sclerosis" from The Doctor Is In series by Films for the Humanities and Sciences. Focus on (1) the adjustment demands of a progressive disability, and (2) the adjustment demands of an invisible disability.

■ View the 24-minute video "A Full Stride: Overcoming the Challenge of Amputation" by Films for the Humanities and Sciences. The producers describe this video as follows: "Focusing on three people, this program shows the many sides of what is often a generic label: disabled or amputee. Old, young, partial loss, complete loss, each story is different. From the time of hospitalization to the triumph of accomplishing small and large tasks, we see the many challenges and the small victories: the psychological pain of losing a limb, the stigma of being 'disabled,' and the vivid 'phantom' pain of a lost limb, but also the process of adjustment to a prosthesis and the freedom and mobility it can bring."

■ View the 19-minute video "Rehabilitation: The Road to Recovery" by Films for the Humanities and Sciences. This program shows both the rehabilitative techniques used with patients who have had a stroke or a spinal cord injury and the techniques and tools available to patients after rehabilitation has proceeded to the maximum physiologically possible. The program stresses the role played by the patient as well as by rehabilitation specialists in the patient's recovery, contrasting the very expensive technologies at the forefront of rehabilitation techniques with the counterbalancing requirement of the patient's commitment and willpower.

■ View the 40-minute video "Misha: Recovery from a Serious Accident" by Films for the Humanities and Sciences. This is the powerful story of 16-year-old Misha Heselwood and her successful fight to regain her life after being seriously injured. The program begins with Misha's hospitalization with severe brain injuries from a car accident and follows Misha, her family, and the medical staff over a 9-month period, charting her recovery from coma as she relearns how to walk, talk, eat, and eventually regain self-reliance and independence.

■ View the 16-minute video "Abilities Taken for Granted: The Disabled." This video profiles a woman who has not allowed her disability to interfere with her successful career or fast-paced lifestyle. It discusses the arduous path a person who is disabled faces in American society and addresses some of the laws and legislation that deal with disabilities.

■ View the 27-minute video "Epilepsy: The Storm Within" by Films for the Humanities and Sciences. Epilepsy is the second most common neurological disorder in the United States. This program examines its causes, what happens in the brain during a seizure, and what should and should not be done to help someone having a seizure. The diagnosis and treatment of the condition are discussed by physicians who present up-to-date information to help families, friends, and coworkers recognize the needs and capabilities of a person with epilepsy. People with epilepsy describe what it is like living with the condition.

■ View the 28-minute video "Dancing from the Inside Out." This video profiles three dancers from AXIS, a troupe of dancers, some disabled and some nondisabled. Members discuss adapting to disabilities and reveal their rediscovery of physical expression in dance. Spliced into the discussion are scenes from the dancers' daily lives, rehearsals, and a performance. "Exuberant! Lends perspective to the unlimited potential in people of differing abilities" (Booklist).

■ View the 25-minute video "Mental Illness in the Family." In this film, Bonnie and members of her family talk about her illness and its impact on all of them. They recall their helplessness and confusion when she became ill and their emotions and reactions in the years that followed. Topics include keeping the illness a secret; "Could I have done something to prevent her illness?"; Bonnie's anger, paranoia, delusions—and guilt; the threat to the marriage; and special problems that affect siblings. Available from Mental Illness Education Project Videos (22-D Hollywood Avenue, Hoboken, NJ 07423, 201-652-1989, 800-343-5540, fax 201-652-1973, www.miepvideos.org).

■ View the 27-minute video "Recovering from Mental Illness." What does it feel like to have schizophrenia? Bonnie talks about learning to cope with her illness, and she and her family discuss her progress (with Andrea Blodgett, MSW, of McLean Hospital, Belmont, MA). Topics include the devastation of realizing you're ill, being written off, the reality of the voices, not wanting to take medications, the difficulty of deciding how much to expect, and recognizing recovery. Available from Mental Illness Education Project Videos (22-D Hollywood Avenue, Hoboken, NJ 07423, 201-652-1989, 800-343-5540, fax 201-652-1973, www.miepvideos .org).

■ View the 22-minute video "My Sister Is Mentally Ill." Bonnie's sister Kathy talks candidly about her emotions and the problems she has faced having a sister with schizophrenia. This is a unique tape on sibling issues that will interest other family members as well as professionals, with Linda Husar, MSW, and including some scenes from "Mental Illness in the Family." Topics include being afraid but not talking about it; guilt; trying to be perfect; and concerns about marriage, having children, estate planning, and the future. The Bonnie tapes are available from Mental Illness Education Project Videos (22-D Hollywood Avenue, Hoboken, NJ 07423, 201-652-1989, 800-343-5540, fax 201-652-1973, www.miepvideos .org).

- View the 25-minute video "Family Challenges: Parenting with a Disability: Exploring Family Relationships When a Parent Has a Disability." When a parent has a disability, everyone in the family is affected. For children, these experiences may profoundly influence their lives and views of the world. In this sensitive film, you will hear about different roles that all the family members take on at varying times. Family Challenges looks at three families coping with different kinds of disabilities. In Family Challenges, the viewer has the opportunity to understand how different families share their stories of accepting and acknowledging the disability. The video explores the relationship with the spouse as well as the insights and perceptions of the children. This film helps the viewer experience firsthand the feelings and emotions of a family that has a parent with a disability. This is an excellent video for those living with a disability and their families, as well as professionals in rehabilitation, mental health counselors, hospitals, and psychology and nursing professionals. Winner of the Silver Award, INTERCOM SuperFest '99 Award. Available from Aquarius Health Care Videos (fax 508-650-4216, www.aquariusproductions.com).

- View the 47-minute video "Beyond the Barriers." Follow sport enthusiast and paraplegic Mark Wellman on his extreme adventures. For too many years, paraplegics, amputees, quadriplegics, and the blind have felt trapped by their disabilities. No more! Mark Wellman and other disabled adventurers rock climb the desert towers of Utah, sail in British Columbia, body-board the big waves of Pipeline and Waimea Bay, scuba dive with sea lions in Mexico, and hang glide the California coast. This film delivers the simple message: Don't give up, and never give in. If you can't ever lose, then you can't ever win. Available from Aquarius Health Care Videos (fax 508-650-4216, www.aquariusproductions.com).

- View the 21-minute video "In the Mind of the Beholder," a film about newly blind adults. This documentary is about newly blind adults making the transition to using their nonvisual senses. In a society in which most people are terrified of losing their vision—and yet know virtually nothing about vision loss—the blind are wrongly viewed as mysterious, pitiful, or courageous. Produced by Karen Brown Davison, this film puts a human face and voice to blindness. By sharing the experience of losing their eyesight and relearning skills they once took for granted, the people in this film demystify blindness and the nonvisual clues they use to navigate the world. "The interviewees talk openly about how they do not allow their vision loss to prevent them from living full lives despite many difficulties and obstacles they face . . . . 'In the Mind of the Beholder' shatters the notion that the blind are helpless or to be pitied" (Samantha J. Gust, *MC Journal: The Journal of Academic Media Librarianship*). Available from Aquarius Health Care Videos (fax 508-650-4216, www.aquariusproductions.com).

- View the 22-minute video "Families and Health: A Child's Voice." Children share their thoughts and fears about having a serious illness in their family. A moving documentary about children communicating their concerns over a family health condition—be it their own, a sibling's, or parent's. These children talk openly about conditions such as HIV, diabetes, asthma, and cancer and how they affect them at home, the hospital, and school. Available from Aquarius Health Care Videos (fax 508-650-4216, www.aquarius productions.com).

- View the 28-minute video "I Am Dekel: Portrait of a Life with Down Syndrome" by Films for the Humanities and Sciences (P.O. Box 2053, Princeton, NJ 08543-2053, 800-257-5126, www .films.com). The language of this video is Hebrew with English subtitles. The producers describe this video: "Dekel Shekarzi, a 21-year-old who defines himself as an actor, a poet, a dancer, and a romantic in love with love itself, is defined by many others not by who he is, but what he was born with: Down syndrome. This engaging documentary follows Dekel in his everyday life, which is anything but 'everyday.' Film of Dekel on stage and at home, candid interviews with his family members, and reflections from this remarkable individual reveal an intriguing personality."

- View the 14-minute video "Freedom Chasers: The Importance of Independence for Teens with a Disability" produced by Aquarius Health Care Media. The producers describe this video: "Living with a disability means that you find yourself both struggling with the need to be independent as well as being dependent upon others at the same time. The teens in this video share great insights on living a challenge like Cerebral Palsy, Spina Bifida, Juvenile Arthritis and Down Syndrome." #83AP8030

- View the 29-minute video "They Don't Come with a Manual" produced by Insight Media. The producers describe this video: "This unsparing look at the difficulties and rewards of raising a disabled child offers hope and compassion for new parents.

Parents of children with autism, Down Syndrome, cerebral palsy, and blindness speak candidly about the daily challenges they face, portraying the psychosocial impact of disability on the family."
#TAD268

Learning Activity
As a class, write some possible questions to ask a PWD. Have several class members interview a PWD using these questions. Report the results of these interviews to the class.

Writing Experience
Using one of the 19 "bullets" listed at the beginning of this chapter, write a response paper.

References

Affleck, G., Tennen, H., Pfeifer, C., & Fifield, J. (1987). Appraisals of control and predictability in adapting to a chronic disease. *Journal of Personality and Social Psychology, 53,* 273–279.

Agich, G. J. (1995). Chronic illness and freedom. In S. K. Toombs, D. Barnard, & R. A. Carson (Eds.), *Chronic illness: From experience to policy* (pp. 129–153). Bloomington, IN: University of Indiana.

Alfano, D. P., Nielsen, P. M., & Fink, M. P. (1993). Long-term psychosocial adjustment following head or spinal cord injury. *Neuropsychiatry, Neuropsychology, and Behavioral Neurology, 6,* 117–125.

Appel, T. (1988). Personal statement: Living in spite of multiple sclerosis. In P. W. Power (Ed.), *Family interventions throughout chronic illness and disability* (pp. 253–257). New York: Springer.

Austin, J. K. (1990). Assessment of coping mechanisms used by parents and children with chronic illness. *Maternal and Child Nursing, 15,* 98–102.

Barnes, C., Mercer, G., & Shakespeare, T. (1999). *Exploring disability: A sociological introduction.* Cambridge, England: Polity.

Batshaw, M. L. (Ed.). (1998). *Children with disabilities* (4th ed.). Baltimore: Brookes.

Bendell, R. D. (1984). Psychological problems of infancy. In M. G. Eisenberg, L. C. Sutkin, & M. A. Jansen (Eds.), *Chronic illness and disability through the life span: Effects on self and the family* (pp. 23–38). New York: Springer.

Bernbaum, J. C., & Batshaw, M. L. (1998). Born too soon, born too small. In M. L. Batshaw (Ed.), *Children with disabilities* (4th ed.) (pp. 115–139). Baltimore: Brookes.

Blackburn, J. (1988). Chronic health problems of the elderly. In C. S. Chilman, E. W. Nunnally, & F. M. Cox (Eds.), *Chronic illness and disability: Families in trouble* (pp. 108–122). Newbury Park, CA: Sage.

Blumberg, B. D., Lewis, M. J., & Susman, E. J. (1984). Adolescence: A time of transition. In M. G. Eisenberg, L. C. Sutkin, & M. A. Jansen (Eds.), *Chronic illness and disability through the life span: Effects on self and the family* (pp. 133–163). New York: Springer.

Bregman, S., & Castles, E. E. (1988). Insights and intervention into the sexual needs of the disabled adolescent. In P. W. Power, A. E. Dell Orto, & M. B. Gibbons (Eds.), *Family interventions throughout chronic illness and disability* (pp. 184–200). New York: Springer.

Breslau, N. (1982). Psychiatric disorder in children with physical disabilities. *Journal of the American Academy of Child Psychiatry, 24,* 87–94.

Breslau, N., & Marshall, I. A. (1985). Psychological disturbances in children with physical disabilities: Continuity and change in a 5-year follow-up study. *Journal of Abnormal Child Psychology, 13,* 199–216.

Brown, D. (1997). Implications of cultural values for cross-cultural consultation with families. *Journal of Counseling and Development, 76,* 29–35.

Campling, J. (1981). *Images of ourselves: Women with disabilities talking.* London: Routledge Kegan Paul.

Chilman, C. S., Nunnally, E. W., & Cox, F. M. (Eds.). (1988). *Chronic illness and disability: Families in trouble.* Newbury Park, CA: Sage.

Cohen, R. B. (2004). *Blindsided: Living a life above illness: A reluctant memoir.* New York: Dutton.

Collins-Moore, M. S. (1984). Birth and diagnosis: A family crisis. In M. G. Eisenberg, L. C. Sutkin, & M. A. Jansen (Eds.), *Chronic illness and disability through the life span: Effects on self and the family* (pp. 39–66). New York: Springer.

Cook, D., & Ferritor, D. (1985). The family: A potential resource in the provision of rehabilitation services. *Journal of Applied Rehabilitation Counseling, 16*(2), 52–53.

Couser, G. T. (1997). *Recovering bodies: Illness, disability, and life writing.* Madison, WI: University of Wisconsin.

Crewe, N. M. (1997). Life stories of people with long-term spinal cord injury. *Rehabilitation Counseling Bulletin, 41,* 26–42.

Cummings, S. (1976). The impact of the child's deficiency on the father: A study of fathers of mentally retarded and of chronically ill children. *American Journal of Orthopsychiatry, 46,* 246–255.

Curry, R. L. (1995). The exceptional family: Walking the edge of tragedy and transformation. In S. K. Toombs, D. Barnard, & R. A. Carlson (Eds.), *Chronic illness: From experience to policy* (pp. 24–37). Bloomington, IN: University of Indiana.

Damrosch, S. P., & Perry, L. A. (1989). Self-reported adjustment, chronic sorrow, and coping of parents of children with Down syndrome. *Nursing Research, 38,* 30.

Danek, M. (1988). Deafness and family impact. In P. W. Power, A. E. Dell Orto, & M. B. Gibbons (Eds.), *Family interventions throughout chronic illness and disability* (pp. 120–135). New York: Springer.

Danek, M. M., & Lawrence, R. E. (1985). Women in rehabilitation: An analysis of state agency services to disabled women. *Journal of Applied Rehabilitation Counseling, 16,* 16–18.

Darling, R. B., & Baxter, C. (1996). *Families in focus: Sociological methods in early intervention.* Austin, TX: PRO-ED.

Davidhizar, R. (1994). The pursuit of illness for secondary gains. *Health Care Supervisor, 13*(3), 49–58.

Deegan, P. E. (1991). Recovery: The lived experience of rehabilitation. In R. P. Martinelli & A. E. Dell Orto (Eds.), *The psychological and social impact of disability* (3rd ed.) (pp. 47–54). New York: Springer.

Dell Orto, A. E. (1988). Respite care: A vehicle for hope, the buffer against desperation. In P. W. Power, A. E. Dell Orto, & M. B. Gibbons (Eds.), *Family interventions throughout chronic illness and disability* (pp. 265–284). New York: Springer.

Donoghue, P. J., & Siegel, M. E. (1992). *Sick and tired of feeling sick and tired: Living with invisible chronic illness.* New York: Norton.

Downey, G., Silver, R. C., & Wortman, C. B. (1990). Reconsidering the attribution-adjustment relation following a major negative event: Coping with the loss of a child. *Journal of Personality and Social Psychology, 59,* 925–940.

Drotar, D., Crawford, P., & Bush, M. (1984). The family context of childhood chronic illness: Implications for psychosocial intervention. In M. G. Eisenberg, L. C. Sutkin, & M. A. Jansen (Eds.), *Chronic illness and disability through the life span: Effects on self and the family* (pp. 103–235). New York: Springer.

Edwards, M. L. (1997). Deaf and dumb in ancient Greece. In L. J. Davis (Ed.), *The disabilities studies reader* (pp. 29–51). New York: Routledge.

Eisenberg, M. G., Sutkin, L. C., & Jansen, M. A. (Eds.). (1984). *Chronic illness and disability through the life span: Effects on self and the family.* New York: Springer.

Elliott, T. R., Shewchuk, R. M., & Richards, J. S. (1999). Caregiver social problem-solving abilities and family member adjustment to recent onset physical disability. *Rehabilitation Psychology, 44,* 104–123.

Erikson, E. (1963). *Childhood and society* (2nd ed.). New York: Norton.

Erikson, E. H. (1968). *Identity and crisis.* New York: Norton.

Evans, A. D., & Falk, W. W. (1986). *Learning to be deaf.* Berlin: Mouton de Gruyter.

Falvo, D. R. (1991). *Medical and psychosocial aspects of chronic illness and disability.* Gaithersburg, MD: Aspen Publishers, Inc.

Farrell, F. Z., & Hutter, J. J. Jr. (1984). The family of the adolescent: A time of challenge. In M. G. Eisenberg, L. C. Sutkin, & M. A. Jansen (Eds.), *Chronic illness and disability through the life span: Effects on self and the family* (pp. 150–163). New York: Springer.

Featherstone, H. (1980). *A difference in the family: Living with a disabled child.* New York: Basic Books.

Fewell, R. (1986). A handicapped child in the family. In R. Fewell & P. Vadasy (Eds.), *Families of handicapped children* (pp. 3–34). Austin, TX: PRO-ED.

Filer, R. D., & Filer, P. A. (2000). Practice considerations for counselors working with hearing children of deaf parents. *Journal of Counseling and Development, 78,* 38–43.

Fine, M., & Asch, A. (1988). *Women with disabilities: Essays in psychology, cultural, and politics.* Philadelphia: Temple University.

Frantz, T. T. (1981). *When your child has a life-threatening illness.* Bethesda, MD: Association for the Care of Children's Health.

Friedberg, F., & Jason, L. A. (1998). *Understanding chronic fatigue syndrome: An empirical guide to assessment and treatment.* Washington, DC: American Psychological Association.

Glueckauf, R. L., & Quittner, A. L. (1984). Facing physical disability as a young adult: Psychological issues and approaches. In M. G. Eisenberg, L. C. Sutkin, & M. A. Jansen (Eds.), *Chronic illness and disability through the life span: Effects on self and the family* (pp. 167–183). New York: Springer.

Goffman, E. (1963). *Stigma: Notes on spoiled identity.* Englewood Cliffs, NJ: Prentice Hall.

Goodheart, C. D., & Lansing, M. H. (1997). *Treating people with chronic disease: A psychological guide.* Washington, DC: American Psychological Association.

Gordon, P. A., Lewis, M. D., & Wong, D. (1994). Multiple sclerosis: Strategies for rehabilitation counselors. *Journal of Rehabilitation, 62,* 34–38.

Graliker, B. V., Fishler, K., & Koch, R. (1962). Teenage reaction to a mentally retarded sibling. *Journal of Mental Deficiency, 66,* 838–843.

Greenberg, M. T. (1980). Hearing families with deaf children: Stress and functioning as related to communication method. *American Annals of the Deaf, 125,* 1063–1071.

Gulati, S. (2003). Psychiatric care of culturally Deaf people. In N. S. Glickman & S. Gulati (Eds.), *Mental health care of deaf people: A culturally affirmative approach* (pp. 33–107). Mahwah, NJ: Lawrence Erlbaum.

Hahn, H. (1993). Can disability be beautiful? In M. Nagler (Ed.), *Perspectives on disability* (2nd ed.) (pp. 213–216). Palo Alto, CA: Health Markets Research.

Harper, D. C. (1999). Social psychology of difference: Stigma, spread, and stereotypes in childhood. *Rehabilitation Psychology, 44,* 131–144.

Havighurst, R. J. (1951). *Developmental tasks and education.* New York: Longman Green.

Head, D. W., Head, B., & Head, J. (1985). Life or death of severely disabled infants: A counseling issue. *Journal of Counseling and Development, 63,* 621–624.

Heller, A., Rafman, S., Zvagulis, I., & Pless, I. B. (1985). Birth defects and psychosocial adjustment. *American Journal of Diseases of Children, 139,* 257–263.

Hersen, M., & Van Hasselt, V. B. (Eds.). (1990). *Psychological aspects of developmental and physical disabilities.* Newbury Park, CA: Sage.

Hillyer, B. (1993). *Feminism and disability.* Norman, OK: University of Oklahoma Press.

Houser, R., & Seligman, R. (1991). Differences in coping strategies used by fathers of adolescents with disabilities and fathers of adolescents without disabilities. *Journal of Applied Rehabilitation Counseling, 22,* 7–10.

Huberty, D. J. (1980). Adapting to illness through family groups. In P. W. Power & A. E. Dell Orto (Eds.), *Role of the family in the rehabilitation of the physically disabled* (pp. 433–443). Austin, TX: PRO-ED.

Ireys, H. T., & Burr, C. K. (1984). Apart and a part: Family issues for young adults with chronic illness and disability. In M. G. Eisenberg, L. C. Sutkin, & M. A. Jansen (Eds.), *Chronic illness and disability through the life span: Effects on self and the family* (pp. 184–206). New York: Springer.

Karchmer, M. A., & Trybus, R. J. (1977). *Who are deaf children in "mainstream" programs?* Washington, DC: Gallaudet College.

Karp, D. A. (2001). *The burden of sympathy: How families cope with mental illness.* Oxford, England: Oxford University.

Keydel, C. (1988). The impact of a handicapped child on adolescent siblings: Implications for professional intervention. In P. W. Power, A. E. Dell Orto, & M. B. Gibbons (Eds.), *Family interventions throughout chronic illness and disability* (pp. 201–215). New York: Springer.

Knoll, J. A. (1992). Being a family: The experience of raising a child with a disability or chronic illness. In V. J. Bradley, J. Knoll, & J. M. Agosta (Eds.), *Emerging issues in family supports* (Monograph Series No. 18, pp. 9–56). Washington, DC: American Association on Mental Retardation.

Knoll, J. A. (1996). Charting unknown territory with families of children with complex medical needs. In G. H. S. Singer, L. E. Powers, & A. L. Olson (Eds.), *Redefining family support: Innovations for public-private partnerships* (pp. 189–223). Baltimore: Brookes.

Kohler, K., Schweikert-Stary, T., & Lubkin, I. (1998). Altered mobility. In I. M. Lubkin & P. D. Larsen (Eds.), *Chronic illness: Impact and interventions* (4th ed.) (pp. 122–148). Sudbury, MA: Jones & Bartlett.

Krause, J. S. (1992). Adjustments to life after spinal cord injury: A comparison among three participant groups based on employment status. *Rehabilitation Counseling Bulletin, 35,* 218–229.

Krause, J. S., & Crewe, N. M. (1991). Chronologic age, time since injury, and time of measurement: Effect on adjustment after spinal cord injury. *Archives of Physical Medicine and Rehabilitation, 72,* 91–100.

Kriegsman, K. H., & Celotta, B. (1981). A program for group counseling for women with physical disabilities. *Journal of Rehabilitation, 47*, 36–39.

Lane, H. L. (1996). The hearing agenda I: To mitigate a disability. In H. Lane, R. Hoffmeister, & B. Bahan (Eds.), *A journey into the deaf-world* (pp. 334–366). San Diego, CA: Dawn Sign Press.

Lane, H., Hoffmeister, R., & Bahan, B. (1996). *A journey into the deaf-world.* San Diego, CA: Dawn Sign Press.

Lawton, M. P. (1996). The aging family in a multigenerational perspective. In G. H. S. Singer, L. E. Powers, & A. L. Olson (Eds.), *Redefining family support: Innovations in public-private partnerships* (pp. 135–149). Baltimore: Brookes.

Lesak, M. D. (1986). Psychological implications of traumatic brain damage for the patient's family. *Rehabilitation Psychology, 31*, 241–250.

Lindenberg, R. E. (1980). Work with families in rehabilitation. In P. W. Power & A. E. Dell Orto (Eds.), *Role of the family in the rehabilitation of the physically disabled* (pp. 516–525). Austin, TX: PRO-ED.

Livneh, H., & Antonak, R. F. (1997). *Psychosocial adaptation to chronic illness and disability.* Gaithersburg, MD: Aspen.

Lubkin, I. M., & Larsen, P. D. (Eds.). (1998). *Chronic illness: Impact and interventions.* Sudbury, MA: Jones & Bartlett.

Mackelprang, R., & Salsgiver, R. (1999). *Disability: A diversity model approach in human service practice.* Pacific Grove, CA: Brooks/Cole.

Mairs, N. (1996) *Waist-high in the world: A life among the nondisabled.* Boston: Beacon.

Maloney, F. P. (1985). Rehabilitation and patients with progressive and remitting disorders. In F. P. Maloney (Ed.), *Interdisciplinary rehabilitation of multiple sclerosis and neuromuscular disorders* (pp. 3–8). Philadelphia: Lippincott.

Mannion, E. (1996). Resilience and burden in spouses with mental illness. *Psychiatric Rehabilitation Journal, 20*, 13–24.

Mannion, E., Mueser, K., & Soloman, P. (1994). Designing psychoeducational services for spouses of persons with serious mental illness. *Community Mental Health Journal, 30*, 177–189.

Marsh, D. T., & Lefly, H. P. (1996). The family experience of mental illness: Evidence for resilience. *Psychiatric Rehabilitation Journal, 20*(2), 3–13.

Meadow-Orlans, K. P. (1996). Socialization of deaf children and youth. In P. C. Higgins & J. E. Nash (Eds.), *Understanding deafness socially: Continuities in research and theory* (pp. 60–70). Springfield, IL: Charles C. Thomas.

Michalko, R. (2002). *The difference disability makes.* Philadelphia: Temple University.

Miller, J. (1988). Personal statement: Mechanisms for coping with the disability of a child—A mother's perspective. In P. W. Power, A. E. Dell Orto, & M. B. Gibbons (Eds.), *Family interventions throughout chronic illness and disability* (pp. 136–147). New York: Springer.

Mitchell, J. M., & Kemp, B. J. (1996). The Older Adult Disability Scale: Development and validation. *Rehabilitation Psychology, 41*, 187–203.

Mitsos, S. B. (1972). The grieving process of parents with atypical children. *Journal of Rehabilitation, 38*(2), 5–7.

Morris, J. (1991). *Pride against prejudice: Transforming attitudes toward disability.* Philadelphia: New Society.

Murphy, R. F. (1987). *The body silent: An anthropologist embarks on the most challenging journey of his life: Into the world of the disabled.* New York: W. W. Norton.

National Public Radio. (May, 1998). Disability History Project. Tomorrow's Children.

Neumann, R. J. (1988). Personal statement experiencing sexuality as an adolescent with rheumatoid arthritis. In P. W. Power, A. E. Dell Orto, & M. B. Gibbons (Eds.), *Family interventions throughout chronic illness and disability* (pp. 156–163). New York: Springer.

Nixon, C. D. (1993). Reducing self-blame and guilt in parents of children with severe disabilities. In G. H. S. Singer & L. E. Powers (Eds.), *Families, disability, and empowerment: Active coping skills and strategies for family interventions* (pp. 175–201). Baltimore: Brookes.

O'Brien, M. T. (1993). Multiple sclerosis: Stressors and coping strategies in spousal caregivers. *Journal of Community Health Nursing, 10,* 123–135.

Olshansky, S. (1962). Chronic sorrow: A response to having a mentally defective child. *Social Casework, 43,* 190–193.

Ouellette, S. E., & Leja, J. A. (1988). Rehabilitation counseling considerations with sensory-impaired persons. In S. E. Rubin & N. M. Rubin (Eds.), *Contemporary challenges to the rehabilitation counseling profession* (pp. 153–182). Baltimore: Brookes.

Patterson, J. M. (1988). Chronic illness in children and the impact upon families. In C. S. Chilman, E. W. Nunnally, & F. M. Cox (Eds.), *Chronic illness and disability* (pp. 69–107). Beverly Hills, CA: Sage.

PBS. (1998) *Paralyzing fear: The story of polio in America.* Item no. PFPA 401.

Pearson, J. E., & Sternberg, A. (1986). A mutual project for families of handicapped children. *Journal of Counseling and Development, 65,* 213–216.

Pelletier, L. (1988). Personal statement: The challenge of cerebral palsy: Familial adaptation and change. In P. W. Power, A. E. Dell Orto, & M. B. Gibbons (Eds.), *Family interventions throughout chronic illness and disability* (pp. 54–59). New York: Springer.

Perlesz, A., Kinsella, G., & Crowe, S. (1999). Impact of traumatic brain injury on the family: A critical review. *Rehabilitation Psychology, 44,* 6–35.

Perrone, K. M., Gordon, P. A., & Tschopp, M. K. (2006). Caregiver marital satisfaction when a spouse has multiple sclerosis. *Journal of Applied Rehabilitation Counseling, 37,* 26–32.

Power, P. W., & Dell Orto, A. E. (1980). Approaches to family interventions. In P. W. Power & A. E. Dell Orto (Eds.), *Role of the family in the rehabilitation of the physically disabled* (pp. 321–330). Austin, TX: PRO-ED.

Power, P. W., & Rogers, S. (1979). Group counseling for multiple sclerosis patients: A preferred mode of treatment for unique adaptive problems. In R. G. Lasky & A. E. Dell Orto (Eds.), *Group counseling and physical disabilities* (pp. 115–127). North Scituate, MA: Duxbury.

Powers, L. E. (1993). Disability and grief: From tragedy to challenge. In G. H. S. Singer & L. E. Powers (Eds.), *Families, disability, and empowerment: Active coping skills and strategies for family interventions* (pp. 119–149). Baltimore: Brookes.

Preston, P. (1994). *Mother father deaf: Living between sound and silence.* Cambridge, MA: Harvard University.

Putnam, M., Greenen, S., Powers, L., Saxton, M., Finney, S., & Dautel, P. (2003). Health and wellness: People with disabilities discuss barriers and facilitators to well-being. *Journal of Rehabilitation, 69,* 37–45.

Rolland, J. S. (1994). *Families, illness, and disability: An integrative treatment model.* New York: Basic Books.

Rubin, S. E., & Rubin, N. M. (Eds.) (1988). *Contemporary challenges to the rehabilitation counseling profession.* Baltimore: Brookes.

Rustad, L. C. (1984). Family adjustment to chronic illness and disability in mid-life. In M. G. Eisenberg, L. C. Sutkin, & M. A. Jansen (Eds.), *Chronic illness and disability through the life span: Effects on self and the family* (pp. 222–242). New York: Springer.

Rutter, M. (1989). Intergenerational continuities and discontinuities in serious parenting difficulties. In D. Cicchetti & V. Carlson (Eds.), *Child maltreatment: Theory and research on causes and consequences of child abuse and neglect* (pp. 317–348). Cambridge, England: Cambridge University.

Sailor, W., Kleinhammer-Tramill, J., Skrtic, T., & Oas, B. K. (1996). Family participation in new community schools. In G. H. S. Singer, L. E. Powers, & A. L. Olson (Eds.), *Redefining family support: Innovations in public-private partnerships* (pp. 313–332). Baltimore: Brookes.

Santelli, B., Turnbull, A. P., Lerner, E., & Marquis, J. (1993). Parent to parent programs: A unique form of mutual support for families of persons with disabilities. In G. H. S. Singer & L. E. Powers (Eds.), *Families, disabilities, and empowerment: Active coping skills and strategies for family interventions* (pp. 27–57). Baltimore: Brookes.

Schienle, D. R., & Eiler, J. M. (1984). Clinical intervention with older adults. In M. G. Eisenberg, L. C. Sutkin, & M. A. Jansen (Eds.), *Chronic illness and disability through the life span: Effects on self and the family* (pp. 245–268). New York: Springer.

Schover, L. R., & Jensen, S. B. (1988). *Sexuality and chronic illness: A comprehensive approach.* New York: Guilford.

Schulz, R., & Decker, S. (1985). Long-term adjustment to physical disability: The role of social support, perceived control, and self-blame. *Journal of Personality and Social Psychology, 48,* 1162–1172.

Shell, M. (2005). *Polio and its aftermath.* Cambridge, MA: Harvard University.

Sidransky, R. (1990). *In silence: Growing up hearing in a deaf world.* New York: St. Martin's.

Singer, G. H. S. (1996). Introduction: Trends affecting home and community care for people with chronic conditions in the United States. In G. H. S. Singer, L. E. Powers, & A. L. Olson (Eds.), *Redefining family support: Innovations in public-private partnerships* (pp. 3–38). Baltimore: Brookes.

Singer, G. H. S., & Irvin, L. K. (1989). Family caregiving, stress, and support. In G. H. S. Singer & L. K. Irvin (Eds.), *Support for caregiving families* (pp. 3–25). Baltimore: Brookes.

Singer, G. H. S., & Powers, L. E. (1993). Contributing to resilience in families: An overview. In G. H. S. Singer & L. E. Powers (Eds.), *Families, disabilities, and empowerment: Active coping skills and strategies for family interventions* (pp. 1–25). Baltimore: Brookes.

Singer, G. H. S., Powers, L. E., & Olson, A. L. (Eds.). (1996). *Redefining family support: Innovations in public-private partnerships.* Baltimore: Brookes.

Smith, S. M., & Kampfe, C. M. (1997). Interpersonal relationship implications of hearing loss in persons who are older. *Journal of Rehabilitation, 63,* 15–20.

Spaniol, L., Zipple, A. M., & Fitzgerald, S. (1985). How professionals can share power with families: A practical approach to working with families of the mentally ill. *Psychosocial Rehabilitation Journal, 8,* 77–84.

Stein, F., & Cutler, S. K. (1998). *Psychosocial occupational therapy: A holistic approach.* San Diego, CA: Singular Publishing Group.

Strauss, A. L. (1981). Chronic illness. In P. Conrad & R. Kerns (Eds.), *The sociology of health and illness: Critical perspectives.* New York: St. Martin's.

Summers, J. A., Behr, S. K., & Turnbull, A. P. (1989). Positive adaptation and coping strengths of families who have children with disabilities. In G. H. S. Singer & L. K. Irvin (Eds.), *Support for caregiving families: Enabling positive adaptation to disabilities* (pp. 27–40). Baltimore: Brookes.

Sutkin, L. C. (1984). Introduction. In M. G. Eisenberg, L. C. Sutkin, & M. A. Jansen (Eds.), *Chronic illness and disability through the life span: Effects on self and the family* (pp. 1–19). New York: Springer.

Szymanski, E. M., & Trueba, H. T. (1994). Castification of people with disabilities: Potential disempowering aspects of classification in disability services. *Journal of Rehabilitation, 60*(3), 12–19.

Tollifson, R. (1997). Imperfection is a beautiful thing: On disability and meditation. In K. Fries (Ed.), *Staring back: The disability experience from the inside out* (pp. 105–112). New York: Plume.

Toombs, S. K. (1995). Sufficient unto the day. In S. K. Toombs, D. Barnard, & R. A. Carson (Eds.), *Chronic illness from experience to policy* (pp. 2–23). Bloomington, IN: University of Indiana.

Trieschmann, R. B. (1987). *Aging with a disability.* New York: Demos.

Tucker, B. P. (1998, July/August). Deaf culture, cochlear implants, and elective disability. *Hastings Center Report, 28*(4), 6–15.

Turnbull, A. P., & Turnbull, H. R. (1991). Understanding families from a systems perspective. In J. M. Williams & T. Kay (Eds.), *Head injury: A family matter* (pp. 37–64). Baltimore: Brookes.

Turner, V. (1979). Betwixt and between: The liminal period in rites of passage. In W. Lessa & E. Z. Vogt (Eds.), *Reader in comparative religion* (4th ed.) (pp. 234–243). New York: Harper & Row.

Vash, C. (1982). Women and employment. In L. Perlman (Ed.), *Women in rehabilitation: The sixth Mary E. Switzer memorial seminar monograph* (pp. 15–24). Alexandria, VA: National Rehabilitation Association.

Vash, C. L. (1981). *The psychology of disability.* New York: Springer.

Verbrugge, L. (1989). Gender, aging, and health. In K. Markides (Ed.), *Aging and health: Perspectives on gender, race, ethnicity, and class* (pp. 55–75). Newbury Park, CA: Sage.

Verbrugge, L. M., & Jette, A. M. (1994). The disablement process. *Social Science and Medicine, 38*, 1–14.

Vermeij, G. (1997). *Privileged hands: A scientific life.* New York: Freeman.

Viney, L. L., & Westbrook, M. T. (1982). Psychological reactions to the onset of chronic illness. *Social Science and Medicine, 16*, 899–905.

Walker, L. A. (1986). *A loss for words: The story of deafness in a family.* New York: Harper.

Wasow, M., & Wilder, L. (1983). Reflections on professionals' attitudes toward the severely mentally retarded and the chronically mentally ill: Implications for parents. *Family Therapy, 10*, 299–308.

Weihenmayer, E. (2001). *Touch the top of the world: A blind man's journey to climb farther than the eye can see.* New York: Dutton.

Wendell, S. (1997). Toward a feminist theory of disability. In L. J. David (Ed.), *The disability studies reader* (pp. 260–278). New York: Routledge.

Westbrook, M. T., & Legge, V. (1993). Health practitioners' perceptions of family attitudes toward children with disabilities: A comparison of six communities in a multicultural society. *Rehabilitation Psychology, 38*, 177–185.

White, N., & Lubkin, I. M. (1998). Illness trajectory. In I. M. Lubkin & P. D. Larsen (Eds.), *Chronic illness: Impact and interventions* (pp. 53–76). Sudbury, MA: Jones & Bartlett.

Whitt, J. K. (1984). Children's adaptation to chronic illness and handicapping conditions. In M. G. Eisenberg, L. C. Sutkin, & M. A. Jansen (Eds.), *Chronic illness and disability through the lifespan: Effects on self and the family* (pp. 69–102). New York: Springer.

Wilkins, S., & Cott, C. (1993). Aging, chronic illness and disability. In M. Nagler (Ed.), *Perspectives on disability* (2nd ed.) (pp. 363–377). Palo Alto, CA: Health Markets Research.

Wilson, D. J. (1990). *Living with polio: The epidemic and its survivors.* Chicago, IL: University of Chicago.

Wolfensberger, W., & Tullman, S. (1991). A brief outline of the principle of normalization. In M. G. Eisenberg & R. S. Glueckauf (Eds.), *Empirical approaches to the psychosocial aspects of disability* (pp. 202–215). New York: Springer.

Woodrich, F., & Patterson, J. B. (1983). Variables related to acceptance of disability in persons with spinal cord injuries. *Journal of Rehabilitation, 49*(3), 26–30.

Wright, D. (1994). *Deafness: An autobiography.* New York: Harper Perennial.

Young, R. K. (1974). Chronic sorrow: Parents' response to the birth of a child with a defect. *Maternal Child Nursing, 3*, 59–76.

Young, R., & Olsen, E. (1991). Introduction. In R. Young & E. Olson (Eds.), *Health, illness, and disability in later life: Practice issues and interventions* (pp. 1–7). Newbury Park, CA: Sage.

Zarit, S. H., & Zarit, J. M. (1984). Psychological approaches to families of the elderly. In M. G. Eisenberg, L. C. Sutkin, & M. A. Jansen (Eds.), *Chronic illness and disability through the life span: Effects on self and the family* (pp. 269–288). New York: Springer.

Ziporyn, T. (1992). *Nameless diseases.* New Brunswick, NJ: Rutgers University.

Zola, I. (1988). Policies and programs concerning aging and disability: Toward a unifying agenda. In S. Sullivan & M. Lewin (Eds.), *The economics and ethics of long-term care and disability* (pp. 90–130). Washington, DC: American Enterprise Institute for Public Policy Research.

Other Factors
of the Disability

- Why can the unpredictable course of a disability be more disturbing than the actual symptoms?
- Why is symptom recognition culturally determined?
- What does this statement mean: "As the course of the disability progresses, social support often disintegrates"?
- What does "temporal disruption" mean in relation to a disability?
- What are the four phases of the course of a disability?
- Is there a relationship between the episodic course of some disabilities and learned helplessness?
- What does this statement mean: "With each level of loss, the individual is faced with adjustment/response demands"?
- Why is the importance of functional losses idiosyncratically and culturally defined?
- Why has the revolution in assistive technology changed the definition of functioning for many people with disabilities (PWDs)?
- What are the factors that determine the level of severity of a disability?
- Is there a clear-cut relationship between severity of disability and psychopathology?
- What is the difference between chronic pain and acute pain?

- With invisible disabilities, why is choosing the point of disclosure important?
- What does the term "social death" mean?
- How is the treatment of disfiguring disabilities different from the treatment of other disabilities?
- What does the phrase "most enabling environment" mean?
- Does society foster dependence and helplessness for PWDs?
- How do PWDs redefine independence, autonomy, and control?
- Why do you think that originally physicians often felt that mutual support groups were a challenge to their authority?
- Do professionals who serve PWDs contribute to prejudice and discrimination at times?
- What are the four resources that professionals can bring to the therapeutic alliance?
- What are the functions of support groups?

You will remember that there are 10 factors of a disability that influence an individual's response:

1. Time of onset
2. Type of onset
3. Course of the disability
4. Functions impaired
5. Severity of the disability
6. Degree of stigma
7. Visibility of the disability
8. Degree (if any) of disfigurement
9. Prognosis
10. Treatment required

Having discussed the onset/diagnosis of the disability and its meaning to the individual in the previous chapter, this chapter will begin with a discussion of the course of a disability, the physiological advancement of the disability, and the emotional and psychological responses to the progression of the disability.

The Course of the Disability

In this section, look for—

- Three factors in the course of a disability
  1. Direction
  2. Pace of movement
  3. Degree of predictability
- In (chronic) disabilities the focus is on the following:
  —Controlling symptoms
  —Preventing secondary disabilities or complications
  —Maintaining the highest quality of life possible

Often termed the trajectory of the disability, the course of a disability includes three factors: (1) the direction (stays the same, improves, or deteriorates), (2) the pace of movement, and (3) the degree of predictability (White & Lubkin, 1998). The course is the way in which a disability or chronic illness advances and, once again, it is the individual's *perception/response* to these stages that is most important (Woog, 1992). Reviewing Chapter 2 and the Biomedical Model of disability, it becomes apparent that the entire concept of the course of a disability is a relatively new approach since, for centuries, the practice of medicine involved only two outcomes—total cure or death. The idea that an individual would manage and treat a disability throughout his or her life span, working for the highest quality of life possible, is a new concept. We have also discussed how many people without disabilities, including physicians, do not consider people with disabilities, especially those with severe and multiple disabilities, to have any kind of quality of life. The concept of a normative "disability role" was derived from Talcott Parson's 1951 idea of a "sick role" (Mechanic, 1978). Inherent in Parson's sick role was the idea that the individual would eventually recover. Therefore, it is not possible to transfer the entire concept of "sick role" to "disability role," simply because disability is chronic and, in most cases, lifelong (Curtin & Lubkin, 1998). Occasionally, PWDs may believe in the capabilities of medicine to cure them. In this excerpt from a professor of English with multiple sclerosis, we can see that it took her some time to come to terms with the chronic, degenerating, and episodic nature of her disability.

> I was not going to get well—ever. Though I might have periods of remission, I would not (and could not) be cured. My expectation had b

that (the profession of) medicine would restore me to health. Now, that expectation was dashed, along with my cherished illusion that I was in control of my life. The future disappeared. (Toombs, 1995, p. 4)

In the disability role, symptom control and prevention of complications and secondary disabilities are important. Further, while this chapter will be discussing the physiological and emotional responses to the stages or phases of the course of the disability, it should be remembered that the individual's developmental stage of life, family resources, and personal resources also affect the course of the disability (Feldman, 1974; Lubkin & Larsen, 1998). Finally, the course of the disability should not be confused with the stages of adaptation; although both involve movement and direction and they certainly influence each other, the course of the disability is thought to be related more to actual physiological changes and symptom manifestation.

We have also discussed the stress, anxiety, and depression associated with ambiguity (Mishel, 1993). The individual with the disability, his or her family, and caregivers feel more in control with a clear-cut, on-schedule, predictable course. The idea of "planning for uncertainty" is difficult to accept. For an individual who cannot explain the cause of his or her disability, or the course, the uncertainty may be more distressing than the actual symptoms of the disability (Strauss et al., 1984; Strauss & Glaser, 1975). Humans demand explanations, and often, in disability, there are no explanations. Despite an inability to know for sure, individuals (both physicians and PWDs) try to predict the phases of the disability, the rate of the course, and symptom manifestation. Support groups can offer a newly diagnosed individual an opportunity to "rehearse" the later stages of his disability by seeing and talking with "veterans" of the same disability (Power & Rogers, 1979). The course of some disabilities is more variable than the course of others.

Complications and secondary disabilities must also be factored into this complex prediction. A straightforward example of unexpected complications is post-polio syndrome. Indeed, polio was considered to be a disability with a stable course in that once an individual reached medical stabilization, it was thought that he or she would continue to function at that level. However, 25% of polio survivors experience new symptoms of muscular weakness, severe fatigue, muscle and joint pain, and respiratory difficulties (Zola, 1988). Many of those who used braces or crutches must now use a many have been required to take early retirement from their sicians could not and did not predict post-polio syndrome, nor ns able to agree on the cause. Falvo (1991) told of the impact of yndrome: "Those who adjusted to and compensated for their ttaining active, independent lives, may find the occurrences of oms and the limitations of post-polio syndrome difficult to accept... ecific treatment is available" (p. 196).

Factors such as the visibility of th... which the course of the disability is per... abilities, symptoms can progress to a ver... may not be aware. High blood pressure... lead to serious disabilities and even dea... (Cott & Wilkins, 1993). Also, symptom... toms, and some individuals may feel th... ity and may terminate treatment/mana... symptom recognition is influenced by... class (Robinson, 1988). Therefore, the c... also culturally determined since it is the individuals recognition of symp-toms and the meaning that he or she ascribes to the symptoms that regulate the course of the disability. In sum, *the individual's assessment* of symptoms is more important than the *physiological course* of symptoms (Dunn, 1996; Sinacore-Guinn, 1995; Spector, 1991).

Another factor in the course of a disability is the degree of social support offered at each phase. Usually, during the acute stage, friends and family rally to the aid of the PWD. However, as the course of the disability progresses, often this support disintegrates. In a study of individuals with brain injuries (Kozloff, 1987), it was found that with the passage of time after the injury, the size of the social network of the individual decreased. Friends disappeared. Kosciulek and Lustig commented, "As a result, the number of multiple relationships increased (i.e., family members served more functions as nonrelatives dropped out of the picture). The ultimate consequences of such changes was the social isolation of families" (1998, p. 8). Randy Souders, a teenager who was paralyzed in a diving accident, describes the gradual, one-by-one loss of friends:

> Of course, there are some things that I wish I could have changed. Ini-tially, everyone rallies around you, you know—they're supportive. All of the friends I had at the time of the accident were right there—right at the beginning. Then, as time went on, one by one they kind of drifted away, slowly. I think it was because they obviously didn't know how to react to me—and I certainly didn't know how to make things easier on them. I was having a hard enough time trying to figure out what was happening to me. I don't know if I pushed them away or if they felt that I wasn't the same person. It was a very gradual thing, but most of them just kind of drifted off. And I drifted off into myself. (Souders, 1993, pp. 153–154)

The course of a disability can be fully known only in retrospect (Lubkin & Larsen, 1998). The course can be predicted, and should be, but even the most predictable disabilities can be unpredictable. Disability scholars term this "temporal disruption," meaning that the PWD cannot accurately predict his or her future or the course of the disability. A disability usually

s the individual's future. "How long will this last?" "Will I be able to
ry?" "Will I be able to have children?" "Will I have to go into a nursing
ome?" For the individual planning medical treatment, lifestyle changes,
and family adaptations, the greater the predictability of the disability's
course, the easier the adjustment. Temporal disruption also is associated
with the predictability of the length of time of each stage.

The Phases or Stages
of the Course of a Disability

In this section, look for—

- The four phases of the course of a disability

1. Onset/diagnosis phase

2. Acute phase

3. Chronic phase

4. Symptom exacerbation phase (sometimes termed "relapse")

Generally speaking, there are four phases of the course of a disability:
(1) the onset and diagnosis; (2) medical stabilization; (3) chronic; and
(4) symptom exacerbation, sometimes referred to as the "crisis" phase or
relapse. Each of these phases or stages may be long or short in duration
(Rolland, 1988). All of these stages involve both a change in self-identity and
role adaptation in addition to medical treatment (Muller-Rohland, 1987).
During the onset phase, the individual is required to think of himself or
herself as a person with a disability; during the medical stabilization phase
the individual is required to think of himself or herself as a compliant pa-
tient/client. And, as we have discussed before, any change in self-identity is
stressful and often viewed as both negative and stressful. During the onset
and medical stabilization phases, the PWD learns to negotiate hospital life
and begins to deal with the symptoms of the disability, which sometimes
include pain (Kohler, Schweikert-Stary, & Lubkin, 1998). Both of these
phases are regarded as acute emergencies, with available resources being
marshaled. These resources include medical treatment and family care and
support (Huberty, 1980). During the chronic stage, however, the PWD is
required to accept his or her permanently changed status and identity. The
chronic stage is the day-to-day living with a disability (Corbin & Strauss,
1988; Feldman, 1974; Power, Dell Orto, & Gibbons, 1988; Robinson, 1988).

The Three Types of Courses

> **In this section, look for—**
> - The three types of courses:
>   1. Stable course
>   2. Episodic course
>   3. Episodic, degenerating course

In rehabilitation, it is generally accepted that there are three broad categories of courses: (1) stable, (2) episodic (sometimes termed recurring or relapsing), and (3) degenerating. A stable course is one in which after medical stabilization, the symptoms are permanent, but they do not vary (assuming good management and treatment) (Trieschmann, 1988). Life is changed, and for most, there are limitations in functioning. Spinal cord injuries, mental retardation, and deafness are considered to be stable disabilities. Disabilities with a progressive or degenerative course exhibit symptoms that worsen over time and require careful monitoring of present symptoms, the exacerbation of old symptoms, and the appearance of new symptoms. Multiple sclerosis and retinitis pigmentosa are types of degenerative disabilities (Gordon, Lewis, & Wong, 1994; Gulick, 1994; McReynolds, Koch, & Rumrill, 1999). Relapsing and episodic disabilities include asthma, seizure disorders, and some types of mental illness. Episodic disabilities, as would be expected, are unpredictable and yet the individual attempts to live a "normal" life. Simple graphs that illustrate each of these three types of courses are provided later in the chapter.

Stable Course Disabilities

It would appear that stable course disabilities would present fewer adjustment demands simply because the individual knows with what he or she is dealing. After diagnosis and medical stabilization, the individual reaches a plateau of functioning and symptom manifestation and is expected to continue at that level indefinitely. However, there are four factors to be considered. First, it is the individual's perception of the disability that determines his or her response to the disability and, as we have discussed, one of the responses to a disability is denial, more specifically the denial of the stability of the disability ("I'm going to walk out of here"). Second, most disabilities are not stable in that secondary disabilities or complications often appear. Perhaps it should be stated that some disabilities have courses that are *more stable* than others. Third, for some disabilities, such as traumatic brain injury, the diagnostic period (even after an acute, traumatic onset such as an automobile accident) may take a long period of time—for some, up to 2 years (see Figure 9–1). Fourth, and perhaps most important, even when the disability is thought to have a stable course, changing life events happen to everyone, and for someone with a disability, minor and even positive variations can require additional coping responses. Disabilities, because they are chronic, do not have quick and easy solutions, nor are they limited.

Spinal cord injuries are considered to be stable course disabilities; however, individuals with these types of injuries experience (1) frequent genitourinary and respiratory infections; (2) sexual dysfunction (especially in males) (Ducharme, Gill, Biener-Bergman, & Fertitta, 1993; Knight, 1989); (3) autonomic hyperreflexia, an abnormal stimulation of the autonomic nervous system that results in headaches, sudden increase in blood pressure, decreased heart rate, sweating, nasal congestion, or blurred vision; (4) spasticity; (5) pain; and (6) decubitus ulcers (pressure sores that can become infected) (Livneh & Antonak, 1997, p. 135). Jubala (1990) described the episodic course of these complications of spinal cord injury and the hospitalizations they require.

Jubala also explained autonomic dysreflexia: "a syndrome where neural stimulation below the level of injury causes dangerous autonomic processes to occur in the body. These include uncontrolled sweating and a significant increase in blood pressure that can lead to death if not treated. Furthermore, uncontrolled spasms of the paralyzed muscles are not uncommon, and at times can be severe enough to throw people from their wheelchairs. The spinal cord injured [*sic*] are very susceptible to skin pressure sores because of the long periods of sitting or lying without movement. Frequent weight shifts are necessary to prevent such complications . . . . [I]t is not unusual for them to have several hospital admissions over the years because of breakdowns in the biological systems outlined above" (1990, p. 230).

Episodic Course Disabilities

Disabilities with an episodic course are ambiguous for the individual, his or her family and friends, and society at large. Stated differently, episodic

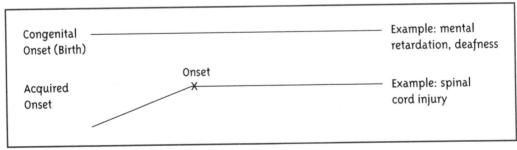

Figure 9–1 Stable course disabilities.

course disabilities usually have a great deal of unpredictability, which acts as a stressor (Gordon, Lewis, & Wong, 1994; Gulick, 1994). Therefore, stress over the prospect of symptom exacerbation may cause symptom exacerbation, and symptom exacerbation causes more stress. The individual feels a loss of control because he or she cannot predict when an episode will occur.

Nancy Mairs (1997) describes the episodic course (and the autoimmune nature) of her disability as "alien invaders." This analogy may also describe her feelings of lack of control:

> I have known that I have multiple sclerosis for about seventeen years now, though the disease probably started long before. The hypothesis is that the disease process, in which the protective covering of the nerves in the brain and in the spinal cord is eaten away and replaced by scar tissue, "hard patches," is caused by an autoimmune reaction to a slow-acting virus. Research suggests that I was infected by this virus, which no one has ever seen and therefore, technically doesn't even "exist," between the ages of four and fifteen. In effect, living with this mysterious mechanism feels like having your present self, and the past selves it embodies, haunted by a capricious and meanspirited ghost, unseen except for its footprints, which trips you even when you're watching where you're going, knocks glassware out of your hand, squeezes urine out of your bladder before you reach the bathroom, and weights your whole body with a weariness that no amount of rest can relieve. An alien invader must be at work. But, of course, it's not. It's your own body. That is, it's you. (pp. 52–53)

A woman with a mental illness described the helpful way in which her physician described her disability and his recommendations for the *management* and *control* (rather than the cure.) Notice that it takes some time for the woman to accept the doctor's assessment:

> A California doctor once compared my mental illness to diabetes. "You have a chronic illness," he said. "You will have to take medication for it, probably for the rest of your life. But it will keep your illness manageable and under control." It took me several years and three more hospitalizations before I heeded that doctor's advice .... I would like to emphasize that only after I accepted the illness as a chronic one could I really do something about improving my life. I had to learn that I could not "wish" the illness: I could not "will it to be so." (Weingarten, 1997, p. 123)

Richard Cohen, a journalist with multiple sclerosis, described the ambiguity as "shadow boxing": "Finally, I had been drafted, only this time into the army of 350,000 Americans who shadowbox with this neurological enemy they cannot see" (2004, p. 23). In a single sentence, Cohen describes the way in which he did not choose multiple sclerosis (he was "drafted"), how he considers his disability an "enemy," and above all the ambiguity— "an enemy that cannot be seen."

Most people try to reduce ambiguity in their lives; however, not *all* ambiguity can be eliminated. Almost everybody likes order, organization, and planning. Indeed, currently in the United States there is an entire industry built around time management and organizational management of one's plans, life, and possessions. Nonetheless, the unpredictable nature of episodic disability, with its intermittent and unpredictable relapses, often instills in the individual, and his or her family, feelings of chaos and lack of control. Two individuals who have spouses with mental illness describe the effect of the ambiguity on their lives:

> Our entire life together has been one big adaptation! I like things organized and planned. Life with mental illness has too many ups and downs with inability to concentrate on planned activities. (Mannion, 1996, p. 22)

> I guess I'm okay with it, but . . . I have tons of anger, not really to him— sometimes to him—but more to, you know, "Why me? Why did this happen to me? Why did my husband happen to be the one who got ill?" Because when we got married, we were the perfect little couple . . . . So yes, I've had to revise a lot . . . . I can't think far in advance any more. That is probably the biggest thing that has changed my life because I used to be a planner, all the time planned—ten years ahead . . . . With an illness like this that runs in cycles . . . . I just think it's too much to put on yourself to expect things when you don't know what's going to happen. (Karp, 2001, p. 143)

However, many individuals with asthma, some types of mental illness, and other disabilities become very skilled in detecting prodromal symptoms (warning signs), such as fatigue and stress. For some disabilities, individuals can become proficient enough to *prevent* some of the relapses, while with other disabilities the individual can only *predict* and therefore plan for the relapse. However, there are disabilities for which it is impossible to either predict or prevent symptom exacerbation.

Vocational placement, family life, and social life all become difficult. Repetitive recurrences of symptoms or relapses become burdensome for professional caregivers and family members. Compassion fatigue or burnout is quite common (Elliott et al., 1996; Maslach & Florian, 1988; Power, Dell Orto, & Gibbons, 1988; Shinn, Rosario, Morch, & Chesnut, 1984). The uncontrollable and unpredictable aspects of these disabilities may lead to learned helplessness (Peterson, Maier, & Seligman, 1993). Kohler, Schweikert-Stary, and Lubkin summarized the emotional response of some PWDs to episodic course disabilities:

Clients have compared times of adjustment to riding a roller coaster; constantly challenged or angered by the uphill struggles, never knowing when another curve will come, and unable to stop the motion. During this period of mixed and conflicting emotions, they have a sense of instability, of bewilderment, and of helplessness. (1998, p. 129)

Individuals with episodic course disabilities often hope for prolonged remissions and stabilization and fewer and shorter relapses. Each relapse or symptom exacerbation requires an emotional response. Will treatment be effective? Will this relapse be severe or moderate? How long will this episode last? Will I have my job when I come home from the hospital? Will there be residual effects? Will I return to my past level of functioning? Will my family take me back? Less serious than full-blown relapses are the fluctuating energy and fatigue levels of some disabilities. Also, chronic pain often varies from day to day. Individuals, their families, and their caregivers can feel overwhelmed by these fluctuations and the resulting lack of control. Family members also live with ongoing and permanent uncertainty (O'Brien, 1993).

Occasionally, family members and friends do not think that the individual with an episodic disability has a disability. The individual often (or most often) seems like herself or himself and can be highly adaptive and functional in periods of remission. Stefan (2001) completed a national survey of people with psychiatric disabilities, asking about their experiences. She summarized one of the findings:

One of the most striking aspects of the survey responses was the percentage of people who described themselves as disabled but said that other people did not regard them as so, saying such things as: "even the people who know of my psychiatric history do not know what a struggle it is for me to maintain my balance." Another wrote, "Friends and family—they don't understand my illness/disability—they think I am getting away with something—that there is nothing wrong with me." (p. 57)

Cohen (2004) referred to the experience of his disability as "a lifetime of ambiguity" (p. 12). Toombs (1995) terms an episodic disability "global uncertainty" (p. 16), explaining:

Our sense of who we are is intimately related to the roles we occupy, professional and personal . . . and to the goals we hold dear. Chronic, progressive disabling disease necessarily disrupted (or threatened to disrupt) my every role in ways that, at the outset, seemed to reduce my worth as a person. Moreover, the uncertainty of the prognosis transformed my goals and aspirations into foolishness. This sense of diminishment was accompanied by a sense of guilt. But still, in my heart of hearts, I felt in a myriad of ways that I was failing to do as I ought. (p. 16)

Even in times of symptom remission, when the individual lives a fairly "normal" life, he or she cannot afford to forget the disability (Douard, 1995). PWDs with episodic disabilities (1) follow treatment regimens closely and (2) control their environment at all times with the understanding that symptom exacerbation could occur at any time. For example, individuals with seizure disorders take their antiseizure medication on time, do not engage in any activity that might trigger a seizure, wear a medical identification bracelet, and do not engage in dangerous activities alone (such as swimming). Naturally, if the PWD is a child, it is the parents who assume these treatment/management regimens.

The following two excerpts provide a clear picture of prodromal symptoms. The first account tells of antidepressants that stop working and describes the relapse as flames and fire. In the second account, Donna Orrin explains how she becomes aware of an impending relapse and then the steps she takes to successfully avoid hospitalization:

> First, I had a mini-anxiety attack . . . and then I had trouble sleeping, and one morning, two weeks into my Kentucky trip, I woke up a madwoman again. The Prozac had simply stopped working. That's impossible. No, it's not. I started to tap and touch things and to have to count until my mind clenched closed. Where are you, Prozac? Come home, come home. Back to my body again . . . . My mental illness came rushing back in. As fast as Prozac had once, like a sexy firefighter, doused the flames of pain, the flames now flared back up, angrier than ever and my potent pill could do nothing to quell the conflagration. (Karp, 2001, pp. 171–172)

> I start to think squirrels are evil when I begin to become psychotic. Whenever I notice any symptoms, I call my therapist and psychiatrist immediately, so I can "nip my illness in the bud" . . . . After a few days of increased medication, I have been able to return to my maintenance dosage. I used to decompensate quickly and my symptoms would escalate rapidly and I would land in the hospital . . . . I now act quickly enough to prevent that escalation . . . . I quickly get to a safe environment that is not overly stimulative and take care of basic needs . . . . After all those years of experience, I am now able to easily identify symptoms and take the appropriate actions quickly. (Orrin, 1997, pp. 142–143)

Read the following account of a woman with rheumatoid arthritis and how she deals with its episodic nature:

> I have a handicap placard . . . . I feel so bad when I park in that spot, then I finally tell myself—I'm talking [about parking in] handicap

spots—that on those days I'm so tired that I wonder how I even got out, it's all right to park in that spot. And on those good days, leave those spots for someone else. (Gordon, Feldman, & Crose, 1998, p. 8)

Another woman with rheumatoid arthritis described her relapses: (This is also an excellent description of an individual's definition of an auto-immune disease.)

> I've been in the hospital every year—for a week or so. It's progressive. I know where it's heading. But I don't really think about it too often. I have termites and they're just eating, having a good time. That's how I describe juvenile rheumatoid arthritis—having termites eating away at my bones and joints. It's not something that can be fixed. You can't slow it down. Gold shots retard it a little bit, but they're still in there having a picnic. They're eating away at the shoulders, so I've lost the rotator cuffs. This hip has to be redone because the termites that eat the bone eat the glue. It just stinks. (Penn, 1993, p. 111)

Episodes are not only unpredictable; they also vary in frequency, duration, and intensity. An individual may have years without a relapse and then experience several relapses within a single year. Therefore, both the frequency and intensity of the relapses must be considered. If relapses occur very infrequently, are not very visible or impairing, or both, there are not many response demands. In summary, three factors of symptom exacerbation contribute to the individual's response: (1) the predictability, (2) the intensity of the symptoms (is the individual hospitalized?), and (3) the frequency (symptom exacerbations that occur once every 10 years would not impair an individual as much as those that occur every 2 weeks). As would be expected, researchers have found that those who expressed the highest degree of disability ambiguity—including course and treatment—were more likely to respond less positively (see Figure 9–2).

Although this chapter is discussing the *individual's* response to a disability, it is important to repeat that episodic disabilities elicit much more societal prejudice and discrimination than do chronic, stable disabilities. A legal scholar, Stefan (2001), summarized:

> Society is most comfortable with disabilities that are permanent and chronic; either one is disabled or not. Even with people who sometimes have to use a wheelchair find themselves regarded with skepticism and suspicion bordering on hostility. (p. 10)

Stefan continued to describe this prejudice and discrimination as part of the larger legal and economic structures of the United States:

> The economic, mental health, and legal structures, however, cannot accommodate the central truth of alternating or concurrent crisis and

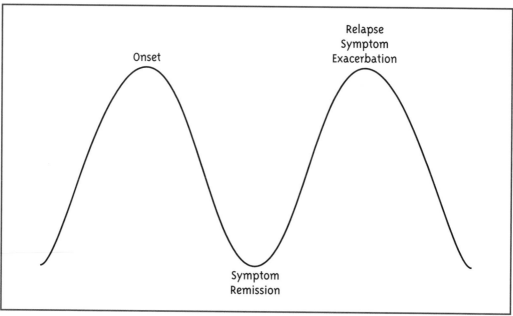

Figure 9–2 Episodic course disabilities (e.g., seizure disorder).

functioning at all. The U.S. legal system, mental health system, and labor market are marked by a static and dichotomous vision: One is either disabled or not, and once identified as disabled, residence in the category is presumed permanent. There is no place for the complexities and contradictions of people's real lives . . . . Defeats . . . are also not seen as temporary, but as permanent. One bad episode can mean the termination of parental rights, an involuntary commitment or involuntary medication. It is all or nothing in American society . . . . (p. 59)

Because an individual's life is directly affected by the health care system and the legal system, a disability of any type, but especially an episodic disability, is difficult to negotiate. In addition, the American workplace is not responsive to individuals with episodic disabilities. As Stefan clearly points out, the lack of a simple dichotomy (disability or no disability) and the resulting ambiguity have created long-standing, institutionalized environmental barriers for individuals with episodic disabilities.

This institutionalized need for a clear-cut dichotomy, in this case, hospitalization or no hospitalization, can be seen in Donna Orrin's experience:

When I think about what I had to go through to get those medication reminder calls, it just infuriates me. I'm a pretty assertive person and, in fact I was on the Community Mental Health Board at the time. Yet they said I was trying to be "taken care of." That's like saying someone with a physical disability is asking to be taken care if they need a wheelchair. No, a wheelchair is a tool or instrument that enables them to have an independent life. A wheelchair is what they need to take care of themselves and move on in life. My medication calls were my tool and extremely cost effective—two one-minute phone calls a day compared to two months of hospitalization. It makes me wonder: if getting those calls was that difficult for me, what is it like for other(s) . . . when they ask for help they know they need. (Orrin, 1999 cf Mackelprang & Salsgiver, 1999, p. 184)

Degenerative Course Disabilities

With each level of loss, the individual is faced with adjustment and response demands and, often, the need to change his or her self-identity. In addition, the "day-to-day" living with a chronic disability must be managed, including the financial costs, costs of time, costs of seeking out accommodations and adaptations, and uncertainty of the future (Corbin & Strauss, 1988). Indeed, the result of several chronic degenerative course disabilities is the death of the individual (Allen & Sawyer, 1983).

Some degenerative disabilities have a steady rate of progression of symptoms without remission, while others have cyclic periods of symptom stability coupled with periods of degeneration. For most of these types of disability, there is no cure and no prevention, only treatment for symptom relief. Many autoimmune disorders, such as rheumatoid arthritis and lupus, are degenerative course disabilities. Not all degenerative course disabilities result in death. With these specific disabilities, the individual's life span is not shortened; however, 50% of those diagnosed with amyotrophic lateral sclerosis (ALS) die within 3 years of disease onset (see Figures 9–3 and 9–4.)

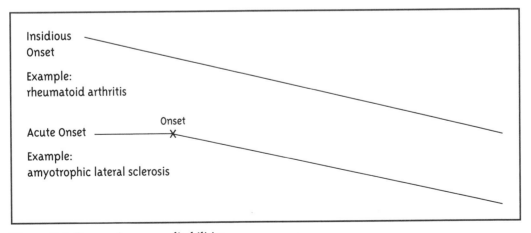

Figure 9–3 Progressive course disabilities.

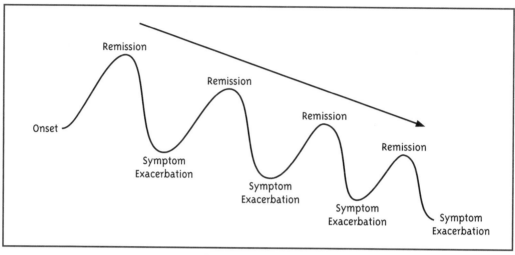

Figure 9–4 Degenerating episodic disabilities.

Robert Neumann described the progression of his rheumatoid arthritis:

> Early in 1960 I went to the Mayo Clinic, where my arthritis was diagnosed at last, and where more appropriate treatment was prescribed. Nonetheless, even this was not able to halt the progression of the disease to my other joints. First, it was my other knee, then my ankles, then my fingers, then my elbows, then my neck, then my hips, then . . . . With a sort of gallows humor, I'd say that I had joined the Joint-of-the-Month Club. But behind this facade, I was terrified at how my body was progressively deteriorating right before my eyes. (1988, p. 157)

A person with a degenerating disability typically is not born with the disability, nor does he or she experience an acute, sudden onset. The course of the disability has a greater impact than the course of other types of disability, and the time of onset may be difficult to pinpoint. The loss of functioning and greater limitation is steady and inevitable. Accepting the realities of a progressive disability requires continual reevaluation at each stage of the loss and possible re-cycling through each the stages of response.

Degenerating disabilities have steady downward courses, and although they are not as ambiguous as degenerating disabilities with a fluctuating course, they may appear ambiguous to others. In J. Morris's book *Pride Against Prejudice* (1991), Edwina Fairchild relates her experience as a young girl in England with degenerating vision. Her parents took her to various doctors, many of whom gave contradictory diagnoses. Nonetheless, over the years, the doctors eventually realized that she was experiencing a gradual vision loss. Edwina was not blind; neither was she fully sighted. Her parents chose to view Edwina as a sighted child:

"Sighted" meant hope, rationality, capability, life. Given these choices, the adults around me tried to force me into the sighted mold. They did this partly by taking me to eye doctors who might be able to "cure" me, but mostly by simply denying that I could be anything but sighted. (p. 89)

Edwina's parents also imputed bad motives to her inability to see. Her family insisted that "she just sees what she wants to see" (p. 89). Fairchild speaks about being unfairly judged:

Some deep part of me must have known it was wrong to be humiliated and punished for something that was a natural and unchangeable part of me . . . . Since I did not fit the acceptable category of "sighted" or even the less acceptable but still comprehensible category of "blind," I threw those who came into contact with me into confusion. I was a creature that existed between two concepts, and they strove to get me to fit into one or the other. (p. 89)

In addition, because her parents wanted to believe that she could see, Edwina probably was not given many accommodations that could have greatly assisted her functioning (especially in school).

As the disability degenerates, the environment becomes less and less accessible. Or stated more accurately, the environment remains inaccessible while the individual's disability degenerates. Michalko (2002) describes his experience:

As my disability becomes worse, I am becoming less and less at home in the world. This is the world of the normal. The world of the normal is the background against which disability stands the figure of blindness . . . . Still, I belong here, but not naturally anymore. Now that I am blind, belonging is a struggle. (p. 38)

Degenerating Episodic Disabilities

> ### In this section, look for—
> - How some disabilities:
>   —Are system-specific
>   —Affect many systems of the body
> - How the degree of impairment of cognitive functioning is important

A disability usually results in loss of function. Some functions, such as respiratory functions, are more important than others. Some disabilities affect many different systems of the body, while other disabilities are system-specific (Livneh & Antonak, 1997). Arthritis affects many different joints and thus affects functioning and mobility to a greater degree than does an amputation. Diabetes, often considered by the general public to not be a very limiting disability, affects all systems of the body and can result in many secondary disabilities and complications. The amputation of an arm is considered to be more disfiguring than the amputation of a leg but less of a loss of function. Of all amputations, 90% are lower-limb amputations (Livneh & Antonak, 1997).

Some disabilities affect functioning in many different areas of the individual's life. Mental retardation, especially severe mental retardation, affects academic, social, and vocational functioning (Hardman, Drew, Egan, & Wolf, 1993). Fatigue, pain, and muscle weakness/numbness, while considered to be invisible to others, can affect functioning in many different areas of the individual's life. Fatigue, which has no direct relationship to physical activity, can render an individual totally immobile. The loss of functioning and greater limitation are steady and inevitable.

Cohen (2004) described the experience of an episodic, degenerating disability: "I felt powerless, a passenger in a speeding car" (p. 26).

Communication Difficulties

> **In this section, look for—**
>
> ■ The problem of loss of communication
>
> —People with communication difficulties are often misdiagnosedashavingmentalretardationorbehavior disorders.
>
> —The Deaf Culture asserts that it is not the impairment ofdeafnessthatpreventscommunicationbutthelackof accommodations.

Communication is an important function that affects many different areas of an individual's daily life. As we have discussed, there are many ways in which to communicate other than via spoken language, but most people consider spoken language to be synonymous with communication. A great deal of learning (both formal and informal) uses spoken language. Daily interactions usually require communication, including interacting with family members. Therefore, parents, siblings, and spouses are affected by their family member's inability to communicate. Individuals with hearing impairments, cerebral palsy, speech disorders, and some developmental disabilities experience functional limitations in speaking and hearing. Often the true cause of the individual's lack of ability to communicate is not diagnosed and the individual is erroneously thought to have mental retardation or behavior disorders. Some individuals are able to hear and understand spoken language but cannot speak, such as those with cerebral palsy, while others can neither hear nor speak, which is the case with individuals who are profoundly deaf.

Those in the Deaf Culture state that it is not the functional limitations of the individual's hearing impairment that renders him or her unable to communicate; it is the lack of accommodations in the environment (Higgins & Nash, 1987). The Deaf Culture believes that people who are deaf can and do communicate; they simply use another language (Higgins, 1980, 1992). Obviously, individuals who experience limitations in speaking, hearing, or both depend on visual channels of communication. Assistive technology, such as communication boards and visual/vibrating warning devices, are helpful.

Individuals who lose their hearing later in life often feel isolated and lonely because they have not learned sign language and they are embarrassed to associate with people who speak. Further, these individuals may feel vulnerable because of their inability to hear sounds that alert them to danger, such as the honking of a car, a fire alarm, and so on. Naturally, those who have been deaf for the greater part of their lives have learned to use assistive devices.

Read the following account of two women in a nursing home. Ann (age 42) can walk but her speech is difficult to understand, so she uses a communication board. Linda (age 52) uses a wheelchair and speaks very slowly. Notice also the lack of privacy.

> The attendants couldn't speak English and our speech is not so good so there was no communication. Also, we had no privacy. Men, women, anyone would just walk in at any time. They treated us like non-persons and I guess they felt that you can't intrude on a non-person. We were going crazy just trying to be sane. Now I just use it (the communication board) when people don't understand me. I
> office where it's important for people to under
> last resort. I know myself and when I get anxiou
> Scherer, 1993, p. 96)*

*Source: Disabled, Female, and Proud!, by Harilyn Rousso
Garvey. Reproduced with permission of Greenwood Pub
CT.

The Meaning of the Loss of Functioning

In this section, look for—

- The idiosyncratic meaning of functioning
- The degree of "intrusiveness"
- The importance of capitalizing on residual functioning and skills
- The revolution in assistive technology for PWDs

The importance of certain functions is also idiosyncratically defined. In other words, the individual's value system and lifestyle determine the importance of certain functions (DeLoach & Greer, 1981). For example, some individuals are adventuresome; enjoy outdoor, physical activities; and like taking risks. For such types of individuals, the loss of mobility may be felt as a great loss. However, the loss of mobility may not seem catastrophic to someone who enjoys intellectual pursuits. Stephen Hawking, an English physicist with ALS, remarked that his disability gave him more time to think, and thinking is obviously an important function for a physicist. Indeed, many individuals with mobility impairments or sensory impairments have reported, "I escaped into my mind."

It is no coincidence that the leaders in the Disability Rights Movement have been intellectually gifted individuals. Justin Dart, Irving Zola, Paul Longmore, Judith Heumann, and Leonard Kriegel were or are survivors of polio, and therefore their disability did not diminish their intellectual functioning. Livneh and Antonak (1997) use the term "intrusiveness" to describe the effects of a disability that interferes with an individual's functioning. The loss of valued activities (or "intrusiveness") is idiosyncratically defined because valued activities are defined by the individual.

The example most often used to describe the importance of the idiosyncratic meaning of function is that of a piano player missing a little finger. For most people, the loss of a single finger would not be defined as a disability or as a loss of function. However, for an individual who had spent his or her life preparing to be a concert pianist, the loss of a single finger would greatly change his or her life. An individual's learning style can affect the unique meaning he or she ascribes to a loss of functioning. For example, auditory learners would experience difficulty in responding to late-onset hearing impairment, just as visual learners would have difficulty in responding to blindness. Personality characteristics, such as privacy and independence needs, also affect the meaning of the loss of certain functions. One woman with multiple sclerosis describes a particularly difficult loss of function:

> The loss of bowel and bladder control is much more than simply a mechanical or neurological dysfunction. Incontinence reduces an adult to the status of a helpless victim. One is no longer the master of even the most basic of bodily functions. So great is the threat of public humiliation that many afflicted patients simply choose to withdraw from society, rather than risk embarrassment. (Toombs, 1995, p. 18)

Functioning is also culturally and gender defined, meaning that both the loss of function and the role expectations of a PWD are, to some extent, determined by his or her culture and gender (Sasao & Sue, 1993; Sinacore-Guinn, 1995; Spector, 1991). For example, Alice Crespo, a court interpreter who is blind, remarked: "My parents came from Puerto Rico . . . . There, women stay at home and raise babies. If you have a disability, it is assumed that you can't or won't have babies, but you stay home anyhow, being taken care of by your family" (Rousso, 1993, p. 101).

Lee Martin's father lost both his arms in a farming accident when Martin was 1 year old; therefore he has no memory of his father with hands. Martin describes trying to imagine his father with hands:

> When I look at photographs of my father before his accident, my eyes go immediately to his hands. I try to figure out whether they resemble my own, but I can never really decide. His appear to be small, his fingers shorter, but that may only be the perspective of the camera. All I can be certain of is the sadness that comes over me whenever I look at those photographs. I want to tell my father about that moment in the cornfield when the shucking box will clog. "Shut off the tractor," I want to tell him, but of course, I can't. He's there in the photographs, and I'm here over forty years later, recalling the cold steel of his hooks. (Martin, 2000, pp. 7–8)

For many individuals it is not the onset of the disability that is most life-changing but the related loss of function that may occur years after the diagnosis/onset of the disability. Many individuals with arthritis, multiple sclerosis, or muscular dystrophy report that the day they began to use a wheelchair was far more life changing than the day they received their diagnosis. Other such functional losses include being required, because of a progressive disability, to move into an assisted living home, or wear hearing aids, or relinquish their driver's license.

Obviously when an individual loses the ability to function in one area, the solution is to use and develop and capitalize on his or her residual skills (Wright, 1960). Generally speaking, therefore, individuals with a broad interests and abilities are capable of responding more positively to ity simply because they have more options. Individuals with unifo-ests, such as athletics and sports, often find responding to a loss ty to be difficult. However, individuals with a great deal of edu-cation, varied work skills and experience, and multifocal interests will be able to shift their functioning to the areas of their residual abilities and capabilities.

An example of a valued function that was idiosyncratically defined is presented in Marcia Scherer's book, *Living in the State of Stuck: How Technology Impacts the Lives of People with Disabilities* (1993). Brian sustained a spinal cord injury in a motorcycle accident at age 17. Note the impact of an idio-syncratically defined function, attending a Grateful Dead concert:

> My friends came up to visit as usual and said that [my favorite group] the Grateful Dead were playing here in November. My mind was back, but I had to get my strength. The doctors said I would have to sit 4 to 5 hours straight if I were to go to the concert. Every time I got into the wheelchair, I blacked right out. Each day for only a short time, I would sit in a semi-reclined position determined to reach my goal. After a couple of days I was up to three hours. The day of the show I reached my goals and I was psyched. The concert was the first time I had been out of the hospital. I had reached my destination. (p. 22)

Before closing this discussion of loss of functioning, it is important to point out that assistive, or adaptive, technology has greatly decreased the loss of functioning that PWDs experience. Until the invention of comput-ers, the design and use of assistive devices for PWDs changed little for literally hundreds of years. Before computers, these devices were simple mechanical equipment that were most often homemade. These included prosthetic devices such as artificial arms or legs, orthotic (straighten-ing) devices such as braces, and mechanical wheelchairs (without power) (Weisgerber, 1991). Now, most assistive technology is either computerized or electromechanical (Scherer, 1993). Examples of these newer technologies include power wheelchairs; Functional Electrical Stimulation (FES) that sends bursts of low-level electricity to paralyzed muscles; augmentative and alternative communication systems; environmental control computers that lock doors, turn on the furnace, and turn off the lights; and voice-activated computers that allow individuals who do not have the use of their hands to type. This revolution in assistive technology has changed the meaning of loss of function.

Severity of the Disability

In this section, look for—

- How some disabilities have clear-cut levels of severity.
- How the level of severity of most disabilities is judged on several factors, including:

  —The number of disabilities the individual experiences

  —The number of areas of functioning affected

  —The treatment necessary

  —The degree of stigma directed at the individual

Some types of disabilities have clear-cut cutoff points between the categories of mild, moderate, and severe. For example, deafness is defined as the loss of hearing 80 decibels or greater; a severe impairment is the loss of hearing within the 60 to 80 decibel range; a moderate loss (sometimes called "hard of hearing") is defined as loss of hearing in the 40 to 60 decibel range, and a mild hearing loss is a loss of 25 to 40 decibels (Hardman, Drew, Egan, & Wolf, 1993). Mental retardation also has categories: an IQ of 55 to 70 is considered to be mild mental retardation; an IQ of 40 to 55 is considered to be moderate mental retardation; an IQ of 25 to 40 is severe mental retardation; and an IQ score below 25 is considered to be profound retardation (American Psychiatric Association, 1994). Vision impairments also have numerical guidelines that designate categories. These types of categories are possible only when there is great diagnostic precision, usually using objective, standardized measuring instruments. Many disabilities do not have this diagnostic precision and, therefore, it is more difficult to determine the medical treatment, educational placement, and living situation for individuals with these types of disabilities.

Disabilities that cannot be measured precisely are usually determined to be severe, moderate, or mild by several different standards. First, the number of disabilities an individual experiences can help to determine level of severity. For example, individuals who are both blind and deaf are considered to have a severe disability. Second, the number of areas of functioning affected can lead to a diagnosis of severity. An individual with quadriplegia would be considered to have a severe disability. Third, the treatment necessary can, in an indirect way, determine the level of severity. For example, an individual whose schizophrenia can be controlled by medication would not be considered to have as severe a disability as someone who must be institutionalized because he or she does not respond to the medication. Finally, the episodic nature of some types of disability often leads to a diagnosis of a severe disability, based on the premise that the individual's functioning is very impaired.

Degree of severity is never based on visibility of the disability; however, degree of severity is sometimes based on the level of prejudice directed toward the individual. Therefore, an individual with a heart condition (an invisible disability) could be considered to have a severe disability because the heart condition limits many different functions (and yet this person appears to not have a disability). Someone with a facial disfigurement, with few or any functional limitations, is also considered to have a severe disability as a result of the stigma and prejudice that limit the individual's functioning. Many people with facial disfigurements report that they stay at home, always. Individuals who wear eyeglasses (which restore their vision to full functioning) experience little prejudice and stigma. However, those who wear hearing aids (which improve their hearing) are subjected to prejudice and discrimination. Finally, it should be remembered that it is the individual's *judgment/assessment/perception* of the disability that is most important. Further, the individual's judgment often differs from that of medical and educational professionals.

Quality of Life

In this section, look for—

- How quality of life is both subjective and multidimensional

- How minimum requirements usually include:

  —Social and economic independence

  —Freedom to function at one's highest level

  —Social support

  —Access to medical and psychological care

- How often it is the lack of accommodations (and not the disability) that lowers the individual's quality of life

---

Disabilities can be categorized according to how much quality of life an individual with that type of disability enjoys. However, the concept of quality of life is subjective and multidimensional (Fabian, 1991; Taylor, Jones, & Burns, 1998). Because there are more PWDs than ever before, and these individuals (like everyone else) continue to live longer, the already vague concept of "quality of life" becomes even cloudier. The chronic, long-term nature of disability coupled with longer life spans has done much to increase the *quantity* of life, and *quantity* can be measured. *Quality* of life cannot be measured but is usually defined in terms of minimum requirements. For PWDs, quality of life is thought to be social and economic independence (within the limits of the disability); the freedom to function at one's highest level; social support, including family life; and the right to medical and psychological care. Others have felt that to have quality of life, an individual should be able to ascribe some sort of meaning or spiritual component to his or her life (Kilpatrick & McCullough, 1999; McCarthy, 1995; Vash, 1981; Yalom, 1980). We can see that included in these definitions are the concepts of having one's basic needs met, economic independence, social support, and self-actualization (Weisgerber, 1991; Whiteneck, 1994).

Often it is the lack of accommodations that diminishes a PWD's quality of life, rather than the disability itself. Accounts of PWDs tell of the day they received their van; their wheelchair; or, for one girl with legal blindness, a magnifying glass. The quality of life changed for these people. The prejudice, discrimination, and limited opportunities that PWODs direct toward PWDs also needlessly reduce the quality of life for PWDs. Accounts of PWDs tell of their first day at the neighborhood school, their first time in a movie theater, their first day on the job, their first paycheck, and their first date. Many PWODs cannot remember most of these "firsts," probably because these opportunities were automatically given to them. For many PWDs, these are memorable events and, occasionally, some PWDs thought that they would never be able to experience them. Quality of life for PWDs can be limited by the disability itself, but it is safe to state that quality of life is more likely to be limited needlessly by PWODs. Sexual intimacy, considered to be a component of adult quality of life, may be altered or the PWD's partner may leave after the onset of the disability (Ducharme et al., 1993). Partners who do stay in the relationship often report that they are hesitant to resume the sexual relationship.

Many PWDs report an increase in self-esteem and feelings of mastery and control because they are able to manage their disability. Barbara Waxman (J. Morris, 1991) reported that she is "quite skilled at being a disabled person."

> I don't think society understands anything about disability. People look at me and they ask me how do I live my life. I think what they're really saying is *why* do I live my life? They believe that the p
> ence is derived from my functional limitations. What t
> stand is that the pain and rejection I've experienced l
> socially based. I'm not depressed about being disabled.
> at being a disabled person. I'm quite proud of my iden
> person. But the pain is social. (p. 62)

In contrast, read the following excerpt:

I was born, educated, broke my neck, and I'll die and be buried just down the road here about half a mile, so my life hasn't been that much .... My life had no value. [The interviewer then asks, "Not even to you?"] No, because I didn't get a chance to do anything with it. It was not mine when I was a kid; it belonged to the parents. By the time I got to be 16, getting ready to go out and do something for myself, you break your neck, and that's it. You can't do anything. I suppose that a person could go to work; I mean, a lot of people do work that are handicapped [*sic*]; they earn money and have families—stuff like that. But once I was hurt, none of that applied to me any longer. I didn't care about it or think about it or nothing. I just kind of hunkered down for the long pull, I guess. You make the best of what you've got. There's nothing going to happen to me in life after that—not to me there wasn't. I knew that. (Crewe, 1997, p. 38)

The following are two more PWDs speaking of the quality of their lives.

I look at it like this, I was a 25-year-old hellion with a shaved head before my accident. I think I'm a better person than what I was then. I took life for granted, and boom, I got a big awakening. (Boswell, Dawson, & Heininger, 1998, p. 30)

It's like a gift . . . over the years, I've evolved into thinking about the greater scheme and believing, that we all exist in our pigeonholes for a reason. And believing that, you can take this [disability] and be a burden with it. You can live with it as a burden or you can live with it as a gift. (Boswell et al., 1998, p. 30)

Pain and Trauma of the Disability

In this section, look for—

- How some disabilities involve or require:
  —Pain
  —Frequent surgeries
  —Loss of income
  —Loss of valued activities
  —Expensive treatment
  —Hospitalization and/or institutionalization

The treatment/management of a disability can be both time consuming and expensive. Often, sleep disturbances are part of the disability. PWDs often have to alter their lifestyle, relinquishing valued activities. If the PWD has been forced to give up his or her employment, there is a substantial loss of income, coupled with expensive medical and rehabilitation costs. Further, the money and time needed to manage the disability often use the PWD's "disposable" income and time. In other words, the individual must give up social opportunities and fun times to find the time and money to deal with the disability.

The treatment and management of some types of disabilities (for example, spina bifida) require repeated surgeries, prolonged medical treatment, and frequent hospitalizations. Indeed, for many PWDs, several hospital stays each year are typical. Fatigue and muscle weakness, both of which are invisible to others, limit the functioning of some PWDs. These individuals learn to conserve their energy for what they consider to be important activities. Read the following account of Zachary, a man with a spinal cord injury. Note the repeated surgeries, his limited functioning, and the goals he has set for himself:

> The rods in my back were dissolving through a process of electrolysis. My doctor had no explanation—he said the metal was turning into bubble gum and axle grease. When we redid the rods, I was playing the perfect quad—I wouldn't get a glass of water; I wouldn't put any stress on them at all, and the second set still broke. The third set was actually a double operation, first anterior and then a week later, posterior . . . . The last 5 years has been "staying alive." I haven't really accomplished much that could be written down on paper except for staying alive. On April 11, I've been a quad for as many days as I was able-bodied. Right now I have no goals in my life other than that I want to leave this life consciously. (Crewe, 1997, p. 36)

Some disabilities result in the eventual death of the individual. For example, ALS is a rapidly progressing motor neuron disease and 50% of diagnosed individuals die within 3 years. However, retinitis pigmentosa, a progressive type of blindness, does result in total blindness but not in death. Some types of disabilities are thought to have both degenerative and episodic courses, meaning that there are episodes of symptom exacerbation. However, when the symptoms remit, the individual does not return to the level of functioning he or she experienced before the relapse. In other words, the person does "get somewhat better," but with each relapse, the individual returns to a lower level of functioning than before.

It would seem reasonable that severity of disability would be associated with psychopathology (Cook, 1991). In other words, those individuals with very severe disabilities would be maladjusted, depressed, lacking social skills, angry, and/or suicidal. Rehabilitation and disability researchers have sought, for more than 30 years, to find a relationship between severity of disability and degree of psychological impairment. Cook (1991) interpreted the research findings: "In his extensive review of the literature, Shontz (1971) concluded that there is little support for the theory that severity of disability causes psychological maladjustment. In his review of research on emotional factors and disability, McDaniel (1976) cautiously concluded that severity of disability was a determinant of psychological adjustment. Based on their review, Roessler and Bolton (1978) also argued for a relationship, albeit complex, between severity of disability and degree of psychological impairment" (Cook, 1991, pp. 85–86). It appears, therefore, that there are few researchers who would state that severity of disability is directly related to degree of psychopathology.

Chronic Pain

> **In this section, look for—**
> - How there is limited knowledge about pain
> - The difference between acute pain and chronic pain
> - How medical professionals often have negative stereotypes of individuals with chronic pain

Pain is a part of many disabilities, yet there is limited medical knowledge about "the specific mechanism for transmission and perception of pain" (Lubkin & Jeffrey, 1998, p. 149). Further clouding the diagnostic picture is the fact that pain is invisible, experienced subjectively, and impossible to measure objectively. Physicians ask patients questions about the location of the pain; the intensity of the pain using a numerical scale of 1 to 10; the onset, duration, variations, and rhythm of the pain; what relieves the pain; what causes or exacerbates the pain; and the effect of the pain on the individual's functioning. In spite of all this specificity, the experience of pain is impossible to describe fully.

Chronic pain, in contrast to acute pain, persists for a period of time, usually 3 to 6 months, or occurs at intervals for months or years (Bonica, 1990). Acute pain is a different experience: first, the individual knows that acute pain is temporary; second, acute pain subsides when healing occurs; and third, acute pain can usually be controlled by medications. Acute pain, therefore, is viewed as "having a purpose" and an end. In contrast, chronic pain usually is not related to any malignancy; rather it is associated with musculoskeletal disabilities, such as lower back pain. There is no end to chronic pain.

Chronic pain can become the central focus of an individual's life, curtailing work, family life, and social activities. "The individual with chronic pain may undergo a change from being someone with multiple roles (worker, friend, family member, and so forth) to someone who only identifies with the pain" (Lubkin & Jeffrey, 1998, p. 153). Individuals often tire of defending themselves and trying to explain their pain to others. Indeed, they may even begin to question their own perceptions of the pain ("Maybe I *am* crazy"). Rereading the descriptions of malingering and secondary gains, it can be seen that chronic pain is often confused with these maladaptive responses. In the United States, the most commonly reported cause of chronic pain is lower back problems. Chronic pain often leads to sleep disturbances, fatigue, depression, and poor concentration (Latham & Davis, 1994; Linton, 1986). Those who experience chronic pain often lead very restricted, dependent lives. Their lives are controlled by the pain. Family members take on additional responsibilities, trying at the same time to understand and respect the experience of chronic pain. Pain is both a physiological experience and an emotional experience. Additionally, like any other symptom, pain is culturally determined, and there have been cross-cultural and cross-national studies that have shown that one's cultural identification plays some part in the recognition and response to pain (Brena, Sanders, & Motoyama, 1990; Carron, DeGood, & Tait 1985). According to Gallagher (2000), individuals who experience chronic pain are at high risk for depression. Gallagher stated the effect of depression: "Depression may lower both the pain threshold and tolerance" (p. 28). Therefore, it would appear that the relationship between pain and depression can become circular.

Medical professionals often have negative stereotypes of individuals with chronic pain. Thus, there is frustration and anger on the part of the physician and on the part of the patient. The physician cannot understand the pain and the patient feels, justifiably, demeaned and devalued. The idea of pain, and the possibility that everyone may experience pain give the individual who does live with chronic pain an unpleasant reminder of an unpleasant possibility. Further, the ambiguity of chronic pain also contributes to the negative stereotypes of individuals who experience it. Pain is a private experience because there is no socially acceptable way to express it. No one wants to hear about someone else's pain and discomfort. Chronic pain often has no clear-cut cause; no end in sight; and, occasionally, no suitable relief (Bowman, 1994; Hadjistavropoulos & Craig, 1994). Everyone involved feels frustrated. Medical professionals often discount patients' reports of pain because of the following factors: (1) "Professionals do not always give credence to pain complaints unless there is some identifiable pathology," (2) "Professionals also often assume that all clients have the same pain perception threshold and therefore perceive the same intensity of pain from the same stimuli," and (3) "Many professionals have become desensitized to the client's pain experience and rate pain as less important than clients do" (Lubkin & Jeffrey, 1998, p. 151).

Psychogenic Pain Disorder

> **In this section, look for—**
>
> - Problems in diagnosing psychogenic pain disorder
>   - —Often there are undiagnosed organic factors
>   - —The diagnosis has no specific treatment
>   - —The diagnosis is demeaning to the patient
>   - —The diagnosis can lead to unjustified loss of insurance benefits
>   - —The diagnosis may conceal an organically based diagnosis

Dr. Gallagher, in a section of his article titled "Problems in Using 'Psychogenic Pain' and Other Related Diagnoses" (2000, p. 24), stated:

> The notion that psychological problems cause pain disorder is speculative and based on unsystematic studies beset by methodological problems. One interpretation of the hardiness of these diagnoses is that they meet a need to label pain patients in a way that explicitly (i.e., "psychogenic") or vaguely (i.e., "somatoform") suggests a psychologic causation to justify psychiatric treatment or to absolve an employer, workers' compensation, or a physician from further responsibility in the case. (p. 24)

Gallagher lists the problems in diagnosing psychogenic pain disorder, including: (1) in case reviews of patients diagnosed with psychogenic pain disorder, "a high prevalence of previously undiagnosed organic factors" were found; (2) the diagnosis of psychogenic pain disorder has no specific treatment or outcomes; (3) the diagnosis of psychogenic pain disorder "may be perceived as hostile to the patient. Suggesting psychological causation is interpreted by patients to mean that their pain is 'not real,' that they are crazy" (pp. 24–25); (4) such diagnoses can lead to unjustified loss of insurance benefits for the patients; and (5) such diagnoses "are useless clinically, for they suggest no specific treatment and always obfuscate a more refined, biopsychosocial, clinical assessment that does lead to specific treatment approaches" (p. 25).

More About Pain

In this section, look for—

- The widespread fear of pain
- How often individuals who experience chronic pain are blamed for the following:

  —The pain itself

  —The management of the pain

  —Reminding others of the human possibility of pain

Pain is invisible. Individuals who appear "normal" often experience chronic pain that effectively curtails many of their life functions. On the one hand, fear of pain can contribute to such problems as drug and alcohol addictions. On the other hand, society frequently lauds individuals, often athletes, who have overcome pain to accomplish some great goal. Neither view of pain— fearing all pain or ascribing hero status to those who overcome pain—is correct or helpful. D. B. Morris (1998) explained the first view of pain:

> Athletes are repeatedly praised by the media for overcoming extreme pain, like the astonishing Olympic gymnast from Japan who completed his dismount with a broken leg. Yet such praise and its implicit meaning (to overcome pain is heroic) leave a difficult legacy for chronic pain patients, who cannot surmount their affliction in a supreme moment of glory but must live with it, unpraised and often unobserved day after day. (p. 129)

Wendell (1997) described the second view of pain—that those who do not experience chronic pain ascribe much more power to the experience:

> People with painful disabilities can teach us about pain, because they can't avoid it and have had to learn how to face it and live with it. The pernicious myth that it is possible to avoid almost all pain by controlling the body gives the fear of pain greater power than it should have and blames the victims of unavoidable pain. The fear of pain is also expressed or displaced as fear of people in pain, which often isolates those with painful disabilities. All this is unnecessary. People in pain and knowledge of pain could be fully integrated into our culture, to everyone's benefit. (p. 270)

In a study conducted with PWDs, Putnam et al. (2003) found that for some individuals, pain was interpreted as a positive sign. "A few individuals who experienced spinal cord injuries mentioned that pain in their lives, while difficult to tolerate, could be interpreted as a sign that their nerves were still working and therefore was a positive sign of health" (p. 39).

Perhaps the best writing on the experience of pain is Reynolds Price's book *A Whole New Life* (1994). Price is a novelist and a professor at Duke University. After being diagnosed with spinal cancer, he underwent three surgeries and weeks of radiation. Price lost the use of his legs and was left in constant pain as a result of the damage caused by the surgeries and the radiation to his central nervous system. Price described his pain in great detail:

> The pain was high and all-pervading from the neck to the feet; it generally peaked in blinding storms late in the day if I was tired. It intensified in conditions of low barometric pressure; and for dozens of other mysterious reasons, by now it had seized frank control of my mind, my moods, and my treatment of friends. Patience had ebbed to its lowest reach. (p. 151)

Eventually, Reynolds Price overcame the pain with biofeedback and self-hypnosis.

The Degree of Stigma Directed Toward the Disability

In this section, look for—

- How the PWD has two tasks:
  1. Manage the disability
  2. Deal with stigma
- Stigma recognition
- Stigma management

...al with a disability has two tasks: he or she must (1) manage/ ...sability and (2) deal with the degree of stigma that others di- ...the disability. All PWDs, regardless of their type or severity ...y, personal achievements, or socioeconomic status, understand ...re members of a stigmatized and devalued group. However, it is ...e that there is more stigma toward certain types of disabilities than toward other disabilities. We learned earlier that there is a hierarchy of stigma: individuals with physical disabilities experience the least degree of stigma, individuals with intellectual and cognitive disabilities experience more stigma, and individuals with psychiatric disabilities experience the most stigma.

Therefore, individuals with physical disabilities, such as blindness, mobility impairments, and chronic illness, experience less prejudice and less segregation and are allowed more choices than are individuals with schizophrenia (Fink & Tasman, 1992; Friesen, 1996; Garske & Stewart, 1999). If medical and rehabilitation care providers were to attempt to quantify the degree of impairment of a mobility impairment and the degree of impairment of schizophrenia, such considerations as functions impaired, residual capacities available to the individual, treatment and hospitalizations required, and impact on the individual's vocational functioning would be examined. However, even with a comprehensive review of these important factors, the experience of living with these two types of disabilities is very different. Probably the greatest difference between these two types of disabilities (orthopaedic impairment and schizophrenia) is the prejudice and stigma that is directed toward one but not toward the other. In Chapters 3, 4, 5, and 6 we discussed the concepts of prejudice, stigma, and discrimination from a societal viewpoint, looking at these concepts as a large group in power (society) holding prejudicial and stigmatizing views toward PWDs. In this chapter, the focus is on the individual's experience of stigma.

Stigma recognition and stigma management are two skills that PWDs are required to develop. Stigma recognition is the simple act of acknowledging that someone's judgments, appraisals, and actions are both inaccurate and hurtful. If the PWD is not able to recognize stigma and prejudice, he or she may be affected in the following ways: (1) engage in self-doubt, (2) feel angry, (3) feel depressed, or (4) feel humiliated (Holzbauer & Berven, 1996). Indeed, Holzbauer and Berven quoted an individual who felt the stigma to be justified, saying, "The worst part about it is that I felt it was my fault" (p. 481). Those PWDs who are adept at recognizing stigma may "forgive" the stigmatizer, thinking that he or she "doesn't know any better" or is "having a bad day." Other PWDs may become angry. Most important, however, is that by recognizing stigma as inaccurate, the PWD does not internalize these types of judgments. In other words, the PWD does not believe the insults and they do not become part of his or her self-concept. Naturally, a great deal of stigma recognition is dependent on the PWD's age (adults are better at stigma recognition than children) and his or her social skills and awareness. Stigma recognition becomes an even more difficult issue when the stigma/handicapism is unintentional. Remember the story of Sharon L., who was told by her high school counselor that she could be an artist because (1) she would not have to associate with others, and she could work alone and (2) those who purchased her art would never realize that it was "disabled art." Such attitudes are stigmatizing and hurtful, and yet, in this particular case, the professional career guidance was intended to be helpful.

w should a PWD respond to such an unintentional stigma? Compare
counselor's view of "handicapped" art with the art of Randy Souders
nd in Chapter 7.

Stigma management can be handled with skillful humor, assertive and
direct responses, or both. Of course, the PWD must be especially proficient
at correcting misconceptions and refusing to be denied his or her rights.
Often, the skillful humor and assertiveness "backfire" and the PWD has
more stigma directed toward him or her. In the video "Irving King Jordan,"
Dr. Jordan, who was president of Gallaudet University, skillfully manages
the stigmatizing questions and comments of the interviewer. For example,
Dr. Jordan prefaced one response with the comment, "May I teach you
something?" Thus, politely teaching and informing the interviewer seemed
a better response than angrily "setting this guy straight." At another point
in the interview, the interviewer asked if Dr. Jordan ever got tired of using
his hands to sign. Dr. Jordan did not respond to the specific question but
instead humorously asked the interviewer, "Doesn't your mouth get tired
of moving?"

Stigma management is important in social situations and even more
important in job interviews or admission interviews. Explaining accommodations (how they work, their expense, and how they would allow the PWD
to do the job), explaining the disability and its impact (or lack of impact) on
the job, or explaining the gap in a résumé because of a hospitalization all
require skillful stigma management. Further, this type of stigma management has clear-cut effects for the PWD. Stigma is hurtful and stressful,
and, in the case of PWDs, it is personally directed toward a single person.
For someone who has been teased and harassed as a child, managing stigma
as an adult can be overwhelming.

Filing formal complaints is a type of stigma management. A study that
reviewed the complaints of discrimination by PWDs under the Americans
with Disabilities Act (ADA) between 1992 and 1996 (McMahon, Shaw, &
Jaet, 1995) found that the two disability categories with the highest numbers of complaints were mental illness and learning disabilities. Examining
the records of the Equal Employment Opportunity Commission (EEOC),
as McMahon and his colleagues did, supports the idea that there is more
stigma directed toward cognitive and psychiatric disabilities. These researchers interpreted their findings: "Members of both groups have been
erroneously perceived as having subaverage intelligence, and this and other
respects are historically misunderstood by the general public . . . . This
makes the matter of disability harassment appear all the more cowardly and
insidious" (p. 11).

Stigma by Association

Families with a member with a disability also experience stigma, only in
this case it is termed "stigma by association." Leah Hager Cohen, Ruth

Sidransky, and Lou Ann Walker wrote books about their deaf parents and all spoke of the stigma of having relatives who are deaf and of the need to conceal their parents' deafness. It was felt that potential boyfriends or husbands did not want deaf in-laws or deaf children and thus, dating and social opportunities for these women, all of whom were hearing, were unnecessarily limited. These authors relate many instances of stigma by association. Families with members with mental illnesses feel stigma by association (Friesen, 1996), and many have responded to this by engaging in advocacy and educational efforts, such as the National Alliance for the Mentally Ill (NAMI). Reread the excerpt in Chapter 8 from the Westbrook and Legge Australian study. These family members thought the presence of a child with a disability in the family decreased the other children's chances of marriage.

Professionals who serve PWDs are often stigmatized by association. Professionals who have chosen to work with stigmatized individuals (PWDs) are thought to "lack initiative, training, and ambition" (Fink & Tasman, 1992, p. 204). Indeed, Fink and Tasman assert that many talented psychiatrists leave the profession because they are aware of the stigmatization, feeling undervalued. Because psychiatrists treat patients with the most stigmatized disabilities (mental illness), these psychiatrists often feel themselves to be stigmatized. Also, professionals who work with individuals with mental retardation are often thought to be less capable than professionals who work with higher functioning clients/students/patients.

The Degree of Visibility of the Disability

> ### In this section, look for—
>
> - How there is no correlation between degree of visibility and degree of impairment
> - How some episodic disabilities can be invisible during times of symptom remission
> - How choosing the point of disclosure requires careful timing
> - How, often, it is the PWD's family who wishes to keep the disability hidden

Some disabilities are readily apparent to others; other disabilities are not apparent to others unless the PWD chooses to disclose; and other types of disabilities are invisible even to the individual himself or herself. Disabilities such as diabetes may be "hidden" from the individual for a prolonged period.

As you will remember from Chapter 5, there is no correlation between degree of visibility and degree of impairment. However, many PWODs, whether consciously or subconsciously, do view the degree of visibility to be related to the degree of severity. In other words, these PWODs mistakenly believe that invisible disabilities are not as severe as visible disabilities. Indeed, many individuals with invisible disabilities report, "You get tired of defending yourself all the time." Or, occasionally, individuals with invisible disabilities become angry and tell others, "It's none of your damned business." Often PWODs do not consider them to have a disability.

In addition, legally (under the ADA) the individual with an invisible disability is required to disclose the disability to receive accommodations. If he or she chooses not to disclose, often functioning is sacrificed. Visibility of assistive technology, such as insulin pumps or hearing aids, can render a disability visible which heretofore was an invisible disability.

Disabilities with an episodic course are often visible only in times of symptom exacerbation or "flare-ups." Nonetheless, because most disabilities with an episodic course are unpredictable, it is difficult for the individual to "hide" the disability. For example, someone with a seizure disorder may have a difficult time explaining why he or she does not have a driver's license. A woman with rheumatoid arthritis, an episodic disability, described how she made daily decisions whether or not to disclose her disability. She said, "I finally broke down and asked my doctor about a handicap sticker [parking sticker]. [Was that a big step for you?] . . . . yeah, well, I still didn't want the handicap license plate. The sticker, I can not use it or hide it or whatever" (Gordon, Feldman, & Crose, 1998, p. 8). Both a parking sticker and a metal license plate are accommodations for the woman with rheumatoid arthritis. However, the parking sticker can be hidden when the woman is experiencing symptom remission.

For many individuals with invisible disabilities, the question is not *whether* to disclose the presence of the disability, but *when* to disclose the disability. This is referred to as "choosing the point of disclosure." Individuals with these types of disabilities can allow relevant characteristics to be displayed, while establishing the relationship, and when they feel the time is right, they can tell others that they have a disability. For instance, the individual can settle into a new job and demonstrate his or her capabilities and productivity before informing his or her supervisor and coworkers of the disability. In this case, the job capabilities and productivity are the relevant characteristics and the individual with an invisible disability has availed himself or herself of the option to be viewed as an ordinary employee (i.e., an employee without a disability). As we have learned, many PWODs regard a disability to be the defining characteristic of the PWD; however, the individual with an invisible disability can avoid much of this labeling and stereotyping. In social relationships, the individual with an invisible disability can establish friendships and other types of relationships without the automatic and erroneous assumptions about disabilities interfering.

The timing of the disclosure requires a careful balance: The individual must judge when he or she has established his or her capabilities but cannot take too long before disclosing because others may feel betrayed. For example, in the case of a dating relationship, the individual with the invisible disability can wait until the relationship has become very serious and then reveal his or her disability. However, the dating partner may be angry that he or she was not told at the very beginning.

Also important in disclosure is *what* and *how much* to disclose. Should the PWD simply state that he or she has a medical condition? Of course, some individuals with invisible disabilities choose not to disclose at all. People with invisible disabilities often become very skilled in passing as someone without a disability. They learn to avoid situations in which their disability might be revealed. They are adept at idiosyncratic compensation methods. Michalko (2002) became legally blind while in high school, but he managed to convince his friends that he was fully sighted. The difficulty came at the time when all of his friends were obtaining driving licenses.

> The problem was having a "good reason" for not driving.... Thankfully, however, the culture that put so much pressure on me to pass as "normal," also presented me with the structure and organization from which I could create a "good reason" for not driving. I lived in a lower working-class area of the city where quasi-delinquent behavior was quite acceptable and even appropriate. It was not difficult for me to create a "good story" from the building blocks of this social context. Caught drunk driving by the police and having the right to hold a learner's permit suspended for a year was a story that worked out well enough. (p. 74)

Even in the case of an individual who has disclosed to his or her employer, the ADA requires that the employer maintain confidentiality. In these cases, the worker would be given accommodations but his or her coworkers and clients would not know about the disability. The ADA provides for locked personnel file cabinets and other safeguards of the individual's privacy. Nonetheless, it is difficult to "pass" as a PWOD. Work absences for hospitalizations, the need to take medication on a strict schedule, or time off for support group meetings become difficult to explain. Further, as many people with invisible disabilities understand, the truth may be better than the negative implications that others often draw. In the case of the individual with a seizure disorder who does not have a driver's license, it may be wise to disclose the reason why he or she does not drive rather than have others "believe the worst."

Refer to the chart on the cost–benefit ratio of disclosure in Chapter 5 (Exhibit 5–2). Perhaps the greatest "cost" of concealing a disability is the stress of hiding a characteristic that is central to one's identity, feeling that no one really "knows" him or her. The person may feel that he or she is always being a "phony" and being untrue to oneself. Reread Cynthia Rich's excerpt in which she refers to hiding a disability as "one of the most serious threats to selfhood."

Some individuals with invisible disabilities experience "heightened marginality" (Whitt, 1984). Speaking of the self-identity of children, Whitt explained, "Some studies . . . report that children with diseases which produce little significant disability (e.g., epilepsy) may have more psychosocial problems than their physically disabled [*sic*] peers. Barker, Wright, Meyerson, and Gonick's (1953) concept of 'marginality' acknowledged the heightened ambiguity experienced by children with minimal disabilities. These youngsters neither enjoy the benefit of being "normal" nor evoke the environmental support and allowances accorded more clearly handicapped [*sic*] children" (Whitt, 1984, p. 83).

A student in our department retired from the Air Force as a colonel. While in the Air Force, he was selected for the highly competitive test-pilot flight school. During the routine physical examination, it was discovered that he had diabetes. He had to withdraw from test-pilot school and, indeed, discontinue his life's work as a pilot. He jokingly referred to this career change as "flying a desk." Diabetes, an invisible disability, is often considered to be a relatively minor disability, one that does not impair an individual's functioning very much. However, for this colonel, it ended his flying career. While we cannot presume to understand the way in which the colonel responded to his disability, we can see that an invisible disability requires a different response and change in self-identity than a visible disability does. Of course, the type of onset—in the colonel's case, an insidious onset—also influences the individual's response.

Occasionally, it is not the PWD who wishes to hide or minimize the disability. Family members may encourage the individual with an invisible disability to keep the disability concealed. The family members understand the advantages of avoiding the "disabled role" for the PWD, and moreover, they may want to avoid the "stigma by association" for themselves. Weinberg and Sterritt (1991) explained the rationale:

> Many parents of children with physical disabilities would like to have their children develop a primary identification with the able-bodied world. Parents of children with disabilities know that society views people with disabilities as less acceptable, and that people with disabilities have difficulty in establishing satisfying social relationships and obtaining jobs . . . . To improve their children's chances of succeeding, parents may encourage their children to appear, and to behave, as able-bodied as possible. To the extent that children can "pass" as able-bodied, these parents believe that the likelihood of their children's being accepted and succeeding is increased . . . . (p. 68)

Finally, if children with disabilities identify with and su
being a part of the able-bodied world, the parents' place in t
bodied world is less disturbed. If, however, the parents have
who are unacceptable to able-bodied society, this reflects negatively
on them, for they inevitably share their children's negative social identity . . . . (p. 69)

Weinberg and Sterritt (1991) also explained the effect on these children:

In stressing the importance of "passing" as able-bodied, parents may
also be communicating that being able-bodied is good and being disabled [*sic*] is bad . . . . Children with disabilities are thus being told,
"As you are, you are inferior, and to the extent that you can emulate
able-bodied people, this is the extent to which you can overcome your
inferiority." Yet achieving full able-bodied status is inherently impossible, so children with disabilities may be condemned to always feel
inferior, always to work to cover up their deficiencies, and always be on
guard lest their disabilities show. They can rarely be at ease with who
they are. (p. 69)

Facial cosmetic surgery for children with Down syndrome is one way
in which parents are able to minimize the appearance of a disability. Proponents of this plastic surgery cite the advantages of social integration and
greater opportunities for marriage. The surgery involves tongue reduction;
implants in the bridge of the nose, chin, cheeks, and jaw; and reduction of
the epicanthal fold in the eyelids. Nonetheless, in a study (Goeke, 2003) of
250 parents of children who have Down syndrome, 88% stated that they
would refuse the surgery. A few parents said that they would refuse the
surgery because the greatest stigma of Down syndrome is associated with
mental retardation and the related behavioral and social characteristics,
none of which plastic surgery could ameliorate. However, most parents refused the surgery on the grounds that "society does not have the right to
decide what is 'normal' or 'beautiful,' and by extension to determine who
is a candidate for physical alteration" (p. 327). Others said that "to reconstruct a child's differences through painful surgery sends a strong message
to both the child and the larger community that the parents do not accept
their child's disability and that they find their child physically unattractive"
(p. 328). Some parents "equated the decision to expose one's child to unnecessary surgery with child abuse." Several parents described it as "revolting"
and "barbaric" (p. 329). This study shows that many parents are rejecting
the societal expectation that PWDs must appear as "normal" as possible
and, perhaps more important, these parents have demonstrated that they
consider their children's appearance as acceptable, many stating that they
thought their children with Down syndrome were beautiful.

The Degree of Disfigurement of the Disability

> **In this section, look for—**
> - How disabilities can be disfiguring
> - How symptoms of the disability can be disfiguring
> - How treatments can be disfiguring

Not all disabilities involve "disfigurement." Amputations, facial disfigurements, and burns are examples of disabilities that are considered to be disfiguring. Others, such as myasthenia gravis, in which the individual's eyelids droop or rheumatoid arthritis, in which the individual's joints are swollen and misshapen, are thought of as having disfiguring symptoms. Treatments can also be disfiguring. Medications often cause weight gain, radiation treatments cause the individual to lose his or her hair, and antipsychotic medications often have unpleasant and unattractive side effects. Disfiguring side effects of antipsychotic medications include perioral tremor ("rabbit syndrome"), in which the individual involuntarily moves his or her lips rapidly in movements that mimic a rabbit, and tardive dyskinesia, involuntary face, trunk, and limb movements, some of which are rocking, twisting, and jerking (Maxmen & Ward, 1995). (It is not difficult to understand why many individuals with psychiatric disabilities quit taking their medication.)

Body Image

> **In this section, look for—**
> - Body image is (partly) the result of how we think others perceive us
> - Body image changes as the individual progresses through development stages

Since the concept of disfigurement is closely related to an individual's image of his or her body, we will briefly discuss body image. An individual's body image is the mental picture of oneself, including the physical self, physical appearance, sexuality, health, and physical skills (Bramble & Cukr, 1998). Stated differently, body image is how the individual's body appears to himself or herself. The body is a reflection of oneself (Berkman, Weissman, & Frielich, 1978). Obviously, multiple senses—visual, tactile, and kinesthetic—are involved in forming an individual's body image. Even more important in forming one's body image, however, is the individual's perception of how others view his or her body. Interacting with others in establishing body image is circular: how we think others perceive us influences our image of our physical self, and our image of our physical self influences how we perceive the world. Indeed, the "bad hair day" theory has been proved in research; individuals who think their hair is a mess feel bad and perform poorly. Much of an individual's self-esteem is tied to his or her body image.

The development of body image changes as the individual progresses through physical and developmental stages of life (Lerner & Jovanovic, 1990; Pruzinsky, 1990). For instance, infants have no body image; children begin to develop a body image (and a sexual identity) (Weinberg, 1982), and "adolescence is a time of exquisite body image sensitivity" (Bramble & Cukr, 1998, p. 285). Indeed, during adolescence, the individual's body image is more influenced by others, especially peers, rather than his or her own judgment (Blumberg, Lewis, & Susman, 1984). Adults have usually come to terms with their body image and because of this, it is very difficult for adults to adjust their body image. Nonetheless, the aging process requires a shift in body image. Fortunately, the aging process is a gradual one, allowing the individual time to redefine his or her body image. The aging process is also a universal one, meaning that one's agemates also are changing in appearance and experiencing sensory loss and loss of functional abilities.

In addition to the developmental stage of the individual, body image is influenced by the gender of the person. Girls and women are more critical of their appearance than are males, but they are more comfortable with body changes than men are (Pruzinsky & Cash, 1990). It is also safe to say that women are judged more on their appearance than are men (Asch & Fine, 1997).

Disfigurements As Social Handicaps

In this section, look for—

- Disfiguring disabilities

—Age of onset (or stage of development) influences the individual's response

—Pace of onset (acute or gradual) influences the individual's response

Since an individual's body image is a reflection of how the individual thinks others perceive him or her, a disfiguring disability is truly a social handicap.

Further, females and males respond differently to disfigurements because each gender thinks of body image in a somewhat different way. Finally, because an individual's body image evolves with each stage of development, the time of onset of a disfigurement is important (Rybarczyk, Nyenhuis, Nicholas, Cash, & Kaiser, 1995).

Disability scholars (Bernstein, 1989; Macgregor, Abel, Bryt, Laver, & Weissmann, 1953) have used the term "social death" to describe the effect of a major disfigurement and the term "closet people" to describe individuals with these types of disfigurements. "Closet people" withdraw from all social contact and stay at home; therefore they have experienced "social death." These individuals feel they have no place in the world. Feminist disability scholars Adrienne Asch and Michelle Fine have asserted that women with disabilities, especially disfiguring disabilities, because they cannot attain the widely accepted standard of feminine beauty, often turn toward "male standards of achievement" (1997, p. 251), which probably means career advancement. Another feminist disability scholar, Rosemarie Garland Thomson (1997b), stated that political subordination is linked "to the cultural valuing and devaluing of bodies on the basis of their appearance" (p. 297). Thomson also asserts that many feel that virtue is linked to feminine beauty and that "beauty brings fulfillment" (p. 299). Further, Thomson stated that many believe that women with disfiguring disabilities must lead tortured, miserable lives (1997a).

Finally, the age of onset of the disfigurement is important. Those with congenital disabilities do not have to adjust their body image. "Children with congenital physical disabilities are only familiar with their already impaired bodies" (Livneh & Antonak, 1997). Generally speaking, it is adolescents who have the most difficulty in responding to a disfiguring disability simply because adolescence is a time when individuals are very concerned about their appearance and the opinions/judgments of others. Indeed, it can take years for adolescents (and some adults) to adjust their body image after the onset of a disfiguring disability. Elderly individuals may not feel a disfiguring disability to be a great challenge simply because they have already come to terms with physical losses and diminished attractiveness.

The pace of onset of the disfiguring disability influences the individual's response. Disabilities that have a slow and gradual onset, such as rheumatoid arthritis, are considered to present fewer adjustment demands on the individual's body image. Robert Neumann described his teenage experience with rheumatoid arthritis. Note the use of the third person—Neumann writes of the person in the mirror as if the person were not himself:

> One day, almost by chance, I could avoid it no longer. I caught a good look at myself in a full-length mirror and was appalled at what I saw. I had remembered myself as having an able body. The person I saw looking back at me had a face swollen from high doses of cortisone, hands with unnaturally bent fingers, and legs that could barely support his weight. (1988, p. 157)

However, the majority of disfiguring disabilities have acute onset, many of them traumatic (Bernstein, 1976, 1989, 1990; Goldstein, 1986; Patterson, Everett, Bombardier, Questad, Lee, & Marvin, 1993). For example, individuals who experience severe burns confront an unexpected, sudden change in body image (Weinberg & Miller, 1983). One little girl with facial burns remembered: "There were no mirrors in my house, so I wouldn't get scared" (Holaday & McPhearson, 1997, p. 354).

The Importance of Social Support

Anyone with any type of disability needs social support. However, individuals with disfiguring disabilities require even greater degrees of social support because their disability elicits a great deal of rejection and avoidance from others (Bernstein, 1990; Bernstein, Breslau, & Graham, 1988; Love, Bryne, Roberts, Browne, & Brown, 1987). During World War II, a group of English Royal Air Force (RAF) pilots who had acquired disfiguring disabilities (mostly burns) formed an organization. They all wore the same blazer and continued to meet 40 years after the end of the war. The importance of group solidarity, common understanding, and shared experiences filled a need for these men. (The blazer may have also served to inform others of the way in which they acquired their disfigurement: combat service in the RAF.)

Read the following excerpts. The first three are from individuals with severe burns. They all express the importance of social support.

> When I got burned at age 18, I found out who my real friends were: They were the ones who came to see me and they still are my friends. (Holaday & McPhearson, 1997, p. 349)

> They [friends] made me use my burned hand to play games like ping-pong, so it wouldn't get stiff. (ibid, p. 349)

> Another severely burned interviewee (now a grandfather) . . . had been given the last rites and was expected to die. Against hospital rules, his wife brought their infant son into his room to say goodbye. It was at that moment the new father decided that he would fight to live despite his injuries because he wanted to watch his son grow up. "My family became my motivation to survive." (ibid, p. 348)

Read the lack of social support these individuals experienced:

> Amy Hagadorn, a 9-year-old girl with cerebral palsy that limited the use of her fingers on her right hand and resulted in a limp and impairment in speech, wrote a letter to Santa Claus sponsored by a local radio station: "Kids laugh at me because of the way I walk and run and talk.

I want just one day where no one laughs at me or makes fun of me."
(Holzbauer & Berven, 1996, p. 479)

A vignette by Henry Viscardi, whose legs were congenitally deformed, on his first day of grade school: "My sister Terry took me to school the first day. Clutching her hand, I hoisted myself up the steps to the school-yard. It was crowded with children . . . . I heard laughter. 'Hey, Louis, looka the ape man.' Three big boys came toward me . . . . The crowd of jeering boys had grown. One of them . . . came over and shoved me. I shoved back against his knee. 'Oh, you wanta fight, kid?' . . . . 'I want to go home.' I hung on Terry's arm, tears rolling down my cheeks. 'Sissy, sissy.' " (ibid, p. 479)

Scapegoating of a family member with a disability can occur, some-times with grisly consequences . . . . [A] young child who had been severely burned became a 'whipping boy' to his poor, alcoholic, and dysfunctional family for many years. Nearly every evening his parents, two siblings, and two cousins would become drunk and make vicious fun of his disfigurement. One evening when the group had been more abusive than usual, he systematically lured each inebriated individual into a different room of the house, bludgeoning each of them to death. (ibid, p. 349)

The Treatment of Individuals With Disfiguring Disabilities

> **In this section, look for—**
>
> - Treatment of disfiguring disabilities:
> - —Is a battle against societal reactions
> - —Usually does not concern itself with loss of function (mobility or sensory)
> - —Takes years of rehabilitation

Treatment of individuals with disfiguring disabilities is different than other types of treatment or interventions. One disability scholar (Bernstein, 1989) described these different treatments and interventions as the result of three factors:

First, treatment is a battle against societal values and community re-actions. Second, it involves a problem of appearance and symbolism rather than a problem of mobility, pain, or sensory loss. And finally, there is an element of chronic grief over the situation. It is critical to be aware of time scale: for most of these individuals adjustment to a disfigurement takes years and rehabilitation takes years more—sometimes a lifetime. (pp. 155–156)

In their interviews, Holaday and McPhearson (1997) found that "burn survivors insisted that patients also be told about normal and predictable emotional distress following a severe burn so that they could be prepared for the possibility of depression, sleep disorders, nightmares, and physical reactions to reminders of the burn or treatments . . . . 'No one told me about the mood swings. I thought I was crazy. They should tell you these things. One of my daycare workers told me I was possessed because I had such terrible nightmares' " (p. 353).

Individuals respond to their disfiguring disabilities in several ways (Goldstein, 1986). Some individuals develop compassion for the strangers who stare; one person with severe facial scars stated, "I'd stare if I saw someone like me too!" (Holaday & McPhearson, 1997, p. 351). Some sequester themselves in their homes, while others decide that cosmetic devices, designed to make them appear more "normal," are not worth the loss of function or the discomfort and inconvenience. Others do not incorporate the disfigurement into their identity, referring to their facial scarring as a "mask"; indeed, one woman insisted that she removed the mask when she was at home with her family (J. Morris, 1991). Wright (1960) included a short excerpt from Katherine Butler Hathaway:

> Over and over I forgot what I had seen in the mirror. It could not penetrate into the interior of my mind and become an integral part of me. I felt as if it had nothing to do with me; it was only a disguise. But it was not the kind of disguise which is put on voluntarily by the person who wears it, and which is intended to confuse other people as to one's identity. My disguise had been put on me without my consent or knowledge like the ones in fairy tales, and it was on me for life. It was there, it was there, it was real. Every one of those encounters was like a blow on the head. They left me dazed and dumb and senseless every time, until slowly and stubbornly my robust persistent illusion of well-being and of personal beauty spread all through me again . . . (p. 157)

Another way in which to respond is explained in the title of the video "My Body Is Not Who I Am." For these individuals, their self-esteem and self-identity are not associated with their physical bodies.

Susan Wendell (1997) theorized that if PWODs were to understand the experience of PWDs, including individuals with disfiguring disabilities, PWODs would no longer be "oppressed" by their bodies. She summarized: "Our physical ideals change from time to time, but we always have ideals. These ideals are not just about appearance; they are also ideals of strength and energy and proper control of the body. We are perpetually bombarded with images of these ideals, demands for them . . . . Idealizing the body prevents everyone, able-bodied and disabled, from identifying with and loving his/her real body" (p. 267).

Prognosis of the Disability

In the strictest sense, the definition of the word "prognosis" is the prospect of a cure or recovery; therefore, since disabilities are long-term, chronic conditions, the concept of a prognosis does not actually apply to most disabilities. As you remember, the idea of a prognosis is that of two outcomes: cure or death. The idea of prognosis is probably considered in those few disabilities that do have a terminal course, such as muscular dystrophy (MD), AIDS, or cystic fibrosis. The key word in the last sentence is "course" because, as a result of the advances in medical science, individuals with these disabilities often live years after the onset.

Nonetheless, there are a few disabilities that eventually result in the individual's death. Some scholars have termed this experience "living with death," and, as would be expected, the tasks of the individual with this type of disability do not include long-term management of the disability or ensuring the highest quality of life, but emotionally preparing oneself and one's family for death (Allen & Sawyer, 1983). Certainly, the time of onset of these terminal disabilities has an impact on the individual's response. For example, MD is usually diagnosed by age 5 and the individual usually does not live beyond age 20 or 30 years. Therefore, the individual preparing for death is a child or a teenager. In contrast, ALS is a disability with a terminal course, but it is a late-onset disability and the individual is usually elderly. Individuals with MD and their families report that emotional and psychological issues are greater concerns than are physical symptoms. This seems reasonable because it generally is more difficult for a child or young adult to die than it is for an elderly person.

In addition to age of onset, the duration of the period between the diagnosis and the death of the individual influences response. It is safe to state that many individuals who experience a period of years between diagnosis and death often deny the reality of their impending death. This long interval also allows the individual to undertake the typical developmental tasks, such as school, work, marriage, and family. For others, the interval between diagnosis and death is relatively short and issues to be confronted are (1) pain, (2) fear of being separated from loved ones, (3) concern about being a burden on family, and (4) concern about family grieving after the death. Also, different types of disabilities require varied treatments during the final stages. Naturally, the living–dying interval is unique to each individual.

For many individuals with terminal disabilities, and their families, religious/spiritual/philosophic questions and answers are of great importance.

However, many professionals are not trained or experienced in supporting the individual's spiritual search for meaning. This is probably a result of the long-held view of the medical, psychological, and counseling professions that the spiritual/religious/philosophical concerns of clients and patients are private, personal matters. Also, Freudian psychology has long been biased against religion, viewing it as an infantile escape from reality. Indeed, until the fourth edition of the *Diagnostic and Statistical Manual* published by the American Psychiatric Association (1994), religious beliefs of patients and clients were either pathologized or ignored (Smart & Smart, 1997). In spite of this, Taylor, Jones, and Burns (1998) stated, "Spirituality is clearly a core dimension and critical determinant of health-related quality of life" (p. 215).

Many professionals (and others) assume that a disability with a terminal course brings only pain, suffering, and despair. However, many individuals with these types of disability experience a high-quality life and report a feeling of mastery and satisfaction, which often includes ascribing religious meaning and purpose to both the disability and their impending death.

Services

In this section, look for—

- Five general types of services
  1. Medical services
  2. Educational services
  3. Vocational services
  4. Residential services
  5. Mutual support groups

The last factor that influences an individual's response to a disability concerns the type of treatment/services the individual receives. As we have discussed, in the past, disability was thought to be a personal or family concern, meaning that the family took care of all of the PWD's needs (Chubon, 1994). Moreover, it is safe to state that there are some people who continue to think that society should not concern itself with provid PWDs. Nonetheless, broadly speaking, these types of servi ceptualized as falling within these categories: (1) medical ser tional services, (3) vocational services, (4) residential servic tual support groups. Because each of these five broad typ provided by different types of individuals and in differer important that services be comprehensive, continuous, and coordinated. As stated before, a perfect world is not a world without disabilities; it is a world in which (1) treatment and accommodations are provided to PWDs, and (2) there is full social, educational, vocational, and political integration of PWDs.

Medical treatment includes hospitals and regional rehabilitation centers where individuals, especially those with spinal cord injuries, learn the various skills and the use of assistive technology (Boswell, Dawson, & Heninger, 1998). Medical treatment also includes psychologists. Some PWDs, after the medical stabilization of their disability, will not use medical services more than anyone else. For other PWDs there are symptom exacerbations, secondary disabilities, and complications that may require careful medical monitoring and treatment throughout the individual's life (Berkman, Weissman, & Frielich, 1978). Other PWDs take medication, thus requiring careful medical monitoring so as to maximize the therapeutic benefit while limiting side effects. As we have stated before, a PWD has two medical goals: (1) to manage and treat the disability, preventing complications, and (2) to maintain the highest quality of life possible. Rereading the section on the Biomedical Model of disability in Chapter 2, we can see that the relationship between the medical profession and PWDs has been ambivalent. On the one hand, medical practitioners and scientists have greatly improved the lives of PWDs, including saving their lives. On the other hand, medical providers have often not viewed their patients as individuals with social, familial, and vocational roles.

The Difference Between Eligibility Programs and Entitlement Programs

Community educational services are a relatively new development. Indeed, the "birth" of special education is considered to have occurred during the 1960s. Of course, there were residential schools for children who were deaf, blind, or both, but other than these there were no educational services available for children with disabilities. Education, for both children with and without disabilities, is an entitlement program, meaning that there are no eligibility requirements to be admitted to school. Continuity of services is often difficult to achieve when children with disabilities leave the public school because of (1) the shift from children's services to adult services, and (2) the shift from an entitlement program to eligibility programs. In the past, individuals with severe disabilities lived their entire lives in institutions, and, therefore, continuity of services was not an issue.

Federal programs, most often, are entitlement programs, and in entitlement programs everyone who meets the eligibility requirements is provided with services, regardless of the availability of funds. Federal entitlement programs for adults include Social Security and medical care programs such as Medicaid and Medicare.

In contrast, most state programs are eligibility programs, and in eligibility programs, people are served only if there are enough funds available. Therefore, when funds are depleted in state eligibility programs, individuals who have been declared eligible may not receive services. To deal with limited funds and the large numbers of eligible individuals who need services, policies such as waiting lists and priority of services are often initiated. Also, because these programs are guided by state policies and regulations, each program will be different from state to state. State entitlement programs include Vocational Rehabilitation (VR) and Independent Living (IL).

As we learned in Chapter 1, each agency and program has differing definitions of disability, and these differing definitions (and therefore eligibility requirements) can make continuity of services complex and difficult. For example, someone may have a disability that would be considered a disability by one agency or program but not considered a disability by another program. Indeed, some of the guiding foundations and purposes of these programs may be contradictory. The most clear-cut examples of these contradictory purposes are Social Security and VR. Social Security, derived from the Biomedical Model of disability, will not allow an individual to receive benefits if he or she earns more than a certain amount of money. Vocational Rehabilitation, derived from the Functional Model of disability, wants individuals to work—both for the benefits to the individual and for the benefits to the American government and economy. Attempts are under way (such as the Ticket-to-Work and Plan to Achieve Self-Support) to dismantle this archaic system of work disincentives.

One of the most interesting examples of work disincentives is the subject of Paul Longmore's (2003) essay, "Why I Burned My Book." Longmore contracted polio as a child and received Social Security Disability Insurance (SSDI). While the SSDI money never amounted to much, receiving SSDI made Longmore eligible for Medicaid, and without Medicaid benefits, he would be forced to live in a nursing home. Therefore, it was extremely important for Longmore to remain on SSDI. Longmore spent 10 years earning a PhD in American history (and he writes of the discrimination he experienced at these universities). Longmore also wrote a book, *The Invention of George Washington*, which was published by the University of California Press. Subsequently, he was offered a research fellowship at the world-renowned Huntington Library. However, the Social Security Administrator, in a letter, informed Longmore that if he accepted any book royalties, he would no longer be eligible for SSDI. Longmore also states in the essay that he would never earn enough as an academic to pay for all of his disability-related expenses. Longmore then carefully stages a book-burning demonstration with Disability Rights activists present and received television and newspaper coverage. Before the actual demonstration, he had practiced burning books because "I didn't want to set *myself* on fire" (p. 251). Paul Longmore described his feelings:

> I somberly watched the fire consume my book. I had planned the protest. I had rehearsed how to burn the book. I had even thought about what sort of expression I should have on my face. But I could never have prepared for the emotional effect on me of the act itself. I was burning my own book, a book I had spent ten years of my life laboring over, a book that had earned me my Ph.D. in history, a book I felt proud of and, in fact, loved. It was a moment of agony. (p. 253)

Longmore concludes the essay:

> We, like all Americans, have talents to use, work to do, our contributions to make to our communities and county. We want the chance to work and marry without jeopardizing our lives. We want access to opportunity. We want access to work. We want access to the American Dream. (p. 258)

The Different Philosophical Orientation of Vocational Rehabilitation and Independent Living

Vocational rehabilitation, a state and federal program, is both an adult program (minimum age for service is 16 years) and an eligibility program. To be eligible, (1) there must be the presence of a disability, (2) the disability must be an impediment to employment, and (3) there must be a reasonable expectation that services will result in job placement. An individual applying for services must meet all three criteria. Because of this, many PWDs were refused services. These individuals had severe disabilities and therefore met the first two criteria but, because of the severity of their disability, were not able to meet the third criterion and consequently were refused services. The members of the Independent Living (IL) movement fought hard against, as they viewed it, considering an individual only in economic terms. Indeed, the state/federal VR system is a program that pays for itself and, moreover, makes a profit for the government. This is to say, when PWDs are placed in jobs, they pay taxes during their working lifetime and do not need public assistance (welfare), thus repaying many times what their VR services cost the government. Individuals in the IL movement have often viewed this as seeing the PWD only as an economic investment. Individuals in VR claim that working and economic empowerment mean more than money. Such factors as self-esteem, social contact, adult status, the chance to use creativity and to learn new things, and the opportunity to make a contribution and serve others are a few of the "rewards" of working. And, as we have seen, Louis Harris polls have shown that most PWDs express a desire to work.

There is a continuum of vocational placement from sheltered employment—supported employment using a job coach—to what is termed "competitive" employment—meaning that the individual "competes" with PWODs for the same job (and is paid the same as PWODs). Sheltered employment—for example, in workshops—is not used as much as it once was and has been the subject of a great deal of criticism. However, there are some PWDs for whom sheltered workshops are the best placement. This continuum of vocational placement is another new concept that has allowed PWDs to work in the community but at the same time receive appropriate support.

Residential services and living arrangements are far different than they were 40 years ago. Indeed, there are many professionals at the point of retirement who remember when individuals with certain types of disabilities were automatically institutionalized for life. In contrast, most individuals entering professions serving PWDs will not see people who have spent decades of their lives in institutions. Of course, for a few PWDs, institutionalization is necessary (Singer, 1996). However, for the majority of PWDs, there is a continuum of living arrangements, beginning at full community integration, to halfway houses, supported living arrangements, and group homes. The rationale of this continuum is to allow the individual as much community integration as possible while providing the support and care necessary. This is often referred to as "the most enabling environment" or "the least restrictive environment." A single individual during his or her lifetime may move from one group home to a supported living arrangement in an apartment and so on. The importance of comprehensive treatment can be seen here. Some PWDs require a great deal of medical care, support, and supervision in their living arrangement and their jobs. All service providers must work together to ensure that the individual has the highest quality of life possible.

The Advantages of Mutual Support Groups for Newcomers and "Veterans"

The last type of treatment to be discussed is provided not by professionals but by mutual support groups. There are all types of mutual support groups, some for children, others for adults. Most mutual support groups are disability-specific—such as individuals with cancer or individuals with mental retardation (Power & Rogers, 1979). Some groups are comprised of PWDs, whereas others are comprised of family members of PWDs. Also, the level of organization and goal attainment varies; some groups have clear-cut goals, while other groups are more informal and simply offer support. Once mutual support groups were viewed as a challenge to the medical profession. Today, however, physicians recognize the value of such groups and encourage their patients to participate. Some of the benefits of these types of groups include the opportunity to learn about and associate with others who are living with the same type of disability. Often, those who have had the disability for a longer period of time are called "veterans." Veterans can describe the likely course of the disability, help others to view their emotional responses as typical (this is referred to as "normalizing"), help others to establish realistic expectations, and assist others in accessing services and other resources in the community. Most medical professionals do not live 24 hours a day with a disability, and it is natural that PWDs, and their families, would seek out others who are living the same experience. A sense of mastery and competence results for the newcomers. Also, the veterans often report that assisting others to deal with a disability helps them to find meaning in their own disability. Commonality and support are the hallmarks of mutual support groups. Read Joan Tollifson's feelings about associating with other PWDs:

> After a lifetime of isolating myself from other disabled [*sic*] people, it was an awakening to be surrounded by them. For the first time in my life, I felt like a real adult member of the human community. Finally, identifying myself as a disabled [*sic*] person was an enormous healing. It was about recognizing, allowing, and acknowledging something that I had been trying to deny, and finding that disability does not equal ugliness, incompetence, and misery. (Tollifson, 1997, p. 107)

Two Perspectives—The Service Provider and the Recipient of Services

For a therapeutic alliance to be established, both the professional and client/consumer should work toward an open and collaborative relationship. However, service providers and recipients of services often do not operate under the same set of assumptions, and these conflicting assumptions work against establishing a collaborative relationship. We shall briefly discuss both the client/consumer's perspective and the perspective of professionals.

The Perspective of the Client/Consumer

In this section, look for—

- The concept of a "rescuer"
- Why some PWDs have felt themselves to be "pawns" in agencies' struggles for survival
- The concept of iatrogenic treatment
- How professionals can contribute to prejudice and discrimination

Disability is expensive. For example, Livneh and Antonak (1997) stated, "It is estimated that the cost of lifelong treatment for an individual with traumatic brain injury may exceed $4.5 million. The cost of traumatic brain injury to society each year was estimated recently . . . to approach a staggering $5 billion for medical intervention, rehabilitation, residential care, and lost earnings and may be several times that amount if consideration is given to the costs incurred by family, friends, and neighbors" (pp. 151–152). Considering the cost of a single disability, traumatic brain injury, it is not remarkable that both disability and rehabilitation are businesses (Albrecht, 1992). The nation spends billions of dollars annually responding to disability (Berkowitz, 1989). Higgins (1992) summarized the effects of this businesslike atmosphere:

> Disability is a business and many people would be unemployed. Disability is big business. Medical professionals, counselors, special educators, and other human service professionals earn their living by serving disabled [*sic*] people . . . . Consequently, we should not be surprised when such organizations expand disability to encompass more conditions and more people or perpetuate people's status as disabled . . . . Many organizational professionals "live off of" disability. Academics do, too. (p. 220)

For the client/consumer, the experience of a disability is both personal and unique to himself or herself. It is easy to see how professionals and clients often work under different assumptions. The following is a brief list of some of the criticisms or concerns that PWDs have expressed about the services and treatments they have received.

The Perspective of the Recipient of Services

1. Many service providers have abused their power, often wanting to control the PWD rather than allow him or her to make decisions and choices. Much, if not most, of this was the result of good intentions. Indeed, the term "rescuer" has been used to describe care providers who see professional services as "rescuing" and thereby controlling the individual. Billy Golfus (1994) was especially outspoken about this: "When you're disabled and these Do-Gooders pull their shit, there is allegedly nothing that you can do. I know. I've suffered years of the Do-Gooders' afflictions. Their game is about wanting to be in control of other people's lives" (cited in Charlton, 1998, p. 167).

2. Some PWDs have felt themselves to be "pawns" in agencies' or programs' struggle for survival. The Disability Rights Movement uses the derisive term "warm bodies" to describe the need for agencies to document the number of PWDs they serve. Therefore,

at times, there was the temptation to pathologize PWDs or, at minimum, to reinforce the disability so the agency or program could remain operating.

3. Some PWDs (and a few care providers) have termed some of the treatments *iatrogenic*. Iatrogenic means that the caregiver or the institution causes the patient harm. PWDs who had been institutionalized for years were not allowed to develop skills and abilities to live in the community, and therefore their lack of skills was not a result of the disability but a result of the treatment (the institutionalization). This is also a criticism that has been leveled at agencies and programs for individuals with psychiatric disabilities (Deegan, 1990). Anthony (cited in Garske & Stewart, 1999) stated, "Recovery from mental illness involves much more than recovery from the illness itself. People with mental illness may have to recover from the stigma they have incorporated into their very being, from the iatrogenic effects of treatment settings" (p. 7).

4. Especially in medical settings, the care providers with whom PWDs have the most contact are the least trained and least paid. Until recently, there were no background checks for criminal records for these types of employees; moreover, employee turnover was high. Attendants, orderlies, and aides provide most of the "treatment" many PWDs receive (Adams & Gentry, 1999). Eisenberg summarized: "Individuals of low social value, such as people with disabilities, are served by providers of low competence and low professional prestige" (Wolfensberger & Tullman, 1991, p. 212).

5. Professionals have, at times, defined the problems and social agenda of PWDs, even to the point of representing PWDs (without their permission) to the world (Stubbins, 1988). Disability rights advocates have been calling for *organization of* PWDs, rather than *organizations for* PWDs.

6. Many PWDs feel that they have not been treated as complete individuals. Their experiences with prejudice, stigma, and discrimination have not been regarded as relevant to their treatment and rehabilitation (Stubbins, 1988). A disability scholar explained: "Concepts such as sick role, prejudice, normalization, the social order, the power elite, and how these concepts shed understanding on issues in disability are regarded as interesting, but deemed only marginal in clinical practice" (Stubbins, 1988, p. 23).

7. PWDs, especially those in the Deaf Culture, feel that professionals have, in the past, contributed to prejudice, discrimination, and their limited choices and reduced opportunities. The most clearcut example of this is that of hearing teachers for deaf children advocating oralism rather than sign language. Teaching oralism, or the ability to speak (and read lips), was an attempt to make the children appear to be hearing children. Decades of this teaching

method left many of the Deaf without a culture and unable to communicate. Other professionals have needlessly limited the range of choices available to PWDs (within their abilities).

8. Finally, some professional care providers view PWDs as objects of charity, and, therefore, the services they provide to PWDs are "gifts" for which the PWDs should have no expectations, and they must be appropriately grateful. Further, these "gift" services should not be questioned or challenged.

What Do PWDs Want From Professional Care Providers?

> ### In this section, look for—
>
> - Four resources that professionals can bring to the therapeutic alliance:
>   1. Hope
>   2. Ideas
>   3. Understanding of the prejudice and discrimination PWDs face
>   4. Willingness to stand by the PWD

Joe Marrone (1997), a rehabilitation counselor, outlined four resources that professionals can bring to the therapeutic relationship: (1) hope, (2) ideas, (3) an understanding of the prejudice and discrimination that PWDs encounter, and (4) a willingness to stand by the person. Hope, according to Marrone, is not ill-informed optimism that everything will be all right. *receive less help* Patricia Deegan, speaking of individuals with psychiatric disabilities, succinctly summarized hope. Deegan tells people with schizophrenia, "People *do* get better." Neither Marrone nor Deegan is saying that recovery is fast or easy; they are simply saying that there is hope and many people do get better. Ideas that professionals bring to the relationship include knowledge of the disability, of adaptive technology, and of the legal mandates against discrimination (Orrin, 1997).

Donna Orrin (1997), who trains mental health workers, also described the importance of hope:

> I think hope is really a major issue. Professionals must instill a sense of hope in people and their families. Always give the individual logical, concrete examples of why they should be hopeful. When I speak to

groups of consumers, I ask them, "In your suicidal days, were you able to hang on because you had one, just one person who believed in you?" I also ask, "How many of you have come farther in your recovery than you thought possible because someone, just one person had hope for you?" When I ask just those questions, almost all the hands in the audience go up. They tell me that they got through suicidal times because someone had hope for them. The best advice I can give to professionals is to encourage people. Provide a sense of hope. You may be saving someone's life. You may be making a lifelong difference to an individual. (Mackelprang & Salsgiver, 1999, p. 186)

As would be expected, PWDs want easy access to services (often difficult in bureaucratic eligibility programs); they want to be treated as people rather than as a disability, and they do not want to be blamed (implicitly or explicitly) for the disability. PWDs know that they have the right to be informed consumers, which includes knowing the training, experience, credentials, and theoretical orientation of professionals. (Some PWDs ask their physicians: "How many people have you treated with a disability like mine?") Even more important, PWDs understand that they have the right to full explanations of the treatment goals, which includes the right to question, challenge, or appeal any part of the treatment or service. Reading the list, these needs of PWDs seem both legitimate and straightforward; nonetheless, until recently PWDs were not accorded these rights.

A study of 99 adults with long-term disabilities asked questions concerning the individuals' perceptions of their medical care (Putnam et al., 2003). These participants included people with cerebral palsy, polio, multiple sclerosis, amputation, and spinal cord injuries, and the study was conducted in three areas: Houston, Texas; Portland, Oregon; and San Francisco, California. A major conclusion of these focus groups was that "when speaking about health and wellness professionals, participants were generally frustrated with the lack of knowledge health care providers have about disability" (p. 41). Participants stated that they wanted doctors and other health care providers who would be willing to listen to them, who would accept the PWD as knowledgeable about his or her disability, and who was willing to get involved in "external issues like insurance disputes." Above all, participants wanted to be able to trust their health care providers.

For many PWDs, the health care market is not a free and open market. Indeed, for PWDs, the number of doctors from which to select may be limited. In addition to the limitations placed by the insurance company, the number of physicians who provide accommodations (such as sign language interpreters) may be small. In contrast, most PWODs have a much greater range of available choices and can, if necessary, switch to a different physician if they feel they are not developing a therapeutic alliance. Many PWODs have a different experience at the doctor's office than PWDs do.

Most people do not pay for their own medical care. Insurers do. Therefore, the consumer of the service is not the payer. This is not a newsflash, but it is probably safe to state that the difficulties of third-party payors are greater for PWDs than for PWODs. As the dual realities of the consolidation of the health care insurance industry and of the need for cost-containment measures continue, these problems of PWDs will likely increase. Once again, the questions arise: Can anything of human value be measured? What is quality medical care for a PWD?

The Perspective of Professionals

If disability and rehabilitation are businesses, they are also political programs. Berkowitz (1989), the foremost authority on government disability programs, described in his book all the government programs designed to respond to disability. Berkowitz stated:

> Disability does not represent an exception to the general pattern of anachronistic and uncoordinated programs that are resistant to change.... Reform has therefore taken place within the existing contours of the program and involved incremental, rather than fundamental change.... In disability, as in social welfare in general, the only avenue of fundamental reform is to add another program to existing programs and to cope with the resulting confusion.... Because of these tendencies, our disability policy, viewed in its historical context, consists of layers of outdated programs. (p. 227)

Professionals must provide services to PWDs under these types of institutional constraints. Professionals bring technical knowledge; years of experience and training; and, for most, a desire to do a good job. There are other difficulties with which professionals deal, including the complexity and uniqueness of each individual and of each disability. Treatment is individualized (rather than standardized) and such individualization requires a high level of skill. Further, while everyone would quickly agree that it is not possible to measure anything of human value in terms of dollars and cents, most professionals must work within financial constraints. Clients/consumers may think of professionals, such as rehabilitation counselors, as controlling a great deal of money and other resources. In contrast, the rehabilitation counselors probably view themselves as operating with very limited budgets and within strict guidelines.

Another difficulty faced by professionals who serve PWDs is the fact that these professionals are not in control of the outcome (Stav & Florian, 1986). Inherent in the relationship is the right of the PWD to make his or her own decisions. Reread the essay by Dr. Krauthammer in Chapter 5 (Exhibit 5–3) of this book. Focus on the individual with a spinal cord injury who decided to lie in bed for 7 years, and if after the 7 years, a cure for spinal cord injuries had not been developed, he planned to commit suicide. Because this man was a hospital-mate of Krauthammer's when Krauthammer first sustained his injury 22 years ago, it is interesting to imagine what happened to this man. Attempting to view this man from a professional caregiver's perspective, he would seem to be the type that does not "engage" the system but allows himself to be "processed" through it. Physicians, psychologists, and rehabilitation counselors probably advised this man to capitalize on his remaining abilities and to make plans for the future. Did he change his mind and try to look forward to a future? Whether he did or not, this man must have been a very difficult individual for service providers.

Medical and rehabilitation providers work in a system that has, for centuries, been pathology oriented. The technical language of these professions is often pathological. In addition, professionals are, to some extent, a product of their training. Read the following excerpt, focusing on what (and whom) this woman with autism considered to be most helpful:

> As I grew older, the people who were of the greatest assistance were always the more creative, unconventional types. Psychiatrists and psychologists were of little help. They were too busy trying to analyze me and discover my deep dark psychological problems. One psychiatrist thought if he could find my "psychic injury," I would be cured. The high school psychologist wanted to stamp out my fixations on things like doors instead of trying to understand them and use them to stimulate learning. (cited in Mackelprang & Salsgiver, 1999, p. 155)

Autonomy, Independence, and Control

In this section, look for—

- The way in which society fosters dependence in PWDs:
  - —Holds low expectations of PWDs
  - —Has institutionalized financial disincentives for work
  - —Often fails to provide accessible environments
  - —Often fails to provide assistive technology
- The way in which many PWDs redefine independence and control
- How PWDs want to define their own needs, including the need for assistance
- The relationship between PWDs and assistive technology

American values often idealize independence and individualism, both on a national and on a personal level. We have also seen that the (false) ideal of total control over one's circumstances and future is so important that, for some individuals, death would appear preferable to losing this control. Asking for help may be viewed as a sign of weakness. Many PWODs cannot understand how PWDs can maintain their self-esteem and self-respect when they need help with so many of life's basic functions. Indeed, many PWDs have commented that it is humiliating to be dependent in a culture that worships independence (J. Morris, 1991). Longmore (2003) summarized:

> Autonomy and dependency and quality of life are highly value-laden concepts. They are rooted in American values that uphold complete physical self-sufficiency and absolute personal autonomy as cultural ideals. They express a myth, a myth that real Americans are rugged individualists who quite literally stand on their own two feet. The ideal, the authentic American is not in any way dependent on others. To become sick or disabled in America is to lose one's social validity. It is to acquire a relentlessly and radically negative identity. It is to become the inversion of what a real American is supposed to be. (p. 190)

Disabilities and their functional losses can and do make people dependent. Nonetheless, many disability scholars are clear in stating that society further and needlessly promotes the dependence and helplessness of PWDs. A society renders their citizens with disabilities helpless and subordinate if it (1) holds low expectations of PWDs; (2) has longstanding, institutionalized financial disincentives for work; and (3) does not provide accessible environments, assistive technology, or personal care attendants. Rather than viewing the needs of PWDs as situated in the relationship between the environment and PWDs, most PWODs consider these needs to be located solely within an individual's body. Considering the great value Americans place on independence and autonomy, it is ironic that American society fosters dependence in a large segment of its population.

Accommodations and accessibility are often provided reluctantly and only after the Americans with Disabilities Act has been invoked. Randy Souders (1993) is an artist who became paralyzed after a diving accident when he was a teenager. He described his experiences shortly after his accident and the way in which lowered expectations (which he refers to as "underchallenge") and obsolete laws can foster dependence.

> It was the art that provided the motivation for me to get up every morning and do something instead of sitting in front of the TV. It's very easy to get sucked into a dependency routine—you know, this "give me, give me, give me" kind of attitude. Society has such limited expectations of the disabled [sic] person. It doesn't expect you to be able do much of anything. It (society) underchallenges us to perform .... And that's what I take the most pride in—the fact that what I'm doing today is well

received all over, even with people who haven't a clue as to my physical condition. Then, when they learn about the paralysis and the story behind it, their mouths just drop and hang open. The gallery owners, for example, are flabbergasted that I can do anything. So that's what I take some measure of pride in: They don't say, "Gee, this is good, considering your condition . . . blah, blah," they say, "Boy, this is good, *period*." And they dig in their pockets and pull out their wallets. That, for me, is a kick. (p. 151)

An English disability scholar, Deborah Marks (1999), gave a straightforward explanation on the ways in which society makes PWDs dependent, subordinate, and helpless:

No person is completely self-reliant. Those people who are identified as being particularly dependent are *made* this way because social organization and distribution of resources are arranged in such a way that discriminates against them. For example, if steps rather than ramps are built at the entrance of buildings, then wheelchair users (or parents pushing prams) are made dependent on the assistance of others to carry them into the building . . . . In contemporary culture, dependence and independence often tend to be thought about in very narrow and mechanistic ways. (p. 96)

Society tends to define autonomy, control, and independence in very narrow ways; however, PWDs redefine these concepts. Indeed, many PWDs who consider themselves to be independent and productive may be seen by PWODs to be dependent and nonproductive (Phillips, 1992). Rather than viewing independence as the ability to perform particular functions, PWDs consider independence to have two components: (1) the capability to have one's needs met and (2) being a valued part of a larger system. J. Morris (1991) explained the first component:

We use the word [independence] in a practical and commonsense way to mean simply being able to achieve our goals. The point is that independent people have control over their lives, not that they perform every task themselves. Independence is not linked to the physical or intellectual capacity to care for oneself without assistance; independence is created by having assistance when and how one requires it, being able to choose when and how care takes place. (p. 140)

Morris is clear in stating the importance of the individual choosing when, where, and how the assistance is provided. PWDs have personally defined criteria and reject socially defined criteria. Not only do PWDs wish to identify their own problems and define their needs; they want to decide *how* these problems and needs will be addressed. In reading accounts of

PWDs describing how they wish their needs to be met, the word "dignity" often appears. Cheryl Wade (1994) lives at home (rather than in an institution or nursing home) and requires the services of a personal care attendant. Wade relates the importance of dignity:

> But if our shame tells us that our needs lack dignity, then the next thing we hear our shame say is that it is more dignified to die than to live with these basic needs that take away our privacy and seem like such a burden. (p. 89)

The provision of personal care attendants in the individual's home has assisted many PWDs in leaving nursing homes and other institutions. Approximately 10 million people use personal care assistants; the majority of these assistants are unpaid family workers. Only 10% of personal care assistants are paid workers (Saxton et al., 2006). Thus, the accommodation of personal care assistants has released millions of individuals from a lifetime of institutionalization. Certainly, most individuals would rather live at home than in an institution.

While the woman in the following excerpt did not use the word "dignity," she does state that accommodations that are dehumanizing will not be used:

> I'd love to be able to get into the spa. And they have a wonderful spa where I swim, but there is not a decent lift to get into it. They have a sling-type, which just doesn't work for us anymore. It's so fatiguing to use. It's so dehumanizing that it's just not worth it. (Putnam et al., 2003, p. 42)

Linton (1998) observed that society does not think PWDs should ask for luxuries or pleasure for three reasons: (1) PWDs are an economic drain on the system and therefore they really should not demand "non-necessities," (2) PWDs should be grateful for medical care, and (3) pleasure is not important for PWDs!

> Society's choice, and I see it as a choice, to exclude disabled [sic] people from social and cultural events that afford pleasure, or deny them sex education, sexual health care and, at times, marriage, privacy, and friendship are indications of the belief that pleasure is less consequential to disabled [sic] people than to nondisabled people. Yet that belief is likely a rationalization for more virulent impulses. Are disabled [sic] people denied access to pleasure by the unspoken notion that they are not entitled to it because they cause displeasure to others? ... How dare we crippled, blind, and crazy folks ask for parity? Shouldn't we be satisfied with the provision of medical care and sustenance, and leave the luxuries for those who are thought to drain fewer resources from society? (Linton, 1998, p. 111)

We have seen how the concept of "normality" has quite literally been [a stum]bling block to PWDs. Many individuals were forced to undergo use[less or] harmful treatments, wear prostheses, and learn to speak and read [li]ps simply because PWODs thought it important that PWDs appear as "normal" as possible. Often, PWDs were subjected to treatment or given assistive technology for very small gains. A recent oral history of Canadian World War II veterans with spinal cord injuries, entitled "Going Back to Civvy Street," told of physicians who wanted the veterans to walk on crutches; however, after they discovered self-propelled wheelchairs, the veterans realized that using crutches was a wasteful expenditure of energy:

> It didn't make much sense spending all that energy covering a short distance (on crutches) . . . when you could do it quickly and easily with a wheelchair . . . . It didn't take long for people to get over the idea that walking was that essential. (Tremblay, 1996, p. 153)

Olivia, a young woman with a double above-knee amputation, related her decision not to use prostheses and the reasons:

> When Tom proposed to me I said, "Yes, I want to marry you, but there is something I must tell you first. I have decided not to try to use these damnable prostheses any more. I'm tired of falling down, and I've finally caught on that the rehab people only want me to use them because it's important for them that I *look* as normal as possible. They don't seem to tune in to the fact that I'm totally unfunctional when I have them on. I like the way I look and if other people don't like it, that's their problem. I'm not making it mine anymore . . . . I will never put on those dumb legs again." (Vash, 1981, p. 133)

Also, we have learned that many parents have refused facial plastic surgery for their children with Down syndrome, arguing that the surgery places the responsibility for adaptation on the individual, rather than on society as a whole. Of the parents surveyed, 88% rejected the cosmetic surgery. One parent stated, "As long as their physical appearance doesn't interfere with breathing, or seeing or eating, etc., then they are who they are. Beautiful people" (Goeke, 2003, p. 326).

When PWDs are in charge, assistance and accommodations are not viewed as undignified. In surveys of PWDs that have sought to determine their self-reported quality of life, many have stated that learning to do new things and learning to do former activities in a new way brought them a sense of self-worth and of autonomy. Indeed, respondents spoke about the need to reevaluate priorities and the perseverance required to retain their newly defined autonomy and independence (Putnam et al., 2003; Reid, 2004).

The second component in many PWDs' conception of independence and autonomy is a feeling of being a highly valued part of a larger system

(Faull et al., 2004). Erik Weihenmayer (2001) climbed Mt. Everest and he is blind. Although climbing Mt. Everest is a rather unusual accomplishment, something that most people never accomplish, it is important to understand that Weihenmayer wished to be a highly valued part of a climbing team:

> I refused to be the weak link of the team. I wanted them to put their lives in my hands, as I would put mine in theirs. I would carry my share. I could contribute as any other team member. I would not be carried up the mountain and spiked on top like a football. If I were to reach the summit, I would reach it with dignity. (p. 5)

Assistive technology can literally be life-saving. Many PWDs speak of their assistive technology in terms of a relationship: the polio survivor who referred to the iron lung he has used for more than 40 years as his "second skin" (O'Brien, cf Fleischer & Zames, 2001, p. 132); the man who said that he "loved his first wheelchair with a passion that embarrasses me, now" (Kriegel); and others who view their wheelchairs and other types of assistive technology "as a replacement for parts of themselves to get the job done" (Reid, 2004, p. 572). Some PWDs mark the date they received their technology as the beginning of their lives.

The Importance of Social Support

In this section, look for—

- The functions of social support:
  - —Reduce isolation
  - —"Normalize" the experience of disability
  - —Provide role models
  - —Provide validity to the experience of disability
  - —Challenge the way in which PWODs falsely view their lives
  - —Improve quality of life

Support Groups Help to Reduce Isolation

Joan Tollifson described her life before she joined a support group of women with disabilities as a "private hell" (1997, p. 107). In a well-known study by

Clausen and Yarrow (1955), one third of the participants said they attempted to conceal the psychiatric disability of their family member by moving away or terminating relationships with extended family and friends. Clausen and Yarrow's study was completed more than 50 years ago, but it safe to say that many families with disabilities of all types feel isolated. In a more recent study with women with various types of disabilities (Crawford, & Ostrove, 2003), the authors reported the main finding:

> Participants spoke poignantly about their pervasive isolation and loneliness. Many participants espoused that their disabilities—or attitudes toward them—at least to some extent limited their ability to access meaningful social interactions. Participants' frustration with this situation was tied to their unwillingness to participate more actively in society at large. Thus a vicious cycle is activated which serves to further isolate individuals with disabilities and solidify stereotypes relating to their social maturity and competence. (p. 191)

It is important to note that the participants used the phrase "meaningful relationships." Obviously PWDs do have relationships with PWODs and other PWDs, but they are stating that they do not have deep and satisfying associations.

One 57-year-old woman who is deaf told of her attempts to integrate herself:

> They [strangers] treat me like a ghost standing there. When I try to get into conversations, and oh this is the worst thing, they say this all the time. When I ask them what they are saying, they say, "Oh nothing, it's okay" and they won't repeat it because to them it is not worth repeating. To me, it is like gold. I still want to know. (p. 187)

Crawford and Ostrove interpret their findings by stating that the lack of social integration of PWDs and their invisibility in the cultural life of the United States have created difficulties for both PWDs and PWODs. In their opinion, "Lack of integration of individuals with disabilities prevents the daily interaction necessary for both disabled [sic] and able-bodied individuals to learn to negotiate the delicate balance between two cultures" (p. 191).

Family members also experience the isolation that a disability can bring. This woman relates her mother's difficulty in dealing with the daughter's psychiatric disability in the days before such support groups as the National Alliance for the Mentally Ill (NAMI) were available.

> At that time, one of the biggest problems was isolation [after her hospitalization]. People didn't know a lot. I couldn't talk to anyone about

mental illness. My mother was frustrated; she didn't know where she could go for help, and she couldn't talk to any family members or friends about it because nobody was willing to talk to her. (Mackelprang & Salsgiver, 1999)

In Stefan's (2001) national survey of individuals with mental illness, the question was asked: "What are some examples of the worst discrimination you have experienced?" One respondent wrote, "I'm sick of losing friends," and another wrote, "friends who have abandoned me" (p. 14). One question asked if the psychiatric disability limited the individual in any way. One respondent simply wrote, "no job, no friends."

However, in the same survey, one woman wrote: "A few years after my illness I met someone who permitted me to talk about my hospitalization. As I described the experience, I cried. A gentle touch that said, 'It doesn't matter; we can still be friends,' was worth years of therapy. That moment was an emotional breakthrough for me." Remarkable in this excerpt is the fact that she did not find someone to whom she could share her experiences until years after her hospitalization, and, furthermore, she considers this conversation to be an unforgettable breakthrough. Stefan found that the most often cited sources of social support and community involvement were churches and synagogues; many respondents wrote that their church or synagogue was welcoming, friendly, and supportive and provided emotional and social sustenance.

Some participants in these surveys told of friends and family they deliberately avoided because they were not supportive or held negative, limited views of disability (Putnam et al., 2003). One woman said, ". . . there are certain people that I love dearly that I have to restrict association with, because they're not positive . . ." (p. 41).

Often, the individual with a newly acquired disability has internalized all of the societal prejudices and discrimination against PWDs and, therefore, does not wish to associate with other PWDs. One individual refused to attend a support group because "sad stories bored him" (Goffman, 1963, p. 21). Polio survivors were encouraged not to associate with other polio survivors (Wilson, 1990). Marc Shell explained: "After release from the hospital, polios [survivors] usually isolated themselves from one another. They had internalized the doctrine that they should not 'fraternize' with one another after discharge but instead should get on with normal lives" (2005, p. 118). Anne Finger had polio as a child and speaks of her first experience associating with other polio survivors at a conference on post-polio:

I sat for the first time in my life in a room filled with other disabled [sic] people. I remember how nervous I felt. I'd always gone to "regular" schools; I had been mainstreamed before there was a word for it. I had moved through the world as a normal person with a limp, and no

thank you, I didn't need help, I manage just fine. And no, I was nothing like "them." I wasn't whiny, or needy, or self-pitying. (Finger, 1990,
pp. 16–17)

Joan Tollifson remarked, "I joined a group of disabled [*sic*] women on
the advice of my therapist. I hated the idea, but to my surprise, they were
marvelous, dynamic women" (1997, p. 107). Leslie Heller has cerebral palsy.
Here she explains her fear of associating with other PWDs: "When I was
growing up, I was terrified of walking into a room of people with disabilities
and admitting that I was one of them. Now, I just love being in a community of people with disabilities" (Fleischer & Zames, 2001, p. 201).

Support Groups "Normalize" the Experience of Disability

Interacting with other PWDs allows individuals to feel "normal." The word
"normal," as it is used here, simply means that the disability is considered
to be ordinary and natural and the individual is not viewed as his or her
disability. Actually, in a support group of individuals with the same type of
disability, it would be impossible to identify a single individual only as his
or her disability! In these types of support groups, PWDs feel comfortable
and accepted as individuals. PWDs report that they feel relaxed around
others who have had the same experiences, feeling that they could speak
about their disability "without elaborate explanation" (Finger, 1990, p. 17).
Carol, a woman who is deaf, was asked to name one PWOD who truly
understood her experience as a deaf woman. The researchers described her
reaction to the question as "bewilderment." Carol replied, "Who really understands my disability? My mother was determined to make me talk and
she succeeded. But to understand deafness? I don't know, I don't know anybody that understands" (Crawford & Ostrove, 2003, p. 190). The authors
summarized: "The vast majority of individuals who highlighted this lack
of awareness coped by affiliating themselves primarily with the disability
community." Support groups provide a setting in which PWDs feel neither
"different" nor isolated.

In these types of support groups, the stress of dealing with the reactions of PWODs, including prejudice and discrimination, is eliminated.
Indeed, often the discussion centers on the socially relevant, shared experience of prejudice and discrimination. Discussing similar experiences allows
individuals to understand that the prejudice and discrimination are not a
result of some personal fault, but that these prejudicial attitudes are widely
held stereotypes. Realizing that other PWDs have experienced prejudice
often results in a greater sense of self-worth and self-empowerment. Joan
Tollifson (1997) tells of "healing conversations" in that group of women
with disabilities:

They shared so many of what I had always thought were my own isolated, personal experiences that I began to realize that my supposedly private hell was a social phenomenon. We had eye-opening, healing conversations. We discovered, for example, that we had all had the experience of being patronized and treated like children even though we were adults. It wasn't simply some horrible flaw in my own character that provoked such reaction, as I had always believed, but rather, this was part of a collective pattern that was much larger than any one of us. It was a stereotype that existed in the culture at large. Suddenly, disability became not just my personal problem, but a social and political issue as well. (p. 107)

A woman who is hearing impaired spoke about how relaxing it was not to worry about hiding her assistive technology.

I remembered how relaxing it was . . . to be with people who took impaired hearing for granted . . . . How restful it would be to adjust the volume control on my transmitter without caring whether or not anyone was looking. To stop thinking, for a while, about whether the cord at the back of my neck was showing. What luxury to say out loud to someone, "Ye gods, my battery's dead!" (Goffman, 1963, p. 20)

Role models often "normalize" some of the emotions experienced by individuals who have recently acquired their disability.

I didn't want to admit that I was also handicapped . . . . She [mentor] tells me that she felt like that, too, and that you get over this feeling. And you know that life goes on and that there's a lot out there that you can do, anything you want to do . . . . You can still be just as much of a person without [your legs]. (Veith, Sherman, Pellino, & Yasui, 2006, p. 293)

Of all the types of disabilities, the Deaf Culture has achieved the greatest group solidarity and common identity. The Deaf Culture also has the longest history of providing support and community for their members and their families. Much of this long history and solidarity are the results of a common language, sign language, and residential schools. Any language is the repository of a rich cultural tradition, and sign language has many expressions and jokes about handicapism and prejudice. Additionally, because most deaf children are born to hearing parents, many children cannot communicate with their families if the families do not learn sign language. Therefore, deaf children feel more at home among those individuals with whom they can communicate. The importance of having a social category, rather than remaining invisible, cannot be exaggerated.

Many PWDs in the Disability Rights Movement have observed that the hierarchy of stigma is reversed in disability groups—the more severe the disability, the greater the individual's stature and prestige.

Support Groups Provide Role Models

There have been few role models for PWDs. In the Disability History Project produced by National Public Radio, an individual recalls:

> One of the first people I saw working with a disability was the crippled newsie on the corner—the guy who couldn't use his legs who had a little knuckle board who dragged himself around to sell newspapers. I knew that except for the money my family had, that could very easily be me and it scared me to death. (Tomorrow's Children, 1998)

Harold Russell lost his arms in World War II and starred in the movie "The Best Years of Our Lives," for which he won an Academy Award. Russell was asked, "When you were a kid, did you ever know someone with a disability who worked?" Russell answered, "I never knew anybody with a disability before the war" (Tomorrow's Children, 1998).

The former Assistant Secretary of the U. S. Department of Education, Judith Heumann, did not meet a role model with a disability until she was in her 20s. Heumann stated, "When we go into most 'establishment' organizations, we hardly meet any disabled [sic] individuals; there are no peers that we can look up. I never met a disabled [sic] professional until I was in my twenties. I had only nondisabled role models—who were not role models to me because I am disabled" (Heumann, 1979, p. 17). It is interesting that Heumann has become a role model for many PWDs. One individual stated, "That was the turning point for me—when I met Judy Heumann and Ed Roberts. They acted and spoke like there was nothing wrong with them; that what was wrong was that doors were too narrow" (McCarthy, 2003).

Role models for PWDs were absent in the media, with the exception of President Roosevelt (who worked very hard to hide his disability and possessed unlimited resources). Michalko (2002) remembers seeing characters who were blind on television and in the movies and reading about people who were blind when he was a teenager.

> They were all portrayed as victims of a misfortune . . . . When I saw blind people in the movies or on television and even when I saw the "real" ones, I saw incompetence, sadness, and poverty. And I saw misfortune. Whether my perception was accurate or not is irrelevant; that is just what I saw. What I did not see when I saw those blind people is

just as significant as what I did see: I did not see me. Still, when I saw them, I experienced a nebulous fear that I later understood was the fear of seeing myself. (p. 24)

Role models can also provide practical information and share their own experiences with a disability. A woman with a spinal cord injury related that she became less frightened as she received answers and information about her specific questions from someone else with a spinal cord injury (her mentor).

> . . . how [the mentor] got around and what had happened to her and how she dealt with cooking and how she dealt with her kids, how she had sex and what kind of bed she had. Lots of different questions [about] life and living . . . . Spasticity and, oh God, just everything . . . . And the more I learned, the less scared I got. (Veith et al., 2006, p. 291)

Other specific questions included "How (can I) go through the day?" "How long might it take to go through my morning routine?" or "What might (I) be doing to cut it shorter?" Another individual stated, "The fear of the unknown was the biggest factor" (Veith et al., 2006, p. 291).

Other individuals who had recently acquired spinal cord injuries spoke of the importance of having a mentor or role model with whom they could identify:

> And then [the hospital staff] are showing people [with a spinal cord injury] in a $2 million yacht or on farms with 40 horses, you know; I mean that was for real? . . . [My mentor] is a real guy, you know, who lives a real life that's not easy and that's different than it was before . . . . Most of those things [in the video] are way out of reach for the average spinal-cord injured person [sic] . . . . It's not many Chris Reeves." (Veith et al., 2006, p. 294)

Conclusion

As these last two chapters have discussed, the many factors of a disability make each disability a unique experience. Even disabilities of the same type and severity will have different courses; the symptoms will present in different ways, may require somewhat different treatment, and will have varied prognoses. Carolyn Vash (1981), a disability scholar, developed a model of the factors that influence an individual's response to a disability, dividing these factors into three broad categories. These three categories are as follows: (1) factors in the individual, (2) factors in the environment, and (3) factors of the disability. As you will remember, factors in the individual include such aspects as the individual's coping abilities, level of education, and financial resources. The environment includes such aspects as family support, other social support, assistive technology available, services provided, and the amount of prejudice and discrimination in society. These last two chapters have focused on the 10 factors in the disability. We have only briefly discussed the three broad types of factor issues; nonetheless, it can be seen that each disability is a unique experience for the individual.

In-Class Activities

- View the 57-minute video "Breaking the Silence Barrier Inside the World of Cognitive Disabilities." The producers describe this video: "This program reports on creative technologies that are being used to help people with autism, traumatic brain injuries, and learning and speech disabilities. Temple Grandin, an autistic woman [sic] with a PhD in animal science, explains her 'squeeze machine' which uses deep pressure therapy to help ease the hyper-acute sensory dysfunction that often accompanies autism. Re-nowned neurologist Oliver Sacks shares his views on how people with autism can find meaning in their own distinctive way. Also profiled is Bob Williams, who is the first person with a significant speech disability to hold a major federal office, and several people with learning disabilities and traumatic brain injuries who have improved their lives by using multimedia software programs."
- View the 29-minute video "Pain Management." The producers describe this video: "Pain, a frequent part of recovery from illness and injury, is actually controllable in the vast majority of cases. This program . . . illustrates approaches to pain control for patients healing after surgery, dealing with cancer, and coping with chronic back and nerve conditions." Available from Films for the Humanities and Sciences (PO Box 2053, Princeton, NJ 08543-2053, 800-257-5126, www.films.com).

In-Class Videos

- View the film "Murderball" about athletes competing on the U.S. wheelchair rugby team in Athens, Greece. Directors Henry Alex Rubin and Dana Adam Shapiro followed these athletes for 3 years to show their training, competitions, and finally the competition in the Olympic arena in Athens. *Sports Illustrated* stated: "Murderball lifts the lid on the ultra-competitive world of quad rugby. As in any class sports story, the rivalry in Murderball plays out at the highest level. There is more laughter than tears . . . . The filmmaker's success arises from such intimacy, and from the preconceptions they turn inside out." Please note that this film is rated R, probably because of sexual references and strong language.

Learning Activities

Read and discuss any of the following books:

- *Staring Back: The Disability Experience from the Inside Out* edited by Kenny Fries (1997, Plume Books, New York). This book is a compilation of writings, nonfiction, poetry, fiction, and drama, by PWDs. Many of these authors are well-known, including John Hockenberry, Adrienne Rich, and Mark O'Brien (who was the subject of the Academy Award winning documentary "Breathing Lessons"). The publisher's "blurb" states, "The passionate, evocative pieces included here help to dispel the myth that disabilities limit insight and productivity, and focus instead on understanding and redefining the experience of disability."

- *Violence and Abuse in the Lives of People with Disabilities: The End of Silent Acceptance?* by Dick Sobsey (1994, Paul H. Brookes Publishing Company, Baltimore). Using both statistical information and case studies, this book clearly describes the violence, abuse, and neglect that PWDs experience. Sobsey also offers some explanations as to why this abuse occurs and then outlines ways in which to (1) detect abuse, (2) combat abuse by altering specific social situations, and (3) help to heal the consequences of abuse.

- *Women with Disabilities: Essays in Psychology, Culture, and Politics* edited by Michelle Fine and Adrienne Asch (1988, Temple University Press, Philadelphia). In their introduction, the editors pose these questions: "How do being female and having a disability interact? How do women with disabilities view their experience? What can we learn about disability from literature, folklore, social science, law, and public policy? How do race, social class, social circumstances, and sexual orientation influence the lives of women with disabilities?" (p. 1). This book answers these questions.

- *The Deaf Way: Perspectives from the International Conference on Deaf Culture* edited by Carol J. Erting, Robert C. Johnson, Dorothy L. Smith, and Bruce D. Snider (1989, Gallaudet University Press, Washington, DC). During the week of July 9–14, 1989, more than 6,000 people with hearing disabilities from all over the world came to Washington, DC, and this book is the compilation of the presentations. We learn about the Deaf in Sweden, Japan, Italy, African nations, the United States, and many more countries. The foreword of the book states, "Most important of all, perhaps, was the sense of peopleness that was everywhere prevalent. This book will provide, in some measure, an enduring documentation of many of the formal presentations. But above and beyond these serious overtones on the reality and vitality of deaf people, on empowerment, advancement, pride, and self-identity, the week was a deaf Woodstock, an exhilarating and unbelievable extravaganza brimming with the wonder of self-fulfillment and realization" (p. 414).

References

Adams, C., & Gentry, C. (1999, December 31). Nurse shortage hurts families of the disabled. *Wall Street Journal*, p. A12.

Albrecht, G. L. (1992). *The disability experience: Rehabilitation in America*. Newbury Park, CA: Sage.

Allen, H. A., & Sawyer, H. W. (1983). Individuals with life-threatening disabilities: A rehabilitation counseling approach. *Journal of Applied Rehabilitation Counseling, 15*, 26–29, 37.

American Psychiatric Association. (1994). *Diagnostic and statistical manual of mental disorder* (4th ed.). Washington, DC: Author.

Asch, A., & Fine, M. (1997). Nurturance, sexuality, and women with disabilities: The example of women and literature. In L. J. Davis (Ed.), *The Disability Studies Reader* (pp. 242–259). New York: Routledge.

Barker, R. G., Wright, B. A., Meyerson, L., & Gonick, M. R. (1953). *Adjustment to physical handicap and illness: A survey of the social psychology of physique and disability* (rev. ed.). New York: Social Science Research Council.

Berkman, A., Weissman, R., & Frielich, M. (1978). Sexual adjustment of spinal cord injured veterans living in the community. *Archives of Physical Medicine and Rehabilitation, 59*, 22–23.

Berkowitz, E. D. (1989). *Disabled policy: America's programs for the handicapped*. Cambridge, England: University of Cambridge.

Bernstein, N. R. (1976). *Emotional care of the facially burned and disfigured*. Boston: Little, Brown.

Bernstein, N. R. (1989). Psychological problems associated with facial disfigurement. In B. W. Heller, L. M. Flohr, & L. S. Zegans, (Eds.), *Psychosocial interventions with physically disabled persons* (pp. 147–161). New Brunswick, NJ: Rutgers University.

Bernstein, N. R. (1990). Objective bodily damage: Disfigurement and dignity. In T. F. Cash & T. Pruzinsky (Eds.), *Body images: Development, deviance, and change* (pp. 131–148). New York: Guilford.

Bernstein, N. R., Breslau, J. J., & Graham, J. A. (Eds.). (1988). *Coping strategies for burn survivors and their families*. New York: Praeger.

Blumberg, B. D., Lewis, M. J., & Susman, E. J. (1984). Adolescence: A time of transition. In M. G. Eisenberg, L. C. Sutkin, & M. A. Jansen (Eds.), *Chronic illness and lifespan: Effects on self and family* (pp. 133–149). New York: Springer.

Bonica, J. J. (Ed.) (1990). *The management of pain*. Philadelphia: Lea & Febiger.

Boswell, B.B., Dawson, M., & Heininger, E. (1998). Quality of life as defined by adults with spinal cord injuries. *Journal of Rehabilitation, 64*, 27–32.

Bowman, J. M. (1994). Experiencing the chronic pain phenomenon: A study. *Rehabilitation Nursing, 19*(2), 91–95.

Bramble, K., & Cukr, P. (1998). Body image. In I. M. Lubkin & P. D. Larsen (Eds.), *Chronic illness: Impact and interventions* (pp. 283–298). Sudbury, MA: Jones & Bartlett.

Brena, S. F., Sanders, S. H., & Motoyama, H. (1990). American and Japanese low back pain patients: Cross cultural similarities and differences. *Clinical Journal of Pain, 6,* 118–124.

Carron, H., DeGood, D., & Tait, R. (1985). A comparison of low back pain patients in the United States and New Zealand: Psychosocial and economic factors affecting severity of disability. *Pain, 21,* 77–89.

Charlton, J. I. (1998). *Nothing about us without us: Disability oppression and empowerment.* Berkeley, CA: University of California.

Chubon, R. A. (1994). *Social and psychosocial foundations of rehabilitation.* Springfield, IL: Charles C. Thomas.

Clausen, J., & Yarrow, M. R. (1955). The impact of mental illness on the family. *Journal of Social Issues, 11,* 1–65.

Cohen, R. M. (2004). *Blindsided: Living a life above illness. A reluctant memoir.* New York: HarperCollins.

Cook, D. W. (1991). Disability, psychopathology, and vocational adjustment. In M. G. Eisenberg & R. L. Glueckauf (Eds.), *Empirical approaches to psychosocial aspects of disability* (pp. 85–105). New York: Springer.

Corbin, J., & Strauss, A. (1988). *Unending work, and care: Managing chronic illness at home.* San Francisco: Jossey-Bass.

Cott, C., & Wilkins, S. (1993). Aging, chronic illness and disability. In M. Nagler (Ed.), *Perspectives on disability* (2nd ed.) (pp. 363–377). Palo Alto, CA: Health Markets Research.

Crawford, D., & Ostrove, J. M. (2003). Representations of disability and the interpersonal relationships of women with disabilities. *Women and Therapy, 26,* 179–194.

Crewe, N. M (1997). Life stories of people with long term spinal cord injury. *Rehabilitation Counseling Bulletin, 41,* 26–42.

Curtin, M., & Lubkin, I. (1998). What is chronicity? In I. M. Lubkin & P. D. Larsen (Eds.), *Chronic illness: Impact and interventions* (4th ed.) (p. 325). Sudbury, MA: Jones & Bartlett.

Deegan, P. (1990). Spirit breaking: When the helping professions hurt. *The Humanistic Psychologist, 18,* 301–313.

DeLoach, C., & Greer, B. G. (1981). *Adjustment to severe physical disability: A metamorphosis.* New York: McGraw-Hill.

Douard, J. W. (1995). Disability and the persistence of the "Normal." In S. K. Toombs, D. Barnard, & R. A. Carson (Eds.), *Chronic illness: From experience to policy* (pp. 154–175). Bloomington: University of Indiana.

Ducharme, S., Gill, K., Biener-Bergman, S., & Fertitta, L. (1993). Sexual functioning: Medical and psychological aspects. In J. DeLisa (Ed.), *Rehabilitation medicine: Principles and practices* (2nd ed.) (pp. 763–782). Philadelphia: Lippincott.

Dunn, D. S. (1996). Well-being following amputation: Salutary effects of positive meaning, optimism, and control. *Rehabilitation Psychology, 41,* 285–301.

Elliott, T. R., Shewchuk, R., Hagglun, K., Rybarczyk, B., & Harkings, S. (1996). Occupational burnout, tolerance for stress, and coping among nurses in rehabilitation units. *Rehabilitation Psychology, 41,* 267–284.

Fabian, E. S. (1991). Using quality of life indicators in rehabilitation program evaluation. *Rehabilitation Counseling Bulletin, 34,* 344–356.

Falvo, D. R. (1991). *Medical and psychosocial aspects of chronic illness and disability*. Gaithersburg, MD: Aspen.

Faull, K., Hills, M. D., Cochrane, G., Gray, J., Hunt M., McKenzie, C., et al. (2004). Investigation of health perspectives of those with physical disabilities. The role of spirituality as a determinant of health. *Disability and Rehabilitation, 26*, 129–144.

Feldman, D. (1974). Chronic disabling illness: A holistic view. *Journal of Chronic Diseases, 27*, 287–291.

Finger, A. (1990). *Past due: A story of disability, pregnancy, and birth*. Seattle, WA: Seal.

Fink, P. J., & Tasman, A. (Eds.). (1992). *Stigma and mental illness*. Washington, DC: American Psychiatric Association.

Fleischer, D. Z., & Zames, F. (2001). *The disability rights movement: From charity to confrontation*. Philadelphia, PA: Temple University.

Friesen, B. J. (1996). Family support in child and adult mental health. In G. H. S. Singer, L. E. Powers, & A. L. Olson (Eds.), *Redefining family support: Innovations in public-private partnerships* (pp. 259–274). Baltimore: Brookes.

Gallagher, R. M. (2000). Treating depression in patients with comorbid chronic pain, Part 1. *Directions in Rehabilitation Counseling, 1*, 15–32.

Garske, G. G., & Stewart, J. R. (1999). Stigmatic and mythical thinking: Barriers to vocational rehabilitation services to persons with severe mental illness. *Journal of Rehabilitation, 65*, 4–8.

Goeke, J. (2003). Parents speak out: Facial plastic surgery for children with Down syndrome. *Education and Training in Developmental Disabilities, 38*, 323–333.

Goffman, E. (1963). *Stigma: Notes on the management of spoiled identity*. Englewood Cliffs, NJ: Prentice Hall.

Goldstein, R. K. (1986). Adjustment of the burned patient. In D. W. Krueger (Ed.), *Emotional rehabilitation of physical trauma and disability* (pp. 87–104). New York: Pergamon.

Gordon, P. A., Feldman, D., & Crose, R. (1998). The meaning of disability: How women with chronic illness view their experiences. *Journal of Rehabilitation, 64*, 5–11.

Gordon, P. A., Lewis, M. D., & Wong, D. (1994). Multiple sclerosis: Strategies for rehabilitation counselors. *Journal of Rehabilitation*, 34–38.

Gulick, E. E. (1994). Social support among persons with multiple sclerosis. *Research in Nursing and Health, 17*(3), 195–206.

Hadjistavropoulos, H. D., & Craig, K. D. (1994). Acute and chronic low back pain: Cognitive, affective, and behavioral dimensions. *Journal of Consulting and Clinical Psychology, 62*, 341–349.

Hardman, M. L., Drew, C. J., Egan, M. W., & Wolf, B. (1993). *Human exceptionality: Society, school, and family*. (4th ed.). Boston: Allyn & Bacon.

Heumann, J. E. (1979). *Disability: Our challenge*. New York: Columbia University.

Higgins, P. C. (1980). *Outsiders in a hearing world: A sociology of deafness*. Newbury Park, CA: Sage.

Higgins, P. C. (1992). *Making disability: Exploring the social transformation of human variation*. Springfield, IL: Charles C. Thomas.

Higgins, P. C., & Nash, J. E. (Eds.). (1987). *Understanding deafness socially*. Springfield, IL: Charles C. Thomas.

Holaday, M., & McPhearson, R. W. (1997). Resilience and severe burns. *Journal of Counseling and Development, 75*, 346–356.

Holzbauer, J. J., & Berven, N. L. (1996). Disability harassment: A new term for a long-standing problem. *Journal of Counseling and Development, 74*, 478–483.

Huberty, D. J. (1980). Adapting to illness through family groups. In P. W. Power & A. E. Dell Orto (Eds.), *Role of the family in the rehabilitation of the physically disabled* (pp. 433–443). Austin, TX: PRO-ED.

Jubala, J. A. (1990). Spinal cord injuries. In M. Hersen & V. B. Van Hasselt (Eds.), *Psychological aspects of developmental and physical disabilities* (pp. 229–245).

Karp, D. A. (2001). *The burden of sympathy: How families cope with mental illness.* Oxford, England: Oxford University.

Kilpatrick, S. D., & McCullough, M. E. (1999). Religion and spirituality in rehabilitation psychology. *Rehabilitation Psychology, 44,* 388–402.

Knight, S. E. (1989). Sexual concerns of the physically disabled. In B. W. Heller, L. M. Flohr, & L. S. Zegans (Eds.), *Psychosocial interventions with physically disabled persons* (pp. 183–199). New Brunswick, NJ: Rutgers University.

Kohler, K., Schweikert-Stary, M. T., & Lubkin, I. (1998). Altered mobility. In I. M. Lubkin & P. D. Larsen (Eds.), *Chronic illness: Impact and interventions* (4th ed.) (pp. 122–148). Sudbury, MA: Jones and Bartlett.

Kosciulek, J. F., & Lustig, D. C. (1998). Predicting family adaptation from brain injury-related family stress. *Journal of Applied Rehabilitation, 29*(1), 8–12.

Kozloff, R. (1987). Networks of social supports and the outcome from severe head injury. *Journal of Head Trauma Rehabilitation, 2,* 14–23.

Latham, J., & Davis, B. D. (1994). The socioeconomic impact of chronic pain. *Disability and Rehabilitation, 16,* 33–44.

Lerner, R. M., & Jovanovic, J. (1990). The role of body image in psychosocial adjustment across the lifespan: A developmental contextual perspective. In T. F. Cash & T. Pruzinsky (Eds.), *Body images, development, deviance, and change* (pp. 110–127). New York: Guilford.

Linton, S. (1998). *Claiming disability: Knowledge and identity.* New York: New York University.

Linton, S. J. (1986). Chronic back pain: Integrating psychological and physical therapy—an overview. *Pain, 24,* 101–104.

Livneh, H., & Antonak, R. F. (1997). *Psychosocial adaptation to chronic illness and disability.* Gaithersburg, MD: Aspen Publishers, Inc.

Longmore, P. K. (2003). *Why I burned my book and other essays on disability.* Philadelphia, PA: Temple University.

Love, B., Bryne, C., Roberts, J., Browne, G., & Brown, B. (1987). Adult psychosocial adjustment following childhood injury: The effect of disfigurement. *Journal of Burn Care and Rehabilitation, 8,* 280–285.

Lubkin, I. M., & Larsen, P. D. (Eds.). (1998). *Chronic illness: Impact and interventions* (4th ed.). Sudbury, MA: Jones and Bartlett.

Lubkin, I., & Jeffrey, J. (1998). Chronic pain. In I. M. Lubkin & P. D. Larsen (Eds.), *Chronic illness: Impact and interventions* (4th ed.) (pp. 149–178). Sudbury, MA: Jones and Bartlett.

Macgregor, F. C., Abel, J. M., Bryt, A., Laver, E., & Weissmann, S. (1953). *Facial deformities and plastic surgery: A psychosocial study.* Springfield, IL: Charles C. Thomas.

Mackelprang, R., & Salsgiver, R. (1999). Disability: A diversity model approach in human service practice. Pacific Grove, CA: Brooks/Cole.

Mairs, N. (1997). Carnal acts. In K. Fries (Ed.), *Staring back: The disability experience from the inside out.* New York: Plume.

Mannion, E. (1996). Resilience and burden in spouses with mental illness. *Psychiatric Rehabilitation, 20,* 13–24.

Marks, D. (1999). *Disability: Controversial debates and psychosocial perspectives.* London: Routledge.

Marrone, J. (1997, May 21). *Job placement for individuals with psychiatric disabilities.* Paper presented at the Utah State Office of Rehabilitation. 75th Anniversary Conference, Provo, Utah.

Martin, L. (2000). *From our house: A memoir.* New York: Dutton.

Maslach, C., & Florian, V. (1988). Burnout, job setting, and self-evaluation among rehabilitation counselors. *Rehabilitation Psychology, 33,* 85–93.

Maxmen, J. S., & Ward, N. G. (1995). *Psychotropic drugs: Fast facts* (2nd ed.). New York: Norton.

McCarthy, H. (2003). The disability rights movement: Experiences and perspectives of selected leaders in the disability community. *Rehabilitation Counseling Bulletin, 46,* 209–223.

McCarthy, H. (1995). Understanding and reversing rehabilitation counseling's neglect of spirituality. *Rehabilitation Education, 9,* 187–199.

McDaniel, J. W. (1976). *Physical disability, antihuman behavior* (2nd ed.). New York: Pergamon.

McMahon, B. T., Shaw, L. R., & Jaet, D. N. (1995). An empirical analysis: Employment and disability from an ADA litigation perspective. *NARPPS Journal and News, 10*(1), 3–14.

McReynolds, C. J., Koch, L.C., & Rumrill, P. D., Jr. (1999). Psychosocial adjustment to multiple sclerosis: Implications for rehabilitation counselors. *Journal of Vocational Rehabilitation, 12,* 83–91.

Mechanic, D. (1978). *Medical sociology* (2nd ed.). New York: Free Press.

Michalko, R. (2002). *The difference that disability makes.* Philadelphia, PA: Temple University.

Mishel, M. (1993). Reconceptualization of the uncertainty in illness theory. *Image: The Journal of Nursing Scholarship, 22*(45), 256–262.

Morris, D. B. (1998). *Illness and culture in the postmodern age.* Berkeley: University of California.

Morris, J. (1991). *Pride against prejudice: Transforming attitudes to disability.* Philadelphia: New Society.

Muller-Rohland, J. (1987). The medical aspects of disabling conditions: An overview. In B. Caplan (Ed.), *Rehabilitation psychology desk reference* (pp. 473–499). Rockville, MD: Aspen Publishers, Inc.

National Public Radio. Disability History Project. Tomorrow's Children.

Neumann, R. J. (1988). Personal statement: Experiencing sexuality as an adolescent with rheumatoid arthritis. In P. W. Power, A. E. Dell Orto, & M. B. Gibbons (Eds.), *Family interventions throughout chronic illness and disability* (pp. 156–163). New York: Springer.

O'Brien, M. T. (1993). Multiple sclerosis: Stressors and coping strategies in spousal caregivers. *Journal of Community Health Nursing, 10,* 123–135.

Orrin, D. (1997). Past the struggles of mental illness, toward the development of quality lives. In L. Spanoil, C. Gagne, & M. Hoehler (Eds.), *Psychological and social aspects of psychiatric disability* (pp. 138–144). Boston: Center for Psychiatric Rehabilitation. Boston University.

Patterson, D. R., Everett, J. J., Bombardier, C. H., Questad, K. A., Lee, V. K., & Marvin, J. A. (1993). Psychological effects of severe burn injuries. *Psychological Bulletin, 113,* 362–368.

Penn, A. (1993). Audrey Penn. In J. K. Smith & G. Plimpton (Eds.), *Chronicles of courage: Very special artists* (pp. 109–117). New York: Random House.

Peterson, C., Maier, S. F., & Seligman, M. E. P. (1993). *Learned helplessness: A theory for the age of personal control.* New York: Oxford University.

Phillips, M. (1992). "Try harder": The experience of disability and the dilemma of normalization. In P. M. Ferguson, D. L. Ferguson, & S. J. Taylor (Eds.), *Interpreting disability: A qualitative reader* (pp. 213–227). New York: Columbia Teachers College.

Power, P. W., Dell Orto, A. E., & Gibbons, M. B. (1988). *Family interventions through chronic illness and disability.* New York: Springer.

Power, P. W., & Rogers, S. (1979). Group counseling for multiple sclerosis patients: A preferred mode of treatment for unique adaptive problems. In R. G. Lasky & A. E. Dell Orto (Eds.), *Group counseling and physical disability* (pp. 115–127). North Scituate, MA: Duxbury.

Price, R. (1994). *A whole new life: An illness and a healing.* New York: Atheneum.

Pruzinsky, T. (1990). Psychopathology of body experience: Expanded perspectives. In T. F. Cash & T. Pruzinsky (Eds.), *Body images: Development, deviance, and change* (pp. 170–189). New York: Guilford.

Pruzinsky, T., & Cash, T. F. (1990). Integrative themes in body-image development, deviance, and change. In T. F. Cash & T. Pruzinsky (Eds.), *Body images: Development, deviance, and change* (pp. 337–347). New York: Guilford.

Putnam, M., Greenen, S., Powers, L., Saxton, M., Finney, S., & Dautel, P. (2003). Health and wellness: People with disabilities discuss barriers and facilitators to well-being. *Journal of Rehabilitation, 69,* 37–45.

Reid, D. (2004, December). Impact of the environment on role performance in older stroke survivors living at home. *International Journal of Therapy and Rehabilitation, 11,* 567–573.

Robinson, I. (1988). Managing symptoms in chronic disease: Some dimensions of patients' experience. *International Disability Studies, 10*(3), 112–119.

Roessler, R., & Bolton, B. (1978). *Psychosocial adjustment to disability.* Baltimore: University Park Press.

Rolland, J. S. (1988). A conceptual model of chronic and life threatening illness and its impact on family. In C. S. Chilman, E. W. Nunnally, & F. M. Cox (Eds.), *Chronic illness and disability: Families in trouble* (pp. 17–68). Newbury Park, CA: Sage.

Rousso, H. (1993). *Disabled, female and proud! Stories of ten women with disabilities.* Westport, CT: Bergin & Garvey.

Rybarczyk, B., Nyenhuis, D. L., Nicholas, J. J., Cash, S. M., & Kaiser, J. (1995). Body image, perceived social stigma, and the prediction of psychosocial adjustment to leg amputation. *Rehabilitation Psychology, 40,* 95–110.

Sasao, T., & Sue, S. (1993). Toward a culturally anchored ecological framework of research in ethnic-cultural communities. *American Journal of Community Psychology, 21,* 705–772.

Saxton, M., Curry, M. A., McNeff, E., Limont, M., Powers, L., & Benson, J. (2006). We're all little John Waynes: A study of disabled men's experience of abuse by personal assistants. *Journal of Rehabilitation, 72*(4), 3–13.

Scherer, M. J. (1993). *Living in the state of stuck: How technology impacts the lives of people with disabilities.* Cambridge, MA: Brookline.

Shell, M. (2005). *Polio and its aftermath.* Cambridge, MA: Harvard University.

Shinn, M., Rosario, M., Morch, H., & Chesnut, D. (1984). Coping with job stress and burnout in the human services. *Journal of Personality and Social Psychology, 46,* 864–876.

Shontz, F. C. (1971). Physical disability and personality. In W. S. Neff (Ed.). *Rehabilitation psychology*. Washington, DC: American Psychological Association.

Sinacore-Guinn, A. L. (1995). The diagnostic window: Culture and gender-sensitive diagnosis and training. *Counselor Education and Supervision, 35,* 18–32.

Singer, G. H. S. (1996). Introduction: Trends affecting home and community care for people with chronic conditions in the United States. In G. H. S. Singer, L. E. Powers, & A. L. Olsen (Eds.). *Redefining family support: Innovations in public private partnerships* (pp. 3–38). Baltimore: Brookes.

Smart, D., & Smart, J. (1997). DSM-IV and culturally sensitive diagnosis: Some observations for counselors. *Journal of Counseling & Development, 75,* 392–397.

Souders, R. (1993). Randy Souders. In J. K. Smith & G. Plimpton, (Eds.). *Chronicles of courage: Very special artists* (pp. 147–155). New York: Random House.

Spector, R. E. (1991). *Cultural diversity in health and illness* (3rd ed.). Norwalk, CT: Appleton & Lange.

Stav, A., & Florian, V. (1986). Burnout among social workers working with physically disabled persons and bereaved families. *Journal of Personality and Social Psychology, 46,* 864–876.

Stefan, S. (2001). *Unequal rights: Discrimination against people with mental disabilities and the Americans with Disabilities Act.* Washington, DC: American Psychological Association.

Strauss, A. L., Corbin, J., Fagerhaugh, S., Glaser, B. G., Maines, D., Suczek, B., & Weiner, C. L. (1984). *Chronic illness and the quality of life* (2nd ed.). St. Louis, MO: Mosby.

Strauss, A., & Glaser, B. (1975). *Chronic illness and the quality of life.* St. Louis, MO: Mosby.

Stubbins, J. (1988). The politics of disability. In A. E. Yuker (Ed.). *Attitudes toward persons with disabilities* (pp. 22–32). New York: Springer.

Taylor, E. J., Jones, P., & Burns, M. (1998). Quality of life. In I. M. Lubkin & P. D. Larsen (Eds.). *Chronic illness: Impact and interventions* (4th ed.) (pp. 207–226). Sudbury, MA: Jones & Bartlett.

Thomson, R. G. (1997a). Feminist theory, the body, and the disabled figure. In L. J. Davis (Ed.), *Disability studies reader* (pp. 279–292). New York: Routledge.

Thomson, R. G. (1997b). Integrating disability studies into the existing curriculum: The example of "Women and Literature" at Howard University. In L. J. Davis (Ed.). *The disability studies reader* (pp. 295–306). New York: Routledge.

Tollifson, J. (1997). Imperfection is a beautiful thing: On disability and meditation. In K. Fries (Ed.). *Staring back: The disability experience from the inside out* (pp. 105–112). New York: Plume.

Toombs, S. K. (1995). Sufficient unto the day: A life with multiple sclerosis. In S. K. Toombs, D. Barnard, & R. A. Carson (Eds.), *Chronic illness: From experience to policy* (pp. 2–23). Bloomington: University of Indiana.

Tremblay, M. (1996). Going back to civvy street: A historical account of the Everest and Jennings wheelchair for Canadian World War II veterans with spinal cord injuries. *Disability and Society, 11,* 149–169.

Trieschmann, R. B. (1988). *Spinal cord injuries: Psychological, social, and vocational rehabilitation* (2nd ed.). New York: Demos.

Vash, C. L. (1981). *The psychology of disability.* New York: Springer.

Veith, E. M., Sherman, J. E., Pellino, T. A., & Yasui, N. Y. (2006). Qualitative analysis of the peer-mentoring relationship among individuals with spinal cord injury. *Rehabilitation Psychology, 51,* 289–298.

Wade, C. (1994). It ain't exactly sexy. *The Ragged Edge,* 89–90.

Weihenmayer, E. (2001). *Touch the top of the world: A blind man's journey to climb farther than the eye can see.* New York: Dutton.

Weinberg, N. (1982). Growing up physically disabled: Factors in the evaluation of disability. *Rehabilitation Counseling Bulletin, 25,* 219–227.

Weinberg, N., & Miller, N. J. (1983). Burn care: A social work perspective. *Health and Social Work, 8,* 97–106.

Weinberg, N., & Sterritt, M. (1991). Disability and identity: A study of identity patterns in adolescents with hearing impairments. In M. G. Eisenberg & R. L. Glueckauf (Eds.), *Empirical approaches to psychosocial aspects of disability* (pp. 68–75). New York: Springer.

Weingarten, R. (1997). How I've managed my mental illness. In L. Spanoil, C. Gagne, & M. Hoehler (Eds.), *Psychological and social aspects of psychiatric disability* (pp. 123–129). Boston: Center for Psychiatric Rehabilitation, Boston University.

Weisgerber, R. S. (1991). *Quality of life for persons with disabilities.* Gaithersburg, MD: Aspen.

Wendell, S. (1997). Toward a feminist theory of disability. In L. J. Davis (Ed.), *The disability studies reader* (pp. 260–278). New York: Routledge.

White, N., & Lubkin, I. (1998). Illness trajectory. In I. M. Lubkin & P. D. Larsen (Eds.), *Chronic illness: Impact and interventions* (4th ed.) (pp. 53–76). Sudbury, MA: Jones & Bartlett.

Whiteneck, O. G. (1994). Measuring what matters: Key rehabilitation outcomes. *Archive of Physical Medicine and Rehabilitation, 75,* 1073–1076.

Whitt, J. K. (1984). Children's adaptation to chronic illness and handicapping conditions. In M. G. Eisenberg, L. C. Sutkin, & M. A. Jansen (Eds.), *Chronic illness and disability through the life span: Effects on self and family* (pp. 69–102). New York: Springer.

Wilson, D. J. (1990). *Living with polio: The epidemic and its survivors.* Chicago, IL: University of Chicago.

Wolfensberger, W., & Tullman, S. (1991). A brief outline of the principle of normalization. In M. G. Eisenberg & R. L. Glueckauf (Eds.), *Empirical approaches to the psychosocial aspects of disability* (pp. 202–215). New York: Springfield.

Woog, P. (1992). *The chronic illness trajectory framework: The Corbin and Strauss nursing model.* New York: Springer.

Wright, B. (1960). *Physical disability: A psychological approach.* New York: Harper & Row.

Yalom, I. D. (1980). *Existential psychotherapy.* New York: Basic Books.

Zola, I. (1988). Policies and programs concerning aging and disability: Toward a unifying agenda. In S. Sullivan & M. Lewin (Eds.), *The economics and ethics of long-term care and disability* (pp. 90–130). American Enterprise Institute for Public Policy Research.

Epilogue

What Is Disability History?

We return to the questions posed at the beginning of this book: "When you walk into any major chain bookstore, do you find any books about people with disabilities? Is there a large section devoted to Disability History?" John Hockenberry, a journalist who is paralyzed, asked: "Why is it that a person would not be considered educated or privileged if he went through school and never learned there was a France or a French language? But if a person went through school and knew nothing about disability, never met a disabled person [*sic*], never heard of American Sign Language, he might be considered not only educated, but also lucky?" (Fleischer & Zames, 2001, p. 205). So it is with disability history. There have always been people with disabilities; however, society has chosen to view their experiences as a narrow, clinical concern, rather than a universal concern.

History gives voice to individuals and self-defined groups of people, typically those who have lived in the past, relating their experiences, accomplishments, contributions, perspectives, and accumulated wisdom and knowledge. PWODs have represented humanity. Disability history, like all history, is ownership of the past (Longmore, 2003). A group identity is necessary to compile and write the history of any collection of people. This last statement appears to be self-evident; however, in the case of PWDs, for centuries the only commonalities among PWDs were thought to be inferiority, prejudice, and discrimination. Because of these mistaken beliefs, PWDs did not form a group identity. Until recently, the persistence of the Biomedical Model of disability and the blame and shame of the larger culture worked in combination to keep individual PWDs from seeking each other out.

Disability scholars are justifiably ambivalent toward the Biomedical Model of disability. Medical professionals and scientists in the biological sciences have made many contributions to the lives of PWDs; however, as a *model* (rather than as specific individuals), the Biomedical Model has created the idea that disability is a *private, individual* concern and is pathological inferiority. These false but widely accepted views of PWDs have isolated

PWDs from each other. Private concerns are not typically considered to be history. Neither is (falsely) perceived inferiority. After all, it is the winners and the ruling powers who write history. In the Disability History Project produced by National Public Radio (1998) it is stated, "History is about successes and heroes. People who are isolated, hidden, incarcerated, and segregated do not write their history, nor are they considered to be heroes or successes." Furthermore, writers of history need institutionalized power, and PWDs have not had access to this type of power (Humphrey, 1999). However, recently, PWDs have been following the lead of African Americans, Hispanic Americans, and women in reclaiming their right to be included in American history.

Of course, there have always been PWDs, so there has always been disability history. However, there has not been *written* and *recorded* history of PWDs written *by* PWDS. As we have seen throughout this book, PWDs do have common purposes; they share many of the same experiences, and many similar patterns and themes are found in diverse autobiographical works. This, then, is what disability history is. Millions of individuals have experienced a wide variety of disabilities throughout centuries, yet disability history is hidden from PWDs and, indeed, from everybody. Until recently, PWDs had no recorded history and, therefore, students have not been required to study a nonexistent history. Both PWDs and PWODs have been deprived of disability history. A great historian (Wecter, 1985) remarked, "Ignorance . . . is bad citizenship" (p. 40).

One of the purposes of any type of history is to build a present and a future that are more equitable and moral. Self-criticism of our culture, society, and legal system is health and growth promoting. Disability history should be an integrated part of American life and of interest to everyone. Indeed, PWDs want their experiences, knowledge, and perspectives to become a valued part of ordinary public life (Young & Quibell, 2000).

As a nation, we observe the birthday of Dr. Martin Luther King, an American hero. Will we celebrate the birthday of Justin Dart? (Justin Dart is considered to be the father of the Americans with Disabilities Act.)

Why Has There Been No Disability History?

The medical professions and the media have dominated in representing PWDs to the public, and the media has used PWDs (or more accurately stated, the media's representations of PWDs) as a medium of exchange. The representation of PWDs to the public has been exploited to make money because disability appears to be deviant, alien, and exotic. The actor's (supposed) disability is never a secondary characteristic. Jenny Morris (1991), an English woman who is paraplegic, wrote:

I could watch television for years, possibly a lifetime, without seeing my experience reflected in its dramas, documentaries, news stories. I could spend a lifetime going to theatres, libraries, bookshops, reading newspapers, without finding any portrayal of a woman's life which speaks to my experience. (p. 84)

Every individual and every group of individuals claims the right to define themselves. Leonard Kriegel (1991), a polio survivor, summarized:

But to be a cripple is to learn that one can be defined from outside . . . . What we invariably discover is that our true selves, our own inner lives, have been auctioned off so that we can be palatable rather than real . . . . [T]he only thing we can be certain of is that the world would prefer to turn a blind eye and a deaf ear to our selves—and that it will do precisely that until we impose those selves on the world. (p. 66)

Anne Emerman, former director of the New York City Office of People with Disabilities, stated: "Our issues are always being discussed by people who are experts about us—politicians, policymakers, doctors, social workers—but not us. It's as if they thought, what do we know about ourselves? With all the enlightened thinking about disability, there's still that residue of paternalism" (Fleischer & Zames, 2001, p. 211).

Susan Wendell (1997) "fell ill overnight with what turned out to be a disabling chronic disease" (p. 160). As part of her attempts to identify as an individual with a disability, she relates:

Some time ago, I decided to delve into what I assumed would be a substantial literature in medical ethics on the nature and experience of disability. I consulted *The Philosopher's Index*, looking under "Disability," "Handicap," "Illness," and "Disease." This was a depressing experience. At least 90 percent of philosophical articles on these topics are concerned with two questions: Under what conditions is it morally permissible/right to kill/let die a disabled person [*sic*] and how potentially disabled does a fetus have to be before it is permissible/right to prevent its being born? (p. 260)

As a university professor, Wendell turned to her research skills to help her learn about "the nature and experience of disability." She found very little disability history.

Marc Shell (2005), a polio survivor, wrote what might be termed a "metapathography" (Hawkins, 1993) of the experiences of hundreds of polio survivors. At the beginning of his book, Shell explained his research methods: "Authors of such autobiographical and biographical works (polio stories) usually seem unaware of one another; yet they often offer the same wise counsel about lifestyle, religion, love, and medical knowledge and the lack thereof" (p. 7). On the next page, Shell continued to describe the difficulties he experienced in simply *finding* these written accounts:

> *Polio and Its Aftermath* makes reference to hundreds of book-length first-person polio narratives .... Dozens of these polio narratives are referenced here for the first time anywhere. (Four dozen are not listed in a single library catalogue *anywhere* in the world. I found most of them at secondhand bookstores in Canada, the United States, Tasmania, Australia, South Africa, Zimbabwe, Singapore, Mexico, France, and Germany.) ... Library materials about polios [survivors] from outside the usual commercial publishers' arena were especially difficult for me to find. Unpublished book manuscripts, self-published books, and even so-called children's books have been strangely "disappeared." Their absence from the libraries, as well as from the general histories of childhood and the sociology of childhood disease, mirrors not merely the commercial publishing practices of the past but also the general reception of polio literature and the general repression of the memory of polio. (p. 7)

Disability is thought of as deviation, not as human diversity or variation, and, because of this, few PWODs identify with PWDs. PWDs are thought to be "the other" and a relatively small and narrow population. Susan Wendell (1997), a disability feminist scholar, summarized: "Our culture idealizes the body and demands that we control it .... [T]he disabled are made 'the other,' who symbolize failure of control and the threat of pain, limitation, dependency, and death" (p. 260). Rather than viewing PWDs as ordinary people who share the concerns of family, education, work, and community life, PWDs are viewed as deviant abnormals who should not be allowed to participate in family, education, work, and community life.

The Importance of Disability History

> **In this section, look for—**
> - PWDs wish to transform society with their accumulated knowledge
> - Disability is a valued human experience
> - Disability is an essential part of life
> - PWDs want their experiences to be an ordinary part of American life
> - Fear of disability is fostered by ignorance
> - Everyone is eligible to acquire a disability

Disability history, written by those who have disabilities, should be integrated into cultural and social life. In other words, the experience of disability should be viewed as a valued, strengthening, and broadening diversity, with much to contribute to the wider culture. Disability is a rich and important part of life. Like any other cultural group, PWDs want their differences to be acknowledged, respected, and valued. They claim the right to self-identity. At the same time, they want others to view their differences and values to be an important part of human life, thus universalizing their experience. They no longer wish to be considered a narrowly defined minority.

Hockenberry (2001) stated that PWODs have been deprived of disability history. Those without disabilities have a great deal to learn from those who do have disabilities. Why haven't PWODs demonstrated interest in the disability experience? Perhaps it is the fear of acquiring a disability, or the idea that all disability is tragedy, or the historical tendency to segregate, institutionalize, and shun PWDs that has led to a lack of knowledge. It is probably a combination of all these factors. Liachowski (1988) thinks that this fear of disability engenders more fear and that institutionalized segregation of PWDs leads to more segregation:

> Obviously, segregation affects people with physical handicaps [sic] and people with able bodies . . . . A major consequence of a segregated educational system is the fear that is fostered by ignorance. This kind of fear among those empowered to construct educational policy almost certainly engenders the justification of more segregation. (p. 111)

Nonetheless, everyone can benefit from the disability experience, including those who never acquire a disability. Joan Tollifson (1997), in a chapter titled "Imperfection Is a Beautiful Thing," explained:

> Imperfection is the essence of being organic and alive. Organic life is vulnerable; it inevitably ends in disintegration. This is part of its beauty. True meditation delves into this mystery of life and death, discovering (not intellectually, but experientially) how porous and momentary every thing is. (p. 106)

While most PWDs identify themselves as someone *with* a disability, most PWODs do not think of themselves as someone *without* a disability. Furthermore, because PWDs have been marginalized, most people without disabilities find it difficult to identify with someone with a disability. Susan Wendell (1997) explained: "Suffering caused by the body and the inability to control the body are despised, pitied, and above all, feared. This fear, experienced individually is also deeply embedded in our culture" (p. 267). Wendell considers this fear to be a barrier for PWODs to identify with PWDs. It will be difficult to integrate PWDs into the social and cultural life of society if the wider society maintains this fear and lack of ability to identify with PWDs.

Paul Longmore (2003) suggests that by learning and studying the disability experience, society will be able "to uncover cultural beliefs regarding such matters as body image, masculinity and femininity, personal autonomy and selfhood" (p. 39). Patricia Deegan (1991) considers it necessary to accept the fact that no one is exempt from acquiring a disability to understand the disability experience and PWDs: "To accept our own vulnerability is the first step to understanding the experience of the person with a disability. In so doing, we discover that we share a common humanity with PWDs and we are not 'worlds apart'" (p. 47).

Certainly, those with disabilities have experience and knowledge that are not available to those without disabilities; furthermore, these experiences and knowledge are important for those without disabilities. Thus, the disability experience is an important source of knowledge. If the experience of PWDs were incorporated into cultural life, the relationship between self and body would be viewed in a different way. By listening to those who have transcended pain, functional limitations, and uncertainty, much can be learned about adaptability, strength, and what it means to be human.

References

Deegan, P. E. (1991). Recovery: The lived experience of rehabilitation (pp. 47–54). In R. Martinelli & A. E. Dell Orto (Eds.), *The psychological and social impact of disability.* New York: Springer.

Fleischer, D. Z., & Zames, F. (2001). *The disability rights movement: From charity to confrontation.* Philadelphia: Temple University.

Hawkins, A. H. (1993). *Reconstructing illness: Studies in pathography.* West Layette, IN: Purdue University.

Hockenberry, J. (1995). *Moving violations: War zones, wheelchairs, and declarations of independence.* New York: Hyperion.

Humphrey, J. C. (1999). Disabled people and the politics of differences. *Disability & Society, 14,* 17–188.

Kriegel, L. (1991). *Falling into life.* Berkeley, CA: The Free Press.

Liachowski, C. H. (1988). *Disability as a social construct: Legislative roots.* Philadelphia: Temple University.

Longmore, P. K. (2003). *Why I burned my book and other essays.* Philadelphia: Temple University.

Morris, J. (1991). *Pride against prejudice.* London: Women's Press.

National Public Radio. (1998, May). The Disability History Project.

Shell, M. (2005). *Polio and its aftermath.* Cambridge, MA: Harvard University.

Tollifson, J. (1997). Imperfection is a beautiful thing. In K. Fries (Ed.), *Staring back: The disability experience from the inside out* (pp. 105–112). New York: Plume.

Wecter, D. (1985). How to write history. In *A sense of history: The best writing from the pages of American Heritage* (pp. 38–45). New York: American Heritage.

Wendell, S. (1997). Toward a feminist theory of disability. In L. Davis (Ed.), *Disability studies reader* (pp. 260–278). New York: Routledge.

Young, D. A., & Quibell, R. (2000). Why rights are never enough: Rights, intellectual disability, and understanding. *Disability & Society, 15*, 747–764.

Index

"PWDs" in index refers to people with disabilities. "PWODs" refers to people without disabilities.

About the Author

Julie Smart, PhD, CRC, LPC, ABDA, CCFC, ABPC, NCC, is professor and director of the Rehabilitation Counseling program at Utah State University. Her first career was as a college teacher of Spanish, and she has continued to utilize her Spanish language skills by translating and field-testing rehabilitation instruments, such as *The Acceptance of Disability Scale* and *Client Satisfaction with Rehabilitation Services Scale.* She has authored or co-authored more than 35 articles in rehabilitation and general counseling journals and also has written 10 book chapters. Her research interests include the rehabilitation of racial/ethnic minority individuals with disabilities and models of disability. In 1989–1990, Dr. Smart was the recipient of a postdoctoral research fellowship, the Mary E. Switzer Award, from the National Institute on Disability and Rehabilitation Research (NIDRR).

The stage theory also assists service providers in understanding the process of response/adaptation and, in so doing, helps service providers to choose the best treatment goals (Livneh, 1986b). Tailoring concrete short-term goals compatible with the stage of adaptation/response can provide a task-oriented approach that does not overwhelm the individual. Conceptualizing the adaptation/response to a disability as a process can also assist service providers in encouraging and supporting the individual to progress to the next stage while not permitting coping mechanisms of one stage to become long-term habits. Caregivers cannot counter maladaptive responses and behaviors unless they understand the demands of each stage. Case management, in which many different professionals provide services to a single individual, is facilitated when there is agreement and understanding concerning the stage in which the PWD is operating. This agreement among members of the treatment team will ensure that all treatment will be coordinated. Furthermore, educating and supporting PWDs and their families can assist in maintaining family equilibrium and help families to avoid making major life changes until they are further along in the process.

Understanding the stages of adaptation/response assists family members in their efforts to support the PWD. For example, family members can be educated about the importance of noncritical acceptance of the PWD's denial. Family members learn that confronting or arguing with the PWD is counterproductive. Another example concerns the individual who is in the anger stage. Often, this anger is expressed toward the most accessible people—family members or care providers. Helping family and caregivers to understand that the anger of the PWD is an attempt to regain balance and control will reduce their stress and help to eliminate compassion fatigue and burnout. Therefore, if caregivers and family members understand the stages of adaptation, it is less likely that the PWD will become socially isolated. The stage theory promotes hope and optimism and provides a starting point for assisting the PWD. Deegan (1991) stated, "Hope is contagious" (p. 53).

Often professional caregivers minimize or purposely avoid certain stages of the adaptation/response process. For example, some professionals are not comfortable with individuals who are experiencing the anger stage (Clanton, Rude, & Taylor, 1992). By understanding the stage theory and developing an awareness of their own responses to certain stages, professional caregivers can develop alternative treatment strategies, such as referring PWDs to other caregivers.

Assisting PWDs to understand the stages of adaptation/responses can allow them to draw on their strengths and capabilities at each stage (Livneh & Antonak, 1990). Of course, such an understanding is more than an intellectual understanding; it is a deep, therapeutic conceptualization of a long-term process. Often, PWDs join support groups with individuals who have experienced the same disability. Because group members may be at different stages in the adaptation/response process, members often learn from the experiences of others. These self-help groups can do much to promote and maintain hope. Further, group members know that others understand their experiences.

Cautions in Implementing the Stage Theory

> **In this section, look for—**
>
> - Some stage theories that are specific to the disability, such as therapeutic amputations
> - How, in some disabilities, the stages progress not in a linear fashion but in a curvilinear fashion
> - How each stage encompasses a wide variety of behavioral characteristics
> - How the stage theory does not consider the prejudice and discrimination of others and how these affect the adjustment/response process
> - How individuals can recycle through the stages, repeat a stage, or skip a stage
> - How disability is not a single event but a process

The stage theory of adaptation/response to disability faces some criticism, even to the point of terming the stage theory "social oppression" (Kendall & Buys, 1998, p. 17). The idea that *every* PWD, and his or her family, regardless of the type or severity of disability, experiences a predictable, orderly, sequential, linear, hierarchical progression through these stages has never been suggested by the proponents of the theory. Nor has the wide variability in behavioral characteristics of each stage been disputed. One critique does, however, have merit. Kendall and Buys argued, "Stage models of adjustment also normalize responses such as denial and distress following acquired disability, which may lead rehabilitation workers to expect, or even encourage, such responses" (p. 17). Nonetheless, proponents of the stage model have noted the following:

> The process of adaptation is not irreversible. Individuals who experience a chronic illness or sustain a permanent disability may regress to an earlier phase or skip one or more phases of psychosocial adaptation.